Key

International Human Rights Law Documents

This accessible collection of important international human rights documents is an essential resource for students and researchers of international human rights law. In addition to standard instruments such as the Universal Declaration, the 1966 United Nations Covenants and the European Convention and its Protocols, the volume also features topics and documents such as all core UN human rights treaties and their protocols, key international labour instruments and the obligations of the global financial organisations and multi-national corporations. Taking a broad and historical approach, the collection also incorporates Inter-American, African, Asian and Arab instruments alongside older UN documents and numerous soft law documents. Its approach reflects the diverse nature of international human rights law and the courses which now seek to teach it. This book is also valuable for students of international law, global governance and other courses which discuss the law of international human rights.

URFAN KHALIQ is Professor of Public International and European Laws at Cardiff University. He is the prize-winning author of *Ethical Dimensions of the Foreign Policies of the EU* (Cambridge, 2008) and has taught international human rights law for over twenty years. Professor Khaliq has advised and worked on international human rights matters with international organisations and NGOs and has also advised a number of governments on international human rights law issues.

International Human Rights Law Documents

EDITED BY **URFAN KHALIQ**
Cardiff University

CAMBRIDGE
UNIVERSITY PRESS

CAMBRIDGE
UNIVERSITY PRESS

University Printing House, Cambridge CB2 8BS, United Kingdom

One Liberty Plaza, 20th Floor, New York, NY 10006, USA

477 Williamstown Road, Port Melbourne, VIC 3207, Australia

314–321, 3rd Floor, Plot 3, Splendor Forum, Jasola District Centre, New Delhi – 110025, India

79 Anson Road, #06–04/06, Singapore 079906

Cambridge University Press is part of the University of Cambridge.

It furthers the University's mission by disseminating knowledge in the pursuit of
education, learning, and research at the highest international levels of excellence.

www.cambridge.org
Information on this title: www.cambridge.org/9781316614792
DOI: 10.1017/9781316677117

First published 2018

Printed and bound in Great Britain by Clays Ltd, Elcograf S.p.A.

A catalogue record for this publication is available from the British Library.

Library of Congress Cataloging-in-Publication Data
Names: Khaliq, Urfan, 1970– editor.
Title: International human rights law documents / edited by Urfan Khaliq,
Cardiff University.
Description: Cambridge [UK] ; New York : Cambridge University Press, 2017.
Identifiers: LCCN 2017024138 | ISBN 9781316614792
Subjects: LCSH: International law and human rights. | Human rights.
Classification: LCC KZ1266 .I579 2017 | DDC 341.4/8–dc23
LC record available at https://lccn.loc.gov/2017024138

ISBN 978-1-316-61479-2 Paperback

Contents

Editor's Preface

When I was first asked by Cambridge University Press to compile a 'documents book' on international human rights law, I was of the view that what was 'needed' was a comprehensive collection that reflected the historical development and breadth of the topic and that this would be of most use to researchers and students in the field alike. It soon became clear, however, that the commercial objectives of the publisher focused primarily on examination use for students and thus their view differed from mine as to 'what was needed' and the imposed constraints with regard to eventual size and price soon required me to substantially limit the scope of the envisaged project. Nevertheless, in light of the peer reviews commissioned by Cambridge University Press and what I felt warranted inclusion, the first manuscript I completed ran to over three quarters of a million words, significantly over twice the limit I was given. Thus hard and some regrettable choices had to be made. The parochial view of international human rights law as a 'law of peace time' had to prevail, and I was unable to include documents on international humanitarian law such as the 1949 Geneva Conventions and the Additional Protocols. Nor was I able to include many important documents which are broadly considered part of international criminal law and thus, for example, the Statute of the International Criminal Court, the ad-hoc tribunals and UN Mechanism for International Criminal Tribunals also had to be excluded. Other documents which are concerned with criminal activity and relate to, for example, trafficking I was able to retain. Equally regrettably, I had to exclude a series of documents which relate to 'international human rights law' as that term is more usually used in university module descriptors. I had hoped to include several older but important General Assembly resolutions, but they do not, from the feedback received at least, seem often to form part of the modern university curriculum and thus these also had to be excluded. I have, however, included a few such resolutions, the most recent being the 2014 General Assembly resolution relating to the reform of the UN Human Rights Treaty Bodies. This resolution is to be found accompanying the said treaties.

Having explained what had to be excluded, there is still all that has been included. I am firmly of the view that a collection of documents on 'international human rights law' needs to reflect the 'international', thus fully encompassing both universal systems and all the regional mechanisms. At the universal level, I sought to include all the major UN human rights treaties and their protocols, as well as the UN complaints mechanisms. I further sought to include Security Council resolutions where they directly relate to human rights issues, albeit only two resolutions made the final edit. I have also included the 'core' International Labour Organization (ILO) conventions as well as relevant extracts relating to documents which establish the World Bank and the International Monetary Fund (IMF). At the regional level, again a number of difficult choices had to be made. Some of the issue-specific treaties that have been adopted under the auspices of the Organization of American States or the African Union reflect important developments and I have thus sought to include examples of each. In the context of the African Union, for instance, I have included the Kampala Convention on internally displaced persons. While such an example may not necessarily be representative of global trends, it does represent an important attempt at the regional level to deal with a pressing issue. In the documents included from regional systems, I have in particular sought to focus where possible on the general protection of civil and political rights and economic and social rights and then include some issue-specific treaties. It has of course not been possible to include many 'regional issue-specific treaties' but I hope the balance struck is an appropriate one.

I have also included a number of 'soft law' documents, such as the Siracusa Principles on the limitations and derogation provisions of the International Covenant on Civil and Political Rights (ICCPR) and the Maastricht Guidelines on Violations of Economic, Social and Cultural Rights. This is not to equate them to multi-lateral treaties but has been done with an eye to ease of reference and relevance, whether being used by a student in the examination hall or not.

I have sought to include some very basic reference details for each document such as date of adoption and, if applicable, treaty reference numbers and when the treaty entered into force. I have corrected any obvious mistakes I spotted in the official versions of documents, such as spelling errors, and in terms of formatting tried, as much as possible, to stay faithful to the formatting, indenting, capitalisation and so forth of the original version of the text. In terms of organisation, I have sought to organise documents by organisation (universal first and then regional in alphabetical order) and in chronological order, with any Protocols to a treaty, however, accompanying the treaty as opposed to being organised by date alone. Soft law instruments either accompany the treaties they relate to – the Siracusa Principles, for example, come after the ICCPR and its Protocols – or stand alone, for example, the 1981 Declaration on Religious Intolerance.

I am sure the balances I have sought to strike and approaches taken could have been done equally validly in other ways and any feedback will be gratefully received and taken account of in any subsequent editions.

Urfan Khaliq
Cardiff

SECTION A
Global Documents

PART I
Treaties and Associated Documents Adopted under the Auspices of or Relating to the League of Nations and United Nations

1

Slavery Convention, 1926

Note: the Convention was signed at Geneva on 25 September 1926, entering into force on 9 March 1927. The Convention was amended by a Protocol signed in New York on 7 December 1953; the amended Convention entered into force on 7 July 1955. The text below is of the 1926 Convention as amended by the 1953 Protocol.

Whereas the signatories of the General Act of the Brussels Conference of 1889–90 declared that they were equally animated by the firm intention of putting an end to the traffic in African slaves,

Whereas the signatories of the Convention of Saint-Germain-en-Laye of 1919, to revise the General Act of Berlin of 1885 and the General Act and Declaration of Brussels of 1890, affirmed their intention of securing the complete suppression of slavery in all its forms and of the slave trade by land and sea,

Taking into consideration the report of the Temporary Slavery Commission appointed by the Council of the League of Nations on June 12th, 1924,

Desiring to complete and extend the work accomplished under the Brussels Act and to find a means of giving practical effect throughout the world to such intentions as were expressed in regard to slave trade and slavery by the signatories of the Convention of Saint-Germain-en-Laye, and recognising that it is necessary to conclude to that end more detailed arrangements than are contained in that Convention,

Considering, moreover, that it is necessary to prevent forced labour from developing into conditions analogous to slavery,

Have decided to conclude a Convention and have … agreed as follows:

Article 1

For the purpose of the present Convention, the following definitions are agreed upon:

(1) Slavery is the status or condition of a person over whom any or all of the powers attaching to the right of ownership are exercised.

(2) The slave trade includes all acts involved in the capture, acquisition or disposal of a person with intent to reduce him to slavery; all acts involved in the acquisition of a slave with a view to selling or exchanging him; all acts of disposal by sale or exchange of a slave acquired with a view to being sold or exchanged, and, in general, every act of trade or transport in slaves.

Article 2

The High Contracting Parties undertake, each in respect of the territories placed under its sovereignty, jurisdiction, protection, suzerainty or tutelage, so far as they have not already taken the necessary steps:
 (a) To prevent and suppress the slave trade;
 (b) To bring about, progressively and as soon as possible, the complete abolition of slavery in all its forms.

Article 3

The High Contracting Parties undertake to adopt all appropriate measures with a view to preventing and suppressing the embarkation, disembarkation and transport of slaves in their territorial waters and upon all vessels flying their respective flags.

The High Contracting Parties undertake to negotiate as soon as possible a general Convention with regard to the slave trade which will give them rights and impose upon them duties of the same nature as those provided for in the Convention of June 17th, 1925, relative to the International Trade in Arms (Articles 12, 20, 21, 22, 23, 24 and paragraphs 3, 4 and 5 of Section II of Annex II), with the necessary adaptations, it being understood that this general Convention will not place the ships (even of small tonnage) of any High Contracting Parties in a position different from that of the other High Contracting Parties.

It is also understood that, before or after the coming into force of this general Convention, the High Contracting Parties are entirely free to conclude between themselves, without, however, derogating from the principles laid down in the preceding paragraph, such special agreements as, by reason of their peculiar situation, might appear to be suitable in order to bring about as soon as possible the complete disappearance of the slave trade.

Article 4

The High Contracting Parties shall give to one another every assistance with the object of securing the abolition of slavery and the slave trade.

Article 5

The High Contracting Parties recognise that recourse to compulsory or forced labour may have grave consequences and undertake, each in respect of the territories placed under its sovereignty, jurisdiction, protection, suzerainty or tutelage, to take all necessary measures to prevent compulsory or forced labour from developing into conditions analogous to slavery.

It is agreed that:
(1) Subject to the transitional provisions laid down in paragraph (2) below, compulsory or forced labour may only be exacted for public purposes.
(2) In territories in which compulsory or forced labour for other than public purposes still survives, the High Contracting Parties shall endeavour progressively and as soon as possible to put an end to the practice. So long as such forced or compulsory labour

exists, this labour shall invariably be of an exceptional character, shall always receive adequate remuneration, and shall not involve the removal of the labourers from their usual place of residence.

(3) In all cases, the responsibility for any recourse to compulsory or forced labour shall rest with the competent central authorities of the territory concerned.

Article 6
Those of the High Contracting Parties whose laws do not at present make adequate provision for the punishment of infractions of laws and regulations enacted with a view to giving effect to the purposes of the present Convention undertake to adopt the necessary measures in order that severe penalties may be imposed in respect of such infractions.

Article 7
The High Contracting Parties undertake to communicate to each other and to the Secretary-General of the United Nations any laws and regulations which they may enact with a view to the application of the provisions of the present Convention.

Article 8
The High Contracting Parties agree that disputes arising between them relating to the interpretation or application of this Convention shall, if they cannot be settled by direct negotiation, be referred for decision to the International Court of Justice. In case either or both of the States Parties to such a dispute should not be Parties to the Statute of the International Court of Justice, the dispute shall be referred, at the choice of the Parties and in accordance with the constitutional procedure of each State, either to the International Court of Justice or to a court of arbitration constituted in accordance with the Convention of October 18th, 1907, for the Pacific Settlement of International Disputes, or to some other court of arbitration.

Article 9
At the time of signature or of ratification or of accession, any High Contracting Party may declare that its acceptance of the present Convention does not bind some or all of the territories placed under its sovereignty, jurisdiction, protection, suzerainty or tutelage in respect of all or any provisions of the Convention; it may subsequently accede separately on behalf of any one of them or in respect of any provision to which any one of them is not a Party.

Article 10
In the event of a High Contracting Party wishing to denounce the present Convention, the denunciation shall be notified in writing to the Secretary-General of the United Nations, who will at once communicate a certified true copy of the notification to all the other High Contracting Parties, informing them of the date on which it was received.

The denunciation shall only have effect in regard to the notifying State, and one year after the notification has reached the Secretary-General of the United Nations.

Denunciation may also be made separately in respect of any territory placed under its sovereignty, jurisdiction, protection, suzerainty or tutelage.

Article 11

The present Convention shall be open to accession by all States, including States which are not Members of the United Nations, to which the Secretary-General of the United Nations shall have communicated a certified copy of the Convention.

Accession shall be effected by the deposit of a formal instrument with the Secretary-General of the United Nations, who shall give notice thereof to all States Parties to the Convention and to all other States contemplated in the present article, informing them of the date on which each such instrument of accession was received in deposit.

Article 12

The present Convention will be ratified and the instruments of ratification shall be deposited in the office of the Secretary-General of the United Nations. The Secretary-General will inform all the High Contracting Parties of such deposit.

The Convention will come into operation for each State on the date of the deposit of its ratification or of its accession.

In faith whereof the Plenipotentiaries signed the present Convention.

Done at Geneva the twenty-fifth day of September, one thousand nine hundred and twenty-six, in one copy … A certified copy shall be forwarded to each signatory State.

2

Charter of the United Nations, 1945 (excerpts only)

PREAMBLE TO THE CHARTER OF THE UNITED NATIONS

WE THE PEOPLES OF THE UNITED NATIONS, DETERMINED

to save succeeding generations from the scourge of war, which twice in our lifetime has brought untold sorrow to mankind, and

to reaffirm faith in fundamental human rights, in the dignity and worth of the human person, in the equal rights of men and women and of nations large and small, and

to establish conditions under which justice and respect for the obligations arising from treaties and other sources of international law can be maintained, and

to promote social progress and better standards of life in larger freedom,

AND FOR THESE ENDS

to practice tolerance and live together in peace with one another as good neighbours, and

to unite our strength to maintain international peace and security, and

to ensure, by the acceptance of principles and the institution of methods, that armed force shall not be used, save in the common interest, and

to employ international machinery for the promotion of the economic and social advancement of all peoples,

HAVE RESOLVED TO COMBINE OUR EFFORTS TO ACCOMPLISH THESE AIMS

Accordingly, our respective Governments, through representatives assembled in the city of San Francisco, who have exhibited their full powers found to be in good and due form, have agreed to the present Charter of the United Nations and do hereby establish an international organization to be known as the United Nations.

Chapter I

Article 1

The Purposes of the United Nations are:

1. To maintain international peace and security, and to that end: to take effective collective measures for the prevention and removal of threats to the peace, and for the suppression of acts of aggression or other breaches of the peace, and to bring about by peaceful means, and in conformity with the principles of justice and international law, adjustment or settlement of international disputes or situations which might lead to a breach of the peace;

2. To develop friendly relations among nations based on respect for the principle of equal rights and self-determination of peoples, and to take other appropriate measures to strengthen universal peace;

3. To achieve international co-operation in solving international problems of an economic, social, cultural, or humanitarian character, and in promoting and encouraging respect for human rights and for fundamental freedoms for all without distinction as to race, sex, language, or religion; and

4. To be a centre for harmonizing the actions of nations in the attainment of these common ends.

Article 2

The Organization and its Members, in pursuit of the Purposes stated in Article 1, shall act in accordance with the following Principles.

1. The Organization is based on the principle of the sovereign equality of all its Members.

2. All Members, in order to ensure to all of them the rights and benefits resulting from membership, shall fulfil in good faith the obligations assumed by them in accordance with the present Charter.

3. All Members shall settle their international disputes by peaceful means in such a manner that international peace and security, and justice, are not endangered.

4. All Members shall refrain in their international relations from the threat or use of force against the territorial integrity or political independence of any state, or in any other manner inconsistent with the Purposes of the United Nations.

5. All Members shall give the United Nations every assistance in any action it takes in accordance with the present Charter, and shall refrain from giving assistance to any state against which the United Nations is taking preventive or enforcement action.

6. The Organization shall ensure that states which are not Members of the United Nations act in accordance with these Principles so far as may be necessary for the maintenance of international peace and security.

7. Nothing contained in the present Charter shall authorize the United Nations to intervene in matters which are essentially within the domestic jurisdiction of any state or shall require the Members to submit such matters to settlement under the present Charter; but this principle shall not prejudice the application of enforcement measures under Chapter VII.

…

Chapter V

Article 25
The Members of the United Nations agree to accept and carry out the decisions of the Security Council in accordance with the present Charter.

...

Chapter VII

Article 39
The Security Council shall determine the existence of any threat to the peace, breach of the peace, or act of aggression and shall make recommendations, or decide what measures shall be taken in accordance with Articles 41 and 42, to maintain or restore international peace and security.

Article 40
In order to prevent an aggravation of the situation, the Security Council may, before making the recommendations or deciding upon the measures provided for in Article 39, call upon the parties concerned to comply with such provisional measures as it deems necessary or desirable. Such provisional measures shall be without prejudice to the rights, claims, or position of the parties concerned. The Security Council shall duly take account of failure to comply with such provisional measures.

Article 41
The Security Council may decide what measures not involving the use of armed force are to be employed to give effect to its decisions, and it may call upon the Members of the United Nations to apply such measures. These may include complete or partial interruption of economic relations and of rail, sea, air, postal, telegraphic, radio, and other means of communication, and the severance of diplomatic relations.

Article 42
Should the Security Council consider that measures provided for in Article 41 would be inadequate or have proved to be inadequate, it may take such action by air, sea, or land forces as may be necessary to maintain or restore international peace and security. Such action may include demonstrations, blockade, and other operations by air, sea, or land forces of Members of the United Nations.

...

Article 51
Nothing in the present Charter shall impair the inherent right of individual or collective self-defence if an armed attack occurs against a Member of the United Nations, until the Security Council has taken measures necessary to maintain international peace and security. Measures taken by Members in the exercise of this right of self-defence shall be immediately reported to the Security Council and shall not in any way affect the authority and responsibility of the Security Council under the present Charter to take at any time such action as it deems necessary in order to maintain or restore international peace and security.

Chapter IX

...

Article 55

With a view to the creation of conditions of stability and well-being which are necessary for peaceful and friendly relations among nations based on respect for the principle of equal rights and self-determination of peoples, the United Nations shall promote:

a. higher standards of living, full employment, and conditions of economic and social progress and development;

b. solutions of international economic, social, health, and related problems; and international cultural and educational co-operation; and

c. universal respect for, and observance of, human rights and fundamental freedoms for all without distinction as to race, sex, language, or religion.

...

Chapter XIV

...

Article 92

The International Court of Justice shall be the principal judicial organ of the United Nations. It shall function in accordance with the annexed Statute, which is based upon the Statute of the Permanent Court of International Justice and forms an integral part of the present Charter.

Article 93

1. All Members of the United Nations are ipso facto parties to the Statute of the International Court of Justice.

2. A state which is not a Member of the United Nations may become a party to the Statute of the International Court of Justice on conditions to be determined in each case by the General Assembly upon the recommendation of the Security Council.

Article 94

1. Each Member of the United Nations undertakes to comply with the decision of the International Court of Justice in any case to which it is a party.

2. If any party to a case fails to perform the obligations incumbent upon it under a judgment rendered by the Court, the other party may have recourse to the Security Council, which may, if it deems necessary, make recommendations or decide upon measures to be taken to give effect to the judgment.

3

Statute of the International Court of Justice (excerpts only)

Note: the Statute of the International Court of Justice is annexed to the Charter of the United Nations, of which it forms an integral part. The main object of the Statute is to organise the composition and the functioning of the Court.

…

Article 1

The International Court of Justice established by the Charter of the United Nations as the principal judicial organ of the United Nations shall be constituted and shall function in accordance with the provisions of the present Statute.

…

Article 34

1. Only states may be parties in cases before the Court.

…

Article 35

1. The Court shall be open to the states parties to the present Statute.

…

Article 36

1. The jurisdiction of the Court comprises all cases which the parties refer to it and all matters specially provided for in the Charter of the United Nations or in treaties and conventions in force.
2. The states parties to the present Statute may at any time declare that they recognize as compulsory ipso facto and without special agreement, in relation to any other state accepting the same obligation, the jurisdiction of the Court in all legal disputes concerning:
   a. the interpretation of a treaty;
   b. any question of international law;
   c. the existence of any fact which, if established, would constitute a breach of an international obligation;
   d. the nature or extent of the reparation to be made for the breach of an international obligation.
3. The declarations referred to above may be made unconditionally or on condition of reciprocity on the part of several or certain states, or for a certain time.
4. Such declarations shall be deposited with the Secretary-General of the United Nations, who shall transmit copies thereof to the parties to the Statute and to the Registrar of the Court.

5. Declarations made under Article 36 of the Statute of the Permanent Court of International Justice and which are still in force shall be deemed, as between the parties to the present Statute, to be acceptances of the compulsory jurisdiction of the International Court of Justice for the period which they still have to run and in accordance with their terms.

6. In the event of a dispute as to whether the Court has jurisdiction, the matter shall be settled by the decision of the Court.

…

Article 38

1. The Court, whose function is to decide in accordance with international law such disputes as are submitted to it, shall apply:
   a. international conventions, whether general or particular, establishing rules expressly recognized by the contesting states;
   b. international custom, as evidence of a general practice accepted as law;
   c. the general principles of law recognized by civilized nations;
   d. subject to the provisions of Article 59, judicial decisions and the teachings of the most highly qualified publicists of the various nations, as subsidiary means for the determination of rules of law.

2. This provision shall not prejudice the power of the Court to decide a case ex aequo et bono, if the parties agree thereto.

…

Article 65

1. The Court may give an advisory opinion on any legal question at the request of whatever body may be authorized by or in accordance with the Charter of the United Nations to make such a request.

2. Questions upon which the advisory opinion of the Court is asked shall be laid before the Court by means of a written request containing an exact statement of the question upon which an opinion is required, and accompanied by all documents likely to throw light upon the question.

4

Convention on the Prevention and Punishment of the Crime of Genocide, 1948

Note: approved and proposed for signature and ratification or accession by General Assembly Resolution 260 A (III) of 9 December 1948. Entry into force: 12 January 1951.

The Contracting Parties,

Having considered the declaration made by the General Assembly of the United Nations in its resolution 96 (I) dated 11 December 1946 that genocide is a crime under international law, contrary to the spirit and aims of the United Nations and condemned by the civilized world,

Recognizing that at all periods of history genocide has inflicted great losses on humanity, and

Being convinced that, in order to liberate mankind from such an odious scourge, international co-operation is required,

HEREBY AGREE AS HEREINAFTER PROVIDED:

Article I
The Contracting Parties confirm that genocide, whether committed in time of peace or in time of war, is a crime under international law which they undertake to prevent and to punish.

Article II
In the present Convention, genocide means any of the following acts committed with intent to destroy, in whole or in part, a national, ethnical, racial or religious group, as such:
  (a) Killing members of the group;
  (b) Causing serious bodily or mental harm to members of the group;
  (c) Deliberately inflicting on the group conditions of life calculated to bring about its physical destruction in whole or in part;
  (d) Imposing measures intended to prevent births within the group;
  (e) Forcibly transferring children of the group to another group.

Article III
The following acts shall be punishable:
  (a) Genocide;
  (b) Conspiracy to commit genocide;
  (c) Direct and public incitement to commit genocide;
  (d) Attempt to commit genocide;
  (e) Complicity in genocide.

Article IV

Persons committing genocide or any of the other acts enumerated in article III shall be punished, whether they are constitutionally responsible rulers, public officials or private individuals.

Article V

The Contracting Parties undertake to enact, in accordance with their respective Constitutions, the necessary legislation to give effect to the provisions of the present Convention, and, in particular, to provide effective penalties for persons guilty of genocide or any of the other acts enumerated in article III.

Article VI

Persons charged with genocide or any of the other acts enumerated in article III shall be tried by a competent tribunal of the State in the territory of which the act was committed, or by such international penal tribunal as may have jurisdiction with respect to those Contracting Parties which shall have accepted its jurisdiction.

Article VII

Genocide and the other acts enumerated in article III shall not be considered as political crimes for the purpose of extradition.

The Contracting Parties pledge themselves in such cases to grant extradition in accordance with their laws and treaties in force.

Article VIII

Any Contracting Party may call upon the competent organs of the United Nations to take such action under the Charter of the United Nations as they consider appropriate for the prevention and suppression of acts of genocide or any of the other acts enumerated in article III.

Article IX

Disputes between the Contracting Parties relating to the interpretation, application or fulfilment of the present Convention, including those relating to the responsibility of a State for genocide or for any of the other acts enumerated in article III, shall be submitted to the International Court of Justice at the request of any of the parties to the dispute.

Article X

The present Convention, of which the Chinese, English, French, Russian and Spanish texts are equally authentic, shall bear the date of 9 December 1948.

Article XI

The present Convention shall be open until 31 December 1949 for signature on behalf of any Member of the United Nations and of any nonmember State to which an invitation to sign has been addressed by the General Assembly.

The present Convention shall be ratified, and the instruments of ratification shall be deposited with the Secretary-General of the United Nations.

After 1 January 1950, the present Convention may be acceded to on behalf of any Member of the United Nations and of any non-member State which has received an invitation as aforesaid. Instruments of accession shall be deposited with the Secretary-General of the United Nations.

Article XII
Any Contracting Party may at any time, by notification addressed to the Secretary-General of the United Nations, extend the application of the present Convention to all or any of the territories for the conduct of whose foreign relations that Contracting Party is responsible.

Article XIII
On the day when the first twenty instruments of ratification or accession have been deposited, the Secretary-General shall draw up a proces-verbal and transmit a copy thereof to each Member of the United Nations and to each of the non-member States contemplated in article XI.

The present Convention shall come into force on the ninetieth day following the date of deposit of the twentieth instrument of ratification or accession.

Any ratification or accession effected, subsequent to the latter date shall become effective on the ninetieth day following the deposit of the instrument of ratification or accession.

Article XIV
The present Convention shall remain in effect for a period of ten years as from the date of its coming into force.

It shall thereafter remain in force for successive periods of five years for such Contracting Parties as have not denounced it at least six months before the expiration of the current period.

Denunciation shall be effected by a written notification addressed to the Secretary-General of the United Nations.

Article XV
If, as a result of denunciations, the number of Parties to the present Convention should become less than sixteen, the Convention shall cease to be in force as from the date on which the last of these denunciations shall become effective.

Article XVI
A request for the revision of the present Convention may be made at any time by any Contracting Party by means of a notification in writing addressed to the Secretary-General.

The General Assembly shall decide upon the steps, if any, to be taken in respect of such request.

Article XVII
The Secretary-General of the United Nations shall notify all Members of the United Nations and the non-member States contemplated in article XI of the following:
(a) Signatures, ratifications and accessions received in accordance with article XI;
(b) Notifications received in accordance with article XII;
(c) The date upon which the present Convention comes into force in accordance with article XIII;

(d) Denunciations received in accordance with article XIV;

(e) The abrogation of the Convention in accordance with article XV;

(f) Notifications received in accordance with article XVI.

Article XVIII

The original of the present Convention shall be deposited in the archives of the United Nations.

A certified copy of the Convention shall be transmitted to each Member of the United Nations and to each of the non-member States contemplated in article XI.

Article XIX

The present Convention shall be registered by the Secretary-General of the United Nations on the date of its coming into force.

5

Convention Relating to the Status of Refugees, 1951

Note: adopted by United Nations General Assembly Resolution 429(V) of 14 December 1950, 189 UNTS 150. Entry into force: 22 April 1954.

PREAMBLE

THE HIGH CONTRACTING PARTIES,

CONSIDERING that the Charter of the United Nations and the Universal Declaration of Human Rights approved on 10 December 1948 by the General Assembly have affirmed the principle that human beings shall enjoy fundamental rights and freedoms without discrimination,

CONSIDERING that the United Nations has, on various occasions, manifested its profound concern for refugees and endeavoured to assure refugees the widest possible exercise of these fundamental rights and freedoms,

CONSIDERING that it is desirable to revise and consolidate previous international agreements relating to the status of refugees and to extend the scope of and the protection accorded by such instruments by means of a new agreement,

CONSIDERING that the grant of asylum may place unduly heavy burdens on certain countries, and that a satisfactory solution of a problem of which the United Nations has recognized the international scope and nature cannot therefore be achieved without international co-operation,

EXPRESSING the wish that all States, recognizing the social and humanitarian nature of the problem of refugees, will do everything within their power to prevent this problem from becoming a cause of tension between States,

NOTING that the United Nations High Commissioner for Refugees is charged with the task of supervising international conventions providing for the protection of refugees, and recognizing that the effective co-ordination of measures taken to deal with this problem will depend upon the co-operation of States with the High Commissioner,

HAVE AGREED as follows:

Chapter I General Provisions

Article 1. Definition of the term "refugee"

A. For the purposes of the present Convention, the term "refugee", shall apply to any person who:

  (1) Has been considered a refugee under the Arrangements of 12 May 1926 and 30 June 1928 or under the Conventions of 28 October 1933 and 10 February 1938, the Protocol of 14 September 1939 or the Constitution of the International Refugee Organization;

   Decisions of non-eligibility taken by the International Refugee Organization during the period of its activities shall not prevent the status of refugee being accorded to persons who fulfil the conditions of paragraph 2 of this section;

  (2) As a result of events occurring before 1 January 1951 and owing to well-founded fear of being persecuted for reasons of race, religion, nationality, membership of a particular social group or political opinion, is outside the country of his nationality and is unable or, owing to such fear, is unwilling to avail himself of the protection of that country; or who, not having a nationality and being outside the country of his former habitual residence as a result of such events, is unable or, owing to such fear, is unwilling to return to it.

   In the case of a person who has more than one nationality, the term "the country of his nationality" shall mean each of the countries of which he is a national, and a person shall not be deemed to be lacking the protection of the country of his nationality if, without any valid reason based on well-founded fear, he has not availed himself of the protection of one of the countries of which he is a national.

B. (1) For the purposes of this Convention, the words "events occurring before I January 1951" in article 1, section A, shall be understood to mean either

   (a) "events occurring in Europe before 1 January 1951"; or

   (b) "events occurring in Europe or elsewhere before 1 January 1951"; and each Contracting State shall make a declaration at the time of signature, ratification or accession, specifying which of these meanings it applies for the purpose of its obligations under this Convention.

  (2) Any Contracting State which has adopted alternative (a) may at any time extend its obligations by adopting alternative (b) by means of a notification addressed to the Secretary-General of the United Nations.

C. This Convention shall cease to apply to any person falling under the terms of section A if:

  (1) He has voluntarily re-availed himself of the protection of the country of his nationality; or

  (2) Having lost his nationality, he has voluntarily reacquired it; or

  (3) He has acquired a new nationality, and enjoys the protection of the country of his new nationality; or

  (4) He has voluntarily re-established himself in the country which he left or outside which he remained owing to fear of persecution; or

  (5) He can no longer, because the circumstances in connection with which he has been recognized as a refugee have ceased to exist, continue to refuse to avail himself of the protection of the country of his nationality;

Provided that this paragraph shall not apply to a refugee falling under section A (I) of this article who is able to invoke compelling reasons arising out of previous persecution for refusing to avail himself of the protection of the country of nationality;

(6) Being a person who has no nationality he is, because the circumstances in connection with which he has been recognized as a refugee have ceased to exist, able to return to the country of his former habitual residence;

Provided that this paragraph shall not apply to a refugee falling under section A (I) of this article who is able to invoke compelling reasons arising out of previous persecution for refusing to return to the country of his former habitual residence.

D. This Convention shall not apply to persons who are at present receiving from organs or agencies of the United Nations other than the United Nations High Commissioner for Refugees protection or assistance.

When such protection or assistance has ceased for any reason, without the position of such persons being definitively settled in accordance with the relevant resolutions adopted by the General Assembly of the United Nations, these persons shall ipso facto be entitled to the benefits of this Convention.

E. This Convention shall not apply to a person who is recognized by the competent authorities of the country in which he has taken residence as having the rights and obligations which are attached to the possession of the nationality of that country.

F. The provisions of this Convention shall not apply to any person with respect to whom there are serious reasons for considering that:

(a) He has committed a crime against peace, a war crime, or a crime against humanity, as defined in the international instruments drawn up to make provision in respect of such crimes;

(b) He has committed a serious non-political crime outside the country of refuge prior to his admission to that country as a refugee;

(c) He has been guilty of acts contrary to the purposes and principles of the United Nations.

Article 2. General obligations
Every refugee has duties to the country in which he finds himself, which require in particular that he conform to its laws and regulations as well as to measures taken for the maintenance of public order.

Article 3. Non-discrimination
The Contracting States shall apply the provisions of this Convention to refugees without discrimination as to race, religion or country of origin.

Article 4. Religion
The Contracting States shall accord to refugees within their territories treatment at least as favourable as that accorded to their nationals with respect to freedom to practise their religion and freedom as regards the religious education of their children.

Article 5. Rights granted apart from this Convention

Nothing in this Convention shall be deemed to impair any rights and benefits granted by a Contracting State to refugees apart from this Convention.

Article 6. The term "in the same circumstances"

For the purposes of this Convention, the term "in the same circumstances" implies that any requirements (including requirements as to length and conditions of sojourn or residence) which the particular individual would have to fulfil for the enjoyment of the right in question, if he were not a refugee, must be fulfilled by him, with the exception of requirements which by their nature a refugee is incapable of fulfilling.

Article 7. Exemption from reciprocity

1. Except where this Convention contains more favourable provisions, a Contracting State shall accord to refugees the same treatment as is accorded to aliens generally.
2. After a period of three years' residence, all refugees shall enjoy exemption from legislative reciprocity in the territory of the Contracting States.
3. Each Contracting State shall continue to accord to refugees the rights and benefits to which they were already entitled, in the absence of reciprocity, at the date of entry into force of this Convention for that State.
4. The Contracting States shall consider favourably the possibility of according to refugees, in the absence of reciprocity, rights and benefits beyond those to which they are entitled according to paragraphs 2 and 3, and to extending exemption from reciprocity to refugees who do not fulfil the conditions provided for in paragraphs 2 and 3.
5. The provisions of paragraphs 2 and 3 apply both to the rights and benefits referred to in articles 13, 18, 19, 21 and 22 of this Convention and to rights and benefits for which this Convention does not provide.

Article 8. Exemption from exceptional measures

With regard to exceptional measures which may be taken against the person, property or interests of nationals of a foreign State, the Contracting States shall not apply such measures to a refugee who is formally a national of the said State solely on account of such nationality. Contracting States which, under their legislation, are prevented from applying the general principle expressed in this article, shall, in appropriate cases, grant exemptions in favour of such refugees.

Article 9. Provisional measures

Nothing in this Convention shall prevent a Contracting State, in time of war or other grave and exceptional circumstances, from taking provisionally measures which it considers to be essential to the national security in the case of a particular person, pending a determination by the Contracting State that that person is in fact a refugee and that the continuance of such measures is necessary in his case in the interests of national security.

Article 10. Continuity of residence

1. Where a refugee has been forcibly displaced during the Second World War and removed to the territory of a Contracting State, and is resident there, the period of such enforced sojourn shall be considered to have been lawful residence within that territory.
2. Where a refugee has been forcibly displaced during the Second World War from the territory of a Contracting State and has, prior to the date of entry into force of this Convention, returned there for the purpose of taking up residence, the period of residence before and after such enforced displacement shall be regarded as one uninterrupted period for any purposes for which uninterrupted residence is required.

Article 11. Refugee seamen

In the case of refugees regularly serving as crew members on board a ship flying the flag of a Contracting State, that State shall give sympathetic consideration to their establishment on its territory and the issue of travel documents to them or their temporary admission to its territory particularly with a view to facilitating their establishment in another country.

Chapter II Juridical Status

Article 12. Personal status

1. The personal status of a refugee shall be governed by the law of the country of his domicile or, if he has no domicile, by the law of the country of his residence.
2. Rights previously acquired by a refugee and dependent on personal status, more particularly rights attaching to marriage, shall be respected by a Contracting State, subject to compliance, if this be necessary, with the formalities required by the law of that State, provided that the right in question is one which would have been recognized by the law of that State had he not become a refugee.

Article 13. Movable and immovable property

The Contracting States shall accord to a refugee treatment as favourable as possible and, in any event, not less favourable than that accorded to aliens generally in the same circumstances, as regards the acquisition of movable and immovable property and other rights pertaining thereto, and to leases and other contracts relating to movable and immovable property.

Article 14. Artistic rights and industrial property

In respect of the protection of industrial property, such as inventions, designs or models, trademarks, trade names, and of rights in literary, artistic and scientific works, a refugee shall be accorded in the country in which he has his habitual residence the same protection as is accorded to nationals of that country. In the territory of any other Contracting States, he shall be accorded the same protection as is accorded in that territory to nationals of the country in which he has his habitual residence.

Article 15. Right of association

As regards non-political and non-profit-making associations and trade unions the Contracting States shall accord to refugees lawfully staying in their territory the most favourable treatment accorded to nationals of a foreign country, in the same circumstances.

Article 16. Access to courts

1. A refugee shall have free access to the courts of law on the territory of all Contracting States.
2. A refugee shall enjoy in the Contracting State in which he has his habitual residence the same treatment as a national in matters pertaining to access to the courts, including legal assistance and exemption from cautio judicatum solvi.
3. A refugee shall be accorded in the matters referred to in paragraph 2 in countries other than that in which he has his habitual residence the treatment granted to a national of the country of his habitual residence.

Chapter III Gainful Employment

Article 17. Wage-earning employment

1. The Contracting States shall accord to refugees lawfully staying in their territory the most favourable treatment accorded to nationals of a foreign country in the same circumstances, as regards the right to engage in wage-earning employment.
2. In any case, restrictive measures imposed on aliens or the employment of aliens for the protection of the national labour market shall not be applied to a refugee who was already exempt from them at the date of entry into force of this Convention for the Contracting State concerned, or who fulfils one of the following conditions:
    (a) He has completed three years' residence in the country;
    (b) He has a spouse possessing the nationality of the country of residence. A refugee may not invoke the benefit of this provision if he has abandoned his spouse;
    (c) He has one or more children possessing the nationality of the country of residence.
3. The Contracting States shall give sympathetic consideration to assimilating the rights of all refugees with regard to wage-earning employment to those of nationals, and in particular of those refugees who have entered their territory pursuant to programmes of labour recruitment or under immigration schemes.

Article 18. Self-employment

The Contracting States shall accord to a refugee lawfully in their territory treatment as favourable as possible and, in any event, not less favourable than that accorded to aliens generally in the same circumstances, as regards the right to engage on his own account in agriculture, industry, handicrafts and commerce and to establish commercial and industrial companies.

Article 19. Liberal professions

1. Each Contracting State shall accord to refugees lawfully staying in their territory who hold diplomas recognized by the competent authorities of that State, and who are desirous of practising a liberal profession, treatment as favourable as possible and, in any event, not less favourable than that accorded to aliens generally in the same circumstances.
2. The Contracting States shall use their best endeavours consistently with their laws and constitutions to secure the settlement of such refugees in the territories, other than the metropolitan territory, for whose international relations they are responsible.

Chapter IV Welfare

Article 20. Rationing

Where a rationing system exists, which applies to the population at large and regulates the general distribution of products in short supply, refugees shall be accorded the same treatment as nationals.

Article 21. Housing

As regards housing, the Contracting States, in so far as the matter is regulated by laws or regulations or is subject to the control of public authorities, shall accord to refugees lawfully staying in their territory treatment as favourable as possible and, in any event, not less favourable than that accorded to aliens generally in the same circumstances.

Article 22. Public education

1. The Contracting States shall accord to refugees the same treatment as is accorded to nationals with respect to elementary education.
2. The Contracting States shall accord to refugees treatment as favourable as possible, and, in any event, not less favourable than that accorded to aliens generally in the same circumstances, with respect to education other than elementary education and, in particular, as regards access to studies, the recognition of foreign school certificates, diplomas and degrees, the remission of fees and charges and the award of scholarships.

Article 23. Public relief

The Contracting States shall accord to refugees lawfully staying in their territory the same treatment with respect to public relief and assistance as is accorded to their nationals.

Article 24. Labour legislation and social security

1. The Contracting States shall accord to refugees lawfully staying in their territory the same treatment as is accorded to nationals in respect of the following matters;
   (a) In so far as such matters are governed by laws or regulations or are subject to the control of administrative authorities: remuneration, including family allowances where these form part of remuneration, hours of work, overtime arrangements, holidays with pay, restrictions on home work, minimum age of employment, apprenticeship and training, women's work and the work of young persons, and the enjoyment of the benefits of collective bargaining;
   (b) Social security (legal provisions in respect of employment injury, occupational diseases, maternity, sickness, disability, old age, death, unemployment, family responsibilities and any other contingency which, according to national laws or regulations, is covered by a social security scheme), subject to the following limitations:
      (i) There may be appropriate arrangements for the maintenance of acquired rights and rights in course of acquisition;
      (ii) National laws or regulations of the country of residence may prescribe special arrangements concerning benefits or portions of benefits which are payable wholly out of public funds, and concerning allowances paid to persons who

do not fulfil the contribution conditions prescribed for the award of a normal pension.

2. The right to compensation for the death of a refugee resulting from employment injury or from occupational disease shall not be affected by the fact that the residence of the beneficiary is outside the territory of the Contracting State.

3. The Contracting States shall extend to refugees the benefits of agreements concluded between them, or which may be concluded between them in the future, concerning the maintenance of acquired rights and rights in the process of acquisition in regard to social security, subject only to the conditions which apply to nationals of the States signatory to the agreements in question.

4. The Contracting States will give sympathetic consideration to extending to refugees so far as possible the benefits of similar agreements which may at any time be in force between such Contracting States and non-contracting States.

Chapter V Administrative Measures

Article 25. Administrative assistance

1. When the exercise of a right by a refugee would normally require the assistance of authorities of a foreign country to whom he cannot have recourse, the Contracting States in whose territory he is residing shall arrange that such assistance be afforded to him by their own authorities or by an international authority.

2. The authority or authorities mentioned in paragraph 1 shall deliver or cause to be delivered under their supervision to refugees such documents or certifications as would normally be delivered to aliens by or through their national authorities.

3. Documents or certifications so delivered shall stand in the stead of the official instruments delivered to aliens by or through their national authorities, and shall be given credence in the absence of proof to the contrary.

4. Subject to such exceptional treatment as may be granted to indigent persons, fees may be charged for the services mentioned herein, but such fees shall be moderate and commensurate with those charged to nationals for similar services.

5. The provisions of this article shall be without prejudice to articles 27 and 28.

Article 26. Freedom of movement

Each Contracting State shall accord to refugees lawfully in its territory the right to choose their place of residence and to move freely within its territory subject to any regulations applicable to aliens generally in the same circumstances.

Article 27. Identity papers

The Contracting States shall issue identity papers to any refugee in their territory who does not possess a valid travel document.

Article 28. Travel documents

1. The Contracting States shall issue to refugees lawfully staying in their territory travel documents for the purpose of travel outside their territory, unless compelling reasons of national security or public order otherwise require, and the provisions of the Schedule to this Convention shall apply with respect to such documents. The Contracting States

may issue such a travel document to any other refugee in their territory; they shall in particular give sympathetic consideration to the issue of such a travel document to refugees in their territory who are unable to obtain a travel document from the country of their lawful residence.

2. Travel documents issued to refugees under previous international agreements by Parties thereto shall be recognized and treated by the Contracting States in the same way as if they had been issued pursuant to this article.

Article 29. Fiscal charges

1. The Contracting States shall not impose upon refugees duties, charges or taxes, of any description whatsoever, other or higher than those which are or may be levied on their nationals in similar situations.

2. Nothing in the above paragraph shall prevent the application to refugees of the laws and regulations concerning charges in respect of the issue to aliens of administrative documents including identity papers.

Article 30. Transfer of assets

1. A Contracting State shall, in conformity with its laws and regulations, permit refugees to transfer assets which they have brought into its territory, to another country where they have been admitted for the purposes of resettlement.

2. A Contracting State shall give sympathetic consideration to the application of refugees for permission to transfer assets wherever they may be and which are necessary for their resettlement in another country to which they have been admitted.

Article 31. Refugees unlawfully in the country of refuge

1. The Contracting States shall not impose penalties, on account of their illegal entry or presence, on refugees who, coming directly from a territory where their life or freedom was threatened in the sense of article 1, enter or are present in their territory without authorization, provided they present themselves without delay to the authorities and show good cause for their illegal entry or presence.

2. The Contracting States shall not apply to the movements of such refugees restrictions other than those which are necessary and such restrictions shall only be applied until their status in the country is regularized or they obtain admission into another country. The Contracting States shall allow such refugees a reasonable period and all the necessary facilities to obtain admission into another country.

Article 32. Expulsion

1. The Contracting States shall not expel a refugee lawfully in their territory save on grounds of national security or public order.

2. The expulsion of such a refugee shall be only in pursuance of a decision reached in accordance with due process of law. Except where compelling reasons of national security otherwise require, the refugee shall be allowed to submit evidence to clear himself, and to appeal to and be represented for the purpose before competent authority or a person or persons specially designated by the competent authority.

3. The Contracting States shall allow such a refugee a reasonable period within which to seek legal admission into another country. The Contracting States reserve the right to apply during that period such internal measures as they may deem necessary.

Article 33. Prohibition of expulsion or return ("refoulement")

1. No Contracting State shall expel or return ("refouler") a refugee in any manner whatsoever to the frontiers of territories where his life or freedom would be threatened on account of his race, religion, nationality, membership of a particular social group or political opinion.
2. The benefit of the present provision may not, however, be claimed by a refugee whom there are reasonable grounds for regarding as a danger to the security of the country in which he is, or who, having been convicted by a final judgement of a particularly serious crime, constitutes a danger to the community of that country.

Article 34. Naturalization

The Contracting States shall as far as possible facilitate the assimilation and naturalization of refugees. They shall in particular make every effort to expedite naturalization proceedings and to reduce as far as possible the charges and costs of such proceedings.

Chapter VI EXECUTORY AND TRANSITORY PROVISIONS

Article 35. Co-operation of the national authorities with the united nations

1. The Contracting States undertake to co-operate with the Office of the United Nations High Commissioner for Refugees, or any other agency of the United Nations which may succeed it, in the exercise of its functions, and shall in particular facilitate its duty of supervising the application of the provisions of this Convention.
2. In order to enable the Office of the High Commissioner or any other agency of the United Nations which may succeed it, to make reports to the competent organs of the United Nations, the Contracting States undertake to provide them in the appropriate form with information and statistical data requested concerning:
   (a) The condition of refugees,
   (b) The implementation of this Convention, and
   (c) Laws, regulations and decrees which are, or may hereafter be, in force relating to refugees.

Article 36. Information on national legislation

The Contracting States shall communicate to the Secretary-General of the United Nations the laws and regulations which they may adopt to ensure the application of this Convention.

Article 37. Relation to previous conventions

Without prejudice to article 28, paragraph 2, of this Convention, this Convention replaces, as between Parties to it, the Arrangements of 5 July 1922, 31 May 1924, 12 May 1926, 30 June 1928 and 30 July 1935, the Conventions of 28 October 1933 and 10 February 1938, the Protocol of 14 September 1939 and the Agreement of 15 October 1946.

Chapter VII **FINAL CLAUSES**

Article 38. Settlement of disputes

Any dispute between Parties to this Convention relating to its interpretation or application, which cannot be settled by other means, shall be referred to the International Court of Justice at the request of any one of the parties to the dispute.

Article 39. Signature, ratification and accession

1. This Convention shall be opened for signature at Geneva on 28 July 1951 and shall thereafter be deposited with the Secretary-General of the United Nations. It shall be open for signature at the European Office of the United Nations from 28 July to 31 August 1951 and shall be re-opened for signature at the Headquarters of the United Nations from 17 September 1951 to 31 December 1952.
2. This Convention shall be open for signature on behalf of all States Members of the United Nations, and also on behalf of any other State invited to attend the Conference of Plenipotentiaries on the Status of Refugees and Stateless Persons or to which an invitation to sign will have been addressed by the General Assembly. It shall be ratified and the instruments of ratification shall be deposited with the Secretary-General of the United Nations.
3. This Convention shall be open from 28 July 1951 for accession by the States referred to in paragraph 2 of this article. Accession shall be effected by the deposit of an instrument of accession with the Secretary-General of the United Nations.

Article 40. Territorial application clause

1. Any State may, at the time of signature, ratification or accession, declare that this Convention shall extend to all or any of the territories for the international relations of which it is responsible. Such a declaration shall take effect when the Convention enters into force for the State concerned.
2. At any time thereafter any such extension shall be made by notification addressed to the Secretary-General of the United Nations and shall take effect as from the ninetieth day after the day of receipt by the Secretary-General of the United Nations of this notification, or as from the date of entry into force of the Convention for the State concerned, whichever is the later.
3. With respect to those territories to which this Convention is not extended at the time of signature, ratification or accession, each State concerned shall consider the possibility of taking the necessary steps in order to extend the application of this Convention to such territories, subject, where necessary for constitutional reasons, to the consent of the Governments of such territories.

Article 41. Federal clause

In the case of a Federal or non-unitary State, the following provisions shall apply:

(a) With respect to those articles of this Convention that come within the legislative jurisdiction of the federal legislative authority, the obligations of the Federal Government shall to this extent be the same as those of parties which are not Federal States;

(b) With respect to those articles of this Convention that come within the legislative jurisdiction of constituent States, provinces or cantons which are not, under the constitutional system of the Federation, bound to take legislative action, the Federal Government shall bring such articles with a favourable recommendation to the notice of the appropriate authorities of States, provinces or cantons at the earliest possible moment;

(c) A Federal State Party to this Convention shall, at the request of any other Contracting State transmitted through the Secretary-General of the United Nations, supply a statement of the law and practice of the Federation and its constituent units in regard to any particular provision of the Convention showing the extent to which effect has been given to that provision by legislative or other action.

Article 42. Reservations

1. At the time of signature, ratification or accession, any State may make reservations to articles of the Convention other than to articles 1, 3, 4, 16 (1), 33, 36–46 inclusive.

2. Any State making a reservation in accordance with paragraph 1 of this article may at any time withdraw the reservation by a communication to that effect addressed to the Secretary-General of the United Nations.

Article 43. Entry into force

1. This Convention shall come into force on the ninetieth day following the day of deposit of the sixth instrument of ratification or accession.

2. For each State ratifying or acceding to the Convention after the deposit of the sixth instrument of ratification or accession, the Convention shall enter into force on the ninetieth day following the date of deposit by such State of its instrument of ratification or accession.

Article 44. Denunciation

1. Any Contracting State may denounce this Convention at any time by a notification addressed to the Secretary-General of the United Nations.

2. Such denunciation shall take effect for the Contracting State concerned one year from the date upon which it is received by the Secretary-General of the United Nations.

3. Any State which has made a declaration or notification under article 40 may, at any time thereafter, by a notification to the Secretary-General of the United Nations, declare that the Convention shall cease to extend to such territory one year after the date of receipt of the notification by the Secretary-General.

Article 45. Revision

1. Any Contracting State may request revision of this Convention at any time by a notification addressed to the Secretary-General of the United Nations.

2. The General Assembly of the United Nations shall recommend the steps, if any, to be taken in respect of such request.

Article 46. Notifications by the Secretary-General of the United Nations

The Secretary-General of the United Nations shall inform all Members of the United Nations and non-member States referred to in article 39:

(a) Of declarations and notifications in accordance with section B of article 1;

(b) Of signatures, ratifications and accessions in accordance with article 39;

(c) Of declarations and notifications in accordance with article 40;

(d) Of reservations and withdrawals in accordance with article 42;

(e) Of the date on which this Convention will come into force in accordance with article 43;

(f) Of denunciations and notifications in accordance with article 44;

(g) Of requests for revision in accordance with article 45.

IN FAITH WHEREOF the undersigned, duly authorized, have signed this Convention on behalf of their respective Governments.

DONE at Geneva, this twenty-eighth day of July, one thousand nine hundred and fifty-one, in a single copy, of which the English and French texts are equally authentic and which shall remain deposited in the archives of the United Nations, and certified true copies of which shall be delivered to all Members of the United Nations and to the non-member States referred to in article 39.

6

Protocol Relating to the Status of Refugees, 1967

Note: the Protocol was 'taken note of with approval' in Economic and Social Council Resolution 1186 (XLI) of 18 November 1966 and was 'taken note of' by General Assembly Resolution 2198 (XXI) of 16 December 1966, 606 UNTS 267. Entry into force: 4 October 1967.

The States Parties to the present Protocol,

Considering that the Convention Relating to the Status of Refugees done at Geneva on 28 July 1951 (hereinafter referred to as the Convention) covers only those persons who have become refugees as a result of events occurring before 1 January 1951,

Considering that new refugee situations have arisen since the Convention was adopted and that the refugees concerned may therefore not fall within the scope of the Convention,

Considering that it is desirable that equal status should be enjoyed by all refugees covered by the definition in the Convention irrespective of the dateline 1 January 1951,

Have agreed as follows:

Article I GENERAL PROVISION

1. The States Parties to the present Protocol undertake to apply articles 2 to 34 inclusive of the Convention to refugees as hereinafter defined.

2. For the purpose of the present Protocol, the term "refugee" shall, except as regards the application of paragraph 3 of this article, mean any person within the definition of article 1 of the Convention as if the words "As a result of events occurring before 1 January 1951 and … " and the words " … as a result of such events", in article 1 A (2) were omitted.

3. The present Protocol shall be applied by the States Parties hereto without any geographic limitation, save that existing declarations made by States already Parties to the Convention in accordance with article 1 B (I) (a) of the Convention, shall, unless extended under article 1 B (2) thereof, apply also under the present Protocol.

Article II CO-OPERATION OF THE NATIONAL AUTHORITIES WITH THE UNITED NATIONS

1. The States Parties to the present Protocol undertake to co-operate with the Office of the United Nations High Commissioner for Refugees, or any other agency of the United Nations which may succeed it, in the exercise of its functions, and shall in particular facilitate its duty of supervising the application of the provisions of the present Protocol.

2. In order to enable the Office of the High Commissioner or any other agency of the United Nations which may succeed it, to make reports to the competent organs of

the United Nations, the States Parties to the present Protocol undertake to provide them with the information and statistical data requested, in the appropriate form, concerning:

(a) The condition of refugees;

(b) The implementation of the present Protocol;

(c) Laws, regulations and decrees which are, or may hereafter be, in force relating to refugees.

Article III INFORMATION ON NATIONAL LEGISLATION

The States Parties to the present Protocol shall communicate to the Secretary-General of the United Nations the laws and regulations which they may adopt to ensure the application of the present Protocol.

Article IV SETTLEMENT OF DISPUTES

Any dispute between States Parties to the present Protocol which relates to its interpretation or application and which cannot be settled by other means shall be referred to the International Court of Justice at the request of any one of the parties to the dispute.

Article V ACCESSION

The present Protocol shall be open for accession on behalf of all States Parties to the Convention and of any other State Member of the United Nations or member of any of the specialized agencies or to which an invitation to accede may have been addressed by the General Assembly of the United Nations. Accession shall be effected by the deposit of an instrument of accession with the Secretary-General of the United Nations.

Article VI FEDERAL CLAUSE

In the case of a Federal or non-unitary State, the following provisions shall apply:

(a) With respect to those articles of the Convention to be applied in accordance with article I, paragraph 1, of the present Protocol that come within the legislative jurisdiction of the federal legislative authority, the obligations of the Federal Government shall to this extent be the same as those of States Parties which are not Federal States;

(b) With respect to those articles of the Convention to be applied in accordance with article I, paragraph 1, of the present Protocol that come within the legislative jurisdiction of constituent States, provinces or cantons which are not, under the constitutional system of the Federation, bound to take legislative action, the Federal Government shall bring such articles with a favourable recommendation to the notice of the appropriate authorities of States, provinces or cantons at the earliest possible moment;

(c) A Federal State Party to the present Protocol shall, at the request of any other State Party hereto transmitted through the Secretary-General of the United Nations, supply a statement of the law and practice of the Federation and its constituent units in regard to any particular provision of the Convention to be applied in accordance with article I, paragraph 1, of the present Protocol, showing the extent to which effect has been given to that provision by legislative or other action.

Article VII RESERVATIONS AND DECLARATIONS

1. At the time of accession, any State may make reservations in respect of article IV of the present Protocol and in respect of the application in accordance with article I of the present Protocol of any provisions of the Convention other than those contained in articles 1, 3, 4, 16(1) and 33 thereof, provided that in the case of a State Party to the Convention reservations made under this article shall not extend to refugees in respect of whom the Convention applies.
2. Reservations made by States Parties to the Convention in accordance with article 42 thereof shall, unless withdrawn, be applicable in relation to their obligations under the present Protocol.
3. Any State making a reservation in accordance with paragraph 1 of this article may at any time withdraw such reservation by a communication to that effect addressed to the Secretary-General of the United Nations.
4. Declarations made under article 40, paragraphs 1 and 2, of the Convention by a State Party thereto which accedes to the present Protocol shall be deemed to apply in respect of the present Protocol, unless upon accession a notification to the contrary is addressed by the State Party concerned to the Secretary-General of the United Nations. The provisions of article 40, paragraphs 2 and 3, and of article 44, paragraph 3, of the Convention shall be deemed to apply mutatis mutandis to the present Protocol.

Article VIII ENTRY INTO PROTOCOL

1. The present Protocol shall come into force on the day of deposit of the sixth instrument of accession.
2. For each State acceding to the Protocol after the deposit of the sixth instrument of accession, the Protocol shall come into force on the date of deposit by such State of its instrument of accession.

Article IX DENUNCIATION

1. Any State Party hereto may denounce this Protocol at any time by a notification addressed to the Secretary-General of the United Nations.
2. Such denunciation shall take effect for the State Party concerned one year from the date on which it is received by the Secretary-General of the United Nations.

Article X NOTIFICATIONS BY THE SECRETARY-GENERAL OF THE UNITED NATIONS

The Secretary-General of the United Nations shall inform the States referred to in article V above of the date of entry into force, accessions, reservations and withdrawals of reservations to and denunciations of the present Protocol, and of declarations and notifications relating hereto.

Article XI DEPOSIT IN THE ARCHIVES OF THE SECRETARIAT OF THE UNITED NATIONS

A copy of the present Protocol, of which the Chinese, English, French, Russian and Spanish texts are equally authentic, signed by the President of the General Assembly and by the Secretary-General of the United Nations, shall be deposited in the archives of the Secretariat of the United Nations. The Secretary-General will transmit certified copies thereof to all States Members of the United Nations and to the other States referred to in article V above.

7

International Convention on the Elimination of All Forms of Racial Discrimination, 1965

Note: adopted by General Assembly Resolution 2106 (XX) 21 December 1965, Annex, 20 U.N. GAOR Supp. (No. 14) at 47, U.N. Doc. A/6014 (1966), 660 UNTS 195. Entry into force: 4 January 1969.

The States Parties to this Convention,

Considering that the Charter of the United Nations is based on the principles of the dignity and equality inherent in all human beings, and that all Member States have pledged themselves to take joint and separate action, in co-operation with the Organization, for the achievement of one of the purposes of the United Nations which is to promote and encourage universal respect for and observance of human rights and fundamental freedoms for all, without distinction as to race, sex, language or religion,

Considering that the Universal Declaration of Human Rights proclaims that all human beings are born free and equal in dignity and rights and that everyone is entitled to all the rights and freedoms set out therein, without distinction of any kind, in particular as to race, colour or national origin,

Considering that all human beings are equal before the law and are entitled to equal protection of the law against any discrimination and against any incitement to discrimination,

Considering that the United Nations has condemned colonialism and all practices of segregation and discrimination associated therewith, in whatever form and wherever they exist, and that the Declaration on the Granting of Independence to Colonial Countries and Peoples of 14 December 1960 (General Assembly resolution 1514 (XV)) has affirmed and solemnly proclaimed the necessity of bringing them to a speedy and unconditional end,

Considering that the United Nations Declaration on the Elimination of All Forms of Racial Discrimination of 20 November 1963 (General Assembly resolution 1904 (XVIII)) solemnly affirms the necessity of speedily eliminating racial discrimination throughout the world in all its forms and manifestations and of securing understanding of and respect for the dignity of the human person,

Convinced that any doctrine of superiority based on racial differentiation is scientifically false, morally condemnable, socially unjust and dangerous, and that there is no justification for racial discrimination, in theory or in practice, anywhere,

Reaffirming that discrimination between human beings on the grounds of race, colour or ethnic origin is an obstacle to friendly and peaceful relations among nations and is capable of disturbing peace and security among peoples and the harmony of persons living side by side even within one and the same State,

Convinced that the existence of racial barriers is repugnant to the ideals of any human society,

Alarmed by manifestations of racial discrimination still in evidence in some areas of the world and by governmental policies based on racial superiority or hatred, such as policies of apartheid, segregation or separation,

Resolved to adopt all necessary measures for speedily eliminating racial discrimination in all its forms and manifestations, and to prevent and combat racist doctrines and practices in order to promote understanding between races and to build an international community free from all forms of racial segregation and racial discrimination,

Bearing in mind the Convention concerning Discrimination in respect of Employment and Occupation adopted by the International Labour Organisation in 1958, and the Convention against Discrimination in Education adopted by the United Nations Educational, Scientific and Cultural Organization in 1960,

Desiring to implement the principles embodied in the United Nations Declaration on the Elimination of All Forms of Racial Discrimination and to secure the earliest adoption of practical measures to that end,

Have agreed as follows:

PART I

Article 1

1. In this Convention, the term "racial discrimination" shall mean any distinction, exclusion, restriction or preference based on race, colour, descent, or national or ethnic origin which has the purpose or effect of nullifying or impairing the recognition, enjoyment or exercise, on an equal footing, of human rights and fundamental freedoms in the political, economic, social, cultural or any other field of public life.
2. This Convention shall not apply to distinctions, exclusions, restrictions or preferences made by a State Party to this Convention between citizens and non-citizens.
3. Nothing in this Convention may be interpreted as affecting in any way the legal provisions of States Parties concerning nationality, citizenship or naturalization, provided that such provisions do not discriminate against any particular nationality.
4. Special measures taken for the sole purpose of securing adequate advancement of certain racial or ethnic groups or individuals requiring such protection as may be necessary in order to ensure such groups or individuals equal enjoyment or exercise of human rights and fundamental freedoms shall not be deemed racial discrimination, provided, however, that such measures do not, as a consequence, lead to the maintenance of separate rights for different racial groups and that they shall not be continued after the objectives for which they were taken have been achieved.

Article 2

1. States Parties condemn racial discrimination and undertake to pursue by all appropriate means and without delay a policy of eliminating racial discrimination in all its forms and promoting understanding among all races, and, to this end:

    (a) Each State Party undertakes to engage in no act or practice of racial discrimination against persons, groups of persons or institutions and to ensure that all public authorities and public institutions, national and local, shall act in conformity with this obligation;

    (b) Each State Party undertakes not to sponsor, defend or support racial discrimination by any persons or organizations;

    (c) Each State Party shall take effective measures to review governmental, national and local policies, and to amend, rescind or nullify any laws and regulations which have the effect of creating or perpetuating racial discrimination wherever it exists;

    (d) Each State Party shall prohibit and bring to an end, by all appropriate means, including legislation as required by circumstances, racial discrimination by any persons, group or organization;

    (e) Each State Party undertakes to encourage, where appropriate, integrationist multiracial organizations and movements and other means of eliminating barriers between races, and to discourage anything which tends to strengthen racial division.

2. States Parties shall, when the circumstances so warrant, take, in the social, economic, cultural and other fields, special and concrete measures to ensure the adequate development and protection of certain racial groups or individuals belonging to them, for the purpose of guaranteeing them the full and equal enjoyment of human rights and fundamental freedoms. These measures shall in no case entail as a consequence the maintenance of unequal or separate rights for different racial groups after the objectives for which they were taken have been achieved.

Article 3

States Parties particularly condemn racial segregation and apartheid and undertake to prevent, prohibit and eradicate all practices of this nature in territories under their jurisdiction.

Article 4

States Parties condemn all propaganda and all organizations which are based on ideas or theories of superiority of one race or group of persons of one colour or ethnic origin, or which attempt to justify or promote racial hatred and discrimination in any form, and undertake to adopt immediate and positive measures designed to eradicate all incitement to, or acts of, such discrimination and, to this end, with due regard to the principles embodied in the Universal Declaration of Human Rights and the rights expressly set forth in article 5 of this Convention, inter alia:

    (a) Shall declare an offence punishable by law all dissemination of ideas based on racial superiority or hatred, incitement to racial discrimination, as well as all acts of violence or incitement to such acts against any race or group of persons of another colour or ethnic origin, and also the provision of any assistance to racist activities, including the financing thereof;

(b) Shall declare illegal and prohibit organizations, and also organized and all other propaganda activities, which promote and incite racial discrimination, and shall recognize participation in such organizations or activities as an offence punishable by law;

(c) Shall not permit public authorities or public institutions, national or local, to promote or incite racial discrimination.

Article 5

In compliance with the fundamental obligations laid down in article 2 of this Convention, States Parties undertake to prohibit and to eliminate racial discrimination in all its forms and to guarantee the right of everyone, without distinction as to race, colour, or national or ethnic origin, to equality before the law, notably in the enjoyment of the following rights:

(a) The right to equal treatment before the tribunals and all other organs administering justice;

(b) The right to security of person and protection by the State against violence or bodily harm, whether inflicted by government officials or by any individual group or institution;

(c) Political rights, in particular the right to participate in elections-to vote and to stand for election-on the basis of universal and equal suffrage, to take part in the Government as well as in the conduct of public affairs at any level and to have equal access to public service;

(d) Other civil rights, in particular:

    (i) The right to freedom of movement and residence within the border of the State;

    (ii) The right to leave any country, including one's own, and to return to one's country;

    (iii) The right to nationality;

    (iv) The right to marriage and choice of spouse;

    (v) The right to own property alone as well as in association with others;

    (vi) The right to inherit;

    (vii) The right to freedom of thought, conscience and religion;

    (viii) The right to freedom of opinion and expression;

    (ix) The right to freedom of peaceful assembly and association;

(e) Economic, social and cultural rights, in particular:

    (i) The rights to work, to free choice of employment, to just and favourable conditions of work, to protection against unemployment, to equal pay for equal work, to just and favourable remuneration;

    (ii) The right to form and join trade unions;

    (iii) The right to housing;

    (iv) The right to public health, medical care, social security and social services;

    (v) The right to education and training;

    (vi) The right to equal participation in cultural activities;

(f) The right of access to any place or service intended for use by the general public, such as transport, hotels, restaurants, cafés, theatres and parks.

Article 6

States Parties shall assure to everyone within their jurisdiction effective protection and remedies, through the competent national tribunals and other State institutions, against any acts of racial discrimination which violate his human rights and fundamental freedoms contrary to this Convention, as well as the right to seek from such tribunals just and adequate reparation or satisfaction for any damage suffered as a result of such discrimination.

Article 7

States Parties undertake to adopt immediate and effective measures, particularly in the fields of teaching, education, culture and information, with a view to combating prejudices which lead to racial discrimination and to promoting understanding, tolerance and friendship among nations and racial or ethnical groups, as well as to propagating the purposes and principles of the Charter of the United Nations, the Universal Declaration of Human Rights, the United Nations Declaration on the Elimination of All Forms of Racial Discrimination, and this Convention.

PART II

Article 8

1. There shall be established a Committee on the Elimination of Racial Discrimination (hereinafter referred to as the Committee) consisting of eighteen experts of high moral standing and acknowledged impartiality elected by States Parties from among their nationals, who shall serve in their personal capacity, consideration being given to equitable geographical distribution and to the representation of the different forms of civilization as well as of the principal legal systems.
2. The members of the Committee shall be elected by secret ballot from a list of persons nominated by the States Parties. Each State Party may nominate one person from among its own nationals.
3. The initial election shall be held six months after the date of the entry into force of this Convention. At least three months before the date of each election the Secretary-General of the United Nations shall address a letter to the States Parties inviting them to submit their nominations within two months. The Secretary-General shall prepare a list in alphabetical order of all persons thus nominated, indicating the States Parties which have nominated them, and shall submit it to the States Parties.
4. Elections of the members of the Committee shall be held at a meeting of States Parties convened by the Secretary-General at United Nations Headquarters. At that meeting, for which two thirds of the States Parties shall constitute a quorum, the persons elected to the Committee shall be nominees who obtain the largest number of votes and an absolute majority of the votes of the representatives of States Parties present and voting.
5. (a) The members of the Committee shall be elected for a term of four years. However, the terms of nine of the members elected at the first election shall expire at the end of two years; immediately after the first election the names of these nine members shall be chosen by lot by the Chairman of the Committee;

(b) For the filling of casual vacancies, the State Party whose expert has ceased to function as a member of the Committee shall appoint another expert from among its nationals, subject to the approval of the Committee.

6. States Parties shall be responsible for the expenses of the members of the Committee while they are in performance of Committee duties.

Article 9

1. States Parties undertake to submit to the Secretary-General of the United Nations, for consideration by the Committee, a report on the legislative, judicial, administrative or other measures which they have adopted and which give effect to the provisions of this Convention:

(a) within one year after the entry into force of the Convention for the State concerned; and

(b) thereafter every two years and whenever the Committee so requests. The Committee may request further information from the States Parties.

2. The Committee shall report annually, through the Secretary General, to the General Assembly of the United Nations on its activities and may make suggestions and general recommendations based on the examination of the reports and information received from the States Parties. Such suggestions and general recommendations shall be reported to the General Assembly together with comments, if any, from States Parties.

Article 10

1. The Committee shall adopt its own rules of procedure.

2. The Committee shall elect its officers for a term of two years.

3. The secretariat of the Committee shall be provided by the Secretary General of the United Nations.

4. The meetings of the Committee shall normally be held at United Nations Headquarters.

Article 11

1. If a State Party considers that another State Party is not giving effect to the provisions of this Convention, it may bring the matter to the attention of the Committee. The Committee shall then transmit the communication to the State Party concerned. Within three months, the receiving State shall submit to the Committee written explanations or statements clarifying the matter and the remedy, if any, that may have been taken by that State.

2. If the matter is not adjusted to the satisfaction of both parties, either by bilateral negotiations or by any other procedure open to them, within six months after the receipt by the receiving State of the initial communication, either State shall have the right to refer the matter again to the Committee by notifying the Committee and also the other State.

3. The Committee shall deal with a matter referred to it in accordance with paragraph 2 of this article after it has ascertained that all available domestic remedies have been invoked and exhausted in the case, in conformity with the generally recognized principles of international law. This shall not be the rule where the application of the remedies is unreasonably prolonged.

4. In any matter referred to it, the Committee may call upon the States Parties concerned to supply any other relevant information.

5. When any matter arising out of this article is being considered by the Committee, the States Parties concerned shall be entitled to send a representative to take part in the proceedings of the Committee, without voting rights, while the matter is under consideration.

Article 12

1. (a) After the Committee has obtained and collated all the information it deems necessary, the Chairman shall appoint an ad hoc Conciliation Commission (hereinafter referred to as the Commission) comprising five persons who may or may not be members of the Committee. The members of the Commission shall be appointed with the unanimous consent of the parties to the dispute, and its good offices shall be made available to the States concerned with a view to an amicable solution of the matter on the basis of respect for this Convention;

   (b) If the States Parties to the dispute fail to reach agreement within three months on all or part of the composition of the Commission, the members of the Commission not agreed upon by the States parties to the dispute shall be elected by secret ballot by a two-thirds majority vote of the Committee from among its own members.

2. The members of the Commission shall serve in their personal capacity. They shall not be nationals of the States parties to the dispute or of a State not Party to this Convention.

3. The Commission shall elect its own Chairman and adopt its own rules of procedure.

4. The meetings of the Commission shall normally be held at United Nations Headquarters or at any other convenient place as determined by the Commission.

5. The secretariat provided in accordance with article 10, paragraph 3, of this Convention shall also service the Commission whenever a dispute among States Parties brings the Commission into being.

6. The States parties to the dispute shall share equally all the expenses of the members of the Commission in accordance with estimates to be provided by the Secretary-General of the United Nations.

7. The Secretary-General shall be empowered to pay the expenses of the members of the Commission, if necessary, before reimbursement by the States parties to the dispute in accordance with paragraph 6 of this article.

8. The information obtained and collated by the Committee shall be made available to the Commission, and the Commission may call upon the States concerned to supply any other relevant information.

Article 13

1. When the Commission has fully considered the matter, it shall prepare and submit to the Chairman of the Committee a report embodying its findings on all questions of fact relevant to the issue between the parties and containing such recommendations as it may think proper for the amicable solution of the dispute.

2. The Chairman of the Committee shall communicate the report of the Commission to each of the States parties to the dispute. These States shall, within three months, inform the Chairman of the Committee whether or not they accept the recommendations contained in the report of the Commission.

3. After the period provided for in paragraph 2 of this article, the Chairman of the Committee shall communicate the report of the Commission and the declarations of the States Parties concerned to the other States Parties to this Convention.

Article 14

1. A State Party may at any time declare that it recognizes the competence of the Committee to receive and consider communications from individuals or groups of individuals within its jurisdiction claiming to be victims of a violation by that State Party of any of the rights set forth in this Convention. No communication shall be received by the Committee if it concerns a State Party which has not made such a declaration.

2. Any State Party which makes a declaration as provided for in paragraph 1 of this article may establish or indicate a body within its national legal order which shall be competent to receive and consider petitions from individuals and groups of individuals within its jurisdiction who claim to be victims of a violation of any of the rights set forth in this Convention and who have exhausted other available local remedies.

3. A declaration made in accordance with paragraph 1 of this article and the name of any body established or indicated in accordance with paragraph 2 of this article shall be deposited by the State Party concerned with the Secretary-General of the United Nations, who shall transmit copies thereof to the other States Parties. A declaration may be withdrawn at any time by notification to the Secretary-General, but such a withdrawal shall not affect communications pending before the Committee.

4. A register of petitions shall be kept by the body established or indicated in accordance with paragraph 2 of this article, and certified copies of the register shall be filed annually through appropriate channels with the Secretary-General on the understanding that the contents shall not be publicly disclosed.

5. In the event of failure to obtain satisfaction from the body established or indicated in accordance with paragraph 2 of this article, the petitioner shall have the right to communicate the matter to the Committee within six months.

6. (a) The Committee shall confidentially bring any communication referred to it to the attention of the State Party alleged to be violating any provision of this Convention, but the identity of the individual or groups of individuals concerned shall not be revealed without his or their express consent. The Committee shall not receive anonymous communications;

   (b) Within three months, the receiving State shall submit to the Committee written explanations or statements clarifying the matter and the remedy, if any, that may have been taken by that State.

7. (a) The Committee shall consider communications in the light of all information made available to it by the State Party concerned and by the petitioner. The Committee shall not consider any communication from a petitioner unless it has ascertained that the petitioner has exhausted all available domestic remedies. However, this shall not be the rule where the application of the remedies is unreasonably prolonged;

   (b) The Committee shall forward its suggestions and recommendations, if any, to the State Party concerned and to the petitioner.

8. The Committee shall include in its annual report a summary of such communications and, where appropriate, a summary of the explanations and statements of the States Parties concerned and of its own suggestions and recommendations.

9. The Committee shall be competent to exercise the functions provided for in this article only when at least ten States Parties to this Convention are bound by declarations in accordance with paragraph 1 of this article.

Article 15

1. Pending the achievement of the objectives of the Declaration on the Granting of Independence to Colonial Countries and Peoples, contained in General Assembly resolution 1514 (XV) of 14 December 1960, the provisions of this Convention shall in no way limit the right of petition granted to these peoples by other international instruments or by the United Nations and its specialized agencies.

2. (a) The Committee established under article 8, paragraph 1, of this Convention shall receive copies of the petitions from, and submit expressions of opinion and recommendations on these petitions to, the bodies of the United Nations which deal with matters directly related to the principles and objectives of this Convention in their consideration of petitions from the inhabitants of Trust and Non-Self-Governing Territories and all other territories to which General Assembly resolution 1514 (XV) applies, relating to matters covered by this Convention which are before these bodies;

   (b) The Committee shall receive from the competent bodies of the United Nations copies of the reports concerning the legislative, judicial, administrative or other measures directly related to the principles and objectives of this Convention applied by the administering Powers within the Territories mentioned in subparagraph (a) of this paragraph, and shall express opinions and make recommendations to these bodies.

3. The Committee shall include in its report to the General Assembly a summary of the petitions and reports it has received from United Nations bodies, and the expressions of opinion and recommendations of the Committee relating to the said petitions and reports.

4. The Committee shall request from the Secretary-General of the United Nations all information relevant to the objectives of this Convention and available to him regarding the Territories mentioned in paragraph 2 (a) of this article.

Article 16

The provisions of this Convention concerning the settlement of disputes or complaints shall be applied without prejudice to other procedures for settling disputes or complaints in the field of discrimination laid down in the constituent instruments of, or conventions adopted by, the United Nations and its specialized agencies, and shall not prevent the States Parties from having recourse to other procedures for settling a dispute in accordance with general or special international agreements in force between them.

PART III

Article 17

1. This Convention is open for signature by any State Member of the United Nations or member of any of its specialized agencies, by any State Party to the Statute of the International Court of Justice, and by any other State which has been invited by the General Assembly of the United Nations to become a Party to this Convention.
2. This Convention is subject to ratification. Instruments of ratification shall be deposited with the Secretary-General of the United Nations.

Article 18

1. This Convention shall be open to accession by any State referred to in article 17, paragraph 1, of the Convention.
2. Accession shall be effected by the deposit of an instrument of accession with the Secretary-General of the United Nations.

Article 19

1. This Convention shall enter into force on the thirtieth day after the date of the deposit with the Secretary-General of the United Nations of the twenty-seventh instrument of ratification or instrument of accession.
2. For each State ratifying this Convention or acceding to it after the deposit of the twenty-seventh instrument of ratification or instrument of accession, the Convention shall enter into force on the thirtieth day after the date of the deposit of its own instrument of ratification or instrument of accession.

Article 20

1. The Secretary-General of the United Nations shall receive and circulate to all States which are or may become Parties to this Convention reservations made by States at the time of ratification or accession. Any State which objects to the reservation shall, within a period of ninety days from the date of the said communication, notify the Secretary-General that it does not accept it.
2. A reservation incompatible with the object and purpose of this Convention shall not be permitted, nor shall a reservation the effect of which would inhibit the operation of any of the bodies established by this Convention be allowed. A reservation shall be considered incompatible or inhibitive if at least two thirds of the States Parties to this Convention object to it.
3. Reservations may be withdrawn at any time by notification to this effect addressed to the Secretary-General. Such notification shall take effect on the date on which it is received.

Article 21

A State Party may denounce this Convention by written notification to the Secretary-General of the United Nations. Denunciation shall take effect one year after the date of receipt of the notification by the Secretary General.

Article 22

Any dispute between two or more States Parties with respect to the interpretation or application of this Convention, which is not settled by negotiation or by the procedures expressly provided for in this Convention, shall, at the request of any of the parties to the dispute, be referred to the International Court of Justice for decision, unless the disputants agree to another mode of settlement.

Article 23

1. A request for the revision of this Convention may be made at any time by any State Party by means of a notification in writing addressed to the Secretary-General of the United Nations.
2. The General Assembly of the United Nations shall decide upon the steps, if any, to be taken in respect of such a request.

Article 24

The Secretary-General of the United Nations shall inform all States referred to in article 17, paragraph 1, of this Convention of the following particulars:

    (a) Signatures, ratifications and accessions under articles 17 and 18;
    (b) The date of entry into force of this Convention under article 19;
    (c) Communications and declarations received under articles 14, 20 and 23;
    (d) Denunciations under article 21.

Article 25

1. This Convention, of which the Chinese, English, French, Russian and Spanish texts are equally authentic, shall be deposited in the archives of the United Nations.
2. The Secretary-General of the United Nations shall transmit certified copies of this Convention to all States belonging to any of the categories mentioned in article 17, paragraph 1, of the Convention.

8

International Covenant on Economic, Social and Cultural Rights, 1966

Note: adopted by General Assembly Resolution 2200A (XXI), 21 U.N.GAOR Supp. (No. 16) at 49, U.N. Doc. A/6316 (1966), 993 UNTS 3. Entry into force: 3 January 1976.

PREAMBLE

The States Parties to the present Covenant,

Considering that, in accordance with the principles proclaimed in the Charter of the United Nations, recognition of the inherent dignity and of the equal and inalienable rights of all members of the human family is the foundation of freedom, justice and peace in the world,

Recognizing that these rights derive from the inherent dignity of the human person,

Recognizing that, in accordance with the Universal Declaration of Human Rights, the ideal of free human beings enjoying freedom from fear and want can only be achieved if conditions are created whereby everyone may enjoy his economic, social and cultural rights, as well as his civil and political rights,

Considering the obligation of States under the Charter of the United Nations to promote universal respect for, and observance of, human rights and freedoms,

Realizing that the individual, having duties to other individuals and to the community to which he belongs, is under a responsibility to strive for the promotion and observance of the rights recognized in the present Covenant,

Agree upon the following articles:

PART I

Article 1

1. All peoples have the right of self-determination. By virtue of that right they freely determine their political status and freely pursue their economic, social and cultural development.
2. All peoples may, for their own ends, freely dispose of their natural wealth and resources without prejudice to any obligations arising out of international economic co-operation, based upon the principle of mutual benefit, and international law. In no case may a people be deprived of its own means of subsistence.
3. The States Parties to the present Covenant, including those having responsibility for the administration of Non-Self-Governing and Trust Territories, shall promote the

realization of the right of self-determination, and shall respect that right, in conformity with the provisions of the Charter of the United Nations.

PART II

Article 2

1. Each State Party to the present Covenant undertakes to take steps, individually and through international assistance and co-operation, especially economic and technical, to the maximum of its available resources, with a view to achieving progressively the full realization of the rights recognized in the present Covenant by all appropriate means, including particularly the adoption of legislative measures.
2. The States Parties to the present Covenant undertake to guarantee that the rights enunciated in the present Covenant will be exercised without discrimination of any kind as to race, colour, sex, language, religion, political or other opinion, national or social origin, property, birth or other status.
3. Developing countries, with due regard to human rights and their national economy, may determine to what extent they would guarantee the economic rights recognized in the present Covenant to non-nationals.

Article 3

The States Parties to the present Covenant undertake to ensure the equal right of men and women to the enjoyment of all economic, social and cultural rights set forth in the present Covenant.

Article 4

The States Parties to the present Covenant recognize that, in the enjoyment of those rights provided by the State in conformity with the present Covenant, the State may subject such rights only to such limitations as are determined by law only in so far as this may be compatible with the nature of these rights and solely for the purpose of promoting the general welfare in a democratic society.

Article 5

1. Nothing in the present Covenant may be interpreted as implying for any State, group or person any right to engage in any activity or to perform any act aimed at the destruction of any of the rights or freedoms recognized herein, or at their limitation to a greater extent than is provided for in the present Covenant.
2. No restriction upon or derogation from any of the fundamental human rights recognized or existing in any country in virtue of law, conventions, regulations or custom shall be admitted on the pretext that the present Covenant does not recognize such rights or that it recognizes them to a lesser extent.

PART III

Article 6

1. The States Parties to the present Covenant recognize the right to work, which includes the right of everyone to the opportunity to gain his living by work which he freely chooses or accepts, and will take appropriate steps to safeguard this right.

2. The steps to be taken by a State Party to the present Covenant to achieve the full realization of this right shall include technical and vocational guidance and training programmes, policies and techniques to achieve steady economic, social and cultural development and full and productive employment under conditions safeguarding fundamental political and economic freedoms to the individual.

Article 7

The States Parties to the present Covenant recognize the right of everyone to the enjoyment of just and favourable conditions of work which ensure, in particular:

  (a) Remuneration which provides all workers, as a minimum, with:
     (i) Fair wages and equal remuneration for work of equal value without distinction of any kind, in particular women being guaranteed conditions of work not inferior to those enjoyed by men, with equal pay for equal work;
    (ii) A decent living for themselves and their families in accordance with the provisions of the present Covenant;
  (b) Safe and healthy working conditions;
  (c) Equal opportunity for everyone to be promoted in his employment to an appropriate higher level, subject to no considerations other than those of seniority and competence;
  (d) Rest, leisure and reasonable limitation of working hours and periodic holidays with pay, as well as remuneration for public holidays.

Article 8

1. The States Parties to the present Covenant undertake to ensure:
  (a) The right of everyone to form trade unions and join the trade union of his choice, subject only to the rules of the organization concerned, for the promotion and protection of his economic and social interests. No restrictions may be placed on the exercise of this right other than those prescribed by law and which are necessary in a democratic society in the interests of national security or public order or for the protection of the rights and freedoms of others;
  (b) The right of trade unions to establish national federations or confederations and the right of the latter to form or join international trade-union organizations;
  (c) The right of trade unions to function freely subject to no limitations other than those prescribed by law and which are necessary in a democratic society in the interests of national security or public order or for the protection of the rights and freedoms of others;
  (d) The right to strike, provided that it is exercised in conformity with the laws of the particular country.

2. This article shall not prevent the imposition of lawful restrictions on the exercise of these rights by members of the armed forces or of the police or of the administration of the State.

3. Nothing in this article shall authorize States Parties to the International Labour Organisation Convention of 1948 concerning Freedom of Association and Protection of the Right to Organize to take legislative measures which would prejudice, or apply the law in such a manner as would prejudice, the guarantees provided for in that Convention.

Article 9
The States Parties to the present Covenant recognize the right of everyone to social security, including social insurance.

Article 10
The States Parties to the present Covenant recognize that:

1. The widest possible protection and assistance should be accorded to the family, which is the natural and fundamental group unit of society, particularly for its establishment and while it is responsible for the care and education of dependent children. Marriage must be entered into with the free consent of the intending spouses.

2. Special protection should be accorded to mothers during a reasonable period before and after childbirth. During such period working mothers should be accorded paid leave or leave with adequate social security benefits.

3. Special measures of protection and assistance should be taken on behalf of all children and young persons without any discrimination for reasons of parentage or other conditions. Children and young persons should be protected from economic and social exploitation. Their employment in work harmful to their morals or health or dangerous to life or likely to hamper their normal development should be punishable by law. States should also set age limits below which the paid employment of child labour should be prohibited and punishable by law.

Article 11
1. The States Parties to the present Covenant recognize the right of everyone to an adequate standard of living for himself and his family, including adequate food, clothing and housing, and to the continuous improvement of living conditions. The States Parties will take appropriate steps to ensure the realization of this right, recognizing to this effect the essential importance of international co-operation based on free consent.

2. The States Parties to the present Covenant, recognizing the fundamental right of everyone to be free from hunger, shall take, individually and through international co-operation, the measures, including specific programmes, which are needed:

   (a) To improve methods of production, conservation and distribution of food by making full use of technical and scientific knowledge, by disseminating knowledge of the principles of nutrition and by developing or reforming agrarian systems in such a way as to achieve the most efficient development and utilization of natural resources;

   (b) Taking into account the problems of both food-importing and food-exporting countries, to ensure an equitable distribution of world food supplies in relation to need.

Article 12

1. The States Parties to the present Covenant recognize the right of everyone to the enjoyment of the highest attainable standard of physical and mental health.
2. The steps to be taken by the States Parties to the present Covenant to achieve the full realization of this right shall include those necessary for:
   (a) The provision for the reduction of the stillbirth-rate and of infant mortality and for the healthy development of the child;
   (b) The improvement of all aspects of environmental and industrial hygiene;
   (c) The prevention, treatment and control of epidemic, endemic, occupational and other diseases;
   (d) The creation of conditions which would assure to all medical service and medical attention in the event of sickness.

Article 13

1. The States Parties to the present Covenant recognize the right of everyone to education. They agree that education shall be directed to the full development of the human personality and the sense of its dignity, and shall strengthen the respect for human rights and fundamental freedoms. They further agree that education shall enable all persons to participate effectively in a free society, promote understanding, tolerance and friendship among all nations and all racial, ethnic or religious groups, and further the activities of the United Nations for the maintenance of peace.
2. The States Parties to the present Covenant recognize that, with a view to achieving the full realization of this right:
   (a) Primary education shall be compulsory and available free to all;
   (b) Secondary education in its different forms, including technical and vocational secondary education, shall be made generally available and accessible to all by every appropriate means, and in particular by the progressive introduction of free education;
   (c) Higher education shall be made equally accessible to all, on the basis of capacity, by every appropriate means, and in particular by the progressive introduction of free education;
   (d) Fundamental education shall be encouraged or intensified as far as possible for those persons who have not received or completed the whole period of their primary education;
   (e) The development of a system of schools at all levels shall be actively pursued, an adequate fellowship system shall be established, and the material conditions of teaching staff shall be continuously improved.
3. The States Parties to the present Covenant undertake to have respect for the liberty of parents and, when applicable, legal guardians to choose for their children schools, other than those established by the public authorities, which conform to such minimum educational standards as may be laid down or approved by the State and to ensure the religious and moral education of their children in conformity with their own convictions.
4. No part of this article shall be construed so as to interfere with the liberty of individuals and bodies to establish and direct educational institutions, subject always

to the observance of the principles set forth in paragraph 1 of this article and to the requirement that the education given in such institutions shall conform to such minimum standards as may be laid down by the State.

Article 14

Each State Party to the present Covenant which, at the time of becoming a Party, has not been able to secure in its metropolitan territory or other territories under its jurisdiction compulsory primary education, free of charge, undertakes, within two years, to work out and adopt a detailed plan of action for the progressive implementation, within a reasonable number of years, to be fixed in the plan, of the principle of compulsory education free of charge for all.

Article 15

1. The States Parties to the present Covenant recognize the right of everyone:
   (a) To take part in cultural life;
   (b) To enjoy the benefits of scientific progress and its applications;
   (c) To benefit from the protection of the moral and material interests resulting from any scientific, literary or artistic production of which he is the author.
2. The steps to be taken by the States Parties to the present Covenant to achieve the full realization of this right shall include those necessary for the conservation, the development and the diffusion of science and culture.
3. The States Parties to the present Covenant undertake to respect the freedom indispensable for scientific research and creative activity.
4. The States Parties to the present Covenant recognize the benefits to be derived from the encouragement and development of international contacts and co-operation in the scientific and cultural fields.

PART IV

Article 16

1. The States Parties to the present Covenant undertake to submit in conformity with this part of the Covenant reports on the measures which they have adopted and the progress made in achieving the observance of the rights recognized herein.
2. (a) All reports shall be submitted to the Secretary-General of the United Nations, who shall transmit copies to the Economic and Social Council for consideration in accordance with the provisions of the present Covenant;
   (b) The Secretary-General of the United Nations shall also transmit to the specialized agencies copies of the reports, or any relevant parts therefrom, from States Parties to the present Covenant which are also members of these specialized agencies in so far as these reports, or parts therefrom, relate to any matters which fall within the responsibilities of the said agencies in accordance with their constitutional instruments.

Article 17

1. The States Parties to the present Covenant shall furnish their reports in stages, in accordance with a programme to be established by the Economic and Social Council

within one year of the entry into force of the present Covenant after consultation with the States Parties and the specialized agencies concerned.

2. Reports may indicate factors and difficulties affecting the degree of fulfilment of obligations under the present Covenant.

3. Where relevant information has previously been furnished to the United Nations or to any specialized agency by any State Party to the present Covenant, it will not be necessary to reproduce that information, but a precise reference to the information so furnished will suffice.

Article 18

Pursuant to its responsibilities under the Charter of the United Nations in the field of human rights and fundamental freedoms, the Economic and Social Council may make arrangements with the specialized agencies in respect of their reporting to it on the progress made in achieving the observance of the provisions of the present Covenant falling within the scope of their activities. These reports may include particulars of decisions and recommendations on such implementation adopted by their competent organs.

Article 19

The Economic and Social Council may transmit to the Commission on Human Rights for study and general recommendation or, as appropriate, for information the reports concerning human rights submitted by States in accordance with articles 16 and 17, and those concerning human rights submitted by the specialized agencies in accordance with article 18.

Article 20

The States Parties to the present Covenant and the specialized agencies concerned may submit comments to the Economic and Social Council on any general recommendation under article 19 or reference to such general recommendation in any report of the Commission on Human Rights or any documentation referred to therein.

Article 21

The Economic and Social Council may submit from time to time to the General Assembly reports with recommendations of a general nature and a summary of the information received from the States Parties to the present Covenant and the specialized agencies on the measures taken and the progress made in achieving general observance of the rights recognized in the present Covenant.

Article 22

The Economic and Social Council may bring to the attention of other organs of the United Nations, their subsidiary organs and specialized agencies concerned with furnishing technical assistance any matters arising out of the reports referred to in this part of the present Covenant which may assist such bodies in deciding, each within its field of competence, on the advisability of international measures likely to contribute to the effective progressive implementation of the present Covenant.

Article 23

The States Parties to the present Covenant agree that international action for the achievement of the rights recognized in the present Covenant includes such methods as the conclusion of conventions, the adoption of recommendations, the furnishing of technical assistance and the holding of regional meetings and technical meetings for the purpose of consultation and study organized in conjunction with the Governments concerned.

Article 24

Nothing in the present Covenant shall be interpreted as impairing the provisions of the Charter of the United Nations and of the constitutions of the specialized agencies which define the respective responsibilities of the various organs of the United Nations and of the specialized agencies in regard to the matters dealt with in the present Covenant.

Article 25

Nothing in the present Covenant shall be interpreted as impairing the inherent right of all peoples to enjoy and utilize fully and freely their natural wealth and resources.

PART V

Article 26

1. The present Covenant is open for signature by any State Member of the United Nations or member of any of its specialized agencies, by any State Party to the Statute of the International Court of Justice, and by any other State which has been invited by the General Assembly of the United Nations to become a party to the present Covenant.
2. The present Covenant is subject to ratification. Instruments of ratification shall be deposited with the Secretary-General of the United Nations.
3. The present Covenant shall be open to accession by any State referred to in paragraph 1 of this article.
4. Accession shall be effected by the deposit of an instrument of accession with the Secretary-General of the United Nations.
5. The Secretary-General of the United Nations shall inform all States which have signed the present Covenant or acceded to it of the deposit of each instrument of ratification or accession.

Article 27

1. The present Covenant shall enter into force three months after the date of the deposit with the Secretary-General of the United Nations of the thirty-fifth instrument of ratification or instrument of accession.
2. For each State ratifying the present Covenant or acceding to it after the deposit of the thirty-fifth instrument of ratification or instrument of accession, the present Covenant shall enter into force three months after the date of the deposit of its own instrument of ratification or instrument of accession.

Article 28

The provisions of the present Covenant shall extend to all parts of federal States without any limitations or exceptions.

Article 29

1. Any State Party to the present Covenant may propose an amendment and file it with the Secretary-General of the United Nations. The Secretary-General shall thereupon communicate any proposed amendments to the States Parties to the present Covenant with a request that they notify him whether they favour a conference of States Parties for the purpose of considering and voting upon the proposals. In the event that at least one third of the States Parties favours such a conference, the Secretary-General shall convene the conference under the auspices of the United Nations. Any amendment adopted by a majority of the States Parties present and voting at the conference shall be submitted to the General Assembly of the United Nations for approval.

2. Amendments shall come into force when they have been approved by the General Assembly of the United Nations and accepted by a two-thirds majority of the States Parties to the present Covenant in accordance with their respective constitutional processes.

3. When amendments come into force they shall be binding on those States Parties which have accepted them, other States Parties still being bound by the provisions of the present Covenant and any earlier amendment which they have accepted.

Article 30

Irrespective of the notifications made under article 26, paragraph 5, the Secretary-General of the United Nations shall inform all States referred to in paragraph 1 of the same article of the following particulars:

    (a) Signatures, ratifications and accessions under article 26;

    (b) The date of the entry into force of the present Covenant under article 27 and the date of the entry into force of any amendments under article 29.

Article 31

1. The present Covenant, of which the Chinese, English, French, Russian and Spanish texts are equally authentic, shall be deposited in the archives of the United Nations.

2. The Secretary-General of the United Nations shall transmit certified copies of the present Covenant to all States referred to in article 26.

9

Optional Protocol to the International Covenant on Economic, Social and Cultural Rights, 2008

Note: adopted by General Assembly Resolution 63/117 (2008), 10 December 2008. Registration No. 14531. Entry into force: 5 May 2013.

PREAMBLE

The States Parties to the present Protocol,

Considering that, in accordance with the principles proclaimed in the Charter of the United Nations, recognition of the inherent dignity and of the equal and inalienable rights of all members of the human family is the foundation of freedom, justice and peace in the world,

Noting that the Universal Declaration of Human Rights proclaims that all human beings are born free and equal in dignity and rights and that everyone is entitled to all the rights and freedoms set forth therein, without distinction of any kind, such as race, colour, sex, language, religion, political or other opinion, national or social origin, property, birth or other status,

Recalling that the Universal Declaration of Human Rights and the International Covenants on Human Rights recognize that the ideal of free human beings enjoying freedom from fear and want can only be achieved if conditions are created whereby everyone may enjoy civil, cultural, economic, political and social rights,

Reaffirming the universality, indivisibility, interdependence and interrelatedness of all human rights and fundamental freedoms,

Recalling that each State Party to the International Covenant on Economic, Social and Cultural Rights (hereinafter referred to as the Covenant) undertakes to take steps, individually and through international assistance and cooperation, especially economic and technical, to the maximum of its available resources, with a view to achieving progressively the full realization of the rights recognized in the Covenant by all appropriate means, including particularly the adoption of legislative measures,

Considering that, in order further to achieve the purposes of the Covenant and the implementation of its provisions, it would be appropriate to enable the Committee on Economic, Social and Cultural Rights (hereinafter referred to as the Committee) to carry out the functions provided for in the present Protocol,

Have agreed as follows:

Article 1
Competence of the Committee to receive and consider communications

1. A State Party to the Covenant that becomes a Party to the present Protocol recognizes the competence of the Committee to receive and consider communications as provided for by the provisions of the present Protocol.
2. No communication shall be received by the Committee if it concerns a State Party to the Covenant which is not a Party to the present Protocol.

Article 2
Communications

Communications may be submitted by or on behalf of individuals or groups of individuals, under the jurisdiction of a State Party, claiming to be victims of a violation of any of the economic, social and cultural rights set forth in the Covenant by that State Party. Where a communication is submitted on behalf of individuals or groups of individuals, this shall be with their consent unless the author can justify acting on their behalf without such consent.

Article 3
Admissibility

1. The Committee shall not consider a communication unless it has ascertained that all available domestic remedies have been exhausted. This shall not be the rule where the application of such remedies is unreasonably prolonged.
2. The Committee shall declare a communication inadmissible when:
   (a) It is not submitted within one year after the exhaustion of domestic remedies, except in cases where the author can demonstrate that it had not been possible to submit the communication within that time limit;
   (b) The facts that are the subject of the communication occurred prior to the entry into force of the present Protocol for the State Party concerned unless those facts continued after that date;
   (c) The same matter has already been examined by the Committee or has been or is being examined under another procedure of international investigation or settlement;
   (d) It is incompatible with the provisions of the Covenant;
   (e) It is manifestly ill-founded, not sufficiently substantiated or exclusively based on reports disseminated by mass media;
   (f) It is an abuse of the right to submit a communication; or when
   (g) It is anonymous or not in writing.

Article 4
Communications not revealing a clear disadvantage

The Committee may, if necessary, decline to consider a communication where it does not reveal that the author has suffered a clear disadvantage, unless the Committee considers that the communication raises a serious issue of general importance.

Article 5
Interim measures

1. At any time after the receipt of a communication and before a determination on the merits has been reached, the Committee may transmit to the State Party concerned for its urgent consideration a request that the State Party take such interim measures as may be necessary in exceptional circumstances to avoid possible irreparable damage to the victim or victims of the alleged violations.

2. Where the Committee exercises its discretion under paragraph 1 of the present article, this does not imply a determination on admissibility or on the merits of the communication.

Article 6
Transmission of the communication

1. Unless the Committee considers a communication inadmissible without reference to the State Party concerned, the Committee shall bring any communication submitted to it under the present Protocol confidentially to the attention of the State Party concerned.

2. Within six months, the receiving State Party shall submit to the Committee written explanations or statements clarifying the matter and the remedy, if any, that may have been provided by that State Party.

Article 7
Friendly settlement

1. The Committee shall make available its good offices to the parties concerned with a view to reaching a friendly settlement of the matter on the basis of the respect for the obligations set forth in the Covenant.

2. An agreement on a friendly settlement closes consideration of the communication under the present Protocol.

Article 8
Examination of communications

1. The Committee shall examine communications received under article 2 of the present Protocol in the light of all documentation submitted to it, provided that this documentation is transmitted to the parties concerned.

2. The Committee shall hold closed meetings when examining communications under the present Protocol.

3. When examining a communication under the present Protocol, the Committee may consult, as appropriate, relevant documentation emanating from other United Nations bodies, specialized agencies, funds, programmes and mechanisms, and other international organizations, including from regional human rights systems, and any observations or comments by the State Party concerned.

4. When examining communications under the present Protocol, the Committee shall consider the reasonableness of the steps taken by the State Party in accordance with Part II of the Covenant. In doing so, the Committee shall bear in mind that the State Party may adopt a range of possible policy measures for the implementation of the rights set forth in the Covenant.

Article 9
Follow-up to the views of the Committee

1. After examining a communication, the Committee shall transmit its views on the communication, together with its recommendations, if any, to the parties concerned.
2. The State Party shall give due consideration to the views of the Committee, together with its recommendations, if any, and shall submit to the Committee, within six months, a written response, including information on any action taken in the light of the views and recommendations of the Committee.
3. The Committee may invite the State Party to submit further information about any measures the State Party has taken in response to its views or recommendations, if any, including as deemed appropriate by the Committee, in the State Party's subsequent reports under articles 16 and 17 of the Covenant.

Article 10
Inter-State communications

1. A State Party to the present Protocol may at any time declare under this article that it recognizes the competence of the Committee to receive and consider communications to the effect that a State Party claims that another State Party is not fulfilling its obligations under the Covenant. Communications under this article may be received and considered only if submitted by a State Party that has made a declaration recognizing in regard to itself the competence of the Committee. No communication shall be received by the Committee if it concerns a State Party which has not made such a declaration. Communications received under this article shall be dealt with in accordance with the following procedure:
   (a) If a State Party to the present Protocol considers that another State Party is not fulfilling its obligations under the Covenant, it may, by written communication, bring the matter to the attention of that State Party. The State Party may also inform the Committee of the matter. Within three months after the receipt of the communication the receiving State shall afford the State that sent the communication an explanation, or any other statement in writing clarifying the matter which should include, to the extent possible and pertinent, reference to domestic procedures and remedies taken, pending or available in the matter;
   (b) If the matter is not settled to the satisfaction of both States Parties concerned within six months after the receipt by the receiving State of the initial communication, either State shall have the right to refer the matter to the Committee, by notice given to the Committee and to the other State;
   (c) The Committee shall deal with a matter referred to it only after it has ascertained that all available domestic remedies have been invoked and exhausted in the matter. This shall not be the rule where the application of the remedies is unreasonably prolonged;
   (d) Subject to the provisions of subparagraph (c) of the present paragraph the Committee shall make available its good offices to the States Parties concerned with a view to a friendly solution of the matter on the basis of the respect for the obligations set forth in the Covenant;
   (e) The Committee shall hold closed meetings when examining communications under the present article;

(f) In any matter referred to it in accordance with subparagraph (b) of the present paragraph, the Committee may call upon the States Parties concerned, referred to in subparagraph (b), to supply any relevant information;

(g) The States Parties concerned, referred to in subparagraph (b) of the present paragraph, shall have the right to be represented when the matter is being considered by the Committee and to make submissions orally and/or in writing;

(h) The Committee shall, with all due expediency after the date of receipt of notice under subparagraph (b) of the present paragraph, submit a report, as follows:

    (i) If a solution within the terms of subparagraph (d) of the present paragraph is reached, the Committee shall confine its report to a brief statement of the facts and of the solution reached;

    (ii) If a solution within the terms of subparagraph (d) is not reached, the Committee shall, in its report, set forth the relevant facts concerning the issue between the States Parties concerned. The written submissions and record of the oral submissions made by the States Parties concerned shall be attached to the report. The Committee may also communicate only to the States Parties concerned any views that it may consider relevant to the issue between them.

In every matter, the report shall be communicated to the States Parties concerned.

2. A declaration under paragraph 1 of the present article shall be deposited by the States Parties with the Secretary-General of the United Nations, who shall transmit copies thereof to the other States Parties. A declaration may be withdrawn at any time by notification to the Secretary-General. Such a withdrawal shall not prejudice the consideration of any matter that is the subject of a communication already transmitted under the present article; no further communication by any State Party shall be received under the present article after the notification of withdrawal of the declaration has been received by the Secretary-General, unless the State Party concerned has made a new declaration.

Article 11
Inquiry procedure

1. A State Party to the present Protocol may at any time declare that it recognizes the competence of the Committee provided for under this article.

2. If the Committee receives reliable information indicating grave or systematic violations by a State Party of any of the economic, social and cultural rights set forth in the Covenant, the Committee shall invite that State Party to cooperate in the examination of the information and to this end to submit observations with regard to the information concerned.

3. Taking into account any observations that may have been submitted by the State Party concerned as well as any other reliable information available to it, the Committee may designate one or more of its members to conduct an inquiry and to report urgently to the Committee. Where warranted and with the consent of the State Party, the inquiry may include a visit to its territory.

4. Such an inquiry shall be conducted confidentially and the cooperation of the State Party shall be sought at all stages of the proceedings.

5. After examining the findings of such an inquiry, the Committee shall transmit these findings to the State Party concerned together with any comments and recommendations.

6. The State Party concerned shall, within six months of receiving the findings, comments and recommendations transmitted by the Committee, submit its observations to the Committee.

7. After such proceedings have been completed with regard to an inquiry made in accordance with paragraph 2, the Committee may, after consultations with the State Party concerned, decide to include a summary account of the results of the proceedings in its annual report provided for in article 15.

8. Any State Party having made a declaration in accordance with paragraph 1 of the present article may, at any time, withdraw this declaration by notification to the Secretary-General.

Article 12
Follow-up to the inquiry procedure

1. The Committee may invite the State Party concerned to include in its report under articles 16 and 17 of the Covenant details of any measures taken in response to an inquiry conducted under article 11 of the present Protocol.

2. The Committee may, if necessary, after the end of the period of six months referred to in article 11, paragraph 6, invite the State Party concerned to inform it of the measures taken in response to such an inquiry.

Article 13
Protection measures

A State Party shall take all appropriate measures to ensure that individuals under its jurisdiction are not subjected to any form of ill-treatment or intimidation as a consequence of communicating with the Committee pursuant to the present Protocol.

Article 14
International assistance and cooperation

1. The Committee shall transmit, as it may consider appropriate, and with the consent of the State Party concerned, to United Nations specialized agencies, funds and programmes and other competent bodies, its views or recommendations concerning communications and inquiries that indicate a need for technical advice or assistance, along with the State Party's observations and suggestions, if any, on these views or recommendations.

2. The Committee may also bring to the attention of such bodies, with the consent of the State Party concerned, any matter arising out of communications considered under the present Protocol which may assist them in deciding, each within its field of competence, on the advisability of international measures likely to contribute to assisting States Parties in achieving progress in implementation of the rights recognized in the Covenant.

3. A trust fund shall be established in accordance with the relevant procedures of the General Assembly, to be administered in accordance with the financial regulations and rules of the United Nations, with a view to providing expert and technical assistance to States Parties, with the consent of the State Party concerned, for the enhanced implementation of the rights contained in the Covenant, thus contributing to building

national capacities in the area of economic, social and cultural rights in the context of the present Protocol.

4. The provisions of this article are without prejudice to the obligations of each State Party to fulfil its obligations under the Covenant.

Article 15
Annual report

The Committee shall include in its annual report a summary of its activities under the present Protocol.

Article 16
Dissemination and information

Each State Party undertakes to make widely known and to disseminate the Covenant and the present Protocol and to facilitate access to information about the views and recommendations of the Committee, in particular, on matters involving that State Party, and to do so in accessible formats for persons with disabilities.

Article 17
Signature, ratification and accession

1. The present Protocol is open for signature by any State that has signed, ratified or acceded to the Covenant.
2. The present Protocol is subject to ratification by any State that has ratified or acceded to the Covenant. Instruments of ratification shall be deposited with the Secretary-General of the United Nations.
3. The present Protocol shall be open to accession by any State that has ratified or acceded to the Covenant.
4. Accession shall be effected by the deposit of an instrument of accession with the Secretary-General of the United Nations.

Article 18
Entry into force

1. The present Protocol shall enter into force three months after the date of the deposit with the Secretary-General of the United Nations of the tenth instrument of ratification or accession.
2. For each State ratifying or acceding to the present Protocol, after the deposit of the tenth instrument of ratification or accession, the protocol shall enter into force three months after the date of the deposit of its instrument of ratification or accession.

Article 19
Amendments

1. Any State Party may propose an amendment to the present Protocol and submit it to the Secretary-General of the United Nations. The Secretary-General shall communicate any proposed amendments to States Parties, with a request to be notified whether they favour a meeting of States Parties for the purpose of considering and deciding upon the proposals. In the event that, within four months from the date of such communication, at least one third of the States Parties favour such a meeting, the

Secretary-General shall convene the meeting under the auspices of the United Nations. Any amendment adopted by a majority of two thirds of the States Parties present and voting shall be submitted by the Secretary-General to the General Assembly for approval and thereafter to all States Parties for acceptance.

2. An amendment adopted and approved in accordance with paragraph 1 of this article shall enter into force on the thirtieth day after the number of instruments of acceptance deposited reaches two thirds of the number of States Parties at the date of adoption of the amendment. Thereafter, the amendment shall enter into force for any State Party on the thirtieth day following the deposit of its own instrument of acceptance. An amendment shall be binding only on those States Parties which have accepted it.

Article 20
Denunciation

1. Any State Party may denounce the present Protocol at any time by written notification addressed to the Secretary-General of the United Nations. Denunciation shall take effect six months after the date of receipt of the notification by the Secretary-General.
2. Denunciation shall be without prejudice to the continued application of the provisions of the present Protocol to any communication submitted under articles 2 and 10 or to any procedure initiated under article 11 before the effective date of denunciation.

Article 21
Notification by the Secretary-General

The Secretary-General of the United Nations shall notify all States referred to in article 26, paragraph 1 of the Covenant of the following particulars:

(a) Signatures, ratifications and accessions under the present Protocol;

(b) The date of entry into force of the present Protocol and of any amendment under article 19;

(c) Any denunciation under article 20.

Article 22
Official languages

1. The present Protocol, of which the Arabic, Chinese, English, French, Russian and Spanish texts are equally authentic, shall be deposited in the archives of the United Nations.
2. The Secretary-General of the United Nations shall transmit certified copies of the present Protocol to all States referred to in article 26 of the Covenant.

10

Maastricht Guidelines on Violations of Economic, Social and Cultural Rights, 1997

Note: the Maastricht Guidelines were adopted by a group of experts meeting at Maastricht, Netherlands between 22 and 26 January 1997 so as to agree what was entailed in the violation of economic, social and cultural rights. They are not legally binding and are now a little dated but still useful in understanding what is meant by some of the terms in treaties protecting such rights.

INTRODUCTION

On the occasion of the 10th anniversary of the Limburg Principles on the Implementation of the International Covenant on Economic, Social and Cultural Rights (hereinafter 'the Limburg Principles'), a group of more than thirty experts met in Maastricht from 22–26 January 1997 at the invitation of the International Commission of Jurists (Geneva, Switzerland), the Urban Morgan Institute on Human Rights (Cincinnati, Ohio, USA) and the Centre for Human Rights of the Faculty of Law of Maastricht University (the Netherlands). The objective of this meeting was to elaborate on the Limburg Principles as regards the nature and scope of violations of economic, social and cultural rights and appropriate responses and remedies.

The participants unanimously agreed on the following guidelines which they understand to reflect the evolution of international law since 1986. These guidelines are designed to be of use to all who are concerned with understanding and determining violations of economic, social and cultural rights and in providing remedies thereto, in particular monitoring and adjudicating bodies at the national, regional and international levels.

THE MAASTRICHT GUIDELINES ON VIOLATIONS OF ECONOMIC, SOCIAL AND CULTURAL RIGHTS

I THE SIGNIFICANCE OF ECONOMIC, SOCIAL AND CULTURAL RIGHTS

1. Since the Limburg Principles were adopted in 1986, the economic and social conditions have declined at alarming rates for over 1.6 billion people, while they have advanced also at a dramatic pace for more than a quarter of the world's population. The gap between rich and poor has doubled in the last three decades, with the poorest fifth of the world's population receiving 1.4% of the global income and the richest fifth 85%. The impact of these disparities on the lives of people – especially the poor – is dramatic and renders the enjoyment of economic, social and cultural rights illusory for a significant portion of humanity.

2. Since the end of the Cold War, there has been a trend in all regions of the world to reduce the role of the state and to rely on the market to resolve problems of human welfare, often in response to conditions generated by international and national financial markets and institutions and in an effort to attract investments from the multinational enterprises whose wealth and power exceed that of many states. It is no longer taken for granted that the realization of economic, social and cultural rights depends significantly on action by the state, although, as a matter of international law, the state remains ultimately responsible for guaranteeing the realization of these rights. While the challenge of addressing violations of economic, social and cultural rights is rendered more complicated by these trends, it is more urgent than ever to take these rights seriously and, therefore, to deal with the accountability of governments for failure to meet their obligations in this area.

3. There have also been significant legal developments enhancing economic, social and cultural rights since 1986, including the emerging jurisprudence of the Committee on Economic, Social and Cultural Rights and the adoption of instruments, such as the revised European Social Charter of 1996 and the Additional Protocol to the European Charter Providing for a System of Collective Complaints, and the San Salvador Protocol to the American Convention on Human Rights in the Area of Economic, Social and Cultural Rights of 1988. Governments have made firm commitments to address more effectively economic, social and cultural rights within the framework of seven UN World Summits conferences (1992–1996). Moreover, the potential exists for improved accountability for violations of economic, social and cultural rights through the proposed Optional Protocols to the International Covenant on Economic, Social and Cultural Rights and the Convention on the Elimination of All Forms of Discrimination Against Women. Significant developments within national civil society movements and regional and international NGOs in the field of economic, social and cultural rights have taken place.

4. It is now undisputed that all human rights are indivisible, interdependent, interrelated and of equal importance for human dignity. Therefore, states are as responsible for violations of economic, social and cultural rights as they are for violations of civil and political rights.

5. As in the case of civil and political rights, the failure by a State Party to comply with a treaty obligation concerning economic, social and cultural rights is, under international law, a violation of that treaty. Building upon the Limburg Principles, the considerations below relate primarily to the International Covenant on Economic, Social and Cultural Rights (hereinafter "the Covenant"). They are equally relevant, however, to the interpretation and application of other norms of international and domestic law in the field of economic, social and cultural rights.

II THE MEANING OF VIOLATIONS OF ECONOMIC, SOCIAL AND CULTURAL RIGHTS

Obligations to respect, protect and fulfil

6. Like civil and political rights, economic, social and cultural rights impose three different types of obligations on States: the obligations to respect, protect and fulfil. Failure to perform any one of these three obligations constitutes a violation of such rights. The obligation to respect requires States to refrain from interfering with the enjoyment of

economic, social and cultural rights. Thus, the right to housing is violated if the State engages in arbitrary forced evictions. The obligation to protect requires States to prevent violations of such rights by third parties. Thus, the failure to ensure that private employers comply with basic labour standards may amount to a violation of the right to work or the right to just and favourable conditions of work. The obligation to fulfil requires States to take appropriate legislative, administrative, budgetary, judicial and other measures towards the full realization of such rights. Thus, the failure of States to provide essential primary health care to those in need may amount to a violation.

Obligations of conduct and of result

7. The obligations to respect, protect and fulfil each contain elements of obligation of conduct and obligation of result. The obligation of conduct requires action reasonably calculated to realize the enjoyment of a particular right. In the case of the right to health, for example, the obligation of conduct could involve the adoption and implementation of a plan of action to reduce maternal mortality. The obligation of result requires States to achieve specific targets to satisfy a detailed substantive standard. With respect to the right to health, for example, the obligation of result requires the reduction of maternal mortality to levels agreed at the 1994 Cairo International Conference on Population and Development and the 1995 Beijing Fourth World Conference on Women.

Margin of discretion

8. As in the case of civil and political rights, States enjoy a margin of discretion in selecting the means for implementing their respective obligations. State practice and the application of legal norms to concrete cases and situations by international treaty monitoring bodies as well as by domestic courts have contributed to the development of universal minimum standards and the common understanding of the scope, nature and limitation of economic, social and cultural rights. The fact that the full realization of most economic, social and cultural rights can only be achieved progressively, which in fact also applies to most civil and political rights, does not alter the nature of the legal obligation of States which requires that certain steps be taken immediately and others as soon as possible. Therefore, the burden is on the State to demonstrate that it is making measurable progress toward the full realization of the rights in question. The State cannot use the "progressive realization" provisions in article 2 of the Covenant as a pretext for non-compliance. Nor can the State justify derogations or limitations of rights recognized in the Covenant because of different social, religious and cultural backgrounds.

Minimum core obligations

9. Violations of the Covenant occur when a State fails to satisfy what the Committee on Economic, Social and Cultural Rights has referred to as "a minimum core obligation to ensure the satisfaction of, at the very least, minimum essential levels of each of the rights … Thus, for example, a State party in which any significant number of individuals is deprived of essential foodstuffs, of essential primary health care, of basic shelter and housing, or of the most basic forms of education is, prima facie, violating the Covenant." Such minimum core obligations apply irrespective of the availability of resources of the country concerned or any other factors and difficulties.

Availability of resources

10. In many cases, compliance with such obligations may be undertaken by most States with relative ease, and without significant resource implications. In other cases, however, full realization of the rights may depend upon the availability of adequate financial and material resources. Nonetheless, as established by Limburg Principles 25–28, and confirmed by the developing jurisprudence of the Committee on Economic, Social and Cultural Rights, resource scarcity does not relieve States of certain minimum obligations in respect of the implementation of economic, social and cultural rights.

State policies

11. A violation of economic, social and cultural rights occurs when a State pursues, by action or omission, a policy or practice which deliberately contravenes or ignores obligations of the Covenant, or fails to achieve the required standard of conduct or result. Furthermore, any discrimination on grounds of race, colour, sex, language, religion, political or other opinion, national or social origin, property, birth or other status with the purpose or effect of nullifying or impairing the equal enjoyment or exercise of economic, social and cultural rights constitutes a violation of the Covenant.

Gender discrimination

12. Discrimination against women in relation to the rights recognized in the Covenant, is understood in light of the standard of equality for women under the Convention on the Elimination of All Forms of Discrimination Against Women. That standard requires the elimination of all forms of discrimination against women including gender discrimination arising out of social, cultural and other structural disadvantages.

Inability to comply

13. In determining which actions or omissions amount to a violation of an economic, social or cultural right, it is important to distinguish the inability from the unwillingness of a State to comply with its treaty obligations. A State claiming that it is unable to carry out its obligation for reasons beyond its control has the burden of proving that this is the case. A temporary closure of an educational institution due to an earthquake, for instance, would be a circumstance beyond the control of the State, while the elimination of a social security scheme without an adequate replacement programme could be an example of unwillingness by the State to fulfil its obligations.

Violations through acts of commission

14. Violations of economic, social and cultural rights can occur through the direct action of States or other entities insufficiently regulated by States. Examples of such violations include:
    (a) The formal removal or suspension of legislation necessary for the continued enjoyment of an economic, social and cultural right that is currently enjoyed;
    (b) The active denial of such rights to particular individuals or groups, whether through legislated or enforced discrimination;
    (c) The active support for measures adopted by third parties which are inconsistent with economic, social and cultural rights;

(d) The adoption of legislation or policies which are manifestly incompatible with pre-existing legal obligations relating to these rights, unless it is done with the purpose and effect of increasing equality and improving the realization of economic, social and cultural rights for the most vulnerable groups;

(e) The adoption of any deliberately retrogressive measure that reduces the extent to which any such right is guaranteed;

(f) The calculated obstruction of, or halt to, the progressive realization of a right protected by the Covenant, unless the State is acting within a limitation permitted by the Covenant or it does so due to a lack of available resources or force majeure;

(g) The reduction or diversion of specific public expenditure, when such reduction or diversion results in the non-enjoyment of such rights and is not accompanied by adequate measures to ensure minimum subsistence rights for everyone.

Violations through acts of omission

15. Violations of economic, social, cultural rights can also occur through the omission or failure of States to take necessary measures stemming from legal obligations. Examples of such violations include:

(a) The failure to take appropriate steps as required under the Covenant;

(b) The failure to reform or repeal legislation which is manifestly inconsistent with an obligation of the Covenant;

(c) The failure to enforce legislation or put into effect policies designed to implement provisions of the Covenant;

(d) The failure to regulate activities of individuals or groups so as to prevent them from violating economic, social and cultural rights;

(e) The failure to utilize the maximum of available resources towards the full realization of the Covenant;

(f) The failure to monitor the realization of economic, social and cultural rights, including the development and application of criteria and indicators for assessing compliance;

(g) The failure to remove promptly obstacles which it is under a duty to remove to permit the immediate fulfilment of a right guaranteed by the Covenant;

(h) The failure to implement without delay a right which it is required by the Covenant to provide immediately;

(i) The failure to meet a generally accepted international minimum standard of achievement, which is within its powers to meet;

(j) The failure of a State to take into account its international legal obligations in the field of economic, social and cultural rights when entering into bilateral or multilateral agreements with other States, international organizations or multinational corporations.

III RESPONSIBILITY FOR VIOLATIONS

State responsibility

16. The violations referred to in section II are in principle imputable to the State within whose jurisdiction they occur. As a consequence, the State responsible must establish mechanisms to correct such violations, including monitoring investigation, prosecution, and remedies for victims.

Alien domination or occupation

17. Under circumstances of alien domination, deprivations of economic, social and cultural rights may be imputable to the conduct of the State exercising effective control over the territory in question. This is true under conditions of colonialism, other forms of alien domination and military occupation. The dominating or occupying power bears responsibility for violations of economic, social and cultural rights. There are also circumstances in which States acting in concert violate economic, social and cultural rights.

Acts by non-state entities

18. The obligation to protect includes the State's responsibility to ensure that private entities or individuals, including transnational corporations over which they exercise jurisdiction, do not deprive individuals of their economic, social and cultural rights. States are responsible for violations of economic, social and cultural rights that result from their failure to exercise due diligence in controlling the behaviour of such non-state actors.

Acts by international organizations

19. The obligations of States to protect economic, social and cultural rights extend also to their participation in international organizations, where they act collectively. It is particularly important for States to use their influence to ensure that violations do not result from the programmes and policies of the organizations of which they are members. It is crucial for the elimination of violations of economic, social and cultural rights for international organizations, including international financial institutions, to correct their policies and practices so that they do not result in deprivation of economic, social and cultural rights. Member States of such organizations, individually or through the governing bodies, as well as the secretariat and nongovernmental organizations should encourage and generalize the trend of several such organizations to revise their policies and programmes to take into account issues of economic, social and cultural rights, especially when these policies and programmes are implemented in countries that lack the resources to resist the pressure brought by international institutions on their decision-making affecting economic, social and cultural rights.

IV VICTIMS OF VIOLATIONS

Individuals and groups

20. As is the case with civil and political rights, both individuals and groups can be victims of violations of economic, social and cultural rights. Certain groups suffer disproportionate harm in this respect such as lower-income groups, women, indigenous and tribal peoples, occupied populations, asylum seekers, refugees and internally displaced persons, minorities, the elderly, children, landless peasants, persons with disabilities and the homeless.

Criminal sanctions

21. Victims of violations of economic, social and cultural rights should not face criminal sanctions purely because of their status as victims, for example, through laws criminalizing persons for being homeless. Nor should anyone be penalized for claiming their economic, social and cultural rights.

V REMEDIES AND OTHER RESPONSES TO VIOLATIONS

Access to remedies

22. Any person or group who is a victim of a violation of an economic, social or cultural right should have access to effective judicial or other appropriate remedies at both national and international levels.

Adequate reparation

23. All victims of violations of economic, social and cultural rights are entitled to adequate reparation, which may take the form of restitution, compensation, rehabilitation and satisfaction or guarantees of non-repetition.

No official sanctioning of violations

24. National judicial and other organs must ensure that any pronouncements they may make do not result in the official sanctioning of a violation of an international obligation of the State concerned. At a minimum, national judiciaries should consider the relevant provisions of international and regional human rights law as an interpretive aide in formulating any decisions relating to violations of economic, social and cultural rights.

National institutions

25. Promotional and monitoring bodies such as national ombudsman institutions and human rights commissions, should address violations of economic, social and cultural rights as vigorously as they address violations of civil and political rights.

Domestic application of international instruments

26. The direct incorporation or application of international instruments recognizing economic, social and cultural rights within the domestic legal order can significantly enhance the scope and effectiveness of remedial measures and should be encouraged in all cases.

Impunity

27. States should develop effective measures to preclude the possibility of impunity of any violation of economic, social and cultural rights and to ensure that no person who may be responsible for violations of such rights has immunity from liability for their actions.

Role of the legal professions

28. In order to achieve effective judicial and other remedies for victims of violations of economic, social and cultural rights, lawyers, judges, adjudicators, bar associations and the legal community generally should pay far greater attention to these violations in the exercise of their professions, as recommended by the International Commission of Jurists in the Bangalore Declaration and Plan of Action of 1995.

Special rapporteurs

29. In order to further strengthen international mechanisms with respect to preventing, early warning, monitoring and redressing violations of economic, social and cultural rights, the UN Commission on Human Rights should appoint thematic Special Rapporteurs in this field.

New standards

30. In order to further clarify the contents of States obligations to respect, protect and fulfil economic, social and cultural rights, States and appropriate international bodies should actively pursue the adoption of new standards on specific economic, social and cultural rights, in particular the right to work, to food, to housing and to health.

Optional protocols

31. The optional protocol providing for individual and group complaints in relation to the rights recognized in the Covenant should be adopted and ratified without delay. The proposed optional protocol to the Convention on the Elimination of All Forms of Discrimination Against Women should ensure that equal attention is paid to violations of economic, social and cultural rights. In addition, consideration should be given to the drafting of an optional complaints procedure under the Convention on the Rights of the Child.

Documenting and monitoring

32. Documenting and monitoring violations of economic, social and cultural rights should be carried out by all relevant actors, including NGOs, national governments and international organizations. It is indispensable that the relevant international organizations provide the support necessary for the implementation of international instruments in this field. The mandate of the United Nations High Commissioner for Human Rights includes the promotion of economic, social and cultural rights and it is essential that effective steps be taken urgently and that adequate staff and financial resources be devoted to this objective. Specialized agencies and other international organizations working in the economic and social spheres should also place appropriate emphasis upon economic, social and cultural rights as rights and, where they do not already do so, should contribute to efforts to respond to violations of these rights.

11

International Covenant on Civil and Political Rights, 1966

Note: adopted by General Assembly Resolution 2200A (XXI), 21 U.N. GAOR Supp. (No. 16) at 52, U.N. Doc. A/6316 (1966), 999 UNTS 17. Entry into force: 23 March 1976.

PREAMBLE

The States Parties to the present Covenant,

Considering that, in accordance with the principles proclaimed in the Charter of the United Nations, recognition of the inherent dignity and of the equal and inalienable rights of all members of the human family is the foundation of freedom, justice and peace in the world,

Recognizing that these rights derive from the inherent dignity of the human person,

Recognizing that, in accordance with the Universal Declaration of Human Rights, the ideal of free human beings enjoying civil and political freedom and freedom from fear and want can only be achieved if conditions are created whereby everyone may enjoy his civil and political rights, as well as his economic, social and cultural rights,

Considering the obligation of States under the Charter of the United Nations to promote universal respect for, and observance of, human rights and freedoms,

Realizing that the individual, having duties to other individuals and to the community to which he belongs, is under a responsibility to strive for the promotion and observance of the rights recognized in the present Covenant,

Agree upon the following articles:

PART I

Article 1

1. All peoples have the right of self-determination. By virtue of that right they freely determine their political status and freely pursue their economic, social and cultural development.
2. All peoples may, for their own ends, freely dispose of their natural wealth and resources without prejudice to any obligations arising out of international economic co-operation, based upon the principle of mutual benefit, and international law. In no case may a people be deprived of its own means of subsistence.
3. The States Parties to the present Covenant, including those having responsibility for the administration of Non-Self-Governing and Trust Territories, shall promote the

realization of the right of self-determination, and shall respect that right, in conformity with the provisions of the Charter of the United Nations.

PART II

Article 2

1. Each State Party to the present Covenant undertakes to respect and to ensure to all individuals within its territory and subject to its jurisdiction the rights recognized in the present Covenant, without distinction of any kind, such as race, colour, sex, language, religion, political or other opinion, national or social origin, property, birth or other status.
2. Where not already provided for by existing legislative or other measures, each State Party to the present Covenant undertakes to take the necessary steps, in accordance with its constitutional processes and with the provisions of the present Covenant, to adopt such legislative or other measures as may be necessary to give effect to the rights recognized in the present Covenant.
3. Each State Party to the present Covenant undertakes:
   (a) To ensure that any person whose rights or freedoms as herein recognized are violated shall have an effective remedy, notwithstanding that the violation has been committed by persons acting in an official capacity;
   (b) To ensure that any person claiming such a remedy shall have his right thereto determined by competent judicial, administrative or legislative authorities, or by any other competent authority provided for by the legal system of the State, and to develop the possibilities of judicial remedy;
   (c) To ensure that the competent authorities shall enforce such remedies when granted.

Article 3

The States Parties to the present Covenant undertake to ensure the equal right of men and women to the enjoyment of all civil and political rights set forth in the present Covenant.

Article 4

1. In time of public emergency which threatens the life of the nation and the existence of which is officially proclaimed, the States Parties to the present Covenant may take measures derogating from their obligations under the present Covenant to the extent strictly required by the exigencies of the situation, provided that such measures are not inconsistent with their other obligations under international law and do not involve discrimination solely on the ground of race, colour, sex, language, religion or social origin.
2. No derogation from articles 6, 7, 8 (paragraphs 1 and 2), 11, 15, 16 and 18 may be made under this provision.
3. Any State Party to the present Covenant availing itself of the right of derogation shall immediately inform the other States Parties to the present Covenant, through the intermediary of the Secretary-General of the United Nations, of the provisions from which it has derogated and of the reasons by which it was actuated. A further communication shall be made, through the same intermediary, on the date on which it terminates such derogation.

Article 5

1. Nothing in the present Covenant may be interpreted as implying for any State, group or person any right to engage in any activity or perform any act aimed at the destruction of any of the rights and freedoms recognized herein or at their limitation to a greater extent than is provided for in the present Covenant.
2. There shall be no restriction upon or derogation from any of the fundamental human rights recognized or existing in any State Party to the present Covenant pursuant to law, conventions, regulations or custom on the pretext that the present Covenant does not recognize such rights or that it recognizes them to a lesser extent.

PART III

Article 6

1. Every human being has the inherent right to life. This right shall be protected by law. No one shall be arbitrarily deprived of his life.
2. In countries which have not abolished the death penalty, sentence of death may be imposed only for the most serious crimes in accordance with the law in force at the time of the commission of the crime and not contrary to the provisions of the present Covenant and to the Convention on the Prevention and Punishment of the Crime of Genocide. This penalty can only be carried out pursuant to a final judgement rendered by a competent court.
3. When deprivation of life constitutes the crime of genocide, it is understood that nothing in this article shall authorize any State Party to the present Covenant to derogate in any way from any obligation assumed under the provisions of the Convention on the Prevention and Punishment of the Crime of Genocide.
4. Anyone sentenced to death shall have the right to seek pardon or commutation of the sentence. Amnesty, pardon or commutation of the sentence of death may be granted in all cases.
5. Sentence of death shall not be imposed for crimes committed by persons below eighteen years of age and shall not be carried out on pregnant women.
6. Nothing in this article shall be invoked to delay or to prevent the abolition of capital punishment by any State Party to the present Covenant.

Article 7

No one shall be subjected to torture or to cruel, inhuman or degrading treatment or punishment. In particular, no one shall be subjected without his free consent to medical or scientific experimentation.

Article 8

1. No one shall be held in slavery; slavery and the slave-trade in all their forms shall be prohibited.
2. No one shall be held in servitude.
3. (a) No one shall be required to perform forced or compulsory labour;
   (b) Paragraph 3 (a) shall not be held to preclude, in countries where imprisonment with hard labour may be imposed as a punishment for a crime, the performance of hard labour in pursuance of a sentence to such punishment by a competent court;

(c) For the purpose of this paragraph the term "forced or compulsory labour" shall not include:

(i) Any work or service, not referred to in subparagraph (b), normally required of a person who is under detention in consequence of a lawful order of a court, or of a person during conditional release from such detention;

(ii) Any service of a military character and, in countries where conscientious objection is recognized, any national service required by law of conscientious objectors;

(iii) Any service exacted in cases of emergency or calamity threatening the life or well-being of the community;

(iv) Any work or service which forms part of normal civil obligations.

Article 9

1. Everyone has the right to liberty and security of person. No one shall be subjected to arbitrary arrest or detention. No one shall be deprived of his liberty except on such grounds and in accordance with such procedure as are established by law.

2. Anyone who is arrested shall be informed, at the time of arrest, of the reasons for his arrest and shall be promptly informed of any charges against him.

3. Anyone arrested or detained on a criminal charge shall be brought promptly before a judge or other officer authorized by law to exercise judicial power and shall be entitled to trial within a reasonable time or to release. It shall not be the general rule that persons awaiting trial shall be detained in custody, but release may be subject to guarantees to appear for trial, at any other stage of the judicial proceedings, and, should occasion arise, for execution of the judgement.

4. Anyone who is deprived of his liberty by arrest or detention shall be entitled to take proceedings before a court, in order that that court may decide without delay on the lawfulness of his detention and order his release if the detention is not lawful.

5. Anyone who has been the victim of unlawful arrest or detention shall have an enforceable right to compensation.

Article 10

1. All persons deprived of their liberty shall be treated with humanity and with respect for the inherent dignity of the human person.

2. (a) Accused persons shall, save in exceptional circumstances, be segregated from convicted persons and shall be subject to separate treatment appropriate to their status as unconvicted persons;

(b) Accused juvenile persons shall be separated from adults and brought as speedily as possible for adjudication.

3. The penitentiary system shall comprise treatment of prisoners the essential aim of which shall be their reformation and social rehabilitation. Juvenile offenders shall be segregated from adults and be accorded treatment appropriate to their age and legal status.

Article 11

No one shall be imprisoned merely on the ground of inability to fulfil a contractual obligation.

Article 12

1. Everyone lawfully within the territory of a State shall, within that territory, have the right to liberty of movement and freedom to choose his residence.
2. Everyone shall be free to leave any country, including his own.
3. The above-mentioned rights shall not be subject to any restrictions except those which are provided by law, are necessary to protect national security, public order (ordre public), public health or morals or the rights and freedoms of others, and are consistent with the other rights recognized in the present Covenant.
4. No one shall be arbitrarily deprived of the right to enter his own country.

Article 13

An alien lawfully in the territory of a State Party to the present Covenant may be expelled therefrom only in pursuance of a decision reached in accordance with law and shall, except where compelling reasons of national security otherwise require, be allowed to submit the reasons against his expulsion and to have his case reviewed by, and be represented for the purpose before, the competent authority or a person or persons especially designated by the competent authority.

Article 14

1. All persons shall be equal before the courts and tribunals. In the determination of any criminal charge against him, or of his rights and obligations in a suit at law, everyone shall be entitled to a fair and public hearing by a competent, independent and impartial tribunal established by law. The press and the public may be excluded from all or part of a trial for reasons of morals, public order (ordre public) or national security in a democratic society, or when the interest of the private lives of the parties so requires, or to the extent strictly necessary in the opinion of the court in special circumstances where publicity would prejudice the interests of justice; but any judgement rendered in a criminal case or in a suit at law shall be made public except where the interest of juvenile persons otherwise requires or the proceedings concern matrimonial disputes or the guardianship of children.
2. Everyone charged with a criminal offence shall have the right to be presumed innocent until proved guilty according to law.
3. In the determination of any criminal charge against him, everyone shall be entitled to the following minimum guarantees, in full equality:
   (a) To be informed promptly and in detail in a language which he understands of the nature and cause of the charge against him;
   (b) To have adequate time and facilities for the preparation of his defence and to communicate with counsel of his own choosing;
   (c) To be tried without undue delay;
   (d) To be tried in his presence, and to defend himself in person or through legal assistance of his own choosing; to be informed, if he does not have legal assistance, of this right; and to have legal assistance assigned to him, in any case where the interests of justice so require, and without payment by him in any such case if he does not have sufficient means to pay for it;
   (e) To examine, or have examined, the witnesses against him and to obtain the attendance and examination of witnesses on his behalf under the same conditions as witnesses against him;

(f) To have the free assistance of an interpreter if he cannot understand or speak the language used in court;

(g) Not to be compelled to testify against himself or to confess guilt.

4. In the case of juvenile persons, the procedure shall be such as will take account of their age and the desirability of promoting their rehabilitation.

5. Everyone convicted of a crime shall have the right to his conviction and sentence being reviewed by a higher tribunal according to law.

6. When a person has by a final decision been convicted of a criminal offence and when subsequently his conviction has been reversed or he has been pardoned on the ground that a new or newly discovered fact shows conclusively that there has been a miscarriage of justice, the person who has suffered punishment as a result of such conviction shall be compensated according to law, unless it is proved that the non-disclosure of the unknown fact in time is wholly or partly attributable to him.

7. No one shall be liable to be tried or punished again for an offence for which he has already been finally convicted or acquitted in accordance with the law and penal procedure of each country.

Article 15

1. No one shall be held guilty of any criminal offence on account of any act or omission which did not constitute a criminal offence, under national or international law, at the time when it was committed. Nor shall a heavier penalty be imposed than the one that was applicable at the time when the criminal offence was committed. If, subsequent to the commission of the offence, provision is made by law for the imposition of the lighter penalty, the offender shall benefit thereby.

2. Nothing in this article shall prejudice the trial and punishment of any person for any act or omission which, at the time when it was committed, was criminal according to the general principles of law recognized by the community of nations.

Article 16

Everyone shall have the right to recognition everywhere as a person before the law.

Article 17

1. No one shall be subjected to arbitrary or unlawful interference with his privacy, family, home or correspondence, nor to unlawful attacks on his honour and reputation.

2. Everyone has the right to the protection of the law against such interference or attacks.

Article 18

1. Everyone shall have the right to freedom of thought, conscience and religion. This right shall include freedom to have or to adopt a religion or belief of his choice, and freedom, either individually or in community with others and in public or private, to manifest his religion or belief in worship, observance, practice and teaching.

2. No one shall be subject to coercion which would impair his freedom to have or to adopt a religion or belief of his choice.

3. Freedom to manifest one's religion or beliefs may be subject only to such limitations as are prescribed by law and are necessary to protect public safety, order, health, or morals or the fundamental rights and freedoms of others.

4. The States Parties to the present Covenant undertake to have respect for the liberty of parents and, when applicable, legal guardians to ensure the religious and moral education of their children in conformity with their own convictions.

Article 19

1. Everyone shall have the right to hold opinions without interference.
2. Everyone shall have the right to freedom of expression; this right shall include freedom to seek, receive and impart information and ideas of all kinds, regardless of frontiers, either orally, in writing or in print, in the form of art, or through any other media of his choice.
3. The exercise of the rights provided for in paragraph 2 of this article carries with it special duties and responsibilities. It may therefore be subject to certain restrictions, but these shall only be such as are provided by law and are necessary:
    (a) For respect of the rights or reputations of others;
    (b) For the protection of national security or of public order (ordre public), or of public health or morals.

Article 20

1. Any propaganda for war shall be prohibited by law.
2. Any advocacy of national, racial or religious hatred that constitutes incitement to discrimination, hostility or violence shall be prohibited by law.

Article 21

The right of peaceful assembly shall be recognized. No restrictions may be placed on the exercise of this right other than those imposed in conformity with the law and which are necessary in a democratic society in the interests of national security or public safety, public order (ordre public), the protection of public health or morals or the protection of the rights and freedoms of others.

Article 22

1. Everyone shall have the right to freedom of association with others, including the right to form and join trade unions for the protection of his interests.
2. No restrictions may be placed on the exercise of this right other than those which are prescribed by law and which are necessary in a democratic society in the interests of national security or public safety, public order (ordre public), the protection of public health or morals or the protection of the rights and freedoms of others. This article shall not prevent the imposition of lawful restrictions on members of the armed forces and of the police in their exercise of this right.
3. Nothing in this article shall authorize States Parties to the International Labour Organisation Convention of 1948 concerning Freedom of Association and Protection of the Right to Organize to take legislative measures which would prejudice, or to apply the law in such a manner as to prejudice, the guarantees provided for in that Convention.

Article 23

1. The family is the natural and fundamental group unit of society and is entitled to protection by society and the State.
2. The right of men and women of marriageable age to marry and to found a family shall be recognized.

3. No marriage shall be entered into without the free and full consent of the intending spouses.

4. States Parties to the present Covenant shall take appropriate steps to ensure equality of rights and responsibilities of spouses as to marriage, during marriage and at its dissolution. In the case of dissolution, provision shall be made for the necessary protection of any children.

Article 24

1. Every child shall have, without any discrimination as to race, colour, sex, language, religion, national or social origin, property or birth, the right to such measures of protection as are required by his status as a minor, on the part of his family, society and the State.

2. Every child shall be registered immediately after birth and shall have a name.

3. Every child has the right to acquire a nationality.

Article 25

Every citizen shall have the right and the opportunity, without any of the distinctions mentioned in article 2 and without unreasonable restrictions:

   (a) To take part in the conduct of public affairs, directly or through freely chosen representatives;
   (b) To vote and to be elected at genuine periodic elections which shall be by universal and equal suffrage and shall be held by secret ballot, guaranteeing the free expression of the will of the electors;
   (c) To have access, on general terms of equality, to public service in his country.

Article 26

All persons are equal before the law and are entitled without any discrimination to the equal protection of the law. In this respect, the law shall prohibit any discrimination and guarantee to all persons equal and effective protection against discrimination on any ground such as race, colour, sex, language, religion, political or other opinion, national or social origin, property, birth or other status.

Article 27

In those States in which ethnic, religious or linguistic minorities exist, persons belonging to such minorities shall not be denied the right, in community with the other members of their group, to enjoy their own culture, to profess and practise their own religion, or to use their own language.

PART IV

Article 28

1. There shall be established a Human Rights Committee (hereafter referred to in the present Covenant as the Committee). It shall consist of eighteen members and shall carry out the functions hereinafter provided.

2. The Committee shall be composed of nationals of the States Parties to the present Covenant who shall be persons of high moral character and recognized competence in

the field of human rights, consideration being given to the usefulness of the participation of some persons having legal experience.

3. The members of the Committee shall be elected and shall serve in their personal capacity.

Article 29

1. The members of the Committee shall be elected by secret ballot from a list of persons possessing the qualifications prescribed in article 28 and nominated for the purpose by the States Parties to the present Covenant.

2. Each State Party to the present Covenant may nominate not more than two persons. These persons shall be nationals of the nominating State.

3. A person shall be eligible for renomination.

Article 30

1. The initial election shall be held no later than six months after the date of the entry into force of the present Covenant.

2. At least four months before the date of each election to the Committee, other than an election to fill a vacancy declared in accordance with article 34, the Secretary-General of the United Nations shall address a written invitation to the States Parties to the present Covenant to submit their nominations for membership of the Committee within three months.

3. The Secretary-General of the United Nations shall prepare a list in alphabetical order of all the persons thus nominated, with an indication of the States Parties which have nominated them, and shall submit it to the States Parties to the present Covenant no later than one month before the date of each election.

4. Elections of the members of the Committee shall be held at a meeting of the States Parties to the present Covenant convened by the Secretary General of the United Nations at the Headquarters of the United Nations. At that meeting, for which two thirds of the States Parties to the present Covenant shall constitute a quorum, the persons elected to the Committee shall be those nominees who obtain the largest number of votes and an absolute majority of the votes of the representatives of States Parties present and voting.

Article 31

1. The Committee may not include more than one national of the same State.

2. In the election of the Committee, consideration shall be given to equitable geographical distribution of membership and to the representation of the different forms of civilization and of the principal legal systems.

Article 32

1. The members of the Committee shall be elected for a term of four years. They shall be eligible for re-election if renominated. However, the terms of nine of the members elected at the first election shall expire at the end of two years; immediately after the first election, the names of these nine members shall be chosen by lot by the Chairman of the meeting referred to in article 30, paragraph 4.

2. Elections at the expiry of office shall be held in accordance with the preceding articles of this part of the present Covenant.

Article 33

1. If, in the unanimous opinion of the other members, a member of the Committee has ceased to carry out his functions for any cause other than absence of a temporary character, the Chairman of the Committee shall notify the Secretary-General of the United Nations, who shall then declare the seat of that member to be vacant.
2. In the event of the death or the resignation of a member of the Committee, the Chairman shall immediately notify the Secretary-General of the United Nations, who shall declare the seat vacant from the date of death or the date on which the resignation takes effect.

Article 34

1. When a vacancy is declared in accordance with article 33 and if the term of office of the member to be replaced does not expire within six months of the declaration of the vacancy, the Secretary-General of the United Nations shall notify each of the States Parties to the present Covenant, which may within two months submit nominations in accordance with article 29 for the purpose of filling the vacancy.
2. The Secretary-General of the United Nations shall prepare a list in alphabetical order of the persons thus nominated and shall submit it to the States Parties to the present Covenant. The election to fill the vacancy shall then take place in accordance with the relevant provisions of this part of the present Covenant.
3. A member of the Committee elected to fill a vacancy declared in accordance with article 33 shall hold office for the remainder of the term of the member who vacated the seat on the Committee under the provisions of that article.

Article 35

The members of the Committee shall, with the approval of the General Assembly of the United Nations, receive emoluments from United Nations resources on such terms and conditions as the General Assembly may decide, having regard to the importance of the Committee's responsibilities.

Article 36

The Secretary-General of the United Nations shall provide the necessary staff and facilities for the effective performance of the functions of the Committee under the present Covenant.

Article 37

1. The Secretary-General of the United Nations shall convene the initial meeting of the Committee at the Headquarters of the United Nations.
2. After its initial meeting, the Committee shall meet at such times as shall be provided in its rules of procedure.
3. The Committee shall normally meet at the Headquarters of the United Nations or at the United Nations Office at Geneva.

Article 38

Every member of the Committee shall, before taking up his duties, make a solemn declaration in open committee that he will perform his functions impartially and conscientiously.

Article 39

1. The Committee shall elect its officers for a term of two years. They may be re-elected.
2. The Committee shall establish its own rules of procedure, but these rules shall provide, inter alia, that:
   (a) Twelve members shall constitute a quorum;
   (b) Decisions of the Committee shall be made by a majority vote of the members present.

Article 40

1. The States Parties to the present Covenant undertake to submit reports on the measures they have adopted which give effect to the rights recognized herein and on the progress made in the enjoyment of those rights:
   (a) Within one year of the entry into force of the present Covenant for the States Parties concerned;
   (b) Thereafter whenever the Committee so requests.
2. All reports shall be submitted to the Secretary-General of the United Nations, who shall transmit them to the Committee for consideration. Reports shall indicate the factors and difficulties, if any, affecting the implementation of the present Covenant.
3. The Secretary-General of the United Nations may, after consultation with the Committee, transmit to the specialized agencies concerned copies of such parts of the reports as may fall within their field of competence.
4. The Committee shall study the reports submitted by the States Parties to the present Covenant. It shall transmit its reports, and such general comments as it may consider appropriate, to the States Parties. The Committee may also transmit to the Economic and Social Council these comments along with the copies of the reports it has received from States Parties to the present Covenant.
5. The States Parties to the present Covenant may submit to the Committee observations on any comments that may be made in accordance with paragraph 4 of this article.

Article 41

1. A State Party to the present Covenant may at any time declare under this article that it recognizes the competence of the Committee to receive and consider communications to the effect that a State Party claims that another State Party is not fulfilling its obligations under the present Covenant. Communications under this article may be received and considered only if submitted by a State Party which has made a declaration recognizing in regard to itself the competence of the Committee. No communication shall be received by the Committee if it concerns a State Party which has not made such a declaration. Communications received under this article shall be dealt with in accordance with the following procedure:
   (a) If a State Party to the present Covenant considers that another State Party is not giving effect to the provisions of the present Covenant, it may, by written communication, bring the matter to the attention of that State Party. Within three months after the receipt of the communication the receiving State shall afford the State which sent the communication an explanation, or any other statement in writing clarifying the matter which should include, to the extent possible and pertinent, reference to domestic procedures and remedies taken, pending, or available in the matter;

(b) If the matter is not adjusted to the satisfaction of both States Parties concerned within six months after the receipt by the receiving State of the initial communication, either State shall have the right to refer the matter to the Committee, by notice given to the Committee and to the other State;

(c) The Committee shall deal with a matter referred to it only after it has ascertained that all available domestic remedies have been invoked and exhausted in the matter, in conformity with the generally recognized principles of international law. This shall not be the rule where the application of the remedies is unreasonably prolonged;

(d) The Committee shall hold closed meetings when examining communications under this article;

(e) Subject to the provisions of subparagraph (c), the Committee shall make available its good offices to the States Parties concerned with a view to a friendly solution of the matter on the basis of respect for human rights and fundamental freedoms as recognized in the present Covenant;

(f) In any matter referred to it, the Committee may call upon the States Parties concerned, referred to in subparagraph (b), to supply any relevant information;

(g) The States Parties concerned, referred to in subparagraph (b), shall have the right to be represented when the matter is being considered in the Committee and to make submissions orally and/or in writing;

(h) The Committee shall, within twelve months after the date of receipt of notice under subparagraph (b), submit a report:

    (i) If a solution within the terms of subparagraph (e) is reached, the Committee shall confine its report to a brief statement of the facts and of the solution reached;

    (ii) If a solution within the terms of subparagraph (e) is not reached, the Committee shall confine its report to a brief statement of the facts; the written submissions and record of the oral submissions made by the States Parties concerned shall be attached to the report. In every matter, the report shall be communicated to the States Parties concerned.

2. The provisions of this article shall come into force when ten States Parties to the present Covenant have made declarations under paragraph 1 of this article. Such declarations shall be deposited by the States Parties with the Secretary-General of the United Nations, who shall transmit copies thereof to the other States Parties. A declaration may be withdrawn at any time by notification to the Secretary-General. Such a withdrawal shall not prejudice the consideration of any matter which is the subject of a communication already transmitted under this article; no further communication by any State Party shall be received after the notification of withdrawal of the declaration has been received by the Secretary-General, unless the State Party concerned has made a new declaration.

Article 42

1. (a) If a matter referred to the Committee in accordance with article 41 is not resolved to the satisfaction of the States Parties concerned, the Committee may, with the prior consent of the States Parties concerned, appoint an ad hoc Conciliation Commission (hereinafter referred to as the Commission). The good offices of the Commission shall be made available to the States Parties concerned with a view to an amicable solution of the matter on the basis of respect for the present Covenant;

(b) The Commission shall consist of five persons acceptable to the States Parties concerned. If the States Parties concerned fail to reach agreement within three months on all or part of the composition of the Commission, the members of the Commission concerning whom no agreement has been reached shall be elected by secret ballot by a two-thirds majority vote of the Committee from among its members.

2. The members of the Commission shall serve in their personal capacity. They shall not be nationals of the States Parties concerned, or of a State not Party to the present Covenant, or of a State Party which has not made a declaration under article 41.

3. The Commission shall elect its own Chairman and adopt its own rules of procedure.

4. The meetings of the Commission shall normally be held at the Headquarters of the United Nations or at the United Nations Office at Geneva. However, they may be held at such other convenient places as the Commission may determine in consultation with the Secretary-General of the United Nations and the States Parties concerned.

5. The secretariat provided in accordance with article 36 shall also service the commissions appointed under this article.

6. The information received and collated by the Committee shall be made available to the Commission and the Commission may call upon the States Parties concerned to supply any other relevant information.

7. When the Commission has fully considered the matter, but in any event not later than twelve months after having been seized of the matter, it shall submit to the Chairman of the Committee a report for communication to the States Parties concerned:

(a) If the Commission is unable to complete its consideration of the matter within twelve months, it shall confine its report to a brief statement of the status of its consideration of the matter;

(b) If an amicable solution to the matter on the basis of respect for human rights as recognized in the present Covenant is reached, the Commission shall confine its report to a brief statement of the facts and of the solution reached;

(c) If a solution within the terms of subparagraph (b) is not reached, the Commission's report shall embody its findings on all questions of fact relevant to the issues between the States Parties concerned, and its views on the possibilities of an amicable solution of the matter. This report shall also contain the written submissions and a record of the oral submissions made by the States Parties concerned;

(d) If the Commission's report is submitted under subparagraph (c), the States Parties concerned shall, within three months of the receipt of the report, notify the Chairman of the Committee whether or not they accept the contents of the report of the Commission.

8. The provisions of this article are without prejudice to the responsibilities of the Committee under article 41.

9. The States Parties concerned shall share equally all the expenses of the members of the Commission in accordance with estimates to be provided by the Secretary-General of the United Nations.

10. The Secretary-General of the United Nations shall be empowered to pay the expenses of the members of the Commission, if necessary, before reimbursement by the States Parties concerned, in accordance with paragraph 9 of this article.

Article 43

The members of the Committee, and of the ad hoc conciliation commissions which may be appointed under article 42, shall be entitled to the facilities, privileges and immunities of experts on mission for the United Nations as laid down in the relevant sections of the Convention on the Privileges and Immunities of the United Nations.

Article 44

The provisions for the implementation of the present Covenant shall apply without prejudice to the procedures prescribed in the field of human rights by or under the constituent instruments and the conventions of the United Nations and of the specialized agencies and shall not prevent the States Parties to the present Covenant from having recourse to other procedures for settling a dispute in accordance with general or special international agreements in force between them.

Article 45

The Committee shall submit to the General Assembly of the United Nations, through the Economic and Social Council, an annual report on its activities.

PART V

Article 46

Nothing in the present Covenant shall be interpreted as impairing the provisions of the Charter of the United Nations and of the constitutions of the specialized agencies which define the respective responsibilities of the various organs of the United Nations and of the specialized agencies in regard to the matters dealt with in the present Covenant.

Article 47

Nothing in the present Covenant shall be interpreted as impairing the inherent right of all peoples to enjoy and utilize fully and freely their natural wealth and resources.

PART VI

Article 48

1. The present Covenant is open for signature by any State Member of the United Nations or member of any of its specialized agencies, by any State Party to the Statute of the International Court of Justice, and by any other State which has been invited by the General Assembly of the United Nations to become a Party to the present Covenant.
2. The present Covenant is subject to ratification. Instruments of ratification shall be deposited with the Secretary-General of the United Nations.
3. The present Covenant shall be open to accession by any State referred to in paragraph 1 of this article.

4. Accession shall be effected by the deposit of an instrument of accession with the Secretary-General of the United Nations.

5. The Secretary-General of the United Nations shall inform all States which have signed this Covenant or acceded to it of the deposit of each instrument of ratification or accession.

Article 49

1. The present Covenant shall enter into force three months after the date of the deposit with the Secretary-General of the United Nations of the thirty-fifth instrument of ratification or instrument of accession.

2. For each State ratifying the present Covenant or acceding to it after the deposit of the thirty-fifth instrument of ratification or instrument of accession, the present Covenant shall enter into force three months after the date of the deposit of its own instrument of ratification or instrument of accession.

Article 50

The provisions of the present Covenant shall extend to all parts of federal States without any limitations or exceptions.

Article 51

1. Any State Party to the present Covenant may propose an amendment and file it with the Secretary-General of the United Nations. The Secretary-General of the United Nations shall thereupon communicate any proposed amendments to the States Parties to the present Covenant with a request that they notify him whether they favour a conference of States Parties for the purpose of considering and voting upon the proposals. In the event that at least one third of the States Parties favours such a conference, the Secretary-General shall convene the conference under the auspices of the United Nations. Any amendment adopted by a majority of the States Parties present and voting at the conference shall be submitted to the General Assembly of the United Nations for approval.

2. Amendments shall come into force when they have been approved by the General Assembly of the United Nations and accepted by a two-thirds majority of the States Parties to the present Covenant in accordance with their respective constitutional processes. 3. When amendments come into force, they shall be binding on those States Parties which have accepted them, other States Parties still being bound by the provisions of the present Covenant and any earlier amendment which they have accepted.

Article 52

Irrespective of the notifications made under article 48, paragraph 5, the Secretary-General of the United Nations shall inform all States referred to in paragraph 1 of the same article of the following particulars:

   (a) Signatures, ratifications and accessions under article 48;
   (b) The date of the entry into force of the present Covenant under article 49 and the date of the entry into force of any amendments under article 51.

Article 53

1. The present Covenant, of which the Chinese, English, French, Russian and Spanish texts are equally authentic, shall be deposited in the archives of the United Nations.

2. The Secretary-General of the United Nations shall transmit certified copies of the present Covenant to all States referred to in article 48.

12

Optional Protocol to the International Covenant on Civil and Political Rights, 1966

Note: General Assembly Resolution 2200A (XXI), 21 U.N. GAOR Supp. (No. 16) at 59, U.N. Doc. A/6316 (1966), 999 UNTS 302. Entry into force: 23 March 1976.

The States Parties to the present Protocol,

Considering that in order further to achieve the purposes of the International Covenant on Civil and Political Rights (hereinafter referred to as the Covenant) and the implementation of its provisions it would be appropriate to enable the Human Rights Committee set up in part IV of the Covenant (hereinafter referred to as the Committee) to receive and consider, as provided in the present Protocol, communications from individuals claiming to be victims of violations of any of the rights set forth in the Covenant.

Have agreed as follows:

Article 1

A State Party to the Covenant that becomes a party to the present Protocol recognizes the competence of the Committee to receive and consider communications from individuals subject to its jurisdiction who claim to be victims of a violation by that State Party of any of the rights set forth in the Covenant.

No communication shall be received by the Committee if it concerns a State Party to the Covenant which is not a party to the present Protocol.

Article 2

Subject to the provisions of article 1, individuals who claim that any of their rights enumerated in the Covenant have been violated and who have exhausted all available domestic remedies may submit a written communication to the Committee for consideration.

Article 3

The Committee shall consider inadmissible any communication under the present Protocol which is anonymous, or which it considers to be an abuse of the right of submission of such communications or to be incompatible with the provisions of the Covenant.

Article 4

1. Subject to the provisions of article 3, the Committee shall bring any communications submitted to it under the present Protocol to the attention of the State Party to the present Protocol alleged to be violating any provision of the Covenant.
2. Within six months, the receiving State shall submit to the Committee written explanations or statements clarifying the matter and the remedy, if any, that may have been taken by that State.

Article 5

1. The Committee shall consider communications received under the present Protocol in the light of all written information made available to it by the individual and by the State Party concerned.
2. The Committee shall not consider any communication from an individual unless it has ascertained that:
   (a) The same matter is not being examined under another procedure of international investigation or settlement;
   (b) The individual has exhausted all available domestic remedies. This shall not be the rule where the application of the remedies is unreasonably prolonged.
3. The Committee shall hold closed meetings when examining communications under the present Protocol.
4. The Committee shall forward its views to the State Party concerned and to the individual.

Article 6

The Committee shall include in its annual report under article 45 of the Covenant a summary of its activities under the present Protocol.

Article 7

Pending the achievement of the objectives of resolution 1514(XV) adopted by the General Assembly of the United Nations on 14 December 1960 concerning the Declaration on the Granting of Independence to Colonial Countries and Peoples, the provisions of the present Protocol shall in no way limit the right of petition granted to these peoples by the Charter of the United Nations and other international conventions and instruments under the United Nations and its specialized agencies.

Article 8

1. The present Protocol is open for signature by any State which has signed the Covenant.
2. The present Protocol is subject to ratification by any State which has ratified or acceded to the Covenant. Instruments of ratification shall be deposited with the Secretary-General of the United Nations.
3. The present Protocol shall be open to accession by any State which has ratified or acceded to the Covenant.
4. Accession shall be effected by the deposit of an instrument of accession with the Secretary-General of the United Nations.
5. The Secretary-General of the United Nations shall inform all States which have signed the present Protocol or acceded to it of the deposit of each instrument of ratification or accession.

Article 9

1. Subject to the entry into force of the Covenant, the present Protocol shall enter into force three months after the date of the deposit with the Secretary-General of the United Nations of the tenth instrument of ratification or instrument of accession.
2. For each State ratifying the present Protocol or acceding to it after the deposit of the tenth instrument of ratification or instrument of accession, the present Protocol shall

enter into force three months after the date of the deposit of its own instrument of ratification or instrument of accession.

Article 10

The provisions of the present Protocol shall extend to all parts of federal States without any limitations or exceptions.

Article 11

1. Any State Party to the present Protocol may propose an amendment and file it with the Secretary-General of the United Nations. The Secretary-General shall thereupon communicate any proposed amendments to the States Parties to the present Protocol with a request that they notify him whether they favour a conference of States Parties for the purpose of considering and voting upon the proposal. In the event that at least one third of the States Parties favours such a conference, the Secretary-General shall convene the conference under the auspices of the United Nations. Any amendment adopted by a majority of the States Parties present and voting at the conference shall be submitted to the General Assembly of the United Nations for approval.
2. Amendments shall come into force when they have been approved by the General Assembly of the United Nations and accepted by a two-thirds majority of the States Parties to the present Protocol in accordance with their respective constitutional processes.
3. When amendments come into force, they shall be binding on those States Parties which have accepted them, other States Parties still being bound by the provisions of the present Protocol and any earlier amendment which they have accepted.

Article 12

1. Any State Party may denounce the present Protocol at any time by written notification addressed to the Secretary-General of the United Nations. Denunciation shall take effect three months after the date of receipt of the notification by the Secretary-General.
2. Denunciation shall be without prejudice to the continued application of the provisions of the present Protocol to any communication submitted under article 2 before the effective date of denunciation.

Article 13

Irrespective of the notifications made under article 8, paragraph 5, of the present Protocol, the Secretary-General of the United Nations shall inform all States referred to in article 48, paragraph 1, of the Covenant of the following particulars:
  (a) Signatures, ratifications and accessions under article 8;
  (b) The date of the entry into force of the present Protocol under article 9 and the date of the entry into force of any amendments under article 11;
  (c) Denunciations under article 12.

Article 14

1. The present Protocol, of which the Chinese, English, French, Russian and Spanish texts are equally authentic, shall be deposited in the archives of the United Nations.
2. The Secretary-General of the United Nations shall transmit certified copies of the present Protocol to all States referred to in article 48 of the Covenant.

13

Second Optional Protocol to the International Covenant on Civil and Political Rights, 1989

Note: Second Optional Protocol to the International Covenant on Civil and Political Rights, Aiming at the Abolition of the Death Penalty, General Assembly Resolution 44/128, annex, 44 U.N. GAOR Supp. (No. 49) at 207, U.N. Doc. A/44/49 (1989), adopted 15 December 1989, 1642 UNTS 414. Entry into force: 11 July 1991.

The States Parties to the present Protocol,

Believing that abolition of the death penalty contributes to enhancement of human dignity and progressive development of human rights,

Recalling article 3 of the Universal Declaration of Human Rights, adopted on 10 December 1948, and article 6 of the International Covenant on Civil and Political Rights, adopted on 16 December 1966,

Noting that article 6 of the International Covenant on Civil and Political Rights refers to abolition of the death penalty in terms that strongly suggest that abolition is desirable,

Convinced that all measures of abolition of the death penalty should be considered as progress in the enjoyment of the right to life,

Desirous to undertake hereby an international commitment to abolish the death penalty,

Have agreed as follows:

Article 1

1. No one within the jurisdiction of a State Party to the present Protocol shall be executed.
2. Each State Party shall take all necessary measures to abolish the death penalty within its jurisdiction.

Article 2

1. No reservation is admissible to the present Protocol, except for a reservation made at the time of ratification or accession that provides for the application of the death penalty in time of war pursuant to a conviction for a most serious crime of a military nature committed during wartime.
2. The State Party making such a reservation shall at the time of ratification or accession communicate to the Secretary-General of the United Nations the relevant provisions of its national legislation applicable during wartime.
3. The State Party having made such a reservation shall notify the Secretary-General of the United Nations of any beginning or ending of a state of war applicable to its territory.

Article 3

The States Parties to the present Protocol shall include in the reports they submit to the Human Rights Committee, in accordance with article 40 of the Covenant, information on the measures that they have adopted to give effect to the present Protocol.

Article 4

With respect to the States Parties to the Covenant that have made a declaration under article 41, the competence of the Human Rights Committee to receive and consider communications when a State Party claims that another State Party is not fulfilling its obligations shall extend to the provisions of the present Protocol, unless the State Party concerned has made a statement to the contrary at the moment of ratification or accession.

Article 5

With respect to the States Parties to the first Optional Protocol to the International Covenant on Civil and Political Rights adopted on 16 December 1966, the competence of the Human Rights Committee to receive and consider communications from individuals subject to its jurisdiction shall extend to the provisions of the present Protocol, unless the State Party concerned has made a statement to the contrary at the moment of ratification or accession.

Article 6

1. The provisions of the present Protocol shall apply as additional provisions to the Covenant.
2. Without prejudice to the possibility of a reservation under article 2 of the present Protocol, the right guaranteed in article 1, paragraph 1, of the present Protocol shall not be subject to any derogation under article 4 of the Covenant.

Article 7

1. The present Protocol is open for signature by any State that has signed the Covenant.
2. The present Protocol is subject to ratification by any State that has ratified the Covenant or acceded to it. Instruments of ratification shall be deposited with the Secretary-General of the United Nations.
3. The present Protocol shall be open to accession by any State that has ratified the Covenant or acceded to it.
4. Accession shall be effected by the deposit of an instrument of accession with the Secretary-General of the United Nations.
5. The Secretary-General of the United Nations shall inform all States that have signed the present Protocol or acceded to it of the deposit of each instrument of ratification or accession.

Article 8

1. The present Protocol shall enter into force three months after the date of the deposit with the Secretary-General of the United Nations of the tenth instrument of ratification or accession.
2. For each State ratifying the present Protocol or acceding to it after the deposit of the tenth instrument of ratification or accession, the present Protocol shall enter into force three months after the date of the deposit of its own instrument of ratification or accession.

Article 9

The provisions of the present Protocol shall extend to all parts of federal States without any limitations or exceptions.

Article 10

The Secretary-General of the United Nations shall inform all States referred to in article 48, paragraph 1, of the Covenant of the following particulars:

(a) Reservations, communications and notifications under article 2 of the present Protocol;

(b) Statements made under articles 4 or 5 of the present Protocol;

(c) Signatures, ratifications and accessions under article 7 of the present Protocol:

(d) The date of the entry into force of the present Protocol under article 8 thereof.

Article 11

1. The present Protocol, of which the Arabic, Chinese, English, French, Russian and Spanish texts are equally authentic, shall be deposited in the archives of the United Nations.

2. The Secretary-General of the United Nations shall transmit certified copies of the present Protocol to all States referred to in article 48 of the Covenant.

14

United Nations, Economic and Social Council, Siracusa Principles on the Limitation and Derogation Provisions in the International Covenant on Civil and Political Rights, 1985

Note: the Siracusa Principles were adopted by the (now defunct) UN Commission on Human Rights on 28 September 1984, they are not legally binding. U.N. Doc. E/CN.4/1985/4, Annex (1985).

I. The Limitation Clauses in the Covenant
    A. General Interpretative Principles Relating to the Justification of Limitations
    B. Interpretative Principles Relating to Specific Limitation Clauses
        i. "prescribed by law"
        ii. "in a democratic society"
        iii. "public order (ordre public)"
        iv. "public health"
        v. "public morals"
        vi. "national security"
        vii. "public safety"
        viii. "rights and freedoms of others," or "rights and reputations of others"
        ix. "restrictions on public trial"
II. Derogations in a Public Emergency
    A. "Public Emergency Which Threatens the Life of the Nation"
    B. Proclamation, Notification, and Termination of a Public Emergency
    C. "Strictly Required by the Exigencies of the Situation"
    D. Non-Derogable Rights
    E. Some General Principles on the Introduction and Application of a Public Emergency and Consequent Derogation Measures
    F. Recommendations Concerning the Functions and Duties of the Human Rights Committee and United Nations Bodies

PART I. THE LIMITATION CLAUSES IN THE COVENANT

A. GENERAL INTERPRETATIVE PRINCIPLES RELATING TO THE JUSTIFICATION OF LIMITATIONS*

(* The term "limitations" in these principles include the term "restrictions" as used in the Covenant.)

1. No limitations or grounds for applying them to rights guaranteed by the Covenant are permitted other than those contained in the terms of the Covenant itself.
2. The scope of a limitation referred to in the Covenant shall not be interpreted so as to jeopardize the essence of the right concerned.
3. All limitation clauses shall be interpreted strictly and in favor of the rights at issue.
4. All limitations shall be interpreted in the light and context of the particular right concerned.
5. All limitations on a right recognized by the Covenant shall be provided for by law and be compatible with the objects and purposes of the Covenant.
6. No limitation referred to in the Covenant shall be applied for any purpose other than that for which it has been prescribed.
7. No limitation shall be applied in an arbitrary manner.
8. Every limitation imposed shall be subject to the possibility of challenge to and remedy against its abusive application.
9. No limitation on a right recognized by the Covenant shall discriminate contrary to Article 2, paragraph 1.
10. Whenever a limitation is required in the terms of the Covenant to be "necessary," this term implies that the limitation:
    (a) is based on one of the grounds justifying limitations recognized by the relevant article of the Covenant,
    (b) responds to a pressing public or social need,
    (c) pursues a legitimate aim, and
    (d) is proportionate to that aim.
Any assessment as to the necessity of a limitation shall be made on objective considerations.
11. In applying a limitation, a state shall use no more restrictive means than are required for the achievement of the purpose of the limitation.
12. The burden of justifying a limitation upon a right guaranteed under the Covenant lies with the state.
13. The requirement expressed in Article 12 of the Covenant, that any restrictions be consistent with other rights recognized in the Covenant, is implicit in limitations to the other rights recognized in the Covenant.
14. The limitation clauses of the Covenant shall not be interpreted to restrict the exercise of any human rights protected to a greater extent by other international obligations binding upon the state.

B. INTERPRETATIVE PRINCIPLES RELATING TO SPECIFIC LIMITATION CLAUSES

i. "prescribed by law"

15. No limitation on the exercise of human rights shall be made unless provided for by national law of general application which is consistent with the Covenant and is in force at the time the limitation is applied.
16. Laws imposing limitations on the exercise of human rights shall not be arbitrary or unreasonable.
17. Legal rules limiting the exercise of human rights shall be clear and accessible to everyone.
18. Adequate safeguards and effective remedies shall be provided by law against illegal or abusive imposition or application of limitations on human rights.

ii. "in a democratic society"

19. The expression "in a democratic society" shall be interpreted as imposing a further restriction on the limitation clauses it qualifies.
20. The burden is upon a state imposing limitations so qualified to demonstrate that the limitations do not impair the democratic functioning of the society.
21. While there is no single model of a democratic society, a society which recognizes and respects the human rights set forth in the United Nations Charter and the Universal Declaration of Human Rights may be viewed as meeting this definition.

iii. "public order (ordre public)"

22. The expression "public order (ordre public)" as used in the Covenant may be defined as the sum of rules which ensure the functioning of society or the set of fundamental principles on which society is founded. Respect for human rights is part of public order (ordre public).
23. Public order (ordre public) shall be interpreted in the context of the purpose of the particular human right which is limited on this ground.
24. State organs or agents responsible for the maintenance of public order (ordre public) shall be subject to controls in the exercise of their power through the parliament, courts, or other competent independent bodies.

iv. "public health"

25. Public health may be invoked as a ground for limiting certain rights in order to allow a state to take measures dealing with a serious threat to the health of the population or individual members of the population. These measures must be specifically aimed at preventing disease or injury or providing care for the sick and injured.
26. Due regard shall be had to the international health regulations of the World Health Organization.

v. "public morals"

27. Since public morality varies over time and from one culture to another, a state which invokes public morality as a ground for restricting human rights, while enjoying a certain margin of discretion, shall demonstrate that the limitation in question is essential to the maintenance of respect for fundamental values of the community.

28. The margin of discretion left to states does not apply to the rule of non-discrimination as defined in the Covenant.

vi. "national security"

29. National security may be invoked to justify measures limiting certain rights only when they are taken to protect the existence of the nation or its territorial integrity or political independence against force or threat of force.

30. National security cannot be invoked as a reason for imposing limitations to prevent merely local or relatively isolated threats to law and order.

31. National security cannot be used as a pretext for imposing vague or arbitrary limitations and may only be invoked when there exists adequate safeguards and effective remedies against abuse.

32. The systematic violation of human rights undermines true national security and may jeopardize international peace and security. A state responsible for such violation shall not invoke national security as a justification for measures aimed at suppressing opposition to such violation or at perpetrating repressive practices against its population.

vii. "public safety"

33. Public safety means protection against danger to the safety of persons, to their life or physical integrity, or serious damage to their property.

34. The need to protect public safety can justify limitations provided by law. It cannot be used for imposing vague or arbitrary limitations and may only be invoked when there exist adequate safeguards and effective remedies against abuse.

viii. "rights and freedoms of others" or the "rights or reputations of others"

35. The scope of the rights and freedoms of others that may act as a limitation upon rights in the Covenant extends beyond the rights and freedoms recognized in the Covenant.

36. When a conflict exists between a right protected in the Covenant and one which is not, recognition and consideration should be given to the fact that the Covenant seeks to protect the most fundamental rights and freedoms. In this context especial weight should be afforded to rights not subject to limitations in the Covenant.

37. A limitation to a human right based upon the reputation of others shall not be used to protect the state and its officials from public opinion or criticism.

ix. "restrictions on public trial"

38. All trials shall be public unless the Court determines in accordance with law that:
   (a) the press or the public should be excluded from all or part of a trial on the basis of specific findings announced in open court showing that the interest of the private lives of the parties or their families or of juveniles so requires; or
   (b) the exclusion is strictly necessary to avoid publicity prejudicial to the fairness of the trial or endangering public morals, public order (ordre public), or national security in a democratic society.

PART II. DEROGATIONS IN A PUBLIC EMERGENCY

A. "PUBLIC EMERGENCY WHICH THREATENS THE LIFE OF THE NATION"

39. A state party may take measures derogating from its obligations under the International Covenant on Civil and Political Rights pursuant to Article 4 (hereinafter called "derogation measures") only when faced with a situation of exceptional and actual or imminent danger which threatens the life of the nation. A threat to the life of the nation is one that:
   (a) affects the whole of the population and either the whole or part of the territory of the State, and
   (b) threatens the physical integrity of the population, the political independence or the territorial integrity of the State or the existence or basic functioning of institutions indispensable to ensure and project the rights recognized in the Covenant.
40. Internal conflict and unrest that do not constitute a grave and imminent threat to the life of the nation cannot justify derogations under Article 4.
41. Economic difficulties per se cannot justify derogation measures.

B. PROCLAMATION, NOTIFICATION, AND TERMINATION OF A PUBLIC EMERGENCY

42. A state party derogating from its obligations under the Covenant shall make an official proclamation of the existence of the public emergency threatening the life of the nation.
43. Procedures under national law for the proclamation of a state of emergency shall be prescribed in advance of the emergency.
44. A state party derogating from its obligations under the Covenant shall immediately notify the other states parties to the Covenant, through the intermediary of the Secretary-General of the United Nations, of the provisions from which it has derogated and the reasons by which it was actuated.
45. The notification shall contain sufficient information to permit the states parties to exercise their rights and discharge their obligations under the Covenant. In particular it shall contain:
   (a) the provisions of the Covenant from which it has derogated;
   (b) a copy of the proclamation of emergency, together with the constitutional provisions, legislation, or decrees governing the state of emergency in order to assist the states parties to appreciate the scope of the derogation;

(c) the effective date of the imposition of the state of emergency and the period for which it has been proclaimed;

(d) an explanation of the reasons which actuated the government's decision to derogate, including a brief description of the factual circumstances leading up to the proclamation of the state of emergency; and

(e) a brief description of the anticipated effect of the derogation measures on the rights recognized by the Covenant, including copies of decrees derogating from these rights issued prior to the notification.

46. States parties may require that further information necessary to enable them to carry out their role under the Covenant be provided through the intermediary of the Secretary-General.

47. A state party which fails to make an immediate notification in due form of its derogation is in breach of its obligations to other states parties and may be deprived of the defenses otherwise available to it in procedures under the Covenant.

48. A state party availing itself of the right of derogation pursuant to Article 4 shall terminate such derogation in the shortest time required to bring to an end the public emergency which threatens the life of the nation.

49. The state party shall on the date on which it terminates such derogation inform the other state parties, through the intermediary of the Secretary-General of the United Nations, of the fact of the termination.

50. On the termination of a derogation pursuant to Article 4 all rights and freedoms protected by the Covenant shall be restored in full. A review of the continuing consequences of derogation measures shall be made as soon as possible. Steps shall be taken to correct injustices and to compensate those who have suffered injustice during or in consequence of the derogation measures.

C. "STRICTLY REQUIRED BY THE EXIGENCIES OF THE SITUATION"

51. The severity, duration, and geographic scope of any derogation measure shall be such only as are strictly necessary to deal with the threat to the life of the nation and are proportionate to its nature and extent.

52. The competent national authorities shall be under a duty to assess individually the necessity of any derogation measure taken or proposed to deal with the specific dangers posed by the emergency.

53. A measure is not strictly required by the exigencies of the situation where ordinary measures permissible under the specific limitations clauses of the Covenant would be adequate to deal with the threat to the life of the nation.

54. The principle of strict necessity shall be applied in an objective manner. Each measure shall be directed to an actual, clear, present, or imminent danger and may not be imposed merely because of an apprehension of potential danger.

55. The national constitution and laws governing states of emergency shall provide for prompt and periodic independent review by the legislature of the necessity for derogation measures.

56. Effective remedies shall be available to persons claiming that derogation measures affecting them are not strictly required by the exigencies of the situation.

57. In determining whether derogation measures are strictly required by the exigencies of the situation the judgment of the national authorities cannot be accepted as conclusive.

D. NON-DEROGABLE RIGHTS

58. No state party shall, even in time of emergency threatening the life of the nation, derogate from the Covenant's guarantees of the right to life; freedom from torture, cruel, inhuman or degrading treatment or punishment, and from medical or scientific experimentation without free consent; freedom from slavery or involuntary servitude; the right not to be imprisoned for contractual debt; the right not to be convicted or sentenced to a heavier penalty by virtue of retroactive criminal legislation; the right to recognition as a person before the law; and freedom of thought, conscience and religion. These rights are not derogable under any conditions even for the asserted purpose of preserving the life of the nation.

59. State parties to the Covenant, as part of their obligation to ensure the enjoyment of these rights to all persons within their jurisdiction (Art. 2(1)) and to adopt measures to secure an effective remedy for violations (Art. 2(3)), shall take special precautions in time of public emergency to ensure that neither official nor semi-official groups engage in a practice of arbitrary and extra-judicial killings or involuntary disappearances, that persons in detention are protected against torture and other forms of cruel, inhuman or degrading treatment or punishment, and that no persons are convicted or punished under laws or decrees with retroactive effect.

60. The ordinary courts shall maintain their jurisdiction, even in a time of public emergency, to adjudicate any complaint that a non-derogable right has been violated.

E. SOME GENERAL PRINCIPLES ON THE INTRODUCTION AND APPLICATION OF A PUBLIC EMERGENCY AND CONSEQUENT DEROGATION MEASURES

61. Derogation from rights recognized under international law in order to respond to a threat to the life of the nation is not exercised in a legal vacuum. It is authorized by law and as such it is subject to several legal principles of general application.

62. A proclamation of a public emergency shall be made in good faith based upon an objective assessment of the situation in order to determine to what extent, if any, it poses a threat to the life of the nation. A proclamation of a public emergency, and consequent derogations from Covenant obligations, that are not made in good faith are violations of international law.

63. The provisions of the Covenant allowing for certain derogations in a public emergency are to be interpreted restrictively.

64. In a public emergency the rule of law shall still prevail. Derogation is an authorized and limited prerogative in order to respond adequately to a threat to the life of the nation. The derogating state shall burden of justifying its actions under law.

65. The Covenant subordinates all procedures to the basic objectives of human rights. Article 5(1) of the Covenant sets definite limits to actions taken under the Covenant:

    Nothing in the present Covenant may be interpreted as implying for any State, group or person any right to engage in any activity or perform any act aimed at the destruction of any of the rights and freedoms recognized herein or at their limitation to a greater extent than is provided for in the present Covenant.

    Article 29(2) of the Universal Declaration of Human Rights sets out the ultimate purpose of law:

In the exercise of his rights and freedoms, everyone shall be subject only to such limitations as are determined by law solely for the purpose of securing due recognition and respect for the rights and freedoms of others and of meeting the just requirements of morality, public order and the general welfare in a democratic society.

These provisions apply with full force to claims that a situation constitutes a threat to the life of a nation and hence enables authorities to derogate.

66. A bona fide proclamation of the public emergency permits derogation from specified obligations in the Covenant, but does not authorize a general departure from international obligations. The Covenant in Article 4(1) and 5(2) expressly prohibits derogations which are inconsistent with other obligations under international law. In this regard, particular note should be taken of international obligations which apply in a public emergency under the Geneva and ILO Conventions.

67. In a situation of a non-international armed conflict a state party to the 1949 Geneva Conventions for the protection of war victims may under no circumstances suspend the right to a trial by a court offering the essential guarantees of independence and impartiality (Article 3 common to the 1949 Conventions). Under the 1977 additional Protocol II, the following rights with respect to penal prosecution shall be respected under all circumstances by state parties to the Protocol:

(a) the duty to give notice of changes without delay and to grant the necessary rights and means of defense;

(b) conviction only on the basis of individual penal responsibility;

(c) the right not to be convicted, or sentenced to a heavier penalty, by virtue of retroactive criminal legislation;

(d) presumption of innocence;

(e) trial in the presence of the accused;

(f) no obligation on the accused to testify against himself or to confess guilt;

(g) the duty to advise the convicted person on judicial and other remedies.

68. The ILO basic human rights conventions contain a number of rights dealing with such matters as forced labor, freedom of association, equality in employment and trade union and workers' rights which are not subject to derogation during an emergency; others permit derogation, but only to the extent strictly necessary to meet the exigencies of the situation.

69. No state, including those that are not parties to the Covenant, may suspend or violate, even in times of public emergency:

(a) the right to life;

(b) freedom from torture or cruel, inhuman or degrading treatment or punishment and from medical or scientific experimentation;

(c) the right not to be held in slavery or involuntary servitude; and,

(d) the right not to be subjected to retroactive criminal penalties as defined in the Covenant.

Customary international law prohibits in all circumstances the denial of such fundamental rights.

70. Although protections against arbitrary arrest and detention (Art. 9) and the right to a fair and public hearing in the determination of a criminal charge (Art. 14) may be subject to legitimate limitations if strictly required by the exigencies of an emergency situation, the denial of certain rights fundamental to human dignity can never

be strictly necessary in any conceivable emergency. Respect for these fundamental rights is essential in order to ensure enjoyment of non-derogable rights and to provide an effective remedy against their violation. In particular:

(a) all arrests and detention and the place of detention shall be recorded, if possible centrally, and make available to the public without delay;

(b) no person shall be detained for an indefinite period of time, whether detained pending judicial investigation or trial or detained without charge;

(c) no person shall be held in isolation without communication with his family, friend, or lawyer for longer than a few days, e.g., three to seven days;

(d) where persons are detained without charge the need of their continued detention shall be considered periodically by an independent review tribunal;

(e) any person charged with an offense shall be entitled to a fair trial by a competent, independent and impartial court established by law;

(f) civilians shall normally be tried by the ordinary courts; where it is found strictly necessary to establish military tribunals or special courts to try civilians, their competence, independence and impartiality shall be ensured and the need for them reviewed periodically by the competent authority;

(g) any person charged with a criminal offense shall be entitled to the presumption of innocence and to at least the following rights to ensure a fair trial:
— the right to be informed of the charges promptly, in detail and in a language he understands,
— the right to have adequate time and facilities to prepare the defense including the right to communicate confidentially with his lawyer,
— the right to a lawyer of his choice, with free legal assistance if he does not have the means to pay for it,
— the right to be present at the trial,
— the right not to be compelled to testify against himself or to make a confession,
— the right to obtain the attendance and examination of defense witnesses,
— the right to be tried in public save where the court orders otherwise on grounds of security with adequate safeguards to prevent abuse,
— the right to appeal to a higher court;

(h) an adequate record of the proceedings shall be kept in all cases; and,

(i) no person shall be tried or punished again for an offense for which he has already been convicted or acquitted.

F. RECOMMENDATIONS CONCERNING THE FUNCTIONS AND DUTIES OF THE HUMAN RIGHTS COMMITTEE AND UNITED NATIONS BODIES

71. In the exercise of its power to study, report, and make general comments on states parties' reports under Article 40 of the Covenant, the Human Rights Committee may and should examine the compliance of states parties with the provisions of Article 4. Likewise it may and should do so when exercising its powers in relevant cases under Article 41 and the Optional Protocol relating, respectively, to interstate and individual communications.

72. In order to determine whether the requirements of Article 4(1) and (2) have been met and for the purpose of supplementing information in states parties' reports, members of the Human Rights Committee, as persons of recognized competence in the field of human rights, may and should have regard to information they consider to be reliable provided by other inter-governmental bodies, non-governmental organizations, and individual communications.

73. The Human Rights Committee should develop a procedure for requesting additional reports under Article 40(1)(b) from states parties which have given notification of derogation under Article 4(3) or which are reasonably believed by the Committee to have imposed emergency measures subject to Article 4 constraints. Such additional reports should relate to questions concerning the emergency insofar as it affects the implementation of the Covenant and should be dealt with by the Committee at the earliest possible date.

74. In order to enable the Human Rights Committee to perform its fact-finding functions more effectively, the committee should develop its procedures for the consideration of communications under the Optional Protocol to permit the hearing of oral submissions and evidence as well as visits to states parties alleged to be in violation of the Covenant. If necessary, the states parties to the Optional Protocol should consider amending it to this effect.

75. The United Nations Commission on Human Rights should request its Sub-Commission on Prevention of Discrimination and Protection of Minorities to prepare an annual list if states, whether parties to the Covenant or not, that proclaim, maintain, or terminate a public emergency together with:
    (a) in the case of a state party, the proclamation and notification; and,
    (b) in the case of other states, any available and apparently reliable information concerning the proclamation, threat to the life of the nation, derogation measures and their proportionality, non-discrimination, and respect for non-derogable rights.

76. The United Nations Commission on Human Rights and its Sub-Commission should continue to utilize the technique of appointment of special rapporteurs and investigatory and fact-finding bodies in relation to prolonged public emergencies.

15

Convention on the Elimination of All Forms of Discrimination Against Women, 1979

Note: adopted by General Assembly Resolution. 34/180, on 18 December 1979, 34 U.N. GAOR Supp. (No. 46) at p.193, U.N. Doc. A/34/46, 1249 UNTS 13. Entry into force: 3 September 1981.

The States Parties to the present Convention,

Noting that the Charter of the United Nations reaffirms faith in fundamental human rights, in the dignity and worth of the human person and in the equal rights of men and women,

Noting that the Universal Declaration of Human Rights affirms the principle of the inadmissibility of discrimination and proclaims that all human beings are born free and equal in dignity and rights and that everyone is entitled to all the rights and freedoms set forth therein, without distinction of any kind, including distinction based on sex,

Noting that the States Parties to the International Covenants on Human Rights have the obligation to ensure the equal rights of men and women to enjoy all economic, social, cultural, civil and political rights,

Considering the international conventions concluded under the auspices of the United Nations and the specialized agencies promoting equality of rights of men and women,

Noting also the resolutions, declarations and recommendations adopted by the United Nations and the specialized agencies promoting equality of rights of men and women,

Concerned, however, that despite these various instruments extensive discrimination against women continues to exist,

Recalling that discrimination against women violates the principles of equality of rights and respect for human dignity, is an obstacle to the participation of women, on equal terms with men, in the political, social, economic and cultural life of their countries, hampers the growth of the prosperity of society and the family and makes more difficult the full development of the potentialities of women in the service of their countries and of humanity,

Concerned that in situations of poverty women have the least access to food, health, education, training and opportunities for employment and other needs,

Convinced that the establishment of the new international economic order based on equity and justice will contribute significantly towards the promotion of equality between men and women,

Emphasizing that the eradication of apartheid, all forms of racism, racial discrimination, colonialism, neo-colonialism, aggression, foreign occupation and domination and interference in the internal affairs of States is essential to the full enjoyment of the rights of men and women,

Affirming that the strengthening of international peace and security, the relaxation of international tension, mutual co-operation among all States irrespective of their social and economic systems, general and complete disarmament, in particular nuclear disarmament under strict and effective international control, the affirmation of the principles of justice, equality and mutual benefit in relations among countries and the realization of the right of peoples under alien and colonial domination and foreign occupation to self-determination and independence, as well as respect for national sovereignty and territorial integrity, will promote social progress and development and as a consequence will contribute to the attainment of full equality between men and women,

Convinced that the full and complete development of a country, the welfare of the world and the cause of peace require the maximum participation of women on equal terms with men in all fields,

Bearing in mind the great contribution of women to the welfare of the family and to the development of society, so far not fully recognized, the social significance of maternity and the role of both parents in the family and in the upbringing of children, and aware that the role of women in procreation should not be a basis for discrimination but that the upbringing of children requires a sharing of responsibility between men and women and society as a whole,

Aware that a change in the traditional role of men as well as the role of women in society and in the family is needed to achieve full equality between men and women,

Determined to implement the principles set forth in the Declaration on the Elimination of Discrimination against Women and, for that purpose, to adopt the measures required for the elimination of such discrimination in all its forms and manifestations,

Have agreed on the following:

PART I

Article 1

For the purposes of the present Convention, the term "discrimination against women" shall mean any distinction, exclusion or restriction made on the basis of sex which has the effect or purpose of impairing or nullifying the recognition, enjoyment or exercise by women, irrespective of their marital status, on a basis of equality of men and women, of human rights and fundamental freedoms in the political, economic, social, cultural, civil or any other field.

Article 2

States Parties condemn discrimination against women in all its forms, agree to pursue by all appropriate means and without delay a policy of eliminating discrimination against women and, to this end, undertake:

(a) To embody the principle of the equality of men and women in their national constitutions or other appropriate legislation if not yet incorporated therein and to ensure, through law and other appropriate means, the practical realization of this principle;

(b) To adopt appropriate legislative and other measures, including sanctions where appropriate, prohibiting all discrimination against women;

(c) To establish legal protection of the rights of women on an equal basis with men and to ensure through competent national tribunals and other public institutions the effective protection of women against any act of discrimination;

(d) To refrain from engaging in any act or practice of discrimination against women and to ensure that public authorities and institutions shall act in conformity with this obligation;

(e) To take all appropriate measures to eliminate discrimination against women by any person, organization or enterprise;

(f) To take all appropriate measures, including legislation, to modify or abolish existing laws, regulations, customs and practices which constitute discrimination against women;

(g) To repeal all national penal provisions which constitute discrimination against women.

Article 3

States Parties shall take in all fields, in particular in the political, social, economic and cultural fields, all appropriate measures, including legislation, to ensure the full development and advancement of women, for the purpose of guaranteeing them the exercise and enjoyment of human rights and fundamental freedoms on a basis of equality with men.

Article 4

1. Adoption by States Parties of temporary special measures aimed at accelerating de facto equality between men and women shall not be considered discrimination as defined in the present Convention, but shall in no way entail as a consequence the maintenance of unequal or separate standards; these measures shall be discontinued when the objectives of equality of opportunity and treatment have been achieved.

2. Adoption by States Parties of special measures, including those measures contained in the present Convention, aimed at protecting maternity shall not be considered discriminatory.

Article 5

States Parties shall take all appropriate measures:

(a) To modify the social and cultural patterns of conduct of men and women, with a view to achieving the elimination of prejudices and customary and all other practices which are based on the idea of the inferiority or the superiority of either of the sexes or on stereotyped roles for men and women;

(b) To ensure that family education includes a proper understanding of maternity as a social function and the recognition of the common responsibility of men and women in the upbringing and development of their children, it being understood that the interest of the children is the primordial consideration in all cases.

Article 6

States Parties shall take all appropriate measures, including legislation, to suppress all forms of traffic in women and exploitation of prostitution of women.

PART II

Article 7
States Parties shall take all appropriate measures to eliminate discrimination against women in the political and public life of the country and, in particular, shall ensure to women, on equal terms with men, the right:
(a) To vote in all elections and public referenda and to be eligible for election to all publicly elected bodies;
(b) To participate in the formulation of government policy and the implementation thereof and to hold public office and perform all public functions at all levels of government;
(c) To participate in non-governmental organizations and associations concerned with the public and political life of the country.

Article 8
States Parties shall take all appropriate measures to ensure to women, on equal terms with men and without any discrimination, the opportunity to represent their Governments at the international level and to participate in the work of international organizations.

Article 9
1. States Parties shall grant women equal rights with men to acquire, change or retain their nationality. They shall ensure in particular that neither marriage to an alien nor change of nationality by the husband during marriage shall automatically change the nationality of the wife, render her stateless or force upon her the nationality of the husband.
2. States Parties shall grant women equal rights with men with respect to the nationality of their children.

PART III

Article 10
States Parties shall take all appropriate measures to eliminate discrimination against women in order to ensure to them equal rights with men in the field of education and in particular to ensure, on a basis of equality of men and women:
(a) The same conditions for career and vocational guidance, for access to studies and for the achievement of diplomas in educational establishments of all categories in rural as well as in urban areas; this equality shall be ensured in pre-school, general, technical, professional and higher technical education, as well as in all types of vocational training;
(b) Access to the same curricula, the same examinations, teaching staff with qualifications of the same standard and school premises and equipment of the same quality;
(c) The elimination of any stereotyped concept of the roles of men and women at all levels and in all forms of education by encouraging coeducation and other types of education which will help to achieve this aim and, in particular, by the revision of textbooks and school programmes and the adaptation of teaching methods;

(d) The same opportunities to benefit from scholarships and other study grants;

(e) The same opportunities for access to programmes of continuing education, including adult and functional literacy programmes, particularly those aimed at reducing, at the earliest possible time, any gap in education existing between men and women;

(f) The reduction of female student drop-out rates and the organization of programmes for girls and women who have left school prematurely;

(g) The same opportunities to participate actively in sports and physical education;

(h) Access to specific educational information to help to ensure the health and well-being of families, including information and advice on family planning.

Article 11

1. States Parties shall take all appropriate measures to eliminate discrimination against women in the field of employment in order to ensure, on a basis of equality of men and women, the same rights, in particular:

(a) The right to work as an inalienable right of all human beings;

(b) The right to the same employment opportunities, including the application of the same criteria for selection in matters of employment;

(c) The right to free choice of profession and employment, the right to promotion, job security and all benefits and conditions of service and the right to receive vocational training and retraining, including apprenticeships, advanced vocational training and recurrent training;

(d) The right to equal remuneration, including benefits, and to equal treatment in respect of work of equal value, as well as equality of treatment in the evaluation of the quality of work;

(e) The right to social security, particularly in cases of retirement, unemployment, sickness, invalidity and old age and other incapacity to work, as well as the right to paid leave;

(f) The right to protection of health and to safety in working conditions, including the safeguarding of the function of reproduction.

2. In order to prevent discrimination against women on the grounds of marriage or maternity and to ensure their effective right to work, States Parties shall take appropriate measures:

(a) To prohibit, subject to the imposition of sanctions, dismissal on the grounds of pregnancy or of maternity leave and discrimination in dismissals on the basis of marital status;

(b) To introduce maternity leave with pay or with comparable social benefits without loss of former employment, seniority or social allowances;

(c) To encourage the provision of the necessary supporting social services to enable parents to combine family obligations with work responsibilities and participation in public life, in particular through promoting the establishment and development of a network of child-care facilities;

(d) To provide special protection to women during pregnancy in types of work proved to be harmful to them.

3. Protective legislation relating to matters covered in this article shall be reviewed periodically in the light of scientific and technological knowledge and shall be revised, repealed or extended as necessary.

Article 12

1. States Parties shall take all appropriate measures to eliminate discrimination against women in the field of health care in order to ensure, on a basis of equality of men and women, access to health care services, including those related to family planning.
2. Notwithstanding the provisions of paragraph 1 of this article, States Parties shall ensure to women appropriate services in connection with pregnancy, confinement and the post-natal period, granting free services where necessary, as well as adequate nutrition during pregnancy and lactation.

Article 13

States Parties shall take all appropriate measures to eliminate discrimination against women in other areas of economic and social life in order to ensure, on a basis of equality of men and women, the same rights, in particular:

   (a) The right to family benefits;
   (b) The right to bank loans, mortgages and other forms of financial credit;
   (c) The right to participate in recreational activities, sports and all aspects of cultural life.

Article 14

1. States Parties shall take into account the particular problems faced by rural women and the significant roles which rural women play in the economic survival of their families, including their work in the non-monetized sectors of the economy, and shall take all appropriate measures to ensure the application of the provisions of the present Convention to women in rural areas.
2. States Parties shall take all appropriate measures to eliminate discrimination against women in rural areas in order to ensure, on a basis of equality of men and women, that they participate in and benefit from rural development and, in particular, shall ensure to such women the right:

   (a) To participate in the elaboration and implementation of development planning at all levels;
   (b) To have access to adequate health care facilities, including information, counselling and services in family planning;
   (c) To benefit directly from social security programmes;
   (d) To obtain all types of training and education, formal and non-formal, including that relating to functional literacy, as well as, inter alia, the benefit of all community and extension services, in order to increase their technical proficiency;
   (e) To organize self-help groups and co-operatives in order to obtain equal access to economic opportunities through employment or self employment;
   (f) To participate in all community activities;
   (g) To have access to agricultural credit and loans, marketing facilities, appropriate technology and equal treatment in land and agrarian reform as well as in land resettlement schemes;
   (h) To enjoy adequate living conditions, particularly in relation to housing, sanitation, electricity and water supply, transport and communications.

PART IV

Article 15

1. States Parties shall accord to women equality with men before the law.
2. States Parties shall accord to women, in civil matters, a legal capacity identical to that of men and the same opportunities to exercise that capacity. In particular, they shall give women equal rights to conclude contracts and to administer property and shall treat them equally in all stages of procedure in courts and tribunals.
3. States Parties agree that all contracts and all other private instruments of any kind with a legal effect which is directed at restricting the legal capacity of women shall be deemed null and void.
4. States Parties shall accord to men and women the same rights with regard to the law relating to the movement of persons and the freedom to choose their residence and domicile.

Article 16

1. States Parties shall take all appropriate measures to eliminate discrimination against women in all matters relating to marriage and family relations and in particular shall ensure, on a basis of equality of men and women:
   (a) The same right to enter into marriage;
   (b) The same right freely to choose a spouse and to enter into marriage only with their free and full consent;
   (c) The same rights and responsibilities during marriage and at its dissolution;
   (d) The same rights and responsibilities as parents, irrespective of their marital status, in matters relating to their children; in all cases the interests of the children shall be paramount;
   (e) The same rights to decide freely and responsibly on the number and spacing of their children and to have access to the information, education and means to enable them to exercise these rights;
   (f) The same rights and responsibilities with regard to guardianship, wardship, trusteeship and adoption of children, or similar institutions where these concepts exist in national legislation; in all cases the interests of the children shall be paramount;
   (g) The same personal rights as husband and wife, including the right to choose a family name, a profession and an occupation;
   (h) The same rights for both spouses in respect of the ownership, acquisition, management, administration, enjoyment and disposition of property, whether free of charge or for a valuable consideration.
2. The betrothal and the marriage of a child shall have no legal effect, and all necessary action, including legislation, shall be taken to specify a minimum age for marriage and to make the registration of marriages in an official registry compulsory.

PART V

Article 17

1. For the purpose of considering the progress made in the implementation of the present Convention, there shall be established a Committee on the Elimination of Discrimination against Women (hereinafter referred to as the Committee) consisting, at the time of entry into force of the Convention, of eighteen and, after ratification of or accession to the Convention by the thirty-fifth State Party, of twenty-three experts of high moral standing and competence in the field covered by the Convention. The experts shall be elected by States Parties from among their nationals and shall serve in their personal capacity, consideration being given to equitable geographical distribution and to the representation of the different forms of civilization as well as the principal legal systems.

2. The members of the Committee shall be elected by secret ballot from a list of persons nominated by States Parties. Each State Party may nominate one person from among its own nationals.

3. The initial election shall be held six months after the date of the entry into force of the present Convention. At least three months before the date of each election the Secretary-General of the United Nations shall address a letter to the States Parties inviting them to submit their nominations within two months. The Secretary-General shall prepare a list in alphabetical order of all persons thus nominated, indicating the States Parties which have nominated them, and shall submit it to the States Parties.

4. Elections of the members of the Committee shall be held at a meeting of States Parties convened by the Secretary-General at United Nations Headquarters. At that meeting, for which two thirds of the States Parties shall constitute a quorum, the persons elected to the Committee shall be those nominees who obtain the largest number of votes and an absolute majority of the votes of the representatives of States Parties present and voting.

5. The members of the Committee shall be elected for a term of four years. However, the terms of nine of the members elected at the first election shall expire at the end of two years; immediately after the first election the names of these nine members shall be chosen by lot by the Chairman of the Committee.

6. The election of the five additional members of the Committee shall be held in accordance with the provisions of paragraphs 2, 3 and 4 of this article, following the thirty-fifth ratification or accession. The terms of two of the additional members elected on this occasion shall expire at the end of two years, the names of these two members having been chosen by lot by the Chairman of the Committee.

7. For the filling of casual vacancies, the State Party whose expert has ceased to function as a member of the Committee shall appoint another expert from among its nationals, subject to the approval of the Committee.

8. The members of the Committee shall, with the approval of the General Assembly, receive emoluments from United Nations resources on such terms and conditions as the Assembly may decide, having regard to the importance of the Committee's responsibilities.

9. The Secretary-General of the United Nations shall provide the necessary staff and facilities for the effective performance of the functions of the Committee under the present Convention.

Article 18

1. States Parties undertake to submit to the Secretary-General of the United Nations, for consideration by the Committee, a report on the legislative, judicial, administrative or other measures which they have adopted to give effect to the provisions of the present Convention and on the progress made in this respect:
   (a) Within one year after the entry into force for the State concerned;
   (b) Thereafter at least every four years and further whenever the Committee so requests.
2. Reports may indicate factors and difficulties affecting the degree of fulfilment of obligations under the present Convention.

Article 19

1. The Committee shall adopt its own rules of procedure.
2. The Committee shall elect its officers for a term of two years.

Article 20

1. The Committee shall normally meet for a period of not more than two weeks annually in order to consider the reports submitted in accordance with article 18 of the present Convention.
2. The meetings of the Committee shall normally be held at United Nations Headquarters or at any other convenient place as determined by the Committee.

Article 21

1. The Committee shall, through the Economic and Social Council, report annually to the General Assembly of the United Nations on its activities and may make suggestions and general recommendations based on the examination of reports and information received from the States Parties. Such suggestions and general recommendations shall be included in the report of the Committee together with comments, if any, from States Parties.
2. The Secretary-General of the United Nations shall transmit the reports of the Committee to the Commission on the Status of Women for its information.

Article 22

The specialized agencies shall be entitled to be represented at the consideration of the implementation of such provisions of the present Convention as fall within the scope of their activities. The Committee may invite the specialized agencies to submit reports on the implementation of the Convention in areas falling within the scope of their activities.

PART VI

Article 23
Nothing in the present Convention shall affect any provisions that are more conducive to the achievement of equality between men and women which may be contained:
  (a) In the legislation of a State Party; or
  (b) In any other international convention, treaty or agreement in force for that State.

Article 24
States Parties undertake to adopt all necessary measures at the national level aimed at achieving the full realization of the rights recognized in the present Convention.

Article 25
1. The present Convention shall be open for signature by all States.
2. The Secretary-General of the United Nations is designated as the depositary of the present Convention.
3. The present Convention is subject to ratification. Instruments of ratification shall be deposited with the Secretary-General of the United Nations.
4. The present Convention shall be open to accession by all States. Accession shall be effected by the deposit of an instrument of accession with the Secretary-General of the United Nations.

Article 26
1. A request for the revision of the present Convention may be made at any time by any State Party by means of a notification in writing addressed to the Secretary-General of the United Nations.
2. The General Assembly of the United Nations shall decide upon the steps, if any, to be taken in respect of such a request.

Article 27
1. The present Convention shall enter into force on the thirtieth day after the date of deposit with the Secretary-General of the United Nations of the twentieth instrument of ratification or accession.
2. For each State ratifying the present Convention or acceding to it after the deposit of the twentieth instrument of ratification or accession, the Convention shall enter into force on the thirtieth day after the date of the deposit of its own instrument of ratification or accession.

Article 28
1. The Secretary-General of the United Nations shall receive and circulate to all States the text of reservations made by States at the time of ratification or accession.
2. A reservation incompatible with the object and purpose of the present Convention shall not be permitted.
3. Reservations may be withdrawn at any time by notification to this effect addressed to the Secretary-General of the United Nations, who shall then inform all States thereof. Such notification shall take effect on the date on which it is received.

Article 29

1. Any dispute between two or more States Parties concerning the interpretation or application of the present Convention which is not settled by negotiation shall, at the request of one of them, be submitted to arbitration. If within six months from the date of the request for arbitration the parties are unable to agree on the organization of the arbitration, any one of those parties may refer the dispute to the International Court of Justice by request in conformity with the Statute of the Court.

2. Each State Party may at the time of signature or ratification of the present Convention or accession thereto declare that it does not consider itself bound by paragraph 1 of this article. The other States Parties shall not be bound by that paragraph with respect to any State Party which has made such a reservation.

3. Any State Party which has made a reservation in accordance with paragraph 2 of this article may at any time withdraw that reservation by notification to the Secretary-General of the United Nations.

Article 30

The present Convention, the Arabic, Chinese, English, French, Russian and Spanish texts of which are equally authentic, shall be deposited with the Secretary-General of the United Nations.

IN WITNESS WHEREOF the undersigned, duly authorized, have signed the present Convention.

16

Optional Protocol to the Convention on the Elimination of Discrimination against Women, 1999

Note: Adopted on 6 October 1999 by G.A. Resolution 54/4, annex, 54 U.N. GAOR Supp. (No. 49) at 5, U.N. Doc. A/54/49 (Vol. I) (2000), 2131 UNTS 83. Entry into force: 22 December 2000.

The States Parties to the present Protocol,

Noting that the Charter of the United Nations reaffirms faith in fundamental human rights, in the dignity and worth of the human person and in the equal rights of men and women,

Also noting that the Universal Declaration of Human Rights Resolution 217 A (III). proclaims that all human beings are born free and equal in dignity and rights and that everyone is entitled to all the rights and freedoms set forth therein, without distinction of any kind, including distinction based on sex,

Recalling that the International Covenants on Human Rights Resolution 2200 A (XXI), annex. and other international human rights instruments prohibit discrimination on the basis of sex,

Also recalling the Convention on the Elimination of All Forms of Discrimination against Women ("the Convention"), in which the States Parties thereto condemn discrimination against women in all its forms and agree to pursue by all appropriate means and without delay a policy of eliminating discrimination against women,

Reaffirming their determination to ensure the full and equal enjoyment by women of all human rights and fundamental freedoms and to take effective action to prevent violations of these rights and freedoms,

Have agreed as follows:

Article 1

A State Party to the present Protocol ("State Party") recognizes the competence of the Committee on the Elimination of Discrimination against Women ("the Committee") to receive and consider communications submitted in accordance with article 2.

Article 2

Communications may be submitted by or on behalf of individuals or groups of individuals, under the jurisdiction of a State Party, claiming to be victims of a violation of any of the rights set forth in the Convention by that State Party. Where a communication is submitted on behalf of individuals or groups of individuals, this shall be with their consent unless the author can justify acting on their behalf without such consent.

Article 3

Communications shall be in writing and shall not be anonymous. No communication shall be received by the Committee if it concerns a State Party to the Convention that is not a party to the present Protocol.

Article 4

1. The Committee shall not consider a communication unless it has ascertained that all available domestic remedies have been exhausted unless the application of such remedies is unreasonably prolonged or unlikely to bring effective relief.
2. The Committee shall declare a communication inadmissible where:
   (a) The same matter has already been examined by the Committee or has been or is being examined under another procedure of international investigation or settlement;
   (b) It is incompatible with the provisions of the Convention;
   (c) It is manifestly ill-founded or not sufficiently substantiated;
   (d) It is an abuse of the right to submit a communication;
   (e) The facts that are the subject of the communication occurred prior to the entry into force of the present Protocol for the State Party concerned unless those facts continued after that date.

Article 5

1. At any time after the receipt of a communication and before a determination on the merits has been reached, the Committee may transmit to the State Party concerned for its urgent consideration a request that the State Party take such interim measures as may be necessary to avoid possible irreparable damage to the victim or victims of the alleged violation.
2. Where the Committee exercises its discretion under paragraph 1 of the present article, this does not imply a determination on admissibility or on the merits of the communication.

Article 6

1. Unless the Committee considers a communication inadmissible without reference to the State Party concerned, and provided that the individual or individuals consent to the disclosure of their identity to that State Party, the Committee shall bring any communication submitted to it under the present Protocol confidentially to the attention of the State Party concerned.
2. Within six months, the receiving State Party shall submit to the Committee written explanations or statements clarifying the matter and the remedy, if any, that may have been provided by that State Party.

Article 7

1. The Committee shall consider communications received under the present Protocol in the light of all information made available to it by or on behalf of individuals or groups of individuals and by the State Party concerned, provided that this information is transmitted to the parties concerned.
2. The Committee shall hold closed meetings when examining communications under the present Protocol.

3. After examining a communication, the Committee shall transmit its views on the communication, together with its recommendations, if any, to the parties concerned.

4. The State Party shall give due consideration to the views of the Committee, together with its recommendations, if any, and shall submit to the Committee, within six months, a written response, including information on any action taken in the light of the views and recommendations of the Committee.

5. The Committee may invite the State Party to submit further information about any measures the State Party has taken in response to its views or recommendations, if any, including as deemed appropriate by the Committee, in the State Party's subsequent reports under article 18 of the Convention.

Article 8

1. If the Committee receives reliable information indicating grave or systematic violations by a State Party of rights set forth in the Convention, the Committee shall invite that State Party to cooperate in the examination of the information and to this end to submit observations with regard to the information concerned.

2. Taking into account any observations that may have been submitted by the State Party concerned as well as any other reliable information available to it, the Committee may designate one or more of its members to conduct an inquiry and to report urgently to the Committee. Where warranted and with the consent of the State Party, the inquiry may include a visit to its territory.

3. After examining the findings of such an inquiry, the Committee shall transmit these findings to the State Party concerned together with any comments and recommendations.

4. The State Party concerned shall, within six months of receiving the findings, comments and recommendations transmitted by the Committee, submit its observations to the Committee.

5. Such an inquiry shall be conducted confidentially and the cooperation of the State Party shall be sought at all stages of the proceedings.

Article 9

1. The Committee may invite the State Party concerned to include in its report under article 18 of the Convention details of any measures taken in response to an inquiry conducted under article 8 of the present Protocol.

2. The Committee may, if necessary, after the end of the period of six months referred to in article 8.4, invite the State Party concerned to inform it of the measures taken in response to such an inquiry.

Article 10

1. Each State Party may, at the time of signature or ratification of the present Protocol or accession thereto, declare that it does not recognize the competence of the Committee provided for in articles 8 and 9.

2. Any State Party having made a declaration in accordance with paragraph 1 of the present article may, at any time, withdraw this declaration by notification to the Secretary-General.

Article 11

A State Party shall take all appropriate steps to ensure that individuals under its jurisdiction are not subjected to ill treatment or intimidation as a consequence of communicating with the Committee pursuant to the present Protocol.

Article 12

The Committee shall include in its annual report under article 21 of the Convention a summary of its activities under the present Protocol.

Article 13

Each State Party undertakes to make widely known and to give publicity to the Convention and the present Protocol and to facilitate access to information about the views and recommendations of the Committee, in particular, on matters involving that State Party.

Article 14

The Committee shall develop its own rules of procedure to be followed when exercising the functions conferred on it by the present Protocol.

Article 15

1. The present Protocol shall be open for signature by any State that has signed, ratified or acceded to the Convention.
2. The present Protocol shall be subject to ratification by any State that has ratified or acceded to the Convention. Instruments of ratification shall be deposited with the Secretary-General of the United Nations.
3. The present Protocol shall be open to accession by any State that has ratified or acceded to the Convention.
4. Accession shall be effected by the deposit of an instrument of accession with the Secretary-General of the United Nations.

Article 16

1. The present Protocol shall enter into force three months after the date of the deposit with the Secretary-General of the United Nations of the tenth instrument of ratification or accession.
2. For each State ratifying the present Protocol or acceding to it after its entry into force, the present Protocol shall enter into force three months after the date of the deposit of its own instrument of ratification or accession.

Article 17

No reservations to the present Protocol shall be permitted.

Article 18

1. Any State Party may propose an amendment to the present Protocol and file it with the Secretary-General of the United Nations. The Secretary-General shall thereupon communicate any proposed amendments to the States Parties with a request that they notify her or him whether they favour a conference of States Parties for the purpose of considering and voting on the proposal. In the event that at least one third of the States

Parties favour such a conference, the Secretary-General shall convene the conference under the auspices of the United Nations. Any amendment adopted by a majority of the States Parties present and voting at the conference shall be submitted to the General Assembly of the United Nations for approval.

2. Amendments shall come into force when they have been approved by the General Assembly of the United Nations and accepted by a two-thirds majority of the States Parties to the present Protocol in accordance with their respective constitutional processes.

3. When amendments come into force, they shall be binding on those States Parties that have accepted them, other States Parties still being bound by the provisions of the present Protocol and any earlier amendments that they have accepted.

Article 19

1. Any State Party may denounce the present Protocol at any time by written notification addressed to the Secretary-General of the United Nations. Denunciation shall take effect six months after the date of receipt of the notification by the Secretary-General.

2. Denunciation shall be without prejudice to the continued application of the provisions of the present Protocol to any communication submitted under article 2 or any inquiry initiated under article 8 before the effective date of denunciation.

Article 20

The Secretary-General of the United Nations shall inform all States of:

   (a) Signatures, ratifications and accessions under the present Protocol;
   (b) The date of entry into force of the present Protocol and of any amendment under article 18;
   (c) Any denunciation under article 19.

Article 21

1. The present Protocol, of which the Arabic, Chinese, English, French, Russian and Spanish texts are equally authentic, shall be deposited in the archives of the United Nations.

2. The Secretary-General of the United Nations shall transmit certified copies of the present Protocol to all States referred to in article 25 of the Convention.

17

Convention against Torture and Other Cruel, Inhuman or Degrading Treatment or Punishment, 1984

Note: Adopted on 10 December 1984 by General Assembly Resolution 39/46, Annex, 39 U.N. GAOR Supp. (No. 51) at 197, U.N. Doc. A/39/51 (1984)], 1465 UNTS 85. Entry into force: 26 June 1987.

The States Parties to this Convention,

Considering that, in accordance with the principles proclaimed in the Charter of the United Nations, recognition of the equal and inalienable rights of all members of the human family is the foundation of freedom, justice and peace in the world,

Recognizing that those rights derive from the inherent dignity of the human person,

Considering the obligation of States under the Charter, in particular Article 55, to promote universal respect for, and observance of, human rights and fundamental freedoms,

Having regard to article 5 of the Universal Declaration of Human Rights and article 7 of the International Covenant on Civil and Political Rights, both of which provide that no one shall be subjected to torture or to cruel, inhuman or degrading treatment or punishment,

Having regard also to the Declaration on the Protection of All Persons from Being Subjected to Torture and Other Cruel, Inhuman or Degrading Treatment or Punishment, adopted by the General Assembly on 9 December 1975,

Desiring to make more effective the struggle against torture and other cruel, inhuman or degrading treatment or punishment throughout the world,

Have agreed as follows:

PART I

Article 1

1. For the purposes of this Convention, the term "torture" means any act by which severe pain or suffering, whether physical or mental, is intentionally inflicted on a person for such purposes as obtaining from him or a third person information or a confession, punishing him for an act he or a third person has committed or is suspected of having committed, or intimidating or coercing him or a third person, or for any reason based on discrimination of any kind, when such pain or suffering is inflicted by or at the instigation of or with the consent or acquiescence of a public official or other person

acting in an official capacity. It does not include pain or suffering arising only from, inherent in or incidental to lawful sanctions.

2. This article is without prejudice to any international instrument or national legislation which does or may contain provisions of wider application.

Article 2

1. Each State Party shall take effective legislative, administrative, judicial or other measures to prevent acts of torture in any territory under its jurisdiction.

2. No exceptional circumstances whatsoever, whether a state of war or a threat of war, internal political instability or any other public emergency, may be invoked as a justification of torture.

3. An order from a superior officer or a public authority may not be invoked as a justification of torture.

Article 3

1. No State Party shall expel, return (*refouler*) or extradite a person to another State where there are substantial grounds for believing that he would be in danger of being subjected to torture.

2. For the purpose of determining whether there are such grounds, the competent authorities shall take into account all relevant considerations including, where applicable, the existence in the State concerned of a consistent pattern of gross, flagrant or mass violations of human rights.

Article 4

1. Each State Party shall ensure that all acts of torture are offences under its criminal law. The same shall apply to an attempt to commit torture and to an act by any person which constitutes complicity or participation in torture.

2. Each State Party shall make these offences punishable by appropriate penalties which take into account their grave nature.

Article 5

1. Each State Party shall take such measures as may be necessary to establish its jurisdiction over the offences referred to in article 4 in the following cases:
   (a)   When the offences are committed in any territory under its jurisdiction or on board a ship or aircraft registered in that State;
   (b)   When the alleged offender is a national of that State;
   (c)   When the victim is a national of that State if that State considers it appropriate.

2. Each State Party shall likewise take such measures as may be necessary to establish its jurisdiction over such offences in cases where the alleged offender is present in any territory under its jurisdiction and it does not extradite him pursuant to article 8 to any of the States mentioned in paragraph 1 of this article.

3. This Convention does not exclude any criminal jurisdiction exercised in accordance with internal law.

Article 6

1. Upon being satisfied, after an examination of information available to it, that the circumstances so warrant, any State Party in whose territory a person alleged to have committed any offence referred to in article 4 is present shall take him into custody or take other legal measures to ensure his presence. The custody and other legal measures shall be as provided in the law of that State but may be continued only for such time as is necessary to enable any criminal or extradition proceedings to be instituted.
2. Such State shall immediately make a preliminary inquiry into the facts.
3. Any person in custody pursuant to paragraph 1 of this article shall be assisted in communicating immediately with the nearest appropriate representative of the State of which he is a national, or, if he is a stateless person, with the representative of the State where he usually resides.
4. When a State, pursuant to this article, has taken a person into custody, it shall immediately notify the States referred to in article 5, paragraph 1, of the fact that such person is in custody and of the circumstances which warrant his detention. The State which makes the preliminary inquiry contemplated in paragraph 2 of this article shall promptly report its findings to the said States and shall indicate whether it intends to exercise jurisdiction.

Article 7

1. The State Party in the territory under whose jurisdiction a person alleged to have committed any offence referred to in article 4 is found shall in the cases contemplated in article 5, if it does not extradite him, submit the case to its competent authorities for the purpose of prosecution.
2. These authorities shall take their decision in the same manner as in the case of any ordinary offence of a serious nature under the law of that State. In the cases referred to in article 5, paragraph 2, the standards of evidence required for prosecution and conviction shall in no way be less stringent than those which apply in the cases referred to in article 5, paragraph 1.
3. Any person regarding whom proceedings are brought in connection with any of the offences referred to in article 4 shall be guaranteed fair treatment at all stages of the proceedings.

Article 8

1. The offences referred to in article 4 shall be deemed to be included as extraditable offences in any extradition treaty existing between States Parties. States Parties undertake to include such offences as extraditable offences in every extradition treaty to be concluded between them.
2. If a State Party which makes extradition conditional on the existence of a treaty receives a request for extradition from another. State Party with which it has no extradition treaty, it may consider this Convention as the legal basis for extradition in respect of such offences. Extradition shall be subject to the other conditions provided by the law of the requested State.
3. States Parties which do not make extradition conditional on the existence of a treaty shall recognize such offences as extraditable offences between themselves subject to the conditions provided by the law of the requested State.

4. Such offences shall be treated, for the purpose of extradition between States Parties, as if they had been committed not only in the place in which they occurred but also in the territories of the States required to establish their jurisdiction in accordance with article 5, paragraph 1.

Article 9

1. States Parties shall afford one another the greatest measure of assistance in connection with criminal proceedings brought in respect of any of the offences referred to in article 4, including the supply of all evidence at their disposal necessary for the proceedings.
2. States Parties shall carry out their obligations under paragraph 1 of this article in conformity with any treaties on mutual judicial assistance that may exist between them.

Article 10

1. Each State Party shall ensure that education and information regarding the prohibition against torture are fully included in the training of law enforcement personnel, civil or military, medical personnel, public officials and other persons who may be involved in the custody, interrogation or treatment of any individual subjected to any form of arrest, detention or imprisonment.
2. Each State Party shall include this prohibition in the rules or instructions issued in regard to the duties and functions of any such person.

Article 11

Each State Party shall keep under systematic review interrogation rules, instructions, methods and practices as well as arrangements for the custody and treatment of persons subjected to any form of arrest, detention or imprisonment in any territory under its jurisdiction, with a view to preventing any cases of torture.

Article 12

Each State Party shall ensure that its competent authorities proceed to a prompt and impartial investigation, wherever there is reasonable ground to believe that an act of torture has been committed in any territory under its jurisdiction.

Article 13

Each State Party shall ensure that any individual who alleges he has been subjected to torture in any territory under its jurisdiction has the right to complain to, and to have his case promptly and impartially examined by, its competent authorities. Steps shall be taken to ensure that the complainant and witnesses are protected against all ill-treatment or intimidation as a consequence of his complaint or any evidence given.

Article 14

1. Each State Party shall ensure in its legal system that the victim of an act of torture obtains redress and has an enforceable right to fair and adequate compensation, including the means for as full rehabilitation as possible. In the event of the death of the victim as a result of an act of torture, his dependants shall be entitled to compensation.
2. Nothing in this article shall affect any right of the victim or other persons to compensation which may exist under national law.

Article 15

Each State Party shall ensure that any statement which is established to have been made as a result of torture shall not be invoked as evidence in any proceedings, except against a person accused of torture as evidence that the statement was made.

Article 16

1. Each State Party shall undertake to prevent in any territory under its jurisdiction other acts of cruel, inhuman or degrading treatment or punishment which do not amount to torture as defined in article 1, when such acts are committed by or at the instigation of or with the consent or acquiescence of a public official or other person acting in an official capacity. In particular, the obligations contained in articles 10, 11, 12 and 13 shall apply with the substitution for references to torture of references to other forms of cruel, inhuman or degrading treatment or punishment.
2. The provisions of this Convention are without prejudice to the provisions of any other international instrument or national law which prohibits cruel, inhuman or degrading treatment or punishment or which relates to extradition or expulsion.

PART II

Article 17

1. There shall be established a Committee against Torture (hereinafter referred to as the Committee) which shall carry out the functions hereinafter provided. The Committee shall consist of ten experts of high moral standing and recognized competence in the field of human rights, who shall serve in their personal capacity. The experts shall be elected by the States Parties, consideration being given to equitable geographical distribution and to the usefulness of the participation of some persons having legal experience.
2. The members of the Committee shall be elected by secret ballot from a list of persons nominated by States Parties. Each State Party may nominate one person from among its own nationals. States Parties shall bear in mind the usefulness of nominating persons who are also members of the Human Rights Committee established under the International Covenant on Civil and Political Rights and who are willing to serve on the Committee against Torture.
3. Elections of the members of the Committee shall be held at biennial meetings of States Parties convened by the Secretary-General of the United Nations. At those meetings, for which two thirds of the States Parties shall constitute a quorum, the persons elected to the Committee shall be those who obtain the largest number of votes and an absolute majority of the votes of the representatives of States Parties present and voting.
4. The initial election shall be held no later than six months after the date of the entry into force of this Convention. At least four months before the date of each election, the Secretary-General of the United Nations shall address a letter to the States Parties inviting them to submit their nominations within three months. The Secretary-General shall prepare a list in alphabetical order of all persons thus nominated, indicating the States Parties which have nominated them, and shall submit it to the States Parties.

5. The members of the Committee shall be elected for a term of four years. They shall be eligible for re-election if renominated. However, the term of five of the members elected at the first election shall expire at the end of two years; immediately after the first election the names of these five members shall be chosen by lot by the chairman of the meeting referred to in paragraph 3 of this article.

6. If a member of the Committee dies or resigns or for any other cause can no longer perform his Committee duties, the State Party which nominated him shall appoint another expert from among its nationals to serve for the remainder of his term, subject to the approval of the majority of the States Parties. The approval shall be considered given unless half or more of the States Parties respond negatively within six weeks after having been informed by the Secretary-General of the United Nations of the proposed appointment.

7. States Parties shall be responsible for the expenses of the members of the Committee while they are in performance of Committee duties.

Article 18

1. The Committee shall elect its officers for a term of two years. They may be re-elected.

2. The Committee shall establish its own rules of procedure, but these rules shall provide, inter alia, that:
   (a) Six members shall constitute a quorum;
   (b) Decisions of the Committee shall be made by a majority vote of the members present.

3. The Secretary-General of the United Nations shall provide the necessary staff and facilities for the effective performance of the functions of the Committee under this Convention.

4. The Secretary-General of the United Nations shall convene the initial meeting of the Committee. After its initial meeting, the Committee shall meet at such times as shall be provided in its rules of procedure.

5. The States Parties shall be responsible for expenses incurred in connection with the holding of meetings of the States Parties and of the Committee, including reimbursement to the United Nations for any expenses, such as the cost of staff and facilities, incurred by the United Nations pursuant to paragraph 3 of this article.

Article 19

1. The States Parties shall submit to the Committee, through the Secretary-General of the United Nations, reports on the measures they have taken to give effect to their undertakings under this Convention, within one year after the entry into force of the Convention for the State Party concerned. Thereafter the States Parties shall submit supplementary reports every four years on any new measures taken and such other reports as the Committee may request.

2. The Secretary-General of the United Nations shall transmit the reports to all States Parties.

3. Each report shall be considered by the Committee which may make such general comments on the report as it may consider appropriate and shall forward these to the State Party concerned. That State Party may respond with any observations it chooses to the Committee.

4. The Committee may, at its discretion, decide to include any comments made by it in accordance with paragraph 3 of this article, together with the observations thereon received from the State Party concerned, in its annual report made in accordance with article 24. If so requested by the State Party concerned, the Committee may also include a copy of the report submitted under paragraph 1 of this article.

Article 20

1. If the Committee receives reliable information which appears to it to contain well-founded indications that torture is being systematically practised in the territory of a State Party, the Committee shall invite that State Party to co-operate in the examination of the information and to this end to submit observations with regard to the information concerned.
2. Taking into account any observations which may have been submitted by the State Party concerned, as well as any other relevant information available to it, the Committee may, if it decides that this is warranted, designate one or more of its members to make a confidential inquiry and to report to the Committee urgently.
3. If an inquiry is made in accordance with paragraph 2 of this article, the Committee shall seek the co-operation of the State Party concerned. In agreement with that State Party, such an inquiry may include a visit to its territory.
4. After examining the findings of its member or members submitted in accordance with paragraph 2 of this article, the Commission shall transmit these findings to the State Party concerned together with any comments or suggestions which seem appropriate in view of the situation.
5. All the proceedings of the Committee referred to in paragraphs I to 4 of this article shall be confidential, and at all stages of the proceedings the co-operation of the State Party shall be sought. After such proceedings have been completed with regard to an inquiry made in accordance with paragraph 2, the Committee may, after consultations with the State Party concerned, decide to include a summary account of the results of the proceedings in its annual report made in accordance with article 24.

Article 21

1. A State Party to this Convention may at any time declare under this article that it recognizes the competence of the Committee to receive and consider communications to the effect that a State Party claims that another State Party is not fulfilling its obligations under this Convention. Such communications may be received and considered according to the procedures laid down in this article only if submitted by a State Party which has made a declaration recognizing in regard to itself the competence of the Committee. No communication shall be dealt with by the Committee under this article if it concerns a State Party which has not made such a declaration. Communications received under this article shall be dealt with in accordance with the following procedure;
   (a) If a State Party considers that another State Party is not giving effect to the provisions of this Convention, it may, by written communication, bring the matter to the attention of that State Party. Within three months after the receipt of the communication the receiving State shall afford the State which

sent the communication an explanation or any other statement in writing clarifying the matter, which should include, to the extent possible and pertinent, reference to domestic procedures and remedies taken, pending or available in the matter;

(b) If the matter is not adjusted to the satisfaction of both States Parties concerned within six months after the receipt by the receiving State of the initial communication, either State shall have the right to refer the matter to the Committee, by notice given to the Committee and to the other State;

(c) The Committee shall deal with a matter referred to it under this article only after it has ascertained that all domestic remedies have been invoked and exhausted in the matter, in conformity with the generally recognized principles of international law. This shall not be the rule where the application of the remedies is unreasonably prolonged or is unlikely to bring effective relief to the person who is the victim of the violation of this Convention;

(d) The Committee shall hold closed meetings when examining communications under this article;

(e) Subject to the provisions of subparagraph (c), the Committee shall make available its good offices to the States Parties concerned with a view to a friendly solution of the matter on the basis of respect for the obligations provided for in this Convention. For this purpose, the Committee may, when appropriate, set up an ad hoc conciliation commission;

(f) In any matter referred to it under this article, the Committee may call upon the States Parties concerned, referred to in subparagraph (b), to supply any relevant information;

(g) The States Parties concerned, referred to in subparagraph (b), shall have the right to be represented when the matter is being considered by the Committee and to make submissions orally and/or in writing;

(h) The Committee shall, within twelve months after the date of receipt of notice under subparagraph (b), submit a report:

(i) If a solution within the terms of subparagraph (e) is reached, the Committee shall confine its report to a brief statement of the facts and of the solution reached;

(ij) If a solution within the terms of subparagraph (e) is not reached, the Committee shall confine its report to a brief statement of the facts; the written submissions and record of the oral submissions made by the States Parties concerned shall be attached to the report. In every matter, the report shall be communicated to the States Parties concerned.

2. The provisions of this article shall come into force when five States Parties to this Convention have made declarations under paragraph 1 of this article. Such declarations shall be deposited by the States Parties with the Secretary-General of the United Nations, who shall transmit copies thereof to the other States Parties. A declaration may be withdrawn at any time by notification to the Secretary-General. Such a withdrawal shall not prejudice the consideration of any matter which is the subject of a communication already transmitted under this article; no further communication by any State Party shall be received under this article after the notification of withdrawal of the declaration has been received by the Secretary-General, unless the State Party concerned has made a new declaration.

Article 22

1. A State Party to this Convention may at any time declare under this article that it recognizes the competence of the Committee to receive and consider communications from or on behalf of individuals subject to its jurisdiction who claim to be victims of a violation by a State Party of the provisions of the Convention. No communication shall be received by the Committee if it concerns a State Party which has not made such a declaration.

2. The Committee shall consider inadmissible any communication under this article which is anonymous or which it considers to be an abuse of the right of submission of such communications or to be incompatible with the provisions of this Convention.

3. Subject to the provisions of paragraph 2, the Committee shall bring any communications submitted to it under this article to the attention of the State Party to this Convention which has made a declaration under paragraph 1 and is alleged to be violating any provisions of the Convention. Within six months, the receiving State shall submit to the Committee written explanations or statements clarifying the matter and the remedy, if any, that may have been taken by that State.

4. The Committee shall consider communications received under this article in the light of all information made available to it by or on behalf of the individual and by the State Party concerned.

5. The Committee shall not consider any communications from an individual under this article unless it has ascertained that:
   (a) The same matter has not been, and is not being, examined under another procedure of international investigation or settlement;
   (b) The individual has exhausted all available domestic remedies; this shall not be the rule where the application of the remedies is unreasonably prolonged or is unlikely to bring effective relief to the person who is the victim of the violation of this Convention.

6. The Committee shall hold closed meetings when examining communications under this article.

7. The Committee shall forward its views to the State Party concerned and to the individual.

8. The provisions of this article shall come into force when five States Parties to this Convention have made declarations under paragraph 1 of this article. Such declarations shall be deposited by the States Parties with the Secretary-General of the United Nations, who shall transmit copies thereof to the other States Parties. A declaration may be withdrawn at any time by notification to the Secretary-General. Such a withdrawal shall not prejudice the consideration of any matter which is the subject of a communication already transmitted under this article; no further communication by or on behalf of an individual shall be received under this article after the notification of withdrawal of the declaration has been received by the Secretary General, unless the State Party has made a new declaration.

Article 23

The members of the Committee and of the ad hoc conciliation commissions which may be appointed under article 21, paragraph 1 (e), shall be entitled to the facilities, privileges and immunities of experts on mission for the United Nations as laid down in the relevant sections of the Convention on the Privileges and Immunities of the United Nations.

Article 24

The Committee shall submit an annual report on its activities under this Convention to the States Parties and to the General Assembly of the United Nations.

PART III

Article 25

1. This Convention is open for signature by all States.
2. This Convention is subject to ratification. Instruments of ratification shall be deposited with the Secretary-General of the United Nations.

Article 26

This Convention is open to accession by all States. Accession shall be effected by the deposit of an instrument of accession with the Secretary General of the United Nations.

Article 27

1. This Convention shall enter into force on the thirtieth day after the date of the deposit with the Secretary-General of the United Nations of the twentieth instrument of ratification or accession.
2. For each State ratifying this Convention or acceding to it after the deposit of the twentieth instrument of ratification or accession, the Convention shall enter into force on the thirtieth day after the date of the deposit of its own instrument of ratification or accession.

Article 28

1. Each State may, at the time of signature or ratification of this Convention or accession thereto, declare that it does not recognize the competence of the Committee provided for in article 20.
2. Any State Party having made a reservation in accordance with paragraph 1 of this article may, at any time, withdraw this reservation by notification to the Secretary-General of the United Nations.

Article 29

1. Any State Party to this Convention may propose an amendment and file it with the Secretary-General of the United Nations. The Secretary General shall thereupon communicate the proposed amendment to the States Parties with a request that they notify him whether they favour a conference of States Parties for the purpose of considering and voting upon the proposal. In the event that within four months from the date of such communication at least one third of the States Parties favours such a conference, the Secretary General shall convene the conference under the auspices of the United Nations. Any amendment adopted by a majority of the States Parties present and voting at the conference shall be submitted by the Secretary-General to all the States Parties for acceptance.
2. An amendment adopted in accordance with paragraph 1 of this article shall enter into force when two thirds of the States Parties to this Convention have notified the Secretary-General of the United Nations that they have accepted it in accordance with their respective constitutional processes.

3. When amendments enter into force, they shall be binding on those States Parties which have accepted them, other States Parties still being bound by the provisions of this Convention and any earlier amendments which they have accepted.

Article 30

1. Any dispute between two or more States Parties concerning the interpretation or application of this Convention which cannot be settled through negotiation shall, at the request of one of them, be submitted to arbitration. If within six months from the date of the request for arbitration the Parties are unable to agree on the organization of the arbitration, any one of those Parties may refer the dispute to the International Court of Justice by request in conformity with the Statute of the Court.
2. Each State may, at the time of signature or ratification of this Convention or accession thereto, declare that it does not consider itself bound by paragraph 1 of this article. The other States Parties shall not be bound by paragraph 1 of this article with respect to any State Party having made such a reservation.
3. Any State Party having made a reservation in accordance with paragraph 2 of this article may at any time withdraw this reservation by notification to the Secretary-General of the United Nations.

Article 31

1. A State Party may denounce this Convention by written notification to the Secretary-General of the United Nations. Denunciation becomes effective one year after the date of receipt of the notification by the Secretary-General.
2. Such a denunciation shall not have the effect of releasing the State Party from its obligations under this Convention in regard to any act or omission which occurs prior to the date at which the denunciation becomes effective, nor shall denunciation prejudice in any way the continued consideration of any matter which is already under consideration by the Committee prior to the date at which the denunciation becomes effective.
3. Following the date at which the denunciation of a State Party becomes effective, the Committee shall not commence consideration of any new matter regarding that State.

Article 32

The Secretary-General of the United Nations shall inform all States Members of the United Nations and all States which have signed this Convention or acceded to it of the following:

(a) Signatures, ratifications and accessions under articles 25 and 26;
(b) The date of entry into force of this Convention under article 27 and the date of the entry into force of any amendments under article 29;
(c) Denunciations under article 31.

Article 33

1. This Convention, of which the Arabic, Chinese, English, French, Russian and Spanish texts are equally authentic, shall be deposited with the Secretary-General of the United Nations.
2. The Secretary-General of the United Nations shall transmit certified copies of this Convention to all States.

18

Optional Protocol to the Convention against Torture and Other Cruel, Inhuman or Degrading Treatment or Punishment, 2002

Note: Adopted on 18 December 2002 by General Assembly Resolution A/RES/57/199, 2375 UNTS 237. Entry into force: 22 June 2006.

PREAMBLE

The States Parties to the present Protocol,

Reaffirming that torture and other cruel, inhuman or degrading treatment or punishment are prohibited and constitute serious violations of human rights,

Convinced that further measures are necessary to achieve the purposes of the Convention against Torture and Other Cruel, Inhuman or Degrading Treatment or Punishment (hereinafter referred to as the Convention) and to strengthen the protection of persons deprived of their liberty against torture and other cruel, inhuman or degrading treatment or punishment,

Recalling that articles 2 and 16 of the Convention oblige each State Party to take effective measures to prevent acts of torture and other cruel, inhuman or degrading treatment or punishment in any territory under its jurisdiction,

Recognizing that States have the primary responsibility for implementing those articles, that strengthening the protection of people deprived of their liberty and the full respect for their human rights is a common responsibility shared by all and that international implementing bodies complement and strengthen national measures,

Recalling that the effective prevention of torture and other cruel, inhuman or degrading treatment or punishment requires education and a combination of various legislative, administrative, judicial and other measures,

Recalling also that the World Conference on Human Rights firmly declared that efforts to eradicate torture should first and foremost be concentrated on prevention and called for the adoption of an optional protocol to the Convention, intended to establish a preventive system of regular visits to places of detention,

Convinced that the protection of persons deprived of their liberty against torture and other cruel, inhuman or degrading treatment or punishment can be strengthened by non-judicial means of a preventive nature, based on regular visits to places of detention, Have agreed as follows:

PART I: GENERAL PRINCIPLES

Article 1
The objective of the present Protocol is to establish a system of regular visits undertaken by independent international and national bodies to places where people are deprived of their liberty, in order to prevent torture and other cruel, inhuman or degrading treatment or punishment.

Article 2
1. A Subcommittee on Prevention of Torture and Other Cruel, Inhuman or Degrading Treatment or Punishment of the Committee against Torture (hereinafter referred to as the Subcommittee on Prevention) shall be established and shall carry out the functions laid down in the present Protocol.
2. The Subcommittee on Prevention shall carry out its work within the framework of the Charter of the United Nations and shall be guided by the purposes and principles thereof, as well as the norms of the United Nations concerning the treatment of people deprived of their liberty.
3. Equally, the Subcommittee on Prevention shall be guided by the principles of confidentiality, impartiality, non-selectivity, universality and objectivity.
4. The Subcommittee on Prevention and the States Parties shall cooperate in the implementation of the present Protocol.

Article 3
Each State Party shall set up, designate or maintain at the domestic level one or several visiting bodies for the prevention of torture and other cruel, inhuman or degrading treatment or punishment (hereinafter referred to as the national preventive mechanism).

Article 4
1. Each State Party shall allow visits, in accordance with the present Protocol, by the mechanisms referred to in articles 2 and 3 to any place under its jurisdiction and control where persons are or may be deprived of their liberty, either by virtue of an order given by a public authority or at its instigation or with its consent or acquiescence (hereinafter referred to as places of detention). These visits shall be undertaken with a view to strengthening, if necessary, the protection of these persons against torture and other cruel, inhuman or degrading treatment or punishment.
2. For the purposes of the present Protocol, deprivation of liberty means any form of detention or imprisonment or the placement of a person in a public or private custodial setting which that person is not permitted to leave at will by order of any judicial, administrative or other authority.

PART II: SUBCOMMITTEE ON PREVENTION

Article 5
1. The Subcommittee on Prevention shall consist of ten members. After the fiftieth ratification of or accession to the present Protocol, the number of the members of the Subcommittee on Prevention shall increase to twenty-five.

2. The members of the Subcommittee on Prevention shall be chosen from among persons of high moral character, having proven professional experience in the field of the administration of justice, in particular criminal law, prison or police administration, or in the various fields relevant to the treatment of persons deprived of their liberty.
3. In the composition of the Subcommittee on Prevention due consideration shall be given to equitable geographic distribution and to the representation of different forms of civilization and legal systems of the States Parties.
4. In this composition consideration shall also be given to balanced gender representation on the basis of the principles of equality and non-discrimination.
5. No two members of the Subcommittee on Prevention may be nationals of the same State.
6. The members of the Subcommittee on Prevention shall serve in their individual capacity, shall be independent and impartial and shall be available to serve the Subcommittee on Prevention efficiently.

Article 6

1. Each State Party may nominate, in accordance with paragraph 2 of the present article, up to two candidates possessing the qualifications and meeting the requirements set out in article 5, and in doing so shall provide detailed information on the qualifications of the nominees.
2. (a) The nominees shall have the nationality of a State Party to the present Protocol;
   (b) At least one of the two candidates shall have the nationality of the nominating State Party;
   (c) No more than two nationals of a State Party shall be nominated;
   (d) Before a State Party nominates a national of another State Party, it shall seek and obtain the consent of that State Party.
3. At least five months before the date of the meeting of the States Parties during which the elections will be held, the Secretary-General of the United Nations shall address a letter to the States Parties inviting them to submit their nominations within three months. The Secretary-General shall submit a list, in alphabetical order, of all persons thus nominated, indicating the States Parties that have nominated them.

Article 7

1. The members of the Subcommittee on Prevention shall be elected in the following manner:
   (a) Primary consideration shall be given to the fulfilment of the requirements and criteria of article 5 of the present Protocol;
   (b) The initial election shall be held no later than six months after the entry into force of the present Protocol;
   (c) The States Parties shall elect the members of the Subcommittee on Prevention by secret ballot;
   (d) Elections of the members of the Subcommittee on Prevention shall be held at biennial meetings of the States Parties convened by the Secretary-General of the United Nations. At those meetings, for which two thirds of the States Parties shall constitute a quorum, the persons elected to the Subcommittee on Prevention shall be those who obtain the largest number of votes and an absolute majority of the votes of the representatives of the States Parties present and voting.

2. If during the election process two nationals of a State Party have become eligible to serve as members of the Subcommittee on Prevention, the candidate receiving the higher number of votes shall serve as the member of the Subcommittee on Prevention. Where nationals have received the same number of votes, the following procedure applies:

(a) Where only one has been nominated by the State Party of which he or she is a national, that national shall serve as the member of the Subcommittee on Prevention;

(b) Where both candidates have been nominated by the State Party of which they are nationals, a separate vote by secret ballot shall be held to determine which national shall become the member;

(c) Where neither candidate has been nominated by the State Party of which he or she is a national, a separate vote by secret ballot shall be held to determine which candidate shall be the member.

Article 8

If a member of the Subcommittee on Prevention dies or resigns, or for any cause can no longer perform his or her duties, the State Party that nominated the member shall nominate another eligible person possessing the qualifications and meeting the requirements set out in article 5, taking into account the need for a proper balance among the various fields of competence, to serve until the next meeting of the States Parties, subject to the approval of the majority of the States Parties. The approval shall be considered given unless half or more of the States Parties respond negatively within six weeks after having been informed by the Secretary-General of the United Nations of the proposed appointment.

Article 9

The members of the Subcommittee on Prevention shall be elected for a term of four years. They shall be eligible for re-election once if renominated. The term of half the members elected at the first election shall expire at the end of two years; immediately after the first election the names of those members shall be chosen by lot by the Chairman of the meeting referred to in article 7, paragraph 1 (d).

Article 10

1. The Subcommittee on Prevention shall elect its officers for a term of two years. They may be re-elected.

2. The Subcommittee on Prevention shall establish its own rules of procedure. These rules shall provide, inter alia, that:

(a) Half the members plus one shall constitute a quorum;

(b) Decisions of the Subcommittee on Prevention shall be made by a majority vote of the members present;

(c) The Subcommittee on Prevention shall meet in camera.

3. The Secretary-General of the United Nations shall convene the initial meeting of the Subcommittee on Prevention. After its initial meeting, the Subcommittee on Prevention shall meet at such times as shall be provided by its rules of procedure. The Subcommittee on Prevention and the Committee against Torture shall hold their sessions simultaneously at least once a year.

PART III: MANDATE OF THE SUBCOMMITTEE ON PREVENTION

Article 11

1. The Subcommittee on Prevention shall:
   (a) Visit the places referred to in article 4 and make recommendations to States Parties concerning the protection of persons deprived of their liberty against torture and other cruel, inhuman or degrading treatment or punishment;
   (b) In regard to the national preventive mechanisms:
      (i) Advise and assist States Parties, when necessary, in their establishment;
      (ii) Maintain direct, and if necessary confidential, contact with the national preventive mechanisms and offer them training and technical assistance with a view to strengthening their capacities;
      (iii) Advise and assist them in the evaluation of the needs and the means necessary to strengthen the protection of persons deprived of their liberty against torture and other cruel, inhuman or degrading treatment or punishment;
      (iv) Make recommendations and observations to the States Parties with a view to strengthening the capacity and the mandate of the national preventive mechanisms for the prevention of torture and other cruel, inhuman or degrading treatment or punishment;
   (c) Cooperate, for the prevention of torture in general, with the relevant United Nations organs and mechanisms as well as with the international, regional and national institutions or organizations working towards the strengthening of the protection of all persons against torture and other cruel, inhuman or degrading treatment or punishment.

Article 12

In order to enable the Subcommittee on Prevention to comply with its mandate as laid down in article 11, the States Parties undertake:
   (a) To receive the Subcommittee on Prevention in their territory and grant it access to the places of detention as defined in article 4 of the present Protocol;
   (b) To provide all relevant information the Subcommittee on Prevention may request to evaluate the needs and measures that should be adopted to strengthen the protection of persons deprived of their liberty against torture and other cruel, inhuman or degrading treatment or punishment;
   (c) To encourage and facilitate contacts between the Subcommittee on Prevention and the national preventive mechanisms;
   (d) To examine the recommendations of the Subcommittee on Prevention and enter into dialogue with it on possible implementation measures.

Article 13

1. The Subcommittee on Prevention shall establish, at first by lot, a programme of regular visits to the States Parties in order to fulfil its mandate as established in article 11.
2. After consultations, the Subcommittee on Prevention shall notify the States Parties of its programme in order that they may, without delay, make the necessary practical arrangements for the visits to be conducted.

3. The visits shall be conducted by at least two members of the Subcommittee on Prevention. These members may be accompanied, if needed, by experts of demonstrated professional experience and knowledge in the fields covered by the present Protocol who shall be selected from a roster of experts prepared on the basis of proposals made by the States Parties, the Office of the United Nations High Commissioner for Human Rights and the United Nations Centre for International Crime Prevention. In preparing the roster, the States Parties concerned shall propose no more than five national experts. The State Party concerned may oppose the inclusion of a specific expert in the visit, whereupon the Subcommittee on Prevention shall propose another expert.

4. If the Subcommittee on Prevention considers it appropriate, it may propose a short follow-up visit after a regular visit.

Article 14

1. In order to enable the Subcommittee on Prevention to fulfil its mandate, the States Parties to the present Protocol undertake to grant it:
   (a) Unrestricted access to all information concerning the number of persons deprived of their liberty in places of detention as defined in article 4, as well as the number of places and their location;
   (b) Unrestricted access to all information referring to the treatment of those persons as well as their conditions of detention;
   (c) Subject to paragraph 2 below, unrestricted access to all places of detention and their installations and facilities;
   (d) The opportunity to have private interviews with the persons deprived of their liberty without witnesses, either personally or with a translator if deemed necessary, as well as with any other person who the Subcommittee on Prevention believes may supply relevant information;
   (e) The liberty to choose the places it wants to visit and the persons it wants to interview.

2. Objection to a visit to a particular place of detention may be made only on urgent and compelling grounds of national defence, public safety, natural disaster or serious disorder in the place to be visited that temporarily prevent the carrying out of such a visit. The existence of a declared state of emergency as such shall not be invoked by a State Party as a reason to object to a visit.

Article 15

No authority or official shall order, apply, permit or tolerate any sanction against any person or organization for having communicated to the Subcommittee on Prevention or to its delegates any information, whether true or false, and no such person or organization shall be otherwise prejudiced in any way.

Article 16

1. The Subcommittee on Prevention shall communicate its recommendations and observations confidentially to the State Party and, if relevant, to the national preventive mechanism.

2. The Subcommittee on Prevention shall publish its report, together with any comments of the State Party concerned, whenever requested to do so by that State Party. If the

State Party makes part of the report public, the Subcommittee on Prevention may publish the report in whole or in part. However, no personal data shall be published without the express consent of the person concerned.

3. The Subcommittee on Prevention shall present a public annual report on its activities to the Committee against Torture.

4. If the State Party refuses to cooperate with the Subcommittee on Prevention according to articles 12 and 14, or to take steps to improve the situation in the light of the recommendations of the Subcommittee on Prevention, the Committee against Torture may, at the request of the Subcommittee on Prevention, decide, by a majority of its members, after the State Party has had an opportunity to make its views known, to make a public statement on the matter or to publish the report of the Subcommittee on Prevention.

PART IV: NATIONAL PREVENTIVE MECHANISMS

Article 17

Each State Party shall maintain, designate or establish, at the latest one year after the entry into force of the present Protocol or of its ratification or accession, one or several independent national preventive mechanisms for the prevention of torture at the domestic level. Mechanisms established by decentralized units may be designated as national preventive mechanisms for the purposes of the present Protocol if they are in conformity with its provisions.

Article 18

1. The States Parties shall guarantee the functional independence of the national preventive mechanisms as well as the independence of their personnel.

2. The States Parties shall take the necessary measures to ensure that the experts of the national preventive mechanism have the required capabilities and professional knowledge. They shall strive for a gender balance and the adequate representation of ethnic and minority groups in the country.

3. The States Parties undertake to make available the necessary resources for the functioning of the national preventive mechanisms.

4. When establishing national preventive mechanisms, States Parties shall give due consideration to the Principles relating to the status of national institutions for the promotion and protection of human rights.

Article 19

The national preventive mechanisms shall be granted at a minimum the power:

(a) To regularly examine the treatment of the persons deprived of their liberty in places of detention as defined in article 4, with a view to strengthening, if necessary, their protection against torture and other cruel, inhuman or degrading treatment or punishment;

(b) To make recommendations to the relevant authorities with the aim of improving the treatment and the conditions of the persons deprived of their liberty and to prevent torture and other cruel, inhuman or degrading treatment or punishment, taking into consideration the relevant norms of the United Nations;

(c) To submit proposals and observations concerning existing or draft legislation.

Article 20

In order to enable the national preventive mechanisms to fulfil their mandate, the States Parties to the present Protocol undertake to grant them:

(a) Access to all information concerning the number of persons deprived of their liberty in places of detention as defined in article 4, as well as the number of places and their location;

(b) Access to all information referring to the treatment of those persons as well as their conditions of detention;

(c) Access to all places of detention and their installations and facilities;

(d) The opportunity to have private interviews with the persons deprived of their liberty without witnesses, either personally or with a translator if deemed necessary, as well as with any other person who the national preventive mechanism believes may supply relevant information;

(e) The liberty to choose the places they want to visit and the persons they want to interview;

(f) The right to have contacts with the Subcommittee on Prevention, to send it information and to meet with it.

Article 21

1. No authority or official shall order, apply, permit or tolerate any sanction against any person or organization for having communicated to the national preventive mechanism any information, whether true or false, and no such person or organization shall be otherwise prejudiced in any way.

2. Confidential information collected by the national preventive mechanism shall be privileged. No personal data shall be published without the express consent of the person concerned.

Article 22

The competent authorities of the State Party concerned shall examine the recommendations of the national preventive mechanism and enter into a dialogue with it on possible implementation measures.

Article 23

The States Parties to the present Protocol undertake to publish and disseminate the annual reports of the national preventive mechanisms.

PART V: DECLARATION

Article 24

1. Upon ratification, States Parties may make a declaration postponing the implementation of their obligations under either part III or part IV of the present Protocol.

2. This postponement shall be valid for a maximum of three years. After due representations made by the State Party and after consultation with the Subcommittee on Prevention, the Committee against Torture may extend that period for an additional two years.

PART VI: FINANCIAL PROVISIONS

Article 25

1. The expenditure incurred by the Subcommittee on Prevention in the implementation of the present Protocol shall be borne by the United Nations.
2. The Secretary-General of the United Nations shall provide the necessary staff and facilities for the effective performance of the functions of the Subcommittee on Prevention under the present Protocol.

Article 26

1. A Special Fund shall be set up in accordance with the relevant procedures of the General Assembly, to be administered in accordance with the financial regulations and rules of the United Nations, to help finance the implementation of the recommendations made by the Subcommittee on Prevention after a visit to a State Party, as well as education programmes of the national preventive mechanisms.
2. The Special Fund may be financed through voluntary contributions made by Governments, intergovernmental and non-governmental organizations and other private or public entities.

PART VII: FINAL PROVISIONS

Article 27

1. The present Protocol is open for signature by any State that has signed the Convention.
2. The present Protocol is subject to ratification by any State that has ratified or acceded to the Convention. Instruments of ratification shall be deposited with the Secretary-General of the United Nations.
3. The present Protocol shall be open to accession by any State that has ratified or acceded to the Convention.
4. Accession shall be effected by the deposit of an instrument of accession with the Secretary-General of the United Nations.
5. The Secretary-General of the United Nations shall inform all States that have signed the present Protocol or acceded to it of the deposit of each instrument of ratification or accession.

Article 28

1. The present Protocol shall enter into force on the thirtieth day after the date of deposit with the Secretary-General of the United Nations of the twentieth instrument of ratification or accession.
2. For each State ratifying the present Protocol or acceding to it after the deposit with the Secretary-General of the United Nations of the twentieth instrument of ratification or accession, the present Protocol shall enter into force on the thirtieth day after the date of deposit of its own instrument of ratification or accession.

Article 29

The provisions of the present Protocol shall extend to all parts of federal States without any limitations or exceptions.

Article 30

No reservations shall be made to the present Protocol.

Article 31

The provisions of the present Protocol shall not affect the obligations of States Parties under any regional convention instituting a system of visits to places of detention. The Subcommittee on Prevention and the bodies established under such regional conventions are encouraged to consult and cooperate with a view to avoiding duplication and promoting effectively the objectives of the present Protocol.

Article 32

The provisions of the present Protocol shall not affect the obligations of States Parties to the four Geneva Conventions of 12 August 1949 and the Additional Protocols thereto of 8 June 1977, nor the opportunity available to any State Party to authorize the International Committee of the Red Cross to visit places of detention in situations not covered by international humanitarian law.

Article 33

1. Any State Party may denounce the present Protocol at any time by written notification addressed to the Secretary-General of the United Nations, who shall thereafter inform the other States Parties to the present Protocol and the Convention. Denunciation shall take effect one year after the date of receipt of the notification by the Secretary-General.
2. Such a denunciation shall not have the effect of releasing the State Party from its obligations under the present Protocol in regard to any act or situation that may occur prior to the date on which the denunciation becomes effective, or to the actions that the Subcommittee on Prevention has decided or may decide to take with respect to the State Party concerned, nor shall denunciation prejudice in any way the continued consideration of any matter already under consideration by the Subcommittee on Prevention prior to the date on which the denunciation becomes effective.
3. Following the date on which the denunciation of the State Party becomes effective, the Subcommittee on Prevention shall not commence consideration of any new matter regarding that State.

Article 34

1. Any State Party to the present Protocol may propose an amendment and file it with the Secretary-General of the United Nations. The Secretary-General shall thereupon communicate the proposed amendment to the States Parties to the present Protocol with a request that they notify him whether they favour a conference of States Parties for the purpose of considering and voting upon the proposal. In the event that within four months from the date of such communication at least one third of the States Parties favour such a conference, the Secretary-General shall convene the conference under the auspices of the United Nations. Any amendment adopted by a majority of two thirds of the States Parties present and voting at the conference shall be submitted by the Secretary-General of the United Nations to all States Parties for acceptance.

2. An amendment adopted in accordance with paragraph 1 of the present article shall come into force when it has been accepted by a two-thirds majority of the States Parties to the present Protocol in accordance with their respective constitutional processes.

3. When amendments come into force, they shall be binding on those States Parties that have accepted them, other States Parties still being bound by the provisions of the present Protocol and any earlier amendment that they have accepted.

Article 35

Members of the Subcommittee on Prevention and of the national preventive mechanisms shall be accorded such privileges and immunities as are necessary for the independent exercise of their functions. Members of the Subcommittee on Prevention shall be accorded the privileges and immunities specified in section 22 of the Convention on the Privileges and Immunities of the United Nations of 13 February 1946, subject to the provisions of section 23 of that Convention.

Article 36

When visiting a State Party, the members of the Subcommittee on Prevention shall, without prejudice to the provisions and purposes of the present Protocol and such privileges and immunities as they may enjoy:

(a) Respect the laws and regulations of the visited State;

(b) Refrain from any action or activity incompatible with the impartial and international nature of their duties.

Article 37

1. The present Protocol, of which the Arabic, Chinese, English, French, Russian and Spanish texts are equally authentic, shall be deposited with the Secretary-General of the United Nations.

2. The Secretary-General of the United Nations shall transmit certified copies of the present Protocol to all States.

19

Convention on the Rights of the Child, 1989

Note: Adopted by General Assembly Resolution 44/25 of 20 November 1989, Official Records of the General Assembly (A/44/49) p. 166, 1577 UNTS 3. Entry into force: 2 September 1990.

PREAMBLE

The States Parties to the present Convention,

Considering that, in accordance with the principles proclaimed in the Charter of the United Nations, recognition of the inherent dignity and of the equal and inalienable rights of all members of the human family is the foundation of freedom, justice and peace in the world,

Bearing in mind that the peoples of the United Nations have, in the Charter, reaffirmed their faith in fundamental human rights and in the dignity and worth of the human person, and have determined to promote social progress and better standards of life in larger freedom,

Recognizing that the United Nations has, in the Universal Declaration of Human Rights and in the International Covenants on Human Rights, proclaimed and agreed that everyone is entitled to all the rights and freedoms set forth therein, without distinction of any kind, such as race, colour, sex, language, religion, political or other opinion, national or social origin, property, birth or other status,

Recalling that, in the Universal Declaration of Human Rights, the United Nations has proclaimed that childhood is entitled to special care and assistance,

Convinced that the family, as the fundamental group of society and the natural environment for the growth and well-being of all its members and particularly children, should be afforded the necessary protection and assistance so that it can fully assume its responsibilities within the community,

Recognizing that the child, for the full and harmonious development of his or her personality, should grow up in a family environment, in an atmosphere of happiness, love and understanding,

Considering that the child should be fully prepared to live an individual life in society, and brought up in the spirit of the ideals proclaimed in the Charter of the United Nations, and in particular in the spirit of peace, dignity, tolerance, freedom, equality and solidarity,

Bearing in mind that the need to extend particular care to the child has been stated in the Geneva Declaration of the Rights of the Child of 1924 and in the Declaration of the Rights of the Child adopted by the General Assembly on 20 November 1959 and recognized in the Universal Declaration of Human Rights, in the International Covenant on Civil and Political Rights (in particular in articles 23 and 24), in the International Covenant on Economic, Social and Cultural Rights (in particular in article 10) and in the statutes and relevant instruments of specialized agencies and international organizations concerned with the welfare of children,

Bearing in mind that, as indicated in the Declaration of the Rights of the Child, "the child, by reason of his physical and mental immaturity, needs special safeguards and care, including appropriate legal protection, before as well as after birth",

Recalling the provisions of the Declaration on Social and Legal Principles relating to the Protection and Welfare of Children, with Special Reference to Foster Placement and Adoption Nationally and Internationally; the United Nations Standard Minimum Rules for the Administration of Juvenile Justice (The Beijing Rules); and the Declaration on the Protection of Women and Children in Emergency and Armed Conflict, Recognizing that, in all countries in the world, there are children living in exceptionally difficult conditions, and that such children need special consideration,

Taking due account of the importance of the traditions and cultural values of each people for the protection and harmonious development of the child,

Recognizing the importance of international co-operation for improving the living conditions of children in every country, in particular in the developing countries,

Have agreed as follows:

PART I

Article 1
For the purposes of the present Convention, a child means every human being below the age of eighteen years unless under the law applicable to the child, majority is attained earlier.

Article 2
1. States Parties shall respect and ensure the rights set forth in the present Convention to each child within their jurisdiction without discrimination of any kind, irrespective of the child's or his or her parent's or legal guardian's race, colour, sex, language, religion, political or other opinion, national, ethnic or social origin, property, disability, birth or other status.
2. States Parties shall take all appropriate measures to ensure that the child is protected against all forms of discrimination or punishment on the basis of the status, activities, expressed opinions, or beliefs of the child's parents, legal guardians, or family members.

Article 3
1. In all actions concerning children, whether undertaken by public or private social welfare institutions, courts of law, administrative authorities or legislative bodies, the best interests of the child shall be a primary consideration.
2. States Parties undertake to ensure the child such protection and care as is necessary for his or her well-being, taking into account the rights and duties of his or her parents, legal guardians, or other individuals legally responsible for him or her, and, to this end, shall take all appropriate legislative and administrative measures.

3. States Parties shall ensure that the institutions, services and facilities responsible for the care or protection of children shall conform with the standards established by competent authorities, particularly in the areas of safety, health, in the number and suitability of their staff, as well as competent supervision.

Article 4

States Parties shall undertake all appropriate legislative, administrative, and other measures for the implementation of the rights recognized in the present Convention. With regard to economic, social and cultural rights, States Parties shall undertake such measures to the maximum extent of their available resources and, where needed, within the framework of international co-operation.

Article 5

States Parties shall respect the responsibilities, rights and duties of parents or, where applicable, the members of the extended family or community as provided for by local custom, legal guardians or other persons legally responsible for the child, to provide, in a manner consistent with the evolving capacities of the child, appropriate direction and guidance in the exercise by the child of the rights recognized in the present Convention.

Article 6

1. States Parties recognize that every child has the inherent right to life.
2. States Parties shall ensure to the maximum extent possible the survival and development of the child.

Article 7

1. The child shall be registered immediately after birth and shall have the right from birth to a name, the right to acquire a nationality and, as far as possible, the right to know and be cared for by his or her parents.
2. States Parties shall ensure the implementation of these rights in accordance with their national law and their obligations under the relevant international instruments in this field, in particular where the child would otherwise be stateless.

Article 8

1. States Parties undertake to respect the right of the child to preserve his or her identity, including nationality, name and family relations as recognized by law without unlawful interference.
2. Where a child is illegally deprived of some or all of the elements of his or her identity, States Parties shall provide appropriate assistance and protection, with a view to re-establishing speedily his or her identity.

Article 9

1. States Parties shall ensure that a child shall not be separated from his or her parents against their will, except when competent authorities subject to judicial review determine, in accordance with applicable law and procedures, that such separation is necessary for the best interests of the child. Such determination may be necessary in a particular case such as one involving abuse or neglect of the child by the parents,

or one where the parents are living separately and a decision must be made as to the child's place of residence.

2. In any proceedings pursuant to paragraph 1 of the present article, all interested parties shall be given an opportunity to participate in the proceedings and make their views known.

3. States Parties shall respect the right of the child who is separated from one or both parents to maintain personal relations and direct contact with both parents on a regular basis, except if it is contrary to the child's best interests.

4. Where such separation results from any action initiated by a State Party, such as the detention, imprisonment, exile, deportation or death (including death arising from any cause while the person is in the custody of the State) of one or both parents or of the child, that State Party shall, upon request, provide the parents, the child or, if appropriate, another member of the family with the essential information concerning the whereabouts of the absent member(s) of the family unless the provision of the information would be detrimental to the well-being of the child. States Parties shall further ensure that the submission of such a request shall of itself entail no adverse consequences for the person(s) concerned.

Article 10

1. In accordance with the obligation of States Parties under article 9, paragraph 1, applications by a child or his or her parents to enter or leave a State Party for the purpose of family reunification shall be dealt with by States Parties in a positive, humane and expeditious manner. States Parties shall further ensure that the submission of such a request shall entail no adverse consequences for the applicants and for the members of their family.

2. A child whose parents reside in different States shall have the right to maintain on a regular basis, save in exceptional circumstances personal relations and direct contacts with both parents. Towards that end and in accordance with the obligation of States Parties under article 9, paragraph 1, States Parties shall respect the right of the child and his or her parents to leave any country, including their own, and to enter their own country. The right to leave any country shall be subject only to such restrictions as are prescribed by law and which are necessary to protect the national security, public order (ordre public), public health or morals or the rights and freedoms of others and are consistent with the other rights recognized in the present Convention.

Article 11

1. States Parties shall take measures to combat the illicit transfer and non-return of children abroad.

2. To this end, States Parties shall promote the conclusion of bilateral or multilateral agreements or accession to existing agreements.

Article 12

1. States Parties shall assure to the child who is capable of forming his or her own views the right to express those views freely in all matters affecting the child, the views of the child being given due weight in accordance with the age and maturity of the child.

2. For this purpose, the child shall in particular be provided the opportunity to be heard in any judicial and administrative proceedings affecting the child, either directly, or

through a representative or an appropriate body, in a manner consistent with the procedural rules of national law.

Article 13

1. The child shall have the right to freedom of expression; this right shall include freedom to seek, receive and impart information and ideas of all kinds, regardless of frontiers, either orally, in writing or in print, in the form of art, or through any other media of the child's choice.
2. The exercise of this right may be subject to certain restrictions, but these shall only be such as are provided by law and are necessary:
   (a) For respect of the rights or reputations of others; or
   (b) For the protection of national security or of public order (ordre public), or of public health or morals.

Article 14

1. States Parties shall respect the right of the child to freedom of thought, conscience and religion.
2. States Parties shall respect the rights and duties of the parents and, when applicable, legal guardians, to provide direction to the child in the exercise of his or her right in a manner consistent with the evolving capacities of the child.
3. Freedom to manifest one's religion or beliefs may be subject only to such limitations as are prescribed by law and are necessary to protect public safety, order, health or morals, or the fundamental rights and freedoms of others.

Article 15

1. States Parties recognize the rights of the child to freedom of association and to freedom of peaceful assembly.
2. No restrictions may be placed on the exercise of these rights other than those imposed in conformity with the law and which are necessary in a democratic society in the interests of national security or public safety, public order (ordre public), the protection of public health or morals or the protection of the rights and freedoms of others.

Article 16

1. No child shall be subjected to arbitrary or unlawful interference with his or her privacy, family, or correspondence, nor to unlawful attacks on his or her honour and reputation.
2. The child has the right to the protection of the law against such interference or attacks.

Article 17

States Parties recognize the important function performed by the mass media and shall ensure that the child has access to information and material from a diversity of national and international sources, especially those aimed at the promotion of his or her social, spiritual and moral well-being and physical and mental health.

   To this end, States Parties shall:
   (a) Encourage the mass media to disseminate information and material of social and cultural benefit to the child and in accordance with the spirit of article 29;

(b) Encourage international co-operation in the production, exchange and dissemination of such information and material from a diversity of cultural, national and international sources;

(c) Encourage the production and dissemination of children's books;

(d) Encourage the mass media to have particular regard to the linguistic needs of the child who belongs to a minority group or who is indigenous;

(e) Encourage the development of appropriate guidelines for the protection of the child from information and material injurious to his or her well-being, bearing in mind the provisions of articles 13 and 18.

Article 18

1. States Parties shall use their best efforts to ensure recognition of the principle that both parents have common responsibilities for the upbringing and development of the child. Parents or, as the case may be, legal guardians, have the primary responsibility for the upbringing and development of the child. The best interests of the child will be their basic concern.

2. For the purpose of guaranteeing and promoting the rights set forth in the present Convention, States Parties shall render appropriate assistance to parents and legal guardians in the performance of their child-rearing responsibilities and shall ensure the development of institutions, facilities and services for the care of children.

3. States Parties shall take all appropriate measures to ensure that children of working parents have the right to benefit from child-care services and facilities for which they are eligible.

Article 19

1. States Parties shall take all appropriate legislative, administrative, social and educational measures to protect the child from all forms of physical or mental violence, injury or abuse, neglect or negligent treatment, maltreatment or exploitation, including sexual abuse, while in the care of parent(s), legal guardian(s) or any other person who has the care of the child.

2. Such protective measures should, as appropriate, include effective procedures for the establishment of social programmes to provide necessary support for the child and for those who have the care of the child, as well as for other forms of prevention and for identification, reporting, referral, investigation, treatment and follow-up of instances of child maltreatment described heretofore, and, as appropriate, for judicial involvement.

Article 20

1. A child temporarily or permanently deprived of his or her family environment, or in whose own best interests cannot be allowed to remain in that environment, shall be entitled to special protection and assistance provided by the State.

2. States Parties shall in accordance with their national laws ensure alternative care for such a child.

3. Such care could include, inter alia, foster placement, kafalah of Islamic law, adoption or if necessary placement in suitable institutions for the care of children. When considering solutions, due regard shall be paid to the desirability of continuity in a child's upbringing and to the child's ethnic, religious, cultural and linguistic background.

Article 21

States Parties that recognize and/or permit the system of adoption shall ensure that the best interests of the child shall be the paramount consideration and they shall:

(a) Ensure that the adoption of a child is authorized only by competent authorities who determine, in accordance with applicable law and procedures and on the basis of all pertinent and reliable information, that the adoption is permissible in view of the child's status concerning parents, relatives and legal guardians and that, if required, the persons concerned have given their informed consent to the adoption on the basis of such counselling as may be necessary;

(b) Recognize that inter-country adoption may be considered as an alternative means of child's care, if the child cannot be placed in a foster or an adoptive family or cannot in any suitable manner be cared for in the child's country of origin;

(c) Ensure that the child concerned by inter-country adoption enjoys safeguards and standards equivalent to those existing in the case of national adoption;

(d) Take all appropriate measures to ensure that, in inter-country adoption, the placement does not result in improper financial gain for those involved in it;

(e) Promote, where appropriate, the objectives of the present article by concluding bilateral or multilateral arrangements or agreements, and endeavour, within this framework, to ensure that the placement of the child in another country is carried out by competent authorities or organs.

Article 22

1. States Parties shall take appropriate measures to ensure that a child who is seeking refugee status or who is considered a refugee in accordance with applicable international or domestic law and procedures shall, whether unaccompanied or accompanied by his or her parents or by any other person, receive appropriate protection and humanitarian assistance in the enjoyment of applicable rights set forth in the present Convention and in other international human rights or humanitarian instruments to which the said States are Parties.

2. For this purpose, States Parties shall provide, as they consider appropriate, co-operation in any efforts by the United Nations and other competent intergovernmental organizations or non-governmental organizations co-operating with the United Nations to protect and assist such a child and to trace the parents or other members of the family of any refugee child in order to obtain information necessary for reunification with his or her family. In cases where no parents or other members of the family can be found, the child shall be accorded the same protection as any other child permanently or temporarily deprived of his or her family environment for any reason, as set forth in the present Convention.

Article 23

1. States Parties recognize that a mentally or physically disabled child should enjoy a full and decent life, in conditions which ensure dignity, promote self-reliance and facilitate the child's active participation in the community.

2. States Parties recognize the right of the disabled child to special care and shall encourage and ensure the extension, subject to available resources, to the eligible child and those responsible for his or her care, of assistance for which application is made and

which is appropriate to the child's condition and to the circumstances of the parents or others caring for the child.

3. Recognizing the special needs of a disabled child, assistance extended in accordance with paragraph 2 of the present article shall be provided free of charge, whenever possible, taking into account the financial resources of the parents or others caring for the child, and shall be designed to ensure that the disabled child has effective access to and receives education, training, health care services, rehabilitation services, preparation for employment and recreation opportunities in a manner conducive to the child's achieving the fullest possible social integration and individual development, including his or her cultural and spiritual development.

4. States Parties shall promote, in the spirit of international cooperation, the exchange of appropriate information in the field of preventive health care and of medical, psychological and functional treatment of disabled children, including dissemination of and access to information concerning methods of rehabilitation, education and vocational services, with the aim of enabling States Parties to improve their capabilities and skills and to widen their experience in these areas. In this regard, particular account shall be taken of the needs of developing countries.

Article 24

1. States Parties recognize the right of the child to the enjoyment of the highest attainable standard of health and to facilities for the treatment of illness and rehabilitation of health. States Parties shall strive to ensure that no child is deprived of his or her right of access to such health care services.

2. States Parties shall pursue full implementation of this right and, in particular, shall take appropriate measures:

   (a) To diminish infant and child mortality;

   (b) To ensure the provision of necessary medical assistance and health care to all children with emphasis on the development of primary health care;

   (c) To combat disease and malnutrition, including within the framework of primary health care, through, inter alia, the application of readily available technology and through the provision of adequate nutritious foods and clean drinking-water, taking into consideration the dangers and risks of environmental pollution;

   (d) To ensure appropriate pre-natal and post-natal health care for mothers;

   (e) To ensure that all segments of society, in particular parents and children, are informed, have access to education and are supported in the use of basic knowledge of child health and nutrition, the advantages of breastfeeding, hygiene and environmental sanitation and the prevention of accidents;

   (f) To develop preventive health care, guidance for parents and family planning education and services.

3. States Parties shall take all effective and appropriate measures with a view to abolishing traditional practices prejudicial to the health of children.

4. States Parties undertake to promote and encourage international co-operation with a view to achieving progressively the full realization of the right recognized in the present article. In this regard, particular account shall be taken of the needs of developing countries.

Article 25

States Parties recognize the right of a child who has been placed by the competent authorities for the purposes of care, protection or treatment of his or her physical or mental health, to a periodic review of the treatment provided to the child and all other circumstances relevant to his or her placement.

Article 26

1. States Parties shall recognize for every child the right to benefit from social security, including social insurance, and shall take the necessary measures to achieve the full realization of this right in accordance with their national law.
2. The benefits should, where appropriate, be granted, taking into account the resources and the circumstances of the child and persons having responsibility for the maintenance of the child, as well as any other consideration relevant to an application for benefits made by or on behalf of the child.

Article 27

1. States Parties recognize the right of every child to a standard of living adequate for the child's physical, mental, spiritual, moral and social development.
2. The parent(s) or others responsible for the child have the primary responsibility to secure, within their abilities and financial capacities, the conditions of living necessary for the child's development.
3. States Parties, in accordance with national conditions and within their means, shall take appropriate measures to assist parents and others responsible for the child to implement this right and shall in case of need provide material assistance and support programmes, particularly with regard to nutrition, clothing and housing.
4. States Parties shall take all appropriate measures to secure the recovery of maintenance for the child from the parents or other persons having financial responsibility for the child, both within the State Party and from abroad. In particular, where the person having financial responsibility for the child lives in a State different from that of the child, States Parties shall promote the accession to international agreements or the conclusion of such agreements, as well as the making of other appropriate arrangements.

Article 28

1. States Parties recognize the right of the child to education, and with a view to achieving this right progressively and on the basis of equal opportunity, they shall, in particular:
    (a) Make primary education compulsory and available free to all;
    (b) Encourage the development of different forms of secondary education, including general and vocational education, make them available and accessible to every child, and take appropriate measures such as the introduction of free education and offering financial assistance in case of need;
    (c) Make higher education accessible to all on the basis of capacity by every appropriate means;
    (d) Make educational and vocational information and guidance available and accessible to all children;
    (e) Take measures to encourage regular attendance at schools and the reduction of drop-out rates.

2. States Parties shall take all appropriate measures to ensure that school discipline is administered in a manner consistent with the child's human dignity and in conformity with the present Convention.

3. States Parties shall promote and encourage international cooperation in matters relating to education, in particular with a view to contributing to the elimination of ignorance and illiteracy throughout the world and facilitating access to scientific and technical knowledge and modern teaching methods. In this regard, particular account shall be taken of the needs of developing countries.

Article 29

1. States Parties agree that the education of the child shall be directed to:
   (a) The development of the child's personality, talents and mental and physical abilities to their fullest potential;
   (b) The development of respect for human rights and fundamental freedoms, and for the principles enshrined in the Charter of the United Nations;
   (c) The development of respect for the child's parents, his or her own cultural identity, language and values, for the national values of the country in which the child is living, the country from which he or she may originate, and for civilizations different from his or her own;
   (d) The preparation of the child for responsible life in a free society, in the spirit of understanding, peace, tolerance, equality of sexes, and friendship among all peoples, ethnic, national and religious groups and persons of indigenous origin;
   (e) The development of respect for the natural environment.

2. No part of the present article or article 28 shall be construed so as to interfere with the liberty of individuals and bodies to establish and direct educational institutions, subject always to the observance of the principle set forth in paragraph 1 of the present article and to the requirements that the education given in such institutions shall conform to such minimum standards as may be laid down by the State.

Article 30

In those States in which ethnic, religious or linguistic minorities or persons of indigenous origin exist, a child belonging to such a minority or who is indigenous shall not be denied the right, in community with other members of his or her group, to enjoy his or her own culture, to profess and practise his or her own religion, or to use his or her own language.

Article 31

1. States Parties recognize the right of the child to rest and leisure, to engage in play and recreational activities appropriate to the age of the child and to participate freely in cultural life and the arts.

2. States Parties shall respect and promote the right of the child to participate fully in cultural and artistic life and shall encourage the provision of appropriate and equal opportunities for cultural, artistic, recreational and leisure activity.

Article 32

1. States Parties recognize the right of the child to be protected from economic exploitation and from performing any work that is likely to be hazardous or to interfere with

the child's education, or to be harmful to the child's health or physical, mental, spiritual, moral or social development.

2. States Parties shall take legislative, administrative, social and educational measures to ensure the implementation of the present article. To this end, and having regard to the relevant provisions of other international instruments, States Parties shall in particular:

    (a) Provide for a minimum age or minimum ages for admission to employment;
    (b) Provide for appropriate regulation of the hours and conditions of employment;
    (c) Provide for appropriate penalties or other sanctions to ensure the effective enforcement of the present article.

Article 33

States Parties shall take all appropriate measures, including legislative, administrative, social and educational measures, to protect children from the illicit use of narcotic drugs and psychotropic substances as defined in the relevant international treaties, and to prevent the use of children in the illicit production and trafficking of such substances.

Article 34

States Parties undertake to protect the child from all forms of sexual exploitation and sexual abuse. For these purposes, States Parties shall in particular take all appropriate national, bilateral and multilateral measures to prevent:

    (a) The inducement or coercion of a child to engage in any unlawful sexual activity;
    (b) The exploitative use of children in prostitution or other unlawful sexual practices;
    (c) The exploitative use of children in pornographic performances and materials.

Article 35

States Parties shall take all appropriate national, bilateral and multilateral measures to prevent the abduction of, the sale of or traffic in children for any purpose or in any form.

Article 36

States Parties shall protect the child against all other forms of exploitation prejudicial to any aspects of the child's welfare.

Article 37

States Parties shall ensure that:

    (a) No child shall be subjected to torture or other cruel, inhuman or degrading treatment or punishment. Neither capital punishment nor life imprisonment without possibility of release shall be imposed for offences committed by persons below eighteen years of age;
    (b) No child shall be deprived of his or her liberty unlawfully or arbitrarily. The arrest, detention or imprisonment of a child shall be in conformity with the law and shall be used only as a measure of last resort and for the shortest appropriate period of time;
    (c) Every child deprived of liberty shall be treated with humanity and respect for the inherent dignity of the human person, and in a manner which takes into account the needs of persons of his or her age. In particular, every child deprived of liberty shall be separated from adults unless it is considered in the child's best interest not

to do so and shall have the right to maintain contact with his or her family through correspondence and visits, save in exceptional circumstances;

(d) Every child deprived of his or her liberty shall have the right to prompt access to legal and other appropriate assistance, as well as the right to challenge the legality of the deprivation of his or her liberty before a court or other competent, independent and impartial authority, and to a prompt decision on any such action.

Article 38

1. States Parties undertake to respect and to ensure respect for rules of international humanitarian law applicable to them in armed conflicts which are relevant to the child.
2. States Parties shall take all feasible measures to ensure that persons who have not attained the age of fifteen years do not take a direct part in hostilities.
3. States Parties shall refrain from recruiting any person who has not attained the age of fifteen years into their armed forces. In recruiting among those persons who have attained the age of fifteen years but who have not attained the age of eighteen years, States Parties shall endeavour to give priority to those who are oldest.
4. In accordance with their obligations under international humanitarian law to protect the civilian population in armed conflicts, States Parties shall take all feasible measures to ensure protection and care of children who are affected by an armed conflict.

Article 39

States Parties shall take all appropriate measures to promote physical and psychological recovery and social reintegration of a child victim of: any form of neglect, exploitation, or abuse; torture or any other form of cruel, inhuman or degrading treatment or punishment; or armed conflicts. Such recovery and reintegration shall take place in an environment which fosters the health, self-respect and dignity of the child.

Article 40

1. States Parties recognize the right of every child alleged as, accused of, or recognized as having infringed the penal law to be treated in a manner consistent with the promotion of the child's sense of dignity and worth, which reinforces the child's respect for the human rights and fundamental freedoms of others and which takes into account the child's age and the desirability of promoting the child's reintegration and the child's assuming a constructive role in society.
2. To this end, and having regard to the relevant provisions of international instruments, States Parties shall, in particular, ensure that:
   (a) No child shall be alleged as, be accused of, or recognized as having infringed the penal law by reason of acts or omissions that were not prohibited by national or international law at the time they were committed;
   (b) Every child alleged as or accused of having infringed the penal law has at least the following guarantees:
      (i) To be presumed innocent until proven guilty according to law;
      (ii) To be informed promptly and directly of the charges against him or her, and, if appropriate, through his or her parents or legal guardians, and to have legal or other appropriate assistance in the preparation and presentation of his or her defence;

(iii) To have the matter determined without delay by a competent, independent and impartial authority or judicial body in a fair hearing according to law, in the presence of legal or other appropriate assistance and, unless it is considered not to be in the best interest of the child, in particular, taking into account his or her age or situation, his or her parents or legal guardians;

(iv) Not to be compelled to give testimony or to confess guilt; to examine or have examined adverse witnesses and to obtain the participation and examination of witnesses on his or her behalf under conditions of equality;

(v) If considered to have infringed the penal law, to have this decision and any measures imposed in consequence thereof reviewed by a higher competent, independent and impartial authority or judicial body according to law;

(vi) To have the free assistance of an interpreter if the child cannot understand or speak the language used;

(vii) To have his or her privacy fully respected at all stages of the proceedings.

3. States Parties shall seek to promote the establishment of laws, procedures, authorities and institutions specifically applicable to children alleged as, accused of, or recognized as having infringed the penal law, and, in particular:

(a) The establishment of a minimum age below which children shall be presumed not to have the capacity to infringe the penal law;

(b) Whenever appropriate and desirable, measures for dealing with such children without resorting to judicial proceedings, providing that human rights and legal safeguards are fully respected.

4. A variety of dispositions, such as care, guidance and supervision orders; counselling; probation; foster care; education and vocational training programmes and other alternatives to institutional care shall be available to ensure that children are dealt with in a manner appropriate to their well-being and proportionate both to their circumstances and the offence.

Article 41

Nothing in the present Convention shall affect any provisions which are more conducive to the realization of the rights of the child and which may be contained in:

(a) The law of a State party; or

(b) International law in force for that State.

PART II

Article 42

States Parties undertake to make the principles and provisions of the Convention widely known, by appropriate and active means, to adults and children alike.

Article 43

1. For the purpose of examining the progress made by States Parties in achieving the realization of the obligations undertaken in the present Convention, there shall be established a Committee on the Rights of the Child, which shall carry out the functions hereinafter provided.

2. The Committee shall consist of eighteen experts of high moral standing and recognized competence in the field covered by this Convention. The members of the Committee shall be elected by States Parties from among their nationals and shall serve in their personal capacity, consideration being given to equitable geographical distribution, as well as to the principal legal systems.

3. The members of the Committee shall be elected by secret ballot from a list of persons nominated by States Parties. Each State Party may nominate one person from among its own nationals.

4. The initial election to the Committee shall be held no later than six months after the date of the entry into force of the present Convention and thereafter every second year. At least four months before the date of each election, the Secretary-General of the United Nations shall address a letter to States Parties inviting them to submit their nominations within two months. The Secretary-General shall subsequently prepare a list in alphabetical order of all persons thus nominated, indicating States Parties which have nominated them, and shall submit it to the States Parties to the present Convention.

5. The elections shall be held at meetings of States Parties convened by the Secretary-General at United Nations Headquarters. At those meetings, for which two thirds of States Parties shall constitute a quorum, the persons elected to the Committee shall be those who obtain the largest number of votes and an absolute majority of the votes of the representatives of States Parties present and voting.

6. The members of the Committee shall be elected for a term of four years. They shall be eligible for re-election if renominated. The term of five of the members elected at the first election shall expire at the end of two years; immediately after the first election, the names of these five members shall be chosen by lot by the Chairman of the meeting.

7. If a member of the Committee dies or resigns or declares that for any other cause he or she can no longer perform the duties of the Committee, the State Party which nominated the member shall appoint another expert from among its nationals to serve for the remainder of the term, subject to the approval of the Committee.

8. The Committee shall establish its own rules of procedure.

9. The Committee shall elect its officers for a period of two years.

10. The meetings of the Committee shall normally be held at United Nations Headquarters or at any other convenient place as determined by the Committee. The Committee shall normally meet annually. The duration of the meetings of the Committee shall be determined, and reviewed, if necessary, by a meeting of the States Parties to the present Convention, subject to the approval of the General Assembly.

11. The Secretary-General of the United Nations shall provide the necessary staff and facilities for the effective performance of the functions of the Committee under the present Convention.

12. With the approval of the General Assembly, the members of the Committee established under the present Convention shall receive emoluments from United Nations resources on such terms and conditions as the Assembly may decide.

Article 44

1. States Parties undertake to submit to the Committee, through the Secretary-General of the United Nations, reports on the measures they have adopted which give effect to the rights recognized herein and on the progress made on the enjoyment of those rights

   (a) Within two years of the entry into force of the Convention for the State Party concerned;

   (b) Thereafter every five years.

2. Reports made under the present article shall indicate factors and difficulties, if any, affecting the degree of fulfilment of the obligations under the present Convention. Reports shall also contain sufficient information to provide the Committee with a comprehensive understanding of the implementation of the Convention in the country concerned.

3. A State Party which has submitted a comprehensive initial report to the Committee need not, in its subsequent reports submitted in accordance with paragraph 1 (b) of the present article, repeat basic information previously provided.

4. The Committee may request from States Parties further information relevant to the implementation of the Convention.

5. The Committee shall submit to the General Assembly, through the Economic and Social Council, every two years, reports on its activities.

6. States Parties shall make their reports widely available to the public in their own countries.

Article 45

In order to foster the effective implementation of the Convention and to encourage international co-operation in the field covered by the Convention:

(a) The specialized agencies, the United Nations Children's Fund, and other United Nations organs shall be entitled to be represented at the consideration of the implementation of such provisions of the present Convention as fall within the scope of their mandate. The Committee may invite the specialized agencies, the United Nations Children's Fund and other competent bodies as it may consider appropriate to provide expert advice on the implementation of the Convention in areas falling within the scope of their respective mandates. The Committee may invite the specialized agencies, the United Nations Children's Fund, and other United Nations organs to submit reports on the implementation of the Convention in areas falling within the scope of their activities;

(b) The Committee shall transmit, as it may consider appropriate, to the specialized agencies, the United Nations Children's Fund and other competent bodies, any reports from States Parties that contain a request, or indicate a need, for technical advice or assistance, along with the Committee's observations and suggestions, if any, on these requests or indications;

(c) The Committee may recommend to the General Assembly to request the Secretary-General to undertake on its behalf studies on specific issues relating to the rights of the child;

(d) The Committee may make suggestions and general recommendations based on information received pursuant to articles 44 and 45 of the present Convention.

Such suggestions and general recommendations shall be transmitted to any State Party concerned and reported to the General Assembly, together with comments, if any, from States Parties.

PART III

Article 46
The present Convention shall be open for signature by all States.

Article 47
The present Convention is subject to ratification. Instruments of ratification shall be deposited with the Secretary-General of the United Nations.

Article 48
The present Convention shall remain open for accession by any State. The instruments of accession shall be deposited with the Secretary-General of the United Nations.

Article 49
1. The present Convention shall enter into force on the thirtieth day following the date of deposit with the Secretary-General of the United Nations of the twentieth instrument of ratification or accession.
2. For each State ratifying or acceding to the Convention after the deposit of the twentieth instrument of ratification or accession, the Convention shall enter into force on the thirtieth day after the deposit by such State of its instrument of ratification or accession.

Article 50
1. Any State Party may propose an amendment and file it with the Secretary-General of the United Nations. The Secretary-General shall thereupon communicate the proposed amendment to States Parties, with a request that they indicate whether they favour a conference of States Parties for the purpose of considering and voting upon the proposals. In the event that, within four months from the date of such communication, at least one third of the States Parties favour such a conference, the Secretary-General shall convene the conference under the auspices of the United Nations. Any amendment adopted by a majority of States Parties present and voting at the conference shall be submitted to the General Assembly for approval.
2. An amendment adopted in accordance with paragraph 1 of the present article shall enter into force when it has been approved by the General Assembly of the United Nations and accepted by a two-thirds majority of States Parties.
3. When an amendment enters into force, it shall be binding on those States Parties which have accepted it, other States Parties still being bound by the provisions of the present Convention and any earlier amendments which they have accepted.

Article 51
1. The Secretary-General of the United Nations shall receive and circulate to all States the text of reservations made by States at the time of ratification or accession.

2. A reservation incompatible with the object and purpose of the present Convention shall not be permitted.

3. Reservations may be withdrawn at any time by notification to that effect addressed to the Secretary-General of the United Nations, who shall then inform all States. Such notification shall take effect on the date on which it is received by the Secretary-General

Article 52

A State Party may denounce the present Convention by written notification to the Secretary-General of the United Nations. Denunciation becomes effective one year after the date of receipt of the notification by the Secretary-General.

Article 53

The Secretary-General of the United Nations is designated as the depositary of the present Convention.

Article 54

The original of the present Convention, of which the Arabic, Chinese, English, French, Russian and Spanish texts are equally authentic, shall be deposited with the Secretary-General of the United Nations. In witness thereof the undersigned plenipotentiaries, being duly authorized thereto by their respective Governments, have signed the present Convention.

20

Optional Protocol to the Convention on the Rights of the Child on the Involvement of Children in Armed Conflict, 2000

Note: Adopted by General Assembly Resolution A/RES/54/263 of 25 May 2000, 2173 UNTS 222. Entry into force: 12 February 2002.

The States Parties to the present Protocol,

Encouraged by the overwhelming support for the Convention on the Rights of the Child, demonstrating the widespread commitment that exists to strive for the promotion and protection of the rights of the child,

Reaffirming that the rights of children require special protection, and calling for continuous improvement of the situation of children without distinction, as well as for their development and education in conditions of peace and security,

Disturbed by the harmful and widespread impact of armed conflict on children and the long-term consequences it has for durable peace, security and development,

Condemning the targeting of children in situations of armed conflict and direct attacks on objects protected under international law, including places that generally have a significant presence of children, such as schools and hospitals,

Noting the adoption of the Rome Statute of the International Criminal Court, in particular, the inclusion therein as a war crime, of conscripting or enlisting children under the age of 15 years or using them to participate actively in hostilities in both international and non-international armed conflict,

Considering therefore that to strengthen further the implementation of rights recognized in the Convention on the Rights of the Child there is a need to increase the protection of children from involvement in armed conflict,

Noting that article 1 of the Convention on the Rights of the Child specifies that, for the purposes of that Convention, a child means every human being below the age of 18 years unless, under the law applicable to the child, majority is attained earlier,

Convinced that an optional protocol to the Convention that raises the age of possible recruitment of persons into armed forces and their participation in hostilities will contribute effectively to the implementation of the principle that the best interests of the child are to be a primary consideration in all actions concerning children,

Noting that the twenty-sixth International Conference of the Red Cross and Red Crescent in December 1995 recommended, inter alia, that parties to conflict take every feasible step to ensure that children below the age of 18 years do not take part in hostilities,

Welcoming the unanimous adoption, in June 1999, of International Labour Organization Convention No. 182 on the Prohibition and Immediate Action for the

Elimination of the Worst Forms of Child Labour, which prohibits, inter alia, forced or compulsory recruitment of children for use in armed conflict,

Condemning with the gravest concern the recruitment, training and use within and across national borders of children in hostilities by armed groups distinct from the armed forces of a State, and recognizing the responsibility of those who recruit, train and use children in this regard,

Recalling the obligation of each party to an armed conflict to abide by the provisions of international humanitarian law,

Stressing that the present Protocol is without prejudice to the purposes and principles contained in the Charter of the United Nations, including Article 51, and relevant norms of humanitarian law,

Bearing in mind that conditions of peace and security based on full respect of the purposes and principles contained in the Charter and observance of applicable human rights instruments are indispensable for the full protection of children, in particular during armed conflict and foreign occupation,

Recognizing the special needs of those children who are particularly vulnerable to recruitment or use in hostilities contrary to the present Protocol owing to their economic or social status or gender,

Mindful of the necessity of taking into consideration the economic, social and political root causes of the involvement of children in armed conflict,

Convinced of the need to strengthen international cooperation in the implementation of the present Protocol, as well as the physical and psychosocial rehabilitation and social reintegration of children who are victims of armed conflict,

Encouraging the participation of the community and, in particular, children and child victims in the dissemination of informational and educational programmes concerning the implementation of the Protocol,

Have agreed as follows:

Article 1

States Parties shall take all feasible measures to ensure that members of their armed forces who have not attained the age of 18 years do not take a direct part in hostilities.

Article 2

States Parties shall ensure that persons who have not attained the age of 18 years are not compulsorily recruited into their armed forces.

Article 3

1. States Parties shall raise the minimum age for the voluntary recruitment of persons into their national armed forces from that set out in article 38, paragraph 3, of the Convention on the Rights of the Child, taking account of the principles contained in that article and recognizing that under the Convention persons under the age of 18 years are entitled to special protection.
2. Each State Party shall deposit a binding declaration upon ratification of or accession to the present Protocol that sets forth the minimum age at which it will permit voluntary recruitment into its national armed forces and a description of the safeguards it has adopted to ensure that such recruitment is not forced or coerced.

3. States Parties that permit voluntary recruitment into their national armed forces under the age of 18 years shall maintain safeguards to ensure, as a minimum, that:
   (a) Such recruitment is genuinely voluntary;
   (b) Such recruitment is carried out with the informed consent of the person's parents or legal guardians;
   (c) Such persons are fully informed of the duties involved in such military service;
   (d) Such persons provide reliable proof of age prior to acceptance into national military service.
4. Each State Party may strengthen its declaration at any time by notification to that effect addressed to the Secretary-General of the United Nations, who shall inform all States Parties. Such notification shall take effect on the date on which it is received by the Secretary-General.
5. The requirement to raise the age in paragraph 1 of the present article does not apply to schools operated by or under the control of the armed forces of the States Parties, in keeping with articles 28 and 29 of the Convention on the Rights of the Child.

Article 4

1. Armed groups that are distinct from the armed forces of a State should not, under any circumstances, recruit or use in hostilities persons under the age of 18 years.
2. States Parties shall take all feasible measures to prevent such recruitment and use, including the adoption of legal measures necessary to prohibit and criminalize such practices.
3. The application of the present article shall not affect the legal status of any party to an armed conflict.

Article 5

Nothing in the present Protocol shall be construed as precluding provisions in the law of a State Party or in international instruments and international humanitarian law that are more conducive to the realization of the rights of the child.

Article 6

1. Each State Party shall take all necessary legal, administrative and other measures to ensure the effective implementation and enforcement of the provisions of the present Protocol within its jurisdiction.
2. States Parties undertake to make the principles and provisions of the present Protocol widely known and promoted by appropriate means, to adults and children alike.
3. States Parties shall take all feasible measures to ensure that persons within their jurisdiction recruited or used in hostilities contrary to the present Protocol are demobilized or otherwise released from service. States Parties shall, when necessary, accord to such persons all appropriate assistance for their physical and psychological recovery and their social reintegration.

Article 7

1. States Parties shall cooperate in the implementation of the present Protocol, including in the prevention of any activity contrary thereto and in the rehabilitation and social reintegration of persons who are victims of acts contrary thereto, including through

technical cooperation and financial assistance. Such assistance and cooperation will be undertaken in consultation with the States Parties concerned and the relevant international organizations.

2. States Parties in a position to do so shall provide such assistance through existing multilateral, bilateral or other programmes or, inter alia, through a voluntary fund established in accordance with the rules of the General Assembly.

Article 8

1. Each State Party shall, within two years following the entry into force of the present Protocol for that State Party, submit a report to the Committee on the Rights of the Child providing comprehensive information on the measures it has taken to implement the provisions of the Protocol, including the measures taken to implement the provisions on participation and recruitment.

2. Following the submission of the comprehensive report, each State Party shall include in the reports it submits to the Committee on the Rights of the Child, in accordance with article 44 of the Convention, any further information with respect to the implementation of the Protocol. Other States Parties to the Protocol shall submit a report every five years.

3. The Committee on the Rights of the Child may request from States Parties further information relevant to the implementation of the present Protocol.

Article 9

1. The present Protocol is open for signature by any State that is a party to the Convention or has signed it.

2. The present Protocol is subject to ratification and is open to accession by any State. Instruments of ratification or accession shall be deposited with the Secretary-General of the United Nations.

3. The Secretary-General, in his capacity as depositary of the Convention and the Protocol, shall inform all States Parties to the Convention and all States that have signed the Convention of each instrument of declaration pursuant to article 3.

Article 10

1. The present Protocol shall enter into force three months after the deposit of the tenth instrument of ratification or accession.

2. For each State ratifying the present Protocol or acceding to it after its entry into force, the Protocol shall enter into force one month after the date of the deposit of its own instrument of ratification or accession.

Article 11

1. Any State Party may denounce the present Protocol at any time by written notification to the Secretary-General of the United Nations, who shall thereafter inform the other States Parties to the Convention and all States that have signed the Convention. The denunciation shall take effect one year after the date of receipt of the notification by the Secretary-General. If, however, on the expiry of that year the denouncing State Party is engaged in armed conflict, the denunciation shall not take effect before the end of the armed conflict.

2. Such a denunciation shall not have the effect of releasing the State Party from its obligations under the present Protocol in regard to any act that occurs prior to the date on which the denunciation becomes effective. Nor shall such a denunciation prejudice in any way the continued consideration of any matter that is already under consideration by the Committee on the Rights of the Child prior to the date on which the denunciation becomes effective.

Article 12

1. Any State Party may propose an amendment and file it with the Secretary-General of the United Nations. The Secretary-General shall thereupon communicate the proposed amendment to States Parties with a request that they indicate whether they favour a conference of States Parties for the purpose of considering and voting upon the proposals. In the event that, within four months from the date of such communication, at least one third of the States Parties favour such a conference, the Secretary-General shall convene the conference under the auspices of the United Nations. Any amendment adopted by a majority of States Parties present and voting at the conference shall be submitted to the General Assembly of the United Nations for approval.
2. An amendment adopted in accordance with paragraph 1 of the present article shall enter into force when it has been approved by the General Assembly and accepted by a two-thirds majority of States Parties.
3. When an amendment enters into force, it shall be binding on those States Parties that have accepted it, other States Parties still being bound by the provisions of the present Protocol and any earlier amendments they have accepted.

Article 13

1. The present Protocol, of which the Arabic, Chinese, English, French, Russian and Spanish texts are equally authentic, shall be deposited in the archives of the United Nations.
2. The Secretary-General of the United Nations shall transmit certified copies of the present Protocol to all States Parties to the Convention and all States that have signed the Convention.

21

Optional Protocol to the Convention on the Rights of the Child on the Sale of Children, Child Prostitution and Child Pornography, 2000

Note: Adopted by General Assembly Resolution A/RES/54/263 of 25 May 2000, 2171 UNTS 227. Entry into force: 18 January 2002.

The States Parties to the present Protocol,

Considering that, in order further to achieve the purposes of the Convention on the Rights of the Child and the implementation of its provisions, especially articles 1, 11, 21, 32, 33, 34, 35 and 36, it would be appropriate to extend the measures that States Parties should undertake in order to guarantee the protection of the child from the sale of children, child prostitution and child pornography,

Considering also that the Convention on the Rights of the Child recognizes the right of the child to be protected from economic exploitation and from performing any work that is likely to be hazardous or to interfere with the child's education, or to be harmful to the child's health or physical, mental, spiritual, moral or social development,

Gravely concerned at the significant and increasing international traffic in children for the purpose of the sale of children, child prostitution and child pornography,

Deeply concerned at the widespread and continuing practice of sex tourism, to which children are especially vulnerable, as it directly promotes the sale of children, child prostitution and child pornography,

Recognizing that a number of particularly vulnerable groups, including girl children, are at greater risk of sexual exploitation and that girl children are disproportionately represented among the sexually exploited,

Concerned about the growing availability of child pornography on the Internet and other evolving technologies, and recalling the International Conference on Combating Child Pornography on the Internet, held in Vienna in 1999, in particular its conclusion calling for the worldwide criminalization of the production, distribution, exportation, transmission, importation, intentional possession and advertising of child pornography, and stressing the importance of closer cooperation and partnership between Governments and the Internet industry,

Believing that the elimination of the sale of children, child prostitution and child pornography will be facilitated by adopting a holistic approach, addressing the contributing factors, including underdevelopment, poverty, economic disparities, inequitable socio-economic structure, dysfunctioning families, lack of education, urban-rural migration, gender discrimination, irresponsible adult sexual behaviour, harmful traditional practices, armed conflicts and trafficking in children,

Believing also that efforts to raise public awareness are needed to reduce consumer demand for the sale of children, child prostitution and child pornography, and believing further in the importance of strengthening global partnership among all actors and of improving law enforcement at the national level,

Noting the provisions of international legal instruments relevant to the protection of children, including the Hague Convention on Protection of Children and Cooperation in Respect of Intercountry Adoption, the Hague Convention on the Civil Aspects of International Child Abduction, the Hague Convention on Jurisdiction, Applicable Law, Recognition, Enforcement and Cooperation in Respect of Parental Responsibility and Measures for the Protection of Children, and International Labour Organization Convention No. 182 on the Prohibition and Immediate Action for the Elimination of the Worst Forms of Child Labour,

Encouraged by the overwhelming support for the Convention on the Rights of the Child, demonstrating the widespread commitment that exists for the promotion and protection of the rights of the child,

Recognizing the importance of the implementation of the provisions of the Programme of Action for the Prevention of the Sale of Children, Child Prostitution and Child Pornography and the Declaration and Agenda for Action adopted at the World Congress against Commercial Sexual Exploitation of Children, held in Stockholm from 27 to 31 August 1996, and the other relevant decisions and recommendations of pertinent international bodies,

Taking due account of the importance of the traditions and cultural values of each people for the protection and harmonious development of the child, Have agreed as follows:

Article 1
States Parties shall prohibit the sale of children, child prostitution and child pornography as provided for by the present Protocol.

Article 2
For the purposes of the present Protocol:
  (a) Sale of children means any act or transaction whereby a child is transferred by any person or group of persons to another for remuneration or any other consideration;
  (b) Child prostitution means the use of a child in sexual activities for remuneration or any other form of consideration;
  (c) Child pornography means any representation, by whatever means, of a child engaged in real or simulated explicit sexual activities or any representation of the sexual parts of a child for primarily sexual purposes.

Article 3
1. Each State Party shall ensure that, as a minimum, the following acts and activities are fully covered under its criminal or penal law, whether such offences are committed domestically or transnationally or on an individual or organized basis:
  (a) In the context of sale of children as defined in article 2:
    (i) Offering, delivering or accepting, by whatever means, a child for the purpose of:
      a. Sexual exploitation of the child;
      b. Transfer of organs of the child for profit;
      c. Engagement of the child in forced labour;
    (ii) Improperly inducing consent, as an intermediary, for the adoption of a child in violation of applicable international legal instruments on adoption;

   (b) Offering, obtaining, procuring or providing a child for child prostitution, as defined in article 2;

   (c) Producing, distributing, disseminating, importing, exporting, offering, selling or possessing for the above purposes child pornography as defined in article 2.

2. Subject to the provisions of the national law of a State Party, the same shall apply to an attempt to commit any of the said acts and to complicity or participation in any of the said acts.

3. Each State Party shall make such offences punishable by appropriate penalties that take into account their grave nature.

4. Subject to the provisions of its national law, each State Party shall take measures, where appropriate, to establish the liability of legal persons for offences established in paragraph 1 of the present article. Subject to the legal principles of the State Party, such liability of legal persons may be criminal, civil or administrative.

5. States Parties shall take all appropriate legal and administrative measures to ensure that all persons involved in the adoption of a child act in conformity with applicable international legal instruments.

Article 4

1. Each State Party shall take such measures as may be necessary to establish its jurisdiction over the offences referred to in article 3, paragraph 1, when the offences are committed in its territory or on board a ship or aircraft registered in that State.

2. Each State Party may take such measures as may be necessary to establish its jurisdiction over the offences referred to in article 3, paragraph 1, in the following cases:

   (a) When the alleged offender is a national of that State or a person who has his habitual residence in its territory;

   (b) When the victim is a national of that State.

3. Each State Party shall also take such measures as may be necessary to establish its jurisdiction over the aforementioned offences when the alleged offender is present in its territory and it does not extradite him or her to another State Party on the ground that the offence has been committed by one of its nationals.

4. The present Protocol does not exclude any criminal jurisdiction exercised in accordance with internal law.

Article 5

1. The offences referred to in article 3, paragraph 1, shall be deemed to be included as extraditable offences in any extradition treaty existing between States Parties and shall be included as extraditable offences in every extradition treaty subsequently concluded between them, in accordance with the conditions set forth in such treaties.

2. If a State Party that makes extradition conditional on the existence of a treaty receives a request for extradition from another State Party with which it has no extradition treaty, it may consider the present Protocol to be a legal basis for extradition in respect of such offences. Extradition shall be subject to the conditions provided by the law of the requested State.

3. States Parties that do not make extradition conditional on the existence of a treaty shall recognize such offences as extraditable offences between themselves subject to the conditions provided by the law of the requested State.

4. Such offences shall be treated, for the purpose of extradition between States Parties, as if they had been committed not only in the place in which they occurred but also in the territories of the States required to establish their jurisdiction in accordance with article 4.

5. If an extradition request is made with respect to an offence described in article 3, paragraph 1, and the requested State Party does not or will not extradite on the basis of the nationality of the offender, that State shall take suitable measures to submit the case to its competent authorities for the purpose of prosecution.

Article 6

1. States Parties shall afford one another the greatest measure of assistance in connection with investigations or criminal or extradition proceedings brought in respect of the offences set forth in article 3, paragraph 1, including assistance in obtaining evidence at their disposal necessary for the proceedings.

2. States Parties shall carry out their obligations under paragraph 1 of the present article in conformity with any treaties or other arrangements on mutual legal assistance that may exist between them. In the absence of such treaties or arrangements, States Parties shall afford one another assistance in accordance with their domestic law.

Article 7

States Parties shall, subject to the provisions of their national law:

(a) Take measures to provide for the seizure and confiscation, as appropriate, of:
   (i) Goods, such as materials, assets and other instrumentalities used to commit or facilitate offences under the present protocol;
   (ii) Proceeds derived from such offences;
(b) Execute requests from another State Party for seizure or confiscation of goods or proceeds referred to in subparagraph (a);
(c) Take measures aimed at closing, on a temporary or definitive basis, premises used to commit such offences.

Article 8

1. States Parties shall adopt appropriate measures to protect the rights and interests of child victims of the practices prohibited under the present Protocol at all stages of the criminal justice process, in particular by:

(a) Recognizing the vulnerability of child victims and adapting procedures to recognize their special needs, including their special needs as witnesses;
(b) Informing child victims of their rights, their role and the scope, timing and progress of the proceedings and of the disposition of their cases;
(c) Allowing the views, needs and concerns of child victims to be presented and considered in proceedings where their personal interests are affected, in a manner consistent with the procedural rules of national law;
(d) Providing appropriate support services to child victims throughout the legal process;
(e) Protecting, as appropriate, the privacy and identity of child victims and taking measures in accordance with national law to avoid the inappropriate dissemination of information that could lead to the identification of child victims;

    (f) Providing, in appropriate cases, for the safety of child victims, as well as that of their families and witnesses on their behalf, from intimidation and retaliation;

    (g) Avoiding unnecessary delay in the disposition of cases and the execution of orders or decrees granting compensation to child victims.

2. States Parties shall ensure that uncertainty as to the actual age of the victim shall not prevent the initiation of criminal investigations, including investigations aimed at establishing the age of the victim.

3. States Parties shall ensure that, in the treatment by the criminal justice system of children who are victims of the offences described in the present Protocol, the best interest of the child shall be a primary consideration.

4. States Parties shall take measures to ensure appropriate training, in particular legal and psychological training, for the persons who work with victims of the offences prohibited under the present Protocol.

5. States Parties shall, in appropriate cases, adopt measures in order to protect the safety and integrity of those persons and/or organizations involved in the prevention and/or protection and rehabilitation of victims of such offences.

6. Nothing in the present article shall be construed to be prejudicial to or inconsistent with the rights of the accused to a fair and impartial trial.

Article 9

1. States Parties shall adopt or strengthen, implement and disseminate laws, administrative measures, social policies and programmes to prevent the offences referred to in the present Protocol. Particular attention shall be given to protect children who are especially vulnerable to such practices.

2. States Parties shall promote awareness in the public at large, including children, through information by all appropriate means, education and training, about the preventive measures and harmful effects of the offences referred to in the present Protocol. In fulfilling their obligations under this article, States Parties shall encourage the participation of the community and, in particular, children and child victims, in such information and education and training programmes, including at the international level.

3. States Parties shall take all feasible measures with the aim of ensuring all appropriate assistance to victims of such offences, including their full social reintegration and their full physical and psychological recovery.

4. States Parties shall ensure that all child victims of the offences described in the present Protocol have access to adequate procedures to seek, without discrimination, compensation for damages from those legally responsible.

5. States Parties shall take appropriate measures aimed at effectively prohibiting the production and dissemination of material advertising the offences described in the present Protocol.

Article 10

1. States Parties shall take all necessary steps to strengthen international cooperation by multilateral, regional and bilateral arrangements for the prevention, detection, investigation, prosecution and punishment of those responsible for acts involving the sale

of children, child prostitution, child pornography and child sex tourism. States Parties shall also promote international cooperation and coordination between their authorities, national and international non-governmental organizations and international organizations.

2. States Parties shall promote international cooperation to assist child victims in their physical and psychological recovery, social reintegration and repatriation.

3. States Parties shall promote the strengthening of international cooperation in order to address the root causes, such as poverty and underdevelopment, contributing to the vulnerability of children to the sale of children, child prostitution, child pornography and child sex tourism.

4. States Parties in a position to do so shall provide financial, technical or other assistance through existing multilateral, regional, bilateral or other programmes.

Article 11

Nothing in the present Protocol shall affect any provisions that are more conducive to the realization of the rights of the child and that may be contained in:

(a) The law of a State Party;

(b) International law in force for that State.

Article 12

1. Each State Party shall, within two years following the entry into force of the present Protocol for that State Party, submit a report to the Committee on the Rights of the Child providing comprehensive information on the measures it has taken to implement the provisions of the Protocol.

2. Following the submission of the comprehensive report, each State Party shall include in the reports they submit to the Committee on the Rights of the Child, in accordance with article 44 of the Convention, any further information with respect to the implementation of the present Protocol. Other States Parties to the Protocol shall submit a report every five years.

3. The Committee on the Rights of the Child may request from States Parties further information relevant to the implementation of the present Protocol.

Article 13

1. The present Protocol is open for signature by any State that is a party to the Convention or has signed it.

2. The present Protocol is subject to ratification and is open to accession by any State that is a party to the Convention or has signed it. Instruments of ratification or accession shall be deposited with the Secretary-General of the United Nations.

Article 14

1. The present Protocol shall enter into force three months after the deposit of the tenth instrument of ratification or accession.

2. For each State ratifying the present Protocol or acceding to it after its entry into force, the Protocol shall enter into force one month after the date of the deposit of its own instrument of ratification or accession.

Article 15

1. Any State Party may denounce the present Protocol at any time by written notification to the Secretary-General of the United Nations, who shall thereafter inform the other States Parties to the Convention and all States that have signed the Convention. The denunciation shall take effect one year after the date of receipt of the notification by the Secretary-General.

2. Such a denunciation shall not have the effect of releasing the State Party from its obligations under the present Protocol in regard to any offence that occurs prior to the date on which the denunciation becomes effective. Nor shall such a denunciation prejudice in any way the continued consideration of any matter that is already under consideration by the Committee on the Rights of the Child prior to the date on which the denunciation becomes effective.

Article 16

1. Any State Party may propose an amendment and file it with the Secretary-General of the United Nations. The Secretary-General shall thereupon communicate the proposed amendment to States Parties with a request that they indicate whether they favour a conference of States Parties for the purpose of considering and voting upon the proposals. In the event that, within four months from the date of such communication, at least one third of the States Parties favour such a conference, the Secretary-General shall convene the conference under the auspices of the United Nations. Any amendment adopted by a majority of States Parties present and voting at the conference shall be submitted to the General Assembly of the United Nations for approval.

2. An amendment adopted in accordance with paragraph 1 of the present article shall enter into force when it has been approved by the General Assembly and accepted by a two-thirds majority of States Parties.

3. When an amendment enters into force, it shall be binding on those States Parties that have accepted it, other States Parties still being bound by the provisions of the present Protocol and any earlier amendments they have accepted.

Article 17

1. The present Protocol, of which the Arabic, Chinese, English, French, Russian and Spanish texts are equally authentic, shall be deposited in the archives of the United Nations.

2. The Secretary-General of the United Nations shall transmit certified copies of the present Protocol to all States Parties to the Convention and all States that have signed the Convention.

22

Optional Protocol to the Convention on the Rights of the Child on a Communications Procedure, 2011

Note: Adopted by General Assembly Resolution 66/138 on 19 December 2011. Registration No. 27531, 14 April 2014. Entry into force: 14 April 2014.

The States parties to the present Protocol,

Considering that, in accordance with the principles proclaimed in the Charter of the United Nations, the recognition of the inherent dignity and the equal and inalienable rights of all members of the human family is the foundation of freedom, justice and peace in the world,

Noting that the States parties to the Convention on the Rights of the Child (hereinafter referred to as "the Convention") recognize the rights set forth in it to each child within their jurisdiction without discrimination of any kind, irrespective of the child's or his or her parent's or legal guardian's race, colour, sex, language, religion, political or other opinion, national, ethnic or social origin, property, disability, birth or other status,

Reaffirming the universality, indivisibility, interdependence and interrelatedness of all human rights and fundamental freedoms,

Reaffirming also the status of the child as a subject of rights and as a human being with dignity and with evolving capacities,

Recognizing that children's special and dependent status may create real difficulties for them in pursuing remedies for violations of their rights,

Considering that the present Protocol will reinforce and complement national and regional mechanisms allowing children to submit complaints for violations of their rights,

Recognizing that the best interests of the child should be a primary consideration to be respected in pursuing remedies for violations of the rights of the child, and that such remedies should take into account the need for child-sensitive procedures at all levels,

Encouraging States parties to develop appropriate national mechanisms to enable a child whose rights have been violated to have access to effective remedies at the domestic level,

Recalling the important role that national human rights institutions and other relevant specialized institutions, mandated to promote and protect the rights of the child, can play in this regard,

Considering that, in order to reinforce and complement such national mechanisms and to further enhance the implementation of the Convention and, where applicable, the Optional Protocols thereto on the sale of children, child prostitution and child pornography and on the involvement of children in armed conflict, it would be appropriate to enable the Committee on the Rights of the Child (hereinafter referred to as "the Committee") to carry out the functions provided for in the present Protocol,

Have agreed as follows:

PART I GENERAL PROVISIONS

Article 1

Competence of the Committee on the Rights of the Child

1. A State party to the present Protocol recognizes the competence of the Committee as provided for by the present Protocol.
2. The Committee shall not exercise its competence regarding a State party to the present Protocol on matters concerning violations of rights set forth in an instrument to which that State is not a party.
3. No communication shall be received by the Committee if it concerns a State that is not a party to the present Protocol.

Article 2

General principles guiding the functions of the Committee

In fulfilling the functions conferred on it by the present Protocol, the Committee shall be guided by the principle of the best interests of the child. It shall also have regard for the rights and views of the child, the views of the child being given due weight in accordance with the age and maturity of the child.

Article 3

Rules of procedure

1. The Committee shall adopt rules of procedure to be followed when exercising the functions conferred on it by the present Protocol. In doing so, it shall have regard, in particular, for article 2 of the present Protocol in order to guarantee child-sensitive procedures.
2. The Committee shall include in its rules of procedure safeguards to prevent the manipulation of the child by those acting on his or her behalf and may decline to examine any communication that it considers not to be in the child's best interests.

Article 4

Protection measures

1. A State party shall take all appropriate steps to ensure that individuals under its jurisdiction are not subjected to any human rights violation, ill-treatment or intimidation as a consequence of communications or cooperation with the Committee pursuant to the present Protocol.
2. The identity of any individual or group of individuals concerned shall not be revealed publicly without their express consent.

PART II COMMUNICATIONS PROCEDURE

Article 5

Individual communications

1. Communications may be submitted by or on behalf of an individual or group of individuals, within the jurisdiction of a State party, claiming to be victims of a violation by that State party of any of the rights set forth in any of the following instruments to which that State is a party:
   (a) The Convention;
   (b) The Optional Protocol to the Convention on the sale of children, child prostitution and child pornography;
   (c) The Optional Protocol to the Convention on the involvement of children in armed conflict.
2. Where a communication is submitted on behalf of an individual or group of individuals, this shall be with their consent unless the author can justify acting on their behalf without such consent.

Article 6

Interim measures

1. At any time after the receipt of a communication and before a determination on the merits has been reached, the Committee may transmit to the State party concerned for its urgent consideration a request that the State party take such interim measures as may be necessary in exceptional circumstances to avoid possible irreparable damage to the victim or victims of the alleged violations.
2. Where the Committee exercises its discretion under paragraph 1 of the present article, this does not imply a determination on admissibility or on the merits of the communication.

Article 7

Admissibility

The Committee shall consider a communication inadmissible when:

(a) The communication is anonymous;

(b) The communication is not in writing;

(c) The communication constitutes an abuse of the right of submission of such communications or is incompatible with the provisions of the Convention and/or the Optional Protocols thereto;

(d) The same matter has already been examined by the Committee or has been or is being examined under another procedure of international investigation or settlement;

(e) All available domestic remedies have not been exhausted. This shall not be the rule where the application of the remedies is unreasonably prolonged or unlikely to bring effective relief;

(f) The communication is manifestly ill-founded or not sufficiently substantiated;

(g) The facts that are the subject of the communication occurred prior to the entry into force of the present Protocol for the State party concerned, unless those facts continued after that date;

(h) The communication is not submitted within one year after the exhaustion of domestic remedies, except in cases where the author can demonstrate that it had not been possible to submit the communication within that time limit.

Article 8

Transmission of the communication

1. Unless the Committee considers a communication inadmissible without reference to the State party concerned, the Committee shall bring any communication submitted to it under the present Protocol confidentially to the attention of the State party concerned as soon as possible.

2. The State party shall submit to the Committee written explanations or statements clarifying the matter and the remedy, if any, that it may have provided. The State party shall submit its response as soon as possible and within six months.

Article 9

Friendly settlement

1. The Committee shall make available its good offices to the parties concerned with a view to reaching a friendly settlement of the matter on the basis of respect for the obligations set forth in the Convention and/or the Optional Protocols thereto.

2. An agreement on a friendly settlement reached under the auspices of the Committee closes consideration of the communication under the present Protocol.

Article 10

Consideration of communications

1. The Committee shall consider communications received under the present Protocol as quickly as possible, in the light of all documentation submitted to it, provided that this documentation is transmitted to the parties concerned.
2. The Committee shall hold closed meetings when examining communications received under the present Protocol.
3. Where the Committee has requested interim measures, it shall expedite the consideration of the communication.
4. When examining communications alleging violations of economic, social or cultural rights, the Committee shall consider the reasonableness of the steps taken by the State party in accordance with article 4 of the Convention. In doing so, the Committee shall bear in mind that the State party may adopt a range of possible policy measures for the implementation of the economic, social and cultural rights in the Convention.
5. After examining a communication, the Committee shall, without delay, transmit its views on the communication, together with its recommendations, if any, to the parties concerned.

Article 11

Follow-up

1. The State party shall give due consideration to the views of the Committee, together with its recommendations, if any, and shall submit to the Committee a written response, including information on any action taken and envisaged in the light of the views and recommendations of the Committee. The State party shall submit its response as soon as possible and within six months.
2. The Committee may invite the State party to submit further information about any measures the State party has taken in response to its views or recommendations or implementation of a friendly settlement agreement, if any, including as deemed appropriate by the Committee, in the State party's subsequent reports under article 44 of the Convention, article 12 of the Optional Protocol to the Convention on the sale of children, child prostitution and child pornography or article 8 of the Optional Protocol to the Convention on the involvement of children in armed conflict, where applicable.

Article 12

Inter-State communications

1. A State party to the present Protocol may, at any time, declare that it recognizes the competence of the Committee to receive and consider communications in which a

State party claims that another State party is not fulfilling its obligations under any of the following instruments to which the State is a party:

(a) The Convention;

(b) The Optional Protocol to the Convention on the sale of children, child prostitution and child pornography;

(c) The Optional Protocol to the Convention on the involvement of children in armed conflict.

2. The Committee shall not receive communications concerning a State party that has not made such a declaration or communications from a State party that has not made such a declaration.

3. The Committee shall make available its good offices to the States parties concerned with a view to a friendly solution of the matter on the basis of the respect for the obligations set forth in the Convention and the Optional Protocols thereto.

4. A declaration under paragraph 1 of the present article shall be deposited by the States parties with the Secretary-General of the United Nations, who shall transmit copies thereof to the other States parties. A declaration may be withdrawn at any time by notification to the Secretary-General. Such a withdrawal shall not prejudice the consideration of any matter that is the subject of a communication already transmitted under the present article; no further communications by any State party shall be received under the present article after the notification of withdrawal of the declaration has been received by the Secretary-General, unless the State party concerned has made a new declaration.

PART III INQUIRY PROCEDURE

Article 13

Inquiry procedure for grave or systematic violations

1. If the Committee receives reliable information indicating grave or systematic violations by a State party of rights set forth in the Convention or in the Optional Protocols thereto on the sale of children, child prostitution and child pornography or on the involvement of children in armed conflict, the Committee shall invite the State party to cooperate in the examination of the information and, to this end, to submit observations without delay with regard to the information concerned.

2. Taking into account any observations that may have been submitted by the State party concerned, as well as any other reliable information available to it, the Committee may designate one or more of its members to conduct an inquiry and to report urgently to the Committee. Where warranted and with the consent of the State party, the inquiry may include a visit to its territory.

3. Such an inquiry shall be conducted confidentially, and the cooperation of the State party shall be sought at all stages of the proceedings.

4. After examining the findings of such an inquiry, the Committee shall transmit without delay these findings to the State party concerned, together with any comments and recommendations.

5. The State party concerned shall, as soon as possible and within six months of receiving the findings, comments and recommendations transmitted by the Committee, submit its observations to the Committee.

6. After such proceedings have been completed with regard to an inquiry made in accordance with paragraph 2 of the present article, the Committee may, after consultation with the State party concerned, decide to include a summary account of the results of the proceedings in its report provided for in article 16 of the present Protocol.

7. Each State party may, at the time of signature or ratification of the present Protocol or accession thereto, declare that it does not recognize the competence of the Committee provided for in the present article in respect of the rights set forth in some or all of the instruments listed in paragraph 1.

8. Any State party having made a declaration in accordance with paragraph 7 of the present article may, at any time, withdraw this declaration by notification to the Secretary-General of the United Nations.

Article 14

Follow-up to the inquiry procedure

1. The Committee may, if necessary, after the end of the period of six months referred to in article 13, paragraph 5, invite the State party concerned to inform it of the measures taken and envisaged in response to an inquiry conducted under article 13 of the present Protocol.

2. The Committee may invite the State party to submit further information about any measures that the State party has taken in response to an inquiry conducted under article 13, including as deemed appropriate by the Committee, in the State party's subsequent reports under article 44 of the Convention, article 12 of the Optional Protocol to the Convention on the sale of children, child prostitution and child pornography or article 8 of the Optional Protocol to the Convention on the involvement of children in armed conflict, where applicable.

PART IV FINAL PROVISIONS

Article 15

International assistance and cooperation

1. The Committee may transmit, with the consent of the State party concerned, to United Nations specialized agencies, funds and programmes and other competent bodies its views or recommendations concerning communications and inquiries that indicate a need for technical advice or assistance, together with the State party's observations and suggestions, if any, on these views or recommendations.

2. The Committee may also bring to the attention of such bodies, with the consent of the State party concerned, any matter arising out of communications considered under the present Protocol that may assist them in deciding, each within its field of competence, on the advisability of international measures likely to contribute to assisting

States parties in achieving progress in the implementation of the rights recognized in the Convention and/or the Optional Protocols thereto.

Article 16

Report to the General Assembly

The Committee shall include in its report submitted every two years to the General Assembly in accordance with article 44, paragraph 5, of the Convention a summary of its activities under the present Protocol.

Article 17

Dissemination of and information on the Optional Protocol

Each State party undertakes to make widely known and to disseminate the present Protocol and to facilitate access to information about the views and recommendations of the Committee, in particular with regard to matters involving the State party, by appropriate and active means and in accessible formats to adults and children alike, including those with disabilities.

Article 18

Signature, ratification and accession

1. The present Protocol is open for signature to any State that has signed, ratified or acceded to the Convention or either of the first two Optional Protocols thereto.
2. The present Protocol is subject to ratification by any State that has ratified or acceded to the Convention or either of the first two Optional Protocols thereto. Instruments of ratification shall be deposited with the Secretary-General of the United Nations.
3. The present Protocol shall be open to accession by any State that has ratified or acceded to the Convention or either of the first two Optional Protocols thereto.
4. Accession shall be effected by the deposit of an instrument of accession with the Secretary-General.

Article 19

Entry into force

1. The present Protocol shall enter into force three months after the deposit of the tenth instrument of ratification or accession.
2. For each State ratifying the present Protocol or acceding to it after the deposit of the tenth instrument of ratification or instrument of accession, the present Protocol shall enter into force three months after the date of the deposit of its own instrument of ratification or accession.

Article 20

Violations occurring after the entry into force

1. The Committee shall have competence solely in respect of violations by the State party of any of the rights set forth in the Convention and/or the first two Optional Protocols thereto occurring after the entry into force of the present Protocol.
2. If a State becomes a party to the present Protocol after its entry into force, the obligations of that State vis-à-vis the Committee shall relate only to violations of the rights set forth in the Convention and/or the first two Optional Protocols thereto occurring after the entry into force of the present Protocol for the State concerned.

Article 21

Amendments

1. Any State party may propose an amendment to the present Protocol and submit it to the Secretary-General of the United Nations. The Secretary-General shall communicate any proposed amendments to States parties with a request to be notified whether they favour a meeting of States parties for the purpose of considering and deciding upon the proposals. In the event that, within four months of the date of such communication, at least one third of the States parties favour such a meeting, the Secretary-General shall convene the meeting under the auspices of the United Nations. Any amendment adopted by a majority of two thirds of the States parties present and voting shall be submitted by the Secretary-General to the General Assembly for approval and, thereafter, to all States parties for acceptance.
2. An amendment adopted and approved in accordance with paragraph 1 of the present article shall enter into force on the thirtieth day after the number of instruments of acceptance deposited reaches two thirds of the number of States parties at the date of adoption of the amendment. Thereafter, the amendment shall enter into force for any State party on the thirtieth day following the deposit of its own instrument of acceptance. An amendment shall be binding only on those States parties that have accepted it.

Article 22

Denunciation

1. Any State party may denounce the present Protocol at any time by written notification to the Secretary-General of the United Nations. The denunciation shall take effect one year after the date of receipt of the notification by the Secretary-General.
2. Denunciation shall be without prejudice to the continued application of the provisions of the present Protocol to any communication submitted under articles 5 or 12 or any inquiry initiated under article 13 before the effective date of denunciation.

Article 23

Depositary and notification by the Secretary-General

1. The Secretary-General of the United Nations shall be the depositary of the present Protocol.
2. The Secretary-General shall inform all States of:
    (a) Signatures, ratifications and accessions under the present Protocol;
    (b) The date of entry into force of the present Protocol and of any amendment thereto under article 21;
    (c) Any denunciation under article 22 of the present Protocol.

Article 24

Languages

1. The present Protocol, of which the Arabic, Chinese, English, French, Russian and Spanish texts are equally authentic, shall be deposited in the archives of the United Nations.
2. The Secretary-General of the United Nations shall transmit certified copies of the present Protocol to all States.

23

International Convention on the Protection of the Rights of All Migrant Workers and Members of Their Families, 1990

Note: Adopted by General Assembly Resolution 45/158 of 18 December 1990, 2220 UNTS 3. Entry into force: 1 July 2003.

PREAMBLE

The States Parties to the present Convention,

Taking into account the principles embodied in the basic instruments of the United Nations concerning human rights, in particular the Universal Declaration of Human Rights, the International Covenant on Economic, Social and Cultural Rights, the International Covenant on Civil and Political Rights, the International Convention on the Elimination of All Forms of Racial Discrimination, the Convention on the Elimination of All Forms of Discrimination against Women and the Convention on the Rights of the Child,

Taking into account also the principles and standards set forth in the relevant instruments elaborated within the framework of the International Labour Organisation, especially the Convention concerning Migration for Employment (No. 97), the Convention concerning Migrations in Abusive Conditions and the Promotion of Equality of Opportunity and Treatment of Migrant Workers (No.143), the Recommendation concerning Migration for Employment (No. 86), the Recommendation concerning Migrant Workers (No. 151), the Convention concerning Forced or Compulsory Labour (No. 29) and the Convention concerning Abolition of Forced Labour (No. 105), Reaffirming the importance of the principles contained in the Convention against Discrimination in Education of the United Nations Educational, Scientific and Cultural Organization,

Recalling the Convention against Torture and Other Cruel, Inhuman or Degrading Treatment or Punishment, the Declaration of the Fourth United Nations Congress on the Prevention of Crime and the Treatment of Offenders, the Code of Conduct for Law Enforcement Officials, and the Slavery Conventions,

Recalling that one of the objectives of the International Labour Organisation, as stated in its Constitution, is the protection of the interests of workers when employed in countries other than their own, and bearing in mind the expertise and experience of that organization in matters related to migrant workers and members of their families,

Recognizing the importance of the work done in connection with migrant workers and members of their families in various organs of the United Nations, in particular in the Commission on Human Rights and the Commission for Social Development, and in the Food and Agriculture Organization of the United Nations, the United Nations Educational, Scientific and Cultural Organization and the World Health Organization, as well as in other international organizations,

Recognizing also the progress made by certain States on a regional or bilateral basis towards the protection of the rights of migrant workers and members of their families, as well as the importance and usefulness of bilateral and multilateral agreements in this field,

Realizing the importance and extent of the migration phenomenon, which involves millions of people and affects a large number of States in the international community,

Aware of the impact of the flows of migrant workers on States and people concerned, and desiring to establish norms which may contribute to the harmonization of the attitudes of States through the acceptance of basic principles concerning the treatment of migrant workers and members of their families,

Considering the situation of vulnerability in which migrant workers and members of their families frequently-find themselves owing, among other things, to their absence from their State of origin and to the difficulties they may encounter arising from their presence in the State of employment,

Convinced that the rights of migrant workers and members of their families have not been sufficiently recognized everywhere and therefore require appropriate international protection,

Taking into account the fact that migration is often the cause of serious problems for the members of the families of migrant workers as well as for the workers themselves, in particular because of the scattering of the family,

Bearing in mind that the human problems involved in migration are even more serious in the case of irregular migration and convinced therefore that appropriate action should be encouraged in order to prevent and eliminate clandestine movements and trafficking in migrant workers, while at the same time assuring the protection of their fundamental human rights,

Considering that workers who are non-documented or in an irregular situation are frequently employed under less favourable conditions of work than other workers and that certain employers find this an inducement to seek such labour in order to reap the benefits of unfair competition,

Considering also that recourse to the employment of migrant workers who are in an irregular situation will be discouraged if the fundamental human rights of all migrant workers are more widely recognized and, moreover, that granting certain additional rights to migrant workers and members of their families in a regular situation will encourage all migrants and employers to respect and comply with the laws and procedures established by the States concerned,

Convinced, therefore, of the need to bring about the international protection of the rights of all migrant workers and members of their families, reaffirming and establishing basic norms in a comprehensive convention which could be applied universally,

Have agreed as follows:

PART I SCOPE AND DEFINITIONS

Article 1

1. The present Convention is applicable, except as otherwise provided hereafter, to all migrant workers and members of their families without distinction of any kind such as sex, race, colour, language, religion or conviction, political or other opinion, national, ethnic or social origin, nationality, age, economic position, property, marital status, birth or other status.

2. The present Convention shall apply during the entire migration process of migrant workers and members of their families, which comprises preparation for migration, departure, transit and the entire period of stay and remunerated activity in the State of employment as well as return to the State of origin or the State of habitual residence.

Article 2

For the purposes of the present Convention:

1. The term "migrant worker" refers to a person who is to be engaged, is engaged or has been engaged in a remunerated activity in a State of which he or she is not a national.

2. (a) The term "frontier worker" refers to a migrant worker who retains his or her habitual residence in a neighbouring State to which he or she normally returns every day or at least once a week;

   (b) The term "seasonal worker" refers to a migrant worker whose work by its character is dependent on seasonal conditions and is performed only during part of the year;

   (c) The term "seafarer", which includes a fisherman, refers to a migrant worker employed on board a vessel registered in a State of which he or she is not a national;

   (d) The term "worker on an offshore installation" refers to a migrant worker employed on an offshore installation that is under the jurisdiction of a State of which he or she is not a national;

   (e) The term "itinerant worker" refers to a migrant worker who, having his or her habitual residence in one State, has to travel to another State or States for short periods, owing to the nature of his or her occupation;

   (f) The term "project-tied worker" refers to a migrant worker admitted to a State of employment for a defined period to work solely on a specific project being carried out in that State by his or her employer;

   (g) The term "specified-employment worker" refers to a migrant worker:

      (i) Who has been sent by his or her employer for a restricted and defined period of time to a State of employment to undertake a specific assignment or duty; or

      (ii) Who engages for a restricted and defined period of time in work that requires professional, commercial, technical or other highly specialized skill; or

      (iii) Who, upon the request of his or her employer in the State of employment, engages for a restricted and defined period of time in work whose nature is transitory or brief; and who is required to depart from the State of employment either at the expiration of his or her authorized period of stay, or earlier if he or she no longer undertakes that specific assignment or duty or engages in that work;

(h) The term "self-employed worker" refers to a migrant worker who is engaged in a remunerated activity otherwise than under a contract of employment and who earns his or her living through this activity normally working alone or together with members of his or her family, and to any other migrant worker recognized as self-employed by applicable legislation of the State of employment or bilateral or multilateral agreements.

Article 3

The present Convention shall not apply to:

(a) Persons sent or employed by international organizations and agencies or persons sent or employed by a State outside its territory to perform official functions, whose admission and status are regulated by general international law or by specific international agreements or conventions;

(b) Persons sent or employed by a State or on its behalf outside its territory who participate in development programmes and other co-operation programmes, whose admission and status are regulated by agreement with the State of employment and who, in accordance with that agreement, are not considered migrant workers;

(c) Persons taking up residence in a State different from their State of origin as investors;

(d) Refugees and stateless persons, unless such application is provided for in the relevant national legislation of, or international instruments in force for, the State Party concerned;

(e) Students and trainees;

(f) Seafarers and workers on an offshore installation who have not been admitted to take up residence and engage in a remunerated activity in the State of employment.

Article 4

For the purposes of the present Convention the term "members of the family" refers to persons married to migrant workers or having with them a relationship that, according to applicable law, produces effects equivalent to marriage, as well as their dependent children and other dependent persons who are recognized as members of the family by applicable legislation or applicable bilateral or multilateral agreements between the States concerned.

Article 5

For the purposes of the present Convention, migrant workers and members of their families:

(a) Are considered as documented or in a regular situation if they are authorized to enter, to stay and to engage in a remunerated activity in the State of employment pursuant to the law of that State and to international agreements to which that State is a party;

(b) Are considered as non-documented or in an irregular situation if they do not comply with the conditions provided for in subparagraph (a) of the present article.

Article 6

For the purposes of the present Convention:

(a) The term "State of origin" means the State of which the person concerned is a national;

(b) The term "State of employment" means a State where the migrant worker is to be engaged, is engaged or has been engaged in a remunerated activity, as the case may be;

(c) The term "State of transit," means any State through which the person concerned passes on any journey to the State of employment or from the State of employment to the State of origin or the State of habitual residence.

PART II NON-DISCRIMINATION WITH RESPECT TO RIGHTS

Article 7

States Parties undertake, in accordance with the international instruments concerning human rights, to respect and to ensure to all migrant workers and members of their families within their territory or subject to their jurisdiction the rights provided for in the present Convention without distinction of any kind such as to sex, race, colour, language, religion or conviction, political or other opinion, national, ethnic or social origin, nationality, age, economic position, property, marital status, birth or other status.

PART III HUMAN RIGHTS OF ALL MIGRANT WORKERS AND MEMBERS OF THEIR FAMILIES

Article 8

1. Migrant workers and members of their families shall be free to leave any State, including their State of origin. This right shall not be subject to any restrictions except those that are provided by law, are necessary to protect national security, public order (ordre public), public health or morals or the rights and freedoms of others and are consistent with the other rights recognized in the present part of the Convention.

2. Migrant workers and members of their families shall have the right at any time to enter and remain in their State of origin.

Article 9

The right to life of migrant workers and members of their families shall be protected by law.

Article 10

No migrant worker or member of his or her family shall be subjected to torture or to cruel, inhuman or degrading treatment or punishment.

Article 11

1. No migrant worker or member of his or her family shall be held in slavery or servitude.

2. No migrant worker or member of his or her family shall be required to perform forced or compulsory labour.

3. Paragraph 2 of the present article shall not be held to preclude, in States where imprisonment with hard labour may be imposed as a punishment for a crime, the performance of hard labour in pursuance of a sentence to such punishment by a competent court.

4. For the purpose of the present article the term "forced or compulsory labour" shall not include:

    (a) Any work or service not referred to in paragraph 3 of the present article normally required of a person who is under detention in consequence of a lawful order of a court or of a person during conditional release from such detention;

    (b) Any service exacted in cases of emergency or calamity threatening the life or well-being of the community;

    (c) Any work or service that forms part of normal civil obligations so far as it is imposed also on citizens of the State concerned.

Article 12

1. Migrant workers and members of their families shall have the right to freedom of thought, conscience and religion. This right shall include freedom to have or to adopt a religion or belief of their choice and freedom either individually or in community with others and in public or private to manifest their religion or belief in worship, observance, practice and teaching.

2. Migrant workers and members of their families shall not be subject to coercion that would impair their freedom to have or to adopt a religion or belief of their choice.

3. Freedom to manifest one's religion or belief may be subject only to such limitations as are prescribed by law and are necessary to protect public safety, order, health or morals or the fundamental rights and freedoms of others.

4. States Parties to the present Convention undertake to have respect for the liberty of parents, at least one of whom is a migrant worker, and, when applicable, legal guardians to ensure the religious and moral education of their children in conformity with their own convictions.

Article 13

1. Migrant workers and members of their families shall have the right to hold opinions without interference.

2. Migrant workers and members of their families shall have the right to freedom of expression; this right shall include freedom to seek, receive and impart information and ideas of all kinds, regardless of frontiers, either orally, in writing or in print, in the form of art or through any other media of their choice.

3. The exercise of the right provided for in paragraph 2 of the present article carries with it special duties and responsibilities. It may therefore be subject to certain restrictions, but these shall only be such as are provided by law and are necessary:

    (a) For respect of the rights or reputation of others;

    (b) For the protection of the national security of the States concerned or of public order (ordre public) or of public health or morals;

    (c) For the purpose of preventing any propaganda for war;

(d) For the purpose of preventing any advocacy of national, racial or religious hatred that constitutes incitement to discrimination, hostility or violence.

Article 14

No migrant worker or member of his or her family shall be subjected to arbitrary or unlawful interference with his or her privacy, family, correspondence or other communications, or to unlawful attacks on his or her honour and reputation. Each migrant worker and member of his or her family shall have the right to the protection of the law against such interference or attacks.

Article 15

No migrant worker or member of his or her family shall be arbitrarily deprived of property, whether owned individually or in association with others. Where, under the legislation in force in the State of employment, the assets of a migrant worker or a member of his or her family are expropriated in whole or in part, the person concerned shall have the right to fair and adequate compensation.

Article 16

1. Migrant workers and members of their families shall have the right to liberty and security of person.
2. Migrant workers and members of their families shall be entitled to effective protection by the State against violence, physical injury, threats and intimidation, whether by public officials or by private individuals, groups or institutions.
3. Any verification by law enforcement officials of the identity of migrant workers or members of their families shall be carried out in accordance with procedure established by law.
4. Migrant workers and members of their families shall not be subjected individually or collectively to arbitrary arrest or detention; they shall not be deprived of their liberty except on such grounds and in accordance with such procedures as are established by law.
5. Migrant workers and members of their families who are arrested shall be informed at the time of arrest as far as possible in a language they understand of the reasons for their arrest and they shall be promptly informed in a language they understand of any charges against them.
6. Migrant workers and members of their families who are arrested or detained on a criminal charge shall be brought promptly before a judge or other officer authorized by law to exercise judicial power and shall be entitled to trial within a reasonable time or to release. It shall not be the general rule that while awaiting trial they shall be detained in custody, but release may be subject to guarantees to appear for trial, at any other stage of the judicial proceedings and, should the occasion arise, for the execution of the judgement.
7. When a migrant worker or a member of his or her family is arrested or committed to prison or custody pending trial or is detained in any other manner:
   (a) The consular or diplomatic authorities of his or her State of origin or of a State representing the interests of that State shall, if he or she so requests, be informed without delay of his or her arrest or detention and of the reasons therefor;
   (b) The person concerned shall have the right to communicate with the said authorities. Any communication by the person concerned to the said authorities shall be

forwarded without delay, and he or she shall also have the right to receive communications sent by the said authorities without delay;

(c) The person concerned shall be informed without delay of this right and of rights deriving from relevant treaties, if any, applicable between the States concerned, to correspond and to meet with representatives of the said authorities and to make arrangements with them for his or her legal representation.

8. Migrant workers and members of their families who are deprived of their liberty by arrest or detention shall be entitled to take proceedings before a court, in order that that court may decide without delay on the lawfulness of their detention and order their release if the detention is not lawful. When they attend such proceedings, they shall have the assistance, if necessary without cost to them, of an interpreter, if they cannot understand or speak the language used.

9. Migrant workers and members of their families who have been victims of unlawful arrest or detention shall have an enforceable right to compensation.

Article 17

1. Migrant workers and members of their families who are deprived of their liberty shall be treated with humanity and with respect for the inherent dignity of the human person and for their cultural identity.

2. Accused migrant workers and members of their families shall, save in exceptional circumstances, be separated from convicted persons and shall be subject to separate treatment appropriate to their status as unconvicted persons. Accused juvenile persons shall be separated from adults and brought as speedily as possible for adjudication.

3. Any migrant worker or member of his or her family who is detained in a State of transit or in a State of employment for violation of provisions relating to migration shall be held, in so far as practicable, separately from convicted persons or persons detained pending trial.

4. During any period of imprisonment in pursuance of a sentence imposed by a court of law, the essential aim of the treatment of a migrant worker or a member of his or her family shall be his or her reformation and social rehabilitation. Juvenile offenders shall be separated from adults and be accorded treatment appropriate to their age and legal status.

5. During detention or imprisonment, migrant workers and members of their families shall enjoy the same rights as nationals to visits by members of their families.

6. Whenever a migrant worker is deprived of his or her liberty, the competent authorities of the State concerned shall pay attention to the problems that may be posed for members of his or her family, in particular for spouses and minor children.

7. Migrant workers and members of their families who are subjected to any form of detention or imprisonment in accordance with the law in force in the State of employment or in the State of transit shall enjoy the same rights as nationals of those States who are in the same situation.

8. If a migrant worker or a member of his or her family is detained for the purpose of verifying any infraction of provisions related to migration, he or she shall not bear any costs arising therefrom.

Article 18

1. Migrant workers and members of their families shall have the right to equality with nationals of the State concerned before the courts and tribunals. In the determination of any criminal charge against them or of their rights and obligations in a suit of law, they shall be entitled to a fair and public hearing by a competent, independent and impartial tribunal established by law.

2. Migrant workers and members of their families who are charged with a criminal offence shall have the right to be presumed innocent until proven guilty according to law.

3. In the determination of any criminal charge against them, migrant workers and members of their families shall be entitled to the following minimum guarantees:

    (a) To be informed promptly and in detail in a language they understand of the nature and cause of the charge against them;

    (b) To have adequate time and facilities for the preparation of their defence and to communicate with counsel of their own choosing;

    (c) To be tried without undue delay;

    (d) To be tried in their presence and to defend themselves in person or through legal assistance of their own choosing; to be informed, if they do not have legal assistance, of this right; and to have legal assistance assigned to them, in any case where the interests of justice so require and without payment by them in any such case if they do not have sufficient means to pay;

    (e) To examine or have examined the witnesses against them and to obtain the attendance and examination of witnesses on their behalf under the same conditions as witnesses against them;

    (f) To have the free assistance of an interpreter if they cannot understand or speak the language used in court;

    (g) Not to be compelled to testify against themselves or to confess guilt.

4. In the case of juvenile persons, the procedure shall be such as will take account of their age and the desirability of promoting their rehabilitation.

5. Migrant workers and members of their families convicted of a crime shall have the right to their conviction and sentence being reviewed by a higher tribunal according to law.

6. When a migrant worker or a member of his or her family has, by a final decision, been convicted of a criminal offence and when subsequently his or her conviction has been reversed or he or she has been pardoned on the ground that a new or newly discovered fact shows conclusively that there has been a miscarriage of justice, the person who has suffered punishment as a result of such conviction shall be compensated according to law, unless it is proved that the non-disclosure of the unknown fact in time is wholly or partly attributable to that person.

7. No migrant worker or member of his or her family shall be liable to be tried or punished again for an offence for which he or she has already been finally convicted or acquitted in accordance with the law and penal procedure of the State concerned.

Article 19

1. No migrant worker or member of his or her family shall be held guilty of any criminal offence on account of any act or omission that did not constitute a criminal offence under national or international law at the time when the criminal offence was

committed, nor shall a heavier penalty be imposed than the one that was applicable at the time when it was committed. If, subsequent to the commission of the offence, provision is made by law for the imposition of a lighter penalty, he or she shall benefit thereby.

2. Humanitarian considerations related to the status of a migrant worker, in particular with respect to his or her right of residence or work, should be taken into account in imposing a sentence for a criminal offence committed by a migrant worker or a member of his or her family.

Article 20

1. No migrant worker or member of his or her family shall be imprisoned merely on the ground of failure to fulfil a contractual obligation.

2. No migrant worker or member of his or her family shall be deprived of his or her authorization of residence or work permit or expelled merely on the ground of failure to fulfil an obligation arising out of a work contract unless fulfilment of that obligation constitutes a condition for such authorization or permit.

Article 21

It shall be unlawful for anyone, other than a public official duly authorized by law, to confiscate, destroy or attempt to destroy identity documents, documents authorizing entry to or stay, residence or establishment in the national territory or work permits. No authorized confiscation of such documents shall take place without delivery of a detailed receipt. In no case shall it be permitted to destroy the passport or equivalent document of a migrant worker or a member of his or her family.

Article 22

1. Migrant workers and members of their families shall not be subject to measures of collective expulsion. Each case of expulsion shall be examined and decided individually.

2. Migrant workers and members of their families may be expelled from the territory of a State Party only in pursuance of a decision taken by the competent authority in accordance with law.

3. The decision shall be communicated to them in a language they understand. Upon their request where not otherwise mandatory, the decision shall be communicated to them in writing and, save in exceptional circumstances on account of national security, the reasons for the decision likewise stated. The persons concerned shall be informed of these rights before or at the latest at the time the decision is rendered.

4. Except where a final decision is pronounced by a judicial authority, the person concerned shall have the right to submit the reason he or she should not be expelled and to have his or her case reviewed by the competent authority, unless compelling reasons of national security require otherwise. Pending such review, the person concerned shall have the right to seek a stay of the decision of expulsion.

5. If a decision of expulsion that has already been executed is subsequently annulled, the person concerned shall have the right to seek compensation according to law and

the earlier decision shall not be used to prevent him or her from re-entering the State concerned.

6. In case of expulsion, the person concerned shall have a reasonable opportunity before or after departure to settle any claims for wages and other entitlements due to him or her and any pending liabilities.

7. Without prejudice to the execution of a decision of expulsion, a migrant worker or a member of his or her family who is subject to such a decision may seek entry into a State other than his or her State of origin.

8. In case of expulsion of a migrant worker or a member of his or her family the costs of expulsion shall not be borne by him or her. The person concerned may be required to pay his or her own travel costs.

9. Expulsion from the State of employment shall not in itself prejudice any rights of a migrant worker or a member of his or her family acquired in accordance with the law of that State, including the right to receive wages and other entitlements due to him or her.

Article 23

Migrant workers and members of their families shall have the right to have recourse to the protection and assistance of the consular or diplomatic authorities of their State of origin or of a State representing the interests of that State whenever the rights recognized in the present Convention are impaired. In particular, in case of expulsion, the person concerned shall be informed of this right without delay and the authorities of the expelling State shall facilitate the exercise of such right.

Article 24

Every migrant worker and every member of his or her family shall have the right to recognition everywhere as a person before the law.

Article 25

1. Migrant workers shall enjoy treatment not less favourable than that which applies to nationals of the State of employment in respect of remuneration and:
   (a) Other conditions of work, that is to say, overtime, hours of work, weekly rest, holidays with pay, safety, health, termination of the employment relationship and any other conditions of work which, according to national law and practice, are covered by these terms;
   (b) Other terms of employment, that is to say, minimum age of employment, restriction on work and any other matters which, according to national law and practice, are considered a term of employment.

2. It shall not be lawful to derogate in private contracts of employment from the principle of equality of treatment referred to in paragraph 1 of the present article.

3. States Parties shall take all appropriate measures to ensure that migrant workers are not deprived of any rights derived from this principle by reason of any irregularity in their stay or employment. In particular, employers shall not be relieved of any legal or contractual obligations, nor shall their obligations be limited in any manner by reason of such irregularity.

Article 26

1. States Parties recognize the right of migrant workers and members of their families:
   (a) To take part in meetings and activities of trade unions and of any other associations established in accordance with law, with a view to protecting their economic, social, cultural and other interests, subject only to the rules of the organization concerned;
   (b) To join freely any trade union and any such association as aforesaid, subject only to the rules of the organization concerned;
   (c) To seek the aid and assistance of any trade union and of any such association as aforesaid.
2. No restrictions may be placed on the exercise of these rights other than those that are prescribed by law and which are necessary in a democratic society in the interests of national security, public order (ordre public) or the protection of the rights and freedoms of others.

Article 27

1. With respect to social security, migrant workers and members of their families shall enjoy in the State of employment the same treatment granted to nationals in so far as they fulfil the requirements provided for by the applicable legislation of that State and the applicable bilateral and multilateral treaties. The competent authorities of the State of origin and the State of employment can at any time establish the necessary arrangements to determine the modalities of application of this norm.
2. Where the applicable legislation does not allow migrant workers and members of their families a benefit, the States concerned shall examine the possibility of reimbursing interested persons the amount of contributions made by them with respect to that benefit on the basis of the treatment granted to nationals who are in similar circumstances.

Article 28

Migrant workers and members of their families shall have the right to receive any medical care that is urgently required for the preservation of their life or the avoidance of irreparable harm to their health on the basis of equality of treatment with nationals of the State concerned. Such emergency medical care shall not be refused them by reason of any irregularity with regard to stay or employment.

Article 29

Each child of a migrant worker shall have the right to a name, to registration of birth and to a nationality.

Article 30

Each child of a migrant worker shall have the basic right of access to education on the basis of equality of treatment with nationals of the State concerned. Access to public pre-school educational institutions or schools shall not be refused or limited by reason of the irregular situation with respect to stay or employment of either parent or by reason of the irregularity of the child's stay in the State of employment.

Article 31

1. States Parties shall ensure respect for the cultural identity of migrant workers and members of their families and shall not prevent them from maintaining their cultural links with their State of origin.
2. States Parties may take appropriate measures to assist and encourage efforts in this respect.

Article 32

Upon the termination of their stay in the State of employment, migrant workers and members of their families shall have the right to transfer their earnings and savings and, in accordance with the applicable legislation of the States concerned, their personal effects and belongings.

Article 33

1. Migrant workers and members of their families shall have the right to be informed by the State of origin, the State of employment or the State of transit as the case may be concerning:
   (a) Their rights arising out of the present Convention;
   (b) The conditions of their admission, their rights and obligations under the law and practice of the State concerned and such other matters as will enable them to comply with administrative or other formalities in that State.
2. States Parties shall take all measures they deem appropriate to disseminate the said information or to ensure that it is provided by employers, trade unions or other appropriate bodies or institutions. As appropriate, they shall co-operate with other States concerned.
3. Such adequate information shall be provided upon request to migrant workers and members of their families, free of charge, and, as far as possible, in a language they are able to understand.

Article 34

Nothing in the present part of the Convention shall have the effect of relieving migrant workers and the members of their families from either the obligation to comply with the laws and regulations of any State of transit and the State of employment or the obligation to respect the cultural identity of the inhabitants of such States.

Article 35

Nothing in the present part of the Convention shall be interpreted as implying the regularization of the situation of migrant workers or members of their families who are non-documented or in an irregular situation or any right to such regularization of their situation, nor shall it prejudice the measures intended to ensure sound and equitable conditions for international migration as provided in part VI of the present Convention.

PART IV OTHER RIGHTS OF MIGRANT WORKERS AND MEMBERS OF THEIR FAMILIES WHO ARE DOCUMENTED OR IN A REGULAR SITUATION

Article 36

Migrant workers and members of their families who are documented or in a regular situation in the State of employment shall enjoy the rights set forth in the present part of the Convention in addition to those set forth in part III.

Article 37

Before their departure, or at the latest at the time of their admission to the State of employment, migrant workers and members of their families shall have the right to be fully informed by the State of origin or the State of employment, as appropriate, of all conditions applicable to their admission and particularly those concerning their stay and the remunerated activities in which they may engage as well as of the requirements they must satisfy in the State of employment and the authority to which they must address themselves for any modification of those conditions.

Article 38

1. States of employment shall make every effort to authorize migrant workers and members of the families to be temporarily absent without effect upon their authorization to stay or to work, as the case may be. In doing so, States of employment shall take into account the special needs and obligations of migrant workers and members of their families, in particular in their States of origin.
2. Migrant workers and members of their families shall have the right to be fully informed of the terms on which such temporary absences are authorized.

Article 39

1. Migrant workers and members of their families shall have the right to liberty of movement in the territory of the State of employment and freedom to choose their residence there.
2. The rights mentioned in paragraph 1 of the present article shall not be subject to any restrictions except those that are provided by law, are necessary to protect national security, public order (ordre public), public health or morals, or the rights and freedoms of others and are consistent with the other rights recognized in the present Convention.

Article 40

1. Migrant workers and members of their families shall have the right to form associations and trade unions in the State of employment for the promotion and protection of their economic, social, cultural and other interests.
2. No restrictions may be placed on the exercise of this right other than those that are prescribed by law and are necessary in a democratic society in the interests of national security, public order (ordre public) or the protection of the rights and freedoms of others.

Article 41

1. Migrant workers and members of their families shall have the right to participate in public affairs of their State of origin and to vote and to be elected at elections of that State, in accordance with its legislation.
2. The States concerned shall, as appropriate and in accordance with their legislation, facilitate the exercise of these rights.

Article 42

1. States Parties shall consider the establishment of procedures or institutions through which account may be taken, both in States of origin and in States of employment, of special needs, aspirations and obligations of migrant workers and members of their families and shall envisage, as appropriate, the possibility for migrant workers and members of their families to have their freely chosen representatives in those institutions.
2. States of employment shall facilitate, in accordance with their national legislation, the consultation or participation of migrant workers and members of their families in decisions concerning the life and administration of local communities.
3. Migrant workers may enjoy political rights in the State of employment if that State, in the exercise of its sovereignty, grants them such rights.

Article 43

1. Migrant workers shall enjoy equality of treatment with nationals of the State of employment in relation to:
   (a) Access to educational institutions and services subject to the admission requirements and other regulations of the institutions and services concerned;
   (b) Access to vocational guidance and placement services;
   (c) Access to vocational training and retraining facilities and institutions;
   (d) Access to housing, including social housing schemes, and protection against exploitation in respect of rents;
   (e) Access to social and health services, provided that the requirements for participation in the respective schemes are met;
   (f) Access to co-operatives and self-managed enterprises, which shall not imply a change of their migration status and shall be subject to the rules and regulations of the bodies concerned;
   (g) Access to and participation in cultural life.
2. States Parties shall promote conditions to ensure effective equality of treatment to enable migrant workers to enjoy the rights mentioned in paragraph 1 of the present article whenever the terms of their stay, as authorized by the State of employment, meet the appropriate requirements.
3. States of employment shall not prevent an employer of migrant workers from establishing housing or social or cultural facilities for them. Subject to article 70 of the present Convention, a State of employment may make the establishment of such facilities subject to the requirements generally applied in that State concerning their installation.

Article 44

1. States Parties, recognizing that the family is the natural and fundamental group unit of society and is entitled to protection by society and the State, shall take appropriate measures to ensure the protection of the unity of the families of migrant workers.
2. States Parties shall take measures that they deem appropriate and that fall within their competence to facilitate the reunification of migrant workers with their spouses or persons who have with the migrant worker a relationship that, according to applicable law, produces effects equivalent to marriage, as well as with their minor dependent unmarried children.
3. States of employment, on humanitarian grounds, shall favourably consider granting equal treatment, as set forth in paragraph 2 of the present article, to other family members of migrant workers.

Article 45

1. Members of the families of migrant workers shall, in the State of employment, enjoy equality of treatment with nationals of that State in relation to:
   (a) Access to educational institutions and services, subject to the admission requirements and other regulations of the institutions and services concerned;
   (b) Access to vocational guidance and training institutions and services, provided that requirements for participation are met;
   (c) Access to social and health services, provided that requirements for participation in the respective schemes are met;
   (d) Access to and participation in cultural life.
2. States of employment shall pursue a policy, where appropriate in collaboration with the States of origin, aimed at facilitating the integration of children of migrant workers in the local school system, particularly in respect of teaching them the local language.
3. States of employment shall endeavour to facilitate for the children of migrant workers the teaching of their mother tongue and culture and, in this regard, States of origin shall collaborate whenever appropriate.
4. States of employment may provide special schemes of education in the mother tongue of children of migrant workers, if necessary in collaboration with the States of origin.

Article 46

Migrant workers and members of their families shall, subject to the applicable legislation of the States concerned, as well as relevant international agreements and the obligations of the States concerned arising out of their participation in customs unions, enjoy exemption from import and export duties and taxes in respect of their personal and household effects as well as the equipment necessary to engage in the remunerated activity for which they were admitted to the State of employment:
   (a) Upon departure from the State of origin or State of habitual residence;
   (b) Upon initial admission to the State of employment;
   (c) Upon final departure from the State of employment;
   (d) Upon final return to the State of origin or State of habitual residence.

Article 47

1. Migrant workers shall have the right to transfer their earnings and savings, in particular those funds necessary for the support of their families, from the State of employment to their State of origin or any other State. Such transfers shall be made in conformity with procedures established by applicable legislation of the State concerned and in conformity with applicable international agreements.
2. States concerned shall take appropriate measures to facilitate such transfers.

Article 48

1. Without prejudice to applicable double taxation agreements, migrant workers and members of their families shall, in the matter of earnings in the State of employment:
   (a) Not be liable to taxes, duties or charges of any description higher or more onerous than those imposed on nationals in similar circumstances;
   (b) Be entitled to deductions or exemptions from taxes of any description and to any tax allowances applicable to nationals in similar circumstances, including tax allowances for dependent members of their families.
2. States Parties shall endeavour to adopt appropriate measures to avoid double taxation of the earnings and savings of migrant workers and members of their families.

Article 49

1. Where separate authorizations to reside and to engage in employment are required by national legislation, the States of employment shall issue to migrant workers authorization of residence for at least the same period of time as their authorization to engage in remunerated activity.
2. Migrant workers who in the State of employment are allowed freely to choose their remunerated activity shall neither be regarded as in an irregular situation nor shall they lose their authorization of residence by the mere fact of the termination of their remunerated activity prior to the expiration of their work permits or similar authorizations.
3. In order to allow migrant workers referred to in paragraph 2 of the present article sufficient time to find alternative remunerated activities, the authorization of residence shall not be withdrawn at least for a period corresponding to that during which they may be entitled to unemployment benefits.

Article 50

1. In the case of death of a migrant worker or dissolution of marriage, the State of employment shall favourably consider granting family members of that migrant worker residing in that State on the basis of family reunion an authorization to stay; the State of employment shall take into account the length of time they have already resided in that State.
2. Members of the family to whom such authorization is not granted shall be allowed before departure a reasonable period of time in order to enable them to settle their affairs in the State of employment.
3. The provisions of paragraphs 1 and 2 of the present article may not be interpreted as adversely affecting any right to stay and work otherwise granted to such family members by the legislation of the State of employment or by bilateral and multilateral treaties applicable to that State.

Article 51

Migrant workers who in the State of employment are not permitted freely to choose their remunerated activity shall neither be regarded as in an irregular situation nor shall they lose their authorization of residence by the mere fact of the termination of their remunerated activity prior to the expiration of their work permit, except where the authorization of residence is expressly dependent upon the specific remunerated activity for which they were admitted. Such migrant workers shall have the right to seek alternative employment, participation in public work schemes and retraining during the remaining period of their authorization to work, subject to such conditions and limitations as are specified in the authorization to work.

Article 52

1. Migrant workers in the State of employment shall have the right freely to choose their remunerated activity, subject to the following restrictions or conditions.
2. For any migrant worker a State of employment may:
   (a) Restrict access to limited categories of employment, functions, services or activities where this is necessary in the interests of this State and provided for by national legislation;
   (b) Restrict free choice of remunerated activity in accordance with its legislation concerning recognition of occupational qualifications acquired outside its territory. However, States Parties concerned shall endeavour to provide for recognition of such qualifications.
3. For migrant workers whose permission to work is limited in time, a State of employment may also:
   (a) Make the right freely to choose their remunerated activities subject to the condition that the migrant worker has resided lawfully in its territory for the purpose of remunerated activity for a period of time prescribed in its national legislation that should not exceed two years;
   (b) Limit access by a migrant worker to remunerated activities in pursuance of a policy of granting priority to its nationals or to persons who are assimilated to them for these purposes by virtue of legislation or bilateral or multilateral agreements. Any such limitation shall cease to apply to a migrant worker who has resided lawfully in its territory for the purpose of remunerated activity for a period of time prescribed in its national legislation that should not exceed five years.

4. States of employment shall prescribe the conditions under which a migrant worker who has been admitted to take up employment may be authorized to engage in work on his or her own account. Account shall be taken of the period during which the worker has already been lawfully in the State of employment.

Article 53

1. Members of a migrant worker's family who have themselves an authorization of residence or admission that is without limit of time or is automatically renewable shall be permitted freely to choose their remunerated activity under the same conditions as are applicable to the said migrant worker in accordance with article 52 of the present Convention.
2. With respect to members of a migrant worker's family who are not permitted freely to choose their remunerated activity, States Parties shall consider favourably granting

them priority in obtaining permission to engage in a remunerated activity over other workers who seek admission to the State of employment, subject to applicable bilateral and multilateral agreements.

Article 54

1. Without prejudice to the terms of their authorization of residence or their permission to work and the rights provided for in articles 25 and 27 of the present Convention, migrant workers shall enjoy equality of treatment with nationals of the State of employment in respect of:
    (a) Protection against dismissal;
    (b) Unemployment benefits;
    (c) Access to public work schemes intended to combat unemployment;
    (d) Access to alternative employment in the event of loss of work or termination of other remunerated activity, subject to article 52 of the present Convention.
2. If a migrant worker claims that the terms of his or her work contract have been violated by his or her employer, he or she shall have the right to address his or her case to the competent authorities of the State of employment, on terms provided for in article 18, paragraph 1, of the present Convention.

Article 55

Migrant workers who have been granted permission to engage in a remunerated activity, subject to the conditions attached to such permission, shall be entitled to equality of treatment with nationals of the State of employment in the exercise of that remunerated activity.

Article 56

1. Migrant workers and members of their families referred to in the present part of the Convention may not be expelled from a State of employment, except for reasons defined in the national legislation of that State, and subject to the safeguards established in part III.
2. Expulsion shall not be resorted to for the purpose of depriving a migrant worker or a member of his or her family of the rights arising out of the authorization of residence and the work permit.
3. In considering whether to expel a migrant worker or a member of his or her family, account should be taken of humanitarian considerations and of the length of time that the person concerned has already resided in the State of employment.

PART V PROVISIONS APPLICABLE TO PARTICULAR CATEGORIES OF MIGRANT WORKERS AND MEMBERS OF THEIR FAMILIES

Article 57

The particular categories of migrant workers and members of their families specified in the present part of the Convention who are documented or in a regular situation shall enjoy the rights set forth in part III and, except as modified below, the rights set forth in part IV.

Article 58

1. Frontier workers, as defined in article 2, paragraph 2 (a), of the present Convention, shall be entitled to the rights provided for in part IV that can be applied to them by reason of their presence and work in the territory of the State of employment, taking into account that they do not have their habitual residence in that State.
2. States of employment shall consider favourably granting frontier workers the right freely to choose their remunerated activity after a specified period of time. The granting of that right shall not affect their status as frontier workers.

Article 59

1. Seasonal workers, as defined in article 2, paragraph 2 (b), of the present Convention, shall be entitled to the rights provided for in part IV that can be applied to them by reason of their presence and work in the territory of the State of employment and that are compatible with their status in that State as seasonal workers, taking into account the fact that they are present in that State for only part of the year.
2. The State of employment shall, subject to paragraph 1 of the present article, consider granting seasonal workers who have been employed in its territory for a significant period of time the possibility of taking up other remunerated activities and giving them priority over other workers who seek admission to that State, subject to applicable bilateral and multilateral agreements.

Article 60

Itinerant workers, as defined in article 2, paragraph 2 (A), of the present Convention, shall be entitled to the rights provided for in part IV that can be granted to them by reason of their presence and work in the territory of the State of employment and that are compatible with their status as itinerant workers in that State.

Article 61

1. Project-tied workers, as defined in article 2, paragraph 2 of the present Convention, and members of their families shall be entitled to the rights provided for in part IV except the provisions of article 43, paragraphs 1 (b) and (c), article 43, paragraph 1 (d), as it pertains to social housing schemes, article 45, paragraph 1 (b), and articles 52 to 55.
2. If a project-tied worker claims that the terms of his or her work contract have been violated by his or her employer, he or she shall have the right to address his or her case to the competent authorities of the State which has jurisdiction over that employer, on terms provided for in article 18, paragraph 1, of the present Convention.
3. Subject to bilateral or multilateral agreements in force for them, the States Parties concerned shall endeavour to enable project-tied workers to remain adequately protected by the social security systems of their States of origin or habitual residence during their engagement in the project. States Parties concerned shall take appropriate measures with the aim of avoiding any denial of rights or duplication of payments in this respect.
4. Without prejudice to the provisions of article 47 of the present Convention and to relevant bilateral or multilateral agreements, States Parties concerned shall permit payment of the earnings of project-tied workers in their State of origin or habitual residence.

Article 62

1. Specified-employment workers as defined in article 2, paragraph 2 (g), of the present Convention, shall be entitled to the rights provided for in part IV, except the provisions of article 43, paragraphs 1 (b) and (c), article 43, paragraph 1 (d), as it pertains to social housing schemes, article 52, and article 54, paragraph 1 (d).
2. Members of the families of specified-employment workers shall be entitled to the rights relating to family members of migrant workers provided for in part IV of the present Convention, except the provisions of article 53.

Article 63

1. Self-employed workers, as defined in article 2, paragraph 2 (h), of the present Convention, shall be entitled to the rights provided for in part IV with the exception of those rights which are exclusively applicable to workers having a contract of employment.
2. Without prejudice to articles 52 and 79 of the present Convention, the termination of the economic activity of the self-employed workers shall not in itself imply the withdrawal of the authorization for them or for the members of their families to stay or to engage in a remunerated activity in the State of employment except where the authorization of residence is expressly dependent upon the specific remunerated activity for which they were admitted.

PART VI PROMOTION OF SOUND, EQUITABLE, HUMANE AND LAWFUL CONDITIONS IN CONNECTION WITH INTERNATIONAL MIGRATION OF WORKERS AND MEMBERS OF THEIR FAMILIES

Article 64

1. Without prejudice to article 79 of the present Convention, the States Parties concerned shall as appropriate consult and co-operate with a view to promoting sound, equitable and humane conditions in connection with international migration of workers and members of their families.
2. In this respect, due regard shall be paid not only to labour needs and resources, but also to the social, economic, cultural and other needs of migrant workers and members of their families involved, as well as to the consequences of such migration for the communities concerned.

Article 65

1. States Parties shall maintain appropriate services to deal with questions concerning international migration of workers and members of their families. Their functions shall include, inter alia:
   (a) The formulation and implementation of policies regarding such migration;
   (b) An exchange of information, consultation and co-operation with the competent authorities of other States Parties involved in such migration;
   (c) The provision of appropriate information, particularly to employers, workers and their organizations on policies, laws and regulations relating to migration and employment, on agreements concluded with other States concerning migration and on other relevant matters;

(d) The provision of information and appropriate assistance to migrant workers and members of their families regarding requisite authorizations and formalities and arrangements for departure, travel, arrival, stay, remunerated activities, exit and return, as well as on conditions of work and life in the State of employment and on customs, currency, tax and other relevant laws and regulations.

2. States Parties shall facilitate as appropriate the provision of adequate consular and other services that are necessary to meet the social, cultural and other needs of migrant workers and members of their families.

Article 66

1. Subject to paragraph 2 of the present article, the right to undertake operations with a view to the recruitment of workers for employment in another State shall be restricted to:

(a) Public services or bodies of the State in which such operations take place;

(b) Public services or bodies of the State of employment on the basis of agreement between the States concerned;

(c) A body established by virtue of a bilateral or multilateral agreement.

2. Subject to any authorization, approval and supervision by the public authorities of the States Parties concerned as may be established pursuant to the legislation and practice of those States, agencies, prospective employers or persons acting on their behalf may also be permitted to undertake the said operations.

Article 67

1. States Parties concerned shall co-operate as appropriate in the adoption of measures regarding the orderly return of migrant workers and members of their families to the State of origin when they decide to return or their authorization of residence or employment expires or when they are in the State of employment in an irregular situation.

2. Concerning migrant workers and members of their families in a regular situation, States Parties concerned shall co-operate as appropriate, on terms agreed upon by those States, with a view to promoting adequate economic conditions for their resettlement and to facilitating their durable social and cultural reintegration in the State of origin.

Article 68

1. States Parties, including States of transit, shall collaborate with a view to preventing and eliminating illegal or clandestine movements and employment of migrant workers in an irregular situation. The measures to be taken to this end within the jurisdiction of each State concerned shall include:

(a) Appropriate measures against the dissemination of misleading information relating to emigration and immigration;

(b) Measures to detect and eradicate illegal or clandestine movements of migrant workers and members of their families and to impose effective sanctions on persons, groups or entities which organize, operate or assist in organizing or operating such movements;

(c) Measures to impose effective sanctions on persons, groups or entities which use violence, threats or intimidation against migrant workers or members of their families in an irregular situation.

2. States of employment shall take all adequate and effective measures to eliminate employment in their territory of migrant workers in an irregular situation, including, whenever appropriate, sanctions on employers of such workers. The rights of migrant workers vis-à-vis their employer arising from employment shall not be impaired by these measures.

Article 69

1. States Parties shall, when there are migrant workers and members of their families within their territory in an irregular situation, take appropriate measures to ensure that such a situation does not persist.

2. Whenever States Parties concerned consider the possibility of regularizing the situation of such persons in accordance with applicable national legislation and bilateral or multilateral agreements, appropriate account shall be taken of the circumstances of their entry, the duration of their stay in the States of employment and other relevant considerations, in particular those relating to their family situation.

Article 70

States Parties shall take measures not less favourable than those applied to nationals to ensure that working and living conditions of migrant workers and members of their families in a regular situation are in keeping with the standards of fitness, safety, health and principles of human dignity.

Article 71

1. States Parties shall facilitate, whenever necessary, the repatriation to the State of origin of the bodies of deceased migrant workers or members of their families.

2. As regards compensation matters relating to the death of a migrant worker or a member of his or her family, States Parties shall, as appropriate, provide assistance to the persons concerned with a view to the prompt settlement of such matters. Settlement of these matters shall be carried out on the basis of applicable national law in accordance with the provisions of the present Convention and any relevant bilateral or multilateral agreements.

PART VII APPLICATION OF THE CONVENTION

Article 72

1. (a) For the purpose of reviewing the application of the present Convention, there shall be established a Committee on the Protection of the Rights of All Migrant Workers and Members of Their Families (hereinafter referred to as "the Committee");

   (b) The Committee shall consist, at the time of entry into force of the present Convention, of ten and, after the entry into force of the Convention for the forty-first State Party, of fourteen experts of high moral standing, impartiality and recognized competence in the field covered by the Convention.

2. (a) Members of the Committee shall be elected by secret ballot by the States Parties from a list of persons nominated by the States Parties, due consideration being given to equitable geographical distribution, including both States of origin and States of employment, and to the representation of the principal legal systems. Each State Party may nominate one person from among its own nationals;

(b) Members shall be elected and shall serve in their personal capacity.

3. The initial election shall be held no later than six months after the date of the entry into force of the present Convention and subsequent elections every second year. At least four months before the date of each election, the Secretary-General of the United Nations shall address a letter to all States Parties inviting them to submit their nominations within two months. The Secretary-General shall prepare a list in alphabetical order of all persons thus nominated, indicating the States Parties that have nominated them, and shall submit it to the States Parties not later than one month before the date of the corresponding election, together with the curricula vitae of the persons thus nominated.

4. Elections of members of the Committee shall be held at a meeting of States Parties convened by the Secretary-General at United Nations Headquarters. At that meeting, for which two thirds of the States Parties shall constitute a quorum, the persons elected to the Committee shall be those nominees who obtain the largest number of votes and an absolute majority of the votes of the States Parties present and voting.

5. (a) The members of the Committee shall serve for a term of four years. However, the terms of five of the members elected in the first election shall expire at the end of two years; immediately after the first election, the names of these five members shall be chosen by lot by the Chairman of the meeting of States Parties;

(b) The election of the four additional members of the Committee shall be held in accordance with the provisions of paragraphs 2, 3 and 4 of the present article, following the entry into force of the Convention for the forty-first State Party. The term of two of the additional members elected on this occasion shall expire at the end of two years; the names of these members shall be chosen by lot by the Chairman of the meeting of States Parties;

(c) The members of the Committee shall be eligible for re-election if renominated.

6. If a member of the Committee dies or resigns or declares that for any other cause he or she can no longer perform the duties of the Committee, the State Party that nominated the expert shall appoint another expert from among its own nationals for the remaining part of the term. The new appointment is subject to the approval of the Committee.

7. The Secretary-General of the United Nations shall provide the necessary staff and facilities for the effective performance of the functions of the Committee.

8. The members of the Committee shall receive emoluments from United Nations resources on such terms and conditions as the General Assembly may decide.

9. The members of the Committee shall be entitled to the facilities, privileges and immunities of experts on mission for the United Nations as laid down in the relevant sections of the Convention on the Privileges and Immunities of the United Nations.

Article 73

1. States Parties undertake to submit to the Secretary-General of the United Nations for consideration by the Committee a report on the legislative, judicial, administrative and other measures they have taken to give effect to the provisions of the present Convention:

   (a) Within one year after the entry into force of the Convention for the State Party concerned;

   (b) Thereafter every five years and whenever the Committee so requests.

2. Reports prepared under the present article shall also indicate factors and difficulties, if any, affecting the implementation of the Convention and shall include information on the characteristics of migration flows in which the State Party concerned is involved.

3. The Committee shall decide any further guidelines applicable to the content of the reports.

4. States Parties shall make their reports widely available to the public in their own countries.

Article 74

1. The Committee shall examine the reports submitted by each State Party and shall transmit such comments as it may consider appropriate to the State Party concerned. This State Party may submit to the Committee observations on any comment made by the Committee in accordance with the present article. The Committee may request supplementary information from States Parties when considering these reports.

2. The Secretary-General of the United Nations shall, in due time before the opening of each regular session of the Committee, transmit to the Director-General of the International Labour Office copies of the reports submitted by States Parties concerned and information relevant to the consideration of these reports, in order to enable the Office to assist the Committee with the expertise the Office may provide regarding those matters dealt with by the present Convention that fall within the sphere of competence of the International Labour Organisation. The Committee shall consider in its deliberations such comments and materials as the Office may provide.

3. The Secretary-General of the United Nations may also, after consultation with the Committee, transmit to other specialized agencies as well as to intergovernmental organizations, copies of such parts of these reports as may fall within their competence.

4. The Committee may invite the specialized agencies and organs of the United Nations, as well as intergovernmental organizations and other concerned bodies to submit, for consideration by the Committee, written information on such matters dealt with in the present Convention as fall within the scope of their activities.

5. The International Labour Office shall be invited by the Committee to appoint representatives to participate, in a consultative capacity, in the meetings of the Committee.

6. The Committee may invite representatives of other specialized agencies and organs of the United Nations, as well as of intergovernmental organizations, to be present and to be heard in its meetings whenever matters falling within their field of competence are considered.

7. The Committee shall present an annual report to the General Assembly of the United Nations on the implementation of the present Convention, containing its own considerations and recommendations, based, in particular, on the examination of the reports and any observations presented by States Parties.

8. The Secretary-General of the United Nations shall transmit the annual reports of the Committee to the States Parties to the present Convention, the Economic and Social Council, the Commission on Human Rights of the United Nations, the Director-General of the International Labour Office and other relevant organizations.

Article 75

1. The Committee shall adopt its own rules of procedure.
2. The Committee shall elect its officers for a term of two years.
3. The Committee shall normally meet annually.
4. The meetings of the Committee shall normally be held at United Nations Headquarters.

Article 76

1. A State Party to the present Convention may at any time declare under this article that it recognizes the competence of the Committee to receive and consider communications to the effect that a State Party claims that another State Party is not fulfilling its obligations under the present Convention. Communications under this article may be received and considered only if submitted by a State Party that has made a declaration recognizing in regard to itself the competence of the Committee. No communication shall be received by the Committee if it concerns a State Party which has not made such a declaration. Communications received under this article shall be dealt with in accordance with the following procedure:

   (a) If a State Party to the present Convention considers that another State Party is not fulfilling its obligations under the present Convention, it may, by written communication, bring the matter to the attention of that State Party. The State Party may also inform the Committee of the matter. Within three months after the receipt of the communication the receiving State shall afford the State that sent the communication an explanation, or any other statement in writing clarifying the matter which should include, to the extent possible and pertinent, reference to domestic procedures and remedies taken, pending or available in the matter;

   (b) If the matter is not adjusted to the satisfaction of both States Parties concerned within six months after the receipt by the receiving State of the initial communication, either State shall have the right to refer the matter to the Committee, by notice given to the Committee and to the other State;

   (c) The Committee shall deal with a matter referred to it only after it has ascertained that all available domestic remedies have been invoked and exhausted in the matter, in conformity with the generally recognized principles of international law. This shall not be the rule where, in the view of the Committee, the application of the remedies is unreasonably prolonged;

(d) Subject to the provisions of subparagraph (c) of the present paragraph, the Committee shall make available its good offices to the States Parties concerned with a view to a friendly solution of the matter on the basis of the respect for the obligations set forth in the present Convention;

(e) The Committee shall hold closed meetings when examining communications under the present article;

(f) In any matter referred to it in accordance with subparagraph (b) of the present paragraph, the Committee may call upon the States Parties concerned, referred to in subparagraph (b), to supply any relevant information;

(g) The States Parties concerned, referred to in subparagraph (b) of the present paragraph, shall have the right to be represented when the matter is being considered by the Committee and to make submissions orally and/or in writing;

(h) The Committee shall, within twelve months after the date of receipt of notice under subparagraph (b) of the present paragraph, submit a report, as follows:

    (i) If a solution within the terms of subparagraph (d) of the present paragraph is reached, the Committee shall confine its report to a brief statement of the facts and of the solution reached;

    (ii) If a solution within the terms of subparagraph (d) is not reached, the Committee shall, in its report, set forth the relevant facts concerning the issue between the States Parties concerned. The written submissions and record of the oral submissions made by the States Parties concerned shall be attached to the report. The Committee may also communicate only to the States Parties concerned any views that it may consider relevant to the issue between them. In every matter, the report shall be communicated to the States Parties concerned.

2. The provisions of the present article shall come into force when ten States Parties to the present Convention have made a declaration under paragraph 1 of the present article. Such declarations shall be deposited by the States Parties with the Secretary-General of the United Nations, who shall transmit copies thereof to the other States Parties. A declaration may be withdrawn at any time by notification to the Secretary-General. Such a withdrawal shall not prejudice the consideration of any matter that is the subject of a communication already transmitted under the present article; no further communication by any State Party shall be received under the present article after the notification of withdrawal of the declaration has been received by the Secretary-General, unless the State Party concerned has made a new declaration.

Article 77

1. A State Party to the present Convention may at any time declare under the present article that it recognizes the competence of the Committee to receive and consider communications from or on behalf of individuals subject to its jurisdiction who claim that their individual rights as established by the present Convention have been violated by that State Party. No communication shall be received by the Committee if it concerns a State Party that has not made such a declaration.

2. The Committee shall consider inadmissible any communication under the present article which is anonymous or which it considers to be an abuse of the right of submission of such communications or to be incompatible with the provisions of the present Convention.

3. The Committee shall not consider any communication from an individual under the present article unless it has ascertained that:

   (a) The same matter has not been, and is not being, examined under another procedure of international investigation or settlement;

   (b) The individual has exhausted all available domestic remedies; this shall not be the rule where, in the view of the Committee, the application of the remedies is unreasonably prolonged or is unlikely to bring effective relief to that individual.

4. Subject to the provisions of paragraph 2 of the present article, the Committee shall bring any communications submitted to it under this article to the attention of the State Party to the present Convention that has made a declaration under paragraph 1 and is alleged to be violating any provisions of the Convention. Within six months, the receiving State shall submit to the Committee written explanations or statements clarifying the matter and the remedy, if any, that may have been taken by that State.

5. The Committee shall consider communications received under the present article in the light of all information made available to it by or on behalf of the individual and by the State Party concerned.

6. The Committee shall hold closed meetings when examining communications under the present article.

7. The Committee shall forward its views to the State Party concerned and to the individual.

8. The provisions of the present article shall come into force when ten States Parties to the present Convention have made declarations under paragraph 1 of the present article. Such declarations shall be deposited by the States Parties with the Secretary-General of the United Nations, who shall transmit copies thereof to the other States Parties. A declaration may be withdrawn at any time by notification to the Secretary-General. Such a withdrawal shall not prejudice the consideration of any matter that is the subject of a communication already transmitted under the present article; no further communication by or on behalf of an individual shall be received under the present article after the notification of withdrawal of the declaration has been received by the Secretary-General, unless the State Party has made a new declaration.

Article 78

The provisions of article 76 of the present Convention shall be applied without prejudice to any procedures for settling disputes or complaints in the field covered by the present Convention laid down in the constituent instruments of, or in conventions adopted by, the United Nations and the specialized agencies and shall not prevent the States Parties from having recourse to any procedures for settling a dispute in accordance with international agreements in force between them.

PART VIII GENERAL PROVISIONS

Article 79
Nothing in the present Convention shall affect the right of each State Party to establish the criteria governing admission of migrant workers and members of their families. Concerning other matters related to their legal situation and treatment as migrant workers and members of their families, States Parties shall be subject to the limitations set forth in the present Convention.

Article 80
Nothing in the present Convention shall be interpreted as impairing the provisions of the Charter of the United Nations and of the constitutions of the specialized agencies which define the respective responsibilities of the various organs of the United Nations and of the specialized agencies in regard to the matters dealt with in the present Convention.

Article 81
1. Nothing in the present Convention shall affect more favourable rights or freedoms granted to migrant workers and members of their families by virtue of:
   (a) The law or practice of a State Party; or
   (b) Any bilateral or multilateral treaty in force for the State Party concerned.
2. Nothing in the present Convention may be interpreted as implying for any State, group or person any right to engage in any activity or perform any act that would impair any of the rights and freedoms as set forth in the present Convention.

Article 82
The rights of migrant workers and members of their families provided for in the present Convention may not be renounced. It shall not be permissible to exert any form of pressure upon migrant workers and members of their families with a view to their relinquishing or foregoing any of the said rights. It shall not be possible to derogate by contract from rights recognized in the present Convention. States Parties shall take appropriate measures to ensure that these principles are respected.

Article 83
Each State Party to the present Convention undertakes:
   (a) To ensure that any person whose rights or freedoms as herein recognized are violated shall have an effective remedy, notwithstanding that the violation has been committed by persons acting in an official capacity;
   (b) To ensure that any persons seeking such a remedy shall have his or her claim reviewed and decided by competent judicial, administrative or legislative authorities, or by any other competent authority provided for by the legal system of the State, and to develop the possibilities of judicial remedy;
   (c) To ensure that the competent authorities shall enforce such remedies when granted.

Article 84

Each State Party undertakes to adopt the legislative and other measures that are necessary to implement the provisions of the present Convention.

PART IX FINAL PROVISIONS

Article 85

The Secretary-General of the United Nations is designated as the depositary of the present Convention.

Article 86

1. The present Convention shall be open for signature by all States. It is subject to ratification.
2. The present Convention shall be open to accession by any State.
3. Instruments of ratification or accession shall be deposited with the Secretary-General of the United Nations.

Article 87

1. The present Convention shall enter into force on the first day of the month following a period of three months after the date of the deposit of the twentieth instrument of ratification or accession.
2. For each State ratifying or acceding to the present Convention after its entry into force, the Convention shall enter into force on the first day of the month following a period of three months after the date of the deposit of its own instrument of ratification or accession.

Article 88

A State ratifying or acceding to the present Convention may not exclude the application of any Part of it, or, without prejudice to article 3, exclude any particular category of migrant workers from its application.

Article 89

1. Any State Party may denounce the present Convention, not earlier than five years after the Convention has entered into force for the State concerned, by means of a notification in writing addressed to the Secretary-General of the United Nations.
2. Such denunciation shall become effective on the first day of the month following the expiration of a period of twelve months after the date of the receipt of the notification by the Secretary-General of the United Nations.
3. Such a denunciation shall not have the effect of releasing the State Party from its obligations under the present Convention in regard to any act or omission which occurs prior to the date at which the denunciation becomes effective, nor shall denunciation prejudice in any way the continued consideration of any matter which is already under

consideration by the Committee prior to the date at which the denunciation becomes effective.

4. Following the date at which the denunciation of a State Party becomes effective, the Committee shall not commence consideration of any new matter regarding that State.

Article 90

1. After five years from the entry into force of the Convention a request for the revision of the Convention may be made at any time by any State Party by means of a notification in writing addressed to the Secretary-General of the United Nations. The Secretary-General shall thereupon communicate any proposed amendments to the States Parties with a request that they notify him whether they favour a conference of States Parties for the purpose of considering and voting upon the proposals. In the event that within four months from the date of such communication at least one third of the States Parties favours such a conference, the Secretary-General shall convene the conference under the auspices of the United Nations. Any amendment adopted by a majority of the States Parties present and voting shall be submitted to the General Assembly for approval.

2. Amendments shall come into force when they have been approved by the General Assembly of the United Nations and accepted by a two-thirds majority of the States Parties in accordance with their respective constitutional processes.

3. When amendments come into force, they shall be binding on those States Parties that have accepted them, other States Parties still being bound by the provisions of the present Convention and any earlier amendment that they have accepted.

Article 91

1. The Secretary-General of the United Nations shall receive and circulate to all States the text of reservations made by States at the time of signature, ratification or accession.

2. A reservation incompatible with the object and purpose of the present Convention shall not be permitted.

3. Reservations may be withdrawn at any time by notification to this effect addressed to the Secretary-General of the United Nations, who shall then inform all States thereof. Such notification shall take effect on the date on which it is received.

Article 92

1. Any dispute between two or more States Parties concerning the interpretation or application of the present Convention that is not settled by negotiation shall, at the request of one of them, be submitted to arbitration. If within six months from the date of the request for arbitration the Parties are unable to agree on the organization of the arbitration, any one of those Parties may refer the dispute to the International Court of Justice by request in conformity with the Statute of the Court.

2. Each State Party may at the time of signature or ratification of the present Convention or accession thereto declare that it does not consider itself bound by paragraph 1 of

the present article. The other States Parties shall not be bound by that paragraph with respect to any State Party that has made such a declaration.

3. Any State Party that has made a declaration in accordance with paragraph 2 of the present article may at any time withdraw that declaration by notification to the Secretary-General of the United Nations.

Article 93

1. The present Convention, of which the Arabic, Chinese, English, French, Russian and Spanish texts are equally authentic, shall be deposited with the Secretary-General of the United Nations.

2. The Secretary-General of the United Nations shall transmit certified copies of the present Convention to all States.

    In witness whereof the undersigned plenipotentiaries, being duly authorized thereto by their respective Governments, have signed the present Convention.

24

Convention on the Rights of Persons with Disabilities, 2006

Note: Adopted on 13 December 2006 by General Assembly Resolution 61/106, Annex I, U.N. GAOR, 61st Session, Supplement. No. 49, at 65, U.N. Doc. A/61/49 (2006), 2515 UNTS 3. Entry into force: 3 May 2008.

PREAMBLE

The States Parties to the present Convention,

(a) Recalling the principles proclaimed in the Charter of the United Nations which recognize the inherent dignity and worth and the equal and inalienable rights of all members of the human family as the foundation of freedom, justice and peace in the world,

(b) Recognizing that the United Nations, in the Universal Declaration of Human Rights and in the International Covenants on Human Rights, has proclaimed and agreed that everyone is entitled to all the rights and freedoms set forth therein, without distinction of any kind,

(c) Reaffirming the universality, indivisibility, interdependence and interrelatedness of all human rights and fundamental freedoms and the need for persons with disabilities to be guaranteed their full enjoyment without discrimination,

(d) Recalling the International Covenant on Economic, Social and Cultural Rights, the International Covenant on Civil and Political Rights, the International Convention on the Elimination of All Forms of Racial Discrimination, the Convention on the Elimination of All Forms of Discrimination against Women, the Convention against Torture and Other Cruel, Inhuman or Degrading Treatment or Punishment, the Convention on the Rights of the Child, and the International Convention on the Protection of the Rights of All Migrant Workers and Members of Their Families,

(e) Recognizing that disability is an evolving concept and that disability results from the interaction between persons with impairments and attitudinal and environmental barriers that hinders their full and effective participation in society on an equal basis with others,

(f) Recognizing the importance of the principles and policy guidelines contained in the World Programme of Action concerning Disabled Persons and in the Standard Rules on the Equalization of Opportunities for Persons with Disabilities in influencing the promotion, formulation and evaluation of the policies, plans, programmes and actions at the national, regional and international levels to further equalize opportunities for persons with disabilities,

(g) Emphasizing the importance of mainstreaming disability issues as an integral part of relevant strategies of sustainable development,

(h) Recognizing also that discrimination against any person on the basis of disability is a violation of the inherent dignity and worth of the human person,

(i) Recognizing further the diversity of persons with disabilities,

(j) Recognizing the need to promote and protect the human rights of all persons with disabilities, including those who require more intensive support,

(k) Concerned that, despite these various instruments and undertakings, persons with disabilities continue to face barriers in their participation as equal members of society and violations of their human rights in all parts of the world,

(l) Recognizing the importance of international cooperation for improving the living conditions of persons with disabilities in every country, particularly in developing countries,

(m) Recognizing the valued existing and potential contributions made by persons with disabilities to the overall well-being and diversity of their communities, and that the promotion of the full enjoyment by persons with disabilities of their human rights and fundamental freedoms and of full participation by persons with disabilities will result in their enhanced sense of belonging and in significant advances in the human, social and economic development of society and the eradication of poverty,

(n) Recognizing the importance for persons with disabilities of their individual autonomy and independence, including the freedom to make their own choices,

(o) Considering that persons with disabilities should have the opportunity to be actively involved in decision-making processes about policies and programmes, including those directly concerning them,

(p) Concerned about the difficult conditions faced by persons with disabilities who are subject to multiple or aggravated forms of discrimination on the basis of race, colour, sex, language, religion, political or other opinion, national, ethnic, indigenous or social origin, property, birth, age or other status,

(q) Recognizing that women and girls with disabilities are often at greater risk, both within and outside the home of violence, injury or abuse, neglect or negligent treatment, maltreatment or exploitation,

(r) Recognizing that children with disabilities should have full enjoyment of all human rights and fundamental freedoms on an equal basis with other children, and recalling obligations to that end undertaken by States Parties to the Convention on the Rights of the Child,

(s) Emphasizing the need to incorporate a gender perspective in all efforts to promote the full enjoyment of human rights and fundamental freedoms by persons with disabilities,

(t) Highlighting the fact that the majority of persons with disabilities live in conditions of poverty, and in this regard recognizing the critical need to address the negative impact of poverty on persons with disabilities,

(u) Bearing in mind that conditions of peace and security based on full respect for the purposes and principles contained in the Charter of the United Nations and observance of applicable human rights instruments are indispensable for the full protection of persons with disabilities, in particular during armed conflicts and foreign occupation,

(v) Recognizing the importance of accessibility to the physical, social, economic and cultural environment, to health and education and to information and communication, in enabling persons with disabilities to fully enjoy all human rights and fundamental freedoms,

(w) Realizing that the individual, having duties to other individuals and to the community to which he or she belongs, is under a responsibility to strive for the promotion and observance of the rights recognized in the International Bill of Human Rights,

(x) Convinced that the family is the natural and fundamental group unit of society and is entitled to protection by society and the State, and that persons with disabilities and their family members should receive the necessary protection and assistance to enable families to contribute towards the full and equal enjoyment of the rights of persons with disabilities,

(y) Convinced that a comprehensive and integral international convention to promote and protect the rights and dignity of persons with disabilities will make a significant contribution to redressing the profound social disadvantage of persons with disabilities and promote their participation in the civil, political, economic, social and cultural spheres with equal opportunities, in both developing and developed countries,

Have agreed as follows:

Article 1

Purpose

The purpose of the present Convention is to promote, protect and ensure the full and equal enjoyment of all human rights and fundamental freedoms by all persons with disabilities, and to promote respect for their inherent dignity.

Persons with disabilities include those who have long-term physical, mental, intellectual or sensory impairments which in interaction with various barriers may hinder their full and effective participation in society on an equal basis with others.

Article 2

Definitions

For the purposes of the present Convention:

"Communication" includes languages, display of text, Braille, tactile communication, large print, accessible multimedia as well as written, audio, plain-language, human-reader and augmentative and alternative modes, means and formats of communication, including accessible information and communication technology;

"Language" includes spoken and signed languages and other forms of non spoken languages;

"Discrimination on the basis of disability" means any distinction, exclusion or restriction on the basis of disability which has the purpose or effect of impairing or nullifying the recognition, enjoyment or exercise, on an equal basis with others, of all human rights and fundamental freedoms in the political, economic, social, cultural, civil or any other field. It includes all forms of discrimination, including denial of reasonable accommodation;

"Reasonable accommodation" means necessary and appropriate modification and adjustments not imposing a disproportionate or undue burden, where needed in a particular case, to ensure to persons with disabilities the enjoyment or exercise on an equal basis with others of all human rights and fundamental freedoms;

"Universal design" means the design of products, environments, programmes and services to be usable by all people, to the greatest extent possible, without the need for adaptation or specialized design. "Universal design" shall not exclude assistive devices for particular groups of persons with disabilities where this is needed.

Article 3

General principles

The principles of the present Convention shall be:
(a) Respect for inherent dignity, individual autonomy including the freedom to make one's own choices, and independence of persons;
(b) Non-discrimination;
(c) Full and effective participation and inclusion in society;
(d) Respect for difference and acceptance of persons with disabilities as part of human diversity and humanity;
(e) Equality of opportunity;
(f) Accessibility;
(g) Equality between men and women;
(h) Respect for the evolving capacities of children with disabilities and respect for the right of children with disabilities to preserve their identities.

Article 4

General obligations

1. States Parties undertake to ensure and promote the full realization of all human rights and fundamental freedoms for all persons with disabilities without discrimination of any kind on the basis of disability. To this end, States Parties undertake:
(a) To adopt all appropriate legislative, administrative and other measures for the implementation of the rights recognized in the present Convention;
(b) To take all appropriate measures, including legislation, to modify or abolish existing laws, regulations, customs and practices that constitute discrimination against persons with disabilities;
(c) To take into account the protection and promotion of the human rights of persons with disabilities in all policies and programmes;
(d) To refrain from engaging in any act or practice that is inconsistent with the present Convention and to ensure that public authorities and institutions act in conformity with the present Convention;

(e) To take all appropriate measures to eliminate discrimination on the basis of disability by any person, organization or private enterprise;

(f) To undertake or promote research and development of universally designed goods, services, equipment and facilities, as defined in article 2 of the present Convention, which should require the minimum possible adaptation and the least cost to meet the specific needs of a person with disabilities, to promote their availability and use, and to promote universal design in the development of standards and guidelines;

(g) To undertake or promote research and development of, and to promote the availability and use of new technologies, including information and communications technologies, mobility aids, devices and assistive technologies, suitable for persons with disabilities, giving priority to technologies at an affordable cost;

(h) To provide accessible information to persons with disabilities about mobility aids, devices and assistive technologies, including new technologies, as well as other forms of assistance, support services and facilities;

(i) To promote the training of professionals and staff working with persons with disabilities in the rights recognized in this Convention so as to better provide the assistance and services guaranteed by those rights.

2. With regard to economic, social and cultural rights, each State Party undertakes to take measures to the maximum of its available resources and, where needed, within the framework of international cooperation, with a view to achieving progressively the full realization of these rights, without prejudice to those obligations contained in the present Convention that are immediately applicable according to international law.

3. In the development and implementation of legislation and policies to implement the present Convention, and in other decision-making processes concerning issues relating to persons with disabilities, States Parties shall closely consult with and actively involve persons with disabilities, including children with disabilities, through their representative organizations.

4. Nothing in the present Convention shall affect any provisions which are more conducive to the realization of the rights of persons with disabilities and which may be contained in the law of a State Party or international law in force for that State. There shall be no restriction upon or derogation from any of the human rights and fundamental freedoms recognized or existing in any State Party to the present Convention pursuant to law, conventions, regulation or custom on the pretext that the present Convention does not recognize such rights or freedoms or that it recognizes them to a lesser extent.

5. The provisions of the present Convention shall extend to all parts of federal states without any limitations or exceptions.

Article 5

Equality and non-discrimination

1. States Parties recognize that all persons are equal before and under the law and are entitled without any discrimination to the equal protection and equal benefit of the law.

2. States Parties shall prohibit all discrimination on the basis of disability and guarantee to persons with disabilities equal and effective legal protection against discrimination on all grounds.

3. In order to promote equality and eliminate discrimination, States Parties shall take all appropriate steps to ensure that reasonable accommodation is provided.

4. Specific measures which are necessary to accelerate or achieve de facto equality of persons with disabilities shall not be considered discrimination under the terms of the present Convention.

Article 6

Women with disabilities

1. States Parties recognize that women and girls with disabilities are subject to multiple discrimination, and in this regard shall take measures to ensure the full and equal enjoyment by them of all human rights and fundamental freedoms.

2. States Parties shall take all appropriate measures to ensure the full development, advancement and empowerment of women, for the purpose of guaranteeing them the exercise and enjoyment of the human rights and fundamental freedoms set out in the present Convention.

Article 7

Children with disabilities

1. States Parties shall take all necessary measures to ensure the full enjoyment by children with disabilities of all human rights and fundamental freedoms on an equal basis with other children.

2. In all actions concerning children with disabilities, the best interests of the child shall be a primary consideration.

3. States Parties shall ensure that children with disabilities have the right to express their views freely on all matters affecting them, their views being given due weight in accordance with their age and maturity, on an equal basis with other children, and to be provided with disability and age-appropriate assistance to realize that right.

Article 8

Awareness-raising

1. States Parties undertake to adopt immediate, effective and appropriate measures:
    (a) To raise awareness throughout society, including at the family level, regarding persons with disabilities, and to foster respect for the rights and dignity of persons with disabilities;
    (b) To combat stereotypes, prejudices and harmful practices relating to persons with disabilities, including those based on sex and age, in all areas of life;
    (c) To promote awareness of the capabilities and contributions of persons with disabilities.

2. Measures to this end include:
   (a) Initiating and maintaining effective public awareness campaigns designed:
       (i) To nurture receptiveness to the rights of persons with disabilities;
       (ii) To promote positive perceptions and greater social awareness towards persons with disabilities;
       (iii) To promote recognition of the skills, merits and abilities of persons with disabilities, and of their contributions to the workplace and the labour market;
   (b) Fostering at all levels of the education system, including in all children from an early age, an attitude of respect for the rights of persons with disabilities;
   (c) Encouraging all organs of the media to portray persons with disabilities in a manner consistent with the purpose of the present Convention;
   (d) Promoting awareness-training programmes regarding persons with disabilities and the rights of persons with disabilities.

Article 9

Accessibility

1. To enable persons with disabilities to live independently and participate fully in all aspects of life, States Parties shall take appropriate measures to ensure to persons with disabilities access, on an equal basis with others, to the physical environment, to transportation, to information and communications, including information and communications technologies and systems, and to other facilities and services open or provided to the public, both in urban and in rural areas. These measures, which shall include the identification and elimination of obstacles and barriers to accessibility, shall apply to, inter alia:
   (a) Buildings, roads, transportation and other indoor and outdoor facilities, including schools, housing, medical facilities and workplaces;
   (b) Information, communications and other services, including electronic services and emergency services.
2. States Parties shall also take appropriate measures to:
   (a) Develop, promulgate and monitor the implementation of minimum standards and guidelines for the accessibility of facilities and services open or provided to the public;
   (b) Ensure that private entities that offer facilities and services which are open or provided to the public take into account all aspects of accessibility for persons with disabilities;
   (c) Provide training for stakeholders on accessibility issues facing persons with disabilities;
   (d) Provide in buildings and other facilities open to the public signage in Braille and in easy to read and understand forms;
   (e) Provide forms of live assistance and intermediaries, including guides, readers and professional sign language interpreters, to facilitate accessibility to buildings and other facilities open to the public;
   (f) Promote other appropriate forms of assistance and support to persons with disabilities to ensure their access to information;

(g) Promote access for persons with disabilities to new information and communications technologies and systems, including the Internet;

(h) Promote the design, development, production and distribution of accessible information and communications technologies and systems at an early stage, so that these technologies and systems become accessible at minimum cost.

Article 10

Right to life

States Parties reaffirm that every human being has the inherent right to life and shall take all necessary measures to ensure its effective enjoyment by persons with disabilities on an equal basis with others.

Article 11

Situations of risk and humanitarian emergencies

States Parties shall take, in accordance with their obligations under international law, including international humanitarian law and international human rights law, all necessary measures to ensure the protection and safety of persons with disabilities in situations of risk, including situations of armed conflict, humanitarian emergencies and the occurrence of natural disasters.

Article 12

Equal recognition before the law

1. States Parties reaffirm that persons with disabilities have the right to recognition everywhere as persons before the law.
2. States Parties shall recognize that persons with disabilities enjoy legal capacity on an equal basis with others in all aspects of life.
3. States Parties shall take appropriate measures to provide access by persons with disabilities to the support they may require in exercising their legal capacity.
4. States Parties shall ensure that all measures that relate to the exercise of legal capacity provide for appropriate and effective safeguards to prevent abuse in accordance with international human rights law. Such safeguards shall ensure that measures relating to the exercise of legal capacity respect the rights, will and preferences of the person, are free of conflict of interest and undue influence, are proportional and tailored to the person's circumstances, apply for the shortest time possible and are subject to regular review by a competent, independent and impartial authority or judicial body. The safeguards shall be proportional to the degree to which such measures affect the person's rights and interests.
5. Subject to the provisions of this article, States Parties shall take all appropriate and effective measures to ensure the equal right of persons with disabilities to own or inherit property, to control their own financial affairs and to have equal access to bank loans, mortgages and other forms of financial credit, and shall ensure that persons with disabilities are not arbitrarily deprived of their property.

Article 13

Access to justice

1. States Parties shall ensure effective access to justice for persons with disabilities on an equal basis with others, including through the provision of procedural and age-appropriate accommodations, in order to facilitate their effective role as direct and indirect participants, including as witnesses, in all legal proceedings, including at investigative and other preliminary stages.

2. In order to help to ensure effective access to justice for persons with disabilities, States Parties shall promote appropriate training for those working in the field of administration of justice, including police and prison staff.

Article 14

Liberty and security of the person

1. States Parties shall ensure that persons with disabilities, on an equal basis with others:
   (a) Enjoy the right to liberty and security of person;
   (b) Are not deprived of their liberty unlawfully or arbitrarily, and that any deprivation of liberty is in conformity with the law, and that the existence of a disability shall in no case justify a deprivation of liberty.

2. States Parties shall ensure that if persons with disabilities are deprived of their liberty through any process, they are, on an equal basis with others, entitled to guarantees in accordance with international human rights law and shall be treated in compliance with the objectives and principles of this Convention, including by provision of reasonable accommodation.

Article 15

Freedom from torture or cruel, inhuman or degrading treatment or punishment

1. No one shall be subjected to torture or to cruel, inhuman or degrading treatment or punishment. In particular, no one shall be subjected without his or her free consent to medical or scientific experimentation.

2. States Parties shall take all effective legislative, administrative, judicial or other measures to prevent persons with disabilities, on an equal basis with others, from being subjected to torture or cruel, inhuman or degrading treatment or punishment.

Article 16

Freedom from exploitation, violence and abuse

1. States Parties shall take all appropriate legislative, administrative, social, educational and other measures to protect persons with disabilities, both within and outside the home, from all forms of exploitation, violence and abuse, including their gender-based aspects.

2. States Parties shall also take all appropriate measures to prevent all forms of exploitation, violence and abuse by ensuring, inter alia, appropriate forms of gender- and age-sensitive assistance and support for persons with disabilities and their families and caregivers, including through the provision of information and education on how to avoid, recognize and report instances of exploitation, violence and abuse. States Parties shall ensure that protection services are age-, gender- and disability-sensitive.

3. In order to prevent the occurrence of all forms of exploitation, violence and abuse, States Parties shall ensure that all facilities and programmes designed to serve persons with disabilities are effectively monitored by independent authorities.

4. States Parties shall take all appropriate measures to promote the physical, cognitive and psychological recovery, rehabilitation and social reintegration of persons with disabilities who become victims of any form of exploitation, violence or abuse, including through the provision of protection services. Such recovery and reintegration shall take place in an environment that fosters the health, welfare, self-respect, dignity and autonomy of the person and takes into account gender- and age-specific needs.

5. States Parties shall put in place effective legislation and policies, including women- and child-focused legislation and policies, to ensure that instances of exploitation, violence and abuse against persons with disabilities are identified, investigated and, where appropriate, prosecuted.

Article 17

Protecting the integrity of the person

Every person with disabilities has a right to respect for his or her physical and mental integrity on an equal basis with others.

Article 18

Liberty of movement and nationality

1. States Parties shall recognize the rights of persons with disabilities to liberty of movement, to freedom to choose their residence and to a nationality, on an equal basis with others, including by ensuring that persons with disabilities:

   (a) Have the right to acquire and change a nationality and are not deprived of their nationality arbitrarily or on the basis of disability;

   (b) Are not deprived, on the basis of disability, of their ability to obtain, possess and utilize documentation of their nationality or other documentation of identification, or to utilize relevant processes such as immigration proceedings, that may be needed to facilitate exercise of the right to liberty of movement;

   (c) Are free to leave any country, including their own;

   (d) Are not deprived, arbitrarily or on the basis of disability, of the right to enter their own country.

2. Children with disabilities shall be registered immediately after birth and shall have the right from birth to a name, the right to acquire a nationality and, as far as possible, the right to know and be cared for by their parents.

Article 19

Living independently and being included in the community

States Parties to this Convention recognize the equal right of all persons with disabilities to live in the community, with choices equal to others, and shall take effective and appropriate measures to facilitate full enjoyment by persons with disabilities of this right and their full inclusion and participation in the community, including by ensuring that:
  (a) Persons with disabilities have the opportunity to choose their place of residence and where and with whom they live on an equal basis with others and are not obliged to live in a particular living arrangement;
  (b) Persons with disabilities have access to a range of in-home, residential and other community support services, including personal assistance necessary to support living and inclusion in the community, and to prevent isolation or segregation from the community;
  (c) Community services and facilities for the general population are available on an equal basis to persons with disabilities and are responsive to their needs.

Article 20

Personal mobility

States Parties shall take effective measures to ensure personal mobility with the greatest possible independence for persons with disabilities, including by:
  (a) Facilitating the personal mobility of persons with disabilities in the manner and at the time of their choice, and at affordable cost;
  (b) Facilitating access by persons with disabilities to quality mobility aids, devices, assistive technologies and forms of live assistance and intermediaries, including by making them available at affordable cost;
  (c) Providing training in mobility skills to persons with disabilities and to specialist staff working with persons with disabilities;
  (d) Encouraging entities that produce mobility aids, devices and assistive technologies to take into account all aspects of mobility for persons with disabilities.

Article 21

Freedom of expression and opinion, and access to information

States Parties shall take all appropriate measures to ensure that persons with disabilities can exercise the right to freedom of expression and opinion, including the freedom to seek, receive and impart information and ideas on an equal basis with others and through all forms of communication of their choice, as defined in article 2 of the present Convention, including by:
  (a) Providing information intended for the general public to persons with disabilities in accessible formats and technologies appropriate to different kinds of disabilities in a timely manner and without additional cost;

(b) Accepting and facilitating the use of sign languages, Braille, augmentative and alternative communication, and all other accessible means, modes and formats of communication of their choice by persons with disabilities in official interactions;

(c) Urging private entities that provide services to the general public, including through the Internet, to provide information and services in accessible and usable formats for persons with disabilities;

(d) Encouraging the mass media, including providers of information through the Internet, to make their services accessible to persons with disabilities;

(e) Recognizing and promoting the use of sign languages.

Article 22

Respect for privacy

1. No person with disabilities, regardless of place of residence or living arrangements, shall be subjected to arbitrary or unlawful interference with his or her privacy, family, home or correspondence or other types of communication or to unlawful attacks on his or her honour and reputation. Persons with disabilities have the right to the protection of the law against such interference or attacks.

2. States Parties shall protect the privacy of personal, health and rehabilitation information of persons with disabilities on an equal basis with others.

Article 23

Respect for home and the family

1. States Parties shall take effective and appropriate measures to eliminate discrimination against persons with disabilities in all matters relating to marriage, family, parenthood and relationships, on an equal basis with others, so as to ensure that:

(a) The right of all persons with disabilities who are of marriageable age to marry and to found a family on the basis of free and full consent of the intending spouses is recognized;

(b) The rights of persons with disabilities to decide freely and responsibly on the number and spacing of their children and to have access to age-appropriate information, reproductive and family planning education are recognized, and the means necessary to enable them to exercise these rights are provided;

(c) Persons with disabilities, including children, retain their fertility on an equal basis with others.

2. States Parties shall ensure the rights and responsibilities of persons with disabilities, with regard to guardianship, wardship, trusteeship, adoption of children or similar institutions, where these concepts exist in national legislation; in all cases the best interests of the child shall be paramount. States Parties shall render appropriate assistance to persons with disabilities in the performance of their child-rearing responsibilities.

3. States Parties shall ensure that children with disabilities have equal rights with respect to family life. With a view to realizing these rights, and to prevent concealment, abandonment, neglect and segregation of children with disabilities, States Parties shall

undertake to provide early and comprehensive information, services and support to children with disabilities and their families.

4. States Parties shall ensure that a child shall not be separated from his or her parents against their will, except when competent authorities subject to judicial review determine, in accordance with applicable law and procedures, that such separation is necessary for the best interests of the child. In no case shall a child be separated from parents on the basis of a disability of either the child or one or both of the parents.

5. States Parties shall, where the immediate family is unable to care for a child with disabilities, undertake every effort to provide alternative care within the wider family, and failing that, within the community in a family setting.

Article 24

Education

1. States Parties recognize the right of persons with disabilities to education. With a view to realizing this right without discrimination and on the basis of equal opportunity, States Parties shall ensure an inclusive education system at all levels and life long learning directed to:

   (a) The full development of human potential and sense of dignity and self-worth, and the strengthening of respect for human rights, fundamental freedoms and human diversity;

   (b) The development by persons with disabilities of their personality, talents and creativity, as well as their mental and physical abilities, to their fullest potential;

   (c) Enabling persons with disabilities to participate effectively in a free society.

2. In realizing this right, States Parties shall ensure that:

   (a) Persons with disabilities are not excluded from the general education system on the basis of disability, and that children with disabilities are not excluded from free and compulsory primary education, or from secondary education, on the basis of disability;

   (b) Persons with disabilities can access an inclusive, quality and free primary education and secondary education on an equal basis with others in the communities in which they live;

   (c) Reasonable accommodation of the individual's requirements is provided;

   (d) Persons with disabilities receive the support required, within the general education system, to facilitate their effective education;

   (e) Effective individualized support measures are provided in environments that maximize academic and social development, consistent with the goal of full inclusion.

3. States Parties shall enable persons with disabilities to learn life and social development skills to facilitate their full and equal participation in education and as members of the community. To this end, States Parties shall take appropriate measures, including:

   (a) Facilitating the learning of Braille, alternative script, augmentative and alternative modes, means and formats of communication and orientation and mobility skills, and facilitating peer support and mentoring;

   (b) Facilitating the learning of sign language and the promotion of the linguistic identity of the deaf community;

(c) Ensuring that the education of persons, and in particular children, who are blind, deaf or deafblind, is delivered in the most appropriate languages and modes and means of communication for the individual, and in environments which maximize academic and social development.

4. In order to help ensure the realization of this right, States Parties shall take appropriate measures to employ teachers, including teachers with disabilities, who are qualified in sign language and/or Braille, and to train professionals and staff who work at all levels of education. Such training shall incorporate disability awareness and the use of appropriate augmentative and alternative modes, means and formats of communication, educational techniques and materials to support persons with disabilities.

5. States Parties shall ensure that persons with disabilities are able to access general tertiary education, vocational training, adult education and lifelong learning without discrimination and on an equal basis with others. To this end, States Parties shall ensure that reasonable accommodation is provided to persons with disabilities.

Article 25

Health

States Parties recognize that persons with disabilities have the right to the enjoyment of the highest attainable standard of health without discrimination on the basis of disability. States Parties shall take all appropriate measures to ensure access for persons with disabilities to health services that are gender-sensitive, including health-related rehabilitation. In particular, States Parties shall:

(a) Provide persons with disabilities with the same range, quality and standard of free or affordable health care and programmes as provided to other persons, including in the area of sexual and reproductive health and population-based public health programmes;

(b) Provide those health services needed by persons with disabilities specifically because of their disabilities, including early identification and intervention as appropriate, and services designed to minimize and prevent further disabilities, including among children and older persons;

(c) Provide these health services as close as possible to people's own communities, including in rural areas;

(d) Require health professionals to provide care of the same quality to persons with disabilities as to others, including on the basis of free and informed consent by, inter alia, raising awareness of the human rights, dignity, autonomy and needs of persons with disabilities through training and the promulgation of ethical standards for public and private health care;

(e) Prohibit discrimination against persons with disabilities in the provision of health insurance, and life insurance where such insurance is permitted by national law, which shall be provided in a fair and reasonable manner;

(f) Prevent discriminatory denial of health care or health services or food and fluids on the basis of disability.

Article 26

Habilitation and rehabilitation

1. States Parties shall take effective and appropriate measures, including through peer support, to enable persons with disabilities to attain and maintain maximum independence, full physical, mental, social and vocational ability, and full inclusion and participation in all aspects of life. To that end, States Parties shall organize, strengthen and extend comprehensive habilitation and rehabilitation services and programmes, particularly in the areas of health, employment, education and social services, in such a way that these services and programmes:

   (a) Begin at the earliest possible stage, and are based on the multidisciplinary assessment of individual needs and strengths;

   (b) Support participation and inclusion in the community and all aspects of society, are voluntary, and are available to persons with disabilities as close as possible to their own communities, including in rural areas.

2. States Parties shall promote the development of initial and continuing training for professionals and staff working in habilitation and rehabilitation services.

3. States Parties shall promote the availability, knowledge and use of assistive devices and technologies, designed for persons with disabilities, as they relate to habilitation and rehabilitation.

Article 27

Work and employment

1. States Parties recognize the right of persons with disabilities to work, on an equal basis with others; this includes the right to the opportunity to gain a living by work freely chosen or accepted in a labour market and work environment that is open, inclusive and accessible to persons with disabilities. States Parties shall safeguard and promote the realization of the right to work, including for those who acquire a disability during the course of employment, by taking appropriate steps, including through legislation, to, inter alia:

   (a) Prohibit discrimination on the basis of disability with regard to all matters concerning all forms of employment, including conditions of recruitment, hiring and employment, continuance of employment, career advancement and safe and healthy working conditions;

   (b) Protect the rights of persons with disabilities, on an equal basis with others, to just and favourable conditions of work, including equal opportunities and equal remuneration for work of equal value, safe and healthy working conditions, including protection from harassment, and the redress of grievances;

   (c) Ensure that persons with disabilities are able to exercise their labour and trade union rights on an equal basis with others;

   (d) Enable persons with disabilities to have effective access to general technical and vocational guidance programmes, placement services and vocational and continuing training;

(e) Promote employment opportunities and career advancement for persons with disabilities in the labour market, as well as assistance in finding, obtaining, maintaining and returning to employment;

(f) Promote opportunities for self-employment, entrepreneurship, the development of cooperatives and starting one's own business;

(g) Employ persons with disabilities in the public sector;

(h) Promote the employment of persons with disabilities in the private sector through appropriate policies and measures, which may include affirmative action programmes, incentives and other measures;

(i) Ensure that reasonable accommodation is provided to persons with disabilities in the workplace;

(j) Promote the acquisition by persons with disabilities of work experience in the open labour market;

(k) Promote vocational and professional rehabilitation, job retention and return-to-work programmes for persons with disabilities.

2. States Parties shall ensure that persons with disabilities are not held in slavery or in servitude, and are protected, on an equal basis with others, from forced or compulsory labour.

Article 28

Adequate standard of living and social protection

1. States Parties recognize the right of persons with disabilities to an adequate standard of living for themselves and their families, including adequate food, clothing and housing, and to the continuous improvement of living conditions, and shall take appropriate steps to safeguard and promote the realization of this right without discrimination on the basis of disability.

2. States Parties recognize the right of persons with disabilities to social protection and to the enjoyment of that right without discrimination on the basis of disability, and shall take appropriate steps to safeguard and promote the realization of this right, including measures:

(a) To ensure equal access by persons with disabilities to clean water services, and to ensure access to appropriate and affordable services, devices and other assistance for disability-related needs;

(b) To ensure access by persons with disabilities, in particular women and girls with disabilities and older persons with disabilities, to social protection programmes and poverty reduction programmes;

(c) To ensure access by persons with disabilities and their families living in situations of poverty to assistance from the State with disability-related expenses, including adequate training, counselling, financial assistance and respite care;

(d) To ensure access by persons with disabilities to public housing programmes;

(e) To ensure equal access by persons with disabilities to retirement benefits and programmes.

Article 29

Participation in political and public life

States Parties shall guarantee to persons with disabilities political rights and the opportunity to enjoy them on an equal basis with others, and shall undertake to:
  (a) Ensure that persons with disabilities can effectively and fully participate in political and public life on an equal basis with others, directly or through freely chosen representatives, including the right and opportunity for persons with disabilities to vote and be elected, inter alia, by:
      (i) Ensuring that voting procedures, facilities and materials are appropriate, accessible and easy to understand and use;
      (ii) Protecting the right of persons with disabilities to vote by secret ballot in elections and public referendums without intimidation, and to stand for elections, to effectively hold office and perform all public functions at all levels of government, facilitating the use of assistive and new technologies where appropriate;
      (iii) Guaranteeing the free expression of the will of persons with disabilities as electors and to this end, where necessary, at their request, allowing assistance in voting by a person of their own choice;
  (b) Promote actively an environment in which persons with disabilities can effectively and fully participate in the conduct of public affairs, without discrimination and on an equal basis with others, and encourage their participation in public affairs, including:
      (i) Participation in non-governmental organizations and associations concerned with the public and political life of the country, and in the activities and administration of political parties;
      (ii) Forming and joining organizations of persons with disabilities to represent persons with disabilities at international, national, regional and local levels.

Article 30

Participation in cultural life, recreation, leisure and sport

1. States Parties recognize the right of persons with disabilities to take part on an equal basis with others in cultural life, and shall take all appropriate measures to ensure that persons with disabilities:
   (a) Enjoy access to cultural materials in accessible formats;
   (b) Enjoy access to television programmes, films, theatre and other cultural activities, in accessible formats;
   (c) Enjoy access to places for cultural performances or services, such as theatres, museums, cinemas, libraries and tourism services, and, as far as possible, enjoy access to monuments and sites of national cultural importance.

2. States Parties shall take appropriate measures to enable persons with disabilities to have the opportunity to develop and utilize their creative, artistic and intellectual potential, not only for their own benefit, but also for the enrichment of society.

3. States Parties shall take all appropriate steps, in accordance with international law, to ensure that laws protecting intellectual property rights do not constitute an unreasonable or discriminatory barrier to access by persons with disabilities to cultural materials.

4. Persons with disabilities shall be entitled, on an equal basis with others, to recognition and support of their specific cultural and linguistic identity, including sign languages and deaf culture.

5. With a view to enabling persons with disabilities to participate on an equal basis with others in recreational, leisure and sporting activities, States Parties shall take appropriate measures:

   (a) To encourage and promote the participation, to the fullest extent possible, of persons with disabilities in mainstream sporting activities at all levels;

   (b) To ensure that persons with disabilities have an opportunity to organize, develop and participate in disability-specific sporting and recreational activities and, to this end, encourage the provision, on an equal basis with others, of appropriate instruction, training and resources;

   (c) To ensure that persons with disabilities have access to sporting, recreational and tourism venues;

   (d) To ensure that children with disabilities have equal access with other children to participation in play, recreation and leisure and sporting activities, including those activities in the school system;

   (e) To ensure that persons with disabilities have access to services from those involved in the organization of recreational, tourism, leisure and sporting activities.

Article 31

Statistics and data collection

1. States Parties undertake to collect appropriate information, including statistical and research data, to enable them to formulate and implement policies to give effect to the present Convention. The process of collecting and maintaining this information shall:

   (a) Comply with legally established safeguards, including legislation on data protection, to ensure confidentiality and respect for the privacy of persons with disabilities;

   (b) Comply with internationally accepted norms to protect human rights and fundamental freedoms and ethical principles in the collection and use of statistics.

2. The information collected in accordance with this article shall be disaggregated, as appropriate, and used to help assess the implementation of States Parties' obligations

under the present Convention and to identify and address the barriers faced by persons with disabilities in exercising their rights.

3. States Parties shall assume responsibility for the dissemination of these statistics and ensure their accessibility to persons with disabilities and others.

Article 32

International cooperation

1. States Parties recognize the importance of international cooperation and its promotion, in support of national efforts for the realization of the purpose and objectives of the present Convention, and will undertake appropriate and effective measures in this regard, between and among States and, as appropriate, in partnership with relevant international and regional organizations and civil society, in particular organizations of persons with disabilities. Such measures could include, inter alia:
   (a) Ensuring that international cooperation, including international development programmes, is inclusive of and accessible to persons with disabilities;
   (b) Facilitating and supporting capacity-building, including through the exchange and sharing of information, experiences, training programmes and best practices;
   (c) Facilitating cooperation in research and access to scientific and technical knowledge;
   (d) Providing, as appropriate, technical and economic assistance, including by facilitating access to and sharing of accessible and assistive technologies, and through the transfer of technologies.

2. The provisions of this article are without prejudice to the obligations of each State Party to fulfil its obligations under the present Convention.

Article 33

National implementation and monitoring

1. States Parties, in accordance with their system of organization, shall designate one or more focal points within government for matters relating to the implementation of the present Convention, and shall give due consideration to the establishment or designation of a coordination mechanism within government to facilitate related action in different sectors and at different levels.

2. States Parties shall, in accordance with their legal and administrative systems, maintain, strengthen, designate or establish within the State Party, a framework, including one or more independent mechanisms, as appropriate, to promote, protect and monitor implementation of the present Convention. When designating or establishing such a mechanism, States Parties shall take into account the principles relating to the status and functioning of national institutions for protection and promotion of human rights.

3. Civil society, in particular persons with disabilities and their representative organizations, shall be involved and participate fully in the monitoring process.

Article 34

Committee on the Rights of Persons with Disabilities

1. There shall be established a Committee on the Rights of Persons with Disabilities (hereafter referred to as "the Committee"), which shall carry out the functions hereinafter provided.
2. The Committee shall consist, at the time of entry into force of the present Convention, of twelve experts. After an additional sixty ratifications or accessions to the Convention, the membership of the Committee shall increase by six members, attaining a maximum number of eighteen members.
3. The members of the Committee shall serve in their personal capacity and shall be of high moral standing and recognized competence and experience in the field covered by the present Convention. When nominating their candidates, States Parties are invited to give due consideration to the provision set out in article 4.3 of the present Convention.
4. The members of the Committee shall be elected by States Parties, consideration being given to equitable geographical distribution, representation of the different forms of civilization and of the principal legal systems, balanced gender representation and participation of experts with disabilities.
5. The members of the Committee shall be elected by secret ballot from a list of persons nominated by the States Parties from among their nationals at meetings of the Conference of States Parties. At those meetings, for which two thirds of States Parties shall constitute a quorum, the persons elected to the Committee shall be those who obtain the largest number of votes and an absolute majority of the votes of the representatives of States Parties present and voting.
6. The initial election shall be held no later than six months after the date of entry into force of the present Convention. At least four months before the date of each election, the Secretary-General of the United Nations shall address a letter to the States Parties inviting them to submit the nominations within two months. The Secretary-General shall subsequently prepare a list in alphabetical order of all persons thus nominated, indicating the State Parties which have nominated them, and shall submit it to the States Parties to the present Convention.
7. The members of the Committee shall be elected for a term of four years. They shall be eligible for re-election once. However, the term of six of the members elected at the first election shall expire at the end of two years; immediately after the first election, the names of these six members shall be chosen by lot by the chairperson of the meeting referred to in paragraph 5 of this article.
8. The election of the six additional members of the Committee shall be held on the occasion of regular elections, in accordance with the relevant provisions of this article.
9. If a member of the Committee dies or resigns or declares that for any other cause she or he can no longer perform her or his duties, the State Party which nominated the member shall appoint another expert possessing the qualifications and meeting the requirements set out in the relevant provisions of this article, to serve for the remainder of the term.
10. The Committee shall establish its own rules of procedure.
11. The Secretary-General of the United Nations shall provide the necessary staff and facilities for the effective performance of the functions of the Committee under the present Convention, and shall convene its initial meeting.

12. With the approval of the General Assembly, the members of the Committee established under the present Convention shall receive emoluments from United Nations resources on such terms and conditions as the Assembly may decide, having regard to the importance of the Committee's responsibilities.

13. The members of the Committee shall be entitled to the facilities, privileges and immunities of experts on mission for the United Nations as laid down in the relevant sections of the Convention on the Privileges and Immunities of the United Nations.

Article 35

Reports by States Parties

1. Each State Party shall submit to the Committee, through the Secretary-General of the United Nations, a comprehensive report on measures taken to give effect to its obligations under the present Convention and on the progress made in that regard, within two years after the entry into force of the present Convention for the State Party concerned.

2. Thereafter, States Parties shall submit subsequent reports at least every four years and further whenever the Committee so requests.

3. The Committee shall decide any guidelines applicable to the content of the reports.

4. A State Party which has submitted a comprehensive initial report to the Committee need not, in its subsequent reports, repeat information previously provided. When preparing reports to the Committee, States Parties are invited to consider doing so in an open and transparent process and to give due consideration to the provision set out in article 4.3 of the present Convention.

5. Reports may indicate factors and difficulties affecting the degree of fulfilment of obligations under the present Convention.

Article 36

Consideration of reports

1. Each report shall be considered by the Committee, which shall make such suggestions and general recommendations on the report as it may consider appropriate and shall forward these to the State Party concerned. The State Party may respond with any information it chooses to the Committee. The Committee may request further information from States Parties relevant to the implementation of the present Convention.

2. If a State Party is significantly overdue in the submission of a report, the Committee may notify the State Party concerned of the need to examine the implementation of the present Convention in that State Party, on the basis of reliable information available to the Committee, if the relevant report is not submitted within three months following the notification. The Committee shall invite the State Party concerned to participate in such examination. Should the State Party respond by submitting the relevant report, the provisions of paragraph 1 of this article will apply.

3. The Secretary-General of the United Nations shall make available the reports to all States Parties.

4. States Parties shall make their reports widely available to the public in their own countries and facilitate access to the suggestions and general recommendations relating to these reports.

5. The Committee shall transmit, as it may consider appropriate, to the specialized agencies, funds and programmes of the United Nations, and other competent bodies, reports from States Parties in order to address a request or indication of a need for technical advice or assistance contained therein, along with the Committee's observations and recommendations, if any, on these requests or indications.

Article 37

Cooperation between States Parties and the Committee

1. Each State Party shall cooperate with the Committee and assist its members in the fulfilment of their mandate.

2. In its relationship with States Parties, the Committee shall give due consideration to ways and means of enhancing national capacities for the implementation of the present Convention, including through international cooperation.

Article 38

Relationship of the Committee with other bodies

In order to foster the effective implementation of the present Convention and to encourage international cooperation in the field covered by the present Convention:

(a) The specialized agencies and other United Nations organs shall be entitled to be represented at the consideration of the implementation of such provisions of the present Convention as fall within the scope of their mandate. The Committee may invite the specialized agencies and other competent bodies as it may consider appropriate to provide expert advice on the implementation of the Convention in areas falling within the scope of their respective mandates. The Committee may invite specialized agencies and other United Nations organs to submit reports on the implementation of the Convention in areas falling within the scope of their activities;

(b) The Committee, as it discharges its mandate, shall consult, as appropriate, other relevant bodies instituted by international human rights treaties, with a view to ensuring the consistency of their respective reporting guidelines, suggestions and general recommendations, and avoiding duplication and overlap in the performance of their functions.

Article 39

Report of the Committee

The Committee shall report every two years to the General Assembly and to the Economic and Social Council on its activities, and may make suggestions and general recommendations based on the examination of reports and information received from the States

Parties. Such suggestions and general recommendations shall be included in the report of the Committee together with comments, if any, from States Parties.

Article 40

Conference of States Parties

1. The States Parties shall meet regularly in a Conference of States Parties in order to consider any matter with regard to the implementation of the present Convention.
2. No later than six months after the entry into force of the present Convention, the Conference of the States Parties shall be convened by the Secretary-General of the United Nations. The subsequent meetings shall be convened by the Secretary-General of the United Nations biennially or upon the decision of the Conference of States Parties.

Article 41

Depositary

The Secretary-General of the United Nations shall be the depositary of the present Convention.

Article 42

Signature

The present Convention shall be open for signature by all States and by regional integration organizations at United Nations Headquarters in New York as of 30 March 2007.

Article 43

Consent to be bound

The present Convention shall be subject to ratification by signatory States and to formal confirmation by signatory regional integration organizations. It shall be open for accession by any State or regional integration organization which has not signed the Convention.

Article 44

Regional integration organizations

1. "Regional integration organization" shall mean an organization constituted by sovereign States of a given region, to which its member States have transferred competence in respect of matters governed by this Convention. Such organizations shall declare, in their instruments of formal confirmation or accession, the extent of their competence

with respect to matters governed by this Convention. Subsequently, they shall inform the depositary of any substantial modification in the extent of their competence.

2. References to "States Parties" in the present Convention shall apply to such organizations within the limits of their competence.

3. For the purposes of article 45, paragraph 1, and article 47, paragraphs 2 and 3, any instrument deposited by a regional integration organization shall not be counted.

4. Regional integration organizations, in matters within their competence, may exercise their right to vote in the Conference of States Parties, with a number of votes equal to the number of their member States that are Parties to this Convention. Such an organization shall not exercise its right to vote if any of its member States exercises its right, and vice versa.

Article 45

Entry into force

1. The present Convention shall enter into force on the thirtieth day after the deposit of the twentieth instrument of ratification or accession.

2. For each State or regional integration organization ratifying, formally confirming or acceding to the Convention after the deposit of the twentieth such instrument, the Convention shall enter into force on the thirtieth day after the deposit of its own such instrument.

Article 46

Reservations

1. Reservations incompatible with the object and purpose of the present Convention shall not be permitted.

2. Reservations may be withdrawn at any time.

Article 47

Amendments

1. Any State Party may propose an amendment to the present Convention and submit it to the Secretary-General of the United Nations. The Secretary-General shall communicate any proposed amendments to States Parties, with a request to be notified whether they favour a conference of States Parties for the purpose of considering and deciding upon the proposals. In the event that, within four months from the date of such communication, at least one third of the States Parties favour such a conference, the Secretary-General shall convene the conference under the auspices of the United Nations. Any amendment adopted by a majority of two thirds of the States Parties present and voting shall be submitted by the Secretary-General to the General Assembly for approval and thereafter to all States Parties for acceptance.

2. An amendment adopted and approved in accordance with paragraph 1 of this article shall enter into force on the thirtieth day after the number of instruments of acceptance deposited reaches two thirds of the number of States Parties at the date of adoption of the amendment. Thereafter, the amendment shall enter into force for any State Party on the thirtieth day following the deposit of its own instrument of acceptance. An amendment shall be binding only on those States Parties which have accepted it.

3. If so decided by the Conference of States Parties by consensus, an amendment adopted and approved in accordance with paragraph 1 of this article which relates exclusively to articles 34, 38, 39 and 40 shall enter into force for all States Parties on the thirtieth day after the number of instruments of acceptance deposited reaches two thirds of the number of States Parties at the date of adoption of the amendment.

Article 48

Denunciation

A State Party may denounce the present Convention by written notification to the Secretary-General of the United Nations. The denunciation shall become effective one year after the date of receipt of the notification by the Secretary-General.

Article 49

Accessible format

The text of the present Convention shall be made available in accessible formats.

Article 50

Authentic texts

The Arabic, Chinese, English, French, Russian and Spanish texts of the present Convention shall be equally authentic.

In witness thereof the undersigned plenipotentiaries, being duly authorized thereto by their respective Governments, have signed the present Convention.

25

Optional Protocol to the Convention on the Rights of Persons with Disabilities, 2006

Note: adopted on 13 December 2006 by General Assembly Resolution 61/016. Registration Number 4490, 3 May 2008. 2518 UNTS 283. Entry into force: 3 May 2008.

The States Parties to the present Protocol have agreed as follows:

Article 1
1. A State Party to the present Protocol ("State Party") recognizes the competence of the Committee on the Rights of Persons with Disabilities ("the Committee") to receive and consider communications from or on behalf of individuals or groups of individuals subject to its jurisdiction who claim to be victims of a violation by that State Party of the provisions of the Convention.
2. No communication shall be received by the Committee if it concerns a State Party to the Convention that is not a party to the present Protocol.

Article 2
The Committee shall consider a communication inadmissible when:
(a) The communication is anonymous;
(b) The communication constitutes an abuse of the right of submission of such communications or is incompatible with the provisions of the Convention;
(c) The same matter has already been examined by the Committee or has been or is being examined under another procedure of international investigation or settlement;
(d) All available domestic remedies have not been exhausted. This shall not be the rule where the application of the remedies is unreasonably prolonged or unlikely to bring effective relief;
(e) It is manifestly ill-founded or not sufficiently substantiated; or when
(f) The facts that are the subject of the communication occurred prior to the entry into force of the present Protocol for the State Party concerned unless those facts continued after that date.

Article 3
Subject to the provisions of article 2 of the present Protocol, the Committee shall bring any communications submitted to it confidentially to the attention of the State Party. Within six months, the receiving State shall submit to the Committee written explanations or statements clarifying the matter and the remedy, if any, that may have been taken by that State.

Article 4

1. At any time after the receipt of a communication and before a determination on the merits has been reached, the Committee may transmit to the State Party concerned for its urgent consideration a request that the State Party take such interim measures as may be necessary to avoid possible irreparable damage to the victim or victims of the alleged violation.
2. Where the Committee exercises its discretion under paragraph 1 of this article, this does not imply a determination on admissibility or on the merits of the communication.

Article 5

The Committee shall hold closed meetings when examining communications under the present Protocol. After examining a communication, the Committee shall forward its suggestions and recommendations, if any, to the State Party concerned and to the petitioner.

Article 6

1. If the Committee receives reliable information indicating grave or systematic violations by a State Party of rights set forth in the Convention, the Committee shall invite that State Party to cooperate in the examination of the information and to this end submit observations with regard to the information concerned.
2. Taking into account any observations that may have been submitted by the State Party concerned as well as any other reliable information available to it, the Committee may designate one or more of its members to conduct an inquiry and to report urgently to the Committee. Where warranted and with the consent of the State Party, the inquiry may include a visit to its territory.
3. After examining the findings of such an inquiry, the Committee shall transmit these findings to the State Party concerned together with any comments and recommendations.
4. The State Party concerned shall, within six months of receiving the findings, comments and recommendations transmitted by the Committee, submit its observations to the Committee.
5. Such an inquiry shall be conducted confidentially and the cooperation of the State Party shall be sought at all stages of the proceedings.

Article 7

1. The Committee may invite the State Party concerned to include in its report under article 35 of the Convention details of any measures taken in response to an inquiry conducted under article 6 of the present Protocol.
2. The Committee may, if necessary, after the end of the period of six months referred to in article 6.4, invite the State Party concerned to inform it of the measures taken in response to such an inquiry.

Article 8

Each State Party may, at the time of signature or ratification of the present Protocol or accession thereto, declare that it does not recognize the competence of the Committee provided for in articles 6 and 7.

Article 9
The Secretary-General of the United Nations shall be the depositary of the present Protocol.

Article 10
The present Protocol shall be open for signature by signatory States and regional integration organizations of the Convention at United Nations Headquarters in New York as of 30 March 2007.

Article 11
The present Protocol shall be subject to ratification by signatory States of this Protocol which have ratified or acceded to the Convention. It shall be subject to formal confirmation by signatory regional integration organizations of this Protocol which have formally confirmed or acceded to the Convention. It shall be open for accession by any State or regional integration organization which has ratified, formally confirmed or acceded to the Convention and which has not signed the Protocol.

Article 12
1. "Regional integration organization" shall mean an organization constituted by sovereign States of a given region, to which its member States have transferred competence in respect of matters governed by the Convention and this Protocol. Such organizations shall declare, in their instruments of formal confirmation or accession, the extent of their competence with respect to matters governed by the Convention and this Protocol. Subsequently, they shall inform the depositary of any substantial modification in the extent of their competence.
2. References to "States Parties" in the present Protocol shall apply to such organizations within the limits of their competence.
3. For the purposes of article 13, paragraph 1, and article 15, paragraph 2, any instrument deposited by a regional integration organization shall not be counted.
4. Regional integration organizations, in matters within their competence, may exercise their right to vote in the meeting of States Parties, with a number of votes equal to the number of their member States that are Parties to this Protocol. Such an organization shall not exercise its right to vote if any of its member States exercises its right, and vice versa.

Article 13
1. Subject to the entry into force of the Convention, the present Protocol shall enter into force on the thirtieth day after the deposit of the tenth instrument of ratification or accession.
2. For each State or regional integration organization ratifying, formally confirming or acceding to the Protocol after the deposit of the tenth such instrument, the Protocol shall enter into force on the thirtieth day after the deposit of its own such instrument.

Article 14
1. Reservations incompatible with the object and purpose of the present Protocol shall not be permitted.
2. Reservations may be withdrawn at any time.

Article 15

1. Any State Party may propose an amendment to the present Protocol and submit it to the Secretary-General of the United Nations. The Secretary-General shall communicate any proposed amendments to States Parties, with a request to be notified whether they favour a meeting of States Parties for the purpose of considering and deciding upon the proposals. In the event that, within four months from the date of such communication, at least one third of the States Parties favour such a meeting, the Secretary-General shall convene the meeting under the auspices of the United Nations. Any amendment adopted by a majority of two thirds of the States Parties present and voting shall be submitted by the Secretary-General to the General Assembly for approval and thereafter to all States Parties for acceptance.

2. An amendment adopted and approved in accordance with paragraph 1 of this article shall enter into force on the thirtieth day after the number of instruments of acceptance deposited reaches two thirds of the number of States Parties at the date of adoption of the amendment. Thereafter, the amendment shall enter into force for any State Party on the thirtieth day following the deposit of its own instrument of acceptance. An amendment shall be binding only on those States Parties which have accepted it.

Article 16

A State Party may denounce the present Protocol by written notification to the Secretary-General of the United Nations. The denunciation shall become effective one year after the date of receipt of the notification by the Secretary-General.

Article 17

The text of the present Protocol shall be made available in accessible formats.

Article 18

The Arabic, Chinese, English, French, Russian and Spanish texts of the present Protocol shall be equally authentic.

IN WITNESS THEREOF the undersigned plenipotentiaries, being duly authorized thereto by their respective Governments, have signed the present Protocol.

26

International Convention for the Protection of All Persons from Enforced Disappearance, 2006

Note: adopted on 20 December 2006, by General Assembly Resolution 61/177, 2716 UNTS 3. Entry into force: 23 December 2010.

The States Parties to this Convention,

Considering the obligation of States under the Charter of the United Nations to promote universal respect for, and observance of, human rights and fundamental freedoms,

Having regard to the Universal Declaration of Human Rights,

Recalling the International Covenant on Economic, Social and Cultural Rights, the International Covenant on Civil and Political Rights and the other relevant international instruments in the fields of human rights, humanitarian law and international criminal law,

Also recalling the Declaration on the Protection of All Persons from Enforced Disappearance adopted by the General Assembly of the United Nations in its resolution 47/133 of 18 December 1992,

Aware of the extreme seriousness of enforced disappearance, which constitutes a crime and, in certain circumstances defined in international law, a crime against humanity,

Determined to prevent enforced disappearances and to combat impunity for the crime of enforced disappearance,

Considering the right of any person not to be subjected to enforced disappearance, the right of victims to justice and to reparation,

Affirming the right of any victim to know the truth about the circumstances of an enforced disappearance and the fate of the disappeared person, and the right to freedom to seek, receive and impart information to this end,

Have agreed on the following articles:

PART I

Article 1

1. No one shall be subjected to enforced disappearance.
2. No exceptional circumstances whatsoever, whether a state of war or a threat of war, internal political instability or any other public emergency, may be invoked as a justification for enforced disappearance.

Article 2

For the purposes of this Convention, "enforced disappearance" is considered to be the arrest, detention, abduction or any other form of deprivation of liberty by agents of the

State or by persons or groups of persons acting with the authorization, support or acquiescence of the State, followed by a refusal to acknowledge the deprivation of liberty or by concealment of the fate or whereabouts of the disappeared person, which place such a person outside the protection of the law.

Article 3
Each State Party shall take appropriate measures to investigate acts defined in article 2 committed by persons or groups of persons acting without the authorization, support or acquiescence of the State and to bring those responsible to justice.

Article 4
Each State Party shall take the necessary measures to ensure that enforced disappearance constitutes an offence under its criminal law.

Article 5
The widespread or systematic practice of enforced disappearance constitutes a crime against humanity as defined in applicable international law and shall attract the consequences provided for under such applicable international law.

Article 6
1. Each State Party shall take the necessary measures to hold criminally responsible at least:
   (a) Any person who commits, orders, solicits or induces the commission of, attempts to commit, is an accomplice to or participates in an enforced disappearance;
   (b) A superior who:
      (i) Knew, or consciously disregarded information which clearly indicated, that subordinates under his or her effective authority and control were committing or about to commit a crime of enforced disappearance;
      (ii) Exercised effective responsibility for and control over activities which were concerned with the crime of enforced disappearance; and
      (iii) Failed to take all necessary and reasonable measures within his or her power to prevent or repress the commission of an enforced disappearance or to submit the matter to the competent authorities for investigation and prosecution;
   (c) Subparagraph (b) above is without prejudice to the higher standards of responsibility applicable under relevant international law to a military commander or to a person effectively acting as a military commander.
2. No order or instruction from any public authority, civilian, military or other, may be invoked to justify an offence of enforced disappearance.

Article 7
1. Each State Party shall make the offence of enforced disappearance punishable by appropriate penalties which take into account its extreme seriousness.
2. Each State Party may establish:
   (a) Mitigating circumstances, in particular for persons who, having been implicated in the commission of an enforced disappearance, effectively contribute to bringing

the disappeared person forward alive or make it possible to clarify cases of enforced disappearance or to identify the perpetrators of an enforced disappearance;

(b) Without prejudice to other criminal procedures, aggravating circumstances, in particular in the event of the death of the disappeared person or the commission of an enforced disappearance in respect of pregnant women, minors, persons with disabilities or other particularly vulnerable persons.

Article 8

Without prejudice to article 5,

1. A State Party which applies a statute of limitations in respect of enforced disappearance shall take the necessary measures to ensure that the term of limitation for criminal proceedings:
   (a) Is of long duration and is proportionate to the extreme seriousness of this offence;
   (b) Commences from the moment when the offence of enforced disappearance ceases, taking into account its continuous nature.
2. Each State Party shall guarantee the right of victims of enforced disappearance to an effective remedy during the term of limitation.

Article 9

1. Each State Party shall take the necessary measures to establish its competence to exercise jurisdiction over the offence of enforced disappearance:
   (a) When the offence is committed in any territory under its jurisdiction or on board a ship or aircraft registered in that State;
   (b) When the alleged offender is one of its nationals;
   (c) When the disappeared person is one of its nationals and the State Party considers it appropriate.
2. Each State Party shall likewise take such measures as may be necessary to establish its competence to exercise jurisdiction over the offence of enforced disappearance when the alleged offender is present in any territory under its jurisdiction, unless it extradites or surrenders him or her to another State in accordance with its international obligations or surrenders him or her to an international criminal tribunal whose jurisdiction it has recognized.
3. This Convention does not exclude any additional criminal jurisdiction exercised in accordance with national law.

Article 10

1. Upon being satisfied, after an examination of the information available to it, that the circumstances so warrant, any State Party in whose territory a person suspected of having committed an offence of enforced disappearance is present shall take him or her into custody or take such other legal measures as are necessary to ensure his or her presence. The custody and other legal measures shall be as provided for in the law of that State Party but may be maintained only for such time as is necessary to ensure the person's presence at criminal, surrender or extradition proceedings.
2. A State Party which has taken the measures referred to in paragraph 1 of this article shall immediately carry out a preliminary inquiry or investigations to establish the facts. It shall notify the States Parties referred to in article 9, paragraph 1, of the

measures it has taken in pursuance of paragraph 1 of this article, including detention and the circumstances warranting detention, and of the findings of its preliminary inquiry or its investigations, indicating whether it intends to exercise its jurisdiction.

3. Any person in custody pursuant to paragraph 1 of this article may communicate immediately with the nearest appropriate representative of the State of which he or she is a national, or, if he or she is a stateless person, with the representative of the State where he or she usually resides.

Article 11

1. The State Party in the territory under whose jurisdiction a person alleged to have committed an offence of enforced disappearance is found shall, if it does not extradite that person or surrender him or her to another State in accordance with its international obligations or surrender him or her to an international criminal tribunal whose jurisdiction it has recognized, submit the case to its competent authorities for the purpose of prosecution.

2. These authorities shall take their decision in the same manner as in the case of any ordinary offence of a serious nature under the law of that State Party. In the cases referred to in article 9, paragraph 2, the standards of evidence required for prosecution and conviction shall in no way be less stringent than those which apply in the cases referred to in article 9, paragraph 1.

3. Any person against whom proceedings are brought in connection with an offence of enforced disappearance shall be guaranteed fair treatment at all stages of the proceedings. Any person tried for an offence of enforced disappearance shall benefit from a fair trial before a competent, independent and impartial court or tribunal established by law.

Article 12

1. Each State Party shall ensure that any individual who alleges that a person has been subjected to enforced disappearance has the right to report the facts to the competent authorities, which shall examine the allegation promptly and impartially and, where necessary, undertake without delay a thorough and impartial investigation. Appropriate steps shall be taken, where necessary, to ensure that the complainant, witnesses, relatives of the disappeared person and their defence counsel, as well as persons participating in the investigation, are protected against all ill-treatment or intimidation as a consequence of the complaint or any evidence given.

2. Where there are reasonable grounds for believing that a person has been subjected to enforced disappearance, the authorities referred to in paragraph 1 of this article shall undertake an investigation, even if there has been no formal complaint.

3. Each State Party shall ensure that the authorities referred to in paragraph 1 of this article:

    (a) Have the necessary powers and resources to conduct the investigation effectively, including access to the documentation and other information relevant to their investigation;

    (b) Have access, if necessary with the prior authorization of a judicial authority, which shall rule promptly on the matter, to any place of detention or any other place where there are reasonable grounds to believe that the disappeared person may be present.

4. Each State Party shall take the necessary measures to prevent and sanction acts that hinder the conduct of an investigation. It shall ensure in particular that persons suspected of having committed an offence of enforced disappearance are not in a position to influence the progress of an investigation by means of pressure or acts of intimidation or reprisal aimed at the complainant, witnesses, relatives of the disappeared person or their defence counsel, or at persons participating in the investigation.

Article 13

1. For the purposes of extradition between States Parties, the offence of enforced disappearance shall not be regarded as a political offence or as an offence connected with a political offence or as an offence inspired by political motives. Accordingly, a request for extradition based on such an offence may not be refused on these grounds alone.
2. The offence of enforced disappearance shall be deemed to be included as an extraditable offence in any extradition treaty existing between States Parties before the entry into force of this Convention.
3. States Parties undertake to include the offence of enforced disappearance as an extraditable offence in any extradition treaty subsequently to be concluded between them.
4. If a State Party which makes extradition conditional on the existence of a treaty receives a request for extradition from another State Party with which it has no extradition treaty, it may consider this Convention as the necessary legal basis for extradition in respect of the offence of enforced disappearance.
5. States Parties which do not make extradition conditional on the existence of a treaty shall recognize the offence of enforced disappearance as an extraditable offence between themselves.
6. Extradition shall, in all cases, be subject to the conditions provided for by the law of the requested State Party or by applicable extradition treaties, including, in particular, conditions relating to the minimum penalty requirement for extradition and the grounds upon which the requested State Party may refuse extradition or make it subject to certain conditions.
7. Nothing in this Convention shall be interpreted as imposing an obligation to extradite if the requested State Party has substantial grounds for believing that the request has been made for the purpose of prosecuting or punishing a person on account of that person's sex, race, religion, nationality, ethnic origin, political opinions or membership of a particular social group, or that compliance with the request would cause harm to that person for any one of these reasons.

Article 14

1. States Parties shall afford one another the greatest measure of mutual legal assistance in connection with criminal proceedings brought in respect of an offence of enforced disappearance, including the supply of all evidence at their disposal that is necessary for the proceedings.
2. Such mutual legal assistance shall be subject to the conditions provided for by the domestic law of the requested State Party or by applicable treaties on mutual legal assistance, including, in particular, the conditions in relation to the grounds upon which the requested State Party may refuse to grant mutual legal assistance or may make it subject to conditions.

Article 15

States Parties shall cooperate with each other and shall afford one another the greatest measure of mutual assistance with a view to assisting victims of enforced disappearance, and in searching for, locating and releasing disappeared persons and, in the event of death, in exhuming and identifying them and returning their remains.

Article 16

1. No State Party shall expel, return ("refouler"), surrender or extradite a person to another State where there are substantial grounds for believing that he or she would be in danger of being subjected to enforced disappearance.
2. For the purpose of determining whether there are such grounds, the competent authorities shall take into account all relevant considerations, including, where applicable, the existence in the State concerned of a consistent pattern of gross, flagrant or mass violations of human rights or of serious violations of international humanitarian law.

Article 17

1. No one shall be held in secret detention.
2. Without prejudice to other international obligations of the State Party with regard to the deprivation of liberty, each State Party shall, in its legislation:
   (a) Establish the conditions under which orders of deprivation of liberty may be given;
   (b) Indicate those authorities authorized to order the deprivation of liberty;
   (c) Guarantee that any person deprived of liberty shall be held solely in officially recognized and supervised places of deprivation of liberty;
   (d) Guarantee that any person deprived of liberty shall be authorized to communicate with and be visited by his or her family, counsel or any other person of his or her choice, subject only to the conditions established by law, or, if he or she is a foreigner, to communicate with his or her consular authorities, in accordance with applicable international law;
   (e) Guarantee access by the competent and legally authorized authorities and institutions to the places where persons are deprived of liberty, if necessary with prior authorization from a judicial authority;
   (f) Guarantee that any person deprived of liberty or, in the case of a suspected enforced disappearance, since the person deprived of liberty is not able to exercise this right, any persons with a legitimate interest, such as relatives of the person deprived of liberty, their representatives or their counsel, shall, in all circumstances, be entitled to take proceedings before a court, in order that the court may decide without delay on the lawfulness of the deprivation of liberty and order the person's release if such deprivation of liberty is not lawful.
3. Each State Party shall assure the compilation and maintenance of one or more up-to-date official registers and/or records of persons deprived of liberty, which shall be made promptly available, upon request, to any judicial or other competent authority or institution authorized for that purpose by the law of the State Party concerned or any relevant international legal instrument to which the State concerned is a party. The information contained therein shall include, as a minimum:
   (a) The identity of the person deprived of liberty;
   (b) The date, time and place where the person was deprived of liberty and the identity of the authority that deprived the person of liberty;

(c) The authority that ordered the deprivation of liberty and the grounds for the deprivation of liberty;

(d) The authority responsible for supervising the deprivation of liberty;

(e) The place of deprivation of liberty, the date and time of admission to the place of deprivation of liberty and the authority responsible for the place of deprivation of liberty;

(f) Elements relating to the state of health of the person deprived of liberty;

(g) In the event of death during the deprivation of liberty, the circumstances and cause of death and the destination of the remains;

(h) The date and time of release or transfer to another place of detention, the destination and the authority responsible for the transfer.

Article 18

1. Subject to articles 19 and 20, each State Party shall guarantee to any person with a legitimate interest in this information, such as relatives of the person deprived of liberty, their representatives or their counsel, access to at least the following information:

(a) The authority that ordered the deprivation of liberty;

(b) The date, time and place where the person was deprived of liberty and admitted to the place of deprivation of liberty;

(c) The authority responsible for supervising the deprivation of liberty;

(d) The whereabouts of the person deprived of liberty, including, in the event of a transfer to another place of deprivation of liberty, the destination and the authority responsible for the transfer;

(e) The date, time and place of release;

(f) Elements relating to the state of health of the person deprived of liberty;

(g) In the event of death during the deprivation of liberty, the circumstances and cause of death and the destination of the remains.

2. Appropriate measures shall be taken, where necessary, to protect the persons referred to in paragraph 1 of this article, as well as persons participating in the investigation, from any ill-treatment, intimidation or sanction as a result of the search for information concerning a person deprived of liberty.

Article 19

1. Personal information, including medical and genetic data, which is collected and/or transmitted within the framework of the search for a disappeared person shall not be used or made available for purposes other than the search for the disappeared person. This is without prejudice to the use of such information in criminal proceedings relating to an offence of enforced disappearance or the exercise of the right to obtain reparation.

2. The collection, processing, use and storage of personal information, including medical and genetic data, shall not infringe or have the effect of infringing the human rights, fundamental freedoms or human dignity of an individual.

Article 20

1. Only where a person is under the protection of the law and the deprivation of liberty is subject to judicial control may the right to information referred to in article 18 be restricted, on an exceptional basis, where strictly necessary and where provided for by

law, and if the transmission of the information would adversely affect the privacy or safety of the person, hinder a criminal investigation, or for other equivalent reasons in accordance with the law, and in conformity with applicable international law and with the objectives of this Convention. In no case shall there be restrictions on the right to information referred to in article 18 that could constitute conduct defined in article 2 or be in violation of article 17, paragraph 1.

2. Without prejudice to consideration of the lawfulness of the deprivation of a person's liberty, States Parties shall guarantee to the persons referred to in article 18, paragraph 1, the right to a prompt and effective judicial remedy as a means of obtaining without delay the information referred to in article 18, paragraph 1. This right to a remedy may not be suspended or restricted in any circumstances.

Article 21

Each State Party shall take the necessary measures to ensure that persons deprived of liberty are released in a manner permitting reliable verification that they have actually been released. Each State Party shall also take the necessary measures to assure the physical integrity of such persons and their ability to exercise fully their rights at the time of release, without prejudice to any obligations to which such persons may be subject under national law.

Article 22

Without prejudice to article 6, each State Party shall take the necessary measures to prevent and impose sanctions for the following conduct:

(a) Delaying or obstructing the remedies referred to in article 17, paragraph 2 (f), and article 20, paragraph 2;

(b) Failure to record the deprivation of liberty of any person, or the recording of any information which the official responsible for the official register knew or should have known to be inaccurate;

(c) Refusal to provide information on the deprivation of liberty of a person, or the provision of inaccurate information, even though the legal requirements for providing such information have been met.

Article 23

1. Each State Party shall ensure that the training of law enforcement personnel, civil or military, medical personnel, public officials and other persons who may be involved in the custody or treatment of any person deprived of liberty includes the necessary education and information regarding the relevant provisions of this Convention, in order to:

(a) Prevent the involvement of such officials in enforced disappearances;

(b) Emphasize the importance of prevention and investigations in relation to enforced disappearances;

(c) Ensure that the urgent need to resolve cases of enforced disappearance is recognized.

2. Each State Party shall ensure that orders or instructions prescribing, authorizing or encouraging enforced disappearance are prohibited. Each State Party shall guarantee that a person who refuses to obey such an order will not be punished.

3. Each State Party shall take the necessary measures to ensure that the persons referred to in paragraph 1 of this article who have reason to believe that an enforced disappearance has occurred or is planned report the matter to their superiors and, where necessary, to the appropriate authorities or bodies vested with powers of review or remedy.

Article 24

1. For the purposes of this Convention, "victim" means the disappeared person and any individual who has suffered harm as the direct result of an enforced disappearance.
2. Each victim has the right to know the truth regarding the circumstances of the enforced disappearance, the progress and results of the investigation and the fate of the disappeared person. Each State Party shall take appropriate measures in this regard.
3. Each State Party shall take all appropriate measures to search for, locate and release disappeared persons and, in the event of death, to locate, respect and return their remains.
4. Each State Party shall ensure in its legal system that the victims of enforced disappearance have the right to obtain reparation and prompt, fair and adequate compensation.
5. The right to obtain reparation referred to in paragraph 4 of this article covers material and moral damages and, where appropriate, other forms of reparation such as:
   (a) Restitution;
   (b) Rehabilitation;
   (c) Satisfaction, including restoration of dignity and reputation;
   (d) Guarantees of non-repetition.
6. Without prejudice to the obligation to continue the investigation until the fate of the disappeared person has been clarified, each State Party shall take the appropriate steps with regard to the legal situation of disappeared persons whose fate has not been clarified and that of their relatives, in fields such as social welfare, financial matters, family law and property rights.
7. Each State Party shall guarantee the right to form and participate freely in organizations and associations concerned with attempting to establish the circumstances of enforced disappearances and the fate of disappeared persons, and to assist victims of enforced disappearance.

Article 25

1. Each State Party shall take the necessary measures to prevent and punish under its criminal law:
   (a) The wrongful removal of children who are subjected to enforced disappearance, children whose father, mother or legal guardian is subjected to enforced disappearance or children born during the captivity of a mother subjected to enforced disappearance;
   (b) The falsification, concealment or destruction of documents attesting to the true identity of the children referred to in subparagraph (a) above.
2. Each State Party shall take the necessary measures to search for and identify the children referred to in paragraph 1 (a) of this article and to return them to their families of origin, in accordance with legal procedures and applicable international agreements.
3. States Parties shall assist one another in searching for, identifying and locating the children referred to in paragraph 1 (a) of this article.

4. Given the need to protect the best interests of the children referred to in paragraph 1 (a) of this article and their right to preserve, or to have re-established, their identity, including their nationality, name and family relations as recognized by law, States Parties which recognize a system of adoption or other form of placement of children shall have legal procedures in place to review the adoption or placement procedure, and, where appropriate, to annul any adoption or placement of children that originated in an enforced disappearance.

5. In all cases, and in particular in all matters relating to this article, the best interests of the child shall be a primary consideration, and a child who is capable of forming his or her own views shall have the right to express those views freely, the views of the child being given due weight in accordance with the age and maturity of the child.

PART II

Article 26

1. A Committee on Enforced Disappearances (hereinafter referred to as "the Committee") shall be established to carry out the functions provided for under this Convention. The Committee shall consist of ten experts of high moral character and recognized competence in the field of human rights, who shall serve in their personal capacity and be independent and impartial. The members of the Committee shall be elected by the States Parties according to equitable geographical distribution. Due account shall be taken of the usefulness of the participation in the work of the Committee of persons having relevant legal experience and of balanced gender representation.

2. The members of the Committee shall be elected by secret ballot from a list of persons nominated by States Parties from among their nationals, at biennial meetings of the States Parties convened by the Secretary-General of the United Nations for this purpose. At those meetings, for which two thirds of the States Parties shall constitute a quorum, the persons elected to the Committee shall be those who obtain the largest number of votes and an absolute majority of the votes of the representatives of States Parties present and voting.

3. The initial election shall be held no later than six months after the date of entry into force of this Convention. Four months before the date of each election, the Secretary-General of the United Nations shall address a letter to the States Parties inviting them to submit nominations within three months. The Secretary-General shall prepare a list in alphabetical order of all persons thus nominated, indicating the State Party which nominated each candidate, and shall submit this list to all States Parties.

4. The members of the Committee shall be elected for a term of four years. They shall be eligible for re-election once. However, the term of five of the members elected at the first election shall expire at the end of two years; immediately after the first election, the names of these five members shall be chosen by lot by the chairman of the meeting referred to in paragraph 2 of this article.

5. If a member of the Committee dies or resigns or for any other reason can no longer perform his or her Committee duties, the State Party which nominated him or her shall, in accordance with the criteria set out in paragraph 1 of this article, appoint another candidate from among its nationals to serve out his or her term, subject to the

approval of the majority of the States Parties. Such approval shall be considered to have been obtained unless half or more of the States Parties respond negatively within six weeks of having been informed by the Secretary-General of the United Nations of the proposed appointment.

6. The Committee shall establish its own rules of procedure.

7. The Secretary-General of the United Nations shall provide the Committee with the necessary means, staff and facilities for the effective performance of its functions. The Secretary-General of the United Nations shall convene the initial meeting of the Committee.

8. The members of the Committee shall be entitled to the facilities, privileges and immunities of experts on mission for the United Nations, as laid down in the relevant sections of the Convention on the Privileges and Immunities of the United Nations.

9. Each State Party shall cooperate with the Committee and assist its members in the fulfilment of their mandate, to the extent of the Committee's functions that the State Party has accepted.

Article 27

A Conference of the States Parties will take place at the earliest four years and at the latest six years following the entry into force of this Convention to evaluate the functioning of the Committee and to decide, in accordance with the procedure described in article 44, paragraph 2, whether it is appropriate to transfer to another body – without excluding any possibility – the monitoring of this Convention, in accordance with the functions defined in articles 28 to 36.

Article 28

1. In the framework of the competencies granted by this Convention, the Committee shall cooperate with all relevant organs, offices and specialized agencies and funds of the United Nations, with the treaty bodies instituted by international instruments, with the special procedures of the United Nations and with the relevant regional intergovernmental organizations or bodies, as well as with all relevant State institutions, agencies or offices working towards the protection of all persons against enforced disappearances.

2. As it discharges its mandate, the Committee shall consult other treaty bodies instituted by relevant international human rights instruments, in particular the Human Rights Committee instituted by the International Covenant on Civil and Political Rights, with a view to ensuring the consistency of their respective observations and recommendations.

Article 29

1. Each State Party shall submit to the Committee, through the Secretary-General of the United Nations, a report on the measures taken to give effect to its obligations under this Convention, within two years after the entry into force of this Convention for the State Party concerned.

2. The Secretary-General of the United Nations shall make this report available to all States Parties.

3. Each report shall be considered by the Committee, which shall issue such comments, observations or recommendations as it may deem appropriate. The comments,

observations or recommendations shall be communicated to the State Party concerned, which may respond to them, on its own initiative or at the request of the Committee.

4. The Committee may also request States Parties to provide additional information on the implementation of this Convention.

Article 30

1. A request that a disappeared person should be sought and found may be submitted to the Committee, as a matter of urgency, by relatives of the disappeared person or their legal representatives, their counsel or any person authorized by them, as well as by any other person having a legitimate interest.

2. If the Committee considers that a request for urgent action submitted in pursuance of paragraph 1 of this article:

   (a) Is not manifestly unfounded;

   (b) Does not constitute an abuse of the right of submission of such requests;

   (c) Has already been duly presented to the competent bodies of the State Party concerned, such as those authorized to undertake investigations, where such a possibility exists;

   (d) Is not incompatible with the provisions of this Convention; and

   (e) The same matter is not being examined under another procedure of international investigation or settlement of the same nature; it shall request the State Party concerned to provide it with information on the situation of the persons sought, within a time limit set by the Committee.

3. In the light of the information provided by the State Party concerned in accordance with paragraph 2 of this article, the Committee may transmit recommendations to the State Party, including a request that the State Party should take all the necessary measures, including interim measures, to locate and protect the person concerned in accordance with this Convention and to inform the Committee, within a specified period of time, of measures taken, taking into account the urgency of the situation. The Committee shall inform the person submitting the urgent action request of its recommendations and of the information provided to it by the State as it becomes available.

4. The Committee shall continue its efforts to work with the State Party concerned for as long as the fate of the person sought remains unresolved. The person presenting the request shall be kept informed.

Article 31

1. A State Party may at the time of ratification of this Convention or at any time afterwards declare that it recognizes the competence of the Committee to receive and consider communications from or on behalf of individuals subject to its jurisdiction claiming to be victims of a violation by this State Party of provisions of this Convention. The Committee shall not admit any communication concerning a State Party which has not made such a declaration.

2. The Committee shall consider a communication inadmissible where:

   (a) The communication is anonymous;

   (b) The communication constitutes an abuse of the right of submission of such communications or is incompatible with the provisions of this Convention;

(c) The same matter is being examined under another procedure of international investigation or settlement of the same nature; or where

(d) All effective available domestic remedies have not been exhausted. This rule shall not apply where the application of the remedies is unreasonably prolonged.

3. If the Committee considers that the communication meets the requirements set out in paragraph 2 of this article, it shall transmit the communication to the State Party concerned, requesting it to provide observations and comments within a time limit set by the Committee.

4. At any time after the receipt of a communication and before a determination on the merits has been reached, the Committee may transmit to the State Party concerned for its urgent consideration a request that the State Party will take such interim measures as may be necessary to avoid possible irreparable damage to the victims of the alleged violation. Where the Committee exercises its discretion, this does not imply a determination on admissibility or on the merits of the communication.

5. The Committee shall hold closed meetings when examining communications under the present article. It shall inform the author of a communication of the responses provided by the State Party concerned. When the Committee decides to finalize the procedure, it shall communicate its views to the State Party and to the author of the communication.

Article 32

A State Party to this Convention may at any time declare that it recognizes the competence of the Committee to receive and consider communications in which a State Party claims that another State Party is not fulfilling its obligations under this Convention. The Committee shall not receive communications concerning a State Party which has not made such a declaration, nor communications from a State Party which has not made such a declaration.

Article 33

1. If the Committee receives reliable information indicating that a State Party is seriously violating the provisions of this Convention, it may, after consultation with the State Party concerned, request one or more of its members to undertake a visit and report back to it without delay.

2. The Committee shall notify the State Party concerned, in writing, of its intention to organize a visit, indicating the composition of the delegation and the purpose of the visit. The State Party shall answer the Committee within a reasonable time.

3. Upon a substantiated request by the State Party, the Committee may decide to postpone or cancel its visit.

4. If the State Party agrees to the visit, the Committee and the State Party concerned shall work together to define the modalities of the visit and the State Party shall provide the Committee with all the facilities needed for the successful completion of the visit.

5. Following its visit, the Committee shall communicate to the State Party concerned its observations and recommendations.

Article 34

If the Committee receives information which appears to it to contain well-founded indications that enforced disappearance is being practised on a widespread or systematic basis in the territory under the jurisdiction of a State Party, it may, after seeking from the State Party concerned all relevant information on the situation, urgently bring the matter to the attention of the General Assembly of the United Nations, through the Secretary-General of the United Nations.

Article 35

1. The Committee shall have competence solely in respect of enforced disappearances which commenced after the entry into force of this Convention.
2. If a State becomes a party to this Convention after its entry into force, the obligations of that State vis-à-vis the Committee shall relate only to enforced disappearances which commenced after the entry into force of this Convention for the State concerned.

Article 36

1. The Committee shall submit an annual report on its activities under this Convention to the States Parties and to the General Assembly of the United Nations.
2. Before an observation on a State Party is published in the annual report, the State Party concerned shall be informed in advance and shall be given reasonable time to answer. This State Party may request the publication of its comments or observations in the report.

PART III

Article 37

Nothing in this Convention shall affect any provisions which are more conducive to the protection of all persons from enforced disappearance and which may be contained in:
(a) The law of a State Party;
(b) International law in force for that State.

Article 38

1. This Convention is open for signature by all Member States of the United Nations.
2. This Convention is subject to ratification by all Member States of the United Nations. Instruments of ratification shall be deposited with the Secretary-General of the United Nations.
3. This Convention is open to accession by all Member States of the United Nations. Accession shall be effected by the deposit of an instrument of accession with the Secretary-General.

Article 39

1. This Convention shall enter into force on the thirtieth day after the date of deposit with the Secretary-General of the United Nations of the twentieth instrument of ratification or accession.
2. For each State ratifying or acceding to this Convention after the deposit of the twentieth instrument of ratification or accession, this Convention shall enter into force on the thirtieth day after the date of the deposit of that State's instrument of ratification or accession.

Article 40

The Secretary-General of the United Nations shall notify all States Members of the United Nations and all States which have signed or acceded to this Convention of the following:

    (a) Signatures, ratifications and accessions under article 38;

    (b) The date of entry into force of this Convention under article 39.

Article 41

The provisions of this Convention shall apply to all parts of federal States without any limitations or exceptions.

Article 42

1. Any dispute between two or more States Parties concerning the interpretation or application of this Convention which cannot be settled through negotiation or by the procedures expressly provided for in this Convention shall, at the request of one of them, be submitted to arbitration. If within six months from the date of the request for arbitration the Parties are unable to agree on the organization of the arbitration, any one of those Parties may refer the dispute to the International Court of Justice by request in conformity with the Statute of the Court.

2. A State may, at the time of signature or ratification of this Convention or accession thereto, declare that it does not consider itself bound by paragraph 1 of this article. The other States Parties shall not be bound by paragraph 1 of this article with respect to any State Party having made such a declaration.

3. Any State Party having made a declaration in accordance with the provisions of paragraph 2 of this article may at any time withdraw this declaration by notification to the Secretary-General of the United Nations.

Article 43

This Convention is without prejudice to the provisions of international humanitarian law, including the obligations of the High Contracting Parties to the four Geneva Conventions of 12 August 1949 and the two Additional Protocols thereto of 8 June 1977, or to the opportunity available to any State Party to authorize the International Committee of the Red Cross to visit places of detention in situations not covered by international humanitarian law.

Article 44

1. Any State Party to this Convention may propose an amendment and file it with the Secretary-General of the United Nations. The Secretary-General shall thereupon communicate the proposed amendment to the States Parties to this Convention with a request that they indicate whether they favour a conference of States Parties for the purpose of considering and voting upon the proposal. In the event that within four months from the date of such communication at least one third of the States Parties favour such a conference, the Secretary-General shall convene the conference under the auspices of the United Nations.

2. Any amendment adopted by a majority of two thirds of the States Parties present and voting at the conference shall be submitted by the Secretary-General of the United Nations to all the States Parties for acceptance.

3. An amendment adopted in accordance with paragraph 2 of this article shall enter into force when two thirds of the States Parties to this Convention have accepted it in accordance with their respective constitutional processes.

4. When amendments enter into force, they shall be binding on those States Parties which have accepted them, other States Parties still being bound by the provisions of this Convention and any earlier amendment which they have accepted.

Article 45

1. This Convention, of which the Arabic, Chinese, English, French, Russian and Spanish texts are equally authentic, shall be deposited with the Secretary-General of the United Nations.

2. The Secretary-General of the United Nations shall transmit certified copies of this Convention to all States referred to in article 38.

27

General Assembly Resolution 68/268 Strengthening and Enhancing the Effective Functioning of the Human Rights Treaty Body System

Note: *General Assembly Resolution 68/268 adopted on 9 April 2014, Strengthening and Enhancing the Effective Functioning of the Human Rights Treaty Body System (A.68/L.37).*

The General Assembly,

Reaffirming the purposes and principles of the Charter of the United Nations, and recalling the Universal Declaration of Human Rights and relevant international human rights instruments,

Underlining the obligation that States have to promote and protect human rights and to carry out the responsibilities that they have undertaken under international law, especially the Charter, as well as various international instruments in the field of human rights, including under international human rights treaties,

Recalling Economic and Social Council resolution 1985/17 of 28 May 1985,

Recalling also its resolution 66/254 of 23 February 2012, by which it launched the intergovernmental process of the General Assembly on strengthening and enhancing the effective functioning of the human rights treaty body system, and its resolutions 66/295 of 17 September 2012 and 68/2 of 20 September 2013, by which it extended the intergovernmental process,

Recalling further its relevant resolutions on the human rights treaty bodies,

Reaffirming that the full and effective implementation of international human rights instruments by States parties is of major importance for the efforts of the United Nations to promote universal respect for and observance of human rights and fundamental freedoms and that the effective functioning of the human rights treaty body system is indispensable for the full and effective implementation of such instruments,

Recognizing the important, valuable and unique role and contribution of each of the human rights treaty bodies in the promotion and protection of human rights and fundamental freedoms, including through their examination of the progress made by States parties to the respective human rights treaties in fulfilling their relevant obligations and their provision of recommendations to States parties on the implementation of such treaties,

Reaffirming the importance of the independence of the human rights treaty bodies,

Reaffirming also that the independence and impartiality of members of the human rights treaty bodies is essential for the performance of their duties and responsibilities in line with the respective treaties, and recalling the requirement that they be individuals of high moral standing serving in their personal capacity,

Recognizing that States have a legal obligation under the international human rights treaties to which they are party to periodically submit to the relevant human rights treaty bodies reports on the measures they have taken to give effect to the provisions of the relevant treaties, and noting the need to increase the level of compliance in this regard,

Recognizing also that the promotion and protection of human rights should be based on the principle of cooperation and genuine dialogue and be aimed at strengthening the capacity of Member States to comply with their human rights obligations for the benefit of all human beings,

Emphasizing the importance of multilingualism in the activities of the United Nations, including those linked to the promotion and protection of human rights, and reaffirming the paramount importance of the equality of the six official languages of the United Nations for the effective functioning of the human rights treaty bodies,

Recognizing that the current allocation of resources has not allowed the human rights treaty body system to work in a sustainable and effective manner, and in this regard also recognizing the importance of providing, under the existing procedures of the General Assembly, adequate funding to the human rights treaty body system from the regular budget of the United Nations,

Recognizing also the importance of continued efforts to improve the efficiency of the working methods of the human rights treaty body system,

Recognizing further the importance and added value of capacity-building and technical assistance provided in consultation with and with the consent of the States parties concerned to ensure the full and effective implementation of and compliance with the international human rights treaties,

Recalling that certain international human rights instruments include provisions regarding the venue of the meetings of the committees, and mindful of the importance of the full engagement of all States parties in the interactive dialogue with the human rights treaty bodies,

Taking note of the reports of the Secretary-General on measures to improve further the effectiveness, harmonization and reform of the human rights treaty body system,

Noting with appreciation the initiative and efforts of the United Nations High Commissioner for Human Rights, in the form of a multi-stakeholder consultation approach for reflecting on how to streamline and strengthen the human rights treaty body system,

Noting that the multi-stakeholder approach consisted of a number of meetings involving representatives of Member States, human rights treaty bodies, national human rights institutions, non-governmental organizations and academia, including events hosted by a number of Member States,

Taking note of the report of the High Commissioner on strengthening the United Nations human rights treaty body system, which includes recommendations addressed to different stakeholders,

Taking note also of the report of the co-facilitators on the open-ended intergovernmental process on how to strengthen and enhance the effective functioning of the human rights treaty body system,

Expressing its appreciation for the efforts of the President of the General Assembly and the co-facilitators in the framework of the intergovernmental process,

Noting the participation and contributions of Member States in the intergovernmental process, as well as experts of the human rights treaty bodies, national human rights institutions, the Office of the United Nations High Commissioner for Human Rights and non governmental organizations,

Emphasizing that strengthening and enhancing the effective functioning of the human rights treaty body system is a common goal shared by stakeholders who have different legal competencies in accordance with the Charter and the international human rights instruments establishing treaty bodies, and recognizing in this regard the ongoing efforts of different treaty bodies towards strengthening and enhancing their effective functioning,

1. *Encourages* the human rights treaty bodies to offer to States parties for their consideration the simplified reporting procedure and to set a limit on the number of the questions included;

2. *Encourages* States parties to consider the possibility of using the simplified reporting procedure, when offered, to facilitate the preparation of their reports and the interactive dialogue on the implementation of their treaty obligations;

3. *Also encourages* States parties to consider submitting a common core document and updating it as appropriate, as a comprehensive document or in the form of an addendum to the original document, bearing in mind the most recent developments in the particular State party, and in this regard encourages the human rights treaty bodies to further elaborate their existing guidelines on the common core document in a clear and consistent manner;

4. *Decides,* without prejudice to the formulation of the annual report of each human rights treaty body as laid out in the respective treaty, that the annual reports of treaty bodies are not to contain documents published separately and referenced therein;

5. *Encourages* the human rights treaty bodies to collaborate towards the elaboration of an aligned methodology for their constructive dialogue with the States parties, bearing in mind the views of States parties as well as the specificity of the respective committees and of their mandates, with the aim of making the dialogue more effective, maximizing the use of the time available and allowing for a more interactive and productive dialogue with States parties;

6. *Also encourages* the human rights treaty bodies to adopt short, focused and concrete concluding observations, including the recommendations therein, that reflect the dialogue with the relevant State party, and to this end further encourages them to develop common guidelines for the elaboration of such concluding observations, bearing in mind the specificity of the respective committees and of their mandates, as well as the views of States parties;

7. *Recommends* the more efficient and effective use of the meetings of States parties, inter alia, by proposing and organizing discussions on matters related to the implementation of each treaty;

8. *Strongly condemns* all acts of intimidation and reprisals against individuals and groups for their contribution to the work of the human rights treaty bodies, and urges States to take all appropriate action, consistent with the Declaration on the Right and Responsibility of Individuals, Groups and Organs of Society to Promote and Protect Universally Recognized Human Rights and Fundamental Freedoms and all other relevant human rights instruments, to prevent and eliminate such human rights violations;

9. *Encourages* the human rights treaty bodies to continue to enhance their efforts towards achieving greater efficiency, transparency, effectiveness and harmonization through their working methods, within their respective mandates, and in this regard

encourages the treaty bodies to continue to review good practices regarding the application of rules of procedure and working methods in their ongoing efforts towards strengthening and enhancing their effective functioning, bearing in mind that these activities should fall under the provisions of the respective treaties, thus not creating new obligations for States parties;

10. *Encourages* States parties to continue their efforts to nominate experts of high moral standing and recognized competence and experience in the field of human rights, in particular in the field covered by the relevant treaty, and, as appropriate, to consider adopting national policies or processes with respect to the nomination of experts as candidates for human rights treaty bodies;

11. *Recommends* that the Economic and Social Council consider replacing the existing procedure for the election of experts to the Committee on Economic, Social and Cultural Rights with a meeting of States parties to the International Covenant on Economic, Social and Cultural Rights, while preserving the current structure, organization and administrative arrangement of the Committee as set forth in Council resolution 1985/17;

12. *Requests* the Office of the United Nations High Commissioner for Human Rights to include in the documentation prepared for elections of members of human rights treaty bodies at meetings of States parties an information note on the current situation with respect to the composition of the treaty body, reflecting the balance in terms of geographical distribution and gender representation, professional background and different legal systems, as well as the tenure of current members;

13. *Encourages* States parties, in the election of treaty body experts, to give due consideration, as stipulated in the relevant human rights instruments, to equitable geographical distribution, the representation of the different forms of civilization and the principal legal systems, balanced gender representation and the participation of experts with disabilities in the membership of the human rights treaty bodies;

14. *Encourages* the human rights treaty bodies to develop an aligned consultation process for the elaboration of general comments that provides for consultation with States parties in particular and bears in mind the views of other stakeholders during the elaboration of new general comments;

15. *Decides*, in line with established practice with respect to other United Nations documentation, to establish a limit of 10,700 words for each document produced by the human rights treaty bodies, and further recommends that word limits also be applied for relevant stakeholders;

16. *Also decides* to establish word limits for all State party documentation submitted to the human rights treaty body system, including State party reports, of 31,800 words for initial reports, 21,200 words for subsequent periodic reports and 42,400 words for common core documents, as endorsed by the human rights treaty bodies, and calls upon the treaty bodies to set a limit on the number of questions posed, focusing on areas seen as priority issues to ensure the ability of States parties to meet the aforementioned word limits;

17. *Requests* the Secretary-General, through the Office of the High Commissioner, to support States parties in building the capacity to implement their treaty obligations and to provide in this regard advisory services, technical assistance and

capacity-building, in line with the mandate of the Office, in consultation with and with the consent of the State concerned, by:

(a) Deploying a dedicated human rights capacity-building officer in every regional office of the Office of the High Commissioner, as required;

(b) Strengthening cooperation with relevant regional human rights mechanisms within regional organizations to provide technical assistance to States in reporting to human rights treaty bodies, including through the training of trainers;

(c) Developing a roster of experts on treaty body reporting, reflecting geographical distribution and gender representation, professional background and different legal systems;

(d) Providing direct assistance to States parties at the national level by building and developing institutional capacity for reporting and strengthening technical knowledge through ad hoc training on reporting guidelines at the national level;

(e) Facilitating the sharing of best practices among States parties;

18. *Underlines* the need to provide further support to States parties through, inter alia, the United Nations Voluntary Fund for Technical Cooperation in the Field of Human Rights and in conjunction with the provision of technical assistance, with a focus on measures to build sustainable capacity in their activities to fulfil their treaty obligations, and encourages all Member States to contribute to the Fund;

19. *Encourages* the Office of the High Commissioner to work with the agencies, funds and programmes of the United Nations system and United Nations country teams, in line with their respective mandates and at the request of States parties, to assist States parties in fulfilling their obligations under international human rights treaties through:

(a) The provision of advisory services, technical assistance and capacity-building to States parties for the preparation of reports to human rights treaty bodies;

(b) The development of programmatic responses, in close coordination with the relevant States parties, to support their compliance with treaty obligations;

20. *Recognizes* that some States parties consider that they would benefit from improved coordination of reporting at the national level, and requests the Office of the High Commissioner to include among its technical assistance activities relevant assistance in this regard, at the request of a State party, based on best practices;

21. *Encourages* Member States to provide voluntary funds to facilitate the engagement of States parties, in particular those without representation in Geneva, with the human rights treaty bodies;

22. *Decides* in principle, with the aim of enhancing the accessibility and visibility of the human rights treaty bodies and in line with the report of the Committee on Information on its thirty-fifth session, to webcast, as soon as feasible, the public meetings of the treaty bodies, and requests the Department of Public Information of the Secretariat to report on the feasibility of providing, in all of the official languages used in the respective committees, live webcasts and video archives that are available, accessible, searchable and secure, including from cyberattacks, of relevant meetings of the treaty bodies;

23. *Requests* the Office of the High Commissioner, with the assistance of United Nations country teams through their existing videoconferencing facilities, as appropriate, to provide, at the request of a State party, the opportunity for members of its official

delegation not present at the meeting to participate in the consideration of the report of that State party by means of videoconference in order to facilitate wider participation in the dialogue;

24. *Underlines* the need for summary records of the dialogue of human rights treaty bodies with States parties, and in this regard decides to issue summary records in one of the working languages of the United Nations and not to translate the pending backlog of summary records, taking into account that these measures will not constitute a precedent, given the special nature of the treaty bodies, and bearing in mind the aim of providing, through alternative methods, verbatim records of the meetings of the treaty bodies in all of the official languages of the United Nations;

25. *Decides* that a summary record of a meeting of a State party with a treaty body, at the request of any State party, shall be translated into the official language of the United Nations used by that State party;

26. *Also decides* that the allocation of meeting time to the treaty bodies will be identified in the following manner, and requests the Secretary-General to provide the corresponding financial and human resources:

    (a) An allocation of the number of weeks that each treaty body requires to review the reports of States parties it can expect annually, using the average number of reports received per committee during the period from 2009 to 2012, on the basis of an assumed attainable rate of review of at least 2.5 reports per week and where relevant at least 5 reports under the Optional Protocols to the human rights treaties per week;

    (b) A further allocation of two weeks of meeting time per committee to allow for mandated activities, plus an allocation of additional meeting time to those committees dealing with individual communications, on the basis of each such communication requiring 1.3 hours of meeting time for review and the average number of such communications received per year by those committees;

    (c) An additional margin to prevent the recurrence of backlogs is established as a target 5 per cent increase in reporting compliance allocated among the committees to address their expected workload, at the beginning of each biennium, with a temporary target increase of 15 per cent for the period from 2015 to 2017;

    (d) An adequate allocation of financial and human resources to those treaty bodies whose main mandated role is to carry out field visits;

27. *Further decides* that the amount of meeting time allocated will be reviewed biennially on the basis of actual reporting during the previous four years and will be amended on this basis at the request of the Secretary-General in line with established budgetary procedures, and decides that the number of weeks allocated to a committee on a permanent basis prior to the adoption of the present resolution will not be reduced;

28. *Requests* the Secretary-General accordingly to take into account the meeting time needed in relation to the increased capacity of States parties to submit reports under the respective human rights instruments and the situation in terms of ratifications and the number of individual communications considered, based on paragraphs 26 and 27 above, in his future biennial programme budget for the human rights treaty body system, including the specific requirements for field visits by treaty bodies mandated to conduct such visits;

29. *Also requests* the Secretary-General to ensure the progressive implementation of relevant accessibility standards with regard to the human rights treaty body system, as appropriate, particularly in connection with the strategic heritage plan being developed for the United Nations Office at Geneva, and to provide reasonable accommodation for treaty body experts with disabilities to ensure their full and effective participation;

30. *Decides* to allocate a maximum of three official working languages for the work of the human rights treaty bodies, with the inclusion, on an exceptional basis, of a fourth official language, when necessary to facilitate communication among the members, as determined by the committee concerned, taking into account that these measures will not constitute a precedent, given the special nature of the treaty bodies, and without prejudice to the right of each State party to interact with the treaty bodies in any of the six official languages of the United Nations;

31. *Requests* the Secretary-General to improve the efficiency of the current arrangement with regard to the travel of treaty body experts in line with section VI of resolution 67/254A of 12 April 2013;

32. *Invites* States parties, as applicable and as an exceptional measure, with a view to achieving greater compliance with reporting obligations by States parties and eliminating the backlog of reports and in agreement with the relevant treaty body, to submit one combined report to satisfy its reporting obligations to the treaty body for the entire period for which reports to that treaty body are outstanding at the time of the adoption of the present resolution;

33. *Invites* the human rights treaty bodies, as an exceptional measure, and with a view to eliminating the current backlog of reports, without prejudice to the existing practices of the human rights treaty bodies or to the right of a State party to provide, or a treaty body to request, a short addendum for the purpose of reflecting significant and relevant recent national developments, to consider all State party reports which at the date of the present resolution have been submitted and are awaiting consideration to satisfy the reporting obligation of the State party concerned to the relevant treaty body until the completion of a reporting cycle starting from the time of the consideration of the report of the State party concerned;

34. *Invites* the human rights treaty bodies and the Office of the High Commissioner, within their respective mandates, to continue to work to increase coordination and predictability in the reporting process, including through cooperation with States parties, with the aim of achieving a clear and regularized schedule for reporting by States parties;

35. *Reaffirms* the importance of the independence and impartiality of members of the human rights treaty bodies, and underlines the importance of all stakeholders of the treaty body system, as well as the Secretariat, respecting fully the independence of treaty body members and the importance of avoiding any act that would interfere with the exercise of their functions;

36. *Notes* the adoption, at the twenty-fourth annual meeting of the Chairs of the human rights treaty bodies, held in Addis Ababa from 25 to 29 June 2012, of the guidelines on the independence and impartiality of members of the human rights treaty bodies (the Addis Ababa guidelines), which are aimed at ensuring objectivity, impartiality and accountability within the treaty body system, in full respect for the independence

of the treaty bodies, and in this regard encourages the treaty bodies to implement the guidelines in accordance with their mandates;

37. *Encourages* the human rights treaty bodies to continue to consider and review the Addis Ababa guidelines, inter alia, by seeking the views of States parties and other stakeholders on their development, and in this regard invites the Chairs of the treaty bodies to keep States parties updated on their implementation;

38. *Also encourages* the human rights treaty bodies, with a view to accelerating the harmonization of the treaty body system, to continue to enhance the role of their Chairs in relation to procedural matters, including with respect to formulating conclusions on issues related to working methods and procedural matters, promptly generalizing good practices and methodologies among all treaty bodies, ensuring coherence across the treaty bodies and standardizing working methods;

39. *Further encourages* the human rights treaty bodies to strengthen the possibilities for interaction during the annual meetings of the Chairs of the treaty bodies with States parties to all human rights treaties, held in Geneva and New York, with a view to ensuring a forum for an open and formal interactive dialogue in which all issues, including those related to the independence and impartiality of treaty body members, may be raised by States parties in a constructive manner;

40. *Requests* the Secretary-General to submit to the General Assembly, on a biennial basis, a comprehensive report on the status of the human rights treaty body system and the progress achieved by the human rights treaty bodies in realizing greater efficiency and effectiveness in their work, including the number of reports submitted and reviewed by the committees, the visits undertaken and the individual communications received and reviewed, where applicable, the state of the backlog, capacity-building efforts and the results achieved, as well as the situation in terms of ratifications, increased reporting and the allocation of meeting time and proposals on measures, including on the basis of information and observations from Member States, to enhance the engagement of all States parties in the dialogue with the treaty bodies;

41. *Decides* to consider the state of the human rights treaty body system no later than six years from the date of adoption of the present resolution, to review the effectiveness of the measures taken in order to ensure their sustainability, and, if appropriate, to decide on further action to strengthen and enhance the effective functioning of the human rights treaty body system.

81st plenary meeting
9 April 2014

PART II

Declarations, Standard Setting and other Relevant Documents Adopted under the Auspices of the United Nations Relating Directly to Human Rights Issues

28

Universal Declaration of Human Rights, 1948

Note: Universal Declaration of Human Rights, adopted on 10 December 1948 by General Assembly Resolution 217A (III), U.N. Doc A/810 at 71 (1948).

PREAMBLE

Whereas recognition of the inherent dignity and of the equal and inalienable rights of all members of the human family is the foundation of freedom, justice and peace in the world,

Whereas disregard and contempt for human rights have resulted in barbarous acts which have outraged the conscience of mankind, and the advent of a world in which human beings shall enjoy freedom of speech and belief and freedom from fear and want has been proclaimed as the highest aspiration of the common people,

Whereas it is essential, if man is not to be compelled to have recourse, as a last resort, to rebellion against tyranny and oppression, that human rights should be protected by the rule of law,

Whereas it is essential to promote the development of friendly relations between nations,

Whereas the peoples of the United Nations have in the Charter reaffirmed their faith in fundamental human rights, in the dignity and worth of the human person and in the equal rights of men and women and have determined to promote social progress and better standards of life in larger freedom,

Whereas Member States have pledged themselves to achieve, in cooperation with the United Nations, the promotion of universal respect for and observance of human rights and fundamental freedoms,

Whereas a common understanding of these rights and freedoms is of the greatest importance for the full realization of this pledge,

Now, therefore,

The General Assembly,

Proclaims this Universal Declaration of Human Rights as a common standard of achievement for all peoples and all nations, to the end that every individual and every organ of society, keeping this Declaration constantly in mind, shall strive by teaching and education to promote respect for these rights and freedoms and by progressive measures, national and international, to secure their universal and effective recognition and observance, both among the peoples of Member States themselves and among the peoples of territories under their jurisdiction.

Article 1

All human beings are born free and equal in dignity and rights. They are endowed with reason and conscience and should act towards one another in a spirit of brotherhood.

Article 2

Everyone is entitled to all the rights and freedoms set forth in this Declaration, without distinction of any kind, such as race, colour, sex, language, religion, political or other opinion, national or social origin, property, birth or other status.

Furthermore, no distinction shall be made on the basis of the political, jurisdictional or international status of the country or territory to which a person belongs, whether it be independent, trust, non-self-governing or under any other limitation of sovereignty.

Article 3

Everyone has the right to life, liberty and security of person.

Article 4

No one shall be held in slavery or servitude; slavery and the slave trade shall be prohibited in all their forms.

Article 5

No one shall be subjected to torture or to cruel, inhuman or degrading treatment or punishment.

Article 6

Everyone has the right to recognition everywhere as a person before the law.

Article 7

All are equal before the law and are entitled without any discrimination to equal protection of the law. All are entitled to equal protection against any discrimination in violation of this Declaration and against any incitement to such discrimination.

Article 8

Everyone has the right to an effective remedy by the competent national tribunals for acts violating the fundamental rights granted him by the constitution or by law.

Article 9

No one shall be subjected to arbitrary arrest, detention or exile.

Article 10

Everyone is entitled in full equality to a fair and public hearing by an independent and impartial tribunal, in the determination of his rights and obligations and of any criminal charge against him.

Article 11

1. Everyone charged with a penal offence has the right to be presumed innocent until proved guilty according to law in a public trial at which he has had all the guarantees necessary for his defence.
2. No one shall be held guilty of any penal offence on account of any act or omission which did not constitute a penal offence, under national or international law, at the time when it was committed. Nor shall a heavier penalty be imposed than the one that was applicable at the time the penal offence was committed.

Article 12

No one shall be subjected to arbitrary interference with his privacy, family, home or correspondence, nor to attacks upon his honour and reputation. Everyone has the right to the protection of the law against such interference or attacks.

Article 13

1. Everyone has the right to freedom of movement and residence within the borders of each State.
2. Everyone has the right to leave any country, including his own, and to return to his country.

Article 14

1. Everyone has the right to seek and to enjoy in other countries asylum from persecution.
2. This right may not be invoked in the case of prosecutions genuinely arising from non-political crimes or from acts contrary to the purposes and principles of the United Nations.

Article 15

1. Everyone has the right to a nationality.
2. No one shall be arbitrarily deprived of his nationality nor denied the right to change his nationality.

Article 16

1. Men and women of full age, without any limitation due to race, nationality or religion, have the right to marry and to found a family. They are entitled to equal rights as to marriage, during marriage and at its dissolution.
2. Marriage shall be entered into only with the free and full consent of the intending spouses.

3. The family is the natural and fundamental group unit of society and is entitled to protection by society and the State.

Article 17

1. Everyone has the right to own property alone as well as in association with others.
2. No one shall be arbitrarily deprived of his property.

Article 18

Everyone has the right to freedom of thought, conscience and religion; this right includes freedom to change his religion or belief, and freedom, either alone or in community with others and in public or private, to manifest his religion or belief in teaching, practice, worship and observance.

Article 19

Everyone has the right to freedom of opinion and expression; this right includes freedom to hold opinions without interference and to seek, receive and impart information and ideas through any media and regardless of frontiers.

Article 20

1. Everyone has the right to freedom of peaceful assembly and association.
2. No one may be compelled to belong to an association.

Article 21

1. Everyone has the right to take part in the government of his country, directly or through freely chosen representatives.
2. Everyone has the right to equal access to public service in his country.
3. The will of the people shall be the basis of the authority of government; this will shall be expressed in periodic and genuine elections which shall be by universal and equal suffrage and shall be held by secret vote or by equivalent free voting procedures.

Article 22

Everyone, as a member of society, has the right to social security and is entitled to realization, through national effort and international co-operation and in accordance with the organization and resources of each State, of the economic, social and cultural rights indispensable for his dignity and the free development of his personality.

Article 23

1. Everyone has the right to work, to free choice of employment, to just and favourable conditions of work and to protection against unemployment.
2. Everyone, without any discrimination, has the right to equal pay for equal work.

3. Everyone who works has the right to just and favourable remuneration ensuring for himself and his family an existence worthy of human dignity, and supplemented, if necessary, by other means of social protection.
4. Everyone has the right to form and to join trade unions for the protection of his interests.

Article 24
Everyone has the right to rest and leisure, including reasonable limitation of working hours and periodic holidays with pay.

Article 25
1. Everyone has the right to a standard of living adequate for the health and well-being of himself and of his family, including food, clothing, housing and medical care and necessary social services, and the right to security in the event of unemployment, sickness, disability, widowhood, old age or other lack of livelihood in circumstances beyond his control.
2. Motherhood and childhood are entitled to special care and assistance. All children, whether born in or out of wedlock, shall enjoy the same social protection.

Article 26
1. Everyone has the right to education. Education shall be free, at least in the elementary and fundamental stages. Elementary education shall be compulsory. Technical and professional education shall be made generally available and higher education shall be equally accessible to all on the basis of merit.
2. Education shall be directed to the full development of the human personality and to the strengthening of respect for human rights and fundamental freedoms. It shall promote understanding, tolerance and friendship among all nations, racial or religious groups, and shall further the activities of the United Nations for the maintenance of peace.
3. Parents have a prior right to choose the kind of education that shall be given to their children.

Article 27
1. Everyone has the right freely to participate in the cultural life of the community, to enjoy the arts and to share in scientific advancement and its benefits.
2. Everyone has the right to the protection of the moral and material interests resulting from any scientific, literary or artistic production of which he is the author.

Article 28
Everyone is entitled to a social and international order in which the rights and freedoms set forth in this Declaration can be fully realized.

Article 29

1. Everyone has duties to the community in which alone the free and full development of his personality is possible.
2. In the exercise of his rights and freedoms, everyone shall be subject only to such limitations as are determined by law solely for the purpose of securing due recognition and respect for the rights and freedoms of others and of meeting the just requirements of morality, public order and the general welfare in a democratic society.
3. These rights and freedoms may in no case be exercised contrary to the purposes and principles of the United Nations.

Article 30

Nothing in this Declaration may be interpreted as implying for any State, group or person any right to engage in any activity or to perform any act aimed at the destruction of any of the rights and freedoms set forth herein.

29

Declaration on the Granting of Independence to Colonial Countries and Peoples, 1960

Note: Adopted by General Assembly Resolution 1514 (XV), of 14 December 1960.

The General Assembly,

Mindful of the determination proclaimed by the peoples of the world in the Charter of the United Nations to reaffirm faith in fundamental human rights, in the dignity and worth of the human person, in the equal rights of men and women and of nations large and small and to promote social progress and better standards of life in larger freedom,

Conscious of the need for the creation of conditions of stability and well-being and peaceful and friendly relations based on respect for the principles of equal rights and self-determination of all peoples, and of universal respect for, and observance of, human rights and fundamental freedoms for all without distinction as to race, sex, language or religion,

Recognizing the passionate yearning for freedom in all dependent peoples and the decisive role of such peoples in the attainment of their independence,

Aware of the increasing conflicts resulting from the denial of or impediments in the way of the freedom of such peoples, which constitute a serious threat to world peace,

Considering the important role of the United Nations in assisting the movement for independence in Trust and Non-Self-Governing Territories,

Recognizing that the peoples of the world ardently desire the end of colonialism in all its manifestations,

Convinced that the continued existence of colonialism prevents the development of international economic co-operation, impedes the social, cultural and economic development of dependent peoples and militates against the United Nations ideal of universal peace,

Affirming that peoples may, for their own ends, freely dispose of their natural wealth and resources without prejudice to any obligations arising out of international economic co-operation, based upon the principle of mutual benefit, and international law,

Believing that the process of liberation is irresistible and irreversible and that, in order to avoid serious crises, an end must be put to colonialism and all practices of segregation and discrimination associated therewith,

Welcoming the emergence in recent years of a large number of dependent territories into freedom and independence, and recognizing the increasingly powerful trends towards freedom in such territories which have not yet attained independence,

Convinced that all peoples have an inalienable right to complete freedom, the exercise of their sovereignty and the integrity of their national territory,

Solemnly proclaims the necessity of bringing to a speedy and unconditional end colonialism in all its forms and manifestations;

And to this end

Declares that:

1. The subjection of peoples to alien subjugation, domination and exploitation constitutes a denial of fundamental human rights, is contrary to the Charter of the United Nations and is an impediment to the promotion of world peace and co-operation.

2. All peoples have the right to self-determination; by virtue of that right they freely determine their political status and freely pursue their economic, social and cultural development.

3. Inadequacy of political, economic, social or educational preparedness should never serve as a pretext for delaying independence.

4. All armed action or repressive measures of all kinds directed against dependent peoples shall cease in order to enable them to exercise peacefully and freely their right to complete independence, and the integrity of their national territory shall be respected.

5. Immediate steps shall be taken, in Trust and Non-Self-Governing Territories or all other territories which have not yet attained independence, to transfer all powers to the peoples of those territories, without any conditions or reservations, in accordance with their freely expressed will and desire, without any distinction as to race, creed or colour, in order to enable them to enjoy complete independence and freedom.

6. Any attempt aimed at the partial or total disruption of the national unity and the territorial integrity of a country is incompatible with the purposes and principles of the Charter of the United Nations.

7. All States shall observe faithfully and strictly the provisions of the Charter of the United Nations, the Universal Declaration of Human Rights and the present Declaration on the basis of equality, non-interference in the internal affairs of all States, and respect for the sovereign rights of all peoples and their territorial integrity.

30

Declaration on the Elimination of All Forms of Intolerance and of Discrimination Based on Religion or Belief, 1981

Note: Declaration on the Elimination of All Forms of Intolerance and of Discrimination Based on Religion or Belief adopted by General Assembly Resolution 36/55 on 25 November 1981.

The General Assembly,

Considering that one of the basic principles of the Charter of the United Nations is that of the dignity and equality inherent in all human beings, and that all Member States have pledged themselves to take joint and separate action in co-operation with the Organization to promote and encourage universal respect for and observance of human rights and fundamental freedoms for all, without distinction as to race, sex, language or religion,

Considering that the Universal Declaration of Human Rights and the International Covenants on Human Rights proclaim the principles of non-discrimination and equality before the law and the right to freedom of thought, conscience, religion and belief,

Considering that the disregard and infringement of human rights and fundamental freedoms, in particular of the right to freedom of thought, conscience, religion or whatever belief, have brought, directly or indirectly, wars and great suffering to mankind, especially where they serve as a means of foreign interference in the internal affairs of other States and amount to kindling hatred between peoples and nations,

Considering that religion or belief, for anyone who professes either, is one of the fundamental elements in his conception of life and that freedom of religion or belief should be fully respected and guaranteed,

Considering that it is essential to promote understanding, tolerance and respect in matters relating to freedom of religion and belief and to ensure that the use of religion or belief for ends inconsistent with the Charter of the United Nations, other relevant instruments of the United Nations and the purposes and principles of the present Declaration is inadmissible,

Convinced that freedom of religion and belief should also contribute to the attainment of the goals of world peace, social justice and friendship among peoples and to the elimination of ideologies or practices of colonialism and racial discrimination,

Noting with satisfaction the adoption of several, and the coming into force of some, conventions, under the aegis of the United Nations and of the specialized agencies, for the elimination of various forms of discrimination,

Concerned by manifestations of intolerance and by the existence of discrimination in matters of religion or belief still in evidence in some areas of the world,

Resolved to adopt all necessary measures for the speedy elimination of such intolerance in all its forms and manifestations and to prevent and combat discrimination on the ground of religion or belief,

Proclaims this Declaration on the Elimination of All Forms of Intolerance and of Discrimination Based on Religion or Belief:

Article 1

1. Everyone shall have the right to freedom of thought, conscience and religion. This right shall include freedom to have a religion or whatever belief of his choice, and freedom, either individually or in community with others and in public or private, to manifest his religion or belief in worship, observance, practice and teaching.
2. No one shall be subject to coercion which would impair his freedom to have a religion or belief of his choice.
3. Freedom to manifest one's religion or beliefs may be subject only to such limitations as are prescribed by law and are necessary to protect public safety, order, health or morals or the fundamental rights and freedoms of others.

Article 2

1. No one shall be subject to discrimination by any State, institution, group of persons, or person on grounds of religion or other beliefs.
2. For the purposes of the present Declaration, the expression "intolerance and discrimination based on religion or belief" means any distinction, exclusion, restriction or preference based on religion or belief and having as its purpose or as its effect nullification or impairment of the recognition, enjoyment or exercise of human rights and fundamental freedoms on an equal basis.

Article 3

Discrimination between human beings on grounds of religion or belief constitutes an affront to human dignity and a disavowal of the principles of the Charter of the United Nations, and shall be condemned as a violation of the human rights and fundamental freedoms proclaimed in the Universal Declaration of Human Rights and enunciated in detail in the International Covenants on Human Rights, and as an obstacle to friendly and peaceful relations between nations.

Article 4

1. All States shall take effective measures to prevent and eliminate discrimination on the grounds of religion or belief in the recognition, exercise and enjoyment of human rights and fundamental freedoms in all fields of civil, economic, political, social and cultural life.
2. All States shall make all efforts to enact or rescind legislation where necessary to prohibit any such discrimination, and to take all appropriate measures to combat intolerance on the grounds of religion or other beliefs in this matter.

Article 5

1. The parents or, as the case may be, the legal guardians of the child have the right to organize the life within the family in accordance with their religion or belief and bearing in mind the moral education in which they believe the child should be brought up.

2. Every child shall enjoy the right to have access to education in the matter of religion or belief in accordance with the wishes of his parents or, as the case may be, legal guardians, and shall not be compelled to receive teaching on religion or belief against the wishes of his parents or legal guardians, the best interests of the child being the guiding principle.

3. The child shall be protected from any form of discrimination on the ground of religion or belief. He shall be brought up in a spirit of understanding, tolerance, friendship among peoples, peace and universal brotherhood, respect for freedom of religion or belief of others, and in full consciousness that his energy and talents should be devoted to the service of his fellow men.

4. In the case of a child who is not under the care either of his parents or of legal guardians, due account shall be taken of their expressed wishes or of any other proof of their wishes in the matter of religion or belief, the best interests of the child being the guiding principle.

5. Practices of a religion or beliefs in which a child is brought up must not be injurious to his physical or mental health or to his full development, taking into account article 1, paragraph 3, of the present Declaration.

Article 6

In accordance with article 1 of the present Declaration, and subject to the provisions of article 1, paragraph 3, the right to freedom of thought, conscience, religion or belief shall include, inter alia, the following freedoms:

(a) To worship or assemble in connexion with a religion or belief, and to establish and maintain places for these purposes;

(b) To establish and maintain appropriate charitable or humanitarian institutions;

(c) To make, acquire and use to an adequate extent the necessary articles and materials related to the rites or customs of a religion or belief;

(d) To write, issue and disseminate relevant publications in these areas;

(e) To teach a religion or belief in places suitable for these purposes;

(f) To solicit and receive voluntary financial and other contributions from individuals and institutions;

(g) To train, appoint, elect or designate by succession appropriate leaders called for by the requirements and standards of any religion or belief;

(h) To observe days of rest and to celebrate holidays and ceremonies in accordance with the precepts of one's religion or belief;

(i) To establish and maintain communications with individuals and communities in matters of religion and belief at the national and international levels.

Article 7

The rights and freedoms set forth in the present Declaration shall be accorded in national legislation in such a manner that everyone shall be able to avail himself of such rights and freedoms in practice.

Article 8

Nothing in the present Declaration shall be construed as restricting or derogating from any right defined in the Universal Declaration of Human Rights and the International Covenants on Human Rights.

31

Declaration on the Right to Development, 1986

Note: The declaration was adopted by General Assembly Resolution, ES/41/128, 4 December 1986.

The General Assembly,

Having considered the question of the right to development,

Decides to adopt the Declaration on the Right to Development, the text of which is annexed to the present resolution.

ANNEX

Declaration on the Right to Development

The General Assembly,

Bearing in mind the purposes and principles of the Charter of the United Nations relating to the achievement of international co-operation in solving international problems of an economic, social, cultural or humanitarian nature, and in promoting and encouraging respect for human rights and fundamental freedoms for all without distinction as to race, sex, language or religion,

Recognizing that development is a comprehensive economic, social, cultural and political process, which aims at the constant improvement of the well-being of the entire population and of all individuals on the basis of their active, free and meaningful participation in development and in the fair distribution of benefits resulting therefrom,

Considering that under the provisions of the Universal Declaration of Human Rights everyone is entitled to a social and international order in which the rights and freedoms set forth in that Declaration can be fully realized,

Recalling the provisions of the International Covenant on Economic, Social and Cultural Rights and of the International Covenant on Civil and Political Rights,

Recalling further the relevant agreements, conventions, resolutions, recommendations and other instruments of the United Nations and its specialized agencies concerning the integral development of the human being, economic and social progress and development of all peoples, including those instruments concerning decolonization, the prevention of discrimination, respect for and observance of, human rights and fundamental freedoms, the maintenance of international peace and security and the further promotion of friendly relations and co-operation among States in accordance with the Charter,

Recalling the right of peoples to self-determination, by virtue of which they have the right freely to determine their political status and to pursue their economic, social and cultural development,

Recalling also the right of peoples to exercise, subject to the relevant provisions of both International Covenants on Human Rights, full and complete sovereignty over all their natural wealth and resources,

Mindful of the obligation of States under the Charter to promote universal respect for and observance of human rights and fundamental freedoms for all without distinction of any kind such as race, colour, sex, language, religion, political or other opinion, national or social origin, property, birth or other status,

Considering that the elimination of the massive and flagrant violations of the human rights of the peoples and individuals affected by situations such as those resulting from colonialism, neo-colonialism, apartheid, all forms of racism and racial discrimination, foreign domination and occupation, aggression and threats against national sovereignty, national unity and territorial integrity and threats of war would contribute to the establishment of circumstances propitious to the development of a great part of mankind,

Concerned at the existence of serious obstacles to development, as well as to the complete fulfilment of human beings and of peoples, constituted, inter alia, by the denial of civil, political, economic, social and cultural rights, and considering that all human rights and fundamental freedoms are indivisible and interdependent and that, in order to promote development, equal attention and urgent consideration should be given to the implementation, promotion and protection of civil, political, economic, social and cultural rights and that, accordingly, the promotion of, respect for and enjoyment of certain human rights and fundamental freedoms cannot justify the denial of other human rights and fundamental freedoms,

Considering that international peace and security are essential elements for the realization of the right to development,

Reaffirming that there is a close relationship between disarmament and development and that progress in the field of disarmament would considerably promote progress in the field of development and that resources released through disarmament measures should be devoted to the economic and social development and well-being of all peoples and, in particular, those of the developing countries,

Recognizing that the human person is the central subject of the development process and that development policy should therefore make the human being the main participant and beneficiary of development,

Recognizing that the creation of conditions favourable to the development of peoples and individuals is the primary responsibility of their States,

Aware that efforts at the international level to promote and protect human rights should be accompanied by efforts to establish a new international economic order,

Confirming that the right to development is an inalienable human right and that equality of opportunity for development is a prerogative both of nations and of individuals who make up nations,

Proclaims the following Declaration on the Right to Development:

Article 1

1. The right to development is an inalienable human right by virtue of which every human person and all peoples are entitled to participate in, contribute to, and enjoy economic, social, cultural and political development, in which all human rights and fundamental freedoms can be fully realized.
2. The human right to development also implies the full realization of the right of peoples to self-determination, which includes, subject to the relevant provisions of both International Covenants on Human Rights, the exercise of their inalienable right to full sovereignty over all their natural wealth and resources.

Article 2

1. The human person is the central subject of development and should be the active participant and beneficiary of the right to development.
2. All human beings have a responsibility for development, individually and collectively, taking into account the need for full respect for their human rights and fundamental freedoms as well as their duties to the community, which alone can ensure the free and complete fulfilment of the human being, and they should therefore promote and protect an appropriate political, social and economic order for development.
3. States have the right and the duty to formulate appropriate national development policies that aim at the constant improvement of the well-being of the entire population and of all individuals, on the basis of their active, free and meaningful participation in development and in the fair distribution of the benefits resulting therefrom.

Article 3

1. States have the primary responsibility for the creation of national and international conditions favourable to the realization of the right to development.
2. The realization of the right to development requires full respect for the principles of international law concerning friendly relations and co-operation among States in accordance with the Charter of the United Nations.
3. States have the duty to co-operate with each other in ensuring development and eliminating obstacles to development. States should realize their rights and fulfil their duties in such a manner as to promote a new international economic order based on sovereign equality, interdependence, mutual interest and co-operation among all States, as well as to encourage the observance and realization of human rights.

Article 4

1. States have the duty to take steps, individually and collectively, to formulate international development policies with a view to facilitating the full realization of the right to development.
2. Sustained action is required to promote more rapid development of developing countries. As a complement to the efforts of developing countries, effective international co-operation is essential in providing these countries with appropriate means and facilities to foster their comprehensive development.

Article 5

States shall take resolute steps to eliminate the massive and flagrant violations of the human rights of peoples and human beings affected by situations such as those resulting from apartheid, all forms of racism and racial discrimination, colonialism, foreign domination and occupation, aggression, foreign interference and threats against national sovereignty, national unity and territorial integrity, threats of war and refusal to recognize the fundamental right of peoples to self-determination.

Article 6

1. All States should co-operate with a view to promoting, encouraging and strengthening universal respect for and observance of all human rights and fundamental freedoms for all without any distinction as to race, sex, language or religion.

2. All human rights and fundamental freedoms are indivisible and interdependent; equal attention and urgent consideration should be given to the implementation, promotion and protection of civil, political, economic, social and cultural rights.
3. States should take steps to eliminate obstacles to development resulting from failure to observe civil and political rights, as well as economic, social and cultural rights.

Article 7
All States should promote the establishment, maintenance and strengthening of international peace and security and, to that end, should do their utmost to achieve general and complete disarmament under effective international control, as well as to ensure that the resources released by effective disarmament measures are used for comprehensive development, in particular that of the developing countries.

Article 8
1. States should undertake, at the national level, all necessary measures for the realization of the right to development and shall ensure, inter alia, equality of opportunity for all in their access to basic resources, education, health services, food, housing, employment and the fair distribution of income. Effective measures should be undertaken to ensure that women have an active role in the development process. Appropriate economic and social reforms should be carried out with a view to eradicating all social injustices.
2. States should encourage popular participation in all spheres as an important factor in development and in the full realization of all human rights.

Article 9
1. All the aspects of the right to development set forth in the present Declaration are indivisible and interdependent and each of them should be considered in the context of the whole.
2. Nothing in the present Declaration shall be construed as being contrary to the purposes and principles of the United Nations, or as implying that any State, group or person has a right to engage in any activity or to perform any act aimed at the violation of the rights set forth in the Universal Declaration of Human Rights and in the International Covenants on Human Rights.

Article 10
Steps should be taken to ensure the full exercise and progressive enhancement of the right to development, including the formulation, adoption and implementation of policy, legislative and other measures at the national and international levels.

32

United Nations Principles for Older Persons, 1991

Note: The United Nations Principles for Older Persons were adopted by General Assembly Resolution 46/91 on 16 December 1991.

The General Assembly,

Appreciating the contribution that older persons make to their societies,

Recognizing that, in the Charter of the United Nations, the peoples of the United Nations declare, inter alia, their determination to reaffirm faith in fundamental human rights, in the dignity and worth of the human person, in the equal rights of men and women and of nations large and small and to promote social progress and better standards of life in larger freedom,

Noting the elaboration of those rights in the Universal Declaration of Human Rights, the International Covenant on Economic, Social and Cultural Rights and the International Covenant on Civil and Political Rights and other declarations to ensure the application of universal standards to particular groups,

In pursuance of the International Plan of Action on Ageing, adopted by the World Assembly on Ageing and endorsed by the General Assembly in its resolution 37/51 of 3 December 1982,

Appreciating the tremendous diversity in the situation of older persons, not only between countries but within countries and between individuals, which requires a variety of policy responses,

Aware that in all countries, individuals are reaching an advanced age in greater numbers and in better health than ever before,

Aware of the scientific research disproving many stereotypes about inevitable and irreversible declines with age,

Convinced that in a world characterized by an increasing number and proportion of older persons, opportunities must be provided for willing and capable older persons to participate in and contribute to the ongoing activities of society,

Mindful that the strains on family life in both developed and developing countries require support for those providing care to frail older persons,

Bearing in mind the standards already set by the International Plan of Action on Ageing and the conventions, recommendations and resolutions of the International Labour Organization, the World Health Organization and other United Nations entities,

Encourages Governments to incorporate the following principles into their national programmes whenever possible:

INDEPENDENCE

1. Older persons should have access to adequate food, water, shelter, clothing and health care through the provision of income, family and community support and self-help.
2. Older persons should have the opportunity to work or to have access to other income-generating opportunities.
3. Older persons should be able to participate in determining when and at what pace withdrawal from the labour force takes place.
4. Older persons should have access to appropriate educational and training programmes.
5. Older persons should be able to live in environments that are safe and adaptable to personal preferences and changing capacities.
6. Older persons should be able to reside at home for as long as possible.

PARTICIPATION

7. Older persons should remain integrated in society, participate actively in the formulation and implementation of policies that directly affect their well-being and share their knowledge and skills with younger generations.
8. Older persons should be able to seek and develop opportunities for service to the community and to serve as volunteers in positions appropriate to their interests and capabilities.
9. Older persons should be able to form movements or associations of older persons.

CARE

10. Older persons should benefit from family and community care and protection in accordance with each society's system of cultural values.
11. Older persons should have access to health care to help them to maintain or regain the optimum level of physical, mental and emotional well-being and to prevent or delay the onset of illness.
12. Older persons should have access to social and legal services to enhance their autonomy, protection and care.
13. Older persons should be able to utilize appropriate levels of institutional care providing protection, rehabilitation and social and mental stimulation in a humane and secure environment.
14. Older persons should be able to enjoy human rights and fundamental freedoms when residing in any shelter, care or treatment facility, including full respect for their dignity, beliefs, needs and privacy and for the right to make decisions about their care and the quality of their lives.

SELF-FULFILMENT

15. Older persons should be able to pursue opportunities for the full development of their potential.
16. Older persons should have access to the educational, cultural, spiritual and recreational resources of society.

DIGNITY

17. Older persons should be able to live in dignity and security and be free of exploitation and physical or mental abuse.
18. Older persons should be treated fairly regardless of age, gender, racial or ethnic background, disability or other status, and be valued independently of their economic contribution.

33

Principles Relating to the Status of National Institutions (The Paris Principles), 1993

Note: The Principles Relating to the Status of National Institutions were adopted by General Assembly Resolution 48/134 on 20 December 1993.

The General Assembly,

Recalling the relevant resolutions concerning national institutions for the protection and promotion of human rights, notably its resolutions 41/129 of 4 December 1986 and 46/124 of 17 December 1991 and Commission on Human Rights resolutions 1987/40 of 10 March 1987, 1988/72 of 10 March 1988, 1989/52 of 7 March 1989, 1990/73 of 7 March 1990, 1991/27 of 5 March 1991 and 1992/54 of 3 March 1992, and taking note of Commission resolution 1993/55 of 9 March 1993,

Emphasizing the importance of the Universal Declaration of Human Rights, the International Covenants on Human Rights and other international instruments for promoting respect for and observance of human rights and fundamental freedoms,

Affirming that priority should be accorded to the development of appropriate arrangements at the national level to ensure the effective implementation of international human rights standards,

Convinced of the significant role that institutions at the national level can play in promoting and protecting human rights and fundamental freedoms and in developing and enhancing public awareness of those rights and freedoms,

Recognizing that the United Nations can play a catalytic role in assisting the development of national institutions by acting as a clearing-house for the exchange of information and experience,

Mindful in this regard of the guidelines on the structure and functioning of national and local institutions for the promotion and protection of human rights endorsed by the General Assembly in its resolution 33/46 of 14 December 1978,

Welcoming the growing interest shown worldwide in the creation and strengthening of national institutions, expressed during the Regional Meeting for Africa of the World Conference on Human Rights, held at Tunis from 2 to 6 November 1992, the Regional Meeting for Latin America and the Caribbean, held at San Jose from 18 to 22 January 1993, the Regional Meeting for Asia, held at Bangkok from 29 March to 2 April 1993, the Commonwealth Workshop on National Human Rights Institutions, held at Ottawa from 30 September to 2 October 1992 and the Workshop for the Asia and Pacific Region on Human Rights Issues, held at Jakarta from 26 to 28 January 1993, and manifested in the decisions announced recently by several Member States to establish national institutions for the promotion and protection of human rights,

Bearing in mind the Vienna Declaration and Programme of Action, in which the World Conference on Human Rights reaffirmed the important and constructive role played by national institutions for the promotion and protection of human rights, in particular in their advisory capacity to the competent authorities, their role in remedying human rights violations, in the dissemination of human rights information and in education in human rights,

Noting the diverse approaches adopted throughout the world for the promotion and protection of human rights at the national level, emphasizing the universality, indivisibility and interdependence of all human rights, and emphasizing and recognizing the value of such approaches to promoting universal respect for and observance of human rights and fundamental freedoms,

1. Takes note with satisfaction of the updated report of the Secretary-General, prepared in accordance with General Assembly resolution 46/124 of 17 December 1991;

2. Reaffirms the importance of developing, in accordance with national legislation, effective national institutions for the promotion and protection of human rights and of ensuring the pluralism of their membership and their independence;

3. Encourages Member States to establish or, where they already exist, to strengthen national institutions for the promotion and protection of human rights and to incorporate those elements in national development plans;

4. Encourages national institutions for the promotion and protection of human rights established by Member States to prevent and combat all violations of human rights as enumerated in the Vienna Declaration and Programme of Action and relevant international instruments;

5. Requests the Centre for Human Rights of the Secretariat to continue its efforts to enhance cooperation between the United Nations and national institutions, particularly in the field of advisory services and technical assistance and of information and education, including within the framework of the World Public Information Campaign for Human Rights;

6. Also requests the Centre for Human Rights to establish, upon the request of States concerned, United Nations centres for human rights documentation and training and to do so on the basis of established procedures for the use of available resources within the United Nations Voluntary Fund for Advisory Services and Technical Assistance in the Field of Human Rights;

7. Requests the Secretary-General to respond favourably to requests from Member States for assistance in the establishment and strengthening of national institutions for the promotion and protection of human rights as part of the programme of advisory services and technical cooperation in the field of human rights, as well as national centres for human rights documentation and training;

8. Encourages all Member States to take appropriate steps to promote the exchange of information and experience concerning the establishment and effective operation of such national institutions;

9. Affirms the role of national institutions as agencies for the dissemination of human rights materials and for other public information activities, prepared or organized under the auspices of the United Nations;

10. Welcomes the organization under the auspices of the Centre for Human Rights of a follow-up meeting at Tunis in December 1993 with a view, in particular, to examining ways and means of promoting technical assistance for the cooperation and

strengthening of national institutions and to continuing to examine all issues relating to the question of national institutions;

11. Welcomes also the Principles relating to the status of national institutions, annexed to the present resolution;

12. Encourages the establishment and strengthening of national institutions having regard to those principles and recognizing that it is the right of each State to choose the framework that is best suited to its particular needs at the national level;

13. Requests the Secretary-General to report to the General Assembly at its fiftieth session on the implementation of the present resolution.

ANNEX

PRINCIPLES RELATING TO THE STATUS OF NATIONAL INSTITUTIONS

Competence and responsibilities

1. A national institution shall be vested with competence to promote and protect human rights.

2. A national institution shall be given as broad a mandate as possible, which shall be clearly set forth in a constitutional or legislative text, specifying its composition and its sphere of competence.

3. A national institution shall, inter alia, have the following responsibilities:

    (a) To submit to the Government, Parliament and any other competent body, on an advisory basis either at the request of the authorities concerned or through the exercise of its power to hear a matter without higher referral, opinions, recommendations, proposals and reports on any matters concerning the promotion and protection of human rights; the national institution may decide to publicize them; these opinions, recommendations, proposals and reports, as well as any prerogative of the national institution, shall relate to the following areas:

        (i) Any legislative or administrative provisions, as well as provisions relating to judicial organizations, intended to preserve and extend the protection of human rights; in that connection, the national institution shall examine the legislation and administrative provisions in force, as well as bills and proposals, and shall make such recommendations as it deems appropriate in order to ensure that these provisions conform to the fundamental principles of human rights; it shall, if necessary, recommend the adoption of new legislation, the amendment of legislation in force and the adoption or amendment of administrative measures;

        (ii) Any situation of violation of human rights which it decides to take up;

        (iii) The preparation of reports on the national situation with regard to human rights in general, and on more specific matters;

        (iv) Drawing the attention of the Government to situations in any part of the country where human rights are violated and making proposals to it for initiatives to put an end to such situations and, where necessary, expressing an opinion on the positions and reactions of the Government;

(b) To promote and ensure the harmonization of national legislation regulations and practices with the international human rights instruments to which the State is a party, and their effective implementation;

(c) To encourage ratification of the above-mentioned instruments or accession to those instruments, and to ensure their implementation;

(d) To contribute to the reports which States are required to submit to United Nations bodies and committees, and to regional institutions, pursuant to their treaty obligations and, where necessary, to express an opinion on the subject, with due respect for their independence;

(e) To cooperate with the United Nations and any other organization in the United Nations system, the regional institutions and the national institutions of other countries that are competent in the areas of the promotion and protection of human rights;

(f) To assist in the formulation of programmes for the teaching of, and research into, human rights and to take part in their execution in schools, universities and professional circles;

(g) To publicize human rights and efforts to combat all forms of discrimination, in particular racial discrimination, by increasing public awareness, especially through information and education and by making use of all press organs.

Composition and guarantees of independence and pluralism

1. The composition of the national institution and the appointment of its members, whether by means of an election or otherwise, shall be established in accordance with a procedure which affords all necessary guarantees to ensure the pluralist representation of the social forces (of civilian society) involved in the promotion and protection of human rights, particularly by powers which will enable effective cooperation to be established with, or through the presence of, representatives of:

   (a) Non-governmental organizations responsible for human rights and efforts to combat racial discrimination, trade unions, concerned social and professional organizations, for example, associations of lawyers, doctors, journalists and eminent scientists;

   (b) Trends in philosophical or religious thought;

   (c) Universities and qualified experts;

   (d) Parliament;

   (e) Government departments (if these are included, their representatives should participate in the deliberations only in an advisory capacity).

2. The national institution shall have an infrastructure which is suited to the smooth conduct of its activities, in particular adequate funding. The purpose of this funding should be to enable it to have its own staff and premises, in order to be independent of the Government and not be subject to financial control which might affect its independence.

3. In order to ensure a stable mandate for the members of the national institution, without which there can be no real independence, their appointment shall be effected by an official act which shall establish the specific duration of the mandate. This mandate may be renewable, provided that the pluralism of the institution's membership is ensured.

Methods of operation

Within the framework of its operation, the national institution shall:

(a) Freely consider any questions falling within its competence, whether they are submitted by the Government or taken up by it without referral to a higher authority, on the proposal of its members or of any petitioner;

(b) Hear any person and obtain any information and any documents necessary for assessing situations falling within its competence;

(c) Address public opinion directly or through any press organ, particularly in order to publicize its opinions and recommendations;

(d) Meet on a regular basis and whenever necessary in the presence of all its members after they have been duly convened;

(e) Establish working groups from among its members as necessary, and set up local or regional sections to assist it in discharging its functions;

(f) Maintain consultation with the other bodies, whether jurisdictional or otherwise, responsible for the promotion and protection of human rights (in particular ombudsmen, mediators and similar institutions);

(g) In view of the fundamental role played by the non-governmental organizations in expanding the work of the national institutions, develop relations with the non-governmental organizations devoted to promoting and protecting human rights, to economic and social development, to combating racism, to protecting particularly vulnerable groups (especially children, migrant workers, refugees, physically and mentally disabled persons) or to specialized areas.

Additional principles concerning the status of commissions with quasi-jurisdictional competence

A national institution may be authorized to hear and consider complaints and petitions concerning individual situations. Cases may be brought before it by individuals, their representatives, third parties, non-governmental organizations, associations of trade unions or any other representative organizations. In such circumstances, and without prejudice to the principles stated above concerning the other powers of the commissions, the functions entrusted to them may be based on the following principles:

(a) Seeking an amicable settlement through conciliation or, within the limits prescribed by the law, through binding decisions or, where necessary, on the basis of confidentiality;

(b) Informing the party who filed the petition of his rights, in particular the remedies available to him, and promoting his access to them;

(c) Hearing any complaints or petitions or transmitting them to any other competent authority within the limits prescribed by the law;

(d) Making recommendations to the competent authorities, especially by proposing amendments or reforms of the laws, regulations and administrative practices, especially if they have created the difficulties encountered by the persons filing the petitions in order to assert their rights.

34

Declaration on the Right and Responsibility of Individuals, Groups and Organs of Society to Promote and Protect Universally Recognized Human Rights and Fundamental Freedoms, 1998

Note: The Declaration was adopted by General Assembly Resolution 53/144 on 9 December 1998.

The General Assembly,

Reaffirming the importance of the observance of the purposes and principles of the Charter of the United Nations for the promotion and protection of all human rights and fundamental freedoms for all persons in all countries of the world,

Reaffirming also the importance of the Universal Declaration of Human Rights and the International Covenants on Human Rights as basic elements of international efforts to promote universal respect for and observance of human rights and fundamental freedoms and the importance of other human rights instruments adopted within the United Nations system, as well as those at the regional level,

Stressing that all members of the international community shall fulfil, jointly and separately, their solemn obligation to promote and encourage respect for human rights and fundamental freedoms for all without distinction of any kind, including distinctions based on race, colour, sex, language, religion, political or other opinion, national or social origin, property, birth or other status, and reaffirming the particular importance of achieving international cooperation to fulfil this obligation according to the Charter,

Acknowledging the important role of international cooperation for, and the valuable work of individuals, groups and associations in contributing to, the effective elimination of all violations of human rights and fundamental freedoms of peoples and individuals, including in relation to mass, flagrant or systematic violations such as those resulting from apartheid, all forms of racial discrimination, colonialism, foreign domination or occupation, aggression or threats to national sovereignty, national unity or territorial integrity and from the refusal to recognize the right of peoples to self-determination and the right of every people to exercise full sovereignty over its wealth and natural resources,

Recognizing the relationship between international peace and security and the enjoyment of human rights and fundamental freedoms, and mindful that the absence of international peace and security does not excuse non-compliance,

Reiterating that all human rights and fundamental freedoms are universal, indivisible, interdependent and interrelated and should be promoted and implemented in a fair and equitable manner, without prejudice to the implementation of each of those rights and freedoms,

Stressing that the prime responsibility and duty to promote and protect human rights and fundamental freedoms lie with the State,

Recognizing the right and the responsibility of individuals, groups and associations to promote respect for and foster knowledge of human rights and fundamental freedoms at the national and international levels,

Declares:

Article 1

Everyone has the right, individually and in association with others, to promote and to strive for the protection and realization of human rights and fundamental freedoms at the national and international levels.

Article 2

1. Each State has a prime responsibility and duty to protect, promote and implement all human rights and fundamental freedoms, inter alia, by adopting such steps as may be necessary to create all conditions necessary in the social, economic, political and other fields, as well as the legal guarantees required to ensure that all persons under its jurisdiction, individually and in association with others, are able to enjoy all those rights and freedoms in practice.
2. Each State shall adopt such legislative, administrative and other steps as may be necessary to ensure that the rights and freedoms referred to in the present Declaration are effectively guaranteed.

Article 3

Domestic law consistent with the Charter of the United Nations and other international obligations of the State in the field of human rights and fundamental freedoms is the juridical framework within which human rights and fundamental freedoms should be implemented and enjoyed and within which all activities referred to in the present Declaration for the promotion, protection and effective realization of those rights and freedoms should be conducted.

Article 4

Nothing in the present Declaration shall be construed as impairing or contradicting the purposes and principles of the Charter of the United Nations or as restricting or derogating from the provisions of the Universal Declaration of Human Rights, the International Covenants on Human Rights and other international instruments and commitments applicable in this field.

Article 5

For the purpose of promoting and protecting human rights and fundamental freedoms, everyone has the right, individually and in association with others, at the national and international levels:

    (a) To meet or assemble peacefully;
    (b) To form, join and participate in non-governmental organizations, associations or groups;
    (c) To communicate with non-governmental or intergovernmental organizations.

Article 6

Everyone has the right, individually and in association with others:

- (a) To know, seek, obtain, receive and hold information about all human rights and fundamental freedoms, including having access to information as to how those rights and freedoms are given effect in domestic legislative, judicial or administrative systems;
- (b) As provided for in human rights and other applicable international instruments, freely to publish, impart or disseminate to others views, information and knowledge on all human rights and fundamental freedoms;
- (c) To study, discuss, form and hold opinions on the observance, both in law and in practice, of all human rights and fundamental freedoms and, through these and other appropriate means, to draw public attention to those matters.

Article 7

Everyone has the right, individually and in association with others, to develop and discuss new human rights ideas and principles and to advocate their acceptance.

Article 8

1. Everyone has the right, individually and in association with others, to have effective access, on a non-discriminatory basis, to participation in the government of his or her country and in the conduct of public affairs.
2. This includes, inter alia, the right, individually and in association with others, to submit to governmental bodies and agencies and organizations concerned with public affairs criticism and proposals for improving their functioning and to draw attention to any aspect of their work that may hinder or impede the promotion, protection and realization of human rights and fundamental freedoms.

Article 9

1. In the exercise of human rights and fundamental freedoms, including the promotion and protection of human rights as referred to in the present Declaration, everyone has the right, individually and in association with others, to benefit from an effective remedy and to be protected in the event of the violation of those rights.
2. To this end, everyone whose rights or freedoms are allegedly violated has the right, either in person or through legally authorized representation, to complain to and have that complaint promptly reviewed in a public hearing before an independent, impartial and competent judicial or other authority established by law and to obtain from such an authority a decision, in accordance with law, providing redress, including any compensation due, where there has been a violation of that person's rights or freedoms, as well as enforcement of the eventual decision and award, all without undue delay.
3. To the same end, everyone has the right, individually and in association with others, inter alia:
   - (a) To complain about the policies and actions of individual officials and governmental bodies with regard to violations of human rights and fundamental freedoms, by petition or other appropriate means, to competent domestic judicial, administrative or legislative authorities or any other competent authority provided for by the legal system of the State, which should render their decision on the complaint without undue delay;

(b) To attend public hearings, proceedings and trials so as to form an opinion on their compliance with national law and applicable international obligations and commitments;

(c) To offer and provide professionally qualified legal assistance or other relevant advice and assistance in defending human rights and fundamental freedoms.

4. To the same end, and in accordance with applicable international instruments and procedures, everyone has the right, individually and in association with others, to unhindered access to and communication with international bodies with general or special competence to receive and consider communications on matters of human rights and fundamental freedoms.

5. The State shall conduct a prompt and impartial investigation or ensure that an inquiry takes place whenever there is reasonable ground to believe that a violation of human rights and fundamental freedoms has occurred in any territory under its jurisdiction.

Article 10

No one shall participate, by act or by failure to act where required, in violating human rights and fundamental freedoms and no one shall be subjected to punishment or adverse action of any kind for refusing to do so.

Article 11

Everyone has the right, individually and in association with others, to the lawful exercise of his or her occupation or profession. Everyone who, as a result of his or her profession, can affect the human dignity, human rights and fundamental freedoms of others should respect those rights and freedoms and comply with relevant national and international standards of occupational and professional conduct or ethics.

Article 12

1. Everyone has the right, individually and in association with others, to participate in peaceful activities against violations of human rights and fundamental freedoms.

2. The State shall take all necessary measures to ensure the protection by the competent authorities of everyone, individually and in association with others, against any violence, threats, retaliation, de facto or de jure adverse discrimination, pressure or any other arbitrary action as a consequence of his or her legitimate exercise of the rights referred to in the present Declaration.

3. In this connection, everyone is entitled, individually and in association with others, to be protected effectively under national law in reacting against or opposing, through peaceful means, activities and acts, including those by omission, attributable to States that result in violations of human rights and fundamental freedoms, as well as acts of violence perpetrated by groups or individuals that affect the enjoyment of human rights and fundamental freedoms.

Article 13

Everyone has the right, individually and in association with others, to solicit, receive and utilize resources for the express purpose of promoting and protecting human rights and fundamental freedoms through peaceful means, in accordance with article 3 of the present Declaration.

Article 14

1. The State has the responsibility to take legislative, judicial, administrative or other appropriate measures to promote the understanding by all persons under its jurisdiction of their civil, political, economic, social and cultural rights.
2. Such measures shall include, inter alia:
   (a) The publication and widespread availability of national laws and regulations and of applicable basic international human rights instruments;
   (b) Full and equal access to international documents in the field of human rights, including the periodic reports by the State to the bodies established by the international human rights treaties to which it is a party, as well as the summary records of discussions and the official reports of these bodies.
3. The State shall ensure and support, where appropriate, the creation and development of further independent national institutions for the promotion and protection of human rights and fundamental freedoms in all territory under its jurisdiction, whether they be ombudsmen, human rights commissions or any other form of national institution.

Article 15

The State has the responsibility to promote and facilitate the teaching of human rights and fundamental freedoms at all levels of education and to ensure that all those responsible for training lawyers, law enforcement officers, the personnel of the armed forces and public officials include appropriate elements of human rights teaching in their training programme.

Article 16

Individuals, non-governmental organizations and relevant institutions have an important role to play in contributing to making the public more aware of questions relating to all human rights and fundamental freedoms through activities such as education, training and research in these areas to strengthen further, inter alia, understanding, tolerance, peace and friendly relations among nations and among all racial and religious groups, bearing in mind the various backgrounds of the societies and communities in which they carry out their activities.

Article 17

In the exercise of the rights and freedoms referred to in the present Declaration, everyone, acting individually and in association with others, shall be subject only to such limitations as are in accordance with applicable international obligations and are determined by law solely for the purpose of securing due recognition and respect for the rights and freedoms of others and of meeting the just requirements of morality, public order and the general welfare in a democratic society.

Article 18

1. Everyone has duties towards and within the community, in which alone the free and full development of his or her personality is possible.
2. Individuals, groups, institutions and non-governmental organizations have an important role to play and a responsibility in safeguarding democracy, promoting human

rights and fundamental freedoms and contributing to the promotion and advancement of democratic societies, institutions and processes.

3. Individuals, groups, institutions and non-governmental organizations also have an important role and a responsibility in contributing, as appropriate, to the promotion of the right of everyone to a social and international order in which the rights and freedoms set forth in the Universal Declaration of Human Rights and other human rights instruments can be fully realized.

Article 19

Nothing in the present Declaration shall be interpreted as implying for any individual, group or organ of society or any State the right to engage in any activity or to perform any act aimed at the destruction of the rights and freedoms referred to in the present Declaration.

Article 20

Nothing in the present Declaration shall be interpreted as permitting States to support and promote activities of individuals, groups of individuals, institutions or non-governmental organizations contrary to the provisions of the Charter of the United Nations.

35

United Nations Millennium Declaration, 2000

Note: The Declaration was adopted by General Assembly Resolution A/55/L.2 on 8 September 2000.

The General Assembly
   Adopts the following Declaration:

UNITED NATIONS MILLENNIUM DECLARATION

I. Values and principles

1. We, heads of State and Government, have gathered at United Nations Headquarters in New York from 6 to 8 September 2000, at the dawn of a new millennium, to reaffirm our faith in the Organization and its Charter as indispensable foundations of a more peaceful, prosperous and just world.
2. We recognize that, in addition to our separate responsibilities to our individual societies, we have a collective responsibility to uphold the principles of human dignity, equality and equity at the global level. As leaders we have a duty therefore to all the world's people, especially the most vulnerable and, in particular, the children of the world, to whom the future belongs.
3. We reaffirm our commitment to the purposes and principles of the Charter of the United Nations, which have proved timeless and universal. Indeed, their relevance and capacity to inspire have increased, as nations and peoples have become increasingly interconnected and interdependent.
4. We are determined to establish a just and lasting peace all over the world in accordance with the purposes and principles of the Charter. We rededicate ourselves to support all efforts to uphold the sovereign equality of all States, respect for their territorial integrity and political independence, resolution of disputes by peaceful means and in conformity with the principles of justice and international law, the right to self-determination of peoples which remain under colonial domination and foreign occupation, non-interference in the internal affairs of States, respect for human rights and fundamental freedoms, respect for the equal rights of all without distinction as to race, sex, language or religion and international cooperation in solving international problems of an economic, social, cultural or humanitarian character.
5. We believe that the central challenge we face today is to ensure that globalization becomes a positive force for all the world's people. For while globalization offers great opportunities, at present its benefits are very unevenly shared, while its costs are unevenly distributed. We recognize that developing countries and countries with

economies in transition face special difficulties in responding to this central challenge. Thus, only through broad and sustained efforts to create a shared future, based upon our common humanity in all its diversity, can globalization be made fully inclusive and equitable. These efforts must include policies and measures, at the global level, which correspond to the needs of developing countries and economies in transition and are formulated and implemented with their effective participation.

6. We consider certain fundamental values to be essential to international relations in the twenty-first century. These include:

- **Freedom.** Men and women have the right to live their lives and raise their children in dignity, free from hunger and from the fear of violence, oppression or injustice. Democratic and participatory governance based on the will of the people best assures these rights.

- **Equality.** No individual and no nation must be denied the opportunity to benefit from development. The equal rights and opportunities of women and men must be assured.

- **Solidarity.** Global challenges must be managed in a way that distributes the costs and burdens fairly in accordance with basic principles of equity and social justice. Those who suffer or who benefit least deserve help from those who benefit most.

- **Tolerance.** Human beings must respect one other, in all their diversity of belief, culture and language. Differences within and between societies should be neither feared nor repressed, but cherished as a precious asset of humanity. A culture of peace and dialogue among all civilizations should be actively promoted.

- **Respect for nature.** Prudence must be shown in the management of all living species and natural resources, in accordance with the precepts of sustainable development. Only in this way can the immeasurable riches provided to us by nature be preserved and passed on to our descendants. The current unsustainable patterns of production and consumption must be changed in the interest of our future welfare and that of our descendants.

- **Shared responsibility.** Responsibility for managing worldwide economic and social development, as well as threats to international peace and security, must be shared among the nations of the world and should be exercised multilaterally. As the most universal and most representative organization in the world, the United Nations must play the central role.

7. In order to translate these shared values into actions, we have identified key objectives to which we assign special significance.

II. Peace, security and disarmament

8. We will spare no effort to free our peoples from the scourge of war, whether within or between States, which has claimed more than 5 million lives in the past decade. We will also seek to eliminate the dangers posed by weapons of mass destruction.

9. We resolve therefore:

- To strengthen respect for the rule of law in international as in national affairs and, in particular, to ensure compliance by Member States with the decisions of the International Court of Justice, in compliance with the Charter of the United Nations, in cases to which they are parties.

- To make the United Nations more effective in maintaining peace and security by giving it the resources and tools it needs for conflict prevention, peaceful resolution of disputes, peacekeeping, post-conflict peace-building and reconstruction. In this context, we take note of the report of the Panel on United Nations Peace Operations and request the General Assembly to consider its recommendations expeditiously.
- To strengthen cooperation between the United Nations and regional organizations, in accordance with the provisions of Chapter VIII of the Charter.
- To ensure the implementation, by States Parties, of treaties in areas such as arms control and disarmament and of international humanitarian law and human rights law, and call upon all States to consider signing and ratifying the Rome Statute of the International Criminal Court.
- To take concerted action against international terrorism, and to accede as soon as possible to all the relevant international conventions.
- To redouble our efforts to implement our commitment to counter the world drug problem.
- To intensify our efforts to fight transnational crime in all its dimensions, including trafficking as well as smuggling in human beings and money laundering.
- To minimize the adverse effects of United Nations economic sanctions on innocent populations, to subject such sanctions regimes to regular reviews and to eliminate the adverse effects of sanctions on third parties.
- To strive for the elimination of weapons of mass destruction, particularly nuclear weapons, and to keep all options open for achieving this aim, including the possibility of convening an international conference to identify ways of eliminating nuclear dangers.
- To take concerted action to end illicit traffic in small arms and light weapons, especially by making arms transfers more transparent and supporting regional disarmament measures, taking account of all the recommendations of the forthcoming United Nations Conference on Illicit Trade in Small Arms and Light Weapons.
- To call on all States to consider acceding to the Convention on the Prohibition of the Use, Stockpiling, Production and Transfer of Anti-personnel Mines and on Their Destruction, as well as the amended mines protocol to the Convention on conventional weapons.

10. We urge Member States to observe the Olympic Truce, individually and collectively, now and in the future, and to support the International Olympic Committee in its efforts to promote peace and human understanding through sport and the Olympic Ideal.

III. Development and poverty eradication

11. We will spare no effort to free our fellow men, women and children from the abject and dehumanizing conditions of extreme poverty, to which more than a billion of them are currently subjected. We are committed to making the right to development a reality for everyone and to freeing the entire human race from want.
12. We resolve therefore to create an environment – at the national and global levels alike – which is conducive to development and to the elimination of poverty.

13. Success in meeting these objectives depends, inter alia, on good governance within each country. It also depends on good governance at the international level and on transparency in the financial, monetary and trading systems. We are committed to an open, equitable, rule-based, predictable and non-discriminatory multilateral trading and financial system.

14. We are concerned about the obstacles developing countries face in mobilizing the resources needed to finance their sustained development. We will therefore make every effort to ensure the success of the High-level International and Intergovernmental Event on Financing for Development, to be held in 2001.

15. We also undertake to address the special needs of the least developed countries. In this context, we welcome the Third United Nations Conference on the Least Developed Countries to be held in May 2001 and will endeavour to ensure its success. We call on the industrialized countries:

   • To adopt, preferably by the time of that Conference, a policy of duty- and quota-free access for essentially all exports from the least developed countries;

   • To implement the enhanced programme of debt relief for the heavily indebted poor countries without further delay and to agree to cancel all official bilateral debts of those countries in return for their making demonstrable commitments to poverty reduction; and

   • To grant more generous development assistance, especially to countries that are genuinely making an effort to apply their resources to poverty reduction.

16. We are also determined to deal comprehensively and effectively with the debt problems of low- and middle-income developing countries, through various national and international measures designed to make their debt sustainable in the long term.

17. We also resolve to address the special needs of small island developing States, by implementing the Barbados Programme of Action and the outcome of the twenty-second special session of the General Assembly rapidly and in full. We urge the international community to ensure that, in the development of a vulnerability index, the special needs of small island developing States are taken into account.

18. We recognize the special needs and problems of the landlocked developing countries, and urge both bilateral and multilateral donors to increase financial and technical assistance to this group of countries to meet their special development needs and to help them overcome the impediments of geography by improving their transit transport systems.

19. We resolve further:

   • To halve, by the year 2015, the proportion of the world's people whose income is less than one dollar a day and the proportion of people who suffer from hunger and, by the same date, to halve the proportion of people who are unable to reach or to afford safe drinking water.

   • To ensure that, by the same date, children everywhere, boys and girls alike, will be able to complete a full course of primary schooling and that girls and boys will have equal access to all levels of education.

   • By the same date, to have reduced maternal mortality by three quarters, and under-five child mortality by two thirds, of their current rates.

- To have, by then, halted, and begun to reverse, the spread of HIV/AIDS, the scourge of malaria and other major diseases that afflict humanity.
- To provide special assistance to children orphaned by HIV/AIDS.
- By 2020, to have achieved a significant improvement in the lives of at least 100 million slum dwellers as proposed in the "Cities Without Slums" initiative.

20. We also resolve:
    - To promote gender equality and the empowerment of women as effective ways to combat poverty, hunger and disease and to stimulate development that is truly sustainable.
    - To develop and implement strategies that give young people everywhere a real chance to find decent and productive work.
    - To encourage the pharmaceutical industry to make essential drugs more widely available and affordable by all who need them in developing countries.
    - To develop strong partnerships with the private sector and with civil society organizations in pursuit of development and poverty eradication.
    - To ensure that the benefits of new technologies, especially information and communication technologies, in conformity with recommendations contained in the ECOSOC 2000 Ministerial Declaration, are available to all.

IV. Protecting our common environment

21. We must spare no effort to free all of humanity, and above all our children and grandchildren, from the threat of living on a planet irredeemably spoilt by human activities, and whose resources would no longer be sufficient for their needs.
22. We reaffirm our support for the principles of sustainable development, including those set out in Agenda 21, agreed upon at the United Nations Conference on Environment and Development.
23. We resolve therefore to adopt in all our environmental actions a new ethic of conservation and stewardship and, as first steps, we resolve:
    - To make every effort to ensure the entry into force of the Kyoto Protocol, preferably by the tenth anniversary of the United Nations Conference on Environment and Development in 2002, and to embark on the required reduction in emissions of greenhouse gases.
    - To intensify our collective efforts for the management, conservation and sustainable development of all types of forests.
    - To press for the full implementation of the Convention on Biological Diversity and the Convention to Combat Desertification in those Countries Experiencing Serious Drought and/or Desertification, particularly in Africa.
    - To stop the unsustainable exploitation of water resources by developing water management strategies at the regional, national and local levels, which promote both equitable access and adequate supplies.
    - To intensify cooperation to reduce the number and effects of natural and man-made disasters.
    - To ensure free access to information on the human genome sequence.

V. Human rights, democracy and good governance

24. We will spare no effort to promote democracy and strengthen the rule of law, as well as respect for all internationally recognized human rights and fundamental freedoms, including the right to development.
25. We resolve therefore:
    - To respect fully and uphold the Universal Declaration of Human Rights.
    - To strive for the full protection and promotion in all our countries of civil, political, economic, social and cultural rights for all.
    - To strengthen the capacity of all our countries to implement the principles and practices of democracy and respect for human rights, including minority rights.
    - To combat all forms of violence against women and to implement the Convention on the Elimination of All Forms of Discrimination against Women.
    - To take measures to ensure respect for and protection of the human rights of migrants, migrant workers and their families, to eliminate the increasing acts of racism and xenophobia in many societies and to promote greater harmony and tolerance in all societies.
    - To work collectively for more inclusive political processes, allowing genuine participation by all citizens in all our countries.
    - To ensure the freedom of the media to perform their essential role and the right of the public to have access to information.

VI. Protecting the vulnerable

26. We will spare no effort to ensure that children and all civilian populations that suffer disproportionately the consequences of natural disasters, genocide, armed conflicts and other humanitarian emergencies are given every assistance and protection so that they can resume normal life as soon as possible. We resolve therefore:
    - To expand and strengthen the protection of civilians in complex emergencies, in conformity with international humanitarian law.
    - To strengthen international cooperation, including burden sharing in, and the coordination of humanitarian assistance to, countries hosting refugees and to help all refugees and displaced persons to return voluntarily to their homes, in safety and dignity and to be smoothly reintegrated into their societies.
    - To encourage the ratification and full implementation of the Convention on the Rights of the Child and its optional protocols on the involvement of children in armed conflict and on the sale of children, child prostitution and child pornography.

VII. Meeting the special needs of Africa

27. We will support the consolidation of democracy in Africa and assist Africans in their struggle for lasting peace, poverty eradication and sustainable development, thereby bringing Africa into the mainstream of the world economy.
28. We resolve therefore:
    - To give full support to the political and institutional structures of emerging democracies in Africa.

- To encourage and sustain regional and subregional mechanisms for preventing conflict and promoting political stability, and to ensure a reliable flow of resources for peacekeeping operations on the continent.
- To take special measures to address the challenges of poverty eradication and sustainable development in Africa, including debt cancellation, improved market access, enhanced Official Development Assistance and increased flows of Foreign Direct Investment, as well as transfers of technology.
- To help Africa build up its capacity to tackle the spread of the HIV/AIDS pandemic and other infectious diseases.

VIII. Strengthening the United Nations

29. We will spare no effort to make the United Nations a more effective instrument for pursuing all of these priorities: the fight for development for all the peoples of the world, the fight against poverty, ignorance and disease; the fight against injustice; the fight against violence, terror and crime; and the fight against the degradation and destruction of our common home.

30. We resolve therefore:
    - To reaffirm the central position of the General Assembly as the chief deliberative, policy-making and representative organ of the United Nations, and to enable it to play that role effectively.
    - To intensify our efforts to achieve a comprehensive reform of the Security Council in all its aspects.
    - To strengthen further the Economic and Social Council, building on its recent achievements, to help it fulfil the role ascribed to it in the Charter.
    - To strengthen the International Court of Justice, in order to ensure justice and the rule of law in international affairs.
    - To encourage regular consultations and coordination among the principal organs of the United Nations in pursuit of their functions.
    - To ensure that the Organization is provided on a timely and predictable basis with the resources it needs to carry out its mandates.
    - To urge the Secretariat to make the best use of those resources, in accordance with clear rules and procedures agreed by the General Assembly, in the interests of all Member States, by adopting the best management practices and technologies available and by concentrating on those tasks that reflect the agreed priorities of Member States.
    - To promote adherence to the Convention on the Safety of United Nations and Associated Personnel.
    - To ensure greater policy coherence and better cooperation between the United Nations, its agencies, the Bretton Woods Institutions and the World Trade Organization, as well as other multilateral bodies, with a view to achieving a fully coordinated approach to the problems of peace and development.
    - To strengthen further cooperation between the United Nations and national parliaments through their world organization, the Inter-Parliamentary Union, in various fields, including peace and security, economic and social development, international law and human rights and democracy and gender issues.

- To give greater opportunities to the private sector, non-governmental organizations and civil society, in general, to contribute to the realization of the Organization's goals and programmes.

31. We request the General Assembly to review on a regular basis the progress made in implementing the provisions of this Declaration, and ask the Secretary-General to issue periodic reports for consideration by the General Assembly and as a basis for further action.

32. We solemnly reaffirm, on this historic occasion, that the United Nations is the indispensable common house of the entire human family, through which we will seek to realize our universal aspirations for peace, cooperation and development. We therefore pledge our unstinting support for these common objectives and our determination to achieve them.

8th plenary meeting
8 September 2000

36

Protocol against the Smuggling of Migrants by Land, Sea and Air, supplementing the United Nations Convention against Transnational Organized Crime, 2000

Note: The Protocol against the Smuggling of Migrants by Land, Sea and Air, supplementing the United Nations Convention against Transnational Organized Crime, 2000 was adopted on 15 November 2000 by General Assembly Resolution 55/25, Annex II, U.N. GAOR, U.N. Doc. A/45/49 (2001). Entry into force: 28 January 2004.

PREAMBLE

The States Parties to this Protocol,

Declaring that effective action to prevent and combat the smuggling of migrants by land, sea and air requires a comprehensive international approach, including cooperation, the exchange of information and other appropriate measures, including socio-economic measures, at the national, regional and international levels,

Recalling General Assembly resolution 54/212 of 22 December 1999, in which the Assembly urged Member States and the United Nations system to strengthen international cooperation in the area of international migration and development in order to address the root causes of migration, especially those related to poverty, and to maximize the benefits of international migration to those concerned, and encouraged, where relevant, interregional, regional and subregional mechanisms to continue to address the question of migration and development,

Convinced of the need to provide migrants with humane treatment and full protection of their rights,

Taking into account the fact that, despite work undertaken in other international forums, there is no universal instrument that addresses all aspects of smuggling of migrants and other related issues,

Concerned at the significant increase in the activities of organized criminal groups in smuggling of migrants and other related criminal activities set forth in this Protocol, which bring great harm to the States concerned,

Also concerned that the smuggling of migrants can endanger the lives or security of the migrants involved,

Recalling General Assembly resolution 53/111 of 9 December 1998, in which the Assembly decided to establish an open-ended intergovernmental ad hoc committee for the purpose of elaborating a comprehensive international convention against transnational organized crime and of discussing the elaboration of, inter alia, an international instrument address-ing illegal trafficking in and transporting of migrants, including by sea,

Convinced that supplementing the United Nations Convention against Transnational Organized Crime with an international instrument against the smuggling of migrants by land, sea and air will be useful in preventing and combating that crime,

Have agreed as follows:

I GENERAL PROVISIONS

Article 1
Relation with the United Nations Convention against Transnational Organized Crime
1. This Protocol supplements the United Nations Convention against Transnational Organized Crime. It shall be interpreted together with the Convention.
2. The provisions of the Convention shall apply, mutatis mutandis, to this Protocol unless otherwise provided herein.
3. The offences established in accordance with article 6 of this Protocol shall be regarded as offences established in accordance with the Convention.

Article 2
Statement of purpose
The purpose of this Protocol is to prevent and combat the smuggling of migrants, as well as to promote cooperation among States Parties to that end, while protecting the rights of smuggled migrants.

Article 3
Use of terms
For the purposes of this Protocol:
(a) "Smuggling of migrants" shall mean the procurement, in order to obtain, directly or indirectly, a financial or other material benefit, of the illegal entry of a person into a State Party of which the person is not a national or a permanent resident;
(b) "Illegal entry" shall mean crossing borders without complying with the necessary requirements for legal entry into the receiving State;
(c) "Fraudulent travel or identity document" shall mean any travel or identity document:
  (i) That has been falsely made or altered in some material way by anyone other than a person or agency lawfully authorized to make or issue the travel or identity document on behalf of a State; or
  (ii) That has been improperly issued or obtained through misrepresentation, corruption or duress or in any other unlawful manner; or
  (iii) That is being used by a person other than the rightful holder;
(d) "Vessel" shall mean any type of water craft, including non-displacement craft and seaplanes, used or capable of being used as a means of transportation on water, except a warship, naval auxiliary or other vessel owned or operated by a Government and used, for the time being, only on government non-commercial service.

Article 4
Scope of application
This Protocol shall apply, except as otherwise stated herein, to the prevention, investigation and prosecution of the offences established in accordance with article 6 of this Protocol, where the offences are transnational in nature and involve an organized criminal group, as well as to the protection of the rights of persons who have been the object of such offences.

Article 5
Criminal liability of migrants
Migrants shall not become liable to criminal prosecution under this Protocol for the fact of having been the object of conduct set forth in article 6 of this Protocol.

Article 6
Criminalization
1. Each State Party shall adopt such legislative and other measures as may be necessary to establish as criminal offences, when committed intentionally and in order to obtain, directly or indirectly, a financial or other material benefit:
   (a) The smuggling of migrants;
   (b) When committed for the purpose of enabling the smuggling of migrants:
      (i)   Producing a fraudulent travel or identity document;
      (ii) Procuring, providing or possessing such a document;
   (c) Enabling a person who is not a national or a permanent resident to remain in the State concerned without complying with the necessary requirements for legally remaining in the State by the means mentioned in subparagraph (b) of this paragraph or any other illegal means.
2. Each State Party shall also adopt such legislative and other measures as may be necessary to establish as criminal offences:
   (a) Subject to the basic concepts of its legal system, attempting to commit an offence established in accordance with paragraph 1 of this article;
   (b) Participating as an accomplice in an offence established in accordance with paragraph 1 (a), (b) (i) or (c) of this article and, subject to the basic concepts of its legal system, participating as an accomplice in an offence established in accordance with paragraph 1 (b) (ii) of this article;
   (c) Organizing or directing other persons to commit an offence established in accordance with paragraph 1 of this article.
3. Each State Party shall adopt such legislative and other measures as may be necessary to establish as aggravating circumstances to the offences established in accordance with paragraph 1 (a), (b) (i) and (c) of this article and, subject to the basic concepts of its legal system, to the offences established in accordance with paragraph 2 (b) and (c) of this article, circumstances:
   (a) That endanger, or are likely to endanger, the lives or safety of the migrants concerned; or
   (b) That entail inhuman or degrading treatment, including for exploitation, of such migrants.
4. Nothing in this Protocol shall prevent a State Party from taking measures against a person whose conduct constitutes an offence under its domestic law.

II SMUGGLING OF MIGRANTS BY SEA

Article 7
Cooperation

States Parties shall cooperate to the fullest extent possible to prevent and suppress the smuggling of migrants by sea, in accordance with the international law of the sea.

Article 8
Measures against the smuggling of migrants by sea

1. A State Party that has reasonable grounds to suspect that a vessel that is flying its flag or claiming its registry, that is without nationality or that, though flying a foreign flag or refusing to show a flag, is in reality of the nationality of the State Party concerned is engaged in the smuggling of migrants by sea may request the assistance of other States Parties in suppressing the use of the vessel for that purpose. The States Parties so requested shall render such assistance to the extent possible within their means.

2. A State Party that has reasonable grounds to suspect that a vessel exercising freedom of navigation in accordance with international law and flying the flag or displaying the marks of registry of another State Party is engaged in the smuggling of migrants by sea may so notify the flag State, request confirmation of registry and, if confirmed, request authorization from the flag State to take appropriate measures with regard to that vessel. The flag State may authorize the requesting State, inter alia:
   (a) To board the vessel;
   (b) To search the vessel; and
   (c) If evidence is found that the vessel is engaged in the smuggling of migrants by sea, to take appropriate measures with respect to the vessel and persons and cargo on board, as authorized by the flag State.

3. A State Party that has taken any measure in accordance with paragraph 2 of this article shall promptly inform the flag State concerned of the results of that measure.

4. A State Party shall respond expeditiously to a request from another State Party to determine whether a vessel that is claiming its registry or flying its flag is entitled to do so and to a request for authorization made in accordance with paragraph 2 of this article.

5. A flag State may, consistent with article 7 of this Protocol, subject its authorization to conditions to be agreed by it and the requesting State, including conditions relating to responsibility and the extent of effective measures to be taken. A State Party shall take no additional measures without the express authorization of the flag State, except those necessary to relieve imminent danger to the lives of persons or those which derive from relevant bilateral or multilateral agreements.

6. Each State Party shall designate an authority or, where necessary, authorities to receive and respond to requests for assistance, for confirmation of registry or of the right of a vessel to fly its flag and for authorization to take appropriate measures. Such designation shall be notified through the Secretary-General to all other States Parties within one month of the designation.

7. A State Party that has reasonable grounds to suspect that a vessel is engaged in the smuggling of migrants by sea and is without nationality or may be assimilated to a

vessel without nationality may board and search the vessel. If evidence confirming the suspicion is found, that State Party shall take appropriate measures in accordance with relevant domestic and international law.

Article 9
Safeguard clauses

1. Where a State Party takes measures against a vessel in accordance with article 8 of this Protocol, it shall:
   (a) Ensure the safety and humane treatment of the persons on board;
   (b) Take due account of the need not to endanger the security of the vessel or its cargo;
   (c) Take due account of the need not to prejudice the commercial or legal interests of the flag State or any other interested State;
   (d) Ensure, within available means, that any measure taken with regard to the vessel is environmentally sound.
2. Where the grounds for measures taken pursuant to article 8 of this Protocol prove to be unfounded, the vessel shall be compensated for any loss or damage that may have been sustained, provided that the vessel has not committed any act justifying the measures taken.
3. Any measure taken, adopted or implemented in accordance with this chapter shall take due account of the need not to interfere with or to affect:
   (a) The rights and obligations and the exercise of jurisdiction of coastal States in accordance with the international law of the sea; or
   (b) The authority of the flag State to exercise jurisdiction and control in administrative, technical and social matters involving the vessel.
4. Any measure taken at sea pursuant to this chapter shall be carried out only by warships or military aircraft, or by other ships or aircraft clearly marked and identifiable as being on government service and authorized to that effect.

III PREVENTION, COOPERATION AND OTHER MEASURES

Article 10
Information

1. Without prejudice to articles 27 and 28 of the Convention, States Parties, in particular those with common borders or located on routes along which migrants are smuggled, shall, for the purpose of achieving the objectives of this Protocol, exchange among themselves, consistent with their respective domestic legal and administrative systems, relevant information on matters such as:
   (a) Embarkation and destination points, as well as routes, carriers and means of transportation, known to be or suspected of being used by an organized criminal group engaged in conduct set forth in article 6 of this Protocol;
   (b) The identity and methods of organizations or organized criminal groups known to be or suspected of being engaged in conduct set forth in article 6 of this Protocol;
   (c) The authenticity and proper form of travel documents issued by a State Party and the theft or related misuse of blank travel or identity documents;
   (d) Means and methods of concealment and transportation of persons, the unlawful alteration, reproduction or acquisition or other misuse of travel or identity

documents used in conduct set forth in article 6 of this Protocol and ways of detecting them;

(e) Legislative experiences and practices and measures to prevent and combat the conduct set forth in article 6 of this Protocol; and

(f) Scientific and technological information useful to law enforcement, so as to enhance each other's ability to prevent, detect and investigate the conduct set forth in article 6 of this Protocol and to prosecute those involved.

2. A State Party that receives information shall comply with any request by the State Party that transmitted the information that places restrictions on its use.

Article 11
Border measures

1. Without prejudice to international commitments in relation to the free movement of people, States Parties shall strengthen, to the extent possible, such border controls as may be necessary to prevent and detect the smuggling of migrants.

2. Each State Party shall adopt legislative or other appropriate measures to prevent, to the extent possible, means of transport operated by commercial carriers from being used in the commission of the offence established in accordance with article 6, paragraph 1 (a), of this Protocol.

3. Where appropriate, and without prejudice to applicable international conventions, such measures shall include establishing the obligation of commercial carriers, including any transportation company or the owner or operator of any means of transport, to ascertain that all passengers are in possession of the travel documents required for entry into the receiving State.

4. Each State Party shall take the necessary measures, in accordance with its domestic law, to provide for sanctions in cases of violation of the obligation set forth in paragraph 3 of this article.

5. Each State Party shall consider taking measures that permit, in accordance with its domestic law, the denial of entry or revocation of visas of persons implicated in the commission of offences established in accordance with this Protocol.

6. Without prejudice to article 27 of the Convention, States Parties shall consider strengthening cooperation among border control agencies by, inter alia, establishing and maintaining direct channels of communication.

Article 12
Security and control of documents

Each State Party shall take such measures as may be necessary, within available means:

(a) To ensure that travel or identity documents issued by it are of such quality that they cannot easily be misused and cannot readily be falsified or unlawfully altered, replicated or issued; and

(b) To ensure the integrity and security of travel or identity documents issued by or on behalf of the State Party and to prevent their unlawful creation, issuance and use.

Article 13
Legitimacy and validity of documents

At the request of another State Party, a State Party shall, in accordance with its domestic law, verify within a reasonable time the legitimacy and validity of travel or identity documents issued or purported to have been issued in its name and suspected of being used for purposes of conduct set forth in article 6 of this Protocol.

Article 14
Training and technical cooperation

1. States Parties shall provide or strengthen specialized training for immigration and other relevant officials in preventing the conduct set forth in article 6 of this Protocol and in the humane treatment of migrants who have been the object of such conduct, while respecting their rights as set forth in this Protocol.
2. States Parties shall cooperate with each other and with competent international organizations, non-governmental organizations, other relevant organizations and other elements of civil society as appropriate to ensure that there is adequate personnel training in their territories to prevent, combat and eradicate the conduct set forth in article 6 of this Protocol and to protect the rights of migrants who have been the object of such conduct. Such training shall include:
   (a) Improving the security and quality of travel documents;
   (b) Recognizing and detecting fraudulent travel or identity documents;
   (c) Gathering criminal intelligence, relating in particular to the identification of organized criminal groups known to be or suspected of being engaged in conduct set forth in article 6 of this Protocol, the methods used to transport smuggled migrants, the misuse of travel or identity documents for purposes of conduct set forth in article 6 and the means of concealment used in the smuggling of migrants;
   (d) Improving procedures for detecting smuggled persons at conventional and non-conventional points of entry and exit; and
   (e) The humane treatment of migrants and the protection of their rights as set forth in this Protocol.
3. States Parties with relevant expertise shall consider providing technical assistance to States that are frequently countries of origin or transit for persons who have been the object of conduct set forth in article 6 of this Protocol. States Parties shall make every effort to provide the necessary resources, such as vehicles, computer systems and document readers, to combat the conduct set forth in article 6.

Article 15
Other prevention measures

1. Each State Party shall take measures to ensure that it provides or strengthens information programmes to increase public awareness of the fact that the conduct set forth in article 6 of this Protocol is a criminal activity frequently perpetrated by organized criminal groups for profit and that it poses serious risks to the migrants concerned.
2. In accordance with article 31 of the Convention, States Parties shall cooperate in the field of public information for the purpose of preventing potential migrants from falling victim to organized criminal groups.
3. Each State Party shall promote or strengthen, as appropriate, development programmes and cooperation at the national, regional and international levels, taking into account the socio-economic realities of migration and paying special attention to economically and socially depressed areas, in order to combat the root socio-economic causes of the smuggling of migrants, such as poverty and underdevelopment.

Article 16
Protection and assistance measures

1. In implementing this Protocol, each State Party shall take, consistent with its obligations under international law, all appropriate measures, including legislation if necessary, to preserve and protect the rights of persons who have been the object of conduct set forth in article 6 of this Protocol as accorded under applicable international law, in particular the right to life and the right not to be subjected to torture or other cruel, inhuman or degrading treatment or punishment.
2. Each State Party shall take appropriate measures to afford migrants appropriate protection against violence that may be inflicted upon them, whether by individuals or groups, by reason of being the object of conduct set forth in article 6 of this Protocol.
3. Each State Party shall afford appropriate assistance to migrants whose lives or safety are endangered by reason of being the object of conduct set forth in article 6 of this Protocol.
4. In applying the provisions of this article, States Parties shall take into account the special needs of women and children.
5. In the case of the detention of a person who has been the object of conduct set forth in article 6 of this Protocol, each State Party shall comply with its obligations under the Vienna Convention on Consular Relations, where applicable, including that of informing the person concerned without delay about the provisions concerning notification to and communication with consular officers.

Article 17
Agreements and arrangements

States Parties shall consider the conclusion of bilateral or regional agreements or operational arrangements or understandings aimed at:

    (a) Establishing the most appropriate and effective measures to prevent and combat the conduct set forth in article 6 of this Protocol; or

    (b) Enhancing the provisions of this Protocol among themselves.

Article 18
Return of smuggled migrants

1. Each State Party agrees to facilitate and accept, without undue or unreasonable delay, the return of a person who has been the object of conduct set forth in article 6 of this Protocol and who is its national or who has the right of permanent residence in its territory at the time of return.
2. Each State Party shall consider the possibility of facilitating and accepting the return of a person who has been the object of conduct set forth in article 6 of this Protocol and who had the right of permanent residence in its territory at the time of entry into the receiving State in accordance with its domestic law.
3. At the request of the receiving State Party, a requested State Party shall, without undue or unreasonable delay, verify whether a person who has been the object of conduct set forth in article 6 of this Protocol is its national or has the right of permanent residence in its territory.

4. In order to facilitate the return of a person who has been the object of conduct set forth in article 6 of this Protocol and is without proper documentation, the State Party of which that person is a national or in which he or she has the right of permanent residence shall agree to issue, at the request of the receiving State Party, such travel documents or other authorization as may be necessary to enable the person to travel to and reenter its territory.

5. Each State Party involved with the return of a person who has been the object of conduct set forth in article 6 of this Protocol shall take all appropriate measures to carry out the return in an orderly manner and with due regard for the safety and dignity of the person.

6. States Parties may cooperate with relevant international organizations in the implementation of this article.

7. This article shall be without prejudice to any right afforded to persons who have been the object of conduct set forth in article 6 of this Protocol by any domestic law of the receiving State Party.

8. This article shall not affect the obligations entered into under any other applicable treaty, bilateral or multilateral, or any other applicable operational agreement or arrangement that governs, in whole or in part, the return of persons who have been the object of conduct set forth in article 6 of this Protocol.

IV FINAL PROVISIONS

Article 19
Saving clause

1. Nothing in this Protocol shall affect the other rights, obligations and responsibilities of States and individuals under international law, including international humanitarian law and international human rights law and, in particular, where applicable, the 1951 Convention and the 1967 Protocol relating to the Status of Refugees and the principle of nonrefoulement as contained therein.

2. The measures set forth in this Protocol shall be interpreted and applied in a way that is not discriminatory to persons on the ground that they are the object of conduct set forth in article 6 of this Protocol. The interpretation and application of those measures shall be consistent with internationally recognized principles of non-discrimination.

Article 20
Settlement of disputes

1. States Parties shall endeavour to settle disputes concerning the interpretation or application of this Protocol through negotiation.

2. Any dispute between two or more States Parties concerning the interpretation or application of this Protocol that cannot be settled through negotiation within a reasonable time shall, at the request of one of those States Parties, be submitted to arbitration. If, six months after the date of the request for arbitration, those States Parties are unable to agree on the organization of the arbitration, any one of those States Parties may refer the dispute to the International Court of Justice by request in accordance with the Statute of the Court.

3. Each State Party may, at the time of signature, ratification, acceptance or approval of or accession to this Protocol, declare that it does not consider itself bound by paragraph 2 of this article. The other States Parties shall not be bound by paragraph 2 of this article with respect to any State Party that has made such a reservation.

4. Any State Party that has made a reservation in accordance with paragraph 3 of this article may at any time withdraw that reservation by notification to the Secretary-General of the United Nations.

Article 21
Signature, ratification, acceptance, approval and accession

1. This Protocol shall be open to all States for signature from 12 to 15 December 2000 in Palermo, Italy, and thereafter at United Nations Headquarters in New York until 12 December 2002.

2. This Protocol shall also be open for signature by regional economic integration organizations provided that at least one member State of such organization has signed this Protocol in accordance with paragraph 1 of this article.

3. This Protocol is subject to ratification, acceptance or approval. Instruments of ratification, acceptance or approval shall be deposited with the Secretary-General of the United Nations. A regional economic integration organization may deposit its instrument of ratification, acceptance or approval if at least one of its member States has done likewise. In that instrument of ratification, acceptance or approval, such organization shall declare the extent of its competence with respect to the matters governed by this Protocol. Such organization shall also inform the depositary of any relevant modification in the extent of its competence.

4. This Protocol is open for accession by any State or any regional economic integration organization of which at least one member State is a Party to this Protocol. Instruments of accession shall be deposited with the Secretary-General of the United Nations. At the time of its accession, a regional economic integration organization shall declare the extent of its competence with respect to matters governed by this Protocol. Such organization shall also inform the depositary of any relevant modification in the extent of its competence.

Article 22
Entry into force

1. This Protocol shall enter into force on the ninetieth day after the date of deposit of the fortieth instrument of ratification, acceptance, approval or accession, except that it shall not enter into force before the entry into force of the Convention. For the purpose of this paragraph, any instrument deposited by a regional economic integration organization shall not be counted as additional to those deposited by member States of such organization.

2. For each State or regional economic integration organization ratifying, accepting, approving or acceding to this Protocol after the deposit of the fortieth instrument of such action, this Protocol shall enter into force on the thirtieth day after the date of deposit by such State or organization of the relevant instrument or on the date this Protocol enters into force pursuant to paragraph 1 of this article, whichever is the later.

Article 23
Amendment

1. After the expiry of five years from the entry into force of this Protocol, a State Party to the Protocol may propose an amendment and file it with the Secretary-General of the United Nations, who shall thereupon communicate the proposed amendment to the States Parties and to the Conference of the Parties to the Convention for the purpose of considering and deciding on the proposal. The States Parties to this Protocol meeting at the Conference of the Parties shall make every effort to achieve consensus on each amendment. If all efforts at consensus have been exhausted and no agreement has been reached, the amendment shall, as a last resort, require for its adoption a two-thirds majority vote of the States Parties to this Protocol present and voting at the meeting of the Conference of the Parties.

2. Regional economic integration organizations, in matters within their competence, shall exercise their right to vote under this article with a number of votes equal to the number of their member States that are Parties to this Protocol. Such organizations shall not exercise their right to vote if their member States exercise theirs and vice versa.

3. An amendment adopted in accordance with paragraph 1 of this article is subject to ratification, acceptance or approval by States Parties.

4. An amendment adopted in accordance with paragraph 1 of this article shall enter into force in respect of a State Party ninety days after the date of the deposit with the Secretary-General of the United Nations of an instrument of ratification, acceptance or approval of such amendment.

5. When an amendment enters into force, it shall be binding on those States Parties which have expressed their consent to be bound by it. Other States Parties shall still be bound by the provisions of this Protocol and any earlier amendments that they have ratified, accepted or approved.

Article 24
Denunciation

1. A State Party may denounce this Protocol by written notification to the Secretary-General of the United Nations. Such denunciation shall become effective one year after the date of receipt of the notification by the Secretary-General.

2. A regional economic integration organization shall cease to be a Party to this Protocol when all of its member States have denounced it.

Article 25
Depositary and languages

1. The Secretary-General of the United Nations is designated depositary of this Protocol.

2. The original of this Protocol, of which the Arabic, Chinese, English, French, Russian and Spanish texts are equally authentic, shall be deposited with the Secretary-General of the United Nations.

IN WITNESS WHEREOF, the undersigned plenipotentiaries, being duly authorized thereto by their respective Governments, have signed this Protocol.

37

Protocol to Prevent, Suppress and Punish Trafficking in Persons, Especially Women and Children, supplementing the United Nations Convention against Transnational Organized Crime, 2000

Note: Adopted on 15 November 2000 by General Assembly Resolution 55/25, Annex II, U.N. GAOR, U.N. Doc. A/45/49 (2001). Entry into force: 25 December 2003.

PREAMBLE

The States Parties to this Protocol,

Declaring that effective action to prevent and combat trafficking in persons, especially women and children, requires a comprehensive international approach in the countries of origin, transit and destination that includes measures to prevent such trafficking, to punish the traffickers and to protect the victims of such trafficking, including by protecting their internationally recognized human rights,

Taking into account the fact that, despite the existence of a variety of international instruments containing rules and practical measures to combat the exploitation of persons, especially women and children, there is no universal instrument that addresses all aspects of trafficking in persons,

Concerned that, in the absence of such an instrument, persons who are vulnerable to trafficking will not be sufficiently protected,

Recalling General Assembly resolution 53/111 of 9 December 1998, in which the Assembly decided to establish an open-ended intergovernmental ad hoc committee for the purpose of elaborating a comprehensive international convention against transnational organized crime and of discussing the elaboration of, inter alia, an international instrument addressing trafficking in women and children,

Convinced that supplementing the United Nations Convention against Transnational Organized Crime with an international instrument for the prevention, suppression and punishment of trafficking in persons, especially women and children, will be useful in preventing and combating that crime,

Have agreed as follows:

I. GENERAL PROVISIONS

Article 1
Relation with the United Nations Convention against Transnational Organized Crime

1. This Protocol supplements the United Nations Convention against Transnational Organized Crime. It shall be interpreted together with the Convention.
2. The provisions of the Convention shall apply, mutatis mutandis, to this Protocol unless otherwise provided herein.
3. The offences established in accordance with article 5 of this Protocol shall be regarded as offences established in accordance with the Convention.

Article 2
Statement of purpose

The purposes of this Protocol are:

(a) To prevent and combat trafficking in persons, paying particular attention to women and children;

(b) To protect and assist the victims of such trafficking, with full respect for their human rights; and

(c) To promote cooperation among States Parties in order to meet those objectives.

Article 3
Use of terms

For the purposes of this Protocol:

(a) "Trafficking in persons" shall mean the recruitment, transportation, transfer, harbouring or receipt of persons, by means of the threat or use of force or other forms of coercion, of abduction, of fraud, of deception, of the abuse of power or of a position of vulnerability or of the giving or receiving of payments or benefits to achieve the consent of a person having control over another person, for the purpose of exploitation. Exploitation shall include, at a minimum, the exploitation of the prostitution of others or other forms of sexual exploitation, forced labour or services, slavery or practices similar to slavery, servitude or the removal of organs;

(b) The consent of a victim of trafficking in persons to the intended exploitation set forth in subparagraph (a) of this article shall be irrelevant where any of the means set forth in subparagraph (a) have been used;

(c) The recruitment, transportation, transfer, harbouring or receipt of a child for the purpose of exploitation shall be considered "trafficking in persons" even if this does not involve any of the means set forth in subparagraph (a) of this article;

(d) "Child" shall mean any person under eighteen years of age.

Article 4
Scope of application

This Protocol shall apply, except as otherwise stated herein, to the prevention, investigation and prosecution of the offences established in accordance with article 5 of this Protocol, where those offences are transnational in nature and involve an organized criminal group, as well as to the protection of victims of such offences.

Article 5
Criminalization

1. Each State Party shall adopt such legislative and other measures as may be necessary to establish as criminal offences the conduct set forth in article 3 of this Protocol, when committed intentionally.

2. Each State Party shall also adopt such legislative and other measures as may be necessary to establish as criminal offences:

    (a) Subject to the basic concepts of its legal system, attempting to commit an offence established in accordance with paragraph 1 of this article;

    (b) Participating as an accomplice in an offence established in accordance with paragraph 1 of this article; and

    (c) Organizing or directing other persons to commit an offence established in accordance with paragraph 1 of this article.

II. PROTECTION OF VICTIMS OF TRAFFICKING IN PERSONS

Article 6
Assistance to and protection of victims of trafficking in persons

1. In appropriate cases and to the extent possible under its domestic law, each State Party shall protect the privacy and identity of victims of trafficking in persons, including, inter alia, by making legal proceedings relating to such trafficking confidential.

2. Each State Party shall ensure that its domestic legal or administrative system contains measures that provide to victims of trafficking in persons, in appropriate cases:

    (a) Information on relevant court and administrative proceedings;

    (b) Assistance to enable their views and concerns to be presented and considered at appropriate stages of criminal proceedings against offenders, in a manner not prejudicial to the rights of the defence.

3. Each State Party shall consider implementing measures to provide for the physical, psychological and social recovery of victims of trafficking in persons, including, in appropriate cases, in cooperation with non-governmental organizations, other relevant organizations and other elements of civil society, and, in particular, the provision of:

    (a) Appropriate housing;

    (b) Counselling and information, in particular as regards their legal rights, in a language that the victims of trafficking in persons can understand;

    (c) Medical, psychological and material assistance; and

    (d) Employment, educational and training opportunities.

4. Each State Party shall take into account, in applying the provisions of this article, the age, gender and special needs of victims of trafficking in persons, in particular the special needs of children, including appropriate housing, education and care.

5. Each State Party shall endeavour to provide for the physical safety of victims of trafficking in persons while they are within its territory.

6. Each State Party shall ensure that its domestic legal system contains measures that offer victims of trafficking in persons the possibility of obtaining compensation for damage suffered.

Article 7
Status of victims of trafficking in persons in receiving States

1. In addition to taking measures pursuant to article 6 of this Protocol, each State Party shall consider adopting legislative or other appropriate measures that permit victims of trafficking in persons to remain in its territory, temporarily or permanently, in appropriate cases.
2. In implementing the provision contained in paragraph 1 of this article, each State Party shall give appropriate consideration to humanitarian and compassionate factors.

Article 8
Repatriation of victims of trafficking in persons

1. The State Party of which a victim of trafficking in persons is a national or in which the person had the right of permanent residence at the time of entry into the territory of the receiving State Party shall facilitate and accept, with due regard for the safety of that person, the return of that person without undue or unreasonable delay.
2. When a State Party returns a victim of trafficking in persons to a State Party of which that person is a national or in which he or she had, at the time of entry into the territory of the receiving State Party, the right of permanent residence, such return shall be with due regard for the safety of that person and for the status of any legal proceedings related to the fact that the person is a victim of trafficking and shall preferably be voluntary.
3. At the request of a receiving State Party, a requested State Party shall, without undue or unreasonable delay, verify whether a person who is a victim of trafficking in persons is its national or had the right of permanent residence in its territory at the time of entry into the territory of the receiving State Party.
4. In order to facilitate the return of a victim of trafficking in persons who is without proper documentation, the State Party of which that person is a national or in which he or she had the right of permanent residence at the time of entry into the territory of the receiving State Party shall agree to issue, at the request of the receiving State Party, such travel documents or other authorization as may be necessary to enable the person to travel to and re-enter its territory.
5. This article shall be without prejudice to any right afforded to victims of trafficking in persons by any domestic law of the receiving State Party.
6. This article shall be without prejudice to any applicable bilateral or multilateral agreement or arrangement that governs, in whole or in part, the return of victims of trafficking in persons.

III. PREVENTION, COOPERATION AND OTHER MEASURES

Article 9
Prevention of trafficking in persons

1. States Parties shall establish comprehensive policies, programmes and other measures:
   (a) To prevent and combat trafficking in persons; and
   (b) To protect victims of trafficking in persons, especially women and children, from revictimization.
2. States Parties shall endeavour to undertake measures such as research, information and mass media campaigns and social and economic initiatives to prevent and combat trafficking in persons.

3. Policies, programmes and other measures established in accordance with this article shall, as appropriate, include cooperation with non-governmental organizations, other relevant organizations and other elements of civil society.

4. States Parties shall take or strengthen measures, including through bilateral or multilateral cooperation, to alleviate the factors that make persons, especially women and children, vulnerable to trafficking, such as poverty, underdevelopment and lack of equal opportunity.

5. States Parties shall adopt or strengthen legislative or other measures, such as educational, social or cultural measures, including through bilateral and multilateral cooperation, to discourage the demand that fosters all forms of exploitation of persons, especially women and children, that leads to trafficking.

Article 10
Information exchange and training

1. Law enforcement, immigration or other relevant authorities of States Parties shall, as appropriate, cooperate with one another by exchanging information, in accordance with their domestic law, to enable them to determine:

   (a) Whether individuals crossing or attempting to cross an international border with travel documents belonging to other persons or without travel documents are perpetrators or victims of trafficking in persons;

   (b) The types of travel document that individuals have used or attempted to use to cross an international border for the purpose of trafficking in persons; and

   (c) The means and methods used by organized criminal groups for the purpose of trafficking in persons, including the recruitment and transportation of victims, routes and links between and among individuals and groups engaged in such trafficking, and possible measures for detecting them.

2. States Parties shall provide or strengthen training for law enforcement, immigration and other relevant officials in the prevention of trafficking in persons. The training should focus on methods used in preventing such trafficking, prosecuting the traffickers and protecting the rights of the victims, including protecting the victims from the traffickers. The training should also take into account the need to consider human rights and child- and gender-sensitive issues and it should encourage cooperation with non-governmental organizations, other relevant organizations and other elements of civil society.

3. A State Party that receives information shall comply with any request by the State Party that transmitted the information that places restrictions on its use.

Article 11
Border measures

1. Without prejudice to international commitments in relation to the free movement of people, States Parties shall strengthen, to the extent possible, such border controls as may be necessary to prevent and detect trafficking in persons.

2. Each State Party shall adopt legislative or other appropriate measures to prevent, to the extent possible, means of transport operated by commercial carriers from being used in the commission of offences established in accordance with article 5 of this Protocol.

3. Where appropriate, and without prejudice to applicable international conventions, such measures shall include establishing the obligation of commercial carriers, including any transportation company or the owner or operator of any means of transport, to ascertain that all passengers are in possession of the travel documents required for entry into the receiving State.

4. Each State Party shall take the necessary measures, in accordance with its domestic law, to provide for sanctions in cases of violation of the obligation set forth in paragraph 3 of this article.

5. Each State Party shall consider taking measures that permit, in accordance with its domestic law, the denial of entry or revocation of visas of persons implicated in the commission of offences established in accordance with this Protocol.

6. Without prejudice to article 27 of the Convention, States Parties shall consider strengthening cooperation among border control agencies by, inter alia, establishing and maintaining direct channels of communication.

Article 12
Security and control of documents

Each State Party shall take such measures as may be necessary, within available means:

   (a) To ensure that travel or identity documents issued by it are of such quality that they cannot easily be misused and cannot readily be falsified or unlawfully altered, replicated or issued; and

   (b) To ensure the integrity and security of travel or identity documents issued by or on behalf of the State Party and to prevent their unlawful creation, issuance and use.

Article 13
Legitimacy and validity of documents

At the request of another State Party, a State Party shall, in accordance with its domestic law, verify within a reasonable time the legitimacy and validity of travel or identity documents issued or purported to have been issued in its name and suspected of being used for trafficking in persons.

IV. FINAL PROVISIONS

Article 14
Saving clause

1. Nothing in this Protocol shall affect the rights, obligations and responsibilities of States and individuals under international law, including international humanitarian law and international human rights law and, in particular, where applicable, the 1951 Convention and the 1967 Protocol relating to the Status of Refugees and the principle of non-refoulement as contained therein.

2. The measures set forth in this Protocol shall be interpreted and applied in a way that is not discriminatory to persons on the ground that they are victims of trafficking in persons. The interpretation and application of those measures shall be consistent with internationally recognized principles of non-discrimination.

Article 15
Settlement of disputes

1. States Parties shall endeavour to settle disputes concerning the interpretation or application of this Protocol through negotiation.
2. Any dispute between two or more States Parties concerning the interpretation or application of this Protocol that cannot be settled through negotiation within a reasonable time shall, at the request of one of those States Parties, be submitted to arbitration. If, six months after the date of the request for arbitration, those States Parties are unable to agree on the organization of the arbitration, any one of those States Parties may refer the dispute to the International Court of Justice by request in accordance with the Statute of the Court.
3. Each State Party may, at the time of signature, ratification, acceptance or approval of or accession to this Protocol, declare that it does not consider itself bound by paragraph 2 of this article. The other States Parties shall not be bound by paragraph 2 of this article with respect to any State Party that has made such a reservation.
4. Any State Party that has made a reservation in accordance with paragraph 3 of this article may at any time withdraw that reservation by notification to the Secretary-General of the United Nations.

Article 16
Signature, ratification, acceptance, approval and accession

1. This Protocol shall be open to all States for signature from 12 to 15 December 2000 in Palermo, Italy, and thereafter at United Nations Headquarters in New York until 12 December 2002.
2. This Protocol shall also be open for signature by regional economic integration organizations provided that at least one member State of such organization has signed this Protocol in accordance with paragraph 1 of this article.
3. This Protocol is subject to ratification, acceptance or approval. Instruments of ratification, acceptance or approval shall be deposited with the Secretary-General of the United Nations. A regional economic integration organization may deposit its instrument of ratification, acceptance or approval if at least one of its member States has done likewise. In that instrument of ratification, acceptance or approval, such organization shall declare the extent of its competence with respect to the matters governed by this Protocol. Such organization shall also inform the depositary of any relevant modification in the extent of its competence.
4. This Protocol is open for accession by any State or any regional economic integration organization of which at least one member State is a Party to this Protocol. Instruments of accession shall be deposited with the Secretary-General of the United Nations. At the time of its accession, a regional economic integration organization shall declare the extent of its competence with respect to matters governed by this Protocol. Such organization shall also inform the depositary of any relevant modification in the extent of its competence.

Article 17
Entry into force

1. This Protocol shall enter into force on the ninetieth day after the date of deposit of the fortieth instrument of ratification, acceptance, approval or accession, except that

it shall not enter into force before the entry into force of the Convention. For the purpose of this paragraph, any instrument deposited by a regional economic integration organization shall not be counted as additional to those deposited by member States of such organization.

2. For each State or regional economic integration organization ratifying, accepting, approving or acceding to this Protocol after the deposit of the fortieth instrument of such action, this Protocol shall enter into force on the thirtieth day after the date of deposit by such State or organization of the relevant instrument or on the date this Protocol enters into force pursuant to paragraph 1 of this article, whichever is the later.

Article 18
Amendment

1. After the expiry of five years from the entry into force of this Protocol, a State Party to the Protocol may propose an amendment and file it with the Secretary-General of the United Nations, who shall thereupon communicate the proposed amendment to the States Parties and to the Conference of the Parties to the Convention for the purpose of considering and deciding on the proposal. The States Parties to this Protocol meeting at the Conference of the Parties shall make every effort to achieve consensus on each amendment. If all efforts at consensus have been exhausted and no agreement has been reached, the amendment shall, as a last resort, require for its adoption a two-thirds majority vote of the States Parties to this Protocol present and voting at the meeting of the Conference of the Parties.

2. Regional economic integration organizations, in matters within their competence, shall exercise their right to vote under this article with a number of votes equal to the number of their member States that are Parties to this Protocol. Such organizations shall not exercise their right to vote if their member States exercise theirs and vice versa.

3. An amendment adopted in accordance with paragraph 1 of this article is subject to ratification, acceptance or approval by States Parties.

4. An amendment adopted in accordance with paragraph 1 of this article shall enter into force in respect of a State Party ninety days after the date of the deposit with the Secretary-General of the United Nations of an instrument of ratification, acceptance or approval of such amendment.

5. When an amendment enters into force, it shall be binding on those States Parties which have expressed their consent to be bound by it. Other States Parties shall still be bound by the provisions of this Protocol and any earlier amendments that they have ratified, accepted or approved.

Article 19
Denunciation

1. A State Party may denounce this Protocol by written notification to the Secretary-General of the United Nations. Such denunciation shall become effective one year after the date of receipt of the notification by the Secretary-General.

2. A regional economic integration organization shall cease to be a Party to this Protocol when all of its member States have denounced it.

Article 20
Depositary and languages
1. The Secretary-General of the United Nations is designated depositary of this Protocol.
2. The original of this Protocol, of which the Arabic, Chinese, English, French, Russian and Spanish texts are equally authentic, shall be deposited with the Secretary-General of the United Nations.

In witness whereof, the undersigned plenipotentiaries, being duly authorized thereto by their respective Governments, have signed this Protocol.

38

Security Council Resolution 1373 (2001)

Note: Adopted by the Security Council at its 4385th meeting, 28 September 2001.

The Security Council,

Reaffirming its resolutions 1269 (1999) of 19 October 1999 and 1368 (2001) of 12 September 2001,

Reaffirming also its unequivocal condemnation of the terrorist attacks which took place in New York, Washington, D.C. and Pennsylvania on 11 September 2001, and expressing its determination to prevent all such acts,

Reaffirming further that such acts, like any act of international terrorism, constitute a threat to international peace and security,

Reaffirming the inherent right of individual or collective self-defence as recognized by the Charter of the United Nations as reiterated in resolution 1368 (2001),

Reaffirming the need to combat by all means, in accordance with the Charter of the United Nations, threats to international peace and security caused by terrorist acts,

Deeply concerned by the increase, in various regions of the world, of acts of terrorism motivated by intolerance or extremism,

Calling on States to work together urgently to prevent and suppress terrorist acts, including through increased cooperation and full implementation of the relevant international conventions relating to terrorism,

Recognizing the need for States to complement international cooperation by taking additional measures to prevent and suppress, in their territories through all lawful means, the financing and preparation of any acts of terrorism,

Reaffirming the principle established by the General Assembly in its declaration of October 1970 (resolution 2625 (XXV)) and reiterated by the Security Council in its resolution 1189 (1998) of 13 August 1998, namely that every State has the duty to refrain from organizing, instigating, assisting or participating in terrorist acts in another State or acquiescing in organized activities within its territory directed towards the commission of such acts,

Acting under Chapter VII of the Charter of the United Nations,

1. *Decides* that all States shall:

   (a) Prevent and suppress the financing of terrorist acts;

   (b) Criminalize the wilful provision or collection, by any means, directly or indirectly, of funds by their nationals or in their territories with the intention that the funds should be used, or in the knowledge that they are to be used, in order to carry out terrorist acts;

   (c) Freeze without delay funds and other financial assets or economic resources of persons who commit, or attempt to commit, terrorist acts or participate in or facilitate the commission of terrorist acts; of entities owned or controlled directly or indirectly by such persons; and of persons and entities acting on behalf of, or at the direction of such persons and entities, including funds derived or generated from property owned or controlled directly or indirectly by such persons and associated persons and entities;

(d) Prohibit their nationals or any persons and entities within their territories from making any funds, financial assets or economic resources or financial or other related services available, directly or indirectly, for the benefit of persons who commit or attempt to commit or facilitate or participate in the commission of terrorist acts, of entities owned or controlled, directly or indirectly, by such persons and of persons and entities acting on behalf of or at the direction of such persons;

2. *Decides* also that all States shall:

(a) Refrain from providing any form of support, active or passive, to entities or persons involved in terrorist acts, including by suppressing recruitment of members of terrorist groups and eliminating the supply of weapons to terrorists;

(b) Take the necessary steps to prevent the commission of terrorist acts, including by provision of early warning to other States by exchange of information;

(c) Deny safe haven to those who finance, plan, support, or commit terrorist acts, or provide safe havens;

(d) Prevent those who finance, plan, facilitate or commit terrorist acts from using their respective territories for those purposes against other States or their citizens;

(e) Ensure that any person who participates in the financing, planning, preparation or perpetration of terrorist acts or in supporting terrorist acts is brought to justice and ensure that, in addition to any other measures against them, such terrorist acts are established as serious criminal offences in domestic laws and regulations and that the punishment duly reflects the seriousness of such terrorist acts;

(f) Afford one another the greatest measure of assistance in connection with criminal investigations or criminal proceedings relating to the financing or support of terrorist acts, including assistance in obtaining evidence in their possession necessary for the proceedings;

(g) Prevent the movement of terrorists or terrorist groups by effective border controls and controls on issuance of identity papers and travel documents, and through measures for preventing counterfeiting, forgery or fraudulent use of identity papers and travel documents;

3. *Calls* upon all States to:

(a) Find ways of intensifying and accelerating the exchange of operational information, especially regarding actions or movements of terrorist persons or networks; forged or falsified travel documents; traffic in arms, explosives or sensitive materials; use of communications technologies by terrorist groups; and the threat posed by the possession of weapons of mass destruction by terrorist groups;

(b) Exchange information in accordance with international and domestic law and cooperate on administrative and judicial matters to prevent the commission of terrorist acts;

(c) Cooperate, particularly through bilateral and multilateral arrangements and agreements, to prevent and suppress terrorist attacks and take action against perpetrators of such acts;

(d) Become parties as soon as possible to the relevant international conventions and protocols relating to terrorism, including the International Convention for the Suppression of the Financing of Terrorism of 9 December 1999;

(e) Increase cooperation and fully implement the relevant international conventions and protocols relating to terrorism and Security Council resolutions 1269 (1999) and 1368 (2001);

(f) Take appropriate measures in conformity with the relevant provisions of national and international law, including international standards of human rights, before granting refugee status, for the purpose of ensuring that the asylum-seeker has not planned, facilitated or participated in the commission of terrorist acts;

(g) Ensure, in conformity with international law, that refugee status is not abused by the perpetrators, organizers or facilitators of terrorist acts, and that claims of political motivation are not recognized as grounds for refusing requests for the extradition of alleged terrorists;

4. *Notes* with concern the close connection between international terrorism and trans-national organized crime, illicit drugs, money-laundering, illegal arms trafficking, and illegal movement of nuclear, chemical, biological and other potentially deadly materials, and in this regard emphasizes the need to enhance coordination of efforts on national, subregional, regional and international levels in order to strengthen a global response to this serious challenge and threat to international security;

5. *Declares* that acts, methods, and practices of terrorism are contrary to the purposes and principles of the United Nations and that knowingly financing, planning and inciting terrorist acts are also contrary to the purposes and principles of the United Nations;

6. *Decides* to establish, in accordance with rule 28 of its provisional rules of procedure, a Committee of the Security Council, consisting of all the members of the Council, to monitor implementation of this resolution, with the assistance of appropriate expertise, and calls upon all States to report to the Committee, no later than 90 days from the date of adoption of this resolution and thereafter according to a timetable to be proposed by the Committee, on the steps they have taken to implement this resolution;

7. *Directs* the Committee to delineate its tasks, submit a work programme within 30 days of the adoption of this resolution, and to consider the support it requires, in consultation with the Secretary-General;

8. *Expresses* its determination to take all necessary steps in order to ensure the full implementation of this resolution, in accordance with its responsibilities under the Charter;

9. *Decides* to remain seized of this matter.

39

Norms on the Responsibilities of Transnational Corporations and Other Business Enterprises with Regard to Human Rights, 2003

Note: The Norms on the Responsibilities of Transnational Corporations and Other Business Enterprises with Regard to Human Rights, 2003, are U.N. Doc. E/CN.4/Sub.2/2003/12/Rev.2 (2003) and were approved on 13 August 2003 by U.N. Sub-Commission on the Promotion and Protection of Human Rights Resolution 2003/16, U.N. Doc. E/CN.4/Sub.2/2003/L.11 at 52 (2003).

PREAMBLE

Bearing in mind the principles and obligations under the Charter of the United Nations, in particular the preamble and Articles 1, 2, 55 and 56, inter alia to promote universal respect for, and observance of, human rights and fundamental freedoms,

Recalling that the Universal Declaration of Human Rights proclaims a common standard of achievement for all peoples and all nations, to the end that Governments, other organs of society and individuals shall strive, by teaching and education to promote respect for human rights and freedoms, and, by progressive measures, to secure universal and effective recognition and observance, including of equal rights of women and men and the promotion of social progress and better standards of life in larger freedom,

Recognizing that even though States have the primary responsibility to promote, secure the fulfilment of, respect, ensure respect of and protect human rights, transnational corporations and other business enterprises, as organs of society, are also responsible for promoting and securing the human rights set forth in the Universal Declaration of Human Rights,

Realizing that transnational corporations and other business enterprises, their officers and persons working for them are also obligated to respect generally recognized responsibilities and norms contained in United Nations treaties and other international instruments such as the Convention on the Prevention and Punishment of the Crime of Genocide; the Convention against Torture and Other Cruel, Inhuman or Degrading Treatment or Punishment; the Slavery Convention and the Supplementary Convention on the Abolition of Slavery, the Slave Trade, and Institutions and Practices Similar to Slavery; the International Convention on the Elimination of All Forms of Racial Discrimination; the Convention on the Elimination of All Forms of Discrimination against Women; the International Covenant on Economic, Social and Cultural Rights; the International Covenant on Civil and Political Rights; the Convention on the Rights of the Child; the International Convention on the Protection of the Rights of All Migrant Workers and

Members of Their Families; the four Geneva Conventions of 12 August 1949 and two Additional Protocols thereto for the protection of victims of war; the Declaration on the Right and Responsibility of Individuals, Groups and Organs of Society to Promote and Protect Universally Recognized Human Rights and Fundamental Freedoms; the Rome Statute of the International Criminal Court; the United Nations Convention against Transnational Organized Crime; the Convention on Biological Diversity; the International Convention on Civil Liability for Oil Pollution Damage; the Convention on Civil Liability for Damage Resulting from Activities Dangerous to the Environment; the Declaration on the Right to Development; the Rio Declaration on the Environment and Development; the Plan of Implementation of the World Summit on Sustainable Development; the United Nations Millennium Declaration; the Universal Declaration on the Human Genome and Human Rights; the International Code of Marketing of Breast milk Substitutes adopted by the World Health Assembly; the Ethical Criteria for Medical Drug Promotion and the "Health for All in the Twenty-First Century" policy of the World Health Organization; the Convention against Discrimination in Education of the United Nations Education, Scientific, and Cultural Organization; conventions and recommendations of the International Labour Organization; the Convention and Protocol relating to the Status of Refugees; the African Charter on Human and Peoples' Rights; the American Convention on Human Rights; the European Convention for the Protection of Human Rights and Fundamental Freedoms; the Charter of Fundamental Rights of the European Union; the Convention on Combating Bribery of Foreign Public Officials in International Business Transactions of the Organization for Economic Cooperation and Development; and other instruments,

Taking into account the standards set forth in the Tripartite Declaration of Principles Concerning Multinational Enterprises and Social Policy and the Declaration on Fundamental Principles and Rights at Work of the International Labour Organization,

Aware of the Guidelines for Multinational Enterprises and the Committee on International Investment and Multinational Enterprises of the Organization for Economic Cooperation and Development,

Aware also of the United Nations Global Compact initiative which challenges business leaders to "embrace and enact" nine basic principles with respect to human rights, including labour rights and the environment,

Conscious of the fact that the Governing Body Subcommittee on Multinational Enterprises and Social Policy, the Committee of Experts on the Application of Standards, as well as the Committee on Freedom of Association of the International Labour Organization, which have named business enterprises implicated in States' failure to comply with Conventions No. 87 concerning the Freedom of Association and Protection of the Right to Organize and No. 98 concerning the Application of the Principles of the Right to Organize and Bargain Collectively, and seeking to supplement and assist their efforts to encourage transnational corporations and other business enterprises to protect human rights,

Conscious also of the Commentary on the Norms on the responsibilities of transnational corporations and other business enterprises with regard to human rights, and finding it a useful interpretation and elaboration of the standards contained in the Norms,

Taking note of global trends which have increased the influence of transnational corporations and other business enterprises on the economies of most countries and in international economic relations, and of the growing number of other business enterprises which operate across national boundaries in a variety of arrangements resulting in economic activities beyond the actual capacities of any one national system,

Noting that transnational corporations and other business enterprises have the capacity to foster economic well-being, development, technological improvement and wealth as well as the capacity to cause harmful impacts on the human rights and lives of individuals through their core business practices and operations, including employment practices, environmental policies, relationships with suppliers and consumers, interactions with Governments and other activities,

Noting also that new international human rights issues and concerns are continually emerging and that transnational corporations and other business enterprises often are involved in these issues and concerns, such that further standard-setting and implementation are required at this time and in the future,

Acknowledging the universality, indivisibility, interdependence and interrelatedness of human rights, including the right to development, which entitles every human person and all peoples to participate in, contribute to and enjoy economic, social, cultural and political development in which all human rights and fundamental freedoms can be fully realized,

Reaffirming that transnational corporations and other business enterprises, their officers – including managers, members of corporate boards or directors and other executives – and persons working for them have, inter alia, human rights obligations and responsibilities and that these human rights norms will contribute to the making and development of international law as to those responsibilities and obligations,

Solemnly proclaims these Norms on the Responsibilities of Transnational Corporations and Other Business Enterprises with Regard to Human Rights and urges that every effort be made so that they become generally known and respected.

A. GENERAL OBLIGATIONS

1. States have the primary responsibility to promote, secure the fulfilment of, respect, ensure respect of and protect human rights recognized in international as well as national law, including ensuring that transnational corporations and other business enterprises respect human rights. Within their respective spheres of activity and influence, transnational corporations and other business enterprises have the obligation to promote, secure the fulfilment of, respect, ensure respect of and protect human rights recognized in international as well as national law, including the rights and interests of indigenous peoples and other vulnerable groups.

B. RIGHT TO EQUAL OPPORTUNITY AND NON-DISCRIMINATORY TREATMENT

2. Transnational corporations and other business enterprises shall ensure equality of opportunity and treatment, as provided in the relevant international instruments and national legislation as well as international human rights law, for the purpose of eliminating discrimination based on race, colour, sex, language, religion, political opinion,

national or social origin, social status, indigenous status, disability, age – except for children, who may be given greater protection – or other status of the individual unrelated to the inherent requirements to perform the job, or of complying with special measures designed to overcome past discrimination against certain groups.

C. RIGHT TO SECURITY OF PERSONS

3. Transnational corporations and other business enterprises shall not engage in nor benefit from war crimes, crimes against humanity, genocide, torture, forced disappearance, forced or compulsory labour, hostage-taking, extrajudicial, summary or arbitrary executions, other violations of humanitarian law and other international crimes against the human person as defined by international law, in particular human rights and humanitarian law.
4. Security arrangements for transnational corporations and other business enterprises shall observe international human rights norms as well as the laws and professional standards of the country or countries in which they operate.

D. RIGHTS OF WORKERS

5. Transnational corporations and other business enterprises shall not use forced or compulsory labour as forbidden by the relevant international instruments and national legislation as well as international human rights and humanitarian law.
6. Transnational corporations and other business enterprises shall respect the rights of children to be protected from economic exploitation as forbidden by the relevant international instruments and national legislation as well as international human rights and humanitarian law.
7. Transnational corporations and other business enterprises shall provide a safe and healthy working environment as set forth in relevant international instruments and national legislation as well as international human rights and humanitarian law.
8. Transnational corporations and other business enterprises shall provide workers with remuneration that ensures an adequate standard of living for them and their families. Such remuneration shall take due account of their needs for adequate living conditions with a view towards progressive improvement.
9. Transnational corporations and other business enterprises shall ensure freedom of association and effective recognition of the right to collective bargaining by protecting the right to establish and, subject only to the rules of the organization concerned, to join organizations of their own choosing without distinction, previous authorization, or interference, for the protection of their employment interests and for other collective bargaining purposes as provided in national legislation and the relevant conventions of the International Labour Organization.

E. RESPECT FOR NATIONAL SOVEREIGNTY AND HUMAN RIGHTS

10. Transnational corporations and other business enterprises shall recognize and respect applicable norms of international law, national laws and regulations, as well as administrative practices, the rule of law, the public interest, development objectives,

social, economic and cultural policies including transparency, accountability and prohibition of corruption, and authority of the countries in which the enterprises operate.

11. Transnational corporations and other business enterprises shall not offer, promise, give, accept, condone, knowingly benefit from, or demand a bribe or other improper advantage, nor shall they be solicited or expected to give a bribe or other improper advantage to any Government, public official, candidate for elective post, any member of the armed forces or security forces, or any other individual or organization. Transnational corporations and other business enterprises shall refrain from any activity which supports, solicits, or encourages States or any other entities to abuse human rights. They shall further seek to ensure that the goods and services they provide will not be used to abuse human rights.

12. Transnational corporations and other business enterprises shall respect economic, social and cultural rights as well as civil and political rights and contribute to their realization, in particular the rights to development, adequate food and drinking water, the highest attainable standard of physical and mental health, adequate housing, privacy, education, freedom of thought, conscience, and religion and freedom of opinion and expression, and shall refrain from actions which obstruct or impede the realization of those rights.

F. OBLIGATIONS WITH REGARD TO CONSUMER PROTECTION

13. Transnational corporations and other business enterprises shall act in accordance with fair business, marketing and advertising practices and shall take all necessary steps to ensure the safety and quality of the goods and services they provide, including observance of the precautionary principle. Nor shall they produce, distribute, market, or advertise harmful or potentially harmful products for use by consumers.

G. OBLIGATIONS WITH REGARD TO ENVIRONMENTAL PROTECTION

14. Transnational corporations and other business enterprises shall carry out their activities in accordance with national laws, regulations, administrative practices and policies relating to the preservation of the environment of the countries in which they operate, as well as in accordance with relevant international agreements, principles, objectives, responsibilities and standards with regard to the environment as well as human rights, public health and safety, bioethics and the precautionary principle, and shall generally conduct their activities in a manner contributing to the wider goal of sustainable development.

H. GENERAL PROVISIONS OF IMPLEMENTATION

15. As an initial step towards implementing these Norms, each transnational corporation or other business enterprise shall adopt, disseminate and implement internal rules of operation in compliance with the Norms. Further, they shall periodically report on and take other measures fully to implement the Norms and to provide at least for the prompt implementation of the protections set forth in the Norms. Each

transnational corporation or other business enterprise shall apply and incorporate these Norms in their contracts or other arrangements and dealings with contractors, subcontractors, suppliers, licensees, distributors, or natural or other legal persons that enter into any agreement with the transnational corporation or business enterprise in order to ensure respect for and implementation of the Norms.

16. Transnational corporations and other businesses enterprises shall be subject to periodic monitoring and verification by United Nations, other international and national mechanisms already in existence or yet to be created, regarding application of the Norms. This monitoring shall be transparent and independent and take into account input from stakeholders (including non governmental organizations) and as a result of complaints of violations of these Norms. Further, transnational corporations and other businesses enterprises shall conduct periodic evaluations concerning the impact of their own activities on human rights under these Norms.

17. States should establish and reinforce the necessary legal and administrative framework for ensuring that the Norms and other relevant national and international laws are implemented by transnational corporations and other business enterprises.

18. Transnational corporations and other business enterprises shall provide prompt, effective and adequate reparation to those persons, entities and communities that have been adversely affected by failures to comply with these Norms through, inter alia, reparations, restitution, compensation and rehabilitation for any damage done or property taken. In connection with determining damages in regard to criminal sanctions, and in all other respects, these Norms shall be applied by national courts and/or international tribunals, pursuant to national and international law.

19. Nothing in these Norms shall be construed as diminishing, restricting, or adversely affecting the human rights obligations of States under national and international law, nor shall they be construed as diminishing, restricting, or adversely affecting more protective human rights norms, nor shall they be construed as diminishing, restricting, or adversely affecting other obligations or responsibilities of transnational corporations and other business enterprises in fields other than human rights.

I. DEFINITIONS

20. The term "transnational corporation" refers to an economic entity operating in more than one country or a cluster of economic entities operating in two or more countries – whatever their legal form, whether in their home country or country of activity, and whether taken individually or collectively.

21. The phrase "other business enterprise" includes any business entity, regardless of the international or domestic nature of its activities, including a transnational corporation, contractor, subcontractor, supplier, licensee or distributor; the corporate, partnership, or other legal form used to establish the business entity; and the nature of the ownership of the entity. These Norms shall be presumed to apply, as a matter of practice, if the business enterprise has any relation with a transnational corporation, the impact of its activities is not entirely local, or the activities involve violations of the right to security as indicated in paragraphs 3 and 4.

22. The term "stakeholder" includes stockholders, other owners, workers and their representatives, as well as any other individual or group that is affected by the activities

of transnational corporations or other business enterprises. The term "stakeholder" shall be interpreted functionally in the light of the objectives of these Norms and include indirect stakeholders when their interests are or will be substantially affected by the activities of the transnational corporation or business enterprise. In addition to parties directly affected by the activities of business enterprises, stakeholders can include parties which are indirectly affected by the activities of transnational corporations or other business enterprises such as consumer groups, customers, Governments, neighbouring communities, indigenous peoples and communities, nongovernmental organizations, public and private lending institutions, suppliers, trade associations, and others.

23. The phrases "human rights" and "international human rights" include civil, cultural, economic, political and social rights, as set forth in the International Bill of Human Rights and other human rights treaties, as well as the right to development and rights recognized by international humanitarian law, international refugee law, international labour law, and other relevant instruments adopted within the United Nations system.

40

United Nations Declaration on the Rights of Indigenous Peoples, 2007

Note: The Declaration on the Rights of Indigenous Peoples, was adopted on 13 September 2007 by General Assembly Resolution 61/295.

The General Assembly,

Taking note of the recommendation of the Human Rights Council contained in its resolution 1/2 of 29 June 2006, by which the Council adopted the text of the United Nations Declaration on the Rights of Indigenous Peoples,

Recalling its resolution 61/178 of 20 December 2006, by which it decided to defer consideration of and action on the Declaration to allow time for further consultations thereon, and also decided to conclude its consideration before the end of the sixty-first session of the General Assembly,

Adopts the United Nations Declaration on the Rights of Indigenous Peoples as contained in the annex to the present resolution.

ANNEX
UNITED NATIONS DECLARATION ON THE RIGHTS OF INDIGENOUS PEOPLES

The General Assembly,

Guided by the purposes and principles of the Charter of the United Nations, and good faith in the fulfilment of the obligations assumed by States in accordance with the Charter,

Affirming that indigenous peoples are equal to all other peoples, while recognizing the right of all peoples to be different, to consider themselves different, and to be respected as such,

Affirming also that all peoples contribute to the diversity and richness of civilizations and cultures, which constitute the common heritage of humankind,

Affirming further that all doctrines, policies and practices based on or advocating superiority of peoples or individuals on the basis of national origin or racial, religious, ethnic or cultural differences are racist, scientifically false, legally invalid, morally condemnable and socially unjust,

Reaffirming that indigenous peoples, in the exercise of their rights, should be free from discrimination of any kind,

Concerned that indigenous peoples have suffered from historic injustices as a result of, inter alia, their colonization and dispossession of their lands, territories and resources, thus preventing them from exercising, in particular, their right to development in accordance with their own needs and interests,

Recognizing the urgent need to respect and promote the inherent rights of indigenous peoples which derive from their political, economic and social structures and from their cultures, spiritual traditions, histories and philosophies, especially their rights to their lands, territories and resources,

Recognizing also the urgent need to respect and promote the rights of indigenous peoples affirmed in treaties, agreements and other constructive arrangements with States,

Welcoming the fact that indigenous peoples are organizing themselves for political, economic, social and cultural enhancement and in order to bring to an end all forms of discrimination and oppression wherever they occur,

Convinced that control by indigenous peoples over developments affecting them and their lands, territories and resources will enable them to maintain and strengthen their institutions, cultures and traditions, and to promote their development in accordance with their aspirations and needs,

Recognizing that respect for indigenous knowledge, cultures and traditional practices contributes to sustainable and equitable development and proper management of the environment,

Emphasizing the contribution of the demilitarization of the lands and territories of indigenous peoples to peace, economic and social progress and development, understanding and friendly relations among nations and peoples of the world,

Recognizing in particular the right of indigenous families and communities to retain shared responsibility for the upbringing, training, education and well-being of their children, consistent with the rights of the child,

Considering that the rights affirmed in treaties, agreements and other constructive arrangements between States and indigenous peoples are, in some situations, matters of international concern, interest, responsibility and character,

Considering also that treaties, agreements and other constructive arrangements, and the relationship they represent, are the basis for a strengthened partnership between indigenous peoples and States,

Acknowledging that the Charter of the United Nations, the International Covenant on Economic, Social and Cultural Rights and the International Covenant on Civil and Political Rights, as well as the Vienna Declaration and Programme of Action affirm the fundamental importance of the right to self-determination of all peoples, by virtue of which they freely determine their political status and freely pursue their economic, social and cultural development,

Bearing in mind that nothing in this Declaration may be used to deny any peoples their right to self-determination, exercised in conformity with international law,

Convinced that the recognition of the rights of indigenous peoples in this Declaration will enhance harmonious and cooperative relations between the State and indigenous peoples, based on principles of justice, democracy, respect for human rights, non-discrimination and good faith,

Encouraging States to comply with and effectively implement all their obligations as they apply to indigenous peoples under international instruments, in particular those related to human rights, in consultation and cooperation with the peoples concerned,

Emphasizing that the United Nations has an important and continuing role to play in promoting and protecting the rights of indigenous peoples,

Believing that this Declaration is a further important step forward for the recognition, promotion and protection of the rights and freedoms of indigenous peoples and in the development of relevant activities of the United Nations system in this field,

Recognizing and reaffirming that indigenous individuals are entitled without discrimination to all human rights recognized in international law, and that indigenous peoples possess collective rights which are indispensable for their existence, well-being and integral development as peoples,

Recognizing that the situation of indigenous peoples varies from region to region and from country to country and that the significance of national and regional particularities and various historical and cultural backgrounds should be taken into consideration,

Solemnly proclaims the following United Nations Declaration on the Rights of Indigenous Peoples as a standard of achievement to be pursued in a spirit of partnership and mutual respect:

Article 1
Indigenous peoples have the right to the full enjoyment, as a collective or as individuals, of all human rights and fundamental freedoms as recognized in the Charter of the United Nations, the Universal Declaration of Human Rights and international human rights law.

Article 2
Indigenous peoples and individuals are free and equal to all other peoples and individuals and have the right to be free from any kind of discrimination, in the exercise of their rights, in particular that based on their indigenous origin or identity.

Article 3
Indigenous peoples have the right to self-determination. By virtue of that right they freely determine their political status and freely pursue their economic, social and cultural development.

Article 4
Indigenous peoples, in exercising their right to self-determination, have the right to autonomy or self-government in matters relating to their internal and local affairs, as well as ways and means for financing their autonomous functions.

Article 5
Indigenous peoples have the right to maintain and strengthen their distinct political, legal, economic, social and cultural institutions, while retaining their right to participate fully, if they so choose, in the political, economic, social and cultural life of the State.

Article 6
Every indigenous individual has the right to a nationality.

Article 7
1. Indigenous individuals have the rights to life, physical and mental integrity, liberty and security of person.
2. Indigenous peoples have the collective right to live in freedom, peace and security as distinct peoples and shall not be subjected to any act of genocide or any other act of violence, including forcibly removing children of the group to another group.

Article 8

1. Indigenous peoples and individuals have the right not to be subjected to forced assimilation or destruction of their culture.
2. States shall provide effective mechanisms for prevention of, and redress for:
   (a) Any action which has the aim or effect of depriving them of their integrity as distinct peoples, or of their cultural values or ethnic identities;
   (b) Any action which has the aim or effect of dispossessing them of their lands, territories or resources;
   (c) Any form of forced population transfer which has the aim or effect of violating or undermining any of their rights;
   (d) Any form of forced assimilation or integration;
   (e) Any form of propaganda designed to promote or incite racial or ethnic discrimination directed against them.

Article 9

Indigenous peoples and individuals have the right to belong to an indigenous community or nation, in accordance with the traditions and customs of the community or nation concerned. No discrimination of any kind may arise from the exercise of such a right.

Article 10

Indigenous peoples shall not be forcibly removed from their lands or territories. No relocation shall take place without the free, prior and informed consent of the indigenous peoples concerned and after agreement on just and fair compensation and, where possible, with the option of return.

Article 11

1. Indigenous peoples have the right to practise and revitalize their cultural traditions and customs. This includes the right to maintain, protect and develop the past, present and future manifestations of their cultures, such as archaeological and historical sites, artefacts, designs, ceremonies, technologies and visual and performing arts and literature.
2. States shall provide redress through effective mechanisms, which may include restitution, developed in conjunction with indigenous peoples, with respect to their cultural, intellectual, religious and spiritual property taken without their free, prior and informed consent or in violation of their laws, traditions and customs.

Article 12

1. Indigenous peoples have the right to manifest, practise, develop and teach their spiritual and religious traditions, customs and ceremonies; the right to maintain, protect, and have access in privacy to their religious and cultural sites; the right to the use and control of their ceremonial objects; and the right to the repatriation of their human remains.
2. States shall seek to enable the access and/or repatriation of ceremonial objects and human remains in their possession through fair, transparent and effective mechanisms developed in conjunction with indigenous peoples concerned.

Article 13

1. Indigenous peoples have the right to revitalize, use, develop and transmit to future generations their histories, languages, oral traditions, philosophies, writing systems and literatures, and to designate and retain their own names for communities, places and persons.
2. States shall take effective measures to ensure that this right is protected and also to ensure that indigenous peoples can understand and be understood in political, legal and administrative proceedings, where necessary through the provision of interpretation or by other appropriate means.

Article 14

1. Indigenous peoples have the right to establish and control their educational systems and institutions providing education in their own languages, in a manner appropriate to their cultural methods of teaching and learning.
2. Indigenous individuals, particularly children, have the right to all levels and forms of education of the State without discrimination.
3. States shall, in conjunction with indigenous peoples, take effective measures, in order for indigenous individuals, particularly children, including those living outside their communities, to have access, when possible, to an education in their own culture and provided in their own language.

Article 15

1. Indigenous peoples have the right to the dignity and diversity of their cultures, traditions, histories and aspirations which shall be appropriately reflected in education and public information.
2. States shall take effective measures, in consultation and cooperation with the indigenous peoples concerned, to combat prejudice and eliminate discrimination and to promote tolerance, understanding and good relations among indigenous peoples and all other segments of society.

Article 16

1. Indigenous peoples have the right to establish their own media in their own languages and to have access to all forms of non-indigenous media without discrimination.
2. States shall take effective measures to ensure that State-owned media duly reflect indigenous cultural diversity. States, without prejudice to ensuring full freedom of expression, should encourage privately owned media to adequately reflect indigenous cultural diversity.

Article 17

1. Indigenous individuals and peoples have the right to enjoy fully all rights established under applicable international and domestic labour law.
2. States shall in consultation and cooperation with indigenous peoples take specific measures to protect indigenous children from economic exploitation and from performing any work that is likely to be hazardous or to interfere with the child's education, or to be harmful to the child's health or physical, mental, spiritual,

moral or social development, taking into account their special vulnerability and the importance of education for their empowerment.

3. Indigenous individuals have the right not to be subjected to any discriminatory conditions of labour and, inter alia, employment or salary.

Article 18

Indigenous peoples have the right to participate in decision-making in matters which would affect their rights, through representatives chosen by themselves in accordance with their own procedures, as well as to maintain and develop their own indigenous decision-making institutions.

Article 19

States shall consult and cooperate in good faith with the indigenous peoples concerned through their own representative institutions in order to obtain their free, prior and informed consent before adopting and implementing legislative or administrative measures that may affect them.

Article 20

1. Indigenous peoples have the right to maintain and develop their political, economic and social systems or institutions, to be secure in the enjoyment of their own means of subsistence and development, and to engage freely in all their traditional and other economic activities.
2. Indigenous peoples deprived of their means of subsistence and development are entitled to just and fair redress.

Article 21

1. Indigenous peoples have the right, without discrimination, to the improvement of their economic and social conditions, including, inter alia, in the areas of education, employment, vocational training and retraining, housing, sanitation, health and social security.
2. States shall take effective measures and, where appropriate, special measures to ensure continuing improvement of their economic and social conditions. Particular attention shall be paid to the rights and special needs of indigenous elders, women, youth, children and persons with disabilities.

Article 22

1. Particular attention shall be paid to the rights and special needs of indigenous elders, women, youth, children and persons with disabilities in the implementation of this Declaration.
2. States shall take measures, in conjunction with indigenous peoples, to ensure that indigenous women and children enjoy the full protection and guarantees against all forms of violence and discrimination.

Article 23

Indigenous peoples have the right to determine and develop priorities and strategies for exercising their right to development. In particular, indigenous peoples have the right to be actively involved in developing and determining health, housing and other economic and social programmes affecting them and, as far as possible, to administer such programmes through their own institutions.

Article 24

1. Indigenous peoples have the right to their traditional medicines and to maintain their health practices, including the conservation of their vital medicinal plants, animals and minerals. Indigenous individuals also have the right to access, without any discrimination, to all social and health services.
2. Indigenous individuals have an equal right to the enjoyment of the highest attainable standard of physical and mental health. States shall take the necessary steps with a view to achieving progressively the full realization of this right.

Article 25

Indigenous peoples have the right to maintain and strengthen their distinctive spiritual relationship with their traditionally owned or otherwise occupied and used lands, territories, waters and coastal seas and other resources and to uphold their responsibilities to future generations in this regard.

Article 26

1. Indigenous peoples have the right to the lands, territories and resources which they have traditionally owned, occupied or otherwise used or acquired.
2. Indigenous peoples have the right to own, use, develop and control the lands, territories and resources that they possess by reason of traditional ownership or other traditional occupation or use, as well as those which they have otherwise acquired.
3. States shall give legal recognition and protection to these lands, territories and resources. Such recognition shall be conducted with due respect to the customs, traditions and land tenure systems of the indigenous peoples concerned.

Article 27

States shall establish and implement, in conjunction with indigenous peoples concerned, a fair, independent, impartial, open and transparent process, giving due recognition to indigenous peoples' laws, traditions, customs and land tenure systems, to recognize and adjudicate the rights of indigenous peoples pertaining to their lands, territories and resources, including those which were traditionally owned or otherwise occupied or used. Indigenous peoples shall have the right to participate in this process.

Article 28

1. Indigenous peoples have the right to redress, by means that can include restitution or, when this is not possible, just, fair and equitable compensation, for the lands, territories and resources which they have traditionally owned or otherwise occupied or used, and which have been confiscated, taken, occupied, used or damaged without their free, prior and informed consent.
2. Unless otherwise freely agreed upon by the peoples concerned, compensation shall take the form of lands, territories and resources equal in quality, size and legal status or of monetary compensation or other appropriate redress.

Article 29

1. Indigenous peoples have the right to the conservation and protection of the environment and the productive capacity of their lands or territories and resources. States shall establish and implement assistance programmes for indigenous peoples for such conservation and protection, without discrimination.

2. States shall take effective measures to ensure that no storage or disposal of hazardous materials shall take place in the lands or territories of indigenous peoples without their free, prior and informed consent.

3. States shall also take effective measures to ensure, as needed, that programmes for monitoring, maintaining and restoring the health of indigenous peoples, as developed and implemented by the peoples affected by such materials, are duly implemented.

Article 30

1. Military activities shall not take place in the lands or territories of indigenous peoples, unless justified by a relevant public interest or otherwise freely agreed with or requested by the indigenous peoples concerned.

2. States shall undertake effective consultations with the indigenous peoples concerned, through appropriate procedures and in particular through their representative institutions, prior to using their lands or territories for military activities.

Article 31

1. Indigenous peoples have the right to maintain, control, protect and develop their cultural heritage, traditional knowledge and traditional cultural expressions, as well as the manifestations of their sciences, technologies and cultures, including human and genetic resources, seeds, medicines, knowledge of the properties of fauna and flora, oral traditions, literatures, designs, sports and traditional games and visual and performing arts. They also have the right to maintain, control, protect and develop their intellectual property over such cultural heritage, traditional knowledge, and traditional cultural expressions.

2. In conjunction with indigenous peoples, States shall take effective measures to recognize and protect the exercise of these rights.

Article 32

1. Indigenous peoples have the right to determine and develop priorities and strategies for the development or use of their lands or territories and other resources.

2. States shall consult and cooperate in good faith with the indigenous peoples concerned through their own representative institutions in order to obtain their free and informed consent prior to the approval of any project affecting their lands or territories and other resources, particularly in connection with the development, utilization or exploitation of mineral, water or other resources.

3. States shall provide effective mechanisms for just and fair redress for any such activities, and appropriate measures shall be taken to mitigate adverse environmental, economic, social, cultural or spiritual impact.

Article 33

1. Indigenous peoples have the right to determine their own identity or membership in accordance with their customs and traditions. This does not impair the right of indigenous individuals to obtain citizenship of the States in which they live.
2. Indigenous peoples have the right to determine the structures and to select the membership of their institutions in accordance with their own procedures.

Article 34

Indigenous peoples have the right to promote, develop and maintain their institutional structures and their distinctive customs, spirituality, traditions, procedures, practices and, in the cases where they exist, juridical systems or customs, in accordance with international human rights standards.

Article 35

Indigenous peoples have the right to determine the responsibilities of individuals to their communities.

Article 36

1. Indigenous peoples, in particular those divided by international borders, have the right to maintain and develop contacts, relations and cooperation, including activities for spiritual, cultural, political, economic and social purposes, with their own members as well as other peoples across borders.
2. States, in consultation and cooperation with indigenous peoples, shall take effective measures to facilitate the exercise and ensure the implementation of this right.

Article 37

1. Indigenous peoples have the right to the recognition, observance and enforcement of treaties, agreements and other constructive arrangements concluded with States or their successors and to have States honour and respect such treaties, agreements and other constructive arrangements.
2. Nothing in this Declaration may be interpreted as diminishing or eliminating the rights of indigenous peoples contained in treaties, agreements and other constructive arrangements.

Article 38

States, in consultation and cooperation with indigenous peoples, shall take the appropriate measures, including legislative measures, to achieve the ends of this Declaration.

Article 39

Indigenous peoples have the right to have access to financial and technical assistance from States and through international cooperation, for the enjoyment of the rights contained in this Declaration.

Article 40

Indigenous peoples have the right to access to and prompt decision through just and fair procedures for the resolution of conflicts and disputes with States or other parties, as well as to effective remedies for all infringements of their individual and collective rights. Such a decision shall give due consideration to the customs, traditions, rules and legal systems of the indigenous peoples concerned and international human rights.

Article 41

The organs and specialized agencies of the United Nations system and other intergovernmental organizations shall contribute to the full realization of the provisions of this Declaration through the mobilization, inter alia, of financial cooperation and technical assistance. Ways and means of ensuring participation of indigenous peoples on issues affecting them shall be established.

Article 42

The United Nations, its bodies, including the Permanent Forum on Indigenous Issues, and specialized agencies, including at the country level, and States shall promote respect for and full application of the provisions of this Declaration and follow up the effectiveness of this Declaration.

Article 43

The rights recognized herein constitute the minimum standards for the survival, dignity and well-being of the indigenous peoples of the world.

Article 44

All the rights and freedoms recognized herein are equally guaranteed to male and female indigenous individuals.

Article 45

Nothing in this Declaration may be construed as diminishing or extinguishing the rights indigenous peoples have now or may acquire in the future.

Article 46

1. Nothing in this Declaration may be interpreted as implying for any State, people, group or person any right to engage in any activity or to perform any act contrary to the Charter of the United Nations or construed as authorizing or encouraging any action which would dismember or impair, totally or in part, the territorial integrity or political unity of sovereign and independent States.
2. In the exercise of the rights enunciated in the present Declaration, human rights and fundamental freedoms of all shall be respected. The exercise of the rights set forth in this Declaration shall be subject only to such limitations as are determined by law and in accordance with international human rights obligations. Any such limitations shall be non-discriminatory and strictly necessary solely for the purpose of securing due recognition and respect for the rights and freedoms of others and for meeting the just and most compelling requirements of a democratic society.

41

Security Council Resolution 1674 (2006)

Note: Adopted by the Security Council at its 5430th meeting, 28 April 2006.

The Security Council,

Reaffirming its resolutions 1265 (1999) and 1296 (2000) on the protection of civilians in armed conflict, its various resolutions on children and armed conflict and on women, peace and security, as well as its resolution 1631 (2005) on cooperation between the United Nations and regional organizations in maintaining international peace and security, and further reaffirming its determination to ensure respect for, and follow-up to, these resolutions,

Reaffirming its commitment to the Purposes of the Charter of the United Nations as set out in Article 1 (1–4) of the Charter, and to the Principles of the Charter as set out in Article 2 (1–7) of the Charter, including its commitment to the principles of the political independence, sovereign equality and territorial integrity of all States, and respect for the sovereignty of all States,

Acknowledging that peace and security, development and human rights are the pillars of the United Nations system and the foundations for collective security and well-being, and recognizing in this regard that development, peace and security and human rights are interlinked and mutually reinforcing,

Expressing its deep regret that civilians account for the vast majority of casualties in situations of armed conflict,

Gravely concerned with the effects of the illicit exploitation and trafficking of natural resources, as well as the illicit trafficking of small arms and light weapons, and the use of such weapons on civilians affected by armed conflict,

Recognizing the important contribution to the protection of civilians in armed conflict by regional organizations, and acknowledging in this regard, the steps taken by the African Union,

Recognizing the important role that education can play in supporting efforts to halt and prevent abuses committed against civilians affected by armed conflict, in particular efforts to prevent sexual exploitation, trafficking in humans, and violations of applicable international law regarding the recruitment and rerecruitment of child soldiers,

Recalling the particular impact which armed conflict has on women and children, including as refugees and internally displaced persons, as well as on other civilians who may have specific vulnerabilities, and stressing the protection and assistance needs of all affected civilian populations,

Reaffirming that parties to armed conflict bear the primary responsibility to take all feasible steps to ensure the protection of affected civilians,

Bearing in mind its primary responsibility under the Charter of the United Nations for the maintenance of international peace and security, and underlining the importance of taking measures aimed at conflict prevention and resolution,

1. *Notes* with appreciation the contribution of the Report of the Secretary General of 28 November 2005 to its understanding of the issues surrounding the protection of civilians in armed conflict, and takes note of its conclusions;

2. *Emphasizes* the importance of preventing armed conflict and its recurrence, and stresses in this context the need for a comprehensive approach through promoting economic growth, poverty eradication, sustainable development, national reconciliation, good governance, democracy, the rule of law, and respect for, and protection of, human rights, and in this regard, urges the cooperation of Member States and underlines the importance of a coherent, comprehensive and coordinated approach by the principal organs of the United Nations, cooperating with one another and within their respective mandates;

3. *Recalls* that deliberately targeting civilians and other protected persons as such in situations of armed conflict is a flagrant violation of international humanitarian law, reiterates its condemnation in the strongest terms of such practices, and demands that all parties immediately put an end to such practices;

4. *Reaffirms* the provisions of paragraphs 138 and 139 of the 2005 World Summit Outcome Document regarding the responsibility to protect populations from genocide, war crimes, ethnic cleansing and crimes against humanity;

5. *Reaffirms* also its condemnation in the strongest terms of all acts of violence or abuses committed against civilians in situations of armed conflict in violation of applicable international obligations with respect in particular to (i) torture and other prohibited treatment, (ii) gender-based and sexual violence, (iii) violence against children, (iv) the recruitment and use of child soldiers, (v) trafficking in humans, (vi) forced displacement, and (vii) the intentional denial of humanitarian assistance, and demands that all parties put an end to such practices;

6. *Demands* that all parties concerned comply strictly with the obligations applicable to them under international law, in particular those contained in the Hague Conventions of 1899 and 1907 and in the Geneva Conventions of 1949 and their Additional Protocols of 1977, as well as with the decisions of the Security Council;

7. *Reaffirms* that ending impunity is essential if a society in conflict or recovering from conflict is to come to terms with past abuses committed against civilians affected by armed conflict and to prevent future such abuses, draws attention to the full range of justice and reconciliation mechanisms to be considered, including national, international and "mixed" criminal courts and tribunals and truth and reconciliation commissions, and notes that such mechanisms can promote not only individual responsibility for serious crimes, but also peace, truth, reconciliation and the rights of the victims;

8. *Emphasizes* in this context the responsibility of States to comply with their relevant obligations to end impunity and to prosecute those responsible for war crimes, genocide, crimes against humanity and serious violations of international humanitarian law, while recognizing, for States in or recovering from armed conflict, the need to restore or build independent national judicial systems and institutions;

9. *Calls* on States that have not already done so to consider ratifying the instruments of international humanitarian, human rights and refugee law, and to take appropriate legislative, judicial and administrative measures to implement their obligations under these instruments;

10. *Demands* that all States fully implement all relevant decisions of the Security Council, and in this regard cooperate fully with United Nations peacekeeping missions and country teams in the follow-up and implementation of these resolutions;

11. *Calls* upon all parties concerned to ensure that all peace processes, peace agreements and post-conflict recovery and reconstruction planning have regard for the special needs of women and children and include specific measures for the protection of civilians including (i) the cessation of attacks on civilians, (ii) the facilitation of the provision of humanitarian assistance, (iii) the creation of conditions conducive to the voluntary, safe, dignified and sustainable return of refugees and internally displaced persons, (iv) the facilitation of early access to education and training, (v) the re-establishment of the rule of law, and (vi) the ending of impunity;

12. *Recalls* the prohibition of the forcible displacement of civilians in situations of armed conflict under circumstances that are in violation of parties' obligations under international humanitarian law;

13. *Urges* the international community to provide support and assistance to enable States to fulfil their responsibilities regarding the protection of refugees and other persons protected under international humanitarian law;

14. *Reaffirms* the need to maintain the security and civilian character of refugee and internally displaced person camps, stresses the primary responsibility of States in this regard, and encourages the Secretary-General where necessary and in the context of existing peacekeeping operations and their respective mandates, to take all feasible measures to ensure security in and around such camps and of their inhabitants;

15. *Expresses* its intention of continuing its collaboration with the United Nations Emergency Relief Coordinator, and invites the Secretary-General to fully associate him from the earliest stages of the planning of United Nations peacekeeping and other relevant missions;

16. *Reaffirms* its practice of ensuring that the mandates of United Nations peacekeeping, political and peacebuilding missions include, where appropriate and on a case-by-case basis, provisions regarding (i) the protection of civilians, particularly those under imminent threat of physical danger within their zones of operation, (ii) the facilitation of the provision of humanitarian assistance, and (iii) the creation of conditions conducive to the voluntary, safe, dignified and sustainable return of refugees and internally displaced persons, and expresses its intention of ensuring that (i) such mandates include clear guidelines as to what missions can and should do to achieve those goals, (ii) the protection of civilians is given priority in decisions about the use of available capacity and resources, including information and intelligence resources, in the implementation of the mandates, and (iii) that protection mandates are implemented;

17. *Reaffirms* that, where appropriate, United Nations peacekeeping and other relevant missions should provide for the dissemination of information about international

humanitarian, human rights and refugee law and the application of relevant Security Council resolutions;

18. *Underscores* the importance of disarmament, demobilization and reintegration of ex-combatants (DDR) in the protection of civilians affected by armed conflict, and, in this regard, emphasizes (i) its support for the inclusion in mandates of United Nations peacekeeping and other relevant missions, where appropriate and on a case-by-case basis, of specific and effective measures for DDR, (ii) the importance of incorporating such activities into specific peace agreements, where appropriate and in consultation with the parties, and (iii) the importance of adequate resources being made available for the full completion of DDR programmes and activities;

19. *Condemns* in the strongest terms all sexual and other forms of violence committed against civilians in armed conflict, in particular women and children, and undertakes to ensure that all peace support operations employ all feasible measures to prevent such violence and to address its impact where it takes place;

20. *Condemns* in equally strong terms all acts of sexual exploitation, abuse and trafficking of women and children by military, police and civilian personnel involved in United Nations operations, welcomes the efforts undertaken by United Nations agencies and peacekeeping operations to implement a zero-tolerance policy in this regard, and requests the Secretary-General and personnel-contributing countries to continue to take all appropriate action necessary to combat these abuses by such personnel, including through the full implementation without delay of those measures adopted in the relevant General Assembly resolutions based upon the recommendations of the report of the Special Committee on Peacekeeping,

21. *Stresses* the importance for all, within the framework of humanitarian assistance, of upholding and respecting the humanitarian principles of humanity, neutrality, impartiality and independence;

22. *Urges* all those concerned as set forth in international humanitarian law, including the Geneva Conventions and the Hague Regulations, to allow full unimpeded access by humanitarian personnel to civilians in need of assistance in situations of armed conflict, and to make available, as far as possible, all necessary facilities for their operations, and to promote the safety, security and freedom of movement of humanitarian personnel and United Nations and its associated personnel and their assets;

23. *Condemns* all attacks deliberately targeting United Nations and associated personnel involved in humanitarian missions, as well as other humanitarian personnel, urges States on whose territory such attacks occur to prosecute or extradite those responsible, and welcomes in this regard the adoption on 8 December 2005 by the General Assembly of the Optional Protocol to the Convention on the Safety of United Nations and Associated Personnel;

24. *Recognizes* the increasingly valuable role that regional organizations and other intergovernmental institutions play in the protection of civilians, and encourages the Secretary-General and the heads of regional and other intergovernmental organizations to continue their efforts to strengthen their partnership in this regard;

25. *Reiterates* its invitation to the Secretary-General to continue to refer to the Council relevant information and analysis regarding the protection of civilians where he believes that such information or analysis could contribute to the resolution of issues before it,

requests him to continue to include in his written reports to the Council on matters of which it is seized, as appropriate, observations relating to the protection of civilians in armed conflict, and encourages him to continue consultations and take concrete steps to enhance the capacity of the United Nations in this regard;

26. *Notes* that the deliberate targeting of civilians and other protected persons, and the commission of systematic, flagrant and widespread violations of international humanitarian and human rights law in situations of armed conflict, may constitute a threat to international peace and security, and, reaffirms in this regard its readiness to consider such situations and, where necessary, to adopt appropriate steps;

27. *Requests* the Secretary-General to submit his next report on the protection of civilians in armed conflict within 18 months of the date of this resolution;

28. *Decides* to remain seized of the matter.

42

UN Guiding Principles on Business and Human Rights: Implementing the United Nations "Protect, Respect and Remedy" Framework, 2011

Note: Report of the Special Representative of the Secretary General on the issue of human rights and transnational corporations and other business enterprises, John Ruggie, 21 March 2011, A/HRC/17/31. The Human Rights Council endorsed the Guiding Principles in Resolution 17/4, 16 June 2011. The principles have been reproduced without the commentary.

GENERAL PRINCIPLES

These Guiding Principles are grounded in recognition of:
  (a) States' existing obligations to respect, protect and fulfil human rights and fundamental freedoms;
  (b) The role of business enterprises as specialized organs of society performing specialized functions, required to comply with all applicable laws and to respect human rights;
  (c) The need for rights and obligations to be matched to appropriate and effective remedies when breached.

These Guiding Principles apply to all States and to all business enterprises, both transnational and others, regardless of their size, sector, location, ownership and structure.

These Guiding Principles should be understood as a coherent whole and should be read, individually and collectively, in terms of their objective of enhancing standards and practices with regard to business and human rights so as to achieve tangible results for affected individuals and communities, and thereby also contributing to a socially sustainable globalization.

Nothing in these Guiding Principles should be read as creating new international law obligations, or as limiting or undermining any legal obligations a State may have undertaken or be subject to under international law with regard to human rights.

These Guiding Principles should be implemented in a non-discriminatory manner, with particular attention to the rights and needs of, as well as the challenges faced by, individuals from groups or populations that may be at heightened risk of becoming vulnerable or marginalized, and with due regard to the different risks that may be faced by women and men.

I. THE STATE DUTY TO PROTECT HUMAN RIGHTS

A. Foundational principles

1. States must protect against human rights abuse within their territory and/or jurisdiction by third parties, including business enterprises. This requires taking appropriate steps to prevent, investigate, punish and redress such abuse through effective policies, legislation, regulations and adjudication.
2. States should set out clearly the expectation that all business enterprises domiciled in their territory and/or jurisdiction respect human rights throughout their operations.

B. Operational principles

General State regulatory and policy functions

3. In meeting their duty to protect, States should:
   (a) Enforce laws that are aimed at, or have the effect of, requiring business enterprises to respect human rights, and periodically to assess the adequacy of such laws and address any gaps;
   (b) Ensure that other laws and policies governing the creation and ongoing operation of business enterprises, such as corporate law, do not constrain but enable business respect for human rights;
   (c) Provide effective guidance to business enterprises on how to respect human rights throughout their operations;
   (d) Encourage, and where appropriate require, business enterprises to communicate how they address their human rights impacts.

The State-business nexus

4. States should take additional steps to protect against human rights abuses by business enterprises that are owned or controlled by the State, or that receive substantial support and services from State agencies such as export credit agencies and official investment insurance or guarantee agencies, including, where appropriate, by requiring human rights due diligence.
5. States should exercise adequate oversight in order to meet their international human rights obligations when they contract with, or legislate for, business enterprises to provide services that may impact upon the enjoyment of human rights.
6. States should promote respect for human rights by business enterprises with which they conduct commercial transactions.

Supporting business respect for human rights in conflict affected areas

7. Because the risk of gross human rights abuses is heightened in conflict affected areas, States should help ensure that business enterprises operating in those contexts are not involved with such abuses, including by:
   (a) Engaging at the earliest stage possible with business enterprises to help them identify, prevent and mitigate the human rights-related risks of their activities and business relationships;
   (b) Providing adequate assistance to business enterprises to assess and address the heightened risks of abuses, paying special attention to both gender-based and sexual violence;

    (c) Denying access to public support and services for a business enterprise that is involved with gross human rights abuses and refuses to cooperate in addressing the situation;

    (d) Ensuring that their current policies, legislation, regulations and enforcement measures are effective in addressing the risk of business involvement in gross human rights abuses.

Ensuring policy coherence

8. States should ensure that governmental departments, agencies and other State-based institutions that shape business practices are aware of and observe the State's human rights obligations when fulfilling their respective mandates, including by providing them with relevant information, training and support.

9. States should maintain adequate domestic policy space to meet their human rights obligations when pursuing business-related policy objectives with other States or business enterprises, for instance through investment treaties or contracts.

10. States, when acting as members of multilateral institutions that deal with business-related issues, should:

    (a) Seek to ensure that those institutions neither restrain the ability of their member States to meet their duty to protect nor hinder business enterprises from respecting human rights;

    (b) Encourage those institutions, within their respective mandates and capacities, to promote business respect for human rights and, where requested, to help States meet their duty to protect against human rights abuse by business enterprises, including through technical assistance, capacity-building and awareness-raising;

    (c) Draw on these Guiding Principles to promote shared understanding and advance international cooperation in the management of business and human rights challenges.

II. THE CORPORATE RESPONSIBILITY TO RESPECT HUMAN RIGHTS

A. Foundational principles

11. Business enterprises should respect human rights. This means that they should avoid infringing on the human rights of others and should address adverse human rights impacts with which they are involved.

12. The responsibility of business enterprises to respect human rights refers to internationally recognized human rights – understood, at a minimum, as those expressed in the International Bill of Human Rights and the principles concerning fundamental rights set out in the International Labour Organization's Declaration on Fundamental Principles and Rights at Work.

13. The responsibility to respect human rights requires that business enterprises:

    (a) Avoid causing or contributing to adverse human rights impacts through their own activities, and address such impacts when they occur;

    (b) Seek to prevent or mitigate adverse human rights impacts that are directly linked to their operations, products or services by their business relationships, even if they have not contributed to those impacts.

14. The responsibility of business enterprises to respect human rights applies to all enterprises regardless of their size, sector, operational context, ownership and structure.

Nevertheless, the scale and complexity of the means through which enterprises meet that responsibility may vary according to these factors and with the severity of the enterprise's adverse human rights impacts.

15. In order to meet their responsibility to respect human rights, business enterprises should have in place policies and processes appropriate to their size and circumstances, including:

   (a) A policy commitment to meet their responsibility to respect human rights;

   (b) A human rights due diligence process to identify, prevent, mitigate and account for how they address their impacts on human rights;

   (c) Processes to enable the remediation of any adverse human rights impacts they cause or to which they contribute.

B. Operational principles

Policy commitment

16. As the basis for embedding their responsibility to respect human rights, business enterprises should express their commitment to meet this responsibility through a statement of policy that:

   (a) Is approved at the most senior level of the business enterprise;

   (b) Is informed by relevant internal and/or external expertise;

   (c) Stipulates the enterprise's human rights expectations of personnel, business partners and other parties directly linked to its operations, products or services;

   (d) Is publicly available and communicated internally and externally to all personnel, business partners and other relevant parties;

   (e) Is reflected in operational policies and procedures necessary to embed it throughout the business enterprise.

Human rights due diligence

17. In order to identify, prevent, mitigate and account for how they address their adverse human rights impacts, business enterprises should carry out human rights due diligence. The process should include assessing actual and potential human rights impacts, integrating and acting upon the findings, tracking responses, and communicating how impacts are addressed. Human rights due diligence:

   (a) Should cover adverse human rights impacts that the business enterprise may cause or contribute to through its own activities, or which may be directly linked to its operations, products or services by its business relationships;

   (b) Will vary in complexity with the size of the business enterprise, the risk of severe human rights impacts, and the nature and context of its operations;

   (c) Should be ongoing, recognizing that the human rights risks may change over time as the business enterprise's operations and operating context evolve.

18. In order to gauge human rights risks, business enterprises should identify and assess any actual or potential adverse human rights impacts with which they may be involved either through their own activities or as a result of their business relationships. This process should:

   (a) Draw on internal and/or independent external human rights expertise;

   (b) Involve meaningful consultation with potentially affected groups and other relevant stakeholders, as appropriate to the size of the business enterprise and the nature and context of the operation.

19. In order to prevent and mitigate adverse human rights impacts, business enterprises should integrate the findings from their impact assessments across relevant internal functions and processes, and take appropriate action.
    (a) Effective integration requires that:
        (i) Responsibility for addressing such impacts is assigned to the appropriate level and function within the business enterprise;
        (ii) Internal decision-making, budget allocations and oversight processes enable effective responses to such impacts.
    (b) Appropriate action will vary according to:
        (i) Whether the business enterprise causes or contributes to an adverse impact, or whether it is involved solely because the impact is directly linked to its operations, products or services by a business relationship;
        (ii) The extent of its leverage in addressing the adverse impact.
20. In order to verify whether adverse human rights impacts are being addressed, business enterprises should track the effectiveness of their response. Tracking should:
    (a) Be based on appropriate qualitative and quantitative indicators;
    (b) Draw on feedback from both internal and external sources, including affected stakeholders.
21. In order to account for how they address their human rights impacts, business enterprises should be prepared to communicate this externally, particularly when concerns are raised by or on behalf of affected stakeholders. Business enterprises whose operations or operating contexts pose risks of severe human rights impacts should report formally on how they address them. In all instances, communications should:
    (a) Be of a form and frequency that reflect an enterprise's human rights impacts and that are accessible to its intended audiences;
    (b) Provide information that is sufficient to evaluate the adequacy of an enterprise's response to the particular human rights impact involved;
    (c) In turn not pose risks to affected stakeholders, personnel or to legitimate requirements of commercial confidentiality.

Remediation
22. Where business enterprises identify that they have caused or contributed to adverse impacts, they should provide for or cooperate in their remediation through legitimate processes.

Issues of context
23. In all contexts, business enterprises should:
    (a) Comply with all applicable laws and respect internationally recognized human rights, wherever they operate;
    (b) Seek ways to honour the principles of internationally recognized human rights when faced with conflicting requirements;
    (c) Treat the risk of causing or contributing to gross human rights abuses as a legal compliance issue wherever they operate.
24. Where it is necessary to prioritize actions to address actual and potential adverse human rights impacts, business enterprises should first seek to prevent and mitigate those that are most severe or where delayed response would make them irremediable.

III. ACCESS TO REMEDY

A. Foundational principle

25. As part of their duty to protect against business-related human rights abuse, States must take appropriate steps to ensure, through judicial, administrative, legislative or other appropriate means, that when such abuses occur within their territory and/or jurisdiction those affected have access to effective remedy.

B. Operational principles

State-based judicial mechanisms

26. States should take appropriate steps to ensure the effectiveness of domestic judicial mechanisms when addressing business-related human rights abuses, including considering ways to reduce legal, practical and other relevant barriers that could lead to a denial of access to remedy.

27. States should provide effective and appropriate non-judicial grievance mechanisms, alongside judicial mechanisms, as part of a comprehensive State-based system for the remedy of business-related human rights abuse.

28. States should consider ways to facilitate access to effective non-State based grievance mechanisms dealing with business-related human rights harms.

29. To make it possible for grievances to be addressed early and remediated directly, business enterprises should establish or participate in effective operational-level grievance mechanisms for individuals and communities who may be adversely impacted.

30. Industry, multi-stakeholder and other collaborative initiatives that are based on respect for human rights-related standards should ensure that effective grievance mechanisms are available.

Effectiveness criteria for non-judicial grievance mechanisms

31. In order to ensure their effectiveness, non-judicial grievance mechanisms, both State-based and non-State-based, should be:
    (a) Legitimate: enabling trust from the stakeholder groups for whose use they are intended, and being accountable for the fair conduct of grievance processes;
    (b) Accessible: being known to all stakeholder groups for whose use they are intended, and providing adequate assistance for those who may face particular barriers to access;
    (c) Predictable: providing a clear and known procedure with an indicative time frame for each stage, and clarity on the types of process and outcome available and means of monitoring implementation;
    (d) Equitable: seeking to ensure that aggrieved parties have reasonable access to sources of information, advice and expertise necessary to engage in a grievance process on fair, informed and respectful terms;
    (e) Transparent: keeping parties to a grievance informed about its progress, and providing sufficient information about the mechanism's performance to build confidence in its effectiveness and meet any public interest at stake;

(f) Rights-compatible: ensuring that outcomes and remedies accord with internationally recognized human rights;

(g) A source of continuous learning: drawing on relevant measures to identify lessons for improving the mechanism and preventing future grievances and harms;

Operational-level mechanisms should also be:

(h) Based on engagement and dialogue: consulting the stakeholder groups for whose use they are intended on their design and performance, and focusing on dialogue as the means to address and resolve grievances.

PART III
UN Human Rights Institutions and Complaints Mechanisms and Procedures

43

Statute of the Office of the United Nations High Commissioner for Refugees, 1950

Note: The Statute of the High Commissioner is the Annex to General Assembly Resolution 428 (V) of 14 December 1950, UN Document A/1775 (1950).

THE GENERAL ASSEMBLY

In view of its resolution 319 A (IV) of 3 December 1949,

1. Adopts the annex to the present resolution, being the Statute of the Office of the United Nations High Commissioner for Refugees;

2. Calls upon Governments to co-operate with the United Nations High Commissioner for Refugees in the performance of his functions concerning refugees falling under the competence of his Office, especially by:

    (a) Becoming parties to international conventions providing for the protection of refugees, and taking the necessary steps of implementation under such conventions;

    (b) Entering into special agreements with the High Commissioner for the execution of measures calculated to improve the situation of refugees and to reduce the number requiring protection;

    (c) Admitting refugees to their territories, not excluding those in the most destitute categories;

    (d) Assisting the High Commissioner in his efforts to promote the voluntary repatriation of refugees;

    (e) Promoting the assimilation of refugees, especially by facilitating their naturalization;

    (f) Providing refugees with travel and other documents such as would normally be provided to other aliens by their national authorities, especially documents which would facilitate their resettlement;

    (g) Permitting refugees to transfer their assets and especially those necessary for their resettlement;

    (h) Providing the High Commissioner with information concerning the number and condition of refugees, and laws and regulations concerning them.

3. Requests the Secretary-General to transmit the present resolution, together with the annex attached thereto, also to States non-members of the United Nations, with a view to obtaining their co-operation in its implementation.

ANNEX
STATUTE OF THE OFFICE OF THE UNITED NATIONS HIGH COMMISSIONER FOR REFUGEES

Chapter I General Provisions

1. The United Nations High Commissioner for Refugees, acting under the authority of the General Assembly, shall assume the function of providing international protection, under the auspices of the United Nations, to refugees who fall within the scope of the present Statute and of seeking permanent solutions for the problem of refugees by assisting Governments and, subject to the approval of the Governments concerned, private organizations to facilitate the voluntary repatriation of such refugees, or their assimilation within new national communities. In the exercise of his functions, more particularly when difficulties arise, and for instance with regard to any controversy concerning the international status of these persons, the High Commissioner shall request the opinion of the advisory committee on refugees if it is created.

2. The work of the High Commissioner shall be of an entirely non-political character; it shall be humanitarian and social and shall relate, as a rule, to groups and categories of refugees.

3. The High Commissioner shall follow policy directives given him by the General Assembly or the Economic and Social Council.

4. The Economic and Social Council may decide, after hearing the views of the High Commissioner on the subject, to establish an advisory committee on refugees, which shall consist of representatives of States Members and States non-members of the United Nations, to be selected by the Council on the basis of their demonstrated interest in and devotion to the solution of the refugee problem.

5. The General Assembly shall review, not later than at its eighth regular session, the arrangements for the Office of the High Commissioner with a view to determining whether the Office should be continued beyond 31 December 1953.

Chapter II Functions of the High Commissioner

6. The competence of the High Commissioner shall extend to:

   A. (i) Any person who has been considered a refugee under the Arrangements of 12 May 1926 and of 30 June 1928 or under the Conventions of 28 October 1933 and 10 February 1938, the Protocol of 14 September 1939 or the Constitution of the International Refugee Organization.

   (ii) Any person who, as a result of events occurring before 1 January 1951 and owing to well-founded fear of being persecuted for reasons of race, religion, nationality or political opinion, is outside the country of his nationality and is unable or, owing to such fear or for reasons other than personal convenience, is unwilling to avail himself of the protection of that country; or who, not having a nationality and being outside the country of his former habitual residence, is unable or, owing to such fear or for reasons other than personal convenience, is unwilling to return to it.

   Decisions as to eligibility taken by the International Refugee Organization during the period of its activities shall not prevent the status of refugee being accorded to persons who fulfil the conditions of the present paragraph;

   The competence of the High Commissioner shall cease to apply to any person defined in section A above if:

(a) He has voluntarily re-availed himself of the protection of the country of his nationality; or

(b) Having lost his nationality, he has voluntarily re-acquired it; or

(c) He has acquired a new nationality, and enjoys the protection of the country of his new nationality; or

(d) He has voluntarily re-established himself in the country which he left or outside which he remained owing to fear of persecution; or

(e) He can no longer, because the circumstances in connexion with which he has been recognized as a refugee have ceased to exist, claim grounds other than those of personal convenience for continuing to refuse to avail himself of the protection of the country of his nationality. Reasons of a purely economic character may not be invoked; or

(f) Being a person who has no nationality, he can no longer, because the circumstances in connexion with which he has been recognized as a refugee have ceased to exist and he is able to return to the country of his former habitual residence, claim grounds other than those of personal convenience for continuing to refuse to return to that country;

B. Any other person who is outside the country of his nationality, or if he has no nationality, the country of his former habitual residence, because he has or had well-founded fear of persecution by reason of his race, religion, nationality or political opinion and is unable or, because of such fear, is unwilling to avail himself of the protection of the government of the country of his nationality, or, if he has no nationality, to return to the country of his former habitual residence.

7. Provided that the competence of the High Commissioner as defined in paragraph 6 above shall not extend to a person:

(a) Who is a national of more than one country unless he satisfies the provisions of the preceding paragraph in relation to each of the countries of which he is a national; or

(b) Who is recognized by the competent authorities of the country in which he has taken residence as having the rights and obligations which are attached to the possession of the nationality of that country; or

(c) Who continues to receive from other organs or agencies of the United Nations protection or assistance; or

(d) In respect of whom there are serious reasons for considering that he has committed a crime covered by the provisions of treaties of extradition or a crime mentioned in article VI of the London Charter of the International Military Tribunal or by the provisions of article 14, paragraph 2, of the Universal Declaration of Human Rights.

8. The High Commissioner shall provide for the protection of refugees falling under the competence of his Office by:

(a) Promoting the conclusion and ratification of international conventions for the protection of refugees, supervising their application and proposing amendments thereto;

(b) Promoting through special agreements with Governments the execution of any measures calculated to improve the situation of refugees and to reduce the number requiring protection;

(c) Assisting governmental and private efforts to promote voluntary repatriation or assimilation within new national communities;

(d) Promoting the admission of refugees, not excluding those in the most destitute categories, to the territories of States;

(e) Endeavouring to obtain permission for refugees to transfer their assets and especially those necessary for their resettlement;

(f) Obtaining from Governments information concerning the number and conditions of refugees in their territories and the laws and regulations concerning them;

(g) Keeping in close touch with the Governments and inter-governmental organizations concerned;

(h) Establishing contact in such manner as he may think best with private organizations dealing with refugee questions;

(i) Facilitating the co-ordination of the efforts of private organizations concerned with the welfare of refugees.

9. The High Commissioner shall engage in such additional activities, including repatriation and resettlement, as the General Assembly may determine, within the limits of the resources placed at his disposal.

10. The High Commissioner shall administer any funds, public or private, which he receives for assistance to refugees, and shall distribute them among the private and, as appropriate, public agencies which he deems best qualified to administer such assistance.

The High Commissioner may reject any offers which he does not consider appropriate or which cannot be utilized.

The High Commissioner shall not appeal to Governments for funds or make a general appeal, without the prior approval of the General Assembly.

The High Commissioner shall include in his annual report a statement of his activities in this field.

11. The High Commissioner shall be entitled to present his views before the General Assembly, the Economic and Social Council and their subsidiary bodies.

The High Commissioner shall report annually to the General Assembly through the Economic and Social Council; his report shall be considered as a separate item on the agenda of the General Assembly.

12. The High Commissioner may invite the co-operation of the various specialized agencies.

Chapter III Organization and finances

13. The High Commissioner shall be elected by the General Assembly on the nomination of the Secretary-General. The terms of appointment of the High Commissioner shall be proposed by the Secretary-General and approved by the General Assembly. The High Commissioner shall be elected for a term of three years, from 1 January 1951.

14. The High Commissioner shall appoint, for the same term, a Deputy High Commissioner of a nationality other than his own.

15. (a) Within the limits of the budgetary appropriations provided, the staff of the Office of the High Commissioner shall be appointed by the High Commissioner and shall be responsible to him in the exercise of their functions.

(b) Such staff shall be chosen from persons devoted to the purposes of the Office of the High Commissioner.

(c) Their conditions of employment shall be those provided under the staff regulations adopted by the General Assembly and the rules promulgated thereunder by the Secretary-General.

(d) Provision may also be made to permit the employment of personnel without compensation.

16. The High Commissioner shall consult the Government of the countries of residence of refugees as to the need for appointing representatives therein.

In any country recognizing such need, there may be appointed a representative approved by the Government of that country. Subject to the foregoing, the same representative may serve in more than one country.

17. The High Commissioner and the Secretary-General shall make appropriate arrangements for liaison and consultation on matters of mutual interest.

18. The Secretary-General shall provide the High Commissioner with all necessary facilities within budgetary limitations.

19. The Office of the High Commissioner shall be located in Geneva, Switzerland.

20. The Office of the High Commissioner shall be financed under the budget of the United Nations. Unless the General Assembly subsequently decides otherwise, no expenditure other than administrative expenditures relating to the functioning of the Office of the High Commissioner shall be borne on the budget of the United Nations and all other expenditures relating to the activities of the High Commissioner shall be financed by voluntary contributions.

21. The administration of the Office of the High Commissioner shall be subject to the Financial Regulations of the United Nations and to the financial rules promulgated thereunder by the Secretary-General.

22. Transactions relating to the High Commissioner's funds shall be subject to audit by the United Nations Board of Auditors, provided that the Board may accept audited accounts from the agencies to which funds have been allocated. Administrative arrangements for the custody of such funds and their allocation shall be agreed between the High Commissioner and the Secretary-General in accordance with the Financial Regulations of the United Nations and rules promulgated thereunder by the Secretary-General.

44

High Commissioner for the Promotion and Protection of All Human Rights, 1993

Note: the post of the High Commissioner for Human Rights was created by General Assembly Resolution A/RES/48/141 adopted on 20 December 1993.

The General Assembly,

Reaffirming its commitment to the purposes and principles of the Charter of the United Nations,

Emphasizing the responsibilities of all States, in conformity with the Charter, to promote and encourage respect for all human rights and fundamental freedoms for all, without distinction as to race, sex, language or religion,

Emphasizing the need to observe the Universal Declaration of Human Rights and for the full implementation of the human rights instruments, including the International Covenant on Civil and Political Rights, the International Covenant on Economic, Social and Cultural Rights, as well as the Declaration on the Right to Development,

Reaffirming that the right to development is a universal and inalienable right which is a fundamental part of the rights of the human person,

Considering that the promotion and the protection of all human rights is one of the priorities of the international community,

Recalling that one of the purposes of the United Nations enshrined in the Charter is to achieve international cooperation in promoting and encouraging respect for human rights,

Reaffirming the commitment made under Article 56 of the Charter to take joint and separate action in cooperation with the United Nations for the achievement of the purposes set forth in Article 55 of the Charter,

Emphasizing the need for the promotion and protection of all human rights to be guided by the principles of impartiality, objectivity and non-selectivity, in the spirit of constructive international dialogue and cooperation,

Aware that all human rights are universal, indivisible, interdependent and interrelated and that as such they should be given the same emphasis,

Affirming its commitment to the Vienna Declaration and Programme of Action, adopted by the World Conference on Human Rights, held at Vienna from 14 to 25 June 1993,

Convinced that the World Conference on Human Rights made an important contribution to the cause of human rights and that its recommendations should be implemented through effective action by all States, the competent organs of the United Nations and the specialized agencies, in cooperation with non-governmental organizations,

Acknowledging the importance of strengthening the provision of advisory services and technical assistance by the Centre for Human Rights of the Secretariat and other relevant programmes and bodies of the United Nations system for the purpose of the promotion and protection of all human rights,

Determined to adapt, strengthen and streamline the existing mechanisms to promote and protect all human rights and fundamental freedoms while avoiding unnecessary duplication,

Recognizing that the activities of the United Nations in the field of human rights should be rationalized and enhanced in order to strengthen the United Nations machinery in this field and to further the objectives of universal respect for observance of international human rights standards,

Reaffirming that the General Assembly, the Economic and Social Council and the Commission on Human Rights are the responsible organs for decision-and policy-making for the promotion and protection of all human rights,

Reaffirming the necessity for a continued adaptation of the United Nations human rights machinery to the current and future needs in the promotion and protection of human rights and the need to improve its coordination, efficiency and effectiveness, as reflected in the Vienna Declaration and Programme of Action and within the framework of a balanced and sustainable development for all people,

Having considered the recommendation contained in paragraph 18 of section II of the Vienna Declaration and Programme of Action,

1. Decides to create the post of the High Commissioner for Human Rights;
2. Decides that the High Commissioner for Human Rights shall:
    (a) Be a person of high moral standing and personal integrity and shall possess expertise, including in the field of human rights, and the general knowledge and understanding of diverse cultures necessary for impartial, objective, non-selective and effective performance of the duties of the High Commissioner;
    (b) Be appointed by the Secretary-General of the United Nations and approved by the General Assembly, with due regard to geographical rotation, and have a fixed term of four years with a possibility of one renewal for another fixed term of four years;
    (c) Be of the rank of Under-Secretary-General;
3. Decides that the High Commissioner for Human Rights shall:
    (a) Function within the framework of the Charter of the United Nations, the Universal Declaration of Human Rights, other international instruments of human rights and international law, including the obligations, within this framework, to respect the sovereignty, territorial integrity and domestic jurisdiction of States and to promote the universal respect for and observance of all human rights, in the recognition that, in the framework of the purposes and principles of the Charter, the promotion and protection of all human rights is a legitimate concern of the international community;
    (b) Be guided by the recognition that all human rights – civil, cultural, economic, political and social – are universal, indivisible, interdependent and interrelated and that, while the significance of national and regional particularities and various historical, cultural and religious backgrounds must be borne in mind, it is the duty of States, regardless of their political, economic and cultural systems, to promote and protect all human rights and fundamental freedoms;
    (c) Recognize the importance of promoting a balanced and sustainable development for all people and of ensuring realization of the right to development, as established in the Declaration on the Right to Development;

4. <u>Decides</u> that the High Commissioner for Human Rights shall be the United Nations official with principal responsibility for United Nations human rights activities under the direction and authority of the Secretary-General; within the framework of the overall competence, authority and decisions of the General Assembly, the Economic and Social Council and the Commission on Human Rights, the High Commissioner's responsibilities shall be:

(a) To promote and protect the effective enjoyment by all of all civil, cultural, economic, political and social rights;

(b) To carry out the tasks assigned to him/her by the competent bodies of the United Nations system in the field of human rights and to make recommendations to them with a view to improving the promotion and protection of all human rights;

(c) To promote and protect the realization of the right to development and to enhance support from relevant bodies of the United Nations system for this purpose;

(d) To provide, through the Centre for Human Rights of the Secretariat and other appropriate institutions, advisory services and technical and financial assistance, at the request of the State concerned and, where appropriate, the regional human rights organizations, with a view to supporting actions and programmes in the field of human rights;

(e) To coordinate relevant United Nations education and public information programmes in the field of human rights;

(f) To play an active role in removing the current obstacles and in meeting the challenges to the full realization of all human rights and in preventing the continuation of human rights violations throughout the world, as reflected in the Vienna Declaration and Programme of Action;

(g) To engage in a dialogue with all Governments in the implementation of his/her mandate with a view to securing respect for all human rights;

(h) To enhance international cooperation for the promotion and protection of all human rights;

(i) To coordinate the human rights promotion and protection activities throughout the United Nations system;

(j) To rationalize, adapt, strengthen and streamline the United Nations machinery in the field of human rights with a view to improving its efficiency and effectiveness;

(k) To carry out overall supervision of the Centre for Human Rights;

5. <u>Requests</u> the High Commissioner for Human Rights to report annually on his/her activities, in accordance with his/her mandate, to the Commission on Human Rights and, through the Economic and Social Council, to the General Assembly;

6. <u>Decides</u> that the Office of the High Commissioner for Human Rights shall be located at Geneva and shall have a liaison office in New York;

7. <u>Requests</u> the Secretary-General to provide appropriate staff and resources, within the existing and future regular budgets of the United Nations, to enable the High Commissioner to fulfil his/her mandate, without diverting resources from the development programmes and activities of the United Nations;

8. <u>Also requests</u> the Secretary-General to report to the General Assembly at its forty-ninth session on the implementation of the present resolution.

45

Establishment of the Human Rights Council, 2006

Note: The Human Rights Council was established by General Assembly Resolution 60/251 which was adopted on 15 March 2006.

The General Assembly,

Reaffirming the purposes and principles contained in the Charter of the United Nations, including developing friendly relations among nations based on respect for the principle of equal rights and self-determination of peoples, and achieving international cooperation in solving international problems of an economic, social, cultural or humanitarian character and in promoting and encouraging respect for human rights and fundamental freedoms for all,

Reaffirming also the Universal Declaration of Human Rights and the Vienna Declaration and Programme of Action, and recalling the International Covenant on Civil and Political Rights, the International Covenant on Economic, Social and Cultural Rights and other human rights instruments,

Reaffirming further that all human rights are universal, indivisible, interrelated, interdependent and mutually reinforcing, and that all human rights must be treated in a fair and equal manner, on the same footing and with the same emphasis,

Reaffirming that, while the significance of national and regional particularities and various historical, cultural and religious backgrounds must be borne in mind, all States, regardless of their political, economic and cultural systems, have the duty to promote and protect all human rights and fundamental freedoms,

Emphasizing the responsibilities of all States, in conformity with the Charter, to respect human rights and fundamental freedoms for all, without distinction of any kind as to race, colour, sex, language or religion, political or other opinion, national or social origin, property, birth or other status,

Acknowledging that peace and security, development and human rights are the pillars of the United Nations system and the foundations for collective security and well-being, and recognizing that development, peace and security and human rights are interlinked and mutually reinforcing,

Affirming the need for all States to continue international efforts to enhance dialogue and broaden understanding among civilizations, cultures and religions, and emphasizing that States, regional organizations, non-governmental organizations, religious bodies and the media have an important role to play in promoting tolerance, respect for and freedom of religion and belief,

Recognizing the work undertaken by the Commission on Human Rights and the need to preserve and build on its achievements and to redress its shortcomings,

Recognizing also the importance of ensuring universality, objectivity and non-selectivity in the consideration of human rights issues, and the elimination of double standards and politicization,

Recognizing further that the promotion and protection of human rights should be based on the principles of cooperation and genuine dialogue and aimed at strengthening the capacity of Member States to comply with their human rights obligations for the benefit of all human beings,

Acknowledging that non-governmental organizations play an important role at the national, regional and international levels, in the promotion and protection of human rights,

Reaffirming the commitment to strengthen the United Nations human rights machinery, with the aim of ensuring effective enjoyment by all of all human rights, civil, political, economic, social and cultural rights, including the right to development, and to that end, the resolve to create a Human Rights Council,

1. *Decides* to establish the Human Rights Council, based in Geneva, in replacement of the Commission on Human Rights, as a subsidiary organ of the General Assembly; the Assembly shall review the status of the Council within five years;

2. *Decides* that the Council shall be responsible for promoting universal respect for the protection of all human rights and fundamental freedoms for all, without distinction of any kind and in a fair and equal manner;

3. *Decides* also that the Council should address situations of violations of human rights, including gross and systematic violations, and make recommendations thereon. It should also promote the effective coordination and the mainstreaming of human rights within the United Nations system;

4. *Decides* further that the work of the Council shall be guided by the principles of universality, impartiality, objectivity and non-selectivity, constructive international dialogue and cooperation, with a view to enhancing the promotion and protection of all human rights, civil, political, economic, social and cultural rights, including the right to development;

5. *Decides* that the Council shall, inter alia:

    (a) Promote human rights education and learning as well as advisory services, technical assistance and capacity-building, to be provided in consultation with and with the consent of Member States concerned;

    (b) Serve as a forum for dialogue on thematic issues on all human rights;

    (c) Make recommendations to the General Assembly for the further development of international law in the field of human rights;

    (d) Promote the full implementation of human rights obligations undertaken by States and follow-up to the goals and commitments related to the promotion and protection of human rights emanating from United Nations conferences and summits;

    (e) Undertake a universal periodic review, based on objective and reliable information, of the fulfilment by each State of its human rights obligations and commitments in a manner which ensures universality of coverage and equal treatment with respect to all States; the review shall be a cooperative mechanism, based on an interactive dialogue, with the full involvement of the country concerned and with consideration given to its capacity-building needs; such a mechanism shall complement and not duplicate the work of treaty bodies; the Council shall develop the modalities and necessary time allocation for the universal periodic review mechanism within one year after the holding of its first session;

(f) Contribute, through dialogue and cooperation, towards the prevention of human rights violations and respond promptly to human rights emergencies;

(g) Assume the role and responsibilities of the Commission on Human Rights relating to the work of the Office of the United Nations High Commissioner for Human Rights, as decided by the General Assembly in its resolution 48/141 of 20 December 1993;

(h) Work in close cooperation in the field of human rights with Governments, regional organizations, national human rights institutions and civil society;

(i) Make recommendations with regard to the promotion and protection of human rights;

(j) Submit an annual report to the General Assembly;

6. *Decides* also that the Council shall assume, review and, where necessary, improve and rationalize all mandates, mechanisms, functions and responsibilities of the Commission on Human Rights in order to maintain a system of special procedures, expert advice and a complaint procedure; the Council shall complete this review within one year after the holding of its first session;

7. *Decides* further that the Council shall consist of forty-seven Member States, which shall be elected directly and individually by secret ballot by the majority of the members of the General Assembly; the membership shall be based on equitable geographical distribution, and seats shall be distributed as follows among regional groups: Group of African States, thirteen; Group of Asian States, thirteen; Group of Eastern European States, six; Group of Latin American and Caribbean States, eight; and Group of Western European and other States, seven; the members of the Council shall serve for a period of three years and shall not be eligible for immediate re-election after two consecutive terms;

8. *Decides* that the membership in the Council shall be open to all States Members of the United Nations; when electing members of the Council, Member States shall take into account the contribution of candidates to the promotion and protection of human rights and their voluntary pledges and commitments made thereto; the General Assembly, by a two-thirds majority of the members present and voting, may suspend the rights of membership in the Council of a member of the Council that commits gross and systematic violations of human rights;

9. *Decides* also that members elected to the Council shall uphold the highest standards in the promotion and protection of human rights, shall fully cooperate with the Council and be reviewed under the universal periodic review mechanism during their term of membership;

10. *Decides* further that the Council shall meet regularly throughout the year and schedule no fewer than three sessions per year, including a main session, for a total duration of no less than ten weeks, and shall be able to hold special sessions, when needed, at the request of a member of the Council with the support of one third of the membership of the Council;

11. *Decides* that the Council shall apply the rules of procedure established for committees of the General Assembly, as applicable, unless subsequently otherwise decided by the Assembly or the Council, and also decides that the participation of and

consultation with observers, including States that are not members of the Council, the specialized agencies, other intergovernmental organizations and national human rights institutions, as well as non-governmental organizations, shall be based on arrangements, including Economic and Social Council resolution 1996/31 of 25 July 1996 and practices observed by the Commission on Human Rights, while ensuring the most effective contribution of these entities;

12. *Decides* also that the methods of work of the Council shall be transparent, fair and impartial and shall enable genuine dialogue, be results oriented, allow for subsequent follow-up discussions to recommendations and their implementation and also allow for substantive interaction with special procedures and mechanisms;

13. *Recommends* that the Economic and Social Council request the Commission on Human Rights to conclude its work at its sixty-second session, and that it abolish the Commission on 16 June 2006;

14. *Decides* to elect the new members of the Council; the terms of membership shall be staggered, and such decision shall be taken for the first election by the drawing of lots, taking into consideration equitable geographical distribution;

15. *Decides* also that elections of the first members of the Council shall take place on 9 May 2006, and that the first meeting of the Council shall be convened on 19 June 2006;

16. *Decides* further that the Council shall review its work and functioning five years after its establishment and report to the General Assembly.

72nd plenary meeting
15 March 2006

46

Human Rights Council Resolution 5/1: Institution Building of the United Nations Human Rights Council, 2007

Note: adopted by the Human Rights Council on 18 June 2007.

The Human Rights Council,

Acting in compliance with the mandate entrusted to it by the United Nations General Assembly in resolution 60/251 of 15 March 2006,

Having considered the draft text on institution-building submitted by the President of the Council,

1. *Adopts* the draft text entitled "United Nations Human Rights Council: Institution Building", as contained in the annex to the present resolution, including its appendix(ces);

2. *Decides* to submit the following draft resolution to the General Assembly for its adoption as a matter of priority in order to facilitate the timely implementation of the text contained thereafter:

"*The General Assembly,*

"*Taking note* of Human Rights Council resolution 5/1 of 18 June 2007,

"1. *Welcomes* the text entitled 'United Nations Human Rights Council: Institution Building', as contained in the annex to the present resolution, including its appendix(ces)."

9th meeting

18 June 2007

[Resolution adopted without a vote.]

Annex

UNITED NATIONS HUMAN RIGHTS COUNCIL: INSTITUTION-BUILDING

I. UNIVERSAL PERIODIC REVIEW MECHANISM

A. Basis of the review

1. The basis of the review is:
   (a) The Charter of the United Nations;
   (b) The Universal Declaration of Human Rights;
   (c) Human rights instruments to which a State is party;

(d) Voluntary pledges and commitments made by States, including those undertaken when presenting their candidatures for election to the Human Rights Council (hereinafter "the Council").

2. In addition to the above and given the complementary and mutually interrelated nature of international human rights law and international humanitarian law, the review shall take into account applicable international humanitarian law.

B. Principles and objectives

1. Principles

3. The universal periodic review should:
   (a) Promote the universality, interdependence, indivisibility and interrelatedness of all human rights;
   (b) Be a cooperative mechanism based on objective and reliable information and on interactive dialogue;
   (c) Ensure universal coverage and equal treatment of all States;
   (d) Be an intergovernmental process, United Nations Member-driven and action oriented;
   (e) Fully involve the country under review;
   (f) Complement and not duplicate other human rights mechanisms, thus representing an added value;
   (g) Be conducted in an objective, transparent, non-selective, constructive, non-confrontational and non-politicized manner;
   (h) Not be overly burdensome to the concerned State or to the agenda of the Council;
   (i) Not be overly long; it should be realistic and not absorb a disproportionate amount of time, human and financial resources;
   (j) Not diminish the Council's capacity to respond to urgent human rights situations;
   (k) Fully integrate a gender perspective;
   (l) Without prejudice to the obligations contained in the elements provided for in the basis of review, take into account the level of development and specificities of countries;
   (m) Ensure the participation of all relevant stakeholders, including non-governmental organizations and national human rights institutions, in accordance with General Assembly resolution 60/251 of 15 March 2006 and Economic and Social Council resolution 1996/31 of 25 July 1996, as well as any decisions that the Council may take in this regard.

2. Objectives

4. The objectives of the review are:
   (a) The improvement of the human rights situation on the ground;
   (b) The fulfilment of the State's human rights obligations and commitments and assessment of positive developments and challenges faced by the State;
   (c) The enhancement of the State's capacity and of technical assistance, in consultation with, and with the consent of, the State concerned;
   (d) The sharing of best practice among States and other stakeholders;
   (e) Support for cooperation in the promotion and protection of human rights;

(f) The encouragement of full cooperation and engagement with the Council, other human rights bodies and the Office of the United Nations High Commissioner for Human Rights.

C. Periodicity and order of the review

5. The review begins after the adoption of the universal periodic review mechanism by the Council.

6. The order of review should reflect the principles of universality and equal treatment.

7. The order of the review should be established as soon as possible in order to allow States to prepare adequately.

8. All member States of the Council shall be reviewed during their term of membership.

9. The initial members of the Council, especially those elected for one or two-year terms, should be reviewed first.

10. A mix of member and observer States of the Council should be reviewed.

11. Equitable geographic distribution should be respected in the selection of countries for review.

12. The first member and observer States to be reviewed will be chosen by the drawing of lots from each Regional Group in such a way as to ensure full respect for equitable geographic distribution. Alphabetical order will then be applied beginning with those countries thus selected, unless other countries volunteer to be reviewed.

13. The period between review cycles should be reasonable so as to take into account the capacity of States to prepare for, and the capacity of other stakeholders to respond to, the requests arising from the review.

14. The periodicity of the review for the first cycle will be of four years. This will imply the consideration of 48 States per year during three sessions of the working group of two weeks each.

D. Process and modalities of the review

1. Documentation

15. The documents on which the review would be based are:

(a) Information prepared by the State concerned, which can take the form of a national report, on the basis of general guidelines to be adopted by the Council at its sixth session (first session of the second cycle), and any other information considered relevant by the State concerned, which could be presented either orally or in writing, provided that the written presentation summarizing the information will not exceed 20 pages, to guarantee equal treatment to all States and not to overburden the mechanism. States are encouraged to prepare the information through a broad consultation process at the national level with all relevant stakeholders;

(b) Additionally a compilation prepared by the Office of the High Commissioner for Human Rights of the information contained in the reports of treaty bodies, special procedures, including observations and comments by the State concerned, and other relevant official United Nations documents, which shall not exceed 10 pages;

(c) Additional, credible and reliable information provided by other relevant stakeholders to the universal periodic review which should also be taken into consideration by the Council in the review. The Office of the High Commissioner for Human Rights will prepare a summary of such information which shall not exceed 10 pages.

16. The documents prepared by the Office of the High Commissioner for Human Rights should be elaborated following the structure of the general guidelines adopted by the Council regarding the information prepared by the State concerned.

17. Both the State's written presentation and the summaries prepared by the Office of the High Commissioner for Human Rights shall be ready six weeks prior to the review by the working group to ensure the distribution of documents simultaneously in the six official languages of the United Nations, in accordance with General Assembly resolution 53/208 of 14 January 1999.

2. Modalities

18. The modalities of the review shall be as follows:

(a) The review will be conducted in one working group, chaired by the President of the Council and composed of the 47 member States of the Council. Each member State will decide on the composition of its delegation;

(b) Observer States may participate in the review, including in the interactive dialogue;

(b) Other relevant stakeholders may attend the review in the Working Group;

(c) A group of three rapporteurs, selected by the drawing of lots among the members of the Council and from different Regional Groups (troika) will be formed to facilitate each review, including the preparation of the report of the working group. The Office of the High Commissioner for Human Rights will provide the necessary assistance and expertise to the rapporteurs.

19. The country concerned may request that one of the rapporteurs be from its own Regional Group and may also request the substitution of a rapporteur on only one occasion.

20. A rapporteur may request to be excused from participation in a specific review process.

21. Interactive dialogue between the country under review and the Council will take place in the working group. The rapporteurs may collate issues or questions to be transmitted to the State under review to facilitate its preparation and focus the interactive dialogue, while guaranteeing fairness and transparency.

22. The duration of the review will be three hours for each country in the working group. Additional time of up to one hour will be allocated for the consideration of the outcome by the plenary of the Council.

23. Half an hour will be allocated for the adoption of the report of each country under review in the working group.

24. A reasonable time frame should be allocated between the review and the adoption of the report of each State in the working group.

25. The final outcome will be adopted by the plenary of the Council.

E. Outcome of the review

1. Format of the outcome

26. The format of the outcome of the review will be a report consisting of a summary of the proceedings of the review process; conclusions and/or recommendations, and the voluntary commitments of the State concerned.

2. Content of the outcome

27. The universal periodic review is a cooperative mechanism. Its outcome may include, inter alia:
    (a) An assessment undertaken in an objective and transparent manner of the human rights situation in the country under review, including positive developments and the challenges faced by the country;
    (b) Sharing of best practices;
    (c) An emphasis on enhancing cooperation for the promotion and protection of human rights;
    (d) The provision of technical assistance and capacity-building in consultation with, and with the consent of, the country concerned;
    (e) Voluntary commitments and pledges made by the country under review.

3. Adoption of the outcome

28. The country under review should be fully involved in the outcome.
29. Before the adoption of the outcome by the plenary of the Council, the State concerned should be offered the opportunity to present replies to questions or issues that were not sufficiently addressed during the interactive dialogue.
30. The State concerned and the member States of the Council, as well as observer States, will be given the opportunity to express their views on the outcome of the review before the plenary takes action on it.
31. Other relevant stakeholders will have the opportunity to make general comments before the adoption of the outcome by the plenary.
32. Recommendations that enjoy the support of the State concerned will be identified as such. Other recommendations, together with the comments of the State concerned thereon, will be noted. Both will be included in the outcome report to be adopted by the Council.

F. Follow-up to the review

33. The outcome of the universal periodic review, as a cooperative mechanism, should be implemented primarily by the State concerned and, as appropriate, by other relevant stakeholders.
34. The subsequent review should focus, inter alia, on the implementation of the preceding outcome.
35. The Council should have a standing item on its agenda devoted to the universal periodic review.
36. The international community will assist in implementing the recommendations and conclusions regarding capacity-building and technical assistance, in consultation with, and with the consent of, the country concerned.

37. In considering the outcome of the universal periodic review, the Council will decide if and when any specific follow up is necessary.

38. After exhausting all efforts to encourage a State to cooperate with the universal periodic review mechanism, the Council will address, as appropriate, cases of persistent non-cooperation with the mechanism.

II. SPECIAL PROCEDURES

A. Selection and appointment of mandate-holders

39. The following general criteria will be of paramount importance while nominating, selecting and appointing mandate-holders: (a) expertise; (b) experience in the field of the mandate; (c) independence; (d) impartiality; (e) personal integrity; and (f) objectivity.

40. Due consideration should be given to gender balance and equitable geographic representation, as well as to an appropriate representation of different legal systems.

41. Technical and objective requirements for eligible candidates for mandate-holders will be approved by the Council at its sixth session (first session of the second cycle), in order to ensure that eligible candidates are highly qualified individuals who possess established competence, relevant expertise and extensive professional experience in the field of human rights.

42. The following entities may nominate candidates as special procedures mandate-holders: (a) Governments; (b) Regional Groups operating within the United Nations human rights system; (c) international organizations or their offices (e.g. the Office of the High Commissioner for Human Rights); (d) non-governmental organizations; (e) other human rights bodies; (f) individual nominations.

43. The Office of the High Commissioner for Human Rights shall immediately prepare, maintain and periodically update a public list of eligible candidates in a standardized format, which shall include personal data, areas of expertise and professional experience. Upcoming vacancies of mandates shall be publicized.

44. The principle of non-accumulation of human rights functions at a time shall be respected.

45. A mandate-holder's tenure in a given function, whether a thematic or country mandate, will be no longer than six years (two terms of three years for thematic mandate-holders).

46. Individuals holding decision-making positions in Government or in any other organization or entity which may give rise to a conflict of interest with the responsibilities inherent to the mandate shall be excluded. Mandate holders will act in their personal capacity.

47. A consultative group would be established to propose to the President, at least one month before the beginning of the session in which the Council would consider the selection of mandate holders, a list of candidates who possess the highest qualifications for the mandates in question and meet the general criteria and particular requirements.

48. The consultative group shall also give due consideration to the exclusion of nominated candidates from the public list of eligible candidates brought to its attention.

49. At the beginning of the annual cycle of the Council, Regional Groups would be invited to appoint a member of the consultative group, who would serve in his/her personal capacity. The Group will be assisted by the Office of the High Commissioner for Human Rights.

50. The consultative group will consider candidates included in the public list; however, under exceptional circumstances and if a particular post justifies it, the Group may consider additional nominations with equal or more suitable qualifications for the post. Recommendations to the President shall be public and substantiated.

51. The consultative group should take into account, as appropriate, the views of stakeholders, including the current or outgoing mandate-holders, in determining the necessary expertise, experience, skills, and other relevant requirements for each mandate.

52. On the basis of the recommendations of the consultative group and following broad consultations, in particular through the regional coordinators, the President of the Council will identify an appropriate candidate for each vacancy. The President will present to member States and observers a list of candidates to be proposed at least two weeks prior to the beginning of the session in which the Council will consider the appointments.

53. If necessary, the President will conduct further consultations to ensure the endorsement of the proposed candidates. The appointment of the special procedures mandate-holders will be completed upon the subsequent approval of the Council. Mandate-holders shall be appointed before the end of the session.

B. Review, rationalization and improvement of mandates

54. The review, rationalization and improvement of mandates, as well as the creation of new ones, must be guided by the principles of universality, impartiality, objectivity and non selectivity, constructive international dialogue and cooperation, with a view to enhancing the promotion and protection of all human rights, civil, political, economic, social and cultural rights, including the right to development.

55. The review, rationalization and improvement of each mandate would take place in the context of the negotiations of the relevant resolutions. An assessment of the mandate may take place in a separate segment of the interactive dialogue between the Council and special procedures mandate-holders.

56. The review, rationalization and improvement of mandates would focus on the relevance, scope and contents of the mandates, having as a framework the internationally recognized human rights standards, the system of special procedures and General Assembly resolution 60/251.

57. Any decision to streamline, merge or possibly discontinue mandates should always be guided by the need for improvement of the enjoyment and protection of human rights.

58. The Council should always strive for improvements:
    (a) Mandates should always offer a clear prospect of an increased level of human rights protection and promotion as well as being coherent within the system of human rights;
    (b) Equal attention should be paid to all human rights. The balance of thematic mandates should broadly reflect the accepted equal importance of civil, political, economic, social and cultural rights, including the right to development;

(c) Every effort should be made to avoid unnecessary duplication;

(d) Areas which constitute thematic gaps will be identified and addressed, including by means other than the creation of special procedures mandates, such as by expanding an existing mandate, bringing a cross-cutting issue to the attention of mandate-holders or by requesting a joint action to the relevant mandate-holders;

(e) Any consideration of merging mandates should have regard to the content and predominant functions of each mandate, as well as to the workload of individual mandate holders;

(f) In creating or reviewing mandates, efforts should be made to identify whether the structure of the mechanism (expert, rapporteur or working group) is the most effective in terms of increasing human rights protection;

(g) New mandates should be as clear and specific as possible, so as to avoid ambiguity.

59. It should be considered desirable to have a uniform nomenclature of mandate-holders, titles of mandates as well as a selection and appointment process, to make the whole system more understandable.

60. Thematic mandate periods will be of three years. Country mandate periods will be of one year.

61. Mandates included in Appendix I, where applicable, will be renewed until the date on which they are considered by the Council according to the programme of work.

62. Current mandate-holders may continue serving, provided they have not exceeded the six year term limit (Appendix II). On an exceptional basis, the term of those mandate-holders who have served more than six years may be extended until the relevant mandate is considered by the Council and the selection and appointment process has concluded.

63. Decisions to create, review or discontinue country mandates should also take into account the principles of cooperation and genuine dialogue aimed at strengthening the capacity of Member States to comply with their human rights obligations.

64. In case of situations of violations of human rights or a lack of cooperation that require the Council's attention, the principles of objectivity, non-selectivity, and the elimination of double standards and politicization should apply.

III. HUMAN RIGHTS COUNCIL ADVISORY COMMITTEE

65. The Human Rights Council Advisory Committee (hereinafter "the Advisory Committee"), composed of 18 experts serving in their personal capacity, will function as a think-tank for the Council and work at its direction. The establishment of this subsidiary body and its functioning will be executed according to the guidelines stipulated below.

A. Nomination

66. All Member States of the United Nations may propose or endorse candidates from their own region. When selecting their candidates, States should consult their national human rights institutions and civil society organizations and, in this regard, include the names of those supporting their candidates.

67. The aim is to ensure that the best possible expertise is made available to the Council. For this purpose, technical and objective requirements for the submission of candidatures will be established and approved by the Council at its sixth session (first session of the second cycle). These should include:

    (a) Recognized competence and experience in the field of human rights;

    (b) High moral standing;

    (c) Independence and impartiality.

68. Individuals holding decision-making positions in Government or in any other organization or entity which might give rise to a conflict of interest with the responsibilities inherent in the mandate shall be excluded. Elected members of the Committee will act in their personal capacity.

69. The principle of non-accumulation of human rights functions at the same time shall be respected.

B. Election

70. The Council shall elect the members of the Advisory Committee, in secret ballot, from the list of candidates whose names have been presented in accordance with the agreed requirements.

71. The list of candidates shall be closed two months prior to the election date. The Secretariat will make available the list of candidates and relevant information to member States and to the public at least one month prior to their election.

72. Due consideration should be given to gender balance and appropriate representation of different civilizations and legal systems.

73. The geographic distribution will be as follows:

    African States: 5

    Asian States: 5

    Eastern European States: 2

    Latin American and Caribbean States: 3

    Western European and other States: 3

74. The members of the Advisory Committee shall serve for a period of three years. They shall be eligible for reelection once. In the first term, one third of the experts will serve for one year and another third for two years. The staggering of terms of membership will be defined by the drawing of lots.

C. Functions

75. The function of the Advisory Committee is to provide expertise to the Council in the manner and form requested by the Council, focusing mainly on studies and research-based advice. Further, such expertise shall be rendered only upon the latter's request, in compliance with its resolutions and under its guidance.

76. The Advisory Committee should be implementation-oriented and the scope of its advice should be limited to thematic issues pertaining to the mandate of the Council; namely promotion and protection of all human rights.

77. The Advisory Committee shall not adopt resolutions or decisions. The Advisory Committee may propose within the scope of the work set out by the Council, for the

latter's consideration and approval, suggestions for further enhancing its procedural efficiency, as well as further research proposals within the scope of the work set out by the Council.

78. The Council shall issue specific guidelines for the Advisory Committee when it requests a substantive contribution from the latter and shall review all or any portion of those guidelines if it deems necessary in the future.

D. Methods of work

79. The Advisory Committee shall convene up to two sessions for a maximum of 10 working days per year. Additional sessions may be scheduled on an ad hoc basis with prior approval of the Council.

80. The Council may request the Advisory Committee to undertake certain tasks that could be performed collectively, through a smaller team or individually. The Advisory Committee will report on such efforts to the Council.

81. Members of the Advisory Committee are encouraged to communicate between sessions, individually or in teams. However, the Advisory Committee shall not establish subsidiary bodies unless the Council authorizes it to do so.

82. In the performance of its mandate, the Advisory Committee is urged to establish interaction with States, national human rights institutions, non-governmental organizations and other civil society entities in accordance with the modalities of the Council.

83. Member States and observers, including States that are not members of the Council, the specialized agencies, other intergovernmental organizations and national human rights institutions, as well as non-governmental organizations shall be entitled to participate in the work of the Advisory Committee based on arrangements, including Economic and Social Council resolution 1996/31 and practices observed by the Commission on Human Rights and the Council, while ensuring the most effective contribution of these entities.

84. The Council will decide at its sixth session (first session of its second cycle) on the most appropriate mechanisms to continue the work of the Working Groups on Indigenous Populations; Contemporary Forms of Slavery; Minorities; and the Social Forum.

IV. COMPLAINT PROCEDURE

A. Objective and scope

85. A complaint procedure is being established to address consistent patterns of gross and reliably attested violations of all human rights and all fundamental freedoms occurring in any part of the world and under any circumstances.

86. Economic and Social Council resolution 1503 (XLVIII) of 27 May 1970 as revised by resolution 2000/3 of 19 June 2000 served as a working basis and was improved where necessary, so as to ensure that the complaint procedure is impartial, objective, efficient, victims oriented and conducted in a timely manner. The procedure will retain its confidential nature, with a view to enhancing cooperation with the State concerned.

B. Admissibility criteria for communications

87. A communication related to a violation of human rights and fundamental freedoms, for the purpose of this procedure, shall be admissible, provided that:
    (a) It is not manifestly politically motivated and its object is consistent with the Charter of the United Nations, the Universal Declaration of Human Rights and other applicable instruments in the field of human rights law;
    (b) It gives a factual description of the alleged violations, including the rights which are alleged to be violated;
    (c) Its language is not abusive. However, such a communication may be considered if it meets the other criteria for admissibility after deletion of the abusive language;
    (d) It is submitted by a person or a group of persons claiming to be the victims of violations of human rights and fundamental freedoms, or by any person or group of persons, including non-governmental organizations, acting in good faith in accordance with the principles of human rights, not resorting to politically motivated stands contrary to the provisions of the Charter of the United Nations and claiming to have direct and reliable knowledge of the violations concerned. Nonetheless, reliably attested communications shall not be inadmissible solely because the knowledge of the individual authors is second-hand, provided that they are accompanied by clear evidence;
    (e) It is not exclusively based on reports disseminated by mass media;
    (f) It does not refer to a case that appears to reveal a consistent pattern of gross and reliably attested violations of human rights already being dealt with by a special procedure, a treaty body or other United Nations or similar regional complaints procedure in the field of human rights;
    (g) Domestic remedies have been exhausted, unless it appears that such remedies would be ineffective or unreasonably prolonged.
88. National human rights institutions, established and operating under the Principles Relating to the Status of National Institutions (the Paris Principles), in particular in regard to quasi-judicial competence, may serve as effective means of addressing individual human rights violations.

C. Working groups

89. Two distinct working groups shall be established with the mandate to examine the communications and to bring to the attention of the Council consistent patterns of gross and reliably attested violations of human rights and fundamental freedoms.
90. Both working groups shall, to the greatest possible extent, work on the basis of consensus. In the absence of consensus, decisions shall be taken by simple majority of the votes. They may establish their own rules of procedure.

1. Working Group on Communications: composition, mandate and powers

91. The Human Rights Council Advisory Committee shall appoint five of its members, one from each Regional Group, with due consideration to gender balance, to constitute the Working Group on Communications.

92. In case of a vacancy, the Advisory Committee shall appoint an independent and highly qualified expert of the same Regional Group from the Advisory Committee.

93. Since there is a need for independent expertise and continuity with regard to the examination and assessment of communications received, the independent and highly qualified experts of the Working Group on Communications shall be appointed for three years. Their mandate is renewable only once.

94. The Chairperson of the Working Group on Communications is requested, together with the secretariat, to undertake an initial screening of communications received, based on the admissibility criteria, before transmitting them to the States concerned. Manifestly ill-founded or anonymous communications shall be screened out by the Chairperson and shall therefore not be transmitted to the State concerned. In a perspective of accountability and transparency, the Chairperson of the Working Group on Communications shall provide all its members with a list of all communications rejected after initial screening. This list should indicate the grounds of all decisions resulting in the rejection of a communication. All other communications, which have not been screened out, shall be transmitted to the State concerned, so as to obtain the views of the latter on the allegations of violations.

95. The members of the Working Group on Communications shall decide on the admissibility of a communication and assess the merits of the allegations of violations, including whether the communication alone or in combination with other communications appear to reveal a consistent pattern of gross and reliably attested violations of human rights and fundamental freedoms. The Working Group on Communications shall provide the Working Group on Situations with a file containing all admissible communications as well as recommendations thereon. When the Working Group on Communications requires further consideration or additional information, it may keep a case under review until its next session and request such information from the State concerned. The Working Group on Communications may decide to dismiss a case. All decisions of the Working Group on Communications shall be based on a rigorous application of the admissibility criteria and duly justified.

2. Working Group on Situations: composition, mandate and powers

96. Each Regional Group shall appoint a representative of a member State of the Council, with due consideration to gender balance, to serve on the Working Group on Situations. Members shall be appointed for one year. Their mandate may be renewed once, if the State concerned is a member of the Council.

97. Members of the Working Group on Situations shall serve in their personal capacity. In order to fill a vacancy, the respective Regional Group to which the vacancy belongs, shall appoint a representative from member States of the same Regional Group.

98. The Working Group on Situations is requested, on the basis of the information and recommendations provided by the Working Group on Communications, to present the Council with a report on consistent patterns of gross and reliably attested violations of human rights and fundamental freedoms and to make recommendations to the Council on the course of action to take, normally in the form of a draft resolution or decision with respect to the situations referred to it. When the Working Group on Situations requires further consideration or additional information, its

members may keep a case under review until its next session. The Working Group on Situations may also decide to dismiss a case.

99. All decisions of the Working Group on Situations shall be duly justified and indicate why the consideration of a situation has been discontinued or action recommended thereon. Decisions to discontinue should be taken by consensus; if that is not possible, by simple majority of the votes.

D. Working modalities and confidentiality

100. Since the complaint procedure is to be, inter alia, victims-oriented and conducted in a confidential and timely manner, both Working Groups shall meet at least twice a year for five working days each session, in order to promptly examine the communications received, including replies of States thereon, and the situations of which the Council is already seized under the complaint procedure.

101. The State concerned shall cooperate with the complaint procedure and make every effort to provide substantive replies in one of the United Nations official languages to any of the requests of the Working Groups or the Council. The State concerned shall also make every effort to provide a reply not later than three months after the request has been made. If necessary, this deadline may however be extended at the request of the State concerned.

102. The Secretariat is requested to make the confidential files available to all members of the Council, at least two weeks in advance, so as to allow sufficient time for the consideration of the files.

103. The Council shall consider consistent patterns of gross and reliably attested violations of human rights and fundamental freedoms brought to its attention by the Working Group on Situations as frequently as needed, but at least once a year.

104. The reports of the Working Group on Situations referred to the Council shall be examined in a confidential manner, unless the Council decides otherwise. When the Working Group on Situations recommends to the Council that it consider a situation in a public meeting, in particular in the case of manifest and unequivocal lack of cooperation, the Council shall consider such recommendation on a priority basis at its next session.

105. So as to ensure that the complaint procedure is victims-oriented, efficient and conducted in a timely manner, the period of time between the transmission of the complaint to the State concerned and consideration by the Council shall not, in principle, exceed 24 months.

E. Involvement of the complainant and of the State concerned

106. The complaint procedure shall ensure that both the author of a communication and the State concerned are informed of the proceedings at the following key stages:

(a) When a communication is deemed inadmissible by the Working Group on Communications or when it is taken up for consideration by the Working Group on Situations; or when a communication is kept pending by one of the Working Groups or by the Council;

(b) At the final outcome.

107. In addition, the complainant shall be informed when his/her communication is registered by the complaint procedure.
108. Should the complainant request that his/her identity be kept confidential, it will not be transmitted to the State concerned.

F. Measures

109. In accordance with established practice the action taken in respect of a particular situation should be one of the following options:
    (a) To discontinue considering the situation when further consideration or action is not warranted;
    (b) To keep the situation under review and request the State concerned to provide further information within a reasonable period of time;
    (c) To keep the situation under review and appoint an independent and highly qualified expert to monitor the situation and report back to the Council;
    (d) To discontinue reviewing the matter under the confidential complaint procedure in order to take up public consideration of the same;
    (e) To recommend to OHCHR to provide technical cooperation, capacity building assistance or advisory services to the State concerned.

V. AGENDA AND FRAMEWORK FOR THE PROGRAMME OF WORK

A. Principles

Universality
Impartiality
Objectivity
Non-selectiveness
Constructive dialogue and cooperation
Predictability
Flexibility
Transparency
Accountability
Balance
Inclusive/comprehensive
Gender perspective
Implementation and follow-up of decisions

B. Agenda

Item 1. Organizational and procedural matters
Item 2. Annual report of the United Nations High Commissioner for Human Rights and reports of the Office of the High Commissioner and the Secretary-General
Item 3. Promotion and protection of all human rights, civil, political, economic, social and cultural rights, including the right to development
Item 4. Human rights situations that require the Council's attention

Item 5.   Human rights bodies and mechanisms

Item 6.   Universal Periodic Review

Item 7.   Human rights situation in Palestine and other occupied Arab territories

Item 8.   Follow-up and implementation of the Vienna Declaration and Programme of Action

Item 9.   Racism, racial discrimination, xenophobia and related forms of intolerance, follow-up and implementation of the Durban Declaration and Programme of Action

Item 10. Technical assistance and capacity-building

C. Framework for the programme of work

Item 1.   Organizational and procedural matters
    Election of the Bureau
    Adoption of the annual programme of work
    Adoption of the programme of work of the session, including other business
    Selection and appointment of mandate-holders
    Election of members of the Human Rights Council Advisory Committee
    Adoption of the report of the session
    Adoption of the annual report

Item 2.   Annual report of the United Nations High Commissioner for Human Rights and reports of the Office of the High Commissioner and the Secretary-General
    Presentation of the annual report and updates

Item 3.   Promotion and protection of all human rights, civil, political, economic, social and cultural rights, including the right to development
    Economic, social and cultural rights
    Civil and political rights
    Rights of peoples, and specific groups and individuals
    Right to development
    Interrelation of human rights and human rights thematic issues

Item 4.   Human rights situations that require the Council's attention

Item 5.   Human rights bodies and mechanisms
    Report of the Human Rights Council Advisory Committee
    Report of the complaint procedure

Item 6.   Universal Periodic Review

Item 7.   Human rights situation in Palestine and other occupied Arab territories
    Human rights violations and implications of the Israeli occupation of Palestine and other occupied Arab territories
    Right to self-determination of the Palestinian people

Item 8.   Follow-up and implementation of the Vienna Declaration and Programme of Action

Item 9.   Racism, racial discrimination, xenophobia and related forms of intolerance, follow--up and implementation of the Durban Declaration and Programme of Action

Item 10. Technical assistance and capacity-building

VI. METHODS OF WORK

110. The methods of work, pursuant to General Assembly resolution 60/251 should be transparent, impartial, equitable, fair, pragmatic; lead to clarity, predictability, and inclusiveness. They may also be updated and adjusted over time.

A. Institutional arrangements

1. Briefings on prospective resolutions or decisions

111. The briefings on prospective resolutions or decisions would be informative only, whereby delegations would be apprised of resolutions and/or decisions tabled or intended to be tabled. These briefings will be organized by interested delegations.

2. President's open-ended information meetings on resolutions, decisions and other related business

112. The President's open-ended information meetings on resolutions, decisions and other related business shall provide information on the status of negotiations on draft resolutions and/or decisions so that delegations may gain a bird's eye view of the status of such drafts. The consultations shall have a purely informational function, combined with information on the extranet, and be held in a transparent and inclusive manner. They shall not serve as a negotiating forum.

3. Informal consultations on proposals convened by main sponsors

113. Informal consultations shall be the primary means for the negotiation of draft resolutions and/or decisions, and their convening shall be the responsibility of the sponsor(s). At least one informal open-ended consultation should be held on each draft resolution and/or decision before it is considered for action by the Council. Consultations should, as much as possible, be scheduled in a timely, transparent and inclusive manner that takes into account the constraints faced by delegations, particularly smaller ones.

4. Role of the Bureau

114. The Bureau shall deal with procedural and organizational matters. The Bureau shall regularly communicate the contents of its meetings through a timely summary report.

5. Other work formats may include panel debates, seminars and round tables

115. Utilization of these other work formats, including topics and modalities, would be decided by the Council on a case-by-case basis. They may serve as tools of the Council for enhancing dialogue and mutual understanding on certain issues. They should be utilized in the context of the Council's agenda and annual programme of work, and reinforce and/or complement its intergovernmental nature. They shall not be used to substitute or replace existing human rights mechanisms and established methods of work.

6. High-Level Segment

116. The High-Level Segment shall be held once a year during the main session of the Council. It shall be followed by a general segment wherein delegations that did not participate in the High-Level Segment may deliver general statements.

B. Working culture

117. There is a need for:
    (a) Early notification of proposals;
    (b) Early submission of draft resolutions and decisions, preferably by the end of the penultimate week of a session;
    (c) Early distribution of all reports, particularly those of special procedures, to be transmitted to delegations in a timely fashion, at least 15 days in advance of their consideration by the Council, and in all official United Nations languages;
    (d) Proposers of a country resolution to have the responsibility to secure the broadest possible support for their initiatives (preferably 15 members), before action is taken;
    (e) Restraint in resorting to resolutions, in order to avoid proliferation of resolutions without prejudice to the right of States to decide on the periodicity of presenting their draft proposals by:
        (i)   Minimizing unnecessary duplication of initiatives with the General Assembly/Third Committee;
        (ii) Clustering of agenda items;
        (iii) Staggering the tabling of decisions and/or resolutions and consideration of action on agenda items/issues.

C. Outcomes other than resolutions and decisions

118. These may include recommendations, conclusions, summaries of discussions and President's Statement. As such outcomes would have different legal implications, they should supplement and not replace resolutions and decisions.

D. Special sessions of the Council

119. The following provisions shall complement the general framework provided by General Assembly resolution 60/251 and the rules of procedure of the Human Rights Council.
120. The rules of procedure of special sessions shall be in accordance with the rules of procedure applicable for regular sessions of the Council.
121. The request for the holding of a special session, in accordance with the requirement established in paragraph 10 of General Assembly resolution 60/251, shall be submitted to the President and to the secretariat of the Council. The request shall specify the item proposed for consideration and include any other relevant information the sponsors may wish to provide.

122. The special session shall be convened as soon as possible after the formal request is communicated, but, in principle, not earlier than two working days, and not later than five working days after the formal receipt of the request. The duration of the special session shall not exceed three days (six working sessions), unless the Council decides otherwise.

123. The secretariat of the Council shall immediately communicate the request for the holding of a special session and any additional information provided by the sponsors in the request, as well as the date for the convening of the special session, to all United Nations Member States and make the information available to the specialized agencies, other intergovernmental organizations and national human rights institutions, as well as to non-governmental organizations in consultative status by the most expedient and expeditious means of communication. Special session documentation, in particular draft resolutions and decisions, should be made available in all official United Nations languages to all States in an equitable, timely and transparent manner.

124. The President of the Council should hold open-ended informative consultations before the special session on its conduct and organization. In this regard, the secretariat may also be requested to provide additional information, including, on the methods of work of previous special sessions.

125. Members of the Council, concerned States, observer States, specialized agencies, other intergovernmental organizations and national human rights institutions, as well as non-governmental organizations in consultative status may contribute to the special session in accordance with the rules of procedure of the Council.

126. If the requesting or other States intend to present draft resolutions or decisions at the special session, texts should be made available in accordance with the Council's relevant rules of procedure. Nevertheless, sponsors are urged to present such texts as early as possible.

127. The sponsors of a draft resolution or decision should hold open-ended consultations on the text of their draft resolution(s) or decision(s) with a view to achieving the widest participation in their consideration and, if possible, achieving consensus on them.

128. A special session should allow participatory debate, be results-oriented and geared to achieving practical outcomes, the implementation of which can be monitored and reported on at the following regular session of the Council for possible follow-up decision.

VII. RULES OF PROCEDURE

Sessions

Rules of procedure
Rule 1
The Human Rights Council shall apply the rules of procedure established for the Main Committees of the General Assembly, as applicable, unless subsequently otherwise decided by the Assembly or the Council.

Regular Sessions

Number of sessions
Rule 2
The Human Rights Council shall meet regularly throughout the year and schedule no fewer than three sessions per Council year, including a main session, for a total duration of no less than 10 weeks.

Assumption of membership
Rule 3
Newly-elected member States of the Human Rights Council shall assume their membership on the first day of the Council year, replacing member States that have concluded their respective membership terms.

Place of meeting
Rule 4
The Human Rights Council shall be based in Geneva.

Special Sessions

Convening of special sessions
Rule 5
The rules of procedure of special sessions of the Human Rights Council will be the same as the rules of procedure applicable for regular sessions of the Human Rights Council.
Rule 6
The Human Rights Council shall hold special sessions, when needed, at the request of a member of the Council with the support of one third of the membership of the Council.

Participation of and Consultation with Observers of the Council

Rule 7
(a) The Council shall apply the rules of procedure established for committees of the General Assembly, as applicable, unless subsequently otherwise decided by the Assembly or the Council, and the participation of and consultation with observers, including States that are not members of the Council, the specialized agencies, other intergovernmental organizations and national human rights institutions, as well as non-governmental organizations, shall be based on arrangements, including Economic and Social Council resolution 1996/31 of 25 July 1996, and practices observed by the Commission on Human Rights, while ensuring the most effective contribution of these entities.

(b) Participation of national human rights institutions shall be based on arrangements and practices agreed upon by the Commission on Human Rights, including resolution 2005/74 of 20 April 2005, while ensuring the most effective contribution of these entities.

Organization of Work and Agenda for Regular Sessions

Organizational meetings
Rule 8

(a) At the beginning of each Council year, the Council shall hold an organizational meeting to elect its Bureau and to consider and adopt the agenda, programme of work, and calendar of regular sessions for the Council year indicating, if possible, a target date for the conclusion of its work, the approximate dates of consideration of items and the number of meetings to be allocated to each item.

(b) The President of the Council shall also convene organizational meetings two weeks before the beginning of each session and, if necessary, during the Council sessions to discuss organizational and procedural issues pertinent to that session.

President and Vice-Presidents

Elections
Rule 9

(a) At the beginning of each Council year, at its organizational meeting, the Council shall elect, from among the representatives of its members, a President and four Vice-Presidents. The President and the Vice Presidents shall constitute the Bureau. One of the Vice-Presidents shall serve as Rapporteur.

(b) In the election of the President of the Council, regard shall be had for the equitable geographical rotation of this office among the following Regional Groups: African States, Asian States, Eastern European States, Latin American and Caribbean States, and Western European and other States. The four Vice-Presidents of the Council shall be elected on the basis of equitable geographical distribution from the Regional Groups other than the one to which the President belongs. The selection of the Rapporteur shall be based on geographic rotation.

Bureau
Rule 10

The Bureau shall deal with procedural and organizational matters.

Term of office
Rule 11

The President and the Vice-Presidents shall, subject to rule 13, hold office for a period of one year. They shall not be eligible for immediate re-election to the same post.

Absence of officers
Rule 12

If the President finds it necessary to be absent during a meeting or any part thereof, he/she shall designate one of the Vice-Presidents to take his/her place. A Vice-President acting as President shall have the same powers and duties as the President. If the President ceases to hold office pursuant to rule 13, the remaining members of the Bureau shall designate one of the Vice Presidents to take his/her place until the election of a new President.

Replacement of the President or a Vice-President
Rule 13
If the President or any Vice-President ceases to be able to carry out his/her functions or ceases to be a representative of a member of the Council, or if the Member of the United Nations of which he/she is a representative ceases to be a member of the Council, he/she shall cease to hold such office and a new President or Vice-President shall be elected for the unexpired term.

Secretariat

Duties of the secretariat
Rule 14
The Office of the United Nations High Commissioner for Human Rights shall act as secretariat for the Council. In this regard, it shall receive, translate, print and circulate in all official United Nations languages, documents, reports and resolutions of the Council, its committees and its organs; interpret speeches made at the meetings; prepare, print and circulate the records of the session; have the custody and proper preservation of the documents in the archives of the Council; distribute all documents of the Council to the members of the Council and observers and, generally, perform all other support functions which the Council may require.

Records and Report

Report to the General Assembly
Rule 15
The Council shall submit an annual report to the General Assembly.

Public and Private Meetings of the Human Rights Council

General principles
Rule 16
The meetings of the Council shall be held in public unless the Council decides that exceptional circumstances require the meeting be held in private.

Private meetings
Rule 17
All decisions of the Council taken at a private meeting shall be announced at an early public meeting of the Council.

Conduct of Business

Working groups and other arrangements
Rule 18
The Council may set up working groups and other arrangements. Participation in these bodies shall be decided upon by the members, based on rule 7. The rules of procedure of

these bodies shall follow those of the Council, as applicable, unless decided otherwise by the Council.

Quorum
Rule 19
The President may declare a meeting open and permit the debate to proceed when at least one third of the members of the Council are present. The presence of a majority of the members shall be required for any decision to be taken.

Majority required
Rule 20
Decisions of the Council shall be made by a simple majority of the members present and voting, subject to rule 19.

(Appendices I and II omitted)

47

Review of the Work and Functioning of the Human Rights Council

Note: Resolution adopted by the Human Rights Council – Review of the work and functioning of the Human Rights Council, A/HRC/RES/16/21. Adopted 25 March 2011.

The Human Rights Council,

   Acting in compliance with the mandate entrusted to it by the General Assembly in paragraph 16 of resolution 60/251 of 15 March 2006, in which the Assembly decided that the Human Rights Council should review its work and functioning five years after its establishment and report to the Assembly,

   Having considered the report of the open-ended intergovernmental working group on the review of work and functioning of the Human Rights Council, established by the Council in its resolution 12/1 of 1 October 2009,

1. *Takes note* of the report of the open-ended intergovernmental working group on the review of work and functioning of the Human Rights Council,

2. *Adopts* the "Outcome of the review of the work and functioning of the United Nations Human Rights Council" as annexed to the present resolution, to be submitted to the General Assembly;

3. *Decides* that the "Outcome of the review of the work and functioning of the United Nations Human Rights Council" shall be a supplement to the institution-building package contained in Human Rights Council resolutions 5/1 and 5/2 of 18 June 2007, as well as in other related Council resolutions, decisions and President's statements;

4. *Also decides* to submit the following draft resolution to the General Assembly for its consideration:

"*The General Assembly,*

"*Taking note* of Human Rights Council resolution 16/21 of 25 March 2011,

"*Endorses* the text entitled "Outcome of the review of the work and functioning of the United Nations Human Rights Council"."

ANNEX

OUTCOME OF THE REVIEW OF THE WORK AND FUNCTIONING OF THE UNITED NATIONS HUMAN RIGHTS COUNCIL

I. UNIVERSAL PERIODIC REVIEW

A. Basis, principles and objectives of the review

1. The basis, principles and objectives of the universal periodic review as set forth in paragraphs 1, 2, 3 and 4 of the annex to Human Rights Council resolution 5/1 shall be reaffirmed.

B. Periodicity and order of the review

2. The second cycle of the review shall begin in June 2012.
3. The periodicity of the review for the second and subsequent cycles will be of four and a half years. This will imply the consideration of 42 States per year during three sessions of the Working Group on the Universal Periodic Review.
4. The order of review established for the first cycle of the review shall be maintained for the second and subsequent cycles.

C. Process and modalities of the review

1. Focus and documentation

5. The review during the second and subsequent cycles will continue to be based on the three documents identified in paragraph 15 of the annex to Council resolution 5/1.
6. The second and subsequent cycles of the review should focus on, inter alia, the implementation of the accepted recommendations and the developments of the human rights situation in the State under review.
7. The general guidelines for universal periodic review reports adopted by the Council in its decision 6/102 shall be adjusted to the focus of the second and subsequent cycles before the eighteenth session of the Council.
8. Other relevant stakeholders are encouraged to include in their contributions information on the follow-up to the preceding review.
9. The summary of the information provided by other relevant stakeholders should contain, where appropriate, a separate section for contributions by the national human rights institution of the State under review that is accredited in full compliance with the Paris Principles. Information provided by other accredited national human rights institutions will be reflected accordingly, as well as information provided by other stakeholders.

2. Modalities

10. The role of the troikas shall be maintained as set forth in the annex to Council resolution 5/1 and in President's statement PRST/8/1.

11. Following the extension of the review cycle to four and a half years and within existing resources and workload, the duration of the Working Group meeting for the review will be extended from the present three hours and the modalities will be agreed upon at the seventeenth session of the Council, including the list of speakers, which shall be based on the modalities as appear in the Appendix.

12. The final outcome of the review will be adopted by the plenary of the Council. The modalities for the organization of the one-hour consideration of the outcome shall be in accordance with President's statement PRST/9/2.

13. The national human rights institution of the State under review consistent with the principles relating to the status of national institutions for the promotion and protection of human rights annexed to General Assembly resolution 48/134 (the Paris Principles) shall be entitled to intervene immediately after the State under review during the adoption of the outcome of the review by the Council plenary.

14. The Universal Periodic Review Voluntary Trust Fund to facilitate the participation of States established by the Council in its resolution 6/17 should be strengthened and operationalized in order to encourage a significant participation of developing countries, particularly least developing countries and small island developing States, in their review.

D. Outcome of the review

15. The recommendations contained in the outcome of the review should preferably be clustered thematically with the full involvement and consent of the State under review and the States that made the recommendations.

16. The State under review should clearly communicate to the Council, in a written format preferably prior to the Council plenary, its positions on all received recommendations, in accordance with the provisions of paragraphs 27 and 32 of the annex to Council resolution 5/1.

E. Follow-up to the review

17. While the outcome of the review, as a cooperative mechanism, should be implemented primarily by the State concerned, States are encouraged to conduct broad consultations with all relevant stakeholders in this regard.

18. States are encouraged to provide the Council, on a voluntary basis, with a midterm update on follow-up to accepted recommendations.

19. The Voluntary Fund for Financial and Technical Assistance, established by the Council in its resolution 6/17, should be strengthened and operationalized in order to provide a source of financial and technical assistance to help countries, in particular least developed countries and small island developing States, to implement the recommendations emanating from their review. A board of trustees should be established in accordance with the rules of the United Nations.

20. States may request the United Nations representation at the national or regional level to assist them in the implementation of follow-up to their review, bearing in mind the provisions of paragraph 36 of the annex to Council resolution 5/1. The Office of the United Nations High Commissioner for Human Rights may act as a clearing house for such assistance.

21. Financial and technical assistance for the implementation of the review should support national needs and priorities, as may be reflected in national implementation plans.

II. SPECIAL PROCEDURES

A. Selection and appointment of mandate holders

22. To further strengthen and enhance transparency in the selection and appointment process of mandate holders envisaged in the annex to Council resolution 5/1, the following provisions will apply:

    (a) In addition to entities specified in paragraph 42, national human rights institutions in compliance with the Paris Principles may also nominate candidates as special procedures mandate holders;

    (b) Individual candidates and candidates nominated by entities shall submit an application for each specific mandate, together with personal data and a motivation letter no longer than 600 words. The Office of the High Commissioner shall prepare a public list of candidates who applied for each vacancy;

    (c) The Consultative Group will consider, in a transparent manner, candidates having applied for each specific mandate. However, under exceptional circumstances and if a particular post justifies it, the Group may consider additional candidates with equal or more suitable qualifications for the post. The Group shall interview shortlisted candidates to ensure equal treatment of all candidates;

    (d) In implementing paragraph 52, the President shall justify his/her decision if he/she decides not to follow the order of priority proposed by the Consultative Group.

B. Working methods

23. In line with Council resolution 5/2, States should cooperate with and assist special procedures in the performance of their tasks and it is incumbent on mandate holders to exercise their functions in accordance with their mandates and in compliance with the code of conduct.

24. The integrity and independence of the special procedures and the principles of cooperation, transparency and accountability are integral to ensuring a robust system of the special procedures that would enhance the capacity of the Council to address human rights situations on the ground.

25. The special procedures shall continue to foster a constructive dialogue with States. The special procedures shall also endeavour to formulate their recommendations in a concrete, comprehensive and action-oriented way and pay attention to the technical assistance and capacity-building needs of States in their thematic and country mission reports. The comments of the State concerned shall be included as an addendum to country mission reports.

26. States are urged to cooperate with and assist special procedures by responding in a timely manner to requests for information and visits, and to study carefully the conclusions and recommendations addressed to them by the special procedures.

27. The Council should streamline its requests to special procedures, in particular with regard to reporting, to ensure meaningful discussion of their reports. The Council should remain as a forum for open, constructive and transparent discussion on cooperation between States and special procedures, allowing for the identification and exchange of good practices and lessons learned.

28. The national human rights institution consistent with the principles relating to the status of national institutions for the promotion and protection of human rights annexed to General Assembly resolution 48/134 (the Paris Principles) of the country concerned shall be entitled to intervene immediately after the country concerned during the interactive dialogue, following the presentation of a country mission report by a special procedure mandate holder.

29. The Office of the High Commissioner will continue to maintain information on special procedures, such as mandates, mandate holders, invitations and country visits and responses thereto, as well as reports presented to the Council and the General Assembly, in a comprehensive and easily accessible manner.

30. The Council strongly rejects any act of intimidation or reprisal against individuals and groups who cooperate or have cooperated with the United Nations, its representatives and mechanisms in the field of human rights, and urges States to prevent and ensure adequate protection against such acts.

C. Resources and funding

31. The Council recognizes the importance of ensuring the provision of adequate and equitable funding, with equal priority accorded to civil and political rights and economic, social and cultural rights, including the right to development, to support all special procedures according to their specific needs, including additional tasks entrusted to them by the General Assembly. This should be achieved through the regular budget of the United Nations.

32. The Council therefore requests the Secretary-General to ensure the availability of adequate resources within the regular budget of the Office of the High Commissioner to support the full implementation by special procedures of their mandates.

33. The Council also recognizes the continued need for extra-budgetary funding to support the work of the special procedures, and welcomes further voluntary contributions by Member States, emphasizing that these contributions should be, to the extent possible, unearmarked.

34. The Council highlights the need for full transparency in the funding of the special procedures.

III. ADVISORY COMMITTEE

35. The Council shall, within existing resources, strengthen its interaction with the Advisory Committee and engage more systematically with it through work formats such as seminars, panels, working groups and sending feedback to the inputs of the Committee.

36. The Council shall endeavour to clarify specific mandates given to the Advisory Committee under relevant resolutions, including indicating thematic priorities and provide specific guidelines for the Advisory Committee with a view to triggering implementation-oriented outputs.

37. In order to provide a proper setting for a better interaction between the Council and its Committee, the first annual session of the Committee shall henceforth be convened immediately prior to the March session of the Council, while the second session shall be held in August.

38. The annual report of the Committee shall be submitted to the Council at its September session, and be the subject of an interactive dialogue with the Committee Chairperson. The present provision does not exclude other interaction with the Committee should such opportunities arise and be deemed appropriate by the Council.

39. The Committee shall endeavour to enhance intersessional work between its members in order to give effect to the provisions of paragraph 81 of the annex to Council resolution 5/1.

IV. AGENDA AND FRAMEWORK FOR THE PROGRAMME OF WORK

40. The Council's agenda and framework for programme of work are as is specified in the annex to Council resolution 5/1.

41. Council cycles will be aligned with the calendar year and be subject to any necessary transitional arrangements decided on by the General Assembly.

V. METHODS OF WORK AND RULES OF PROCEDURE

A. Yearly panel with United Nations agencies and funds

42. The Council shall hold a half-day panel discussion once a year to interact with heads of governing bodies and secretariats of United Nations agencies and funds within their respective mandates on specific human rights themes with the objective of promoting the mainstreaming of human rights throughout the United Nations system. The present provision does not preclude other opportunities that may arise for discussions between the Council and United Nations agencies and funds on the mainstreaming of human rights.

43. State or regional groups may propose issues to be discussed by the panel. On the basis of such proposals and consultation with all regional groups, the President of the Council will propose the theme of the panel discussion for the upcoming year for approval by the Council at its relevant organizational session.

44. The Office of High Commissioner, in its capacity as secretariat of the Council, shall coordinate the preparation of the documentation required for the panel discussion.

B. Voluntary yearly calendar of resolutions

45. The Bureau shall establish a tentative yearly calendar for the thematic resolutions of the Human Rights Council in consultation with the main sponsors. The yearly calendar will be established on a voluntary basis and without prejudice to the right of States as provided for by paragraph 117 of the annex to Council resolution 5/1.

46. The calendar should also contemplate the appropriate synchronization of schedules for resolutions, mandates and presentation of reports by the special procedures, taking into account the need for balance between them.

47. The Bureau shall present a report to the Council in its eighteenth session.

C. Bi- and triennial thematic resolutions

48. In principle and on a voluntary basis, omnibus thematic resolutions should be tabled on a biennial or triennial basis.

49. Thematic resolutions on the same issue to be presented in between the abovementioned intervals are expected to be shorter and focused on addressing the specific question or standard gap that justified their presentation.

D. Transparency and extensive consultations for resolutions and decisions

50. The consultation process on, inter alia, resolutions and decisions of the Council shall observe the principles of transparency and inclusiveness.

E. Documentation

51. There is a need for ensuring the availability of working documents in a timely manner and in all official languages of the United Nations.

F. Deadlines for the notification and submission of draft initiatives and programme budget implication information

52. There is a need for early submission of draft resolutions and decisions by the end of the penultimate week of the Council session.

53. Sponsors of initiatives are encouraged to contact the Office of the High Commissioner before the second week of the session with a view to facilitate the circulation of information on budgetary implications, if any.

G. Establishment of an office of the President

54. In line with the procedural and organizational roles of the President, the Office of the President of the Human Rights Council shall be established, within existing resources, in order to support the President in the fulfilment of his or her tasks and enhance efficiency, continuity and institutional memory in this regard.

55. The Office of the President shall be provided with adequate resources drawn from the regular budget, including staff, office space and necessary equipment required for the fulfilment of their tasks. The appointment of the staff of the Office shall promote equitable geographic distribution and gender balance. The staff of the Office shall be accountable to the President.

56. The composition, modalities and financial implications of the Office of President shall be considered by the Council on the basis of the report of the secretariat, at its seventeenth session.

H. Human Rights Council secretariat service

57. The secretariat service to the Council and its mechanisms should continue to be improved to enhance the efficiency of the work of the Council.

I. Accessibility for persons with disabilities

58. There is a need to enhance accessibility for persons with disabilities to the Council and the work of its mechanisms, including its information and communication technology, Internet resources and documents, in accordance with international standards on accessibility for persons with disabilities.

J. Use of information technology

59. The Council shall explore the feasibility of the use of information technology, such as videoconferencing or video messaging, in order to enhance access and participation by non-resident State delegations, specialized agencies, other intergovernmental organizations and national human rights institutions consistent with the principles relating to the status of national institutions for the promotion and protection of human rights annexed to General Assembly resolution 48/134 (the Paris Principles), as well as by non-governmental organizations in consultative status, bearing in mind the need to ensure full compliance of such participation with its rules of procedure and rules concerning accreditation.

60. The use of modern information technology, such as the electronic circulation of copies, is encouraged in order to reduce the circulation of paper.

K. Task force

61. The Council decides to establish a task force to study the issues envisaged in paragraphs 57, 58, 59 and 60 in consultation with Government representatives, the Office of the High Commissioner and the United Nations Office at Geneva and all relevant stakeholders, and to submit concrete recommendations to the Council at its nineteenth session.

L. Technical assistance trust fund

62. The Council will consider modalities for the establishment of a technical assistance trust fund to support the participation of least developed countries and small island developing States in the work of the Council at its nineteenth session.

APPENDIX

MODALITIES FOR ESTABLISHING THE LIST OF SPEAKERS FOR THE WORKING GROUP ON THE UNIVERSAL PERIODIC REVIEW

The established procedures, which allow speaking time of three minutes for Member States and two minutes for observer States, will continue to apply when all speakers can be accommodated within – minutes available to Member and observer States.

Should it not be possible to accommodate all speakers within – minutes based on three minutes of speaking time for Member States and two minutes for observer States, the speaking time will be reduced to two minutes for all.

If all speakers still cannot be accommodated, the speaking time will be divided among all delegations inscribed so as to enable each and every speaker to take the floor.

STEPS FOR DRAWING UP THE LIST OF SPEAKERS

1. The list of speakers will open at 10 a.m. on the Monday of the week preceding the beginning of the session of the Working Group on the Universal Periodic Review and remain open for a period of four days. It will close on the Thursday at 6 p.m. A registration desk will be set up at the Palais des Nations. The exact location will be communicated to all permanent missions by the secretariat.

2. In all cases, regardless of speaking time, the delegations inscribed on the list of speakers will be arranged in alphabetical order of the country names in English. On the Friday morning preceding the beginning of the session, the President, in the presence of the Bureau, will draw by lot the first speaker on the list. The list of speakers will continue from the State drawn onward. On the Friday afternoon, all delegations will be informed of the speaking order and of the speaking time available to delegations.

3. Speaking time limits during the review will be strictly enforced. Speakers who exceed their speaking time will have their microphones cut off. Speakers may therefore wish to deliver the essential part at the beginning of their statements.

4. All speakers will retain the possibility of swapping place on the speakers list under bilateral arrangement between speakers.

PART IV
UN World Conferences and Summits

48

Proclamation of Teheran, 1968

Note: Proclamation of Teheran, Final Act of the International Conference on Human Rights, Teheran, 22 April to 13 May 1968, U.N. Doc. A/CONF. 32/41 at 3 (1968).

The International Conference on Human Rights,

Having met at Teheran from April 22 to May 13, 1968 to review the progress made in the twenty years since the adoption of the Universal Declaration of Human Rights and to formulate a programme for the future,

Having considered the problems relating to the activities of the United Nations for the promotion and encouragement of respect for human rights and fundamental freedoms,

Bearing in mind the resolutions adopted by the Conference,

Noting that the observance of the International Year for Human Rights takes place at a time when the world is undergoing a process of unprecedented change,

Having regard to the new opportunities made available by the rapid progress of science and technology,

Believing that, in an age when conflict and violence prevail in many parts of the world, the fact of human interdependence and the need for human solidarity are more evident than ever before,

Recognizing that peace is the universal aspiration of mankind and that peace and justice are indispensable to the full realization of human rights and fundamental freedoms,

Solemnly proclaims that:

1. It is imperative that the members of the international community fulfil their solemn obligations to promote and encourage respect for human rights and fundamental freedoms for all without distinctions of any kind such as race, colour, sex, language, religion, political or other opinions;

2. The Universal Declaration of Human Rights states a common understanding of the peoples of the world concerning the inalienable and inviolable rights of all members of the human family and constitutes an obligation for the members of the international community;

3. The International Covenant on Civil and Political Rights, the International Covenant on Economic, Social and Cultural Rights, the Declaration on the Granting of Independence to Colonial Countries and Peoples, the International Convention on the Elimination of All Forms of Racial Discrimination as well as other conventions and declarations in the field of human rights adopted under the auspices of the United Nations, the specialized agencies and the regional intergovernmental organizations, have created new standards and obligations to which States should conform;

4. Since the adoption of the Universal Declaration of Human Rights the United Nations has made substantial progress in defining standards for the enjoyment and protection

of human rights and fundamental freedoms. During this period many important international instruments were adopted but much remains to be done in regard to the implementation of those rights and freedoms;

5. The primary aim of the United Nations in the sphere of human rights is the achievement by each individual of the maximum freedom and dignity. For the realization of this objective, the laws of every country should grant each individual, irrespective of race, language, religion or political belief, freedom of expression, of information, of conscience and of religion, as well as the right to participate in the political, economic, cultural and social life of his country;

6. States should reaffirm their determination effectively to enforce the principles enshrined in the Charter of the United Nations and in other international instruments that concern human rights and fundamental freedoms;

7. Gross denials of human rights under the repugnant policy of apartheid is a matter of the gravest concern to the international community. This policy of apartheid, condemned as a crime against humanity, continues seriously to disturb international peace and security. It is therefore imperative for the international community to use every possible means to eradicate this evil. The struggle against apartheid is recognized as legitimate;

8. The peoples of the world must be made fully aware of the evils of racial discrimination and must join in combating them. The implementation of this principle of non-discrimination, embodied in the Charter of the United Nations, the Universal Declaration of Human Rights, and other international instruments in the field of human rights, constitutes a most urgent task of mankind at the international as well as at the national level. All ideologies based on racial superiority and intolerance must be condemned and resisted;

9. Eight years after the General Assembly's Declaration on the Granting of Independence to Colonial Countries and Peoples the problems of colonialism continue to preoccupy the international community. It is a matter of urgency that all Member States should co-operate with the appropriate organs of the United Nations so that effective measures can be taken to ensure that the Declaration is fully implemented;

10. Massive denials of human rights, arising out of aggression or any armed conflict with their tragic consequences, and resulting in untold human misery, engender reactions which could engulf the world in ever growing hostilities. It is the obligation of the international community to co-operate in eradicating such scourges;

11. Gross denials of human rights arising from discrimination on grounds of race, religion, belief or expressions of opinion outrage the conscience of mankind and endanger the foundations of freedom, justice and peace in the world;

12. The widening gap between the economically developed and developing countries impedes the realization of human rights in the international community. The failure of the Development Decade to reach its modest objectives makes it all the more imperative for every nation, according to its capacities, to make the maximum possible effort to close this gap;

13. Since human rights and fundamental freedoms are indivisible, the full realization of civil and political rights without the enjoyment of economic, social and cultural rights is impossible. The achievement of lasting progress in the implementation of

human rights is dependent upon sound and effective national and international policies of economic and social development;

14. The existence of over seven hundred million illiterates throughout the world is an enormous obstacle to all efforts at realizing the aims and purposes of the Charter of the United Nations and the provisions of the Universal Declaration of Human Rights. International action aimed at eradicating illiteracy from the face of the earth and promoting education at all levels requires urgent attention;

15. The discrimination of which women are still victims in various regions of the world must be eliminated. An inferior status for women is contrary to the Charter of the United Nations as well as the provisions of the Universal Declaration of Human Rights. The full implementation of the Declaration on the Elimination of Discrimination against Women is a necessity for the progress of mankind;

16. The protection of the family and of the child remains the concern of the international community. Parents have a basic human right to determine freely and responsibly the number and the spacing of their children;

17. The aspirations of the younger generation for a better world, in which human rights and fundamental freedoms are fully implemented, must be given the highest encouragement. It is imperative that youth participate in shaping the future of mankind;

18. While recent scientific discoveries and technological advances have opened vast prospects for economic, social and cultural progress, such developments may nevertheless endanger the rights and freedoms of individuals and will require continuing attention;

19. Disarmament would release immense human and material resources now devoted to military purposes. These resources should be used for the promotion of human rights and fundamental freedoms. General and complete disarmament is one of the highest aspirations of all peoples;

Therefore,

The International Conference on Human Rights,

1. Affirming its faith in the principles of the Universal Declaration of Human Rights and other international instruments in this field,

2. Urges all peoples and governments to dedicate themselves to the principles enshrined in the Universal Declaration of Human Rights and to redouble their efforts to provide for all human beings a life consonant with freedom and dignity and conducive to physical, mental, social and spiritual welfare.

49

Vienna Declaration and Programme of Action, 1993

Note: Adopted by the World Conference on Human Rights in Vienna on 25 June 1993.

The World Conference on Human Rights,

Considering that the promotion and protection of human rights is a matter of priority for the international community, and that the Conference affords a unique opportunity to carry out a comprehensive analysis of the international human rights system and of the machinery for the protection of human rights, in order to enhance and thus promote a fuller observance of those rights, in a just and balanced manner,

Recognizing and affirming that all human rights derive from the dignity and worth inherent in the human person, and that the human person is the central subject of human rights and fundamental freedoms, and consequently should be the principal beneficiary and should participate actively in the realization of these rights and freedoms,

Reaffirming their commitment to the purposes and principles contained in the Charter of the United Nations and the Universal Declaration of Human Rights,

Reaffirming the commitment contained in Article 56 of the Charter of the United Nations to take joint and separate action, placing proper emphasis on developing effective international cooperation for the realization of the purposes set out in Article 55, including universal respect for, and observance of, human rights and fundamental freedoms for all,

Emphasizing the responsibilities of all States, in conformity with the Charter of the United Nations, to develop and encourage respect for human rights and fundamental freedoms for all, without distinction as to race, sex, language or religion,

Recalling the Preamble to the Charter of the United Nations, in particular the determination to reaffirm faith in fundamental human rights, in the dignity and worth of the human person, and in the equal rights of men and women and of nations large and small,

Recalling also the determination expressed in the Preamble of the Charter of the United Nations to save succeeding generations from the scourge of war, to establish conditions under which justice and respect for obligations arising from treaties and other sources of international law can be maintained, to promote social progress and better standards of life in larger freedom, to practice tolerance and good neighbourliness, and to employ international machinery for the promotion of the economic and social advancement of all peoples,

Emphasizing that the Universal Declaration of Human Rights, which constitutes a common standard of achievement for all peoples and all nations, is the source of inspiration and has been the basis for the United Nations in making advances in standard setting as contained in the existing international human rights instruments, in particular the

International Covenant on Civil and Political Rights and the International Covenant on Economic, Social and Cultural Rights,

<u>Considering</u> the major changes taking place on the international scene and the aspirations of all the peoples for an international order based on the principles enshrined in the Charter of the United Nations, including promoting and encouraging respect for human rights and fundamental freedoms for all and respect for the principle of equal rights and self-determination of peoples, peace, democracy, justice, equality, rule of law, pluralism, development, better standards of living and solidarity,

<u>Deeply concerned</u> by various forms of discrimination and violence, to which women continue to be exposed all over the world,

<u>Recognizing</u> that the activities of the United Nations in the field of human rights should be rationalized and enhanced in order to strengthen the United Nations machinery in this field and to further the objectives of universal respect for observance of international human rights standards,

<u>Having taken into account</u> the Declarations adopted by the three regional meetings at Tunis, San José and Bangkok and the contributions made by Governments, and bearing in mind the suggestions made by intergovernmental and non-governmental organizations, as well as the studies prepared by independent experts during the preparatory process leading to the World Conference on Human Rights,

<u>Welcoming</u> the International Year of the World's Indigenous People 1993 as a reaffirmation of the commitment of the international community to ensure their enjoyment of all human rights and fundamental freedoms and to respect the value and diversity of their cultures and identities,

<u>Recognizing also</u> that the international community should devise ways and means to remove the current obstacles and meet challenges to the full realization of all human rights and to prevent the continuation of human rights violations resulting therefrom throughout the world,

<u>Invoking</u> the spirit of our age and the realities of our time which call upon the peoples of the world and all States Members of the United Nations to rededicate themselves to the global task of promoting and protecting all human rights and fundamental freedoms so as to secure full and universal enjoyment of these rights,

<u>Determined</u> to take new steps forward in the commitment of the international community with a view to achieving substantial progress in human rights endeavours by an increased and sustained effort of international cooperation and solidarity,

<u>Solemnly adopts</u> the Vienna Declaration and Programme of Action.

I

1. The World Conference on Human Rights reaffirms the solemn commitment of all States to fulfil their obligations to promote universal respect for, and observance and protection of, all human rights and fundamental freedoms for all in accordance with the Charter of the United Nations, other instruments relating to human rights, and international law. The universal nature of these rights and freedoms is beyond question. In this framework, enhancement of international cooperation in the field of human rights is essential for the full achievement of the purposes of the United

Nations. Human rights and fundamental freedoms are the birthright of all human beings; their protection and promotion is the first responsibility of Governments.

2. All peoples have the right of self-determination. By virtue of that right they freely determine their political status, and freely pursue their economic, social and cultural development. Taking into account the particular situation of peoples under colonial or other forms of alien domination or foreign occupation, the World Conference on Human Rights recognizes the right of peoples to take any legitimate action, in accordance with the Charter of the United Nations, to realize their inalienable right of self-determination. The World Conference on Human Rights considers the denial of the right of self-determination as a violation of human rights and underlines the importance of the effective realization of this right.

In accordance with the Declaration on Principles of International Law concerning Friendly Relations and Cooperation Among States in accordance with the Charter of the United Nations, this shall not be construed as authorizing or encouraging any action which would dismember or impair, totally or in part, the territorial integrity or political unity of sovereign and independent States conducting themselves in compliance with the principle of equal rights and self-determination of peoples and thus possessed of a Government representing the whole people belonging to the territory without distinction of any kind.

3. Effective international measures to guarantee and monitor the implementation of human rights standards should be taken in respect of people under foreign occupation, and effective legal protection against the violation of their human rights should be provided, in accordance with human rights norms and international law, particularly the Geneva Convention relative to the Protection of Civilian Persons in Time of War, of 14 August 1949, and other applicable norms of humanitarian law.

4. The promotion and protection of all human rights and fundamental freedoms must be considered as a priority objective of the United Nations in accordance with its purposes and principles, in particular the purpose of international cooperation. In the framework of these purposes and principles, the promotion and protection of all human rights is a legitimate concern of the international community. The organs and specialized agencies related to human rights should therefore further enhance the coordination of their activities based on the consistent and objective application of international human rights instruments.

5. All human rights are universal, indivisible and interdependent and interrelated. The international community must treat human rights globally in a fair and equal manner, on the same footing, and with the same emphasis. While the significance of national and regional particularities and various historical, cultural and religious backgrounds must be borne in mind, it is the duty of States, regardless of their political, economic and cultural systems, to promote and protect all human rights and fundamental freedoms.

6. The efforts of the United Nations system towards the universal respect for, and observance of, human rights and fundamental freedoms for all, contribute to the stability and well-being necessary for peaceful and friendly relations among nations, and to improved conditions for peace and security as well as social and economic development, in conformity with the Charter of the United Nations.

7. The processes of promoting and protecting human rights should be conducted in conformity with the purposes and principles of the Charter of the United Nations, and international law.

8. Democracy, development and respect for human rights and fundamental freedoms are interdependent and mutually reinforcing. Democracy is based on the freely expressed will of the people to determine their own political, economic, social and cultural systems and their full participation in all aspects of their lives. In the context of the above, the promotion and protection of human rights and fundamental freedoms at the national and international levels should be universal and conducted without conditions attached. The international community should support the strengthening and promoting of democracy, development and respect for human rights and fundamental freedoms in the entire world.

9. The World Conference on Human Rights reaffirms that least developed countries committed to the process of democratization and economic reforms, many of which are in Africa, should be supported by the international community in order to succeed in their transition to democracy and economic development.

10. The World Conference on Human Rights reaffirms the right to development, as established in the Declaration on the Right to Development, as a universal and inalienable right and an integral part of fundamental human rights.

   As stated in the Declaration on the Right to Development, the human person is the central subject of development.

   While development facilitates the enjoyment of all human rights, the lack of development may not be invoked to justify the abridgement of internationally recognized human rights.

   States should cooperate with each other in ensuring development and eliminating obstacles to development. The international community should promote an effective international cooperation for the realization of the right to development and the elimination of obstacles to development.

   Lasting progress towards the implementation of the right to development requires effective development policies at the national level, as well as equitable economic relations and a favourable economic environment at the international level.

11. The right to development should be fulfilled so as to meet equitably the developmental and environmental needs of present and future generations. The World Conference on Human Rights recognizes that illicit dumping of toxic and dangerous substances and waste potentially constitutes a serious threat to the human rights to life and health of everyone.

   Consequently, the World Conference on Human Rights calls on all States to adopt and vigorously implement existing conventions relating to the dumping of toxic and dangerous products and waste and to cooperate in the prevention of illicit dumping.

   Everyone has the right to enjoy the benefits of scientific progress and its applications. The World Conference on Human Rights notes that certain advances, notably in the biomedical and life sciences as well as in information technology, may have potentially adverse consequences for the integrity, dignity and human rights of the individual, and calls for international cooperation to ensure that human rights and dignity are fully respected in this area of universal concern.

12. The World Conference on Human Rights calls upon the international community to make all efforts to help alleviate the external debt burden of developing countries, in order to supplement the efforts of the Governments of such countries to attain the full realization of the economic, social and cultural rights of their people.

13. There is a need for States and international organizations, in cooperation with non-governmental organizations, to create favourable conditions at the national, regional and international levels to ensure the full and effective enjoyment of human rights. States should eliminate all violations of human rights and their causes, as well as obstacles to the enjoyment of these rights.

14. The existence of widespread extreme poverty inhibits the full and effective enjoyment of human rights; its immediate alleviation and eventual elimination must remain a high priority for the international community.

15. Respect for human rights and for fundamental freedoms without distinction of any kind is a fundamental rule of international human rights law. The speedy and comprehensive elimination of all forms of racism and racial discrimination, xenophobia and related intolerance is a priority task for the international community. Governments should take effective measures to prevent and combat them. Groups, institutions, intergovernmental and non-governmental organizations and individuals are urged to intensify their efforts in cooperating and coordinating their activities against these evils.

16. The World Conference on Human Rights welcomes the progress made in dismantling apartheid and calls upon the international community and the United Nations system to assist in this process.

    The World Conference on Human Rights also deplores the continuing acts of violence aimed at undermining the quest for a peaceful dismantling of apartheid.

17. The acts, methods and practices of terrorism in all its forms and manifestations as well as linkage in some countries to drug trafficking are activities aimed at the destruction of human rights, fundamental freedoms and democracy, threatening territorial integrity, security of States and destabilizing legitimately constituted Governments. The international community should take the necessary steps to enhance cooperation to prevent and combat terrorism.

18. The human rights of women and of the girl-child are an inalienable, integral and indivisible part of universal human rights. The full and equal participation of women in political, civil, economic, social and cultural life, at the national, regional and international levels, and the eradication of all forms of discrimination on grounds of sex are priority objectives of the international community.

    Gender-based violence and all forms of sexual harassment and exploitation, including those resulting from cultural prejudice and international trafficking, are incompatible with the dignity and worth of the human person, and must be eliminated. This can be achieved by legal measures and through national action and international cooperation in such fields as economic and social development, education, safe maternity and health care, and social support.

    The human rights of women should form an integral part of the United Nations human rights activities, including the promotion of all human rights instruments relating to women.

The World Conference on Human Rights urges Governments, institutions, inter-governmental and non-governmental organizations to intensify their efforts for the protection and promotion of human rights of women and the girl-child.

19. Considering the importance of the promotion and protection of the rights of persons belonging to minorities and the contribution of such promotion and protection to the political and social stability of the States in which such persons live,

The World Conference on Human Rights reaffirms the obligation of States to ensure that persons belonging to minorities may exercise fully and effectively all human rights and fundamental freedoms without any discrimination and in full equality before the law in accordance with the Declaration on the Rights of Persons Belonging to National or Ethnic, Religious and Linguistic Minorities.

The persons belonging to minorities have the right to enjoy their own culture, to profess and practise their own religion and to use their own language in private and in public, freely and without interference or any form of discrimination.

20. The World Conference on Human Rights recognizes the inherent dignity and the unique contribution of indigenous people to the development and plurality of society and strongly reaffirms the commitment of the international community to their economic, social and cultural well-being and their enjoyment of the fruits of sustainable development. States should ensure the full and free participation of indigenous people in all aspects of society, in particular in matters of concern to them. Considering the importance of the promotion and protection of the rights of indigenous people, and the contribution of such promotion and protection to the political and social stability of the States in which such people live, States should, in accordance with international law, take concerted positive steps to ensure respect for all human rights and fundamental freedoms of indigenous people, on the basis of equality and non-discrimination, and recognize the value and diversity of their distinct identities, cultures and social organization.

21. The World Conference on Human Rights, welcoming the early ratification of the Convention on the Rights of the Child by a large number of States and noting the recognition of the human rights of children in the World Declaration on the Survival, Protection and Development of Children and Plan of Action adopted by the World Summit for Children, urges universal ratification of the Convention by 1995 and its effective implementation by States parties through the adoption of all the necessary legislative, administrative and other measures and the allocation to the maximum extent of the available resources. In all actions concerning children, non-discrimi-nation and the best interest of the child should be primary considerations and the views of the child given due weight. National and international mechanisms and programmes should be strengthened for the defence and protection of children, in particular, the girl-child, abandoned children, street children, economically and sex-ually exploited children, including through child pornography, child prostitution or sale of organs, children victims of diseases including acquired immunodeficiency syndrome, refugee and displaced children, children in detention, children in armed conflict, as well as children victims of famine and drought and other emergencies. International cooperation and solidarity should be promoted to support the imple-mentation of the Convention and the rights of the child should be a priority in the United Nations system-wide action on human rights.

The World Conference on Human Rights also stresses that the child for the full and harmonious development of his or her personality should grow up in a family environment which accordingly merits broader protection.

22. Special attention needs to be paid to ensuring non-discrimination, and the equal enjoyment of all human rights and fundamental freedoms by disabled persons, including their active participation in all aspects of society.

23. The World Conference on Human Rights reaffirms that everyone, without distinction of any kind, is entitled to the right to seek and to enjoy in other countries asylum from persecution, as well as the right to return to one's own country. In this respect it stresses the importance of the Universal Declaration of Human Rights, the 1951 Convention relating to the Status of Refugees, its 1967 Protocol and regional instruments. It expresses its appreciation to States that continue to admit and host large numbers of refugees in their territories, and to the Office of the United Nations High Commissioner for Refugees for its dedication to its task. It also expresses its appreciation to the United Nations Relief and Works Agency for Palestine Refugees in the Near East.

The World Conference on Human Rights recognizes that gross violations of human rights, including in armed conflicts, are among the multiple and complex factors leading to displacement of people.

The World Conference on Human Rights recognizes that, in view of the complexities of the global refugee crisis and in accordance with the Charter of the United Nations, relevant international instruments and international solidarity and in the spirit of burden-sharing, a comprehensive approach by the international community is needed in coordination and cooperation with the countries concerned and relevant organizations, bearing in mind the mandate of the United Nations High Commissioner for Refugees. This should include the development of strategies to address the root causes and effects of movements of refugees and other displaced persons, the strengthening of emergency preparedness and response mechanisms, the provision of effective protection and assistance, bearing in mind the special needs of women and children, as well as the achievement of durable solutions, primarily through the preferred solution of dignified and safe voluntary repatriation, including solutions such as those adopted by the international refugee conferences. The World Conference on Human Rights underlines the responsibilities of States, particularly as they relate to the countries of origin.

In the light of the comprehensive approach, the World Conference on Human Rights emphasizes the importance of giving special attention including through intergovernmental and humanitarian organizations and finding lasting solutions to questions related to internally displaced persons including their voluntary and safe return and rehabilitation.

In accordance with the Charter of the United Nations and the principles of humanitarian law, the World Conference on Human Rights further emphasizes the importance of and the need for humanitarian assistance to victims of all natural and man-made disasters.

24. Great importance must be given to the promotion and protection of the human rights of persons belonging to groups which have been rendered vulnerable, including migrant workers, the elimination of all forms of discrimination against them,

and the strengthening and more effective implementation of existing human rights instruments. States have an obligation to create and maintain adequate measures at the national level, in particular in the fields of education, health and social support, for the promotion and protection of the rights of persons in vulnerable sectors of their populations and to ensure the participation of those among them who are interested in finding a solution to their own problems.

25. The World Conference on Human Rights affirms that extreme poverty and social exclusion constitute a violation of human dignity and that urgent steps are necessary to achieve better knowledge of extreme poverty and its causes, including those related to the problem of development, in order to promote the human rights of the poorest, and to put an end to extreme poverty and social exclusion and to promote the enjoyment of the fruits of social progress. It is essential for States to foster participation by the poorest people in the decision-making process by the community in which they live, the promotion of human rights and efforts to combat extreme poverty.

26. The World Conference on Human Rights welcomes the progress made in the codification of human rights instruments, which is a dynamic and evolving process, and urges the universal ratification of human rights treaties. All States are encouraged to accede to these international instruments; all States are encouraged to avoid, as far as possible, the resort to reservations.

27. Every State should provide an effective framework of remedies to redress human rights grievances or violations. The administration of justice, including law enforcement and prosecutorial agencies and, especially, an independent judiciary and legal profession in full conformity with applicable standards contained in international human rights instruments, are essential to the full and non-discriminatory realization of human rights and indispensable to the processes of democracy and sustainable development. In this context, institutions concerned with the administration of justice should be properly funded, and an increased level of both technical and financial assistance should be provided by the international community. It is incumbent upon the United Nations to make use of special programmes of advisory services on a priority basis for the achievement of a strong and independent administration of justice.

28. The World Conference on Human Rights expresses its dismay at massive violations of human rights especially in the form of genocide, "ethnic cleansing" and systematic rape of women in war situations, creating mass exodus of refugees and displaced persons. While strongly condemning such abhorrent practices it reiterates the call that perpetrators of such crimes be punished and such practices immediately stopped.

29. The World Conference on Human Rights expresses grave concern about continuing human rights violations in all parts of the world in disregard of standards as contained in international human rights instruments and international humanitarian law and about the lack of sufficient and effective remedies for the victims.

The World Conference on Human Rights is deeply concerned about violations of human rights during armed conflicts, affecting the civilian population, especially women, children, the elderly and the disabled. The Conference therefore calls upon States and all parties to armed conflicts strictly to observe international humanitarian law, as set forth in the Geneva Conventions of 1949 and other rules and principles of international law, as well as minimum standards for protection of human rights, as laid down in international conventions.

The World Conference on Human Rights reaffirms the right of the victims to be assisted by humanitarian organizations, as set forth in the Geneva Conventions of 1949 and other relevant instruments of international humanitarian law, and calls for the safe and timely access for such assistance.

30. The World Conference on Human Rights also expresses its dismay and condemnation that gross and systematic violations and situations that constitute serious obstacles to the full enjoyment of all human rights continue to occur in different parts of the world. Such violations and obstacles include, as well as torture and cruel, inhuman and degrading treatment or punishment, summary and arbitrary executions, disappearances, arbitrary detentions, all forms of racism, racial discrimination and apartheid, foreign occupation and alien domination, xenophobia, poverty, hunger and other denials of economic, social and cultural rights, religious intolerance, terrorism, discrimination against women and lack of the rule of law.

31. The World Conference on Human Rights calls upon States to refrain from any unilateral measure not in accordance with international law and the Charter of the United Nations that creates obstacles to trade relations among States and impedes the full realization of the human rights set forth in the Universal Declaration of Human Rights and international human rights instruments, in particular the rights of everyone to a standard of living adequate for their health and well-being, including food and medical care, housing and the necessary social services. The World Conference on Human Rights affirms that food should not be used as a tool for political pressure.

32. The World Conference on Human Rights reaffirms the importance of ensuring the universality, objectivity and non-selectivity of the consideration of human rights issues.

33. The World Conference on Human Rights reaffirms that States are duty-bound, as stipulated in the Universal Declaration of Human Rights and the International Covenant on Economic, Social and Cultural Rights and in other international human rights instruments, to ensure that education is aimed at strengthening the respect of human rights and fundamental freedoms. The World Conference on Human Rights emphasizes the importance of incorporating the subject of human rights education programmes and calls upon States to do so. Education should promote understanding, tolerance, peace and friendly relations between the nations and all racial or religious groups and encourage the development of United Nations activities in pursuance of these objectives. Therefore, education on human rights and the dissemination of proper information, both theoretical and practical, play an important role in the promotion and respect of human rights with regard to all individuals without distinction of any kind such as race, sex, language or religion, and this should be integrated in the education policies at the national as well as international levels. The World Conference on Human Rights notes that resource constraints and institutional inadequacies may impede the immediate realization of these objectives.

34. Increased efforts should be made to assist countries which so request to create the conditions whereby each individual can enjoy universal human rights and fundamental freedoms. Governments, the United Nations system as well as other multilateral organizations are urged to increase considerably the resources allocated

to programmes aiming at the establishment and strengthening of national legislation, national institutions and related infrastructures which uphold the rule of law and democracy, electoral assistance, human rights awareness through training, teaching and education, popular participation and civil society.

The programmes of advisory services and technical cooperation under the Centre for Human Rights should be strengthened as well as made more efficient and transparent and thus become a major contribution to improving respect for human rights. States are called upon to increase their contributions to these programmes, both through promoting a larger allocation from the United Nations regular budget, and through voluntary contributions.

35. The full and effective implementation of United Nations activities to promote and protect human rights must reflect the high importance accorded to human rights by the Charter of the United Nations and the demands of the United Nations human rights activities, as mandated by Member States. To this end, United Nations human rights activities should be provided with increased resources.

36. The World Conference on Human Rights reaffirms the important and constructive role played by national institutions for the promotion and protection of human rights, in particular in their advisory capacity to the competent authorities, their role in remedying human rights violations, in the dissemination of human rights information, and education in human rights.

The World Conference on Human Rights encourages the establishment and strengthening of national institutions, having regard to the "Principles relating to the status of national institutions" and recognizing that it is the right of each State to choose the framework which is best suited to its particular needs at the national level.

37. Regional arrangements play a fundamental role in promoting and protecting human rights. They should reinforce universal human rights standards, as contained in international human rights instruments, and their protection. The World Conference on Human Rights endorses efforts under way to strengthen these arrangements and to increase their effectiveness, while at the same time stressing the importance of cooperation with the United Nations human rights activities.

The World Conference on Human Rights reiterates the need to consider the possibility of establishing regional and subregional arrangements for the promotion and protection of human rights where they do not already exist.

38. The World Conference on Human Rights recognizes the important role of non-governmental organizations in the promotion of all human rights and in humanitarian activities at national, regional and international levels. The World Conference on Human Rights appreciates their contribution to increasing public awareness of human rights issues, to the conduct of education, training and research in this field, and to the promotion and protection of all human rights and fundamental freedoms. While recognizing that the primary responsibility for standard-setting lies with States, the conference also appreciates the contribution of non-governmental organizations to this process. In this respect, the World Conference on Human Rights emphasizes the importance of continued dialogue and cooperation between Governments and non-governmental organizations. Non-governmental organizations and their members genuinely involved in the field of human rights should enjoy the rights and freedoms recognized in the

Universal Declaration of Human Rights, and the protection of the national law. These rights and freedoms may not be exercised contrary to the purposes and principles of the United Nations. Non-governmental organizations should be free to carry out their human rights activities, without interference, within the framework of national law and the Universal Declaration of Human Rights.

39. Underlining the importance of objective, responsible and impartial information about human rights and humanitarian issues, the World Conference on Human Rights encourages the increased involvement of the media, for whom freedom and protection should be guaranteed within the framework of national law.

II

A. INCREASED COORDINATION ON HUMAN RIGHTS WITHIN THE UNITED NATIONS SYSTEM

1. The World Conference on Human Rights recommends increased coordination in support of human rights and fundamental freedoms within the United Nations system. To this end, the World Conference on Human Rights urges all United Nations organs, bodies and the specialized agencies whose activities deal with human rights to cooperate in order to strengthen, rationalize and streamline their activities, taking into account the need to avoid unnecessary duplication. The World Conference on Human Rights also recommends to the Secretary-General that high-level officials of relevant United Nations bodies and specialized agencies at their annual meeting, besides coordinating their activities, also assess the impact of their strategies and policies on the enjoyment of all human rights.

2. Furthermore, the World Conference on Human Rights calls on regional organizations and prominent international and regional finance and development institutions to assess also the impact of their policies and programmes on the enjoyment of human rights.

3. The World Conference on Human Rights recognizes that relevant specialized agencies and bodies and institutions of the United Nations system as well as other relevant intergovernmental organizations whose activities deal with human rights play a vital role in the formulation, promotion and implementation of human rights standards, within their respective mandates, and should take into account the outcome of the World Conference on Human Rights within their fields of competence.

4. The World Conference on Human Rights strongly recommends that a concerted effort be made to encourage and facilitate the ratification of and accession or succession to international human rights treaties and protocols adopted within the framework of the United Nations system with the aim of universal acceptance. The Secretary-General, in consultation with treaty bodies, should consider opening a dialogue with States not having acceded to these human rights treaties, in order to identify obstacles and to seek ways of overcoming them.

5. The World Conference on Human Rights encourages States to consider limiting the extent of any reservations they lodge to international human rights instruments, formulate any reservations as precisely and narrowly as possible, ensure that none is

incompatible with the object and purpose of the relevant treaty and regularly review any reservations with a view to withdrawing them.

6. The World Conference on Human Rights, recognizing the need to maintain consistency with the high quality of existing international standards and to avoid proliferation of human rights instruments, reaffirms the guidelines relating to the elaboration of new international instruments contained in General Assembly resolution 41/120 of 4 December 1986 and calls on the United Nations human rights bodies, when considering the elaboration of new international standards, to keep those guidelines in mind, to consult with human rights treaty bodies on the necessity for drafting new standards and to request the Secretariat to carry out technical reviews of proposed new instruments.

7. The World Conference on Human Rights recommends that human rights officers be assigned if and when necessary to regional offices of the United Nations Organization with the purpose of disseminating information and offering training and other technical assistance in the field of human rights upon the request of concerned Member States. Human rights training for international civil servants who are assigned to work relating to human rights should be organized.

8. The World Conference on Human Rights welcomes the convening of emergency sessions of the Commission on Human Rights as a positive initiative and that other ways of responding to acute violations of human rights be considered by the relevant organs of the United Nations system.

Resources

9. The World Conference on Human Rights, concerned by the growing disparity between the activities of the Centre for Human Rights and the human, financial and other resources available to carry them out, and bearing in mind the resources needed for other important United Nations programmes, requests the Secretary-General and the General Assembly to take immediate steps to increase substantially the resources for the human rights programme from within the existing and future regular budgets of the United Nations, and to take urgent steps to seek increased extra-budgetary resources.

10. Within this framework, an increased proportion of the regular budget should be allocated directly to the Centre for Human Rights to cover its costs and all other costs borne by the Centre for Human Rights, including those related to the United Nations human rights bodies. Voluntary funding of the Centre's technical cooperation activities should reinforce this enhanced budget; the World Conference on Human Rights calls for generous contributions to the existing trust funds.

11. The World Conference on Human Rights requests the Secretary-General and the General Assembly to provide sufficient human, financial and other resources to the Centre for Human Rights to enable it effectively, efficiently and expeditiously to carry out its activities.

12. The World Conference on Human Rights, noting the need to ensure that human and financial resources are available to carry out the human rights activities, as mandated by intergovernmental bodies, urges the Secretary-General, in accordance with Article 101 of the Charter of the United Nations, and Member States to adopt a

coherent approach aimed at securing that resources commensurate to the increased mandates are allocated to the Secretariat. The World Conference on Human Rights invites the Secretary-General to consider whether adjustments to procedures in the programme budget cycle would be necessary or helpful to ensure the timely and effective implementation of human rights activities as mandated by Member States.

Centre for Human Rights

13. The World Conference on Human Rights stresses the importance of strengthening the United Nations Centre for Human Rights.
14. The Centre for Human Rights should play an important role in coordinating system-wide attention for human rights. The focal role of the Centre can best be realized if it is enabled to cooperate fully with other United Nations bodies and organs. The coordinating role of the Centre for Human Rights also implies that the office of the Centre for Human Rights in New York is strengthened.
15. The Centre for Human Rights should be assured adequate means for the system of thematic and country rapporteurs, experts, working groups and treaty bodies. Follow-up on recommendations should become a priority matter for consideration by the Commission on Human Rights.
16. The Centre for Human Rights should assume a larger role in the promotion of human rights. This role could be given shape through cooperation with Member States and by an enhanced programme of advisory services and technical assistance. The existing voluntary funds will have to be expanded substantially for these purposes and should be managed in a more efficient and coordinated way. All activities should follow strict and transparent project management rules and regular programme and project evaluations should be held periodically. To this end, the results of such evaluation exercises and other relevant information should be made available regularly. The Centre should, in particular, organize at least once a year information meetings open to all Member States and organizations directly involved in these projects and programmes.

Adaptation and strengthening of the United Nations machinery for human rights, including the question of the establishment of a United Nations High Commissioner for Human Rights

17. The World Conference on Human Rights recognizes the necessity for a continuing adaptation of the United Nations human rights machinery to the current and future needs in the promotion and protection of human rights, as reflected in the present Declaration and within the framework of a balanced and sustainable development for all people. In particular, the United Nations human rights organs should improve their coordination, efficiency and effectiveness.
18. The World Conference on Human Rights recommends to the General Assembly that when examining the report of the Conference at its forty-eighth session, it begin, as a matter of priority, consideration of the question of the establishment of a High Commissioner for Human Rights for the promotion and protection of all human rights.

B. EQUALITY, DIGNITY AND TOLERANCE

1. Racism, racial discrimination, xenophobia and other forms of intolerance

19. The World Conference on Human Rights considers the elimination of racism and racial discrimination, in particular in their institutionalized forms such as apartheid or resulting from doctrines of racial superiority or exclusivity or contemporary forms and manifestations of racism, as a primary objective for the international community and a worldwide promotion programme in the field of human rights. United Nations organs and agencies should strengthen their efforts to implement such a programme of action related to the third decade to combat racism and racial discrimination as well as subsequent mandates to the same end. The World Conference on Human Rights strongly appeals to the international community to contribute generously to the Trust Fund for the Programme for the Decade for Action to Combat Racism and Racial Discrimination.

20. The World Conference on Human Rights urges all Governments to take immediate measures and to develop strong policies to prevent and combat all forms and manifestations of racism, xenophobia or related intolerance, where necessary by enactment of appropriate legislation, including penal measures, and by the establishment of national institutions to combat such phenomena.

21. The World Conference on Human Rights welcomes the decision of the Commission on Human Rights to appoint a Special Rapporteur on contemporary forms of racism, racial discrimination, xenophobia and related intolerance. The World Conference on Human Rights also appeals to all States parties to the International Convention on the Elimination of All Forms of Racial Discrimination to consider making the declaration under article 14 of the Convention.

22. The World Conference on Human Rights calls upon all Governments to take all appropriate measures in compliance with their international obligations and with due regard to their respective legal systems to counter intolerance and related violence based on religion or belief, including practices of discrimination against women and including the desecration of religious sites, recognizing that every individual has the right to freedom of thought, conscience, expression and religion. The Conference also invites all States to put into practice the provisions of the Declaration on the Elimination of All Forms of Intolerance and of Discrimination Based on Religion or Belief.

23. The World Conference on Human Rights stresses that all persons who perpetrate or authorize criminal acts associated with ethnic cleansing are individually responsible and accountable for such human rights violations, and that the international community should exert every effort to bring those legally responsible for such violations to justice.

24. The World Conference on Human Rights calls on all States to take immediate measures, individually and collectively, to combat the practice of ethnic cleansing to bring it quickly to an end. Victims of the abhorrent practice of ethnic cleansing are entitled to appropriate and effective remedies.

2. Persons belonging to national or ethnic, religious and linguistic minorities

25. The World Conference on Human Rights calls on the Commission on Human Rights to examine ways and means to promote and protect effectively the rights of persons belonging to minorities as set out in the Declaration on the Rights of Persons belonging to National or Ethnic, Religious and Linguistic Minorities. In this context, the World Conference on Human Rights calls upon the Centre for Human Rights to provide, at the request of Governments concerned and as part of its programme of advisory services and technical assistance, qualified expertise on minority issues and human rights, as well as on the prevention and resolution of disputes, to assist in existing or potential situations involving minorities.

26. The World Conference on Human Rights urges States and the international community to promote and protect the rights of persons belonging to national or ethnic, religious and linguistic minorities in accordance with the Declaration on the Rights of Persons belonging to National or Ethnic, Religious and Linguistic Minorities.

27. Measures to be taken, where appropriate, should include facilitation of their full participation in all aspects of the political, economic, social, religious and cultural life of society and in the economic progress and development in their country.

Indigenous people

28. The World Conference on Human Rights calls on the Working Group on Indigenous Populations of the Sub-Commission on Prevention of Discrimination and Protection of Minorities to complete the drafting of a declaration on the rights of indigenous people at its eleventh session.

29. The World Conference on Human Rights recommends that the Commission on Human Rights consider the renewal and updating of the mandate of the Working Group on Indigenous Populations upon completion of the drafting of a declaration on the rights of indigenous people.

30. The World Conference on Human Rights also recommends that advisory services and technical assistance programmes within the United Nations system respond positively to requests by States for assistance which would be of direct benefit to indigenous people. The World Conference on Human Rights further recommends that adequate human and financial resources be made available to the Centre for Human Rights within the overall framework of strengthening the Centre's activities as envisaged by this document.

31. The World Conference on Human Rights urges States to ensure the full and free participation of indigenous people in all aspects of society, in particular in matters of concern to them.

32. The World Conference on Human Rights recommends that the General Assembly proclaim an international decade of the world's indigenous people, to begin from January 1994, including action-orientated programmes, to be decided upon in partnership with indigenous people. An appropriate voluntary trust fund should be set up for this purpose. In the framework of such a decade, the establishment of a permanent forum for indigenous people in the United Nations system should be considered.

Migrant workers

33. The World Conference on Human Rights urges all States to guarantee the protection of the human rights of all migrant workers and their families.

34. The World Conference on Human Rights considers that the creation of conditions to foster greater harmony and tolerance between migrant workers and the rest of the society of the State in which they reside is of particular importance.

35. The World Conference on Human Rights invites States to consider the possibility of signing and ratifying, at the earliest possible time, the International Convention on the Rights of All Migrant Workers and Members of Their Families.

3. The equal status and human rights of women

36. The World Conference on Human Rights urges the full and equal enjoyment by women of all human rights and that this be a priority for Governments and for the United Nations. The World Conference on Human Rights also underlines the importance of the integration and full participation of women as both agents and beneficiaries in the development process, and reiterates the objectives established on global action for women towards sustainable and equitable development set forth in the Rio Declaration on Environment and Development and chapter 24 of Agenda 21, adopted by the United Nations Conference on Environment and Development (Rio de Janeiro, Brazil, 3–14 June 1992).

37. The equal status of women and the human rights of women should be integrated into the mainstream of United Nations system-wide activity. These issues should be regularly and systematically addressed throughout relevant United Nations bodies and mechanisms. In particular, steps should be taken to increase cooperation and promote further integration of objectives and goals between the Commission on the Status of Women, the Commission on Human Rights, the Committee for the Elimination of Discrimination against Women, the United Nations Development Fund for Women, the United Nations Development Programme and other United Nations agencies. In this context, cooperation and coordination should be strengthened between the Centre for Human Rights and the Division for the Advancement of Women.

38. In particular, the World Conference on Human Rights stresses the importance of working towards the elimination of violence against women in public and private life, the elimination of all forms of sexual harassment, exploitation and trafficking in women, the elimination of gender bias in the administration of justice and the eradication of any conflicts which may arise between the rights of women and the harmful effects of certain traditional or customary practices, cultural prejudices and religious extremism. The World Conference on Human Rights calls upon the General Assembly to adopt the draft declaration on violence against women and urges States to combat violence against women in accordance with its provisions. Violations of the human rights of women in situations of armed conflict are violations of the fundamental principles of international human rights and humanitarian law. All violations of this kind, including in particular murder, systematic rape, sexual slavery, and forced pregnancy, require a particularly effective response.

39. The World Conference on Human Rights urges the eradication of all forms of discrimination against women, both hidden and overt. The United Nations should encourage the goal of universal ratification by all States of the Convention on the Elimination of All Forms of Discrimination against Women by the year 2000. Ways and means of addressing the particularly large number of reservations to the Convention should be encouraged. Inter alia, the Committee on the Elimination of Discrimination against Women should continue its review of reservations to the Convention. States are urged to withdraw reservations that are contrary to the object and purpose of the Convention or which are otherwise incompatible with international treaty law.

40. Treaty monitoring bodies should disseminate necessary information to enable women to make more effective use of existing implementation procedures in their pursuit of full and equal enjoyment of human rights and non-discrimination. New procedures should also be adopted to strengthen implementation of the commitment to women's equality and the human rights of women. The Commission on the Status of Women and the Committee on the Elimination of Discrimination against Women should quickly examine the possibility of introducing the right of petition through the preparation of an optional protocol to the Convention on the Elimination of All Forms of Discrimination against Women. The World Conference on Human Rights welcomes the decision of the Commission on Human Rights to consider the appointment of a special rapporteur on violence against women at its fiftieth session.

41. The World Conference on Human Rights recognizes the importance of the enjoyment by women of the highest standard of physical and mental health throughout their life span. In the context of the World Conference on Women and the Convention on the Elimination of All Forms of Discrimination against Women, as well as the Proclamation of Tehran of 1968, the World Conference on Human Rights reaffirms, on the basis of equality between women and men, a woman's right to accessible and adequate health care and the widest range of family planning services, as well as equal access to education at all levels.

42. Treaty monitoring bodies should include the status of women and the human rights of women in their deliberations and findings, making use of gender-specific data. States should be encouraged to supply information on the situation of women de jure and de facto in their reports to treaty monitoring bodies. The World Conference on Human Rights notes with satisfaction that the Commission on Human Rights adopted at its forty-ninth session resolution 1993/46 of 8 March 1993 stating that rapporteurs and working groups in the field of human rights should also be encouraged to do so. Steps should also be taken by the Division for the Advancement of Women in cooperation with other United Nations bodies, specifically the Centre for Human Rights, to ensure that the human rights activities of the United Nations regularly address violations of women's human rights, including gender-specific abuses. Training for United Nations human rights and humanitarian relief personnel to assist them to recognize and deal with human rights abuses particular to women and to carry out their work without gender bias should be encouraged.

43. The World Conference on Human Rights urges Governments and regional and international organizations to facilitate the access of women to decision-making posts and their greater participation in the decision-making process. It encourages further steps within the United Nations Secretariat to appoint and promote women staff members in accordance with the Charter of the United Nations, and encourages other principal and subsidiary organs of the United Nations to guarantee the participation of women under conditions of equality.

44. The World Conference on Human Rights welcomes the World Conference on Women to be held in Beijing in 1995 and urges that human rights of women should play an important role in its deliberations, in accordance with the priority themes of the World Conference on Women of equality, development and peace.

4. The rights of the child

45. The World Conference on Human Rights reiterates the principle of "First Call for Children" and, in this respect, underlines the importance of major national and international efforts, especially those of the United Nations Children's Fund, for promoting respect for the rights of the child to survival, protection, development and participation.

46. Measures should be taken to achieve universal ratification of the Convention on the Rights of the Child by 1995 and the universal signing of the World Declaration on the Survival, Protection and Development of Children and Plan of Action adopted by the World Summit for Children, as well as their effective implementation. The World Conference on Human Rights urges States to withdraw reservations to the Convention on the Rights of the Child contrary to the object and purpose of the Convention or otherwise contrary to international treaty law.

47. The World Conference on Human Rights urges all nations to undertake measures to the maximum extent of their available resources, with the support of international cooperation, to achieve the goals in the World Summit Plan of Action. The Conference calls on States to integrate the Convention on the Rights of the Child into their national action plans. By means of these national action plans and through international efforts, particular priority should be placed on reducing infant and maternal mortality rates, reducing malnutrition and illiteracy rates and providing access to safe drinking water and to basic education. Whenever so called for, national plans of action should be devised to combat devastating emergencies resulting from natural disasters and armed conflicts and the equally grave problem of children in extreme poverty.

48. The World Conference on Human Rights urges all States, with the support of international cooperation, to address the acute problem of children under especially difficult circumstances. Exploitation and abuse of children should be actively combated, including by addressing their root causes. Effective measures are required against female infanticide, harmful child labour, sale of children and organs, child prostitution, child pornography, as well as other forms of sexual abuse.

49. The World Conference on Human Rights supports all measures by the United Nations and its specialized agencies to ensure the effective protection and promotion of human rights of the girl child. The World Conference on Human Rights urges

States to repeal existing laws and regulations and remove customs and practices which discriminate against and cause harm to the girl child.

50. The World Conference on Human Rights strongly supports the proposal that the Secretary-General initiate a study into means of improving the protection of children in armed conflicts. Humanitarian norms should be implemented and measures taken in order to protect and facilitate assistance to children in war zones. Measures should include protection for children against indiscriminate use of all weapons of war, especially anti-personnel mines. The need for aftercare and rehabilitation of children traumatized by war must be addressed urgently. The Conference calls on the Committee on the Rights of the Child to study the question of raising the minimum age of recruitment into armed forces.

51. The World Conference on Human Rights recommends that matters relating to human rights and the situation of children be regularly reviewed and monitored by all relevant organs and mechanisms of the United Nations system and by the supervisory bodies of the specialized agencies in accordance with their mandates.

52. The World Conference on Human Rights recognizes the important role played by non-governmental organizations in the effective implementation of all human rights instruments and, in particular, the Convention on the Rights of the Child.

53. The World Conference on Human Rights recommends that the Committee on the Rights of the Child, with the assistance of the Centre for Human Rights, be enabled expeditiously and effectively to meet its mandate, especially in view of the unprecedented extent of ratification and subsequent submission of country reports.

5. Freedom from torture

54. The World Conference on Human Rights welcomes the ratification by many Member States of the Convention against Torture and Other Cruel, Inhuman or Degrading Treatment or Punishment and encourages its speedy ratification by all other Member States.

55. The World Conference on Human Rights emphasizes that one of the most atrocious violations against human dignity is the act of torture, the result of which destroys the dignity and impairs the capability of victims to continue their lives and their activities.

56. The World Conference on Human Rights reaffirms that under human rights law and international humanitarian law, freedom from torture is a right which must be protected under all circumstances, including in times of internal or international disturbance or armed conflicts.

57. The World Conference on Human Rights therefore urges all States to put an immediate end to the practice of torture and eradicate this evil forever through full implementation of the Universal Declaration of Human Rights as well as the relevant conventions and, where necessary, strengthening of existing mechanisms. The World Conference on Human Rights calls on all States to cooperate fully with the Special Rapporteur on the question of torture in the fulfilment of his mandate.

58. Special attention should be given to ensure universal respect for, and effective implementation of, the Principles of Medical Ethics relevant to the Role of Health Personnel, particularly Physicians, in the Protection of Prisoners and Detainees

against Torture and other Cruel, Inhuman or Degrading Treatment or Punishment adopted by the General Assembly of the United Nations.

59. The World Conference on Human Rights stresses the importance of further concrete action within the framework of the United Nations with the view to providing assistance to victims of torture and ensuring more effective remedies for their physical, psychological and social rehabilitation. Providing the necessary resources for this purpose should be given high priority, inter alia, by additional contributions to the United Nations Voluntary Fund for Victims of Torture.

60. States should abrogate legislation leading to impunity for those responsible for grave violations of human rights such as torture and prosecute such violations, thereby providing a firm basis for the rule of law.

61. The World Conference on Human Rights reaffirms that efforts to eradicate torture should, first and foremost, be concentrated on prevention and, therefore, calls for the early adoption of an optional protocol to the Convention against Torture and Other Cruel, Inhuman and Degrading Treatment or Punishment, which is intended to establish a preventive system of regular visits to places of detention.

Enforced disappearances

62. The World Conference on Human Rights, welcoming the adoption by the General Assembly of the Declaration on the Protection of All Persons from Enforced Disappearance, calls upon all States to take effective legislative, administrative, judicial or other measures to prevent, terminate and punish acts of enforced disappearance. The World Conference on Human Rights reaffirms that it is the duty of all States, under any circumstances, to make investigations whenever there is reason to believe that an enforced disappearance has taken place on a territory under their jurisdiction and, if allegations are confirmed, to prosecute its perpetrators.

6. The rights of the disabled person

63. The World Conference on Human Rights reaffirms that all human rights and fundamental freedoms are universal and thus unreservedly include persons with disabilities. Every person is born equal and has the same rights to life and welfare, education and work, living independently and active participation in all aspects of society. Any direct discrimination or other negative discriminatory treatment of a disabled person is therefore a violation of his or her rights. The World Conference on Human Rights calls on Governments, where necessary, to adopt or adjust legislation to assure access to these and other rights for disabled persons.

64. The place of disabled persons is everywhere. Persons with disabilities should be guaranteed equal opportunity through the elimination of all socially determined barriers, be they physical, financial, social or psychological, which exclude or restrict full participation in society.

65. Recalling the World Programme of Action concerning Disabled Persons, adopted by the General Assembly at its thirty-seventh session, the World Conference on Human Rights calls upon the General Assembly and the Economic and Social Council to adopt the draft standard rules on the equalization of opportunities for persons with disabilities, at their meetings in 1993.

C. COOPERATION, DEVELOPMENT AND STRENGTHENING OF HUMAN RIGHTS

66. The World Conference on Human Rights recommends that priority be given to national and international action to promote democracy, development and human rights.

67. Special emphasis should be given to measures to assist in the strengthening and building of institutions relating to human rights, strengthening of a pluralistic civil society and the protection of groups which have been rendered vulnerable. In this context, assistance provided upon the request of Governments for the conduct of free and fair elections, including assistance in the human rights aspects of elections and public information about elections, is of particular importance. Equally important is the assistance to be given to the strengthening of the rule of law, the promotion of freedom of expression and the administration of justice, and to the real and effective participation of the people in the decision-making processes.

68. The World Conference on Human Rights stresses the need for the implementation of strengthened advisory services and technical assistance activities by the Centre for Human Rights. The Centre should make available to States upon request assistance on specific human rights issues, including the preparation of reports under human rights treaties as well as for the implementation of coherent and comprehensive plans of action for the promotion and protection of human rights. Strengthening the institutions of human rights and democracy, the legal protection of human rights, training of officials and others, broad-based education and public information aimed at promoting respect for human rights should all be available as components of these programmes.

69. The World Conference on Human Rights strongly recommends that a comprehensive programme be established within the United Nations in order to help States in the task of building and strengthening adequate national structures which have a direct impact on the overall observance of human rights and the maintenance of the rule of law. Such a programme, to be coordinated by the Centre for Human Rights, should be able to provide, upon the request of the interested Government, technical and financial assistance to national projects in reforming penal and correctional establishments, education and training of lawyers, judges and security forces in human rights, and any other sphere of activity relevant to the good functioning of the rule of law. That programme should make available to States assistance for the implementation of plans of action for the promotion and protection of human rights.

70. The World Conference on Human Rights requests the Secretary-General of the United Nations to submit proposals to the United Nations General Assembly, containing alternatives for the establishment, structure, operational modalities and funding of the proposed programme.

71. The World Conference on Human Rights recommends that each State consider the desirability of drawing up a national action plan identifying steps whereby that State would improve the promotion and protection of human rights.

72. The World Conference on Human Rights reaffirms that the universal and inalienable right to development, as established in the Declaration on the Right to Development, must be implemented and realized. In this context, the World Conference on Human Rights welcomes the appointment by the Commission on Human Rights of

a thematic working group on the right to development and urges that the Working Group, in consultation and cooperation with other organs and agencies of the United Nations system, promptly formulate, for early consideration by the United Nations General Assembly, comprehensive and effective measures to eliminate obstacles to the implementation and realization of the Declaration on the Right to Development and recommending ways and means towards the realization of the right to development by all States.

73. The World Conference on Human Rights recommends that non-governmental and other grass-roots organizations active in development and/or human rights should be enabled to play a major role on the national and international levels in the debate, activities and implementation relating to the right to development and, in cooperation with Governments, in all relevant aspects of development cooperation.

74. The World Conference on Human Rights appeals to Governments, competent agencies and institutions to increase considerably the resources devoted to building well-functioning legal systems able to protect human rights, and to national institutions working in this area. Actors in the field of development cooperation should bear in mind the mutually reinforcing interrelationship between development, democracy and human rights. Cooperation should be based on dialogue and transparency. The World Conference on Human Rights also calls for the establishment of comprehensive programmes, including resource banks of information and personnel with expertise relating to the strengthening of the rule of law and of democratic institutions.

75. The World Conference on Human Rights encourages the Commission on Human Rights, in cooperation with the Committee on Economic, Social and Cultural Rights, to continue the examination of optional protocols to the International Covenant on Economic, Social and Cultural Rights.

76. The World Conference on Human Rights recommends that more resources be made available for the strengthening or the establishment of regional arrangements for the promotion and protection of human rights under the programmes of advisory services and technical assistance of the Centre for Human Rights. States are encouraged to request assistance for such purposes as regional and subregional workshops, seminars and information exchanges designed to strengthen regional arrangements for the promotion and protection of human rights in accord with universal human rights standards as contained in international human rights instruments.

77. The World Conference on Human Rights supports all measures by the United Nations and its relevant specialized agencies to ensure the effective promotion and protection of trade union rights, as stipulated in the International Covenant on Economic, Social and Cultural Rights and other relevant international instruments. It calls on all States to abide fully by their obligations in this regard contained in international instruments.

D. HUMAN RIGHTS EDUCATION

78. The World Conference on Human Rights considers human rights education, training and public information essential for the promotion and achievement of stable and harmonious relations among communities and for fostering mutual understanding, tolerance and peace.

79. States should strive to eradicate illiteracy and should direct education towards the full development of the human personality and to the strengthening of respect for human rights and fundamental freedoms. The World Conference on Human Rights calls on all States and institutions to include human rights, humanitarian law, democracy and rule of law as subjects in the curricula of all learning institutions in formal and non-formal settings.

80. Human rights education should include peace, democracy, development and social justice, as set forth in international and regional human rights instruments, in order to achieve common understanding and awareness with a view to strengthening universal commitment to human rights.

81. Taking into account the World Plan of Action on Education for Human Rights and Democracy, adopted in March 1993 by the International Congress on Education for Human Rights and Democracy of the United Nations Educational, Scientific and Cultural Organization, and other human rights instruments, the World Conference on Human Rights recommends that States develop specific programmes and strategies for ensuring the widest human rights education and the dissemination of public information, taking particular account of the human rights needs of women.

82. Governments, with the assistance of intergovernmental organizations, national institutions and non-governmental organizations, should promote an increased awareness of human rights and mutual tolerance. The World Conference on Human Rights underlines the importance of strengthening the World Public Information Campaign for Human Rights carried out by the United Nations. They should initiate and support education in human rights and undertake effective dissemination of public information in this field. The advisory services and technical assistance programmes of the United Nations system should be able to respond immediately to requests from States for educational and training activities in the field of human rights as well as for special education concerning standards as contained in international human rights instruments and in humanitarian law and their application to special groups such as military forces, law enforcement personnel, police and the health profession. The proclamation of a United Nations decade for human rights education in order to promote, encourage and focus these educational activities should be considered.

E. IMPLEMENTATION AND MONITORING METHODS

83. The World Conference on Human Rights urges Governments to incorporate standards as contained in international human rights instruments in domestic legislation and to strengthen national structures, institutions and organs of society which play a role in promoting and safeguarding human rights.

84. The World Conference on Human Rights recommends the strengthening of United Nations activities and programmes to meet requests for assistance by States which want to establish or strengthen their own national institutions for the promotion and protection of human rights.

85. The World Conference on Human Rights also encourages the strengthening of cooperation between national institutions for the promotion and protection of human rights, particularly through exchanges of information and experience, as well as cooperation with regional organizations and the United Nations.

86. The World Conference on Human Rights strongly recommends in this regard that representatives of national institutions for the promotion and protection of human rights convene periodic meetings under the auspices of the Centre for Human Rights to examine ways and means of improving their mechanisms and sharing experiences.

87. The World Conference on Human Rights recommends to the human rights treaty bodies, to the meetings of chairpersons of the treaty bodies and to the meetings of States parties that they continue to take steps aimed at coordinating the multiple reporting requirements and guidelines for preparing State reports under the respective human rights conventions and study the suggestion that the submission of one overall report on treaty obligations undertaken by each State would make these procedures more effective and increase their impact.

88. The World Conference on Human Rights recommends that the States parties to international human rights instruments, the General Assembly and the Economic and Social Council should consider studying the existing human rights treaty bodies and the various thematic mechanisms and procedures with a view to promoting greater efficiency and effectiveness through better coordination of the various bodies, mechanisms and procedures, taking into account the need to avoid unnecessary duplication and overlapping of their mandates and tasks.

89. The World Conference on Human Rights recommends continued work on the improvement of the functioning, including the monitoring tasks, of the treaty bodies, taking into account multiple proposals made in this respect, in particular those made by the treaty bodies themselves and by the meetings of the chairpersons of the treaty bodies. The comprehensive national approach taken by the Committee on the Rights of the Child should also be encouraged.

90. The World Conference on Human Rights recommends that States parties to human rights treaties consider accepting all the available optional communication procedures.

91. The World Conference on Human Rights views with concern the issue of impunity of perpetrators of human rights violations, and supports the efforts of the Commission on Human Rights and the Sub-Commission on Prevention of Discrimination and Protection of Minorities to examine all aspects of the issue.

92. The World Conference on Human Rights recommends that the Commission on Human Rights examine the possibility for better implementation of existing human rights instruments at the international and regional levels and encourages the International Law Commission to continue its work on an international criminal court.

93. The World Conference on Human Rights appeals to States which have not yet done so to accede to the Geneva Conventions of 12 August 1949 and the Protocols thereto, and to take all appropriate national measures, including legislative ones, for their full implementation.

94. The World Conference on Human Rights recommends the speedy completion and adoption of the draft declaration on the right and responsibility of individuals, groups and organs of society to promote and protect universally recognized human rights and fundamental freedoms.

95. The World Conference on Human Rights underlines the importance of preserving and strengthening the system of special procedures, rapporteurs, representatives, experts and working groups of the Commission on Human Rights and the Sub-Commission on the Prevention of Discrimination and Protection of Minorities, in order to enable them to carry out their mandates in all countries throughout the world, providing them with the necessary human and financial resources. The procedures and mechanisms should be enabled to harmonize and rationalize their work through periodic meetings. All States are asked to cooperate fully with these procedures and mechanisms.

96. The World Conference on Human Rights recommends that the United Nations assume a more active role in the promotion and protection of human rights in ensuring full respect for international humanitarian law in all situations of armed conflict, in accordance with the purposes and principles of the Charter of the United Nations.

97. The World Conference on Human Rights, recognizing the important role of human rights components in specific arrangements concerning some peace-keeping operations by the United Nations, recommends that the Secretary-General take into account the reporting, experience and capabilities of the Centre for Human Rights and human rights mechanisms, in conformity with the Charter of the United Nations.

98. To strengthen the enjoyment of economic, social and cultural rights, additional approaches should be examined, such as a system of indicators to measure progress in the realization of the rights set forth in the International Covenant on Economic, Social and Cultural Rights. There must be a concerted effort to ensure recognition of economic, social and cultural rights at the national, regional and international levels.

F. FOLLOW-UP TO THE WORLD CONFERENCE ON HUMAN RIGHTS

99. The World Conference on Human Rights on Human Rights recommends that the General Assembly, the Commission on Human Rights and other organs and agencies of the United Nations system related to human rights consider ways and means for the full implementation, without delay, of the recommendations contained in the present Declaration, including the possibility of proclaiming a United Nations decade for human rights. The World Conference on Human Rights further recommends that the Commission on Human Rights annually review the progress towards this end.

100. The World Conference on Human Rights requests the Secretary-General of the United Nations to invite on the occasion of the fiftieth anniversary of the Universal Declaration of Human Rights all States, all organs and agencies of the United Nations system related to human rights, to report to him on the progress made in the implementation of the present Declaration and to submit a report to the General Assembly at its fifty-third session, through the Commission on Human Rights and the Economic and Social Council. Likewise, regional and, as appropriate, national human rights institutions, as well as non-governmental organizations, may present their views to the Secretary-General on the progress made in the implementation of the present Declaration. Special attention should be paid to assessing the progress towards the goal of universal ratification of international human rights treaties and protocols adopted within the framework of the United Nations system.

50

Beijing Declaration and Platform for Action, Fourth World Conference on Women: Action for Equality, Development and Peace, 1995

Note: the Conference was held 4–15 September 1995, in Beijing.

BEIJING DECLARATION

1. We, the Governments participating in the Fourth World Conference on Women,
2. Gathered here in Beijing in September 1995, the year of the fiftieth anniversary of the founding of the United Nations,
3. Determined to advance the goals of equality, development and peace for all women everywhere in the interest of all humanity,
4. Acknowledging the voices of all women everywhere and taking note of the diversity of women and their roles and circumstances, honouring the women who paved the way and inspired by the hope present in the world's youth,
5. Recognize that the status of women has advanced in some important respects in the past decade but that progress has been uneven, inequalities between women and men have persisted and major obstacles remain, with serious consequences for the well-being of all people,
6. Also recognize that this situation is exacerbated by the increasing poverty that is affecting the lives of the majority of the world's people, in particular women and children, with origins in both the national and international domains,
7. Dedicate ourselves unreservedly to addressing these constraints and obstacles and thus enhancing further the advancement and empowerment of women all over the world, and agree that this requires urgent action in the spirit of determination, hope, cooperation and solidarity, now and to carry us forward into the next century.
   We reaffirm our commitment to:
8. The equal rights and inherent human dignity of women and men and other purposes and principles enshrined in the Charter of the United Nations, to the Universal Declaration of Human Rights and other international human rights instruments, in particular the Convention on the Elimination of All Forms of Discrimination against Women and the Convention on the Rights of the Child, as well as the Declaration on the Elimination of Violence against Women and the Declaration on the Right to Development;
9. Ensure the full implementation of the human rights of women and of the girl child as an inalienable, integral and indivisible part of all human rights and fundamental freedoms;
10. Build on consensus and progress made at previous United Nations conferences and summits – on women in Nairobi in 1985, on children in New York in 1990,

on environment and development in Rio de Janeiro in 1992, on human rights in Vienna in 1993, on population and development in Cairo in 1994 and on social development in Copenhagen in 1995 with the objective of achieving equality, development and peace;

11. Achieve the full and effective implementation of the Nairobi Forward looking Strategies for the Advancement of Women;

12. The empowerment and advancement of women, including the right to freedom of thought, conscience, religion and belief, thus contributing to the moral, ethical, spiritual and intellectual needs of women and men, individually or in community with others and thereby guaranteeing them the possibility of realizing their full potential in society and shaping their lives in accordance with their own aspirations.

We are convinced that:

13. Women's empowerment and their full participation on the basis of equality in all spheres of society, including participation in the decision-making process and access to power, are fundamental for the achievement of equality, development and peace;

14. Women's rights are human rights;

15. Equal rights, opportunities and access to resources, equal sharing of responsibilities for the family by men and women, and a harmonious partnership between them are critical to their well-being and that of their families as well as to the consolidation of democracy;

16. Eradication of poverty based on sustained economic growth, social development, environmental protection and social justice requires the involvement of women in economic and social development, equal opportunities and the full and equal partic-ipation of women and men as agents and beneficiaries of people-centred sustainable development;

17. The explicit recognition and reaffirmation of the right of all women to control all aspects of their health, in particular their own fertility, is basic to their empowerment;

18. Local, national, regional and global peace is attainable and is inextricably linked with the advancement of women, who are a fundamental force for leadership, conflict resolution and the promotion of lasting peace at all levels;

19. It is essential to design, implement and monitor, with the full participation of women, effective, efficient and mutually reinforcing gender-sensitive policies and programmes, including development policies and programmes, at all levels that will foster the empowerment and advancement of women;

20. The participation and contribution of all actors of civil society, particularly women's groups and networks and other non-governmental organizations and community-based organizations, with full respect for their autonomy, in cooperation with Governments, are important to the effective implementation and follow-up of the Platform for Action;

21. The implementation of the Platform for Action requires commitment from Governments and the international community. By making national and international commitments for action, including those made at the Conference, Governments and the international community recognize the need to take priority action for the empowerment and advancement of women.

We are determined to:

22. Intensify efforts and actions to achieve the goals of the Nairobi Forward looking Strategies for the Advancement of Women by the end of this century;

23. Ensure the full enjoyment by women and the girl child of all human rights and fundamental freedoms and take effective action against violations of these rights and freedoms;

24. Take all necessary measures to eliminate all forms of discrimination against women and the girl child and remove all obstacles to gender equality and the advancement and empowerment of women;

25. Encourage men to participate fully in all actions towards equality;

26. Promote women's economic independence, including employment, and eradicate the persistent and increasing burden of poverty on women by addressing the structural causes of poverty through changes in economic structures, ensuring equal access for all women, including those in rural areas, as vital development agents, to productive resources, opportunities and public services;

27. Promote people-centred sustainable development, including sustained economic growth, through the provision of basic education, life-long education, literacy and training, and primary health care for girls and women;

28. Take positive steps to ensure peace for the advancement of women and, recognizing the leading role that women have played in the peace movement, work actively towards general and complete disarmament under strict and effective international control, and support negotiations on the conclusion, without delay, of a universal and multilaterally and effectively verifiable comprehensive nuclear-test-ban treaty which contributes to nuclear disarmament and the prevention of the proliferation of nuclear weapons in all its aspects;

29. Prevent and eliminate all forms of violence against women and girls;

30. Ensure equal access to and equal treatment of women and men in education and health care and enhance women's sexual and reproductive health as well as education;

31. Promote and protect all human rights of women and girls;

32. Intensify efforts to ensure equal enjoyment of all human rights and fundamental freedoms for all women and girls who face multiple barriers to their empowerment and advancement because of such factors as their race, age, language, ethnicity, culture, religion, or disability, or because they are indigenous people;

33. Ensure respect for international law, including humanitarian law, in order to protect women and girls in particular;

34. Develop the fullest potential of girls and women of all ages, ensure their full and equal participation in building a better world for all and enhance their role in the development process.

    We are determined to:

35. Ensure women's equal access to economic resources, including land, credit, science and technology, vocational training, information, communication and markets, as a means to further the advancement and empowerment of women and girls, including through the enhancement of their capacities to enjoy the benefits of equal access to these resources, inter alia, by means of international cooperation;

36. Ensure the success of the Platform for Action, which will require a strong commitment on the part of Governments, international organizations and institutions at all levels. We are deeply convinced that economic development, social development and

environmental protection are interdependent and mutually reinforcing components of sustainable development, which is the framework for our efforts to achieve a higher quality of life for all people. Equitable social development that recognizes empowering the poor, particularly women living in poverty, to utilize environmental resources sustainably is a necessary foundation for sustainable development. We also recognize that broad-based and sustained economic growth in the context of sustainable development is necessary to sustain social development and social justice. The success of the Platform for Action will also require adequate mobilization of resources at the national and international levels as well as new and additional resources to the developing countries from all available funding mechanisms, including multilateral, bilateral and private sources for the advancement of women; financial resources to strengthen the capacity of national, subregional, regional and international institutions; a commitment to equal rights, equal responsibilities and equal opportunities and to the equal participation of women and men in all national, regional and international bodies and policy-making processes; and the establishment or strengthening of mechanisms at all levels for accountability to the world's women;

37. Ensure also the success of the Platform for Action in countries with economies in transition, which will require continued international cooperation and assistance;

38. We hereby adopt and commit ourselves as Governments to implement the following Platform for Action, ensuring that a gender perspective is reflected in all our policies and programmes. We urge the United Nations system, regional and international financial institutions, other relevant regional and international institutions and all women and men, as well as non-governmental organizations, with full respect for their autonomy, and all sectors of civil society, in cooperation with Governments, to fully commit themselves and contribute to the implementation of this Platform for Action.

51

World Summit Outcome, 2005

Note: Adopted by General Assembly Resolution 60/1 on 16 September 2005

The General Assembly,

Adopts the following 2005 World Summit Outcome:

2005 WORLD SUMMIT OUTCOME

I. VALUES AND PRINCIPLES

1. We, Heads of State and Government, have gathered at United Nations Headquarters in New York from 14 to 16 September 2005.
2. We reaffirm our faith in the United Nations and our commitment to the purposes and principles of the Charter of the United Nations and international law, which are indispensable foundations of a more peaceful, prosperous and just world, and reiterate our determination to foster strict respect for them.
3. We reaffirm the United Nations Millennium Declaration, which we adopted at the dawn of the twenty-first century. We recognize the valuable role of the major United Nations conferences and summits in the economic, social and related fields, including the Millennium Summit, in mobilizing the international community at the local, national, regional and global levels and in guiding the work of the United Nations.
4. We reaffirm that our common fundamental values, including freedom, equality, solidarity, tolerance, respect for all human rights, respect for nature and shared responsibility, are essential to international relations.
5. We are determined to establish a just and lasting peace all over the world in accordance with the purposes and principles of the Charter. We rededicate ourselves to support all efforts to uphold the sovereign equality of all States, respect their territorial integrity and political independence, to refrain in our international relations from the threat or use of force in any manner inconsistent with the purposes and principles of the United Nations, to uphold resolution of disputes by peaceful means and in conformity with the principles of justice and international law, the right to self-determination of peoples which remain under colonial domination and foreign occupation, non-interference in the internal affairs of States, respect for human rights and fundamental freedoms, respect for the equal rights of all without distinction as to race, sex, language or religion, international cooperation in solving international problems of an economic, social, cultural or humanitarian character and the fulfilment in good faith of the obligations assumed in accordance with the Charter.

6. We reaffirm the vital importance of an effective multilateral system, in accordance with international law, in order to better address the multifaceted and interconnected challenges and threats confronting our world and to achieve progress in the areas of peace and security, development and human rights, underlining the central role of the United Nations, and commit ourselves to promoting and strengthening the effectiveness of the Organization through the implementation of its decisions and resolutions.

7. We believe that today, more than ever before, we live in a global and interdependent world. No State can stand wholly alone. We acknowledge that collective security depends on effective cooperation, in accordance with international law, against transnational threats.

8. We recognize that current developments and circumstances require that we urgently build consensus on major threats and challenges. We commit ourselves to translating that consensus into concrete action, including addressing the root causes of those threats and challenges with resolve and determination.

9. We acknowledge that peace and security, development and human rights are the pillars of the United Nations system and the foundations for collective security and well-being. We recognize that development, peace and security and human rights are interlinked and mutually reinforcing.

10. We reaffirm that development is a central goal in itself and that sustainable development in its economic, social and environmental aspects constitutes a key element of the overarching framework of United Nations activities.

11. We acknowledge that good governance and the rule of law at the national and international levels are essential for sustained economic growth, sustainable development and the eradication of poverty and hunger.

12. We reaffirm that gender equality and the promotion and protection of the full enjoyment of all human rights and fundamental freedoms for all are essential to advance development and peace and security. We are committed to creating a world fit for future generations, which takes into account the best interests of the child.

13. We reaffirm the universality, indivisibility, interdependence and interrelatedness of all human rights.

14. Acknowledging the diversity of the world, we recognize that all cultures and civilizations contribute to the enrichment of humankind. We acknowledge the importance of respect and understanding for religious and cultural diversity throughout the world. In order to promote international peace and security, we commit ourselves to advancing human welfare, freedom and progress everywhere, as well as to encouraging tolerance, respect, dialogue and cooperation among different cultures, civilizations and peoples.

15. We pledge to enhance the relevance, effectiveness, efficiency, accountability and credibility of the United Nations system. This is our shared responsibility and interest.

16. We therefore resolve to create a more peaceful, prosperous and democratic world and to undertake concrete measures to continue finding ways to implement the outcome of the Millennium Summit and the other major United Nations conferences and summits so as to provide multilateral solutions to problems in the four following areas:
   • Development
   • Peace and collective security
   • Human rights and the rule of law
   • Strengthening of the United Nations

II. DEVELOPMENT

17. We strongly reiterate our determination to ensure the timely and full realization of the development goals and objectives agreed at the major United Nations conferences and summits, including those agreed at the Millennium Summit that are described as the Millennium Development Goals, which have helped to galvanize efforts towards poverty eradication.

18. We emphasize the vital role played by the major United Nations conferences and summits in the economic, social and related fields in shaping a broad development vision and in identifying commonly agreed objectives, which have contributed to improving human life in different parts of the world.

19. We reaffirm our commitment to eradicate poverty and promote sustained economic growth, sustainable development and global prosperity for all. We are encouraged by reductions in poverty in some countries in the recent past and are determined to reinforce and extend this trend to benefit people worldwide. We remain concerned, however, about the slow and uneven progress towards poverty eradication and the realization of other development goals in some regions. We commit ourselves to promoting the development of the productive sectors in developing countries to enable them to participate more effectively in and benefit from the process of globalization. We underline the need for urgent action on all sides, including more ambitious national development strategies and efforts backed by increased international support.

Global partnership for development

20. We reaffirm our commitment to the global partnership for development set out in the Millennium Declaration, the Monterrey Consensus and the Johannesburg Plan of Implementation.

21. We further reaffirm our commitment to sound policies, good governance at all levels and the rule of law, and to mobilize domestic resources, attract international flows, promote international trade as an engine for development and increase international financial and technical cooperation for development, sustainable debt financing and external debt relief and to enhance the coherence and consistency of the international monetary, financial and trading systems.

22. We reaffirm that each country must take primary responsibility for its own development and that the role of national policies and development strategies cannot be overemphasized in the achievement of sustainable development. We also recognize that national efforts should be complemented by supportive global programmes, measures and policies aimed at expanding the development opportunities of developing countries, while taking into account national conditions and ensuring respect for national ownership, strategies and sovereignty. To this end, we resolve:

    (a) To adopt, by 2006, and implement comprehensive national development strategies to achieve the internationally agreed development goals and objectives, including the Millennium Development Goals;

    (b) To manage public finances effectively to achieve and maintain macroeconomic stability and long-term growth and to make effective and transparent use of public funds and ensure that development assistance is used to build national capacities;

(c) To support efforts by developing countries to adopt and implement national development policies and strategies through increased development assistance, the promotion of international trade as an engine for development, the transfer of technology on mutually agreed terms, increased investment flows and wider and deeper debt relief, and to support developing countries by providing a substantial increase in aid of sufficient quality and arriving in a timely manner to assist them in achieving the internationally agreed development goals, including the Millennium Development Goals;

(d) That the increasing interdependence of national economies in a globalizing world and the emergence of rule-based regimes for international economic relations have meant that the space for national economic policy, that is, the scope for domestic policies, especially in the areas of trade, investment and industrial development, is now often framed by international disciplines, commitments and global market considerations. It is for each Government to evaluate the trade-off between the benefits of accepting international rules and commitments and the constraints posed by the loss of policy space. It is particularly important for developing countries, bearing in mind development goals and objectives, that all countries take into account the need for appropriate balance between national policy space and international disciplines and commitments;

(e) To enhance the contribution of non-governmental organizations, civil society, the private sector and other stakeholders in national development efforts, as well as in the promotion of the global partnership for development;

(f) To ensure that the United Nations funds and programmes and the specialized agencies support the efforts of developing countries through the common country assessment and United Nations Development Assistance Framework process, enhancing their support for capacity-building;

(g) To protect our natural resource base in support of development.

Financing for development

23. We reaffirm the Monterrey Consensus and recognize that mobilizing financial resources for development and the effective use of those resources in developing countries and countries with economies in transition are central to a global partnership for development in support of the achievement of the internationally agreed development goals, including the Millennium Development Goals. In this regard:

(a) We are encouraged by recent commitments to substantial increases in official development assistance and the Organization for Economic Cooperation and Development estimate that official development assistance to all developing countries will now increase by around 50 billion United States dollars a year by 2010, while recognizing that a substantial increase in such assistance is required to achieve the internationally agreed goals, including the Millennium Development Goals, within their respective time frames;

(b) We welcome the increased resources that will become available as a result of the establishment of timetables by many developed countries to achieve the target of 0.7 per cent of gross national product for official development assistance by 2015 and to reach at least 0.5 per cent of gross national product for official development assistance by 2010 as well as, pursuant to the Brussels Programme of Action for the Least Developed Countries for the Decade 2001–2010, 0.15 per cent to 0.20 per cent for the least developed countries no later than 2010, and urge those developed countries that have not yet done so to make concrete efforts in this regard in accordance with their commitments;

(c) We further welcome recent efforts and initiatives to enhance the quality of aid and to increase its impact, including the Paris Declaration on Aid Effectiveness, and resolve to take concrete, effective and timely action in implementing all agreed commitments on aid effectiveness, with clear monitoring and deadlines, including through further aligning assistance with countries' strategies, building institutional capacities, reducing transaction costs and eliminating bureaucratic procedures, making progress on untying aid, enhancing the absorptive capacity and financial management of recipient countries and strengthening the focus on development results;

(d) We recognize the value of developing innovative sources of financing, provided those sources do not unduly burden developing countries. In that regard, we take note with interest of the international efforts, contributions and discussions, such as the Action against Hunger and Poverty, aimed at identifying innovative and additional sources of financing for development on a public, private, domestic or external basis to increase and supplement traditional sources of financing. Some countries will implement the International Finance Facility. Some countries have launched the International Finance Facility for immunization. Some countries will implement in the near future, utilizing their national authorities, a contribution on airline tickets to enable the financing of development projects, in particular in the health sector, directly or through financing of the International Finance Facility. Other countries are considering whether and to what extent they will participate in these initiatives;

(e) We acknowledge the vital role the private sector can play in generating new investments, employment and financing for development;

(f) We resolve to address the development needs of low-income developing countries by working in competent multilateral and international forums, to help them meet, inter alia, their financial, technical and technological requirements;

(g) We resolve to continue to support the development efforts of middle-income developing countries by working, in competent multilateral and international forums and also through bilateral arrangements, on measures to help them meet, inter alia, their financial, technical and technological requirements;

(h) We resolve to operationalize the World Solidarity Fund established by the General Assembly and invite those countries in a position to do so to make voluntary contributions to the Fund;

(i) We recognize the need for access to financial services, in particular for the poor, including through microfinance and microcredit.

Domestic resource mobilization

24. In our common pursuit of growth, poverty eradication and sustainable development, a critical challenge is to ensure the necessary internal conditions for mobilizing domestic savings, both public and private, sustaining adequate levels of productive

investment, increasing human capacity, reducing capital flight, curbing the illicit transfer of funds and enhancing international cooperation for creating an enabling domestic environment. We undertake to support the efforts of developing countries to create a domestic enabling environment for mobilizing domestic resources. To this end, we therefore resolve:

(a) To pursue good governance and sound macroeconomic policies at all levels and support developing countries in their efforts to put in place the policies and investments to drive sustained economic growth, promote small and medium sized enterprises, promote employment generation and stimulate the private sector;

(b) To reaffirm that good governance is essential for sustainable development; that sound economic policies, solid democratic institutions responsive to the needs of the people and improved infrastructure are the basis for sustained economic growth, poverty eradication and employment creation; and that freedom, peace and security, domestic stability, respect for human rights, including the right to development, the rule of law, gender equality and market-oriented policies and an overall commitment to just and democratic societies are also essential and mutually reinforcing;

(c) To make the fight against corruption a priority at all levels and we welcome all actions taken in this regard at the national and international levels, including the adoption of policies that emphasize accountability, transparent public sector management and corporate responsibility and accountability, including efforts to return assets transferred through corruption, consistent with the United Nations Convention against Corruption. We urge all States that have not done so to consider signing, ratifying and implementing the Convention;

(d) To channel private capabilities and resources into stimulating the private sector in developing countries through actions in the public, public/private and private spheres to create an enabling environment for partnership and innovation that contributes to accelerated economic development and hunger and poverty eradication;

(e) To support efforts to reduce capital flight and measures to curb the illicit transfer of funds.

Investment

25. We resolve to encourage greater direct investment, including foreign investment, in developing countries and countries with economies in transition to support their development activities and to enhance the benefits they can derive from such investments. In this regard:

(a) We continue to support efforts by developing countries and countries with economies in transition to create a domestic environment conducive to attracting investments through, inter alia, achieving a transparent, stable and predictable investment climate with proper contract enforcement and respect for property rights and the rule of law and pursuing appropriate policy and regulatory frameworks that encourage business formation;

(b) We will put into place policies to ensure adequate investment in a sustainable manner in health, clean water and sanitation, housing and education and in the provision of public goods and social safety nets to protect vulnerable and disadvantaged sectors of society;

(c) We invite national Governments seeking to develop infrastructure projects and generate foreign direct investment to pursue strategies with the involvement of both the public and private sectors and, where appropriate, international donors;

(d) We call upon international financial and banking institutions to consider enhancing the transparency of risk rating mechanisms. Sovereign risk assessments, made by the private sector should maximize the use of strict, objective and transparent parameters, which can be facilitated by high-quality data and analysis;

(e) We underscore the need to sustain sufficient and stable private financial flows to developing countries and countries with economies in transition. It is important to promote measures in source and destination countries to improve transparency and the information about financial flows to developing countries, particularly countries in Africa, the least developed countries, small island developing States and landlocked developing countries. Measures that mitigate the impact of excessive volatility of short-term capital flows are important and must be considered.

Debt

26. We emphasize the high importance of a timely, effective, comprehensive and durable solution to the debt problems of developing countries, since debt financing and relief can be an important source of capital for development. To this end:

(a) We welcome the recent proposals of the Group of Eight to cancel 100 per cent of the outstanding debt of eligible heavily indebted poor countries owed to the International Monetary Fund, the International Development Association and African Development Fund and to provide additional resources to ensure that the financing capacity of the international financial institutions is not reduced;

(b) We emphasize that debt sustainability is essential for underpinning growth and underline the importance of debt sustainability to the efforts to achieve national development goals, including the Millennium Development Goals, recognizing the key role that debt relief can play in liberating resources that can be directed towards activities consistent with poverty eradication, sustained economic growth and sustainable development;

(c) We further stress the need to consider additional measures and initiatives aimed at ensuring long-term debt sustainability through increased grant-based financing, cancellation of 100 per cent of the official multilateral and bilateral debt of heavily indebted poor countries and, where appropriate, and on a case-by-case basis, to consider significant debt relief or restructuring for low- and middle-income developing countries with an unsustainable debt burden that are not part of the Heavily Indebted Poor Countries Initiative, as well as the exploration of mechanisms to comprehensively address the debt problems of those countries. Such mechanisms may include debt for sustainable development swaps or multicreditor debt swap arrangements, as appropriate. These initiatives could include further efforts by the International Monetary Fund and the World Bank to develop the debt sustainability framework for low-income countries. This should be achieved in a fashion that does not detract from official development assistance resources, while maintaining the financial integrity of the multilateral financial institutions.

Trade

27. A universal, rule-based, open, non-discriminatory and equitable multilateral trading system, as well as meaningful trade liberalization, can substantially stimulate development worldwide, benefiting countries at all stages of development. In that regard, we reaffirm our commitment to trade liberalization and to ensure that trade plays its full part in promoting economic growth, employment and development for all.

28. We are committed to efforts designed to ensure that developing countries, especially the least-developed countries, participate fully in the world trading system in order to meet their economic development needs, and reaffirm our commitment to enhanced and predictable market access for the exports of developing countries.

29. We will work towards the objective, in accordance with the Brussels Programme of Action, of duty-free and quota-free market access for all least developed countries' products to the markets of developed countries, as well as to the markets of developing countries in a position to do so, and support their efforts to overcome their supply-side constraints.

30. We are committed to supporting and promoting increased aid to build productive and trade capacities of developing countries and to taking further steps in that regard, while welcoming the substantial support already provided.

31. We will work to accelerate and facilitate the accession of developing countries and countries with economies in transition to the World Trade Organization consistent with its criteria, recognizing the importance of universal integration in the rules-based global trading system.

32. We will work expeditiously towards implementing the development dimensions of the Doha work programme.

Commodities

33. We emphasize the need to address the impact of weak and volatile commodity prices and support the efforts of commodity-dependent countries to restructure, diversify and strengthen the competitiveness of their commodity sectors.

Quick-impact initiatives

34. Given the need to accelerate progress immediately in countries where current trends make the achievement of the internationally agreed development goals unlikely, we resolve to urgently identify and implement country-led initiatives with adequate international support, consistent with long-term national development strategies, that promise immediate and durable improvements in the lives of people and renewed hope for the achievement of the development goals. In this regard, we will take such actions as the distribution of malaria bed nets, including free distribution,

where appropriate, and effective anti-malarial treatments, the expansion of local school meal programmes, using home-grown foods where possible, and the elimination of user fees for primary education and, where appropriate, health-care services.

Systemic issues and global economic decision-making

35. We reaffirm the commitment to broaden and strengthen the participation of developing countries and countries with economies in transition in international economic decision-making and norm-setting, and to that end stress the importance of continuing efforts to reform the international financial architecture, noting that enhancing the voice and participation of developing countries and countries with economies in transition in the Bretton Woods institutions remains a continuous concern.

36. We reaffirm our commitment to governance, equity and transparency in the financial, monetary and trading systems. We are also committed to open, equitable, rule-based, predictable and non-discriminatory multilateral trading and financial systems.

37. We also underscore our commitment to sound domestic financial sectors, which make a vital contribution to national development efforts, as an important component of an international financial architecture that is supportive of development.

38. We further reaffirm the need for the United Nations to play a fundamental role in the promotion of international cooperation for development and the coherence, coordination and implementation of development goals and actions agreed upon by the international community, and we resolve to strengthen coordination within the United Nations system in close cooperation with all other multilateral financial, trade and development institutions in order to support sustained economic growth, poverty eradication and sustainable development.

39. Good governance at the international level is fundamental for achieving sustainable development. In order to ensure a dynamic and enabling international economic environment, it is important to promote global economic governance through addressing the international finance, trade, technology and investment patterns that have an impact on the development prospects of developing countries. To this effect, the international community should take all necessary and appropriate measures, including ensuring support for structural and macroeconomic reform, a comprehensive solution to the external debt problem and increasing the market access of developing countries.

South–South cooperation

40. We recognize the achievements and great potential of South–South cooperation and encourage the promotion of such cooperation, which complements North–South cooperation as an effective contribution to development and as a means to share best practices and provide enhanced technical cooperation. In this context, we note the recent decision of the leaders of the South, adopted at the Second South Summit and contained in the Doha Declaration and the Doha Plan of Action, to intensify their efforts at South–South cooperation, including through the establishment of the New Asian–African Strategic Partnership and other regional cooperation mechanisms, and encourage the international community, including the

international financial institutions, to support the efforts of developing countries, inter alia, through triangular cooperation. We also take note with appreciation of the launching of the third round of negotiations on the Global System of Trade Preferences among Developing Countries as an important instrument to stimulate South-South cooperation.

41. We welcome the work of the United Nations High-Level Committee on South–South Cooperation and invite countries to consider supporting the Special Unit for South–South Cooperation within the United Nations Development Programme in order to respond effectively to the development needs of developing countries.

42. We recognize the considerable contribution of arrangements such as the Organization of Petroleum Exporting Countries Fund initiated by a group of developing countries, as well as the potential contribution of the South Fund for Development and Humanitarian Assistance, to development activities in developing countries.

Education

43. We emphasize the critical role of both formal and informal education in the achievement of poverty eradication and other development goals as envisaged in the Millennium Declaration, in particular basic education and training for eradicating illiteracy, and strive for expanded secondary and higher education as well as vocational education and technical training, especially for girls and women, the creation of human resources and infrastructure capabilities and the empowerment of those living in poverty. In this context, we reaffirm the Dakar Framework for Action adopted at the World Education Forum in 2009 and recognize the importance of the United Nations Educational, Scientific and Cultural Organization strategy for the eradication of poverty, especially extreme poverty, in supporting the Education for All programmes as a tool to achieve the millennium development goal of universal primary education by 2015.

44. We reaffirm our commitment to support developing country efforts to ensure that all children have access to and complete free and compulsory primary education of good quality, to eliminate gender inequality and imbalance and to renew efforts to improve girls' education. We also commit ourselves to continuing to support the efforts of developing countries in the implementation of the Education for All initiative, including with enhanced resources of all types through the Education for All fast-track initiative in support of country-led national education plans.

45. We commit ourselves to promoting education for peace and human development.

Rural and agricultural development

46. We reaffirm that food security and rural and agricultural development must be adequately and urgently addressed in the context of national development and response strategies and, in this context, will enhance the contributions of indigenous and local communities, as appropriate. We are convinced that the eradication of poverty, hunger and malnutrition, particularly as they affect children, is crucial for the achievement of the Millennium Development Goals. Rural and agricultural development should be an integral part of national and international development

policies. We deem it necessary to increase productive investment in rural and agricultural development to achieve food security. We commit ourselves to increasing support for agricultural development and trade capacity-building in the agricultural sector in developing countries. Support for commodity development projects, especially market-based projects, and for their preparation under the Second Account of the Common Fund for Commodities should be encouraged.

Employment

47. We strongly support fair globalization and resolve to make the goals of full and productive employment and decent work for all, including for women and young people, a central objective of our relevant national and international policies as well as our national development strategies, including poverty reduction strategies, as part of our efforts to achieve the Millennium Development Goals. These measures should also encompass the elimination of the worst forms of child labour, as defined in International Labour Organization Convention No. 182, and forced labour. We also resolve to ensure full respect for the fundamental principles and rights at work.

Sustainable development: managing and protecting our common environment

48. We reaffirm our commitment to achieve the goal of sustainable development, including through the implementation of Agenda 2110 and the Johannesburg Plan of Implementation. To this end, we commit ourselves to undertaking concrete actions and measures at all levels and to enhancing international cooperation, taking into account the Rio principles. These efforts will also promote the integration of the three components of sustainable development – economic development, social development and environmental protection – as interdependent and mutually reinforcing pillars. Poverty eradication, changing unsustainable patterns of production and consumption and protecting and managing the natural resource base of economic and social development are overarching objectives of and essential requirements for sustainable development.

49. We will promote sustainable consumption and production patterns, with the developed countries taking the lead and all countries benefiting from the process, as called for in the Johannesburg Plan of Implementation. In that context, we support developing countries in their efforts to promote a recycling economy.

50. We face serious and multiple challenges in tackling climate change, promoting clean energy, meeting energy needs and achieving sustainable development, and we will act with resolve and urgency in this regard.

51. We recognize that climate change is a serious and long-term challenge that has the potential to affect every part of the globe. We emphasize the need to meet all the commitments and obligations we have undertaken in the United Nations Framework Convention on Climate Change and other relevant international agreements, including, for many of us, the Kyoto Protocol. The Convention is the appropriate framework for addressing future action on climate change at the global level.

52. We reaffirm our commitment to the ultimate objective of the Convention: to stabilize greenhouse gas concentrations in the atmosphere at a level that prevents dangerous anthropogenic interference with the climate system.

53. We acknowledge that the global nature of climate change calls for the widest possible cooperation and participation in an effective and appropriate international response, in accordance with the principles of the Convention. We are committed to moving forward the global discussion on long-term cooperative action to address climate change, in accordance with these principles. We stress the importance of the eleventh session of the Conference of the Parties to the Convention, to be held in Montreal in November 2005.

54. We acknowledge various partnerships that are under way to advance action on clean energy and climate change, including bilateral, regional and multilateral initiatives.

55. We are committed to taking further action through practical international cooperation, inter alia:

    (a) To promote innovation, clean energy and energy efficiency and conservation; improve policy, regulatory and financing frameworks; and accelerate the deployment of cleaner technologies;

    (b) To enhance private investment, transfer of technologies and capacity building to developing countries, as called for in the Johannesburg Plan of Implementation, taking into account their own energy needs and priorities;

    (c) To assist developing countries to improve their resilience and integrate adaptation goals into their sustainable development strategies, given that adaptation to the effects of climate change due to both natural and human factors is a high priority for all nations, particularly those most vulnerable, namely, those referred to in article 4.8 of the Convention;

    (d) To continue to assist developing countries, in particular small island developing States, least developed countries and African countries, including those that are particularly vulnerable to climate change, in addressing their adaptation needs relating to the adverse effects of climate change.

56. In pursuance of our commitment to achieve sustainable development, we further resolve:

    (a) To promote the United Nations Decade of Education for Sustainable Development and the International Decade for Action, "Water for Life";

    (b) To support and strengthen the implementation of the United Nations Convention to Combat Desertification in Those Countries Experiencing Serious Drought and/ or Desertification, Particularly in Africa, to address causes of desertification and land degradation, as well as poverty resulting from land degradation, through, inter alia, the mobilization of adequate and predictable financial resources, the transfer of technology and capacity-building at all levels;

    (c) That the States parties to the Convention on Biological Diversity and the Cartagena Protocol on Biosafety should support the implementation of the Convention and the Protocol, as well as other biodiversity-related agreements and the Johannesburg commitment for a significant reduction in the rate of loss of biodiversity by 2010. The States parties will continue to negotiate within the framework of the Convention on Biological Diversity, bearing in mind the Bonn Guidelines, an international regime to promote and safeguard the fair and equitable sharing of benefits arising out of the utilization of genetic resources. All States will fulfil commitments and significantly reduce the rate of loss of biodiversity by 2010 and continue ongoing efforts towards elaborating and negotiating an international regime on access to genetic resources and benefit sharing;

(d) To recognize that the sustainable development of indigenous peoples and their communities is crucial in our fight against hunger and poverty;

(e) To reaffirm our commitment, subject to national legislation, to respect, preserve and maintain the knowledge, innovations and practices of indigenous and local communities embodying traditional lifestyles relevant to the conservation and sustainable use of biological diversity, promote their wider application with the approval and involvement of the holders of such knowledge, innovations and practices and encourage the equitable sharing of the benefits arising from their utilization;

(f) To work expeditiously towards the establishment of a worldwide early warning system for all natural hazards with regional nodes, building on existing national and regional capacity such as the newly established Indian Ocean Tsunami Warning and Mitigation System;

(g) To fully implement the Hyogo Declaration18 and the Hyogo Framework for Action 2005–2015 adopted at the World Conference on Disaster Reduction, in particular those commitments related to assistance for developing countries that are prone to natural disasters and disaster-stricken States in the transition phase towards sustainable physical, social and economic recovery, for risk-reduction activities in post-disaster recovery and for rehabilitation processes;

(h) To assist developing countries' efforts to prepare integrated water resources management and water efficiency plans as part of their national development strategies and to provide access to safe drinking water and basic sanitation in accordance with the Millennium Declaration and the Johannesburg Plan of Implementation, including halving by 2015 the proportion of people who are unable to reach or afford safe drinking water and who do not have access to basic sanitation;

(i) To accelerate the development and dissemination of affordable and cleaner energy efficiency and energy conservation technologies, as well as the transfer of such technologies, in particular to developing countries, on favourable terms, including on concessional and preferential terms, as mutually agreed, bearing in mind that access to energy facilitates the eradication of poverty;

(j) To strengthen the conservation, sustainable management and development of all types of forests for the benefit of current and future generations, including through enhanced international cooperation, so that trees and forests may contribute fully to the achievement of the internationally agreed development goals, including those contained in the Millennium Declaration, taking full account of the linkages between the forest sector and other sectors. We look forward to the discussions at the sixth session of the United Nations Forum on Forests;

(k) To promote the sound management of chemicals and hazardous wastes throughout their life cycle, in accordance with Agenda 21 and the Johannesburg Plan of Implementation, aiming to achieve that by 2020 chemicals are used and produced in ways that lead to the minimization of significant adverse effects on human health and the environment using transparent and science-based risk assessment and risk management procedures, by adopting and implementing a voluntary strategic approach to international management of chemicals, and to support developing countries in strengthening their capacity for the sound management of chemicals and hazardous wastes by providing technical and financial assistance, as appropriate;

(l) To improve cooperation and coordination at all levels in order to address issues related to oceans and seas in an integrated manner and promote integrated management and sustainable development of the oceans and seas;

(m) To achieve significant improvement in the lives of at least 100 million slum-dwellers by 2020, recognizing the urgent need for the provision of increased resources for affordable housing and housing-related infrastructure, prioritizing slum prevention and slum upgrading, and to encourage support for the United Nations Habitat and Human Settlements Foundation and its Slum Upgrading Facility;

(n) To acknowledge the invaluable role of the Global Environment Facility in facilitating cooperation with developing countries; we look forward to a successful replenishment this year along with the successful conclusion of all outstanding commitments from the third replenishment;

(o) To note that cessation of the transport of radioactive materials through the regions of small island developing States is an ultimate desired goal of small island developing States and some other countries and recognize the right of freedom of navigation in accordance with international law. States should maintain dialogue and consultation, in particular under the aegis of the International Atomic Energy Agency and the International Maritime Organization, with the aim of improved mutual understanding, confidence-building and enhanced communication in relation to the safe maritime transport of radioactive materials. States involved in the transport of such materials are urged to continue to engage in dialogue with small island developing States and other States to address their concerns. These concerns include the further development and strengthening, within the appropriate forums, of international regulatory regimes to enhance safety, disclosure, liability, security and compensation in relation to such transport.

HIV/AIDS, malaria, tuberculosis and other health issues

57. We recognize that HIV/AIDS, malaria, tuberculosis and other infectious diseases pose severe risks for the entire world and serious challenges to the achievement of development goals. We acknowledge the substantial efforts and financial contributions made by the international community, while recognizing that these diseases and other emerging health challenges require a sustained international response. To this end, we commit ourselves to:

(a) Increasing investment, building on existing mechanisms and through partnership, to improve health systems in developing countries and those with economies in transition with the aim of providing sufficient health workers, infrastructure, management systems and supplies to achieve the health-related Millennium Development Goals by 2015;

(b) Implementing measures to increase the capacity of adults and adolescents to protect themselves from the risk of HIV infection;

(c) Fully implementing all commitments established by the Declaration of Commitment on HIV/AIDS 20 through stronger leadership, the scaling up of a comprehensive response to achieve broad multisectoral coverage for prevention, care, treatment and support, the mobilization of additional resources from national, bilateral, multilateral and private sources and the substantial funding of the Global Fund to Fight AIDS, Tuberculosis and Malaria as well as of the HIV/AIDS component of the work programmes of the United Nations system agencies and programmes engaged in the fight against HIV/AIDS;

(d) Developing and implementing a package for HIV prevention, treatment and care with the aim of coming as close as possible to the goal of universal access to treatment by 2010 for all those who need it, including through increased resources, and working towards the elimination of stigma and discrimination, enhanced access to affordable medicines and the reduction of vulnerability of persons affected by HIV/AIDS and other health issues, in particular orphaned and vulnerable children and older persons;

(e) Ensuring the full implementation of our obligations under the International Health Regulations adopted by the fifty-eighth World Health Assembly in May 2005, including the need to support the Global Outbreak Alert and Response Network of the World Health Organization;

(f) Working actively to implement the "Three Ones" principles in all countries, including by ensuring that multiple institutions and international partners all work under one agreed HIV/AIDS framework that provides the basis for coordinating the work of all partners, with one national AIDS coordinating authority having a broad-based multisectoral mandate, and under one agreed country-level monitoring and evaluation system. We welcome and support the important recommendations of the Global Task Team on Improving AIDS Coordination among Multilateral Institutions and International Donors;

(g) Achieving universal access to reproductive health by 2015, as set out at the International Conference on Population and Development, integrating this goal in strategies to attain the internationally agreed development goals, including those contained in the Millennium Declaration, aimed at reducing maternal mortality, improving maternal health, reducing child mortality, promoting gender equality, combating HIV/AIDS and eradicating poverty;

(h) Promoting long-term funding, including public–private partnerships where appropriate, for academic and industrial research as well as for the development of new vaccines and microbicides, diagnostic kits, drugs and treatments to address major pandemics, tropical diseases and other diseases, such as avian flu and severe acute respiratory syndrome, and taking forward work on market incentives, where appropriate through such mechanisms as advance purchase commitments;

(i) Stressing the need to urgently address malaria and tuberculosis, in particular in the most affected countries, and welcoming the scaling up, in this regard, of bilateral and multilateral initiatives.

Gender equality and empowerment of women

58. We remain convinced that progress for women is progress for all. We reaffirm that the full and effective implementation of the goals and objectives of the Beijing Declaration and Platform for Action and the outcome of the twenty-third special session of the General Assembly is an essential contribution to achieving the internationally agreed development goals, including those contained in the Millennium Declaration, and we resolve to promote gender equality and eliminate pervasive gender discrimination by:

    (a) Eliminating gender inequalities in primary and secondary education by the earliest possible date and at all educational levels by 2015;

    (b) Guaranteeing the free and equal right of women to own and inherit property and ensuring secure tenure of property and housing by women;

    (c) Ensuring equal access to reproductive health;

    (d) Promoting women's equal access to labour markets, sustainable employment and adequate labour protection;

    (e) Ensuring equal access of women to productive assets and resources, including land, credit and technology;

    (f) Eliminating all forms of discrimination and violence against women and the girl child, including by ending impunity and by ensuring the protection of civilians, in particular women and the girl child, during and after armed conflicts in accordance with the obligations of States under international humanitarian law and international human rights law;

    (g) Promoting increased representation of women in Government decision-making bodies, including through ensuring their equal opportunity to participate fully in the political process.

59. We recognize the importance of gender mainstreaming as a tool for achieving gender equality. To that end, we undertake to actively promote the mainstreaming of a gender perspective in the design, implementation, monitoring and evaluation of policies and programmes in all political, economic and social spheres, and further undertake to strengthen the capabilities of the United Nations system in the area of gender.

Science and technology for development

60. We recognize that science and technology, including information and communication technology, are vital for the achievement of the development goals and that international support can help developing countries to benefit from technological advancements and enhance their productive capacity. We therefore commit ourselves to:

    (a) Strengthening and enhancing existing mechanisms and supporting initiatives for research and development, including through voluntary partnerships between the public and private sectors, to address the special needs of developing countries in the areas of health, agriculture, conservation, sustainable use of natural resources and environmental management, energy, forestry and the impact of climate change;

(b) Promoting and facilitating, as appropriate, access to and the development, transfer and diffusion of technologies, including environmentally sound technologies and corresponding know-how, to developing countries;

(c) Assisting developing countries in their efforts to promote and develop national strategies for human resources and science and technology, which are primary drivers of national capacity-building for development;

(d) Promoting and supporting greater efforts to develop renewable sources of energy, such as solar, wind and geothermal;

(e) Implementing policies at the national and international levels to attract both public and private investment, domestic and foreign, that enhances knowledge, transfers technology on mutually agreed terms and raises productivity;

(f) Supporting the efforts of developing countries, individually and collectively, to harness new agricultural technologies in order to increase agricultural productivity through environmentally sustainable means;

(g) Building a people-centred and inclusive information society so as to enhance digital opportunities for all people in order to help bridge the digital divide, putting the potential of information and communication technologies at the service of development and addressing new challenges of the information society by implementing the outcomes of the Geneva phase of the World Summit on the Information Society and ensuring the success of the second phase of the Summit, to be held in Tunis in November 2005; in this regard, we welcome the establishment of the Digital Solidarity Fund and encourage voluntary contributions to its financing.

Migration and development

61. We acknowledge the important nexus between international migration and development and the need to deal with the challenges and opportunities that migration presents to countries of origin, destination and transit. We recognize that international migration brings benefits as well as challenges to the global community. We look forward to the high-level dialogue of the General Assembly on international migration and development to be held in 2006, which will offer an opportunity to discuss the multidimensional aspects of international migration and development in order to identify appropriate ways and means to maximize their development benefits and minimize their negative impacts.

62. We reaffirm our resolve to take measures to ensure respect for and protection of the human rights of migrants, migrant workers and members of their families.

63. We reaffirm the need to adopt policies and undertake measures to reduce the cost of transferring migrant remittances to developing countries and welcome efforts by Governments and stakeholders in this regard.

Countries with special needs

64. We reaffirm our commitment to address the special needs of the least developed countries and urge all countries and all relevant organizations of the United Nations system, including the Bretton Woods institutions, to make concerted efforts and

adopt speedy measures for meeting in a timely manner the goals and targets of the Brussels Programme of Action for the Least Developed Countries for the Decade 2001–2010.

65. We recognize the special needs of and challenges faced by landlocked developing countries and therefore reaffirm our commitment to urgently address those needs and challenges through the full, timely and effective implementation of the Almaty Programme of Action: Addressing the Special Needs of Landlocked Developing Countries within a New Global Framework for Transit Transport Cooperation for Landlocked and Transit Developing Countries and the São Paulo Consensus adopted at the eleventh session of the United Nations Conference on Trade and Development. We encourage the work undertaken by United Nations regional commissions and organizations towards establishing a time-cost methodology for indicators to measure the progress in implementation of the Almaty Programme of Action. We also recognize the special difficulties and concerns of landlocked developing countries in their efforts to integrate their economies into the multilateral trading system. In this regard, priority should be given to the full and timely implementation of the Almaty Declaration and the Almaty Programme of Action.

66. We recognize the special needs and vulnerabilities of small island developing States and reaffirm our commitment to take urgent and concrete action to address those needs and vulnerabilities through the full and effective implementation of the Mauritius Strategy adopted by the International Meeting to Review the Implementation of the Programme of Action for the Sustainable Development of Small Island Developing States, the Barbados Programme of Action and the outcome of the twenty-second special session of the General Assembly. We further undertake to promote greater international cooperation and partnership for the implementation of the Mauritius Strategy through, inter alia, the mobilization of domestic and international resources, the promotion of international trade as an engine for development and increased international financial and technical cooperation.

67. We emphasize the need for continued, coordinated and effective international support for achieving the development goals in countries emerging from conflict and in those recovering from natural disasters.

Meeting the special needs of Africa

68. We welcome the substantial progress made by the African countries in fulfilling their commitments and emphasize the need to carry forward the implementation of the New Partnership for Africa's Development to promote sustainable growth and development and deepen democracy, human rights, good governance and sound economic management and gender equality and encourage African countries, with the participation of civil society and the private sector, to continue their efforts in this regard by developing and strengthening institutions for governance and the development of the region, and also welcome the recent decisions taken by Africa's partners, including the Group of Eight and the European Union, in support of Africa's development efforts, including commitments that will lead to an increase in official development assistance to Africa of 25 billion dollars per year by 2010. We reaffirm our commitment to address the special needs of Africa,

which is the only continent not on track to meet any of the goals of the Millennium Declaration by 2015, to enable it to enter the mainstream of the world economy, and resolve:

(a) To strengthen cooperation with the New Partnership for Africa's Development by providing coherent support for the programmes drawn up by African leaders within that framework, including by mobilizing internal and external financial resources and facilitating approval of such programmes by the multilateral financial institutions;

(b) To support the African commitment to ensure that by 2015 all children have access to complete, free and compulsory primary education of good quality, as well as to basic health care;

(c) To support the building of an international infrastructure consortium involving the African Union, the World Bank and the African Development Bank, with the New Partnership for Africa's Development as the main framework, to facilitate public and private infrastructure investment in Africa;

(d) To promote a comprehensive and durable solution to the external debt problems of African countries, including through the cancellation of 100 per cent of multilateral debt consistent with the recent Group of Eight proposal for the heavily indebted poor countries, and, on a case-by-case basis, where appropriate, significant debt relief, including, inter alia, cancellation or restructuring for heavily indebted African countries not part of the Heavily Indebted Poor Countries Initiative that have unsustainable debt burdens;

(e) To make efforts to fully integrate African countries in the international trading system, including through targeted trade capacity-building programmes;

(f) To support the efforts of commodity-dependent African countries to restructure, diversify and strengthen the competitiveness of their commodity sectors and decide to work towards market-based arrangements with the participation of the private sector for commodity price-risk management;

(g) To supplement the efforts of African countries, individually and collectively, to increase agricultural productivity, in a sustainable way, as set out in the Comprehensive Africa Agriculture Development Programme of the New Partnership for Africa's Development as part of an African "Green Revolution";

(h) To encourage and support the initiatives of the African Union and subregional organizations to prevent, mediate and resolve conflicts with the assistance of the United Nations, and in this regard welcomes the proposals from the Group of Eight countries to provide support for African peacekeeping;

(i) To provide, with the aim of an AIDS-, malaria- and tuberculosis-free generation in Africa, assistance for prevention and care and to come as close as possible to achieving the goal of universal access by 2010 to HIV/AIDS treatment in African countries, to encourage pharmaceutical companies to make drugs, including antiretroviral drugs, affordable and accessible in Africa and to ensure increased bilateral and multilateral assistance, where possible on a grant basis, to combat malaria, tuberculosis and other infectious diseases in Africa through the strengthening of health systems.

III. PEACE AND COLLECTIVE SECURITY

69. We recognize that we are facing a whole range of threats that require our urgent, collective and more determined response.

70. We also recognize that, in accordance with the Charter, addressing such threats requires cooperation among all the principal organs of the United Nations within their respective mandates.

71. We acknowledge that we are living in an interdependent and global world and that many of today's threats recognize no national boundaries, are interlinked and must be tackled at the global, regional and national levels in accordance with the Charter and international law.

72. We therefore reaffirm our commitment to work towards a security consensus based on the recognition that many threats are interlinked, that development, peace, security and human rights are mutually reinforcing, that no State can best protect itself by acting entirely alone and that all States need an effective and efficient collective security system pursuant to the purposes and principles of the Charter.

Pacific settlement of disputes

73. We emphasize the obligation of States to settle their disputes by peaceful means in accordance with Chapter VI of the Charter, including, when appropriate, by the use of the International Court of Justice. All States should act in accordance with the Declaration on Principles of International Law concerning Friendly Relations and Cooperation among States in accordance with the Charter of the United Nations.

74. We stress the importance of prevention of armed conflict in accordance with the purposes and principles of the Charter and solemnly renew our commitment to promote a culture of prevention of armed conflict as a means of effectively addressing the interconnected security and development challenges faced by peoples throughout the world, as well as to strengthen the capacity of the United Nations for the prevention of armed conflict.

75. We further stress the importance of a coherent and integrated approach to the prevention of armed conflicts and the settlement of disputes and the need for the Security Council, the General Assembly, the Economic and Social Council and the Secretary-General to coordinate their activities within their respective Charter mandates.

76. Recognizing the important role of the good offices of the Secretary-General, including in the mediation of disputes, we support the Secretary-General's efforts to strengthen his capacity in this area.

Use of force under the Charter of the United Nations

77. We reiterate the obligation of all Member States to refrain in their international relations from the threat or use of force in any manner inconsistent with the Charter. We reaffirm that the purposes and principles guiding the United Nations are, inter alia, to maintain international peace and security, to develop friendly relations among

nations based on respect for the principles of equal rights and self-determination of peoples and to take other appropriate measures to strengthen universal peace, and to that end we are determined to take effective collective measures for the prevention and removal of threats to the peace and for the suppression of acts of aggression or other breaches of the peace, and to bring about by peaceful means, in conformity with the principles of justice and international law, the adjustment or settlement of international disputes or situations that might lead to a breach of the peace.

78. We reiterate the importance of promoting and strengthening the multilateral process and of addressing international challenges and problems by strictly abiding by the Charter and the principles of international law, and further stress our commitment to multilateralism.

79. We reaffirm that the relevant provisions of the Charter are sufficient to address the full range of threats to international peace and security. We further reaffirm the authority of the Security Council to mandate coercive action to maintain and restore international peace and security. We stress the importance of acting in accordance with the purposes and principles of the Charter.

80. We also reaffirm that the Security Council has primary responsibility in the maintenance of international peace and security. We also note the role of the General Assembly relating to the maintenance of international peace and security in accordance with the relevant provisions of the Charter.

Terrorism

81. We strongly condemn terrorism in all its forms and manifestations, committed by whomever, wherever and for whatever purposes, as it constitutes one of the most serious threats to international peace and security.

82. We welcome the Secretary-General's identification of elements of a counterterrorism strategy. These elements should be developed by the General Assembly without delay with a view to adopting and implementing a strategy to promote comprehensive, coordinated and consistent responses, at the national, regional and international levels, to counter terrorism, which also takes into account the conditions conducive to the spread of terrorism. In this context, we commend the various initiatives to promote dialogue, tolerance and understanding among civilizations.

83. We stress the need to make every effort to reach an agreement on and conclude a comprehensive convention on international terrorism during the sixtieth session of the General Assembly.

84. We acknowledge that the question of convening a high-level conference under the auspices of the United Nations to formulate an international response to terrorism in all its forms and manifestations could be considered.

85. We recognize that international cooperation to fight terrorism must be conducted in conformity with international law, including the Charter and relevant international conventions and protocols. States must ensure that any measures taken to combat terrorism comply with their obligations under international law, in particular human rights law, refugee law and international humanitarian law.

86. We reiterate our call upon States to refrain from organizing, financing, encouraging, providing training for or otherwise supporting terrorist activities and to

take appropriate measures to ensure that their territories are not used for such activities.

87. We acknowledge the important role played by the United Nations in combating terrorism and also stress the vital contribution of regional and bilateral cooperation, particularly at the practical level of law enforcement cooperation and technical exchange.

88. We urge the international community, including the United Nations, to assist States in building national and regional capacity to combat terrorism. We invite the Secretary-General to submit proposals to the General Assembly and the Security Council, within their respective mandates, to strengthen the capacity of the United Nations system to assist States in combating terrorism and to enhance the coordination of United Nations activities in this regard.

89. We stress the importance of assisting victims of terrorism and of providing them and their families with support to cope with their loss and their grief.

90. We encourage the Security Council to consider ways to strengthen its monitoring and enforcement role in counter-terrorism, including by consolidating State reporting requirements, taking into account and respecting the different mandates of its counter-terrorism subsidiary bodies. We are committed to cooperating fully with the three competent subsidiary bodies in the fulfilment of their tasks, recognizing that many States continue to require assistance in implementing relevant Security Council resolutions.

91. We support efforts for the early entry into force of the International Convention for the Suppression of Acts of Nuclear Terrorism and strongly encourage States to consider becoming parties to it expeditiously and acceding without delay to the twelve other international conventions and protocols against terrorism and implementing them.

Peacekeeping

92. Recognizing that United Nations peacekeeping plays a vital role in helping parties to conflict end hostilities and commending the contribution of United Nations peacekeepers in that regard, noting improvements made in recent years in United Nations peacekeeping, including the deployment of integrated missions in complex situations, and stressing the need to mount operations with adequate capacity to counter hostilities and fulfil effectively their mandates, we urge further development of proposals for enhanced rapidly deployable capacities to reinforce peacekeeping operations in crises. We endorse the creation of an initial operating capability for a standing police capacity to provide coherent, effective and responsive start-up capability for the policing component of the United Nations peacekeeping missions and to assist existing missions through the provision of advice and expertise.

93. Recognizing the important contribution to peace and security by regional organizations as provided for under Chapter VIII of the Charter and the importance of forging predictable partnerships and arrangements between the United Nations and regional organizations, and noting in particular, given the special needs of Africa, the importance of a strong African Union:

(a) We support the efforts of the European Union and other regional entities to develop capacities such as for rapid deployment, standby and bridging arrangements;

(b) We support the development and implementation of a ten-year plan for capacity-building with the African Union.

94. We support implementation of the 2001 Programme of Action to Prevent, Combat and Eradicate the Illicit Trade in Small Arms and Light Weapons in All Its Aspects.

95. We urge States parties to the Anti-Personnel Mine Ban Convention and Amended Protocol II to the Convention on Certain Conventional Weapons to fully implement their respective obligations. We call upon States in a position to do so to provide greater technical assistance to mine-affected States.

96. We underscore the importance of the recommendations of the Adviser to the Secretary-General on Sexual Exploitation and Abuse by United Nations Peacekeeping Personnel, and urge that those measures adopted in the relevant General Assembly resolutions based upon the recommendations be fully implemented without delay.

Peacebuilding

97. Emphasizing the need for a coordinated, coherent and integrated approach to post-conflict peacebuilding and reconciliation with a view to achieving sustainable peace, recognizing the need for a dedicated institutional mechanism to address the special needs of countries emerging from conflict towards recovery, reintegration and reconstruction and to assist them in laying the foundation for sustainable development, and recognizing the vital role of the United Nations in that regard, we decide to establish a Peacebuilding Commission as an intergovernmental advisory body.

98. The main purpose of the Peacebuilding Commission is to bring together all relevant actors to marshal resources and to advise on and propose integrated strategies for post-conflict peacebuilding and recovery. The Commission should focus attention on the reconstruction and institution-building efforts necessary for recovery from conflict and support the development of integrated strategies in order to lay the foundation for sustainable development. In addition, it should provide recommendations and information to improve the coordination of all relevant actors within and outside the United Nations, develop best practices, help to ensure predictable financing for early recovery activities and extend the period of attention by the international community to post-conflict recovery. The Commission should act in all matters on the basis of consensus of its members.

99. The Peacebuilding Commission should make the outcome of its discussions and recommendations publicly available as United Nations documents to all relevant bodies and actors, including the international financial institutions. The Peacebuilding Commission should submit an annual report to the General Assembly.

100. The Peacebuilding Commission should meet in various configurations. Country-specific meetings of the Commission, upon invitation of the Organizational Committee referred to in paragraph 101 below, should include as members, in addition to members of the Organizational Committee, representatives from:

(a) The country under consideration;

(b) Countries in the region engaged in the post-conflict process and other countries that are involved in relief efforts and/or political dialogue, as well as relevant regional and subregional organizations;

(c) The major financial, troop and civilian police contributors involved in the recovery effort;

(d) The senior United Nations representative in the field and other relevant United Nations representatives;

(e) Such regional and international financial institutions as may be relevant.

101. The Peacebuilding Commission should have a standing Organizational Committee, responsible for developing its procedures and organizational matters, comprising:

(a) Members of the Security Council, including permanent members;

(b) Members of the Economic and Social Council, elected from regional groups, giving due consideration to those countries that have experienced post conflict recovery;

(c) Top providers of assessed contributions to the United Nations budgets and voluntary contributions to the United Nations funds, programmes and agencies, including the standing Peacebuilding Fund, that are not among those selected in (a) or (b) above;

(d) Top providers of military personnel and civilian police to United Nations missions that are not among those selected in (a), (b) or (c) above.

102. Representatives from the World Bank, the International Monetary Fund and other institutional donors should be invited to participate in all meetings of the Peacebuilding Commission in a manner suitable to their governing arrangements, in addition to a representative of the Secretary-General.

103. We request the Secretary-General to establish a multi-year standing Peacebuilding Fund for post-conflict peacebuilding, funded by voluntary contributions and taking due account of existing instruments. The objectives of the Peacebuilding Fund will include ensuring the immediate release of resources needed to launch peacebuilding activities and the availability of appropriate financing for recovery.

104. We also request the Secretary-General to establish, within the Secretariat and from within existing resources, a small peacebuilding support office staffed by qualified experts to assist and support the Peacebuilding Commission. The office should draw on the best expertise available.

105. The Peacebuilding Commission should begin its work no later than 31 December 2005.

Sanctions

106. We underscore that sanctions remain an important tool under the Charter in our efforts to maintain international peace and security without recourse to the use of force, and resolve to ensure that sanctions are carefully targeted in support of clear objectives, to comply with sanctions established by the Security Council and to ensure that sanctions are implemented in ways that balance effectiveness to achieve the desired results against the possible adverse consequences, including socioeconomic and humanitarian consequences, for populations and third States.

107. Sanctions should be implemented and monitored effectively with clear benchmarks and should be periodically reviewed, as appropriate, and remain for as limited a period as necessary to achieve their objectives and should be terminated once the objectives have been achieved.

108. We call upon the Security Council, with the support of the Secretary-General, to improve its monitoring of the implementation and effects of sanctions, to ensure that sanctions are implemented in an accountable manner, to review regularly the results of such monitoring and to develop a mechanism to address special economic problems arising from the application of sanctions in accordance with the Charter.

109. We also call upon the Security Council, with the support of the Secretary General, to ensure that fair and clear procedures exist for placing individuals and entities on sanctions lists and for removing them, as well as for granting humanitarian exemptions.

110. We support efforts through the United Nations to strengthen State capacity to implement sanctions provisions.

Transnational crime

111. We express our grave concern at the negative effects on development, peace and security and human rights posed by transnational crime, including the smuggling of and trafficking in human beings, the world narcotic drug problem and the illicit trade in small arms and light weapons, and at the increasing vulnerability of States to such crime. We reaffirm the need to work collectively to combat transnational crime.

112. We recognize that trafficking in persons continues to pose a serious challenge to humanity and requires a concerted international response. To that end, we urge all States to devise, enforce and strengthen effective measures to combat and eliminate all forms of trafficking in persons to counter the demand for trafficked victims and to protect the victims.

113. We urge all States that have not yet done so to consider becoming parties to the relevant international conventions on organized crime and corruption and, following their entry into force, to implement them effectively, including by incorporating the provisions of those conventions into national legislation and by strengthening criminal justice systems.

114. We reaffirm our unwavering determination and commitment to overcome the world narcotic drug problem through international cooperation and national strategies to eliminate both the illicit supply of and demand for illicit drugs.

115. We resolve to strengthen the capacity of the United Nations Office on Drugs and Crime, within its existing mandates, to provide assistance to Member States in those tasks upon request.

Women in the prevention and resolution of conflicts

116. We stress the important role of women in the prevention and resolution of conflicts and in peacebuilding. We reaffirm our commitment to the full and effective implementation of Security Council resolution 1325 (2000) of 31 October 2000 on women and peace and security. We also underline the importance of integrating a gender perspective and of women having the opportunity for equal participation and full involvement in all efforts to maintain and promote peace and security, as well as the need to increase their role in decision-making at all levels. We strongly

condemn all violations of the human rights of women and girls in situations of armed conflict and the use of sexual exploitation, violence and abuse, and we commit ourselves to elaborating and implementing strategies to report on, prevent and punish gender-based violence.

Protecting children in situations of armed conflict

117. We reaffirm our commitment to promote and protect the rights and welfare of children in armed conflicts. We welcome the significant advances and innovations that have been achieved over the past several years. We welcome in particular the adoption of Security Council resolution 1612 (2005) of 26 July 2005. We call upon States to consider ratifying the Convention on the Rights of the Child and the Optional Protocol to the Convention on the Rights of the Child on the involvement of children in armed conflict. We also call upon States to take effective measures, as appropriate, to prevent the recruitment and use of children in armed conflict, contrary to international law, by armed forces and groups, and to prohibit and criminalize such practices.

118. We therefore call upon all States concerned to take concrete measures to ensure accountability and compliance by those responsible for grave abuses against children. We also reaffirm our commitment to ensure that children in armed conflicts receive timely and effective humanitarian assistance, including education, for their rehabilitation and reintegration into society.

IV. HUMAN RIGHTS AND THE RULE OF LAW

119. We recommit ourselves to actively protecting and promoting all human rights, the rule of law and democracy and recognize that they are interlinked and mutually reinforcing and that they belong to the universal and indivisible core values and principles of the United Nations, and call upon all parts of the United Nations to promote human rights and fundamental freedoms in accordance with their mandates.

120. We reaffirm the solemn commitment of our States to fulfil their obligations to promote universal respect for and the observance and protection of all human rights and fundamental freedoms for all in accordance with the Charter, the Universal Declaration of Human Rights and other instruments relating to human rights and international law. The universal nature of these rights and freedoms is beyond question.

Human rights

121. We reaffirm that all human rights are universal, indivisible, interrelated, interdependent and mutually reinforcing and that all human rights must be treated in a fair and equal manner, on the same footing and with the same emphasis. While the significance of national and regional particularities and various historical, cultural and religious backgrounds must be borne in mind, all States, regardless of their political, economic and cultural systems, have the duty to promote and protect all human rights and fundamental freedoms.

122. We emphasize the responsibilities of all States, in conformity with the Charter, to respect human rights and fundamental freedoms for all, without distinction of any kind as to race, colour, sex, language or religion, political or other opinion, national or social origin, property, birth or other status.

123. We resolve further to strengthen the United Nations human rights machinery with the aim of ensuring effective enjoyment by all of all human rights and civil, political, economic, social and cultural rights, including the right to development.

124. We resolve to strengthen the Office of the United Nations High Commissioner for Human Rights, taking note of the High Commissioner's plan of action, to enable it to effectively carry out its mandate to respond to the broad range of human rights challenges facing the international community, particularly in the areas of technical assistance and capacity-building, through the doubling of its regular budget resources over the next five years with a view to progressively setting a balance between regular budget and voluntary contributions to its resources, keeping in mind other priority programmes for developing countries and the recruitment of highly competent staff on a broad geographical basis and with gender balance, under the regular budget, and we support its closer cooperation with all relevant United Nations bodies, including the General Assembly, the Economic and Social Council and the Security Council.

125. We resolve to improve the effectiveness of the human rights treaty bodies, including through more timely reporting, improved and streamlined reporting procedures and technical assistance to States to enhance their reporting capacities and further enhance the implementation of their recommendations.

126. We resolve to integrate the promotion and protection of human rights into national policies and to support the further mainstreaming of human rights throughout the United Nations system, as well as closer cooperation between the Office of the United Nations High Commissioner for Human Rights and all relevant United Nations bodies.

127. We reaffirm our commitment to continue making progress in the advancement of the human rights of the world's indigenous peoples at the local, national, regional and international levels, including through consultation and collaboration with them, and to present for adoption a final draft United Nations declaration on the rights of indigenous peoples as soon as possible.

128. We recognize the need to pay special attention to the human rights of women and children and undertake to advance them in every possible way, including by bringing gender and child-protection perspectives into the human rights agenda.

129. We recognize the need for persons with disabilities to be guaranteed full enjoyment of their rights without discrimination. We also affirm the need to finalize a comprehensive draft convention on the rights of persons with disabilities.

130. We note that the promotion and protection of the rights of persons belonging to national or ethnic, religious and linguistic minorities contribute to political and social stability and peace and enrich the cultural diversity and heritage of society.

131. We support the promotion of human rights education and learning at all levels, including through the implementation of the World Programme for Human Rights Education, as appropriate, and encourage all States to develop initiatives in this regard.

Internally displaced persons

132. We recognize the Guiding Principles on Internal Displacement as an important international framework for the protection of internally displaced persons and resolve to take effective measures to increase the protection of internally displaced persons.

Refugee protection and assistance

133. We commit ourselves to safeguarding the principle of refugee protection and to upholding our responsibility in resolving the plight of refugees, including through the support of efforts aimed at addressing the causes of refugee movement, bringing about the safe and sustainable return of those populations, finding durable solutions for refugees in protracted situations and preventing refugee movement from becoming a source of tension among States. We reaffirm the principle of solidarity and burden-sharing and resolve to support nations in assisting refugee populations and their host communities.

Rule of law

134. Recognizing the need for universal adherence to and implementation of the rule of law at both the national and international levels, we:
    (a) Reaffirm our commitment to the purposes and principles of the Charter and international law and to an international order based on the rule of law and international law, which is essential for peaceful coexistence and cooperation among States;
    (b) Support the annual treaty event;
    (c) Encourage States that have not yet done so to consider becoming parties to all treaties that relate to the protection of civilians;
    (d) Call upon States to continue their efforts to eradicate policies and practices that discriminate against women and to adopt laws and promote practices that protect the rights of women and promote gender equality;
    (e) Support the idea of establishing a rule of law assistance unit within the Secretariat, in accordance with existing relevant procedures, subject to a report by the Secretary-General to the General Assembly, so as to strengthen United Nations activities to promote the rule of law, including through technical assistance and capacity-building;
    (f) Recognize the important role of the International Court of Justice, the principal judicial organ of the United Nations, in adjudicating disputes among States and the value of its work, call upon States that have not yet done so to consider accepting the jurisdiction of the Court in accordance with its Statute and consider means of strengthening the Court's work, including by supporting the Secretary General's Trust Fund to Assist States in the Settlement of Disputes through the International Court of Justice on a voluntary basis.

Democracy

135. We reaffirm that democracy is a universal value based on the freely expressed will of people to determine their own political, economic, social and cultural systems and their full participation in all aspects of their lives. We also reaffirm that while democracies share common features, there is no single model of democracy, that it does not belong to any country or region, and reaffirm the necessity of due respect for sovereignty and the right of self-determination. We stress that democracy, development and respect for all human rights and fundamental freedoms are interdependent and mutually reinforcing.

136. We renew our commitment to support democracy by strengthening countries' capacity to implement the principles and practices of democracy and resolve to strengthen the capacity of the United Nations to assist Member States upon their request. We welcome the establishment of a Democracy Fund at the United Nations. We note that the advisory board to be established should reflect diverse geographical representation. We invite the Secretary-General to help to ensure that practical arrangements for the Democracy Fund take proper account of existing United Nations activity in this field.

137. We invite interested Member States to give serious consideration to contributing to the Fund.

Responsibility to protect populations from genocide, war crimes, ethnic cleansing and crimes against humanity

138. Each individual State has the responsibility to protect its populations from genocide, war crimes, ethnic cleansing and crimes against humanity. This responsibility entails the prevention of such crimes, including their incitement, through appropriate and necessary means. We accept that responsibility and will act in accordance with it. The international community should, as appropriate, encourage and help States to exercise this responsibility and support the United Nations in establishing an early warning capability.

139. The international community, through the United Nations, also has the responsibility to use appropriate diplomatic, humanitarian and other peaceful means, in accordance with Chapters VI and VIII of the Charter, to help to protect populations from genocide, war crimes, ethnic cleansing and crimes against humanity. In this context, we are prepared to take collective action, in a timely and decisive manner, through the Security Council, in accordance with the Charter, including Chapter VII, on a case-by-case basis and in cooperation with relevant regional organizations as appropriate, should peaceful means be inadequate and national authorities are manifestly failing to protect their populations from genocide, war crimes, ethnic cleansing and crimes against humanity. We stress the need for the General Assembly to continue consideration of the responsibility to protect populations from genocide, war crimes, ethnic cleansing and crimes against humanity and its implications, bearing in mind the principles of the Charter and international law. We also intend to

commit ourselves, as necessary and appropriate, to helping States build capacity to protect their populations from genocide, war crimes, ethnic cleansing and crimes against humanity and to assisting those which are under stress before crises and conflicts break out.

140. We fully support the mission of the Special Adviser of the Secretary-General on the Prevention of Genocide.

Children's rights

141. We express dismay at the increasing number of children involved in and affected by armed conflict, as well as all other forms of violence, including domestic violence, sexual abuse and exploitation and trafficking. We support cooperation policies aimed at strengthening national capacities to improve the situation of those children and to assist in their rehabilitation and reintegration into society.

142. We commit ourselves to respecting and ensuring the rights of each child without discrimination of any kind, irrespective of the race, colour, sex, language, religion, political or other opinion, national, ethnic or social origin, property, disability, birth or other status of the child or his or her parent(s) or legal guardian(s). We call upon States to consider as a priority becoming a party to the Convention on the Rights of the Child.

Human security

143. We stress the right of people to live in freedom and dignity, free from poverty and despair. We recognize that all individuals, in particular vulnerable people, are entitled to freedom from fear and freedom from want, with an equal opportunity to enjoy all their rights and fully develop their human potential. To this end, we commit ourselves to discussing and defining the notion of human security in the General Assembly.

Culture of peace and initiatives on dialogue among cultures, civilizations and religions

144. We reaffirm the Declaration and Programme of Action on a Culture of Peace as well as the Global Agenda for Dialogue among Civilizations and its Programme of Action adopted by the General Assembly and the value of different initiatives on dialogue among cultures and civilizations, including the dialogue on interfaith cooperation. We commit ourselves to taking action to promote a culture of peace and dialogue at the local, national, regional and international levels and request the Secretary-General to explore enhancing implementation mechanisms and to follow up on those initiatives. In this regard, we also welcome the Alliance of Civilizations initiative announced by the Secretary-General on 14 July 2005.

145. We underline that sports can foster peace and development and can contribute to an atmosphere of tolerance and understanding, and we encourage discussions in the General Assembly for proposals leading to a plan of action on sport and development.

V. STRENGTHENING THE UNITED NATIONS

146. We reaffirm our commitment to strengthen the United Nations with a view to enhancing its authority and efficiency, as well as its capacity to address effectively, and in accordance with the purposes and principles of the Charter, the full range of challenges of our time. We are determined to reinvigorate the intergovernmental organs of the United Nations and to adapt them to the needs of the twenty-first century.

147. We stress that, in order to efficiently perform their respective mandates as provided under the Charter, United Nations bodies should develop good cooperation and coordination in the common endeavour of building a more effective United Nations.

148. We emphasize the need to provide the United Nations with adequate and timely resources with a view to enabling it to carry out its mandates. A reformed United Nations must be responsive to the entire membership, faithful to its founding principles and adapted to carrying out its mandate.

General Assembly

149. We reaffirm the central position of the General Assembly as the chief deliberative, policymaking and representative organ of the United Nations, as well as the role of the Assembly in the process of standard-setting and the codification of international law.

150. We welcome the measures adopted by the General Assembly with a view to strengthening its role and authority and the role and leadership of the President of the Assembly and, to that end, we call for their full and speedy implementation.

151. We call for strengthening the relationship between the General Assembly and the other principal organs to ensure better coordination on topical issues that require coordinated action by the United Nations, in accordance with their respective mandates.

Security Council

152. We reaffirm that Member States have conferred on the Security Council primary responsibility for the maintenance of international peace and security, acting on their behalf, as provided for by the Charter.

153. We support early reform of the Security Council – an essential element of our overall effort to reform the United Nations – in order to make it more broadly representative, efficient and transparent and thus to further enhance its effectiveness and the legitimacy and implementation of its decisions. We commit ourselves to continuing our efforts to achieve a decision to this end and request the General Assembly to review progress on the reform set out above by the end of 2005.

154. We recommend that the Security Council continue to adapt its working methods so as to increase the involvement of States not members of the Council in its work, as appropriate, enhance its accountability to the membership and increase the transparency of its work.

Economic and Social Council

155. We reaffirm the role that the Charter and the General Assembly have vested in the Economic and Social Council and recognize the need for a more effective Economic and Social Council as a principal body for coordination, policy review, policy dialogue and recommendations on issues of economic and social development, as well as for implementation of the international development goals agreed at the major United Nations conferences and summits, including the Millennium Development Goals. To achieve these objectives, the Council should:

   (a) Promote global dialogue and partnership on global policies and trends in the economic, social, environmental and humanitarian fields. For this purpose, the Council should serve as a quality platform for high-level engagement among Member States and with the international financial institutions, the private sector and civil society on emerging global trends, policies and action and develop its ability to respond better and more rapidly to developments in the international economic, environmental and social fields;

   (b) Hold a biennial high-level Development Cooperation Forum to review trends in international development cooperation, including strategies, policies and financing, promote greater coherence among the development activities of different development partners and strengthen the links between the normative and operational work of the United Nations;

   (c) Ensure follow-up of the outcomes of the major United Nations conferences and summits, including the internationally agreed development goals, and hold annual ministerial-level substantive reviews to assess progress, drawing on its functional and regional commissions and other international institutions, in accordance with their respective mandates;

   (d) Support and complement international efforts aimed at addressing humanitarian emergencies, including natural disasters, in order to promote an improved, coordinated response from the United Nations;

   (e) Play a major role in the overall coordination of funds, programmes and agencies, ensuring coherence among them and avoiding duplication of mandates and activities.

156. We stress that in order to fully perform the above functions, the organization of work, the agenda and the current methods of work of the Economic and Social Council should be adapted.

Human Rights Council

157. Pursuant to our commitment to further strengthen the United Nations human rights machinery, we resolve to create a Human Rights Council.

158. The Council will be responsible for promoting universal respect for the protection of all human rights and fundamental freedoms for all, without distinction of any kind and in a fair and equal manner.

159. The Council should address situations of violations of human rights, including gross and systematic violations, and make recommendations thereon. It should also

promote effective coordination and the mainstreaming of human rights within the United Nations system.

160. We request the President of the General Assembly to conduct open, transparent and inclusive negotiations, to be completed as soon as possible during the sixtieth session, with the aim of establishing the mandate, modalities, functions, size, composition, membership, working methods and procedures of the Council.

Secretariat and management reform

161. We recognize that in order to effectively comply with the principles and objectives of the Charter, we need an efficient, effective and accountable Secretariat. Its staff shall act in accordance with Article 100 of the Charter, in a culture of organizational accountability, transparency and integrity. Consequently we:

(a) Recognize the ongoing reform measures carried out by the Secretary General to strengthen accountability and oversight, improve management performance and transparency and reinforce ethical conduct, and invite him to report to the General Assembly on the progress made in their implementation;

(b) Emphasize the importance of establishing effective and efficient mechanisms for responsibility and accountability of the Secretariat;

(c) Urge the Secretary-General to ensure that the highest standards of efficiency, competence, and integrity shall be the paramount consideration in the employment of the staff, with due regard to the principle of equitable geographical distribution, in accordance with Article 101 of the Charter;

(d) Welcome the Secretary-General's efforts to ensure ethical conduct, more extensive financial disclosure for United Nations officials and enhanced protection for those who reveal wrongdoing within the Organization. We urge the Secretary General to scrupulously apply the existing standards of conduct and develop a system-wide code of ethics for all United Nations personnel. In this regard, we request the Secretary-General to submit details on an ethics office with independent status, which he intends to create, to the General Assembly at its sixtieth session;

(e) Pledge to provide the United Nations with adequate resources, on a timely basis, to enable the Organization to implement its mandates and achieve its objectives, having regard to the priorities agreed by the General Assembly and the need to respect budget discipline. We stress that all Member States should meet their obligations with regard to the expenses of the Organization;

(f) Strongly urge the Secretary-General to make the best and most efficient use of resources in accordance with clear rules and procedures agreed by the General Assembly, in the interest of all Member States, by adopting the best management practices, including effective use of information and communication technologies, with a view to increasing efficiency and enhancing organizational capacity, concentrating on those tasks that reflect the agreed priorities of the Organization.

162. We reaffirm the role of the Secretary-General as the chief administrative officer of the Organization, in accordance with Article 97 of the Charter. We request the Secretary-General to make proposals to the General Assembly for its consideration

on the conditions and measures necessary for him to carry out his managerial responsibilities effectively.

163. We commend the Secretary-General's previous and ongoing efforts to enhance the effective management of the United Nations and his commitment to update the Organization. Bearing in mind our responsibility as Member States, we emphasize the need to decide on additional reforms in order to make more efficient use of the financial and human resources available to the Organization and thus better comply with its principles, objectives and mandates. We call on the Secretary-General to submit proposals for implementing management reforms to the General Assembly for consideration and decision in the first quarter of 2006, which will include the following elements:

(a) We will ensure that the United Nations budgetary, financial and human resource policies, regulations and rules respond to the current needs of the Organization and enable the efficient and effective conduct of its work, and request the Secretary-General to provide an assessment and recommendations to the General Assembly for decision during the first quarter of 2006. The assessment and recommendations of the Secretary-General should take account of the measures already under way for the reform of human resources management and the budget process;

(b) We resolve to strengthen and update the programme of work of the United Nations so that it responds to the contemporary requirements of Member States. To this end, the General Assembly and other relevant organs will review all mandates older than five years originating from resolutions of the General Assembly and other organs, which would be complementary to the existing periodic reviews of activities. The General Assembly and the other organs should complete and take the necessary decisions arising from this review during 2006. We request the Secretary General to facilitate this review with analysis and recommendations, including on the opportunities for programmatic shifts that could be considered for early General Assembly consideration;

(c) A detailed proposal on the framework for a one-time staff buyout to improve personnel structure and quality, including an indication of costs involved and mechanisms to ensure that it achieves its intended purpose.

164. We recognize the urgent need to substantially improve the United Nations oversight and management processes. We emphasize the importance of ensuring the operational independence of the Office of Internal Oversight Services. Therefore:

(a) The expertise, capacity and resources of the Office of Internal Oversight Services in respect of audit and investigations will be significantly strengthened as a matter of urgency;

(b) We request the Secretary-General to submit an independent external evaluation of the auditing and oversight system of the United Nations, including the specialized agencies, including the roles and responsibilities of management, with due regard to the nature of the auditing and oversight bodies in question. This evaluation will take place within the context of the comprehensive review of the governance arrangements. We ask the General Assembly to adopt measures during its sixtieth session at the earliest possible stage, based on the consideration of recommendations of the evaluation and those made by the Secretary-General;

(c) We recognize that additional measures are needed to enhance the independence of the oversight structures. We therefore request the Secretary General to submit detailed proposals to the General Assembly at its sixtieth session for its early consideration on the creation of an independent oversight advisory committee, including its mandate, composition, selection process and qualification of experts;

(d) We authorize the Office of Internal Oversight Services to examine the feasibility of expanding its services to provide internal oversight to United Nations agencies that request such services in such a way as to ensure that the provision of internal oversight services to the Secretariat will not be compromised.

165. We insist on the highest standards of behaviour from all United Nations personnel and support the considerable efforts under way with respect to the implementation of the Secretary-General's policy of zero tolerance regarding sexual exploitation and abuse by United Nations personnel, both at Headquarters and in the field. We encourage the Secretary-General to submit proposals to the General Assembly leading to a comprehensive approach to victims' assistance by 31 December 2005.

166. We encourage the Secretary-General and all decision-making bodies to take further steps in mainstreaming a gender perspective in the policies and decisions of the Organization.

167. We strongly condemn all attacks against the safety and security of personnel engaged in United Nations activities. We call upon States to consider becoming parties to the Convention on the Safety of United Nations and Associated Personnel and stress the need to conclude negotiations on a protocol expanding the scope of legal protection during the sixtieth session of the General Assembly.

System-wide coherence

168. We recognize that the United Nations brings together a unique wealth of expertise and resources on global issues. We commend the extensive experience and expertise of the various development-related organizations, agencies, funds and programmes of the United Nations system in their diverse and complementary fields of activity and their important contributions to the achievement of the Millennium Development Goals and the other development objectives established by various United Nations conferences.

169. We support stronger system-wide coherence by implementing the following measures:

Policy

- Strengthening linkages between the normative work of the United Nations system and its operational activities
- Coordinating our representation on the governing boards of the various development and humanitarian agencies so as to ensure that they pursue a coherent policy in assigning mandates and allocating resources throughout the system

- Ensuring that the main horizontal policy themes, such as sustainable development, human rights and gender, are taken into account in decision making throughout the United Nations

Operational activities
- Implementing current reforms aimed at a more effective, efficient, coherent, coordinated and better-performing United Nations country presence with a strengthened role for the senior resident official, whether special representative, resident coordinator or humanitarian coordinator, including appropriate authority, resources and accountability, and a common management, programming and monitoring framework
- Inviting the Secretary-General to launch work to further strengthen the management and coordination of United Nations operational activities so that they can make an even more effective contribution to the achievement of the internationally agreed development goals, including the Millennium Development Goals, including proposals for consideration by Member States for more tightly managed entities in the fields of development, humanitarian assistance and the environment

Humanitarian assistance
- Upholding and respecting the humanitarian principles of humanity, neutrality, impartiality and independence and ensuring that humanitarian actors have safe and unhindered access to populations in need in conformity with the relevant provisions of international law and national laws
- Supporting the efforts of countries, in particular developing countries, to strengthen their capacities at all levels in order to prepare for and respond rapidly to natural disasters and mitigate their impact
- Strengthening the effectiveness of the United Nations humanitarian response, inter alia, by improving the timeliness and predictability of humanitarian funding, in part by improving the Central Emergency Revolving Fund
- Further developing and improving, as required, mechanisms for the use of emergency standby capacities, under the auspices of the United Nations, for a timely response to humanitarian emergencies

Environmental activities
- Recognizing the need for more efficient environmental activities in the United Nations system, with enhanced coordination, improved policy advice and guidance, strengthened scientific knowledge, assessment and cooperation, better treaty compliance, while respecting the legal autonomy of the treaties, and better integration of environmental activities in the broader sustainable development framework at the operational level, including through capacity building, we agree to explore the possibility of a more coherent institutional framework to address this need, including a more integrated structure, building on existing institutions and internationally agreed instruments, as well as the treaty bodies and the specialized agencies

Regional organizations

170. We support a stronger relationship between the United Nations and regional and subregional organizations, pursuant to Chapter VIII of the Charter, and therefore resolve:

    (a) To expand consultation and cooperation between the United Nations and regional and subregional organizations through formalized agreements between the respective secretariats and, as appropriate, involvement of regional organizations in the work of the Security Council;

    (b) To ensure that regional organizations that have a capacity for the prevention of armed conflict or peacekeeping consider the option of placing such capacity in the framework of the United Nations Standby Arrangements System;

    (c) To strengthen cooperation in the economic, social and cultural fields.

Cooperation between the United Nations and parliaments

171. We call for strengthened cooperation between the United Nations and national and regional parliaments, in particular through the Inter-Parliamentary Union, with a view to furthering all aspects of the Millennium Declaration in all fields of the work of the United Nations and ensuring the effective implementation of United Nations reform.

Participation of local authorities, the private sector and civil society, including non-governmental organizations

172. We welcome the positive contributions of the private sector and civil society, including non-governmental organizations, in the promotion and implementation of development and human rights programmes and stress the importance of their continued engagement with Governments, the United Nations and other international organizations in these key areas.

173. We welcome the dialogue between those organizations and Member States, as reflected in the first informal interactive hearings of the General Assembly with representatives of non-governmental organizations, civil society and the private sector.

174. We underline the important role of local authorities in contributing to the achievement of the internationally agreed development goals, including the Millennium Development Goals.

175. We encourage responsible business practices, such as those promoted by the Global Compact.

Charter of the United Nations

176. Considering that the Trusteeship Council no longer meets and has no remaining functions, we should delete Chapter XIII of the Charter and references to the Council in Chapter XII.

177. Taking into account General Assembly resolution 50/52 of 11 December 1995 and recalling the related discussions conducted in the General Assembly, bearing in

mind the profound cause for the founding of the United Nations and looking to our common future, we resolve to delete references to "enemy States" in Articles 53, 77 and 107 of the Charter.

178. We request the Security Council to consider the composition, mandate and working methods of the Military Staff Committee.

8th plenary meeting
16 September 2005

PART V
International Labour Organization Documents

52

Forced Labour Convention, 1930 (No. 29)

Note: Convention Concerning Forced or Compulsory Labour. Adopted Geneva, 14th ILC session, 28 June 1930. Entry into force: 1 May 1932.

PREAMBLE

The General Conference of the International Labour Organisation,

Having been convened at Geneva by the Governing Body of the International Labour Office, and having met in its Fourteenth Session on 10 June 1930, and

Having decided upon the adoption of certain proposals with regard to forced or compulsory labour, which is included in the first item on the agenda of the Session, and

Having determined that these proposals shall take the form of an international Convention, adopts this twenty-eighth day of June of the year one thousand nine hundred and thirty the following Convention, which may be cited as the Forced Labour Convention, 1930, for ratification by the Members of the International Labour Organisation in accordance with the provisions of the Constitution of the International Labour Organisation:

Article 1
1. Each Member of the International Labour Organisation which ratifies this Convention undertakes to suppress the use of forced or compulsory labour in all its forms within the shortest possible period.
2. With a view to this complete suppression, recourse to forced or compulsory labour may be had, during the transitional period, for public purposes only and as an exceptional measure, subject to the conditions and guarantees hereinafter provided.
3. At the expiration of a period of five years after the coming into force of this Convention, and when the Governing Body of the International Labour Office prepares the report provided for in Article 31 below, the said Governing Body shall consider the possibility of the suppression of forced or compulsory labour in all its forms without a further transitional period and the desirability of placing this question on the agenda of the Conference.

Article 2
1. For the purposes of this Convention the term forced or compulsory labour shall mean all work or service which is exacted from any person under the menace of any penalty and for which the said person has not offered himself voluntarily.

2. Nevertheless, for the purposes of this Convention, the term forced or compulsory labour shall not include–
    (a) any work or service exacted in virtue of compulsory military service laws for work of a purely military character;
    (b) any work or service which forms part of the normal civic obligations of the citizens of a fully self-governing country;
    (c) any work or service exacted from any person as a consequence of a conviction in a court of law, provided that the said work or service is carried out under the supervision and control of a public authority and that the said person is not hired to or placed at the disposal of private individuals, companies or associations;
    (d) any work or service exacted in cases of emergency, that is to say, in the event of war or of a calamity or threatened calamity, such as fire, flood, famine, earthquake, violent epidemic or epizootic diseases, invasion by animal, insect or vegetable pests, and in general any circumstance that would endanger the existence or the well-being of the whole or part of the population;
    (e) minor communal services of a kind which, being performed by the members of the community in the direct interest of the said community, can therefore be considered as normal civic obligations incumbent upon the members of the community, provided that the members of the community or their direct representatives shall have the right to be consulted in regard to the need for such services.

Article 3
For the purposes of this Convention the term competent authority shall mean either an authority of the metropolitan country or the highest central authority in the territory concerned.

Article 4
1. The competent authority shall not impose or permit the imposition of forced or compulsory labour for the benefit of private individuals, companies or associations.
2. Where such forced or compulsory labour for the benefit of private individuals, companies or associations exists at the date on which a Member's ratification of this Convention is registered by the Director-General of the International Labour Office, the Member shall completely suppress such forced or compulsory labour from the date on which this Convention comes into force for that Member.

Article 5
1. No concession granted to private individuals, companies or associations shall involve any form of forced or compulsory labour for the production or the collection of products which such private individuals, companies or associations utilise or in which they trade.
2. Where concessions exist containing provisions involving such forced or compulsory labour, such provisions shall be rescinded as soon as possible, in order to comply with Article 1 of this Convention.

Article 6
Officials of the administration, even when they have the duty of encouraging the populations under their charge to engage in some form of labour, shall not put constraint

upon the said populations or upon any individual members thereof to work for private individuals, companies or associations.

Article 7

1. Chiefs who do not exercise administrative functions shall not have recourse to forced or compulsory labour.
2. Chiefs who exercise administrative functions may, with the express permission of the competent authority, have recourse to forced or compulsory labour, subject to the provisions of Article 10 of this Convention.
3. Chiefs who are duly recognised and who do not receive adequate remuneration in other forms may have the enjoyment of personal services, subject to due regulation and provided that all necessary measures are taken to prevent abuses.

Article 8

1. The responsibility for every decision to have recourse to forced or compulsory labour shall rest with the highest civil authority in the territory concerned.
2. Nevertheless, that authority may delegate powers to the highest local authorities to exact forced or compulsory labour which does not involve the removal of the workers from their place of habitual residence. That authority may also delegate, for such periods and subject to such conditions as may be laid down in the regulations provided for in Article 23 of this Convention, powers to the highest local authorities to exact forced or compulsory labour which involves the removal of the workers from their place of habitual residence for the purpose of facilitating the movement of officials of the administration, when on duty, and for the transport of Government stores.

Article 9

Except as otherwise provided for in Article 10 of this Convention, any authority competent to exact forced or compulsory labour shall, before deciding to have recourse to such labour, satisfy itself–

    (a) that the work to be done or the service to be rendered is of important direct interest for the community called upon to do work or render the service;

    (b) that the work or service is of present or imminent necessity;

    (c) that it has been impossible to obtain voluntary labour for carrying out the work or rendering the service by the offer of rates of wages and conditions of labour not less favourable than those prevailing in the area concerned for similar work or service; and

    (d) that the work or service will not lay too heavy a burden upon the present population, having regard to the labour available and its capacity to undertake the work.

Article 10

1. Forced or compulsory labour exacted as a tax and forced or compulsory labour to which recourse is had for the execution of public works by chiefs who exercise administrative functions shall be progressively abolished.
2. Meanwhile, where forced or compulsory labour is exacted as a tax, and where recourse is had to forced or compulsory labour for the execution of public works by chiefs who exercise administrative functions, the authority concerned shall first satisfy itself–

(a) that the work to be done or the service to be rendered is of important direct interest for the community called upon to do the work or render the service;
(b) that the work or the service is of present or imminent necessity;
(c) that the work or service will not lay too heavy a burden upon the present population, having regard to the labour available and its capacity to undertake the work;
(d) that the work or service will not entail the removal of the workers from their place of habitual residence;
(e) that the execution of the work or the rendering of the service will be directed in accordance with the exigencies of religion, social life and agriculture.

Article 11

1. Only adult able-bodied males who are of an apparent age of not less than 18 and not more than 45 years may be called upon for forced or compulsory labour. Except in respect of the kinds of labour provided for in Article 10 of this Convention, the following limitations and conditions shall apply:
   (a) whenever possible prior determination by a medical officer appointed by the administration that the persons concerned are not suffering from any infectious or contagious disease and that they are physically fit for the work required and for the conditions under which it is to be carried out;
   (b) exemption of school teachers and pupils and officials of the administration in general;
   (c) the maintenance in each community of the number of adult able-bodied men indispensable for family and social life;
   (d) respect for conjugal and family ties.
2. For the purposes of subparagraph (c) of the preceding paragraph, the regulations provided for in Article 23 of this Convention shall fix the proportion of the resident adult able-bodied males who may be taken at any one time for forced or compulsory labour, provided always that this proportion shall in no case exceed 25 per cent. In fixing this proportion the competent authority shall take account of the density of the population, of its social and physical development, of the seasons, and of the work which must be done by the persons concerned on their own behalf in their locality, and, generally, shall have regard to the economic and social necessities of the normal life of the community concerned.

Article 12

1. The maximum period for which any person may be taken for forced or compulsory labour of all kinds in any one period of twelve months shall not exceed sixty days, including the time spent in going to and from the place of work.
2. Every person from whom forced or compulsory labour is exacted shall be furnished with a certificate indicating the periods of such labour which he has completed.

Article 13

1. The normal working hours of any person from whom forced or compulsory labour is exacted shall be the same as those prevailing in the case of voluntary labour, and the hours worked in excess of the normal working hours shall be remunerated at the rates prevailing in the case of overtime for voluntary labour.

2. A weekly day of rest shall be granted to all persons from whom forced or compulsory labour of any kind is exacted and this day shall coincide as far as possible with the day fixed by tradition or custom in the territories or regions concerned.

Article 14

1. With the exception of the forced or compulsory labour provided for in Article 10 of this Convention, forced or compulsory labour of all kinds shall be remunerated in cash at rates not less than those prevailing for similar kinds of work either in the district in which the labour is employed or in the district from which the labour is recruited, whichever may be the higher.
2. In the case of labour to which recourse is had by chiefs in the exercise of their administrative functions, payment of wages in accordance with the provisions of the preceding paragraph shall be introduced as soon as possible.
3. The wages shall be paid to each worker individually and not to his tribal chief or to any other authority.
4. For the purpose of payment of wages the days spent in travelling to and from the place of work shall be counted as working days.
5. Nothing in this Article shall prevent ordinary rations being given as a part of wages, such rations to be at least equivalent in value to the money payment they are taken to represent, but deductions from wages shall not be made either for the payment of taxes or for special food, clothing or accommodation supplied to a worker for the purpose of maintaining him in a fit condition to carry on his work under the special conditions of any employment, or for the supply of tools.

Article 15

1. Any laws or regulations relating to workmen's compensation for accidents or sickness arising out of the employment of the worker and any laws or regulations providing compensation for the dependants of deceased or incapacitated workers which are or shall be in force in the territory concerned shall be equally applicable to persons from whom forced or compulsory labour is exacted and to voluntary workers.
2. In any case it shall be an obligation on any authority employing any worker on forced or compulsory labour to ensure the subsistence of any such worker who, by accident or sickness arising out of his employment, is rendered wholly or partially incapable of providing for himself, and to take measures to ensure the maintenance of any persons actually dependent upon such a worker in the event of his incapacity or decease arising out of his employment.

Article 16

1. Except in cases of special necessity, persons from whom forced or compulsory labour is exacted shall not be transferred to districts where the food and climate differ so considerably from those to which they have been accustomed as to endanger their health.
2. In no case shall the transfer of such workers be permitted unless all measures relating to hygiene and accommodation which are necessary to adapt such workers to the conditions and to safeguard their health can be strictly applied.
3. When such transfer cannot be avoided, measures of gradual habituation to the new conditions of diet and of climate shall be adopted on competent medical advice.

4. In cases where such workers are required to perform regular work to which they are not accustomed, measures shall be taken to ensure their habituation to it, especially as regards progressive training, the hours of work and the provision of rest intervals, and any increase or amelioration of diet which may be necessary.

Article 17

Before permitting recourse to forced or compulsory labour for works of construction or maintenance which entail the workers remaining at the workplaces for considerable periods, the competent authority shall satisfy itself –

(1) that all necessary measures are taken to safeguard the health of the workers and to guarantee the necessary medical care, and, in particular, (a) that the workers are medically examined before commencing the work and at fixed intervals during the period of service, (b) that there is an adequate medical staff, provided with the dispensaries, infirmaries, hospitals and equipment necessary to meet all requirements, and (c) that the sanitary conditions of the workplaces, the supply of drinking water, food, fuel, and cooking utensils, and, where necessary, of housing and clothing, are satisfactory;

(2) that definite arrangements are made to ensure the subsistence of the families of the workers, in particular by facilitating the remittance, by a safe method, of part of the wages to the family, at the request or with the consent of the workers;

(3) that the journeys of the workers to and from the workplaces are made at the expense and under the responsibility of the administration, which shall facilitate such journeys by making the fullest use of all available means of transport;

(4) that, in case of illness or accident causing incapacity to work of a certain duration, the worker is repatriated at the expense of the administration;

(5) that any worker who may wish to remain as a voluntary worker at the end of his period of forced or compulsory labour is permitted to do so without, for a period of two years, losing his right to repatriation free of expense to himself.

Article 18

1. Forced or compulsory labour for the transport of persons or goods, such as the labour of porters or boatmen, shall be abolished within the shortest possible period. Meanwhile the competent authority shall promulgate regulations determining, inter alia, (a) that such labour shall only be employed for the purpose of facilitating the movement of officials of the administration, when on duty, or for the transport of Government stores, or, in cases of very urgent necessity, the transport of persons other than officials, (b) that the workers so employed shall be medically certified to be physically fit, where medical examination is possible, and that where such medical examination is not practicable the person employing such workers shall be held responsible for ensuring that they are physically fit and not suffering from any infectious or contagious disease, (c) the maximum load which these workers may carry, (d) the maximum distance from their homes to which they may be taken, (e) the maximum number of days per month or other period for which they may be taken, including the days spent in returning to their homes, and (f) the persons entitled to demand this form of forced or compulsory labour and the extent to which they are entitled to demand it.

2. In fixing the maxima referred to under (c), (d) and (e) in the foregoing paragraph, the competent authority shall have regard to all relevant factors, including the physical development of the population from which the workers are recruited, the nature of the country through which they must travel and the climatic conditions.

3. The competent authority shall further provide that the normal daily journey of such workers shall not exceed a distance corresponding to an average working day of eight hours, it being understood that account shall be taken not only of the weight to be carried and the distance to be covered, but also of the nature of the road, the season and all other relevant factors, and that, where hours of journey in excess of the normal daily journey are exacted, they shall be remunerated at rates higher than the normal rates.

Article 19

1. The competent authority shall only authorise recourse to compulsory cultivation as a method of precaution against famine or a deficiency of food supplies and always under the condition that the food or produce shall remain the property of the individuals or the community producing it.

2. Nothing in this Article shall be construed as abrogating the obligation on members of a community, where production is organised on a communal basis by virtue of law or custom and where the produce or any profit accruing from the sale thereof remain the property of the community, to perform the work demanded by the community by virtue of law or custom.

Article 20

Collective punishment laws under which a community may be punished for crimes committed by any of its members shall not contain provisions for forced or compulsory labour by the community as one of the methods of punishment.

Article 21

Forced or compulsory labour shall not be used for work underground in mines.

Article 22

The annual reports that Members which ratify this Convention agree to make to the International Labour Office, pursuant to the provisions of Article 22 of the Constitution of the International Labour Organisation, on the measures they have taken to give effect to the provisions of this Convention, shall contain as full information as possible, in respect of each territory concerned, regarding the extent to which recourse has been had to forced or compulsory labour in that territory, the purposes for which it has been employed, the sickness and death rates, hours of work, methods of payment of wages and rates of wages, and any other relevant information.

Article 23

1. To give effect to the provisions of this Convention the competent authority shall issue complete and precise regulations governing the use of forced or compulsory labour.

2. These regulations shall contain, inter alia, rules permitting any person from whom forced or compulsory labour is exacted to forward all complaints relative to the

conditions of labour to the authorities and ensuring that such complaints will be examined and taken into consideration.

Article 24

Adequate measures shall in all cases be taken to ensure that the regulations governing the employment of forced or compulsory labour are strictly applied, either by extending the duties of any existing labour inspectorate which has been established for the inspection of voluntary labour to cover the inspection of forced or compulsory labour or in some other appropriate manner. Measures shall also be taken to ensure that the regulations are brought to the knowledge of persons from whom such labour is exacted.

Article 25

The illegal exaction of forced or compulsory labour shall be punishable as a penal offence, and it shall be an obligation on any Member ratifying this Convention to ensure that the penalties imposed by law are really adequate and are strictly enforced.

Article 26

1. Each Member of the International Labour Organisation which ratifies this Convention undertakes to apply it to the territories placed under its sovereignty, jurisdiction, protection, suzerainty, tutelage or authority, so far as it has the right to accept obligations affecting matters of internal jurisdiction; provided that, if such Member may desire to take advantage of the provisions of article 35 of the Constitution of the International Labour Organisation, it shall append to its ratification a declaration stating –
   (1) the territories to which it intends to apply the provisions of this Convention without modification;
   (2) the territories to which it intends to apply the provisions of this Convention with modifications, together with details of the said modifications;
   (3) the territories in respect of which it reserves its decision.
2. The aforesaid declaration shall be deemed to be an integral part of the ratification and shall have the force of ratification. It shall be open to any Member, by a subsequent declaration, to cancel in whole or in part the reservations made, in pursuance of the provisions of subparagraphs (2) and (3) of this Article, in the original declaration.

Article 27

The formal ratifications of this Convention under the conditions set forth in the Constitution of the International Labour Organisation shall be communicated to the Director-General of the International Labour Office for registration.

Article 28

1. This Convention shall be binding only upon those Members whose ratifications have been registered with the International Labour Office.
2. It shall come into force twelve months after the date on which the ratifications of two Members of the International Labour Organisation have been registered with the Director-General.
3. Thereafter, this Convention shall come into force for any Member twelve months after the date on which the ratification has been registered.

Article 29

As soon as the ratifications of two Members of the International Labour Organisation have been registered with the International Labour Office, the Director-General of the International Labour Office shall so notify all the Members of the International Labour Organisation. He shall likewise notify them of the registration of ratifications which may be communicated subsequently by other Members of the Organisation.

Article 30

1. A Member which has ratified this Convention may denounce it after the expiration of ten years from the date on which the Convention first comes into force, by an act communicated to the Director-General of the International Labour Office for registration. Such denunciation shall not take effect until one year after the date on which it is registered with the International Labour Office.
2. Each Member which has ratified this Convention and which does not, within the year following the expiration of the period of ten years mentioned in the preceding paragraph, exercise the right of denunciation provided for in this Article, will be bound for another period of five years and, thereafter, may denounce this Convention at the expiration of each period of five years under the terms provided for in this Article.

Article 31

At such times as it may consider necessary the Governing Body of the International Labour Office shall present to the General Conference a report on the working of this Convention and shall examine the desirability of placing on the agenda of the Conference the question of its revision in whole or in part.

Article 32

1. Should the Conference adopt a new Convention revising this Convention in whole or in part, the ratification by a Member of the new revising Convention shall ipso jure involve denunciation of this Convention without any requirement of delay, notwithstanding the provisions of Article 30 above, if and when the new revising Convention shall have come into force.
2. As from the date of the coming into force of the new revising Convention, the present Convention shall cease to be open to ratification by the Members.
3. Nevertheless, this Convention shall remain in force in its actual form and content for those Members which have ratified it but have not ratified the revising convention.

Article 33

The French and English texts of this Convention shall both be authentic.

53

Freedom of Association and Protection of the Right to Organise Convention, 1948 (No. 87)

Note: Convention Concerning Freedom of Association and Protection of the Right to Organise. Adopted San Francisco, 31st ILC session, 9 July 1948. Entry into force: 4 July 1950.

PREAMBLE

The General Conference of the International Labour Organisation,

Having been convened at San Francisco by the Governing Body of the International Labour Office, and having met in its Thirty-first Session on 17 June 1948;

Having decided to adopt, in the form of a Convention, certain proposals concerning freedom of association and protection of the right to organise, which is the seventh item on the agenda of the session;

Considering that the Preamble to the Constitution of the International Labour Organisation declares "recognition of the principle of freedom of association" to be a means of improving conditions of labour and of establishing peace;

Considering that the Declaration of Philadelphia reaffirms that "freedom of expression and of association are essential to sustained progress";

Considering that the International Labour Conference, at its Thirtieth Session, unanimously adopted the principles which should form the basis for international regulation;

Considering that the General Assembly of the United Nations, at its Second Session, endorsed these principles and requested the International Labour Organisation to continue every effort in order that it may be possible to adopt one or several international Conventions;

adopts this ninth day of July of the year one thousand nine hundred and forty-eight the following Convention, which may be cited as the Freedom of Association and Protection of the Right to Organise Convention, 1948:

PART I. FREEDOM OF ASSOCIATION

Article 1
Each Member of the International Labour Organisation for which this Convention is in force undertakes to give effect to the following provisions.

Article 2

Workers and employers, without distinction whatsoever, shall have the right to establish and, subject only to the rules of the organisation concerned, to join organisations of their own choosing without previous authorisation.

Article 3

1. Workers' and employers' organisations shall have the right to draw up their constitutions and rules, to elect their representatives in full freedom, to organise their administration and activities and to formulate their programmes.
2. The public authorities shall refrain from any interference which would restrict this right or impede the lawful exercise thereof.

Article 4

Workers' and employers' organisations shall not be liable to be dissolved or suspended by administrative authority.

Article 5

Workers' and employers' organisations shall have the right to establish and join federations and confederations and any such organisation, federation or confederation shall have the right to affiliate with international organisations of workers and employers.

Article 6

The provisions of Articles 2, 3 and 4 hereof apply to federations and confederations of workers' and employers' organisations.

Article 7

The acquisition of legal personality by workers' and employers' organisations, federations and confederations shall not be made subject to conditions of such a character as to restrict the application of the provisions of Articles 2, 3 and 4 hereof.

Article 8

1. In exercising the rights provided for in this Convention workers and employers and their respective organisations, like other persons or organised collectivities, shall respect the law of the land.
2. The law of the land shall not be such as to impair, nor shall it be so applied as to impair, the guarantees provided for in this Convention.

Article 9

1. The extent to which the guarantees provided for in this Convention shall apply to the armed forces and the police shall be determined by national laws or regulations.
2. In accordance with the principle set forth in paragraph 8 of Article 19 of the Constitution of the International Labour Organisation the ratification of this Convention by any Member shall not be deemed to affect any existing law, award, custom or agreement in virtue of which members of the armed forces or the police enjoy any right guaranteed by this Convention.

Article 10

In this Convention the term organisation means any organisation of workers or of employers for furthering and defending the interests of workers or of employers.

PART II. PROTECTION OF THE RIGHT TO ORGANISE

Article 11

Each Member of the International Labour Organisation for which this Convention is in force undertakes to take all necessary and appropriate measures to ensure that workers and employers may exercise freely the right to organise.

PART III. MISCELLANEOUS PROVISIONS

Article 12

1. In respect of the territories referred to in Article 35 of the Constitution of the International Labour Organisation as amended by the Constitution of the International Labour Organisation Instrument of Amendment 1946, other than the territories referred to in paragraphs 4 and 5 of the said article as so amended, each Member of the Organisation which ratifies this Convention shall communicate to the Director-General of the International Labour Office with or as soon as possible after its ratification a declaration stating:
    (a) the territories in respect of which it undertakes that the provisions of the Convention shall be applied without modification;
    (b) the territories in respect of which it undertakes that the provisions of the Convention shall be applied subject to modifications, together with details of the said modifications;
    (c) the territories in respect of which the Convention is inapplicable and in such cases the grounds on which it is inapplicable;
    (d) the territories in respect of which it reserves its decision.
2. The undertakings referred to in subparagraphs (a) and (b) of paragraph 1 of this Article shall be deemed to be an integral part of the ratification and shall have the force of ratification.
3. Any Member may at any time by a subsequent declaration cancel in whole or in part any reservations made in its original declaration in virtue of subparagraphs (b), (c) or (d) of paragraph 1 of this Article.
4. Any Member may, at any time at which the Convention is subject to denunciation in accordance with the provisions of Article 16, communicate to the Director-General a declaration modifying in any other respect the terms of any former declaration and stating the present position in respect of such territories as it may specify.

Article 13

1. Where the subject-matter of this Convention is within the self-governing powers of any non-metropolitan territory, the Member responsible for the international relations of that territory may, in agreement with the government of the territory, communicate to the Director-General of the International Labour Office a declaration accepting on behalf of the territory the obligations of this Convention.

2. A declaration accepting the obligations of this Convention may be communicated to the Director-General of the International Labour Office:

   (a) by two or more Members of the Organisation in respect of any territory which is under their joint authority; or

   (b) by any international authority responsible for the administration of any territory, in virtue of the Charter of the United Nations or otherwise, in respect of any such territory.

3. Declarations communicated to the Director-General of the International Labour Office in accordance with the preceding paragraphs of this Article shall indicate whether the provisions of the Convention will be applied in the territory concerned without modification or subject to modifications; when the declaration indicates that the provisions of the Convention will be applied subject to modifications it shall give details of the said modifications.

4. The Member, Members or international authority concerned may at any time by a subsequent declaration renounce in whole or in part the right to have recourse to any modification indicated in any former declaration.

5. The Member, Members or international authority concerned may, at any time at which this Convention is subject to denunciation in accordance with the provisions of Article 16, communicate to the Director-General a declaration modifying in any other respect the terms of any former declaration and stating the present position in respect of the application of the Convention.

PART IV. FINAL PROVISIONS

Article 14

The formal ratifications of this Convention shall be communicated to the Director-General of the International Labour Office for registration.

Article 15

1. This Convention shall be binding only upon those Members of the International Labour Organisation whose ratifications have been registered with the Director-General.

2. It shall come into force twelve months after the date on which the ratifications of two Members have been registered with the Director-General.

3. Thereafter, this Convention shall come into force for any Member twelve months after the date on which its ratifications has been registered.

Article 16

1. A Member which has ratified this Convention may denounce it after the expiration of ten years from the date on which the Convention first comes into force, by an act communicated to the Director-General of the International Labour Office for registration. Such denunciation shall not take effect until one year after the date on which it is registered.

2. Each Member which has ratified this Convention and which does not, within the year following the expiration of the period of ten years mentioned in the preceding paragraph, exercise the right of denunciation provided for in this Article, will be bound

for another period of ten years and, thereafter, may denounce this Convention at the expiration of each period of ten years under the terms provided for in this Article.

Article 17

1. The Director-General of the International Labour Office shall notify all Members of the International Labour Organisation of the registration of all ratifications, declarations and denunciations communicated to him by the Members of the Organisation.
2. When notifying the Members of the Organisation of the registration of the second ratification communicated to him, the Director-General shall draw the attention of the Members of the Organisation to the date upon which the Convention will come into force.

Article 18

The Director-General of the International Labour Office shall communicate to the Secretary-General of the United Nations for registration in accordance with Article 102 of the Charter of the United Nations full particulars of all ratifications, declarations and acts of denunciation registered by him in accordance with the provisions of the preceding articles.

Article 19

At such times as it may consider necessary the Governing Body of the International Labour Office shall present to the General Conference a report on the working of this Convention and shall examine the desirability of placing on the agenda of the Conference the question of its revision in whole or in part.

Article 20

1. Should the Conference adopt a new Convention revising this Convention in whole or in part, then, unless the new Convention otherwise provides:
   (a) the ratification by a Member of the new revising Convention shall ipso jure involve the immediate denunciation of this Convention, notwithstanding the provisions of Article 16 above, if and when the new revising Convention shall have come into force;
   (b) as from the date when the new revising Convention comes into force this Convention shall cease to be open to ratification by the Members.
2. This Convention shall in any case remain in force in its actual form and content for those Members which have ratified it but have not ratified the revising Convention.

Article 21

The English and French versions of the text of this Convention are equally authoritative.

54

Right to Organise and Collective Bargaining Convention, 1949 (No. 98)

Note: Convention Concerning the Application of the Principles of the Right to Organise and to Bargain Collectively. Adopted Geneva, 32nd ILC session, 1 July 1949. Entry into force: 18 July 1951.

PREAMBLE

The General Conference of the International Labour Organisation,

Having been convened at Geneva by the Governing Body of the International Labour Office, and having met in its Thirty-second Session on 8 June 1949, and

Having decided upon the adoption of certain proposals concerning the application of the principles of the right to organise and to bargain collectively, which is the fourth item on the agenda of the session, and

Having determined that these proposals shall take the form of an international Convention, adopts this first day of July of the year one thousand nine hundred and forty-nine the following Convention, which may be cited as the Right to Organise and Collective Bargaining Convention, 1949:

Article 1

1. Workers shall enjoy adequate protection against acts of anti-union discrimination in respect of their employment.
2. Such protection shall apply more particularly in respect of acts calculated to –
   (a) make the employment of a worker subject to the condition that he shall not join a union or shall relinquish trade union membership;
   (b) cause the dismissal of or otherwise prejudice a worker by reason of union membership or because of participation in union activities outside working hours or, with the consent of the employer, within working hours.

Article 2

1. Workers' and employers' organisations shall enjoy adequate protection against any acts of interference by each other or each other's agents or members in their establishment, functioning or administration.
2. In particular, acts which are designed to promote the establishment of workers' organisations under the domination of employers or employers' organisations, or to support workers' organisations by financial or other means, with the object of placing such

organisations under the control of employers or employers' organisations, shall be deemed to constitute acts of interference within the meaning of this Article.

Article 3

Machinery appropriate to national conditions shall be established, where necessary, for the purpose of ensuring respect for the right to organise as defined in the preceding Articles.

Article 4

Measures appropriate to national conditions shall be taken, where necessary, to encourage and promote the full development and utilisation of machinery for voluntary negotiation between employers or employers' organisations and workers' organisations, with a view to the regulation of terms and conditions of employment by means of collective agreements.

Article 5

1. The extent to which the guarantees provided for in this Convention shall apply to the armed forces and the police shall be determined by national laws or regulations.
2. In accordance with the principle set forth in paragraph 8 of Article 19 of the Constitution of the International Labour Organisation the ratification of this Convention by any Member shall not be deemed to affect any existing law, award, custom or agreement in virtue of which members of the armed forces or the police enjoy any right guaranteed by this Convention.

Article 6

This Convention does not deal with the position of public servants engaged in the administration of the State, nor shall it be construed as prejudicing their rights or status in any way.

Article 7

The formal ratifications of this Convention shall be communicated to the Director-General of the International Labour Office for registration.

Article 8

1. This Convention shall be binding only upon those Members of the International Labour Organisation whose ratifications have been registered with the Director-General.
2. It shall come into force twelve months after the date on which the ratifications of two Members have been registered with the Director-General.
3. Thereafter, this Convention shall come into force for any Member twelve months after the date on which its ratification has been registered.

Article 9

1. Declarations communicated to the Director-General of the International Labour Office in accordance with paragraph 2 of Article 35 of the Constitution of the International Labour Organisation shall indicate –
   (a) the territories in respect of which the Member concerned undertakes that the provisions of the Convention shall be applied without modification;

(b) the territories in respect of which it undertakes that the provisions of the Convention shall be applied subject to modifications, together with details of the said modifications;

(c) the territories in respect of which the Convention is inapplicable and in such cases the grounds on which it is inapplicable;

(d) the territories in respect of which it reserves its decision pending further consideration of the position.

2. The undertakings referred to in subparagraphs (a) and (b) of paragraph 1 of this Article shall be deemed to be an integral part of the ratification and shall have the force of ratification.

3. Any Member may at any time by a subsequent declaration cancel in whole or in part any reservation made in its original declaration in virtue of subparagraph (b), (c) or (d) of paragraph 1 of this Article.

4. Any Member may, at any time at which the Convention is subject to denunciation in accordance with the provisions of Article 11, communicate to the Director-General a declaration modifying in any other respect the terms of any former declaration and stating the present position in respect of such territories as it may specify.

Article 10

1. Declarations communicated to the Director-General of the International Labour Office in accordance with paragraph 4 or 5 of Article 35 of the Constitution of the International Labour Organisation shall indicate whether the provisions of the Convention will be applied in the territory concerned without modification or subject to modifications; when the declaration indicates that the provisions of the Convention will be applied subject to modifications, it shall give details of the said modifications.

2. The Member, Members or international authority concerned may at any time by a subsequent declaration renounce in whole or in part the right to have recourse to any modification indicated in any former declaration.

3. The Member, Members or international authority concerned may, at any time at which this Convention is subject to denunciation in accordance with the provisions of Article 11, communicate to the Director-General a declaration modifying in any other respect the terms of any former declaration and stating the present position in respect of the application of the Convention.

Article 11

1. A Member which has ratified this Convention may denounce it after the expiration of ten years from the date on which the Convention first comes into force, by an act communicated to the Director-General of the International Labour Office for registration. Such denunciation shall not take effect until one year after the date on which it is registered.

2. Each Member which has ratified this Convention and which does not, within the year following the expiration of the period of ten years mentioned in the preceding paragraph, exercise the right of denunciation provided for in this Article, will be bound for another period of ten years and, thereafter, may denounce this

Convention at the expiration of each period of ten years under the terms provided for in this Article.

Article 12

1. The Director-General of the International Labour Office shall notify all Members of the International Labour Organisation of the registration of all ratifications, declarations and denunciations communicated to him by the Members of the Organisation.
2. When notifying the Members of the Organisation of the registration of the second ratification communicated to him, the Director-General shall draw the attention of the Members of the Organisation to the date upon which the Convention will come into force.

Article 13

The Director-General of the International Labour Office shall communicate to the Secretary-General of the United Nations for registration in accordance with Article 102 of the Charter of the United Nations full particulars of all ratifications, declarations and acts of denunciation registered by him in accordance with the provisions of the preceding articles.

Article 14

At such times as it may consider necessary the Governing Body of the International Labour Office shall present to the General Conference a report on the working of this Convention and shall examine the desirability of placing on the agenda of the Conference the question of its revision in whole or in part.

Article 15

1. Should the Conference adopt a new Convention revising this Convention in whole or in part, then, unless the new Convention otherwise provides,
   (a) the ratification by a Member of the new revising Convention shall ipso jure involve the immediate denunciation of this Convention, notwithstanding the provisions of Article 11 above, if and when the new revising Convention shall have come into force;
   (b) as from the date when the new revising Convention comes into force, this Convention shall cease to be open to ratification by the Members.
2. This Convention shall in any case remain in force in its actual form and content for those Members which have ratified it but have not ratified the revising Convention.

Article 16

The English and French versions of the text of this Convention are equally authoritative.

55

Equal Remuneration Convention, 1951 (No. 100)

Note: Equal Remuneration Convention, 1951. Adopted Geneva, 34th ILC session, 29 June 1951. Entry into force: 23 May 1953.

PREAMBLE

The General Conference of the International Labour Organisation,

Having been convened at Geneva by the Governing Body of the International Labour Office, and having met in its Thirty-fourth Session on 6 June 1951, and

Having decided upon the adoption of certain proposals with regard to the principle of equal remuneration for men and women workers for work of equal value, which is the seventh item on the agenda of the session, and

Having determined that these proposals shall take the form of an international Convention, adopts this twenty-ninth day of June of the year one thousand nine hundred and fifty-one the following Convention, which may be cited as the Equal Remuneration Convention, 1951:

Article 1

For the purpose of this Convention–
  (a) the term remuneration includes the ordinary, basic or minimum wage or salary and any additional emoluments whatsoever payable directly or indirectly, whether in cash or in kind, by the employer to the worker and arising out of the worker's employment;
  (b) the term equal remuneration for men and women workers for work of equal value refers to rates of remuneration established without discrimination based on sex.

Article 2

1. Each Member shall, by means appropriate to the methods in operation for determining rates of remuneration, promote and, in so far as is consistent with such methods, ensure the application to all workers of the principle of equal remuneration for men and women workers for work of equal value.
2. This principle may be applied by means of–
  (a) national laws or regulations;

(b) legally established or recognised machinery for wage determination;
(c) collective agreements between employers and workers; or
(d) a combination of these various means.

Article 3

1. Where such action will assist in giving effect to the provisions of this Convention measures shall be taken to promote objective appraisal of jobs on the basis of the work to be performed.
2. The methods to be followed in this appraisal may be decided upon by the authorities responsible for the determination of rates of remuneration, or, where such rates are determined by collective agreements, by the parties thereto.
3. Differential rates between workers which correspond, without regard to sex, to differences, as determined by such objective appraisal, in the work to be performed shall not be considered as being contrary to the principle of equal remuneration for men and women workers for work of equal value.

Article 4

Each Member shall co-operate as appropriate with the employers' and workers' organisations concerned for the purpose of giving effect to the provisions of this Convention.

Article 5

The formal ratifications of this Convention shall be communicated to the Director-General of the International Labour Office for registration.

Article 6

1. This Convention shall be binding only upon those Members of the International Labour Organisation whose ratifications have been registered with the Director-General.
2. It shall come into force twelve months after the date on which the ratifications of two Members have been registered with the Director-General.
3. Thereafter, this Convention shall come into force for any Member twelve months after the date on which its ratification has been registered.

Article 7

1. Declarations communicated to the Director-General of the International Labour Office in accordance with paragraph 2 of Article 35 of the Constitution of the International Labour Organisation shall indicate–
   (a) the territories in respect of which the Member concerned undertakes that the provisions of the Convention shall be applied without modification;
   (b) the territories in respect of which it undertakes that the provisions of the Convention shall be applied subject to modifications, together with details of the said modifications;
   (c) the territories in respect of which the Convention is inapplicable and in such cases the grounds on which it is inapplicable;
   (d) the territories in respect of which it reserves its decision pending further consideration of the position.

2. The undertakings referred to in subparagraphs (a) and (b) of paragraph 1 of this Article shall be deemed to be an integral part of the ratification and shall have the force of ratification.

3. Any Member may at any time by a subsequent declaration cancel in whole or in part any reservation made in its original declaration in virtue of subparagraph (b), (c) or (d) of paragraph 1 of this Article.

4. Any Member may, at any time at which the Convention is subject to denunciation in accordance with the provisions of Article 9, communicate to the Director-General a declaration modifying in any other respect the terms of any former declaration and stating the present position in respect of such territories as it may specify.

Article 8

1. Declarations communicated to the Director-General of the International Labour Office in accordance with paragraph 4 or 5 of Article 35 of the Constitution of the International Labour Organisation shall indicate whether the provisions of the Convention will be applied in the territory concerned without modification or subject to modifications; when the declaration indicates that the provisions of the Convention will be applied subject to modifications, it shall give details of the said modifications.

2. The Member, Members or international authority concerned may at any time by a subsequent declaration renounce in whole or in part the right to have recourse to any modification indicated in any former declaration.

3. The Member, Members or international authority concerned may, at any time at which this Convention is subject to denunciation in accordance with the provisions of Article 9, communicate to the Director-General a declaration modifying in any other respect the terms of any former declaration and stating the present position in respect of the application of the Convention.

Article 9

1. A Member which has ratified this Convention may denounce it after the expiration of ten years from the date on which the Convention first comes into force, by an act communicated to the Director-General of the International Labour Office for registration. Such denunciation shall not take effect until one year after the date on which it is registered.

2. Each Member which has ratified this Convention and which does not, within the year following the expiration of the period of ten years mentioned in the preceding paragraph, exercise the right of denunciation provided for in this Article, will be bound for another period of ten years and, thereafter, may denounce this Convention at the expiration of each period of ten years under the terms provided for in this Article.

Article 10

1. The Director-General of the International Labour Office shall notify all Members of the International Labour Organisation of the registration of all ratifications, declarations and denunciations communicated to him by the Members of the Organisation.

2. When notifying the Members of the Organisation of the registration of the second ratification communicated to him, the Director-General shall draw the attention of the

Members of the Organisation to the date upon which the Convention will come into force.

Article 11
The Director-General of the International Labour Office shall communicate to the Secretary-General of the United Nations for registration in accordance with Article 102 of the Charter of the United Nations full particulars of all ratifications, declarations and acts of denunciation registered by him in accordance with the provisions of the preceding articles.

Article 12
At such times as may consider necessary the Governing Body of the International Labour Office shall present to the General Conference a report on the working of this Convention and shall examine the desirability of placing on the agenda of the Conference the question of its revision in whole or in part.

Article 13
1. Should the Conference adopt a new Convention revising this Convention in whole or in part, then, unless the new Convention otherwise provides–
   (a) the ratification by a Member of the new revising Convention shall ipso jure involve the immediate denunciation of this Convention, notwithstanding the provisions of Article 9 above, if and when the new revising Convention shall have come into force;
   (b) as from the date when the new revising Convention comes into force this Convention shall cease to be open to ratification by the Members.
2. This Convention shall in any case remain in force in its actual form and content for those Members which have ratified it but have not ratified the revising Convention.

Article 14
The English and French versions of the text of this Convention are equally authoritative.

56

Abolition of Forced Labour Convention, 1957 (No. 105)

Note: Convention Concerning the Abolition of Forced Labour. Adopted Geneva, 40th ILC session, 25 June 1957. Entry into force: 17 January 1959.

PREAMBLE

The General Conference of the International Labour Organisation,

Having been convened at Geneva by the Governing Body of the International Labour Office, and having met in its Fortieth Session on 5 June 1957, and

Having considered the question of forced labour, which is the fourth item on the agenda of the session, and

Having noted the provisions of the Forced Labour Convention, 1930, and

Having noted that the Slavery Convention, 1926, provides that all necessary measures shall be taken to prevent compulsory or forced labour from developing into conditions analogous to slavery and that the Supplementary Convention on the Abolition of Slavery, the Slave Trade and Institutions and Practices Similar to Slavery, 1956, provides for the complete abolition of debt bondage and serfdom, and

Having noted that the Protection of Wages Convention, 1949, provides that wages shall be paid regularly and prohibits methods of payment which deprive the worker of a genuine possibility of terminating his employment, and

Having decided upon the adoption of further proposals with regard to the abolition of certain forms of forced or compulsory labour constituting a violation of the rights of man referred to in the Charter of the United Nations and enunciated by the Universal Declaration of Human Rights, and

Having determined that these proposals shall take the form of an international Convention, adopts this twenty-fifth day of June of the year one thousand nine hundred and fifty-seven the following Convention, which may be cited as the Abolition of Forced Labour Convention, 1957:

Article 1

Each Member of the International Labour Organisation which ratifies this Convention undertakes to suppress and not to make use of any form of forced or compulsory labour–

    (a) as a means of political coercion or education or as a punishment for holding or expressing political views or views ideologically opposed to the established political, social or economic system;

    (b) as a method of mobilising and using labour for purposes of economic development;

(c) as a means of labour discipline;

(d) as a punishment for having participated in strikes;

(e) as a means of racial, social, national or religious discrimination.

Article 2

Each Member of the International Labour Organisation which ratifies this Convention undertakes to take effective measures to secure the immediate and complete abolition of forced or compulsory labour as specified in Article 1 of this Convention.

Article 3

The formal ratifications of this Convention shall be communicated to the Director-General of the International Labour Office for registration.

Article 4

1. This Convention shall be binding only upon those Members of the International Labour Organisation whose ratifications have been registered with the Director-General.
2. It shall come into force twelve months after the date on which the ratifications of two Members have been registered with the Director-General.
3. Thereafter, this Convention shall come into force for any Member twelve months after the date on which its ratification has been registered.

Article 5

1. A Member which has ratified this Convention may denounce it after the expiration of ten years from the date on which the Convention first comes into force, by an act communicated to the Director-General of the International Labour Office for registration. Such denunciation shall not take effect until one year after the date on which it is registered.
2. Each Member which has ratified this Convention and which does not, within the year following the expiration of the period of ten years mentioned in the preceding paragraph, exercise the right of denunciation provided for in this Article, will be bound for another period of ten years and, thereafter, may denounce this Convention at the expiration of each period of ten years under the terms provided for in this Article.

Article 6

1. The Director-General of the International Labour Office shall notify all Members of the International Labour Organisation of the registration of all ratifications and denunciations communicated to him by the Members of the Organisation.
2. When notifying the Members of the Organisation of the registration of the second ratification communicated to him, the Director-General shall draw the attention of the Members of the Organisation to the date upon which the Convention will come into force.

Article 7

The Director-General of the International Labour Office shall communicate to the Secretary-General of the United Nations for registration in accordance with Article 102 of the Charter of the United Nations full particulars of all ratifications and acts of denunciation registered by him in accordance with the provisions of the preceding Articles.

Article 8

At such times as it may consider necessary the Governing Body of the International Labour Office shall present to the General Conference a report on the working of this Convention and shall examine the desirability of placing on the agenda of the Conference the question of its revision in whole or in part.

Article 9

1. Should the Conference adopt a new Convention revising this Convention in whole or in part, then, unless the new Convention otherwise provides:
   (a) the ratification by a Member of the new revising Convention shall ipso jure involve the immediate denunciation of this Convention, notwithstanding the provisions of Article 5 above, if and when the new revising Convention shall have come into force;
   (b) as from the date when the new revising Convention comes into force this Convention shall cease to be open to ratification by the Members.
2. This Convention shall in any case remain in force in its actual form and content for those Members which have ratified it but have not ratified the revising Convention.

Article 10

The English and French versions of the text of this Convention are equally authoritative.

57

Discrimination (Employment and Occupation) Convention, 1958 (No. 111)

Note: Convention Concerning Discrimination in Respect of Employment and Occupation. Adopted Geneva, 42nd ILC session, 25 June 1958. Entry into force: 15 June 1960.

PREAMBLE

The General Conference of the International Labour Organisation,

Having been convened at Geneva by the Governing Body of the International Labour Office, and having met in its Forty-second Session on 4 June 1958, and

Having decided upon the adoption of certain proposals with regard to discrimination in the field of employment and occupation, which is the fourth item on the agenda of the session, and

Having determined that these proposals shall take the form of an international Convention, and

Considering that the Declaration of Philadelphia affirms that all human beings, irrespective of race, creed or sex, have the right to pursue both their material well-being and their spiritual development in conditions of freedom and dignity, of economic security and equal opportunity, and

Considering further that discrimination constitutes a violation of rights enunciated by the Universal Declaration of Human Rights, adopts this twenty-fifth day of June of the year one thousand nine hundred and fifty-eight the following Convention, which may be cited as the Discrimination (Employment and Occupation) Convention, 1958:

Article 1

1. For the purpose of this Convention the term discrimination includes–
    (a) any distinction, exclusion or preference made on the basis of race, colour, sex, religion, political opinion, national extraction or social origin, which has the effect of nullifying or impairing equality of opportunity or treatment in employment or occupation;
    (b) such other distinction, exclusion or preference which has the effect of nullifying or impairing equality of opportunity or treatment in employment or occupation as may be determined by the Member concerned after consultation with representative employers' and workers' organisations, where such exist, and with other appropriate bodies.
2. Any distinction, exclusion or preference in respect of a particular job based on the inherent requirements thereof shall not be deemed to be discrimination.
3. For the purpose of this Convention the terms employment and occupation include access to vocational training, access to employment and to particular occupations, and terms and conditions of employment.

Article 2

Each Member for which this Convention is in force undertakes to declare and pursue a national policy designed to promote, by methods appropriate to national conditions and practice, equality of opportunity and treatment in respect of employment and occupation, with a view to eliminating any discrimination in respect thereof.

Article 3

Each Member for which this Convention is in force undertakes, by methods appropriate to national conditions and practice–

(a) to seek the co-operation of employers' and workers' organisations and other appropriate bodies in promoting the acceptance and observance of this policy;

(b) to enact such legislation and to promote such educational programmes as may be calculated to secure the acceptance and observance of the policy;

(c) to repeal any statutory provisions and modify any administrative instructions or practices which are inconsistent with the policy;

(d) to pursue the policy in respect of employment under the direct control of a national authority;

(e) to ensure observance of the policy in the activities of vocational guidance, vocational training and placement services under the direction of a national authority;

(f) to indicate in its annual reports on the application of the Convention the action taken in pursuance of the policy and the results secured by such action.

Article 4

Any measures affecting an individual who is justifiably suspected of, or engaged in, activities prejudicial to the security of the State shall not be deemed to be discrimination, provided that the individual concerned shall have the right to appeal to a competent body established in accordance with national practice.

Article 5

1. Special measures of protection or assistance provided for in other Conventions or Recommendations adopted by the International Labour Conference shall not be deemed to be discrimination.

2. Any Member may, after consultation with representative employers' and workers' organisations, where such exist, determine that other special measures designed to meet the particular requirements of persons who, for reasons such as sex, age, disablement, family responsibilities or social or cultural status, are generally recognised to require special protection or assistance, shall not be deemed to be discrimination.

Article 6

Each Member which ratifies this Convention undertakes to apply it to non-metropolitan territories in accordance with the provisions of the Constitution of the International Labour Organisation.

Article 7
The formal ratifications of this Convention shall be communicated to the Director-General of the International Labour Office for registration.

Article 8
1. This Convention shall be binding only upon those Members of the International Labour Organisation whose ratifications have been registered with the Director-General.
2. It shall come into force twelve months after the date on which the ratifications of two Members have been registered with the Director-General.
3. Thereafter, this Convention shall come into force for any Member twelve months after the date on which its ratification has been registered.

Article 9
1. A Member which has ratified this Convention may denounce it after the expiration of ten years from the date on which the Convention first comes into force, by an act communicated to the Director-General of the International Labour Office for registration. Such denunciation shall not take effect until one year after the date on which it is registered.
2. Each Member which has ratified this Convention and which does not, within the year following the expiration of the period of ten years mentioned in the preceding paragraph, exercise the right of denunciation provided for in this Article, will be bound for another period of ten years and, thereafter, may denounce this Convention at the expiration of each period of ten years under the terms provided for in this Article.

Article 10
1. The Director-General of the International Labour Office shall notify all Members of the International Labour Organisation of the registration of all ratifications and denunciations communicated to him by the Members of the Organisation.
2. When notifying the Members of the Organisation of the registration of the second ratification communicated to him, the Director-General shall draw the attention of the Members of the Organisation to the date upon which the Convention will come into force.

Article 11
The Director-General of the International Labour Office shall communicate to the Secretary-General of the United Nations for registration in accordance with Article 102 of the Charter of the United Nations full particulars of all ratifications and acts of denunciation registered by him in accordance with the provisions of the preceding Articles.

Article 12
At such times as it may consider necessary the Governing Body of the International Labour Office shall present to the General Conference a report on the working of this Convention and shall examine the desirability of placing on the agenda of the Conference the question of its revision in whole or in part.

Article 13

1. Should the Conference adopt a new Convention revising this Convention in whole or in part, then, unless the new Convention otherwise provides:

   (a) the ratification by a Member of the new revising Convention shall ipso jure involve the immediate denunciation of this Convention, notwithstanding the provisions of Article 9 above, if and when the new revising Convention shall have come into force;

   (b) as from the date when the new revising Convention comes into force, this Convention shall cease to be open to ratification by the Members.

2. This Convention shall in any case remain in force in its actual form and content for those Members which have ratified it but have not ratified the revising Convention.

Article 14

The English and French versions of the text of this Convention are equally authoritative.

58

Minimum Age Convention, 1973 (No. 138)

Note: Convention Concerning Minimum Age for Admission to Employment. Adopted Geneva, 58th ILC session, 26 June 1973. Entry into force: 19 June 1976.

PREAMBLE

The General Conference of the International Labour Organisation,

Having been convened at Geneva by the Governing Body of the International Labour Office, and having met in its Fifty-eighth Session on 6 June 1973, and

Having decided upon the adoption of certain proposals with regard to minimum age for admission to employment, which is the fourth item on the agenda of the session, and

Noting the terms of the Minimum Age (Industry) Convention, 1919, the Minimum Age (Sea) Convention, 1920, the Minimum Age (Agriculture) Convention, 1921, the Minimum Age (Trimmers and Stokers) Convention, 1921, the Minimum Age (Non-Industrial Employment) Convention, 1932, the Minimum Age (Sea) Convention (Revised), 1936, the Minimum Age (Industry) Convention (Revised), 1937, the Minimum Age (Non-Industrial Employment) Convention (Revised), 1937, the Minimum Age (Fishermen) Convention, 1959, and the Minimum Age (Underground Work) Convention, 1965, and

Considering that the time has come to establish a general instrument on the subject, which would gradually replace the existing ones applicable to limited economic sectors, with a view to achieving the total abolition of child labour, and

Having determined that these proposals shall take the form of an international Convention, adopts this twenty-sixth day of June of the year one thousand nine hundred and seventy-three the following Convention, which may be cited as the Minimum Age Convention, 1973:

Article 1

Each Member for which this Convention is in force undertakes to pursue a national policy designed to ensure the effective abolition of child labour and to raise progressively the minimum age for admission to employment or work to a level consistent with the fullest physical and mental development of young persons.

Article 2

1. Each Member which ratifies this Convention shall specify, in a declaration appended to its ratification, a minimum age for admission to employment or work within its territory and on means of transport registered in its territory; subject to Articles 4 to 8 of this Convention, no one under that age shall be admitted to employment or work in any occupation.

2. Each Member which has ratified this Convention may subsequently notify the Director-General of the International Labour Office, by further declarations, that it specifies a minimum age higher than that previously specified.

3. The minimum age specified in pursuance of paragraph 1 of this Article shall not be less than the age of completion of compulsory schooling and, in any case, shall not be less than 15 years.

4. Notwithstanding the provisions of paragraph 3 of this Article, a Member whose economy and educational facilities are insufficiently developed may, after consultation with the organisations of employers and workers concerned, where such exist, initially specify a minimum age of 14 years.

5. Each Member which has specified a minimum age of 14 years in pursuance of the provisions of the preceding paragraph shall include in its reports on the application of this Convention submitted under article 22 of the Constitution of the International Labour Organisation a statement—

   (a) that its reason for doing so subsists; or

   (b) that it renounces its right to avail itself of the provisions in question as from a stated date.

Article 3

1. The minimum age for admission to any type of employment or work which by its nature or the circumstances in which it is carried out is likely to jeopardise the health, safety or morals of young persons shall not be less than 18 years.

2. The types of employment or work to which paragraph 1 of this Article applies shall be determined by national laws or regulations or by the competent authority, after consultation with the organisations of employers and workers concerned, where such exist.

3. Notwithstanding the provisions of paragraph 1 of this Article, national laws or regulations or the competent authority may, after consultation with the organisations of employers and workers concerned, where such exist, authorise employment or work as from the age of 16 years on condition that the health, safety and morals of the young persons concerned are fully protected and that the young persons have received adequate specific instruction or vocational training in the relevant branch of activity.

Article 4

1. In so far as necessary, the competent authority, after consultation with the organisations of employers and workers concerned, where such exist, may exclude from the application of this Convention limited categories of employment or work in respect of which special and substantial problems of application arise.

2. Each Member which ratifies this Convention shall list in its first report on the application of the Convention submitted under article 22 of the Constitution of the International Labour Organisation any categories which may have been excluded in pursuance of paragraph 1 of this Article, giving the reasons for such exclusion, and shall state in subsequent reports the position of its law and practice in respect of the categories excluded and the extent to which effect has been given or is proposed to be given to the Convention in respect of such categories.

3. Employment or work covered by Article 3 of this Convention shall not be excluded from the application of the Convention in pursuance of this Article.

Article 5

1. A Member whose economy and administrative facilities are insufficiently developed may, after consultation with the organisations of employers and workers concerned, where such exist, initially limit the scope of application of this Convention.

2. Each Member which avails itself of the provisions of paragraph 1 of this Article shall specify, in a declaration appended to its ratification, the branches of economic activity or types of undertakings to which it will apply the provisions of the Convention.

3. The provisions of the Convention shall be applicable as a minimum to the following: mining and quarrying; manufacturing; construction; electricity, gas and water; sanitary services; transport, storage and communication; and plantations and other agricultural undertakings mainly producing for commercial purposes, but excluding family and small-scale holdings producing for local consumption and not regularly employing hired workers.

4. Any Member which has limited the scope of application of this Convention in pursuance of this Article–

   (a) shall indicate in its reports under Article 22 of the Constitution of the International Labour Organisation the general position as regards the employment or work of young persons and children in the branches of activity which are excluded from the scope of application of this Convention and any progress which may have been made towards wider application of the provisions of the Convention;

   (b) may at any time formally extend the scope of application by a declaration addressed to the Director-General of the International Labour Office.

Article 6

This Convention does not apply to work done by children and young persons in schools for general, vocational or technical education or in other training institutions, or to work done by persons at least 14 years of age in undertakings, where such work is carried out in accordance with conditions prescribed by the competent authority, after consultation with the organisations of employers and workers concerned, where such exist, and is an integral part of–

   (a) a course of education or training for which a school or training institution is primarily responsible;

   (b) a programme of training mainly or entirely in an undertaking, which programme has been approved by the competent authority; or

   (c) a programme of guidance or orientation designed to facilitate the choice of an occupation or of a line of training.

Article 7

1. National laws or regulations may permit the employment or work of persons 13 to 15 years of age on light work which is–

   (a) not likely to be harmful to their health or development; and

   (b) not such as to prejudice their attendance at school, their participation in vocational orientation or training programmes approved by the competent authority or their capacity to benefit from the instruction received.

2. National laws or regulations may also permit the employment or work of persons who are at least 15 years of age but have not yet completed their compulsory schooling

on work which meets the requirements set forth in sub-paragraphs (a) and (b) of paragraph 1 of this Article.

3. The competent authority shall determine the activities in which employment or work may be permitted under paragraphs 1 and 2 of this Article and shall prescribe the number of hours during which and the conditions in which such employment or work may be undertaken.

4. Notwithstanding the provisions of paragraphs 1 and 2 of this Article, a Member which has availed itself of the provisions of paragraph 4 of Article 2 may, for as long as it continues to do so, substitute the ages 12 and 14 for the ages 13 and 15 in paragraph 1 and the age 14 for the age 15 in paragraph 2 of this Article.

Article 8

1. After consultation with the organisations of employers and workers concerned, where such exist, the competent authority may, by permits granted in individual cases, allow exceptions to the prohibition of employment or work provided for in Article 2 of this Convention, for such purposes as participation in artistic performances.

2. Permits so granted shall limit the number of hours during which and prescribe the conditions in which employment or work is allowed.

Article 9

1. All necessary measures, including the provision of appropriate penalties, shall be taken by the competent authority to ensure the effective enforcement of the provisions of this Convention.

2. National laws or regulations or the competent authority shall define the persons responsible for compliance with the provisions giving effect to the Convention.

3. National laws or regulations or the competent authority shall prescribe the registers or other documents which shall be kept and made available by the employer; such registers or documents shall contain the names and ages or dates of birth, duly certified wherever possible, of persons whom he employs or who work for him and who are less than 18 years of age.

Article 10

1. This Convention revises, on the terms set forth in this Article, the Minimum Age (Industry) Convention, 1919, the Minimum Age (Sea) Convention, 1920, the Minimum Age (Agriculture) Convention, 1921, the Minimum Age (Trimmers and Stokers) Convention, 1921, the Minimum Age (Non-Industrial Employment) Convention, 1932, the Minimum Age (Sea) Convention (Revised), 1936, the Minimum Age (Industry) Convention (Revised), 1937, the Minimum Age (Non-Industrial Employment) Convention (Revised), 1937, the Minimum Age (Fishermen) Convention, 1959, and the Minimum Age (Underground Work) Convention, 1965.

2. The coming into force of this Convention shall not close the Minimum Age (Sea) Convention (Revised), 1936, the Minimum Age (Industry) Convention (Revised), 1937, the Minimum Age (Non-Industrial Employment) Convention (Revised), 1937, the Minimum Age (Fishermen) Convention, 1959, or the Minimum Age (Underground Work) Convention, 1965, to further ratification.

3. The Minimum Age (Industry) Convention, 1919, the Minimum Age (Sea) Convention, 1920, the Minimum Age (Agriculture) Convention, 1921, and the Minimum Age (Trimmers and Stokers) Convention, 1921, shall be closed to further ratification when all the parties thereto have consented to such closing by ratification of this Convention or by a declaration communicated to the Director-General of the International Labour Office.

4. When the obligations of this Convention are accepted–
   (a) by a Member which is a party to the Minimum Age (Industry) Convention (Revised), 1937, and a minimum age of not less than 15 years is specified in pursuance of Article 2 of this Convention, this shall ipso jure involve the immediate denunciation of that Convention,
   (b) in respect of non-industrial employment as defined in the Minimum Age (Non-Industrial Employment) Convention, 1932, by a Member which is a party to that Convention, this shall ipso jure involve the immediate denunciation of that Convention,
   (c) in respect of non-industrial employment as defined in the Minimum Age (Non-Industrial Employment) Convention (Revised), 1937, by a Member which is a party to that Convention, and a minimum age of not less than 15 years is specified in pursuance of Article 2 of this Convention, this shall ipso jure involve the immediate denunciation of that Convention,
   (d) in respect of maritime employment, by a Member which is a party to the Minimum Age (Sea) Convention (Revised), 1936, and a minimum age of not less than 15 years is specified in pursuance of Article 2 of this Convention or the Member specifies that Article 3 of this Convention applies to maritime employment, this shall ipso jure involve the immediate denunciation of that Convention,
   (e) in respect of employment in maritime fishing, by a Member which is a party to the Minimum Age (Fishermen) Convention, 1959, and a minimum age of not less than 15 years is specified in pursuance of Article 2 of this Convention or the Member specifies that Article 3 of this Convention applies to employment in maritime fishing, this shall ipso jure involve the immediate denunciation of that Convention,
   (f) by a Member which is a party to the Minimum Age (Underground Work) Convention, 1965, and a minimum age of not less than the age specified in pursuance of that Convention is specified in pursuance of Article 2 of this Convention or the Member specifies that such an age applies to employment underground in mines in virtue of Article 3 of this Convention, this shall ipso jure involve the immediate denunciation of that Convention, if and when this Convention shall have come into force.

5. Acceptance of the obligations of this Convention–
   (a) shall involve the denunciation of the Minimum Age (Industry) Convention, 1919, in accordance with Article 12 thereof,
   (b) in respect of agriculture shall involve the denunciation of the Minimum Age (Agriculture) Convention, 1921, in accordance with Article 9 thereof,
   (c) in respect of maritime employment shall involve the denunciation of the Minimum Age (Sea) Convention, 1920, in accordance with Article 10 thereof, and of the Minimum Age (Trimmers and Stokers) Convention, 1921, in accordance with Article 12 thereof, if and when this Convention shall have come into force.

Article 11

The formal ratifications of this Convention shall be communicated to the Director-General of the International Labour Office for registration.

Article 12

1. This Convention shall be binding only upon those Members of the International Labour Organisation whose ratifications have been registered with the Director-General.
2. It shall come into force twelve months after the date on which the ratifications of two Members have been registered with the Director-General.
3. Thereafter, this Convention shall come into force for any Member twelve months after the date on which its ratifications has been registered.

Article 13

1. A Member which has ratified this Convention may denounce it after the expiration of ten years from the date on which the Convention first comes into force, by an act communicated to the Director-General of the International Labour Office for registration. Such denunciation shall not take effect until one year after the date on which it is registered.
2. Each Member which has ratified this Convention and which does not, within the year following the expiration of the period of ten years mentioned in the preceding paragraph, exercise the right of denunciation provided for in this Article, will be bound for another period of ten years and, thereafter, may denounce this Convention at the expiration of each period of ten years under the terms provided for in this Article.

Article 14

1. The Director-General of the International Labour Office shall notify all Members of the International Labour Organisation of the registration of all ratifications and denunciations communicated to him by the Members of the Organisation.
2. When notifying the Members of the Organisation of the registration of the second ratification communicated to him, the Director-General shall draw the attention of the Members of the Organisation to the date upon which the Convention will come into force.

Article 15

The Director-General of the International Labour Office shall communicate to the Secretary-General of the United Nations for registration in accordance with Article 102 of the Charter of the United Nations full particulars of all ratifications and acts of denunciation registered by him in accordance with the provisions of the preceding Articles.

Article 16

At such times as it may consider necessary the Governing Body of the International Labour Office shall present to the General Conference a report on the working of this Convention and shall examine the desirability of placing on the agenda of the Conference the question of its revision in whole or in part.

Article 17

1. Should the Conference adopt a new Convention revising this Convention in whole or in part, then, unless the new Convention otherwise provides:
   (a) the ratification by a Member of the new revising Convention shall ipso jure involve the immediate denunciation of this Convention, notwithstanding the provisions of Article 13 above, if and when the new revising Convention shall have come into force;
   (b) as from the date when the new revising Convention comes into force this Convention shall cease to be open to ratification by the Members.
2. This Convention shall in any case remain in force in its actual form and content for those Members which have ratified it but have not ratified the revising Convention.

Article 18

The English and French versions of the text of this Convention are equally authoritative.

59

Convention Concerning Indigenous and Tribal Peoples in Independent Countries, 1989 (No. 169)

Note: Convention Concerning Indigenous and Tribal Peoples in Independent Countries. Adopted Geneva, 76th ILC session, 27 June 1989. Entry into force: 5 September 1991.

PREAMBLE

The General Conference of the International Labour Organisation,

Having been convened at Geneva by the Governing Body of the International Labour Office, and having met in its 76th Session on 7 June 1989, and

Noting the international standards contained in the Indigenous and Tribal Populations Convention and Recommendation, 1957, and

Recalling the terms of the Universal Declaration of Human Rights, the International Covenant on Economic, Social and Cultural Rights, the International Covenant on Civil and Political Rights, and the many international instruments on the prevention of discrimination, and

Considering that the developments which have taken place in international law since 1957, as well as developments in the situation of indigenous and tribal peoples in all regions of the world, have made it appropriate to adopt new international standards on the subject with a view to removing the assimilationist orientation of the earlier standards, and

Recognising the aspirations of these peoples to exercise control over their own institutions, ways of life and economic development and to maintain and develop their identities, languages and religions, within the framework of the States in which they live, and

Noting that in many parts of the world these peoples are unable to enjoy their fundamental human rights to the same degree as the rest of the population of the States within which they live, and that their laws, values, customs and perspectives have often been eroded, and

Calling attention to the distinctive contributions of indigenous and tribal peoples to the cultural diversity and social and ecological harmony of humankind and to international co-operation and understanding, and

Noting that the following provisions have been framed with the co-operation of the United Nations, the Food and Agriculture Organisation of the United Nations, the

United Nations Educational, Scientific and Cultural Organisation and the World Health Organisation, as well as of the Inter-American Indian Institute, at appropriate levels and in their respective fields, and that it is proposed to continue this co-operation in promoting and securing the application of these provisions, and

Having decided upon the adoption of certain proposals with regard to the partial revision of the Indigenous and Tribal Populations Convention, 1957 (No. 107), which is the fourth item on the agenda of the session, and

Having determined that these proposals shall take the form of an international Convention revising the Indigenous and Tribal Populations Convention, 1957;

adopts this twenty-seventh day of June of the year one thousand nine hundred and eighty-nine the following Convention, which may be cited as the Indigenous and Tribal Peoples Convention, 1989;

PART I. GENERAL POLICY

Article 1

1. This Convention applies to:
   (a) tribal peoples in independent countries whose social, cultural and economic conditions distinguish them from other sections of the national community, and whose status is regulated wholly or partially by their own customs or traditions or by special laws or regulations;
   (b) peoples in independent countries who are regarded as indigenous on account of their descent from the populations which inhabited the country, or a geographical region to which the country belongs, at the time of conquest or colonisation or the establishment of present state boundaries and who, irrespective of their legal status, retain some or all of their own social, economic, cultural and political institutions.
2. Self-identification as indigenous or tribal shall be regarded as a fundamental criterion for determining the groups to which the provisions of this Convention apply.
3. The use of the term peoples in this Convention shall not be construed as having any implications as regards the rights which may attach to the term under international law.

Article 2

1. Governments shall have the responsibility for developing, with the participation of the peoples concerned, co-ordinated and systematic action to protect the rights of these peoples and to guarantee respect for their integrity.
2. Such action shall include measures for:
   (a) ensuring that members of these peoples benefit on an equal footing from the rights and opportunities which national laws and regulations grant to other members of the population;
   (b) promoting the full realisation of the social, economic and cultural rights of these peoples with respect for their social and cultural identity, their customs and traditions and their institutions;
   (c) assisting the members of the peoples concerned to eliminate socio-economic gaps that may exist between indigenous and other members of the national community, in a manner compatible with their aspirations and ways of life.

Article 3

1. Indigenous and tribal peoples shall enjoy the full measure of human rights and fundamental freedoms without hindrance or discrimination. The provisions of the Convention shall be applied without discrimination to male and female members of these peoples.
2. No form of force or coercion shall be used in violation of the human rights and fundamental freedoms of the peoples concerned, including the rights contained in this Convention.

Article 4

1. Special measures shall be adopted as appropriate for safeguarding the persons, institutions, property, labour, cultures and environment of the peoples concerned.
2. Such special measures shall not be contrary to the freely-expressed wishes of the peoples concerned.
3. Enjoyment of the general rights of citizenship, without discrimination, shall not be prejudiced in any way by such special measures.

Article 5

In applying the provisions of this Convention:
   (a) the social, cultural, religious and spiritual values and practices of these peoples shall be recognised and protected, and due account shall be taken of the nature of the problems which face them both as groups and as individuals;
   (b) the integrity of the values, practices and institutions of these peoples shall be respected;
   (c) policies aimed at mitigating the difficulties experienced by these peoples in facing new conditions of life and work shall be adopted, with the participation and co-operation of the peoples affected.

Article 6

1. In applying the provisions of this Convention, governments shall:
   (a) consult the peoples concerned, through appropriate procedures and in particular through their representative institutions, whenever consideration is being given to legislative or administrative measures which may affect them directly;
   (b) establish means by which these peoples can freely participate, to at least the same extent as other sectors of the population, at all levels of decision-making in elective institutions and administrative and other bodies responsible for policies and programmes which concern them;
   (c) establish means for the full development of these peoples' own institutions and initiatives, and in appropriate cases provide the resources necessary for this purpose.
2. The consultations carried out in application of this Convention shall be undertaken, in good faith and in a form appropriate to the circumstances, with the objective of achieving agreement or consent to the proposed measures.

Article 7

1. The peoples concerned shall have the right to decide their own priorities for the process of development as it affects their lives, beliefs, institutions and spiritual well-being and the lands they occupy or otherwise use, and to exercise control, to the extent possible, over their own economic, social and cultural development. In addition, they shall participate in the formulation, implementation and evaluation of plans and programmes for national and regional development which may affect them directly.
2. The improvement of the conditions of life and work and levels of health and education of the peoples concerned, with their participation and co-operation, shall be a matter of priority in plans for the overall economic development of areas they inhabit. Special projects for development of the areas in question shall also be so designed as to promote such improvement.
3. Governments shall ensure that, whenever appropriate, studies are carried out, in co-operation with the peoples concerned, to assess the social, spiritual, cultural and environmental impact on them of planned development activities. The results of these studies shall be considered as fundamental criteria for the implementation of these activities.
4. Governments shall take measures, in co-operation with the peoples concerned, to protect and preserve the environment of the territories they inhabit.

Article 8

1. In applying national laws and regulations to the peoples concerned, due regard shall be had to their customs or customary laws.
2. These peoples shall have the right to retain their own customs and institutions, where these are not incompatible with fundamental rights defined by the national legal system and with internationally recognised human rights. Procedures shall be established, whenever necessary, to resolve conflicts which may arise in the application of this principle.
3. The application of paragraphs 1 and 2 of this Article shall not prevent members of these peoples from exercising the rights granted to all citizens and from assuming the corresponding duties.

Article 9

1. To the extent compatible with the national legal system and internationally recognised human rights, the methods customarily practised by the peoples concerned for dealing with offences committed by their members shall be respected.
2. The customs of these peoples in regard to penal matters shall be taken into consideration by the authorities and courts dealing with such cases.

Article 10

1. In imposing penalties laid down by general law on members of these peoples account shall be taken of their economic, social and cultural characteristics.
2. Preference shall be given to methods of punishment other than confinement in prison.

Article 11

The exaction from members of the peoples concerned of compulsory personal services in any form, whether paid or unpaid, shall be prohibited and punishable by law, except in cases prescribed by law for all citizens.

Article 12

The peoples concerned shall be safeguarded against the abuse of their rights and shall be able to take legal proceedings, either individually or through their representative bodies, for the effective protection of these rights. Measures shall be taken to ensure that members of these peoples can understand and be understood in legal proceedings, where necessary through the provision of interpretation or by other effective means.

PART II. LAND

Article 13

1. In applying the provisions of this Part of the Convention governments shall respect the special importance for the cultures and spiritual values of the peoples concerned of their relationship with the lands or territories, or both as applicable, which they occupy or otherwise use, and in particular the collective aspects of this relationship.
2. The use of the term lands in Articles 15 and 16 shall include the concept of territories, which covers the total environment of the areas which the peoples concerned occupy or otherwise use.

Article 14

1. The rights of ownership and possession of the peoples concerned over the lands which they traditionally occupy shall be recognised. In addition, measures shall be taken in appropriate cases to safeguard the right of the peoples concerned to use lands not exclusively occupied by them, but to which they have traditionally had access for their subsistence and traditional activities. Particular attention shall be paid to the situation of nomadic peoples and shifting cultivators in this respect.
2. Governments shall take steps as necessary to identify the lands which the peoples concerned traditionally occupy, and to guarantee effective protection of their rights of ownership and possession.
3. Adequate procedures shall be established within the national legal system to resolve land claims by the peoples concerned.

Article 15

1. The rights of the peoples concerned to the natural resources pertaining to their lands shall be specially safeguarded. These rights include the right of these peoples to participate in the use, management and conservation of these resources.
2. In cases in which the State retains the ownership of mineral or sub-surface resources or rights to other resources pertaining to lands, governments shall establish or maintain procedures through which they shall consult these peoples, with a view to ascertaining whether and to what degree their interests would be prejudiced, before undertaking or permitting any programmes for the exploration or exploitation of such resources pertaining to their lands. The peoples concerned shall wherever possible participate in the benefits of such activities, and shall receive fair compensation for any damages which they may sustain as a result of such activities.

Article 16

1. Subject to the following paragraphs of this Article, the peoples concerned shall not be removed from the lands which they occupy.
2. Where the relocation of these peoples is considered necessary as an exceptional measure, such relocation shall take place only with their free and informed consent. Where their consent cannot be obtained, such relocation shall take place only following appropriate procedures established by national laws and regulations, including public inquiries where appropriate, which provide the opportunity for effective representation of the peoples concerned.
3. Whenever possible, these peoples shall have the right to return to their traditional lands, as soon as the grounds for relocation cease to exist.
4. When such return is not possible, as determined by agreement or, in the absence of such agreement, through appropriate procedures, these peoples shall be provided in all possible cases with lands of quality and legal status at least equal to that of the lands previously occupied by them, suitable to provide for their present needs and future development. Where the peoples concerned express a preference for compensation in money or in kind, they shall be so compensated under appropriate guarantees.
5. Persons thus relocated shall be fully compensated for any resulting loss or injury.

Article 17

1. Procedures established by the peoples concerned for the transmission of land rights among members of these peoples shall be respected.
2. The peoples concerned shall be consulted whenever consideration is being given to their capacity to alienate their lands or otherwise transmit their rights outside their own community.
3. Persons not belonging to these peoples shall be prevented from taking advantage of their customs or of lack of understanding of the laws on the part of their members to secure the ownership, possession or use of land belonging to them.

Article 18

Adequate penalties shall be established by law for unauthorised intrusion upon, or use of, the lands of the peoples concerned, and governments shall take measures to prevent such offences.

Article 19

National agrarian programmes shall secure to the peoples concerned treatment equivalent to that accorded to other sectors of the population with regard to:
   (a) the provision of more land for these peoples when they have not the area necessary for providing the essentials of a normal existence, or for any possible increase in their numbers;
   (b) the provision of the means required to promote the development of the lands which these peoples already possess.

PART III. RECRUITMENT AND CONDITIONS OF EMPLOYMENT

Article 20

1. Governments shall, within the framework of national laws and regulations, and in co-operation with the peoples concerned, adopt special measures to ensure the effective protection with regard to recruitment and conditions of employment of workers belonging to these peoples, to the extent that they are not effectively protected by laws applicable to workers in general.

2. Governments shall do everything possible to prevent any discrimination between workers belonging to the peoples concerned and other workers, in particular as regards:
   (a) admission to employment, including skilled employment, as well as measures for promotion and advancement;
   (b) equal remuneration for work of equal value;
   (c) medical and social assistance, occupational safety and health, all social security benefits and any other occupationally related benefits, and housing;
   (d) the right of association and freedom for all lawful trade union activities, and the right to conclude collective agreements with employers or employers' organisations.

3. The measures taken shall include measures to ensure:
   (a) that workers belonging to the peoples concerned, including seasonal, casual and migrant workers in agricultural and other employment, as well as those employed by labour contractors, enjoy the protection afforded by national law and practice to other such workers in the same sectors, and that they are fully informed of their rights under labour legislation and of the means of redress available to them;
   (b) that workers belonging to these peoples are not subjected to working conditions hazardous to their health, in particular through exposure to pesticides or other toxic substances;
   (c) that workers belonging to these peoples are not subjected to coercive recruitment systems, including bonded labour and other forms of debt servitude;
   (d) that workers belonging to these peoples enjoy equal opportunities and equal treatment in employment for men and women, and protection from sexual harassment.

4. Particular attention shall be paid to the establishment of adequate labour inspection services in areas where workers belonging to the peoples concerned undertake wage employment, in order to ensure compliance with the provisions of this Part of this Convention.

PART IV. VOCATIONAL TRAINING, HANDICRAFTS AND RURAL INDUSTRIES

Article 21

Members of the peoples concerned shall enjoy opportunities at least equal to those of other citizens in respect of vocational training measures.

Article 22

1. Measures shall be taken to promote the voluntary participation of members of the peoples concerned in vocational training programmes of general application.

2. Whenever existing programmes of vocational training of general application do not meet the special needs of the peoples concerned, governments shall, with the participation of these peoples, ensure the provision of special training programmes and facilities.

3. Any special training programmes shall be based on the economic environment, social and cultural conditions and practical needs of the peoples concerned. Any studies made in this connection shall be carried out in co-operation with these peoples, who shall be consulted on the organisation and operation of such programmes. Where feasible, these peoples shall progressively assume responsibility for the organisation and operation of such special training programmes, if they so decide.

Article 23

1. Handicrafts, rural and community-based industries, and subsistence economy and traditional activities of the peoples concerned, such as hunting, fishing, trapping and gathering, shall be recognised as important factors in the maintenance of their cultures and in their economic self-reliance and development. Governments shall, with the participation of these people and whenever appropriate, ensure that these activities are strengthened and promoted.
2. Upon the request of the peoples concerned, appropriate technical and financial assistance shall be provided wherever possible, taking into account the traditional technologies and cultural characteristics of these peoples, as well as the importance of sustainable and equitable development.

PART V. SOCIAL SECURITY AND HEALTH

Article 24

Social security schemes shall be extended progressively to cover the peoples concerned, and applied without discrimination against them.

Article 25

1. Governments shall ensure that adequate health services are made available to the peoples concerned, or shall provide them with resources to allow them to design and deliver such services under their own responsibility and control, so that they may enjoy the highest attainable standard of physical and mental health.
2. Health services shall, to the extent possible, be community-based. These services shall be planned and administered in co-operation with the peoples concerned and take into account their economic, geographic, social and cultural conditions as well as their traditional preventive care, healing practices and medicines.
3. The health care system shall give preference to the training and employment of local community health workers, and focus on primary health care while maintaining strong links with other levels of health care services.
4. The provision of such health services shall be co-ordinated with other social, economic and cultural measures in the country.

PART VI. EDUCATION AND MEANS OF COMMUNICATION

Article 26

Measures shall be taken to ensure that members of the peoples concerned have the opportunity to acquire education at all levels on at least an equal footing with the rest of the national community.

Article 27

1. Education programmes and services for the peoples concerned shall be developed and implemented in co-operation with them to address their special needs, and shall incorporate their histories, their knowledge and technologies, their value systems and their further social, economic and cultural aspirations.
2. The competent authority shall ensure the training of members of these peoples and their involvement in the formulation and implementation of education programmes, with a view to the progressive transfer of responsibility for the conduct of these programmes to these peoples as appropriate.
3. In addition, governments shall recognise the right of these peoples to establish their own educational institutions and facilities, provided that such institutions meet minimum standards established by the competent authority in consultation with these peoples. Appropriate resources shall be provided for this purpose.

Article 28

1. Children belonging to the peoples concerned shall, wherever practicable, be taught to read and write in their own indigenous language or in the language most commonly used by the group to which they belong. When this is not practicable, the competent authorities shall undertake consultations with these peoples with a view to the adoption of measures to achieve this objective.
2. Adequate measures shall be taken to ensure that these peoples have the opportunity to attain fluency in the national language or in one of the official languages of the country.
3. Measures shall be taken to preserve and promote the development and practice of the indigenous languages of the peoples concerned.

Article 29

The imparting of general knowledge and skills that will help children belonging to the peoples concerned to participate fully and on an equal footing in their own community and in the national community shall be an aim of education for these peoples.

Article 30

1. Governments shall adopt measures appropriate to the traditions and cultures of the peoples concerned, to make known to them their rights and duties, especially in regard to labour, economic opportunities, education and health matters, social welfare and their rights deriving from this Convention.
2. If necessary, this shall be done by means of written translations and through the use of mass communications in the languages of these peoples.

Article 31

Educational measures shall be taken among all sections of the national community, and particularly among those that are in most direct contact with the peoples concerned, with the object of eliminating prejudices that they may harbour in respect of these peoples. To this end, efforts shall be made to ensure that history textbooks and other educational materials provide a fair, accurate and informative portrayal of the societies and cultures of these peoples.

PART VII. CONTACTS AND CO-OPERATION ACROSS BORDERS

Article 32
Governments shall take appropriate measures, including by means of international agreements, to facilitate contacts and co-operation between indigenous and tribal peoples across borders, including activities in the economic, social, cultural, spiritual and environmental fields.

PART VIII. ADMINISTRATION

Article 33
1. The governmental authority responsible for the matters covered in this Convention shall ensure that agencies or other appropriate mechanisms exist to administer the programmes affecting the peoples concerned, and shall ensure that they have the means necessary for the proper fulfilment of the functions assigned to them.
2. These programmes shall include:
   (a) the planning, co-ordination, execution and evaluation, in co-operation with the peoples concerned, of the measures provided for in this Convention;
   (b) the proposing of legislative and other measures to the competent authorities and supervision of the application of the measures taken, in co-operation with the peoples concerned.

PART IX. GENERAL PROVISIONS

Article 34
The nature and scope of the measures to be taken to give effect to this Convention shall be determined in a flexible manner, having regard to the conditions characteristic of each country.

Article 35
The application of the provisions of this Convention shall not adversely affect rights and benefits of the peoples concerned pursuant to other Conventions and Recommendations, international instruments, treaties, or national laws, awards, custom or agreements.

PART X. FINAL PROVISIONS

Article 36
This Convention revises the Indigenous and Tribal Populations Convention, 1957.

Article 37
The formal ratifications of this Convention shall be communicated to the Director-General of the International Labour Office for registration.

Article 38
1. This Convention shall be binding only upon those Members of the International Labour Organisation whose ratifications have been registered with the Director-General.

2. It shall come into force twelve months after the date on which the ratifications of two Members have been registered with the Director-General.

3. Thereafter, this Convention shall come into force for any Member twelve months after the date on which its ratification has been registered.

Article 39

1. A Member which has ratified this Convention may denounce it after the expiration of ten years from the date on which the Convention first comes into force, by an act communicated to the Director-General of the International Labour Office for registration. Such denunciation shall not take effect until one year after the date on which it is registered.

2. Each Member which has ratified this Convention and which does not, within the year following the expiration of the period of ten years mentioned in the preceding paragraph, exercise the right of denunciation provided for in this Article, will be bound for another period of ten years and, thereafter, may denounce this Convention at the expiration of each period of ten years under the terms provided for in this Article.

Article 40

1. The Director-General of the International Labour Office shall notify all Members of the International Labour Organisation of the registration of all ratifications and denunciations communicated to him by the Members of the Organisation.

2. When notifying the Members of the Organisation of the registration of the second ratification communicated to him, the Director-General shall draw the attention of the Members of the Organisation to the date upon which the Convention will come into force.

Article 41

The Director-General of the International Labour Office shall communicate to the Secretary-General of the United Nations for registration in accordance with Article 102 of the Charter of the United Nations full particulars of all ratifications and acts of denunciation registered by him in accordance with the provisions of the preceding Articles.

Article 42

At such times as it may consider necessary the Governing Body of the International Labour Office shall present to the General Conference a report on the working of this Convention and shall examine the desirability of placing on the agenda of the Conference the question of its revision in whole or in part.

Article 43

1. Should the Conference adopt a new Convention revising this Convention in whole or in part, then, unless the new Convention otherwise provides–

    (a) the ratification by a Member of the new revising Convention shall ipso jure involve the immediate denunciation of this Convention, notwithstanding the provisions of Article 39 above, if and when the new revising Convention shall have come into force;

(b) as from the date when the new revising Convention comes into force this Convention shall cease to be open to ratification by the Members.

2. This Convention shall in any case remain in force in its actual form and content for those Members which have ratified it but have not ratified the revising Convention.

Article 44
The English and French versions of the text of this Convention are equally authoritative.

60

ILO Declaration on Fundamental Principles and Rights at Work, 1998

Note: ILO Declaration on Fundamental Principles and Rights at Work and its Follow-up. Adopted by the International Labour Conference, 86th Session, Geneva, 18 June 1998. Annex revised 15 June 2010.

Whereas the ILO was founded in the conviction that social justice is essential to universal and lasting peace;

Whereas economic growth is essential but not sufficient to ensure equity, social progress and the eradication of poverty, confirming the need for the ILO to promote strong social policies, justice and democratic institutions;

Whereas the ILO should, now more than ever, draw upon all its standard-setting, technical cooperation and research resources in all its areas of competence, in particular employment, vocational training and working conditions, to ensure that, in the context of a global strategy for economic and social development, economic and social policies are mutually reinforcing components in order to create broad-based sustainable development;

Whereas the ILO should give special attention to the problems of persons with special social needs, particularly the unemployed and migrant workers, and mobilize and encourage international, regional and national efforts aimed at resolving their problems, and promote effective policies aimed at job creation;

Whereas, in seeking to maintain the link between social progress and economic growth, the guarantee of fundamental principles and rights at work is of particular significance in that it enables the persons concerned, to claim freely and on the basis of equality of opportunity, their fair share of the wealth which they have helped to generate, and to achieve fully their human potential;

Whereas the ILO is the constitutionally mandated international organization and the competent body to set and deal with international labour standards, and enjoys universal support and acknowledgement in promoting Fundamental Rights at Work as the expression of its constitutional principles;

Whereas it is urgent, in a situation of growing economic interdependence, to reaffirm the immutable nature of the fundamental principles and rights embodied in the Constitution of the Organization and to promote their universal application;

THE INTERNATIONAL LABOUR CONFERENCE
1. Recalls:
   (a) that in freely joining the ILO, all Members have endorsed the principles and rights set out in its Constitution and in the Declaration of Philadelphia, and have undertaken to work towards attaining the overall objectives of the Organization to the best of their resources and fully in line with their specific circumstances;

(b) that these principles and rights have been expressed and developed in the form of specific rights and obligations in Conventions recognized as fundamental both inside and outside the Organization.

2. Declares that all Members, even if they have not ratified the Conventions in question, have an obligation arising from the very fact of membership in the Organization to respect, to promote and to realize, in good faith and in accordance with the Constitution, the principles concerning the fundamental rights which are the subject of those Conventions, namely:

(a) freedom of association and the effective recognition of the right to collective bargaining;

(b) the elimination of all forms of forced or compulsory labour;

(c) the effective abolition of child labour; and

(d) the elimination of discrimination in respect of employment and occupation.

3. Recognizes the obligation on the Organization to assist its Members, in response to their established and expressed needs, in order to attain these objectives by making full use of its constitutional, operational and budgetary resources, including, by the mobilization of external resources and support, as well as by encouraging other international organizations with which the ILO has established relations, pursuant to article 12 of its Constitution, to support these efforts:

(a) by offering technical cooperation and advisory services to promote the ratification and implementation of the fundamental Conventions;

(b) by assisting those Members not yet in a position to ratify some or all of these Conventions in their efforts to respect, to promote and to realize the principles concerning fundamental rights which are the subject of these Conventions; and

(c) by helping the Members in their efforts to create a climate for economic and social development.

4. Decides that, to give full effect to this Declaration, a promotional follow-up, which is meaningful and effective, shall be implemented in accordance with the measures specified in the annex hereto, which shall be considered as an integral part of this Declaration.

5. Stresses that labour standards should not be used for protectionist trade purposes, and that nothing in this Declaration and its follow-up shall be invoked or otherwise used for such purposes; in addition, the comparative advantage of any country should in no way be called into question by this Declaration and its follow-up.

ANNEX (REVISED)

FOLLOW-UP TO THE DECLARATION

I. OVERALL PURPOSE

1. The aim of the follow-up described below is to encourage the efforts made by the Members of the Organization to promote the fundamental principles and rights enshrined in the Constitution of the ILO and the Declaration of Philadelphia and reaffirmed in this Declaration.

2. In line with this objective, which is of a strictly promotional nature, this follow up will allow the identification of areas in which the assistance of the Organization through its

technical cooperation activities may prove useful to its Members to help them implement these fundamental principles and rights. It is not a substitute for the established supervisory mechanisms, nor shall it impede their functioning; consequently, specific situations within the purview of those mechanisms shall not be examined or re-examined within the framework of this follow-up.

3. The two aspects of this follow-up, described below, are based on existing procedures: the annual follow-up concerning non-ratified fundamental Conventions will entail merely some adaptation of the present modalities of application of article 19, paragraph 5(e), of the Constitution; and the Global Report on the effect given to the promotion of the fundamental principles and rights at work that will serve to inform the recurrent discussion at the Conference on the needs of the Members, the ILO action undertaken, and the results achieved in the promotion of the fundamental principles and rights at work.

II. ANNUAL FOLLOW-UP CONCERNING NON-RATIFIED FUNDAMENTAL CONVENTIONS

A. Purpose and scope

1. The purpose is to provide an opportunity to review each year, by means of simplified procedures, the efforts made in accordance with the Declaration by Members which have not yet ratified all the fundamental Conventions.
2. The follow-up will cover the four categories of fundamental principles and rights specified in the Declaration.

B. Modalities

1. The follow-up will be based on reports requested from Members under article 19, paragraph 5(e), of the Constitution. The report forms will be drawn up so as to obtain information from governments which have not ratified one or more of the fundamental Conventions, on any changes which may have taken place in their law and practice, taking due account of article 23 of the Constitution and established practice.
2. These reports, as compiled by the Office, will be reviewed by the Governing Body.
3. Adjustments to the Governing Body's existing procedures should be examined to allow Members which are not represented on the Governing Body to provide, in the most appropriate way, clarifications which might prove necessary or useful during Governing Body discussions to supplement the information contained in their reports.

III. GLOBAL REPORT ON FUNDAMENTAL PRINCIPLES AND RIGHTS AT WORK

A. Purpose and scope

1. The purpose of the Global Report is to provide a dynamic global picture relating to the four categories of fundamental principles and rights at work noted during the preceding period, and to serve as a basis for assessing the effectiveness of the assistance

provided by the Organization, and for determining priorities for the following period, including in the form of action plans for technical cooperation designed in particular to mobilize the internal and external resources necessary to carry them out.

B. Modalities

1. The report will be drawn up under the responsibility of the Director-General on the basis of official information, or information gathered and assessed in accordance with established procedures. In the case of States which have not ratified the fundamental Conventions, it will be based in particular on the findings of the aforementioned annual follow-up. In the case of Members which have ratified the Conventions concerned, the report will be based in particular on reports as dealt with pursuant to article 22 of the Constitution. It will also refer to the experience gained from technical cooperation and other relevant activities of the ILO.

2. This report will be submitted to the Conference for a recurrent discussion on the strategic objective of fundamental principles and rights at work based on the modalities agreed by the Governing Body. It will then be for the Conference to draw conclusions from this discussion on all available ILO means of action, including the priorities and plans of action for technical cooperation to be implemented for the following period, and to guide the Governing Body and the Office in their responsibilities.

IV. IT IS UNDERSTOOD THAT

1. The Conference shall, in due course, review the operation of this follow-up in the light of the experience acquired to assess whether it has adequately fulfilled the overall purpose articulated in Part I.

61

Worst Forms of Child Labour Convention, 1999 (No. 182)

Note: Convention Concerning the Prohibition and Immediate Action for the Elimination of the Worst Forms of Child Labour. Adopted Geneva, 87th session of the ILC, 17 June 1999. Entry into force: 19 November 2000.

PREAMBLE

The General Conference of the International Labour Organization,

Having been convened at Geneva by the Governing Body of the International Labour Office, and having met in its 87th Session on 1 June 1999, and

Considering the need to adopt new instruments for the prohibition and elimination of the worst forms of child labour, as the main priority for national and international action, including international cooperation and assistance, to complement the Convention and the Recommendation concerning Minimum Age for Admission to Employment, 1973, which remain fundamental instruments on child labour, and

Considering that the effective elimination of the worst forms of child labour requires immediate and comprehensive action, taking into account the importance of free basic education and the need to remove the children concerned from all such work and to provide for their rehabilitation and social integration while addressing the needs of their families, and

Recalling the resolution concerning the elimination of child labour adopted by the International Labour Conference at its 83rd Session in 1996, and

Recognizing that child labour is to a great extent caused by poverty and that the long-term solution lies in sustained economic growth leading to social progress, in particular poverty alleviation and universal education, and

Recalling the Convention on the Rights of the Child adopted by the United Nations General Assembly on 20 November 1989, and

Recalling the ILO Declaration on Fundamental Principles and Rights at Work and its Follow-up, adopted by the International Labour Conference at its 86th Session in 1998, and

Recalling that some of the worst forms of child labour are covered by other international instruments, in particular the Forced Labour Convention, 1930, and the United Nations Supplementary Convention on the Abolition of Slavery, the Slave Trade, and Institutions and Practices Similar to Slavery, 1956, and

Having decided upon the adoption of certain proposals with regard to child labour, which is the fourth item on the agenda of the session, and

Having determined that these proposals shall take the form of an international Convention; adopts this seventeenth day of June of the year one thousand nine hundred and ninety-nine the following Convention, which may be cited as the Worst Forms of Child Labour Convention, 1999.

Article 1

Each Member which ratifies this Convention shall take immediate and effective measures to secure the prohibition and elimination of the worst forms of child labour as a matter of urgency.

Article 2

For the purposes of this Convention, the term child shall apply to all persons under the age of 18.

Article 3

For the purposes of this Convention, the term the worst forms of child labour comprises:

(a) all forms of slavery or practices similar to slavery, such as the sale and trafficking of children, debt bondage and serfdom and forced or compulsory labour, including forced or compulsory recruitment of children for use in armed conflict;

(b) the use, procuring or offering of a child for prostitution, for the production of pornography or for pornographic performances;

(c) the use, procuring or offering of a child for illicit activities, in particular for the production and trafficking of drugs as defined in the relevant international treaties;

(d) work which, by its nature or the circumstances in which it is carried out, is likely to harm the health, safety or morals of children.

Article 4

1. The types of work referred to under Article 3(d) shall be determined by national laws or regulations or by the competent authority, after consultation with the organizations of employers and workers concerned, taking into consideration relevant international standards, in particular Paragraphs 3 and 4 of the Worst Forms of Child Labour Recommendation, 1999.

2. The competent authority, after consultation with the organizations of employers and workers concerned, shall identify where the types of work so determined exist.

3. The list of the types of work determined under paragraph 1 of this Article shall be periodically examined and revised as necessary, in consultation with the organizations of employers and workers concerned.

Article 5

Each Member shall, after consultation with employers' and workers' organizations, establish or designate appropriate mechanisms to monitor the implementation of the provisions giving effect to this Convention.

Article 6

1. Each Member shall design and implement programmes of action to eliminate as a priority the worst forms of child labour.
2. Such programmes of action shall be designed and implemented in consultation with relevant government institutions and employers' and workers' organizations, taking into consideration the views of other concerned groups as appropriate.

Article 7

1. Each Member shall take all necessary measures to ensure the effective implementation and enforcement of the provisions giving effect to this Convention including the provision and application of penal sanctions or, as appropriate, other sanctions.
2. Each Member shall, taking into account the importance of education in eliminating child labour, take effective and time-bound measures to:
   (a) prevent the engagement of children in the worst forms of child labour;
   (b) provide the necessary and appropriate direct assistance for the removal of children from the worst forms of child labour and for their rehabilitation and social integration;
   (c) ensure access to free basic education, and, wherever possible and appropriate, vocational training, for all children removed from the worst forms of child labour;
   (d) identify and reach out to children at special risk; and
   (e) take account of the special situation of girls.
3. Each Member shall designate the competent authority responsible for the implementation of the provisions giving effect to this Convention.

Article 8

Members shall take appropriate steps to assist one another in giving effect to the provisions of this Convention through enhanced international cooperation and/or assistance including support for social and economic development, poverty eradication programmes and universal education.

Article 9

The formal ratifications of this Convention shall be communicated to the Director-General of the International Labour Office for registration.

Article 10

1. This Convention shall be binding only upon those Members of the International Labour Organization whose ratifications have been registered with the Director-General of the International Labour Office.
2. It shall come into force 12 months after the date on which the ratifications of two Members have been registered with the Director-General.
3. Thereafter, this Convention shall come into force for any Member 12 months after the date on which its ratification has been registered.

Article 11

1. A Member which has ratified this Convention may denounce it after the expiration of ten years from the date on which the Convention first comes into force, by an act

communicated to the Director-General of the International Labour Office for registration. Such denunciation shall not take effect until one year after the date on which it is registered.

2. Each Member which has ratified this Convention and which does not, within the year following the expiration of the period of ten years mentioned in the preceding paragraph, exercise the right of denunciation provided for in this Article, will be bound for another period of ten years and, thereafter, may denounce this Convention at the expiration of each period of ten years under the terms provided for in this Article.

Article 12

1. The Director-General of the International Labour Office shall notify all Members of the International Labour Organization of the registration of all ratifications and acts of denunciation communicated by the Members of the Organization.

2. When notifying the Members of the Organization of the registration of the second ratification, the Director-General shall draw the attention of the Members of the Organization to the date upon which the Convention shall come into force.

Article 13

The Director-General of the International Labour Office shall communicate to the Secretary-General of the United Nations, for registration in accordance with article 102 of the Charter of the United Nations, full particulars of all ratifications and acts of denunciation registered by the Director-General in accordance with the provisions of the preceding Articles.

Article 14

At such times as it may consider necessary, the Governing Body of the International Labour Office shall present to the General Conference a report on the working of this Convention and shall examine the desirability of placing on the agenda of the Conference the question of its revision in whole or in part.

Article 15

1. Should the Conference adopt a new Convention revising this Convention in whole or in part, then, unless the new Convention otherwise provides –
   (a) the ratification by a Member of the new revising Convention shall ipso jure involve the immediate denunciation of this Convention, notwithstanding the provisions of Article 11 above, if and when the new revising Convention shall have come into force;
   (b) as from the date when the new revising Convention comes into force, this Convention shall cease to be open to ratification by the Members.

2. This Convention shall in any case remain in force in its actual form and content for those Members which have ratified it but have not ratified the revising Convention.

Article 16

The English and French versions of the text of this Convention are equally authoritative.

62

ILO Declaration on Social Justice for a Fair Globalization, 2008

Note: Adopted by the International Labour Conference, Geneva, 97th session, 10 June 2008.

The International Labour Conference, meeting in Geneva on the occasion of its Ninety-seventh Session,

Considering that the present context of globalization, characterized by the diffusion of new technologies, the flow of ideas, the exchange of goods and services, the increase in capital and financial flows, the internationalization of business and business processes and dialogue as well as the movement of persons, especially working women and men, is reshaping the world of work in profound ways:

- on the one hand, the process of economic cooperation and integration has helped a number of countries to benefit from high rates of economic growth and employment creation, to absorb many of the rural poor into the modern urban economy, to advance their developmental goals, and to foster innovation in product development and the circulation of ideas;
- on the other hand, global economic integration has caused many countries and sectors to face major challenges of income inequality, continuing high levels of unemployment and poverty, vulnerability of economies to external shocks, and the growth of both unprotected work and the informal economy, which impact on the employment relationship and the protections it can offer;

Recognizing that achieving an improved and fair outcome for all has become even more necessary in these circumstances to meet the universal aspiration for social justice, to reach full employment, to ensure the sustainability of open societies and the global economy, to achieve social cohesion and to combat poverty and rising inequalities;

Convinced that the International Labour Organization has a key role to play in helping to promote and achieve progress and social justice in a constantly changing environment:

- based on the mandate contained in the ILO Constitution, including the Declaration of Philadelphia (1944), which continues to be fully relevant in the twenty-first century and should inspire the policy of its Members and which, among other aims, purposes and principles:
  - affirms that labour is not a commodity and that poverty anywhere constitutes a danger to prosperity everywhere;
  - recognizes that the ILO has the solemn obligation to further among the nations of the world programmes which will achieve the objectives of full employment and the raising of standards of living, a minimum living wage and the extension

of social security measures to provide a basic income to all in need, along with all the other objectives set out in the Declaration of Philadelphia;

– provides the ILO with the responsibility to examine and consider all international economic and financial policies in the light of the fundamental objective of social justice; and

- drawing on and reaffirming the ILO Declaration on Fundamental Principles and Rights at Work and its Follow-up (1998) in which Members recognized, in the discharge of the Organization's mandate, the particular significance of the fundamental rights, namely: freedom of association and the effective recognition of the right to collective bargaining, the elimination of all forms of forced or compulsory labour, the effective abolition of child labour, and the elimination of discrimination in respect of employment and occupation;

Encouraged by the international community's recognition of Decent Work as an effective response to the challenges of globalization, having regard to:

- the outcomes of the 1995 World Summit for Social Development in Copenhagen;
- the wide support, repeatedly expressed at global and regional levels, for the decent work concept developed by the ILO; and
- the endorsement by Heads of State and Government at the 2005 World Summit of the United Nations of fair globalization and the goals of full and productive employment and decent work for all, as central objectives of their relevant national and international policies;

Convinced that in a world of growing interdependence and complexity and the internationalization of production:

- the fundamental values of freedom, human dignity, social justice, security and non-discrimination are essential for sustainable economic and social development and efficiency;
- social dialogue and the practice of tripartism between governments and the representative organizations of workers and employers within and across borders are now more relevant to achieving solutions and to building up social cohesion and the rule of law through, among other means, international labour standards;
- the importance of the employment relationship should be recognized as a means of providing legal protection to workers;
- productive, profitable and sustainable enterprises, together with a strong social economy and a viable public sector, are critical to sustainable economic development and employment opportunities; and
- the Tripartite Declaration of Principles concerning Multinational Enterprises and Social Policy (1977), as revised, which addresses the growing role of such actors in the realization of the Organization's objectives, has particular relevance; and

Recognizing that the present challenges call for the Organization to intensify its efforts and to mobilize all its means of action to promote its constitutional objectives, and that, to make these efforts effective and strengthen the ILO's capacity to assist its Members' efforts to reach the ILO's objectives in the context of globalization, the Organization must:

- ensure coherence and collaboration in its approach to advancing its development of a global and integrated approach, in line with the Decent Work Agenda and the four strategic objectives of the ILO, drawing upon the synergies among them;

- adapt its institutional practices and governance to improve effectiveness and efficiency while fully respecting the existing constitutional framework and procedures;
- assist constituents to meet the needs they have expressed at country level based on full tripartite discussion, through the provision of high-quality information, advice and technical programmes that help them meet those needs in the context of the ILO's constitutional objectives; and
- promote the ILO's standard-setting policy as a cornerstone of ILO activities by enhancing its relevance to the world of work, and ensure the role of standards as a useful means of achieving the constitutional objectives of the Organization;

Therefore adopts this tenth day of June of the year two thousand and eight the present Declaration.

I. SCOPE AND PRINCIPLES

The Conference recognizes and declares that:

A. In the context of accelerating change, the commitments and efforts of Members and the Organization to implement the ILO's constitutional mandate, including through international labour standards, and to place full and productive employment and decent work at the centre of economic and social policies, should be based on the four equally important strategic objectives of the ILO, through which the Decent Work Agenda is expressed and which can be summarized as follows:

(i) promoting employment by creating a sustainable institutional and economic environment in which:
  - individuals can develop and update the necessary capacities and skills they need to enable them to be productively occupied for their personal fulfilment and the common well-being;
  - all enterprises, public or private, are sustainable to enable growth and the generation of greater employment and income opportunities and prospects for all; and
  - societies can achieve their goals of economic development, good living standards and social progress;

(ii) developing and enhancing measures of social protection – social security and labour protection – which are sustainable and adapted to national circumstances, including:
  - the extension of social security to all, including measures to provide basic income to all in need of such protection, and adapting its scope and coverage to meet the new needs and uncertainties generated by the rapidity of technological, societal, demographic and economic changes;
  - healthy and safe working conditions; and
  - policies in regard to wages and earnings, hours and other conditions of work, designed to ensure a just share of the fruits of progress to all and a minimum living wage to all employed and in need of such protection;

(iii) promoting social dialogue and tripartism as the most appropriate methods for:
  - adapting the implementation of the strategic objectives to the needs and circumstances of each country;
  - translating economic development into social progress, and social progress into economic development;

- facilitating consensus building on relevant national and international policies that impact on employment and decent work strategies and programmes; and
- making labour law and institutions effective, including in respect of the recognition of the employment relationship, the promotion of good industrial relations and the building of effective labour inspection systems; and

(iv) respecting, promoting and realizing the fundamental principles and rights at work, which are of particular significance, as both rights and enabling conditions that are necessary for the full realization of all of the strategic objectives, noting:
  - that freedom of association and the effective recognition of the right to collective bargaining are particularly important to enable the attainment of the four strategic objectives; and
  - that the violation of fundamental principles and rights at work cannot be invoked or otherwise used as a legitimate comparative advantage and that labour standards should not be used for protectionist trade purposes.

B. The four strategic objectives are inseparable, interrelated and mutually supportive. The failure to promote any one of them would harm progress towards the others. To optimize their impact, efforts to promote them should be part of an ILO global and integrated strategy for decent work. Gender equality and non-discrimination must be considered to be cross-cutting issues in the abovementioned strategic objectives.

C. How Members achieve the strategic objectives is a question that must be determined by each Member subject to its existing international obligations and the fundamental principles and rights at work with due regard, among others, to:
  (i) the national conditions and circumstances, and needs as well as priorities expressed by representative organizations of employers and workers;
  (ii) the interdependence, solidarity and cooperation among all Members of the ILO that are more pertinent than ever in the context of a global economy; and
  (iii) the principles and provisions of international labour standards.

II. METHOD OF IMPLEMENTATION

The Conference further recognizes that, in a globalized economy:

A. The implementation of Part I of this Declaration requires that the ILO effectively assist its Members in their efforts.

To that end, the Organization should review and adapt its institutional practices to enhance governance and capacity building in order to make the best use of its human and financial resources and of the unique advantage of its tripartite structure and standards system, with a view to:

  (i) better understanding its Members' needs, with respect to each of the strategic objectives, as well as past ILO action to meet them in the framework of a recurring item on the agenda of the Conference, so as to:
  - determine how the ILO can more efficiently address these needs through coordinated use of all its means of action;
  - determine the necessary resources to address these needs and, if appropriate, to attract additional resources; and
  - guide the Governing Body and the Office in their responsibilities;

    (ii) strengthening and streamlining its technical cooperation and expert advice in order to:
- support and assist efforts by individual Members to make progress on a tripartite basis towards all the strategic objectives, through country programmes for decent work, where appropriate, and within the framework of the United Nations system; and
- help, wherever necessary, the institutional capacity of member States, as well as representative organizations of employers and workers, to facilitate meaningful and coherent social policy and sustainable development;

    (iii) promoting shared knowledge and understanding of the synergies between the strategic objectives through empirical analysis and tripartite discussion of concrete experiences, with the voluntary cooperation of countries concerned, and with a view to informing Members' decision-making in relation to the opportunities and challenges of globalization;

    (iv) upon request, providing assistance to Members who wish to promote strategic objectives jointly within the framework of bilateral or multilateral agreements, subject to their compatibility with ILO obligations; and

    (v) developing new partnerships with non-state entities and economic actors, such as multinational enterprises and trade unions operating at the global sectoral level in order to enhance the effectiveness of ILO operational programmes and activities, enlist their support in any appropriate way, and otherwise promote the ILO strategic objectives. This will be done in consultation with representative national and international organizations of workers and employers.

B. At the same time, Members have a key responsibility to contribute, through their social and economic policy, to the realization of a global and integrated strategy for the implementation of the strategic objectives, which encompass the Decent Work Agenda outlined in Part I of this Declaration. Implementation of the Decent Work Agenda at national level will depend on national needs and priorities and it will be for member States, in consultation with the representative organizations of workers and employers, to determine how to discharge that responsibility. To that end, they may consider, among other steps:

    (i) the adoption of a national or regional strategy for decent work, or both, targeting a set of priorities for the integrated pursuit of the strategic objectives;

    (ii) the establishment of appropriate indicators or statistics, if necessary with the assistance of the ILO, to monitor and evaluate the progress made;

    (iii) the review of their situation as regards the ratification or implementation of ILO instruments with a view to achieving a progressively increasing coverage of each of the strategic objectives, with special emphasis on the instruments classified as core labour standards as well as those regarded as most significant from the viewpoint of governance covering tripartism, employment policy and labour inspection;

    (iv) the taking of appropriate steps for an adequate coordination between positions taken on behalf of the member State concerned in relevant international forums and any steps they may take under the present Declaration;

    (v) the promotion of sustainable enterprises;

(vi) where appropriate, sharing national and regional good practice gained from the successful implementation of national or regional initiatives with a decent work element; and

(vii) the provision on a bilateral, regional or multilateral basis, in so far as their resources permit, of appropriate support to other Members' efforts to give effect to the principles and objectives referred to in this Declaration.

C. Other international and regional organizations with mandates in closely related fields can have an important contribution to make to the implementation of the integrated approach. The ILO should invite them to promote decent work, bearing in mind that each agency will have full control of its mandate. As trade and financial market policy both affect employment, it is the ILO's role to evaluate those employment effects to achieve its aim of placing employment at the heart of economic policies.

III. FINAL PROVISIONS

A. The Director-General of the International Labour Office will ensure that the present Declaration is communicated to all Members and, through them, to representative organizations of employers and workers, to international organizations with competence in related fields at the international and regional levels, and to such other entities as the Governing Body may identify. Governments, as well as employers' and workers' organizations at the national level, shall make the Declaration known in all relevant forums where they may participate or be represented, or otherwise disseminate it to any other entities that may be concerned.

B. The Governing Body and the Director-General of the International Labour Office will have the responsibility for establishing appropriate modalities for the expeditious implementation of Part II of this Declaration.

C. At such time(s) as the Governing Body may find appropriate, and in accordance with modalities to be established, the impact of the present Declaration, and in particular the steps taken to promote its implementation, will be the object of a review by the International Labour Conference with a view to assessing what action might be appropriate.

ANNEX

FOLLOW-UP TO THE DECLARATION

I. Overall purpose and scope

A. The aim of this follow-up is to address the means by which the Organization will assist the efforts of its Members to give effect to their commitment to pursue the four strategic objectives important for implementing the constitutional mandate of the Organization.

B. This follow-up seeks to make the fullest possible use of all the means of action provided under the Constitution of the ILO to fulfil its mandate. Some of the measures to assist the Members may entail some adaptation of existing modalities of application of article 19, paragraphs 5(e) and 6(d), of the ILO Constitution, without increasing the reporting obligations of member States.

II. ACTION BY THE ORGANIZATION TO ASSIST ITS MEMBERS

Administration, resources and external relations

A. The Director-General will take all necessary steps, including making proposals to the Governing Body as appropriate, to ensure the means by which the Organization will assist the Members in their efforts under this Declaration. Such steps will include reviewing and adapting the ILO's institutional practices and governance as set out in the Declaration and should take into account the need to ensure:

   (i)   coherence, coordination and collaboration within the International Labour Office for its efficient conduct;

   (ii) building and maintaining policy and operational capacity;

   (iii) efficient and effective resource use, management processes and institutional structures;

   (iv) adequate competencies and knowledge base, and effective governance structures;

   (v)   the promotion of effective partnerships within the United Nations and the multi-lateral system to strengthen ILO operational programmes and activities or otherwise promote ILO objectives; and

   (vi) the identification, updating and promotion of the list of standards that are the most significant from the viewpoint of governance.

Understanding and responding to Members' realities and needs

B. The Organization will introduce a scheme of recurrent discussions by the International Labour Conference based on modalities agreed by the Governing Body, without duplicating the ILO's supervisory mechanisms, so as to:

   (i)   understand better the diverse realities and needs of its Members with respect to each of the strategic objectives, respond more effectively to them, using all the means of action at its disposal, including standards related action, technical cooperation, and the technical and research capacity of the Office, and adjust its priorities and programmes of action accordingly; and

   (ii) assess the results of the ILO's activities with a view to informing programme, budget and other governance decisions.

Technical assistance and advisory services

C. The Organization will provide, upon request of governments and representative organizations of workers and employers, all appropriate assistance within its mandate to support Members' efforts to make progress towards the strategic objectives through an integrated and coherent national or regional strategy, including by:

   (i)   strengthening and streamlining its technical cooperation activities within the framework of country programmes for decent work and that of the United Nations system;

   (ii) providing general expertise and assistance which each Member may request for the purpose of adopting a national strategy and exploring innovative partnerships for implementation;

(iii) developing appropriate tools for effectively evaluating the progress made and assessing the impact that other factors and policies may have on the Members' efforts; and

(iv) addressing the special needs and capacities of developing countries and of the representative organizations of workers and employers, including by seeking resource mobilization.

Research, information collection and sharing

D. The Organization will take appropriate steps to strengthen its research capacity, empirical knowledge and understanding of how the strategic objectives interact with each other and contribute to social progress, sustainable enterprises, sustainable development and the eradication of poverty in the global economy. These steps may include the tripartite sharing of experiences and good practices at the international, regional and national levels in the framework of:

(i) studies conducted on an ad hoc basis with the voluntary cooperation of the governments and representative organizations of employers and workers in the countries concerned; or

(ii) any common schemes such as peer reviews which interested Members may wish to establish or join on a voluntary basis.

III. EVALUATION BY THE CONFERENCE

A. The impact of the Declaration, in particular the extent to which it has contributed to promoting, among Members, the aims and purposes of the Organization through the integrated pursuit of the strategic objectives, will be the subject of evaluation by the Conference, which may be repeated from time to time, within the framework of an item placed on its agenda.

B. The Office will prepare a report to the Conference for evaluation of the impact of the Declaration, which will contain information on:

(i) actions or steps taken as a result of the present Declaration, which may be provided by tripartite constituents through the services of the ILO, notably in the regions, and by any other reliable source;

(ii) steps taken by the Governing Body and the Office to follow up on relevant governance, capacity and knowledge-base issues relating to the pursuit of the strategic objectives, including programmes and activities of the ILO and their impact; and

(iii) the possible impact of the Declaration in relation to other interested international organizations.

C. Interested multilateral organizations will be given the opportunity to participate in the evaluation of the impact and in the discussion. Other interested entities may attend and participate in the discussion at the invitation of the Governing Body.

D. In the light of its evaluation, the Conference will draw conclusions regarding the desirability of further evaluations or the opportunity of engaging in any appropriate course of action.

The foregoing is the ILO Declaration on Social Justice for a Fair Globalization duly adopted by the General Conference of the International Labour Organization during its Ninety seventh Session which was held at Geneva and declared closed on 13 June 2008.

IN FAITH WHEREOF we have appended our signatures this thirteenth day of June 2008:

The President of the Conference,

EDWIN SALAMIN JAEN

The Director-General of the International Labour Office,

JUAN SOMAVIA

PART VI
International Financial Institutions

63

International Bank of Reconstruction and Development (World Bank), Articles of Agreement, 1944 (excerpts only)

Note: Introductory Article and Article I only. Adopted by the United Nations Monetary and Financial Conference; Bretton Woods, 1–22 July 1944, as amended with effect 16 February 1989.

IBRD ARTICLES OF AGREEMENT

Introductory Article
The International Bank for Reconstruction and Development is established and shall operate in accordance with the following provisions:

Article I

Purposes

The purposes of the Bank are:
  (i) To assist in the reconstruction and development of territories of members by facilitating the investment of capital for productive purposes, including the restoration of economies destroyed or disrupted by war, the reconversion of productive facilities to peacetime needs and the encouragement of the development of productive facilities and resources in less developed countries.
  (ii) To promote private foreign investment by means of guarantees or participations in loans and other investments made by private investors; and when private capital is not available on reasonable terms, to supplement private investment by providing, on suitable conditions, finance for productive purposes out of its own capital, funds raised by it and its other resources.
  (iii) To promote the long-range balanced growth of international trade and the maintenance of equilibrium in balances of payments by encouraging international investment for the development of the productive resources of members, thereby assisting in raising productivity, the standard of living and conditions of labor in their territories.
  (iv) To arrange the loans made or guaranteed by it in relation to international loans through other channels so that the more useful and urgent projects, large and small alike, will be dealt with first.

(v) To conduct its operations with due regard to the effect of international investment on business conditions in the territories of members and, in the immediate postwar years, to assist in bringing about a smooth transition from a wartime to a peacetime economy.

The Bank shall be guided in all its decisions by the purposes set forth above.

64

International Monetary Fund, Articles of Agreement, 1944 (excerpts only)

Note: Introductory Article and Article I only. Adopted by the United Nations Monetary and Financial Conference, Bretton Woods, 1–22 July 1944.

Introductory Article

(i) The International Monetary Fund is established and shall operate in accordance with the provisions of this Agreement as originally adopted and subsequently amended.

(ii) To enable the Fund to conduct its operations and transactions, the Fund shall maintain a General Department and a Special Drawing Rights Department. Membership in the Fund shall give the right to participation in the Special Drawing Rights Department.

(iii) Operations and transactions authorized by this Agreement shall be conducted through the General Department, consisting in accordance with the provisions of this Agreement of the General Resources Account, the Special Disbursement Account, and the Investment Account; except that operations and transactions involving special drawing rights shall be conducted through the Special Drawing Rights Department.

Article I: Purposes

The purposes of the International Monetary Fund are:

(i) To promote international monetary cooperation through a permanent institution which provides the machinery for consultation and collaboration on international monetary problems.

(ii) To facilitate the expansion and balanced growth of international trade, and to contribute thereby to the promotion and maintenance of high levels of employment and real income and to the development of the productive resources of all members as primary objectives of economic policy.

(iii) To promote exchange stability, to maintain orderly exchange arrangements among members, and to avoid competitive exchange depreciation.

(iv) To assist in the establishment of a multilateral system of payments in respect of current transactions between members and in the elimination of foreign exchange restrictions which hamper the growth of world trade.

(v) To give confidence to members by making the general resources of the Fund temporarily available to them under adequate safeguards, thus providing them with opportunity to correct maladjustments in their balance of payments without resorting to measures destructive of national or international prosperity.

(vi) In accordance with the above, to shorten the duration and lessen the degree of disequilibrium in the international balances of payments of members.

The Fund shall be guided in all its policies and decisions by the purposes set forth in this Article.

SECTION B
Regional Documents

PART VII
African Union Documents

65

African Charter on Human and Peoples' Rights, 1981

Note: African [Banjul] Charter on Human and Peoples' Rights. Adopted Banjul, The Gambia, 27 June 1981. OAU Document CAB/LEG/67/3 rev. 5; 1520 UNTS 217. Entry into force: 21 October 1986.

PREAMBLE

The African States members of the Organisation of African Unity, parties to the present Convention entitled "African Charter on Human and Peoples' Rights"

Recalling Decision 115 (XVI) of the Assembly of Heads of State and Government at its Sixteenth Ordinary Session held in Monrovia, Liberia, from 17 to 20 July 1979 on the preparation of "a preliminary draft on an African Charter on Human and Peoples' Rights, providing inter alia for the establishment of bodies to promote and protect human and peoples' rights";

Considering the Charter of the Organisation of African Unity, which stipulates that "freedom, equality, justice and dignity are essential objectives for the achievement of the legitimate aspirations of the African peoples";

Reaffirming the pledge they solemnly made in Article 2 of the said Charter to eradicate all forms of colonialism from Africa, to coordinate and intensify their cooperation and efforts to achieve a better life for the peoples of Africa and to promote international cooperation having due regard to the Charter of the United Nations and the Universal Declaration of Human Rights;

Taking into consideration the virtues of their historical tradition and the values of African civilization which should inspire and characterize their reflection on the concept of human and peoples' rights;

Recognizing on the one hand, that fundamental human rights stem from the attitudes of human beings, which justifies their international protection and on the other hand that the reality and respect of peoples' rights should necessarily guarantee human rights;

Considering that the enjoyment of rights and freedoms also implies the performance of duties on the part of everyone;

Convinced that it is henceforth essential to pay particular attention to the right to development and that civil and political rights cannot be dissociated from economic, social and cultural rights in their conception as well as universality and that the satisfaction of economic, social and cultural rights is a guarantee for the enjoyment of civil and political rights;

Conscious of their duty to achieve the total liberation of Africa, the peoples of which are still struggling for their dignity and genuine independence, and undertaking to eliminate colonialism, neo-colonialism, apartheid, zionism and to dismantle aggressive foreign military bases and all forms of discrimination, language, religion or political opinions;

Reaffirming their adherence to the principles of human and peoples' rights and freedoms contained in the declarations, conventions and other instruments adopted by the Organisation of African Unity, the Movement of Non-Aligned Countries and the United Nations;

Firmly convinced of their duty to promote and protect human and peoples' rights and freedoms and taking into account the importance traditionally attached to these rights and freedoms in Africa;

HAVE AGREED AS FOLLOWS:

PART I. RIGHTS AND DUTIES

Chapter I. Human and Peoples' Rights

Article 1
The Member States of the Organisation of African Unity, parties to the present Charter shall recognise the rights, duties and freedoms enshrined in the Charter and shall undertake to adopt legislative or other measures to give effect to them.

Article 2
Every individual shall be entitled to the enjoyment of the rights and freedoms recognised and guaranteed in the present Charter without distinction of any kind such as race, ethnic group, colour, sex, language, religion, political or any other opinion, national and social origin, fortune, birth or any status.

Article 3
1. Every individual shall be equal before the law.
2. Every individual shall be entitled to equal protection of the law.

Article 4
Human beings are inviolable. Every human being shall be entitled to respect for his life and the integrity of his person. No one may be arbitrarily deprived of this right.

Article 5
Every individual shall have the right to the respect of the dignity inherent in a human being and to the recognition of his legal status. All forms of exploitation and degradation of man, particularly slavery, slave trade, torture, cruel, inhuman or degrading punishment and treatment shall be prohibited.

Article 6

Every individual shall have the right to liberty and to the security of his person. No one may be deprived of his freedom except for reasons and conditions previously laid down by law. In particular, no one may be arbitrarily arrested or detained.

Article 7

1. Every individual shall have the right to have his cause heard. This comprises:
   a. The right to an appeal to competent national organs against acts of violating his fundamental rights as recognized and guaranteed by conventions, laws, regulations and customs in force;
   b. The right to be presumed innocent until proved guilty by a competent court or tribunal;
   c. The right to defence, including the right to be defended by counsel of his choice;
   d. The right to be tried within a reasonable time by an impartial court or tribunal.
2. No one may be condemned for an act or omission which did not constitute a legally punishable offence at the time it was committed. No penalty may be inflicted for an offence for which no provision was made at the time it was committed. Punishment is personal and can be imposed only on the offender.

Article 8

Freedom of conscience, the profession and free practice of religion shall be guaranteed. No one may, subject to law and order, be submitted to measures restricting the exercise of these freedoms.

Article 9

1. Every individual shall have the right to receive information.
2. Every individual shall have the right to express and disseminate his opinions within the law.

Article 10

1. Every individual shall have the right to free association provided that he abides by the law.
2. Subject to the obligation of solidarity provided for in Article 29, no one may be compelled to join an association.

Article 11

Every individual shall have the right to assemble freely with others. The exercise of this right shall be subject only to necessary restrictions provided for by law, in particular those enacted in the interest of national security, the safety, health, ethics and rights and freedoms of others.

Article 12

1. Every individual shall have the right to freedom of movement and residence within the borders of a State provided he abides by the law.
2. Every individual shall have the right to leave any country including his own, and to return to his country. This right may only be subject to restrictions, provided for by law for the protection of national security, law and order, public health or morality.

3. Every individual shall have the right, when persecuted, to seek and obtain asylum in other countries in accordance with the law of those countries and international conventions.

4. A non-national legally admitted in a territory of a State Party to the present Charter, may only be expelled from it by virtue of a decision taken in accordance with the law.

5. The mass expulsion of non-nationals shall be prohibited. Mass expulsion shall be that which is aimed at national, racial, ethnic or religious groups.

Article 13

1. Every citizen shall have the right to participate freely in the government of his country, either directly or through freely chosen representatives in accordance with the provisions of the law.

2. Every citizen shall have the right of equal access to the public service of the country.

3. Every individual shall have the right of access to public property and services in strict equality of all persons before the law.

Article 14

The right to property shall be guaranteed. It may only be encroached upon in the interest of public need or in the general interest of the community and in accordance with the provisions of appropriate laws.

Article 15

Every individual shall have the right to work under equitable and satisfactory conditions, and shall receive equal pay for equal work.

Article 16

1. Every individual shall have the right to enjoy the best attainable state of physical and mental health.

2. State Parties to the present Charter shall take the necessary measures to protect the health of their people and to ensure that they receive medical attention when they are sick.

Article 17

1. Every individual shall have the right to education.

2. Every individual may freely take part in the cultural life of his community.

3. The promotion and protection of morals and traditional values recognized by the community shall be the duty of the State.

Article 18

1. The family shall be the natural unit and basis of society. It shall be protected by the State which shall take care of its physical health and moral.

2. The State shall have the duty to assist the family which is the custodian of morals and traditional values recognized by the community.

3. The State shall ensure the elimination of every discrimination against women and also ensure the protection of the rights of women and the child as stipulated in international declarations and conventions.

4. The aged and the disabled shall also have the right to special measures of protection in keeping with their physical or moral needs.

Article 19

All peoples shall be equal; they shall enjoy the same respect and shall have the same rights. Nothing shall justify the domination of a people by another.

Article 20

1. All peoples shall have the right to existence. They shall have the unquestionable and inalienable right to self-determination. They shall freely determine their political status and shall pursue their economic and social development according to the policy they have freely chosen.
2. Colonized or oppressed peoples shall have the right to free themselves from the bonds of domination by resorting to any means recognized by the international community.
3. All peoples shall have the right to the assistance of the State Parties to the present Charter in their liberation struggle against foreign domination, be it political, economic or cultural.

Article 21

1. All peoples shall freely dispose of their wealth and natural resources. This right shall be exercised in the exclusive interest of the people. In no case shall a people be deprived of it.
2. In case of spoilation, the dispossessed people shall have the right to the lawful recovery of its property as well as to an adequate compensation.
3. The free disposal of wealth and natural resources shall be exercised without prejudice to the obligation of promoting international economic cooperation based on mutual respect, equitable exchange and the principles of international law.
4. State Parties to the present Charter shall individually and collectively exercise the right to free disposal of their wealth and natural resources with a view to strengthening African Unity and solidarity.
5. State Parties to the present Charter shall undertake to eliminate all forms of foreign exploitation particularly that practised by international monopolies so as to enable their peoples to fully benefit from the advantages derived from their national resources.

Article 22

1. All peoples shall have the right to their economic, social and cultural development with due regard to their freedom and identity and in the equal enjoyment of the common heritage of mankind.
2. States shall have the duty, individually or collectively, to ensure the exercise of the right to development.

Article 23

1. All peoples shall have the right to national and international peace and security. The principles of solidarity and friendly relations implicitly affirmed by the Charter of the

United Nations and reaffirmed by that of the Organisation of African Unity shall govern relations between States.

2. For the purpose of strengthening peace, solidarity and friendly relations, State Parties to the present Charter shall ensure that:

   a. any individual enjoying the right of asylum under Article 12 of the present Charter shall not engage in subversive activities against his country of origin or any other State Party to the present Charter;

   b. their territories shall not be used as bases for subversive or terrorist activities against the people of any other State Party to the present Charter.

Article 24

All peoples shall have the right to a general satisfactory environment favourable to their development.

Article 25

State Parties to the present Charter shall have the duty to promote and ensure through teaching, education and publication, the respect of the rights and freedoms contained in the present Charter and to see to it that these freedoms and rights as well as corresponding obligations and duties are understood.

Article 26

State Parties to the present Charter shall have the duty to guarantee the independence of the Courts and shall allow the establishment and improvement of appropriate national institutions entrusted with the promotion and protection of the rights and freedoms guaranteed by the present Charter.

Chapter II. Duties

Article 27

1. Every individual shall have duties towards his family and society, the State and other legally recognised communities and the international community.

2. The rights and freedoms of each individual shall be exercised with due regard to the rights of others, collective security, morality and common interest.

Article 28

Every individual shall have the duty to respect and consider his fellow beings without discrimination, and to maintain relations aimed at promoting, safeguarding and reinforcing mutual respect and tolerance.

Article 29

The individual shall also have the duty:

1. To preserve the harmonious development of the family and to work for the cohesion and respect of the family; to respect his parents at all times, to maintain them in case of need.

2. To serve his national community by placing his physical and intellectual abilities at its service;

3. Not to compromise the security of the State whose national or resident he is;
4. To preserve and strengthen social and national solidarity, particularly when the latter is strengthened;
5. To preserve and strengthen the national independence and the territorial integrity of his country and to contribute to his defence in accordance with the law;
6. To work to the best of his abilities and competence, and to pay taxes imposed by law in the interest of the society;
7. To preserve and strengthen positive African cultural values in his relations with other members of the society, in the spirit of tolerance, dialogue and consultation and, in general, to contribute to the promotion of the moral well-being of society;
8. To contribute to the best of his abilities, at all times and at all levels, to the promotion and achievement of African unity.

PART II. MEASURES OF SAFEGUARD

Chapter I. Establishment and Organisation of the African Commission on Human and Peoples' Rights

Article 30
An African Commission on Human and Peoples' Rights, hereinafter called "the Commission", shall be established within the Organisation of African Unity to promote human and peoples' rights and ensure their protection in Africa.

Article 31
1. The Commission shall consist of eleven members chosen from amongst African personalities of the highest reputation, known for their high morality, integrity, impartiality and competence in matters of human and peoples' rights; particular consideration being given to persons having legal experience.
2. The members of the Commission shall serve in their personal capacity.

Article 32
The Commission shall not include more than one national of the same State.

Article 33
The members of the Commission shall be elected by secret ballot by the Assembly of Heads of State and Government, from a list of persons nominated by the State Parties to the present Charter.

Article 34
Each State Party to the present Charter may not nominate more than two candidates. The candidates must have the nationality of one of the State Parties to the present Charter. When two candidates are nominated by a State, one of them may not be a national of that State.

Article 35

1. The Secretary General of the Organisation of African Unity shall invite State Parties to the present Charter at least four months before the elections to nominate candidates;
2. The Secretary General of the Organisation of African Unity shall make an alphabetical list of the persons thus nominated and communicate it to the Heads of State and Government at least one month before the elections;

Article 36

The members of the Commission shall be elected for a six year period and shall be eligible for re-election. However, the term of office of four of the members elected at the first election shall terminate after two years and the term of office of three others, at the end of four years.

Article 37

Immediately after the first election, the Chairman of the Assembly of Heads of State and Government of the Organisation of African Unity shall draw lots to decide the names of those members referred to in Article 36.

Article 38

After their election, the members of the Commission shall make a solemn declaration to discharge their duties impartially and faithfully.

Article 39

1. In case of death or resignation of a member of the Commission, the Chairman of the Commission shall immediately inform the Secretary General of the Organisation of African Unity, who shall declare the seat vacant from the date of death or from the date on which the resignation takes effect.
2. If, in the unanimous opinion of other members of the Commission, a member has stopped discharging his duties for any reason other than a temporary absence, the Chairman of the Commission shall inform the Secretary General of the Organisation of African Unity, who shall then declare the seat vacant.
3. In each of the cases anticipated above, the Assembly of Heads of State and Government shall replace the member whose seat became vacant for the remaining period of his term, unless the period is less than six months.

Article 40

Every member of the Commission shall be in office until the date his successor assumes office.

Article 41

The Secretary General of the Organisation of African Unity shall appoint the Secretary of the Commission. He shall provide the staff and services necessary for the effective discharge of the duties of the Commission. The Organisation of African Unity shall bear the cost of the staff and services.

Article 42

1. The Commission shall elect its Chairman and Vice Chairman for a two-year period. They shall be eligible for re-election.
2. The Commission shall lay down its rules of procedure.
3. Seven members shall form the quorum.
4. In case of an equality of votes, the Chairman shall have a casting vote.
5. The Secretary General may attend the meetings of the Commission. He shall neither participate in deliberations nor shall he be entitled to vote. The Chairman of the Commission may, however, invite him to speak.

Article 43

In discharging their duties, members of the Commission shall enjoy diplomatic privileges and immunities provided for in the General Convention on the Privileges and Immunities of the Organisation of African Unity.

Article 44

Provision shall be made for the emoluments and allowances of the members of the Commission in the Regular Budget of the Organisation of African Unity.

Chapter II. Mandate of the Commission

Article 45

The functions of the Commission shall be:
1. To promote human and peoples' rights and in particular:
   a. to collect documents, undertake studies and researches on African problems in the field of human and peoples' rights, organise seminars, symposia and conferences, disseminate information, encourage national and local institutions concerned with human and peoples' rights and, should the case arise, give its views or make recommendations to Governments.
   b. to formulate and lay down, principles and rules aimed at solving legal problems relating to human and peoples' rights and fundamental freedoms upon which African Governments may base their legislation.
   c. cooperate with other African and international institutions concerned with the promotion and protection of human and peoples' rights.
2. Ensure the protection of human and peoples' rights under conditions laid down by the present Charter.
3. Interpret all the provisions of the present Charter at the request of a State Party, an institution of the OAU or an African Organisation recognised by the OAU.
4. Perform any other tasks which may be entrusted to it by the Assembly of Heads of State and Government.

Chapter III. Procedure of the Commission

Article 46

The Commission may resort to any appropriate method of investigation; it may hear from the Secretary General of the Organisation of African Unity or any other person capable of enlightening it.

Communication From States

Article 47
If a State Party to the present Charter has good reasons to believe that another State Party to this Charter has violated the provisions of the Charter, it may draw, by written communication, the attention of that State to the matter. This Communication shall also be addressed to the Secretary General of the OAU and to the Chairman of the Commission. Within three months of the receipt of the Communication, the State to which the Communication is addressed shall give the enquiring State, written explanation or statement elucidating the matter. This should include as much as possible, relevant information relating to the laws and rules of procedure applied and applicable and the redress already given or course of action available.

Article 48
If within three months from the date on which the original communication is received by the State to which it is addressed, the issue is not settled to the satisfaction of the two States involved through bilateral negotiation or by any other peaceful procedure, either State shall have the right to submit the matter to the Commission through the Chairman and shall notify the other States involved.

Article 49
Notwithstanding the provisions of Article 47, if a State Party to the present Charter considers that another State Party has violated the provisions of the Charter, it may refer the matter directly to the Commission by addressing a communication to the Chairman, to the Secretary General of the Organisation of African unity and the State concerned.

Article 50
The Commission can only deal with a matter submitted to it after making sure that all local remedies, if they exist, have been exhausted, unless it is obvious to the Commission that the procedure of achieving these remedies would be unduly prolonged.

Article 51
1. The Commission may ask the State concerned to provide it with all relevant information.
2. When the Commission is considering the matter, States concerned may be represented before it and submit written or oral representation.

Article 52
After having obtained from the States concerned and from other sources all the information it deems necessary and after having tried all appropriate means to reach an amicable solution based on the respect of human and peoples' rights, the Commission shall prepare, within a reasonable period of time from the notification referred to in Article 48, a report to the States concerned and communicated to the Assembly of Heads of State and Government.

Article 53

While transmitting its report, the Commission may make to the Assembly of Heads of State and Government such recommendations as it deems useful.

Article 54

The Commission shall submit to each Ordinary Session of the Assembly of Heads of State and Government a report on its activities.

Other Communications

Article 55

1. Before each Session, the Secretary of the Commission shall make a list of the Communications other than those of State Parties to the present Charter and transmit them to Members of the Commission, who shall indicate which Communications should be considered by the Commission.
2. A Communication shall be considered by the Commission if a simple majority of its members so decide.

Article 56

Communications relating to Human and Peoples' rights referred to in Article 55 received by the Commission, shall be considered if they:

1. Indicate their authors even if the latter requests anonymity,
2. Are compatible with the Charter of the Organisation of African Unity or with the present Charter,
3. Are not written in disparaging or insulting language directed against the State concerned and its institutions or to the Organisation of African Unity,
4. Are not based exclusively on news disseminated through the mass media,
5. Are sent after exhausting local remedies, if any, unless it is obvious that this procedure is unduly prolonged,
6. Are submitted within a reasonable period from the time local remedies are exhausted or from the date the Commission is seized with the matter, and
7. Do not deal with cases which have been settled by those States involved in accordance with the principles of the Charter of the United Nations, or the Charter of the Organisation of African Unity or the provisions of the present Charter.

Article 57

Prior to any substantive consideration, all communications shall be brought to the knowledge of the State concerned by the Chairman of the Commission.

Article 58

1. When it appears after deliberations of the Commission that one or more Communications apparently relate to special cases which reveal the existence of a series of serious or massive violations of human and peoples' rights, the Commission shall draw the attention of the Assembly of Heads of State and Government to these special cases.

2. The Assembly of Heads of State and Government may then request the Commission to undertake an in-depth study of these cases and make a factual report, accompanied by its finding and recommendations.

3. A case of emergency duly noticed by the Commission shall be submitted by the latter to the Chairman of the Assembly of Heads of State and Government who may request an in-depth study.

Article 59

1. All measures taken within the provisions of the present Chapter shall remain confidential until the Assembly of Heads of State and Government shall otherwise decide.

2. However the report shall be published by the Chairman of the Commission upon the decision of the Assembly of Heads of State and Government.

3. The report on the activities of the Commission shall be published by its Chairman after it has been considered by the Assembly of Heads of State and Government.

Chapter IV. Applicable Principles

Article 60

The Commission shall draw inspiration from international law on human and peoples' rights, particularly from the provisions of various African instruments on Human and Peoples' Rights, the Charter of the United Nations, the Charter of the Organisation of African Unity, the Universal Declaration of Human Rights, other instruments adopted by the United Nations and by African countries in the field of Human and Peoples' Rights, as well as from the provisions of various instruments adopted within the Specialised Agencies of the United Nations of which the Parties to the present Charter are members.

Article 61

The Commission shall also take into consideration, as subsidiary measures to determine the principles of law, other general or special international conventions, laying down rules expressly recognised by Member States of the Organisation of African Unity, African practices consistent with international norms on Human and Peoples' Rights, customs generally accepted as law, general principles of law recognised by African States as well as legal precedents and doctrine.

Article 62

Each State Party shall undertake to submit every two years, from the date the present Charter comes into force, a report on the legislative or other measures taken, with a view to giving effect to the rights and freedoms recognised and guaranteed by the present Charter.

Article 63

1. The present Charter shall be open to signature, ratification or adherence of the Member States of the Organisation of African Unity.

2. The instruments of ratification or adherence to the present Charter shall be deposited with the Secretary General of the Organisation of African Unity.

3. The present Charter shall come into force three months after the reception by the Secretary General of the instruments of ratification or adherence of a simple majority of the Member States of the Organisation of African Unity.

PART III. GENERAL PROVISIONS

Article 64

1. After the coming into force of the present Charter, members of the Commission shall be elected in accordance with the relevant Articles of the present Charter.

2. The Secretary General of the Organisation of African Unity shall convene the first meeting of the Commission at the Headquarters of the Organisation within three months of the constitution of the Commission. Thereafter, the Commission shall be convened by its Chairman whenever necessary but at least once a year.

Article 65

For each of the States that will ratify or adhere to the present Charter after its coming into force, the Charter shall take effect three months after the date of the deposit by that State of the instrument of ratification or adherence.

Article 66

Special protocols or agreements may, if necessary, supplement the provisions of the present Charter.

Article 67

The Secretary General of the Organisation of African Unity shall inform members of the Organisation of the deposit of each instrument of ratification or adherence.

Article 68

The present Charter may be amended if a State Party makes a written request to that effect to the Secretary General of the Organisation of African Unity. The Assembly of Heads of State and Government may only consider the draft amendment after all the State Parties have been duly informed of it and the Commission has given its opinion on it at the request of the sponsoring State. The amendment shall be approved by a simple majority of the State Parties. It shall come into force for each State which has accepted it in accordance with its constitutional procedure three months after the Secretary General has received notice of the acceptance.

Adopted by the eighteenth Assembly of Heads of State and Government, June 1981 – Nairobi, Kenya

66

Protocol to the African Charter on Human And Peoples' Rights on the Establishment of an African Court on Human and Peoples' Rights, 1998

Note: Protocol to the African Charter on Human and Peoples' Rights on the Establishment of an African Court on Human and Peoples' Rights. Adopted at Ouagadougou, Burkina Faso, 10 June 1998, OAU/LEG/MIN/AFCHPR/PROT.1 rev.2 (1997). Entry into force: 25 January 2004.

The Member States of the Organization of African Unity hereinafter referred to as the OAU, States Parties to the African Charter on Human and Peoples Rights.

Considering that the Charter of the Organization of African Unity recognizes that freedom, equality, justice, peace and dignity are essential objectives for the achievement of the legitimate aspirations of the African Peoples;

Noting that the African Charter on Human and Peoples' Rights reaffirms adherence to the principles of Human and Peoples' Rights, freedoms and duties contained in the declarations, conventions and other instruments adopted by the Organization of African Unity, and other international organizations;

Recognizing that the twofold objective of the African Commission on Human and Peoples' Rights is to ensure on the one hand promotion and on the other protection of Human and Peoples' Rights, freedom and duties;

Recognizing further, the efforts of the African Charter on Human and Peoples' Rights in the promotion and protection of Human and Peoples' Rights since its inception in 1987;

Recalling resolution AHGéRes.230 (XXX) adopted by the Assembly of Heads of State and Government in June 1994 in Tunis, Tunisia, requesting the Secretary-General to convene a Government experts' meeting to ponder, in conjunction with the African Commission, over the means to enhance the efficiency of the African commission and to consider in particular the establishment of an African Court on Human and Peoples' Rights;

Noting the first and second Government legal experts' meeting held respectively in Cape Town, South Africa (September, 1995) and Nouakchott, Mauritania (April 1997), and the third Government Legal Experts meeting held in Addis Ababa, Ethiopia (December, 1997), which was enlarged to include Diplomats;

Firmly convinced that the attainment of the objectives of the African Charter on Human and Peoples' Rights requires the establishment of an African Court on Human and Peoples' Rights to complement and reinforce the functions of the African Commission on Human and Peoples' Rights.

HAVE AGREED AS FOLLOWS:

Article 1 Establishment of the Court

There shall be established within the Organization of African Unity an African Court of Human and Peoples' Rights hereinafter referred to as "the Court", the organization, jurisdiction and functioning of which shall be governed by the present Protocol.

Article 2 Relationship between the Court and the Commission

The Court shall, bearing in mind the provisions of this Protocol, complement the protective mandate of the African Commission on Human and Peoples' Rights hereinafter referred to as "the Commission", conferred upon it by the African Charter on Human and Peoples' Rights, hereinafter referred to as "the Charter".

Article 3 Jurisdiction

1. The jurisdiction of the Court shall extend to all cases and disputes submitted to it concerning the interpretation and application of the Charter, this Protocol and any other relevant Human Rights instrument ratified by the States concerned.
2. In the event of a dispute as to whether the Court has jurisdiction, the Court shall decide.

Article 4 Advisory Opinions

1. At the request of a Member State of the OAU, the OAU, any of its organs, or any African organization recognized by the OAU, the Court may provide an opinion on any legal matter relating to the Charter or any other relevant human rights instruments, provided that the subject matter of the opinion is not related to a matter being examined by the Commission.
2. The Court shall give reasons for its advisory opinions provided that every judge shall be entitled to deliver a separate or dissenting decision.

Article 5 Access to the Court

1. The following are entitled to submit cases to the Court:
   a) The Commission
   b) The State Party which had lodged a complaint to the Commission
   c) The State Party against which the complaint has been lodged at the Commission
   d) The State Party whose citizen is a victim of a human rights violation
   e) African Intergovernmental Organizations
2. When a State Party has an interest in a case, it may submit a request to the Court to be permitted to join.
3. The Court may entitle relevant Non-Governmental organizations (NGOs) with observer status before the Commission, and individuals to institute cases directly before it, in accordance with article 34 (6) of this Protocol.

Article 6 Admissibility of Cases

1. The Court, when deciding on the admissibility of a case instituted under article 5 (3) of this Protocol, may request the opinion of the Commission which shall give it as soon as possible.

2. The Court shall rule on the admissibility of cases taking into account the provisions of article 56 of the Charter.
3. The Court may consider cases or transfer them to the Commission.

Article 7 Sources of Law

The Court shall apply the provision of the Charter and any other relevant human rights instruments ratified by the States concerned.

Article 8 Consideration of Cases

The Rules of Procedure of the Court shall lay down the detailed conditions under which the Court shall consider cases brought before it, bearing in mind the complementarity between the Commission and the Court.

Article 9 Amicable Settlement

The Court may try to reach an amicable settlement in a case pending before it in accordance with the provisions of the Charter.

Article 10 Hearings and Representation

1. The Court shall conduct its proceedings in public. The Court may, however, conduct proceedings in camera as may be provided for in the Rules of Procedure.
2. Any party to a case shall be entitled to be represented by a legal representative of the party's choice. Free legal representation may be provided where the interests of justice so require.
3. Any person, witness or representative of the parties, who appears before the Court, shall enjoy protection and all facilities, in accordance with international law, necessary for the discharging of their functions, tasks and duties in relation to the Court.

Article 11 Composition

1. The Court shall consist of eleven judges, nationals of Member States of the OAU, elected in an individual capacity from among jurists of high moral character and of recognized practical, judicial or academic competence and experience in the field of human and peoples' rights.
2. No two judges shall be nationals of the same State.

Article 12 Nominations

1. States Parties to the Protocol may each propose up to three candidates, at least two of whom shall be nationals of that State.
2. Due consideration shall be given to adequate gender representation in the nomination process.

Article 13 List of Candidates

1. Upon entry into force of this Protocol, the Secretary-General of the OAU shall request each State Party to the Protocol to present, within ninety (90) days of such a request, its nominees for the office of judge of the Court.

2. The Secretary-General of the OAU shall prepare a list in alphabetical order of the candidates nominated and transmit it to the Member States of the OAU at least thirty days prior to the next session of the Assembly of Heads of State and Government of the OAU hereinafter referred to as "the Assembly".

Article 14 Elections

1. The judges of the Court shall be elected by secret ballot by the Assembly from the list referred to in Article 13 (2) of the present Protocol.
2. The Assembly shall ensure that in the Court as a whole there is representation of the main regions of Africa and of their principal legal traditions.
3. In the election of the judges, the Assembly shall ensure that there is adequate gender representation.

Article 15 Term of Office

1. The judges of the Court shall be elected for a period of six years and may be re-elected only once. The terms of four judges elected at the first election shall expire at the end of two years, and the terms of four more judges shall expire at the end of four years.
2. The judges whose terms are to expire at the end of the initial periods of two and four years shall be chosen by lot to be drawn by the Secretary-General of the OAU immediately after the first election has been completed.
3. A judge elected to replace a judge whose term of office has not expired shall hold office for the remainder of the predecessor's term.
4. All judges except the President shall perform their functions on a part-time basis. However, the Assembly may change this arrangement as it deems appropriate.

Article 16 Oath of Office

After their election, the judges of the Court shall make a solemn declaration to discharge their duties impartially and faithfully.

Article 17 Independence

1. The independence of the judges shall be fully ensured in accordance with international law.
2. No judge may hear any case in which the same judge has previously taken part as agent, counsel or advocate for one of the parties or as a member of a national or international court or a commission of enquiry or in any other capacity. Any doubt on this point shall be settled by decision of the Court.
3. The judges of the Court shall enjoy, from the moment of their election and throughout their term of office, the immunities extended to diplomatic agents in accordance with international law.
4. At no time shall the judges of the Court be held liable for any decision or opinion issued in the exercise of their functions.

Article 18 Incompatibility

The position of judge of the court is incompatible with any activity that might interfere with the independence or impartiality of such a judge or the demands of the office as determined in the Rules of Procedure of the Court.

Article 19 Cessation of Office

1. A judge shall not be suspended or removed from office unless, by the unanimous decision of the other judges of the Court, the judge concerned has been found to be no longer fulfilling the required conditions to be a judge of the Court.
2. Such a decision of the Court shall become final unless it is set aside by the Assembly at its next session.

Article 20 Vacancies

1. In case of death or resignation of a judge of the Court, the President of the Court shall immediately inform the Secretary General of the Organization of African Unity, who shall declare the seat vacant from the date of death or from the date on which the resignation takes effect.
2. The Assembly shall replace the judge whose office became vacant unless the remaining period of the term is less than one hundred and eighty (180) days.
3. The same procedure and considerations as set out in Articles 12, 13 and 14 shall be followed for the filling of vacancies.

Article 21 Presidency of the Court

1. The Court shall elect its President and one Vice-President for a period of two years. They may be re-elected only once.
2. The President shall perform judicial functions on a full-time basis and shall reside at the seat of the Court.
3. The functions of the President and the Vice-President shall be set out in the Rules of Procedure of the Court.

Article 22 Exclusion

If the judge is a national of any State which is a party to a case submitted to the Court, that judge shall not hear the case.

Article 23 Quorum

The Court shall examine cases brought before it, if it has a quorum of at least seven judges.

Article 24 Registry of the Court

1. The Court shall appoint its own Registrar and other staff of the registry from among nationals of Member States of the OAU according to the Rules of Procedure.
2. The office and residence of the Registrar shall be at the place where the Court has its seat.

Article 25 Seat of the Court

1. The Court shall have its seat at the place determined by the Assembly from among States parties to this Protocol. However, it may convene in the territory of any Member State of the OAU when the majority of the Court considers it desirable, and with the prior consent of the State concerned.
2. The seat of the Court may be changed by the Assembly after due consultation with the Court.

Article 26 Evidence

1. The Court shall hear submissions by all parties and if deemed necessary, hold an enquiry. The States concerned shall assist by providing relevant facilities for the efficient handling of the case.
2. The Court may receive written and oral evidence including expert testimony and shall make its decision on the basis of such evidence.

Article 27 Findings

1. If the Court finds that there has been violation of a human or peoples' rights, it shall make appropriate orders to remedy the violation, including the payment of fair compensation or reparation.
2. In cases of extreme gravity and urgency, and when necessary to avoid irreparable harm to persons, the Court shall adopt such provisional measures as it deems necessary.

Article 28 Judgment

1. The Court shall render its judgment within ninety (90) days of having completed its deliberations.
2. The judgment of the Court decided by majority shall be final and not subject to appeal.
3. Without prejudice to sub-article 2 above, the Court may review its decision in the light of new evidence under conditions to be set out in the Rules of Procedure.
4. The Court may interpret its own decision.
5. The judgment of the Court shall be read in open court, due notice having been given to the parties.
6. Reasons shall be given for the judgment of the Court.
7. If the judgment of the court does not represent, in whole or in part, the unanimous decision of the judges, any judge shall be entitled to deliver a separate or dissenting opinion.

Article 29 Notification of Judgment

1. The parties to the case shall be notified of the judgment of the Court and it shall be transmitted to the Member States of the OAU and the Commission.
2. The Council of Ministers shall also be notified of the judgment and shall monitor its execution on behalf of the Assembly.

Article 30 Execution of Judgment

The States Parties to the present Protocol undertake to comply with the judgment in any case to which they are parties within the time stipulated by the Court and to guarantee its execution.

Article 31 Report

The Court shall submit to each regular session of the Assembly, a report on its work during the previous year. The report shall specify, in particular, the cases in which a State has not complied with the Court's judgment.

Article 32 Budget

Expenses of the Court, emoluments and allowances for judges and the budget of its registry, shall be determined and borne by the OAU, in accordance with criteria laid down by the OAU in consultation with the Court.

Article 33 Rules of Procedure

The Court shall draw up its Rules and determine its own procedures. The Court shall consult the Commission as appropriate.

Article 34 Ratification

1. This Protocol shall be open for signature and ratification or accession by any State Party to the Charter.
2. The instrument of ratification or accession to the present Protocol shall be deposited with the Secretary-General of the OAU.
3. The Protocol shall come into force thirty days after fifteen instruments of ratification or accession have been deposited.
4. For any State Party ratifying or acceding subsequently, the present Protocol shall come into force in respect of that State on the date of the deposit of its instrument of ratification or accession.
5. The Secretary-General of the OAU shall inform all Member States of the entry into force of the present Protocol.
6. At the time of the ratification of this Protocol or any time thereafter, the State shall make a declaration accepting the competence of the Court to receive cases under article 5 (3) of this Protocol. The Court shall not receive any petition under article 5 (3) involving a State Party which has not made such a declaration.
7. Declarations made under sub-article (6) above shall be deposited with the Secretary-General, who shall transmit copies thereof to the State parties.

Article 35 Amendments

1. The present Protocol may be amended if a State Party to the Protocol makes a written request to that effect to the Secretary-General of the OAU. The Assembly may adopt, by simple majority, the draft amendment after all the State Parties to the present Protocol have been duly informed of it and the Court has given its opinion on the amendment.
2. The Court shall also be entitled to propose such amendments to the present Protocol as it may deem necessary, through the Secretary-General of the OAU.
3. The amendment shall come into force for each State Party which has accepted it thirty days after the Secretary-General of the OAU has received notice of the acceptance.

67

Protocol on the Statute of the African Court of Justice and Human Rights, 2008

Note: Adopted Sharm-El-Sheikh, Egypt. 1 July 2008. Not yet in force.

PROTOCOL ON THE STATUTE OF THE AFRICAN COURT OF JUSTICE AND HUMAN RIGHTS

The Member States of the African Union, Parties to this Protocol,

RECALLING the objectives and principles enunciated in the Constitutive Act of the African Union, adopted on 11 July 2000 in Lomé, Togo, in particular the commitment to settle their disputes through peaceful means;

BEARING IN MIND their commitment to promote peace, security and stability on the Continent and to protect human and peoples' rights in accordance with the African Charter on Human and Peoples' Rights and other relevant instruments relating to human rights;

CONSIDERING that the Constitutive Act of the African Union provides for the establishment of a Court of Justice charged with hearing, among other things, all cases relating to interpretation or application of the said Act or of all other Treaties adopted within the framework of the Union;

FURTHER CONSIDERING Decisions Assembly/AU/Dec.45 (III) and Assembly/AU/Dec.83 (V) of the Assembly of the Union, adopted respectively at its Third (6–8 July 2004, Addis Ababa, Ethiopia) and Fifth (4–5 July 2005, Sirte, Libya), Ordinary Sessions, to merge the African Court on Human and Peoples' Rights and the Court of Justice of the African Union into a single Court,

FIRMLY CONVINCED that the establishment of an African Court of Justice and Human Rights shall assist in the achievement of the goals pursued by the African Union and that the attainment of the objectives of the African Charter on Human and Peoples' Rights requires the establishment of a judicial organ to supplement and strengthen the mission of the African Commission on Human and Peoples' Rights as well as the African Committee of Experts on the Rights and Welfare of the Child;

TAKING DUE ACCOUNT of the Protocol to the African Charter on Human and Peoples' Rights on the Establishment of an African Court on Human and Peoples' Rights, adopted by the Assembly of Heads of States and Governments of the Organization of African Unity on 10 June 1998 at Ouagadougou, Burkina Faso, and which entered into force on 25 January 2004;

TAKING DUE ACCOUNT ALSO of the Protocol of the Court of Justice of the African Union, adopted by the Assembly of the Union on 11 July 2003 in Maputo Mozambique;

RECALLING their commitment to take all necessary measures to strengthen their common institutions and to endow them with the necessary powers and resources to carry out their missions effectively;

COGNIZANT of the Protocol to the African Charter on Human and Peoples' Rights on the Rights of Women in Africa, and the commitments contained in the Solemn Declaration on the gender equality in Africa (Assembly/AU/Decl.12 (III) adopted by the Assembly of the Union respectively at its Second and Third ordinary sessions held in July 2003 and 2004, in Maputo, Mozambique and in Addis Ababa, Ethiopia);

Convinced that that the present Protocol shall supplement the mandate and efforts of other continental treaty bodies as well as national institutions in protecting human rights:

HAVE AGREED AS FOLLOWS:

Chapter I Merger of the African Court on Human and Peoples' Rights and the Court of Justice of the African Union

Article 1
Replacement of the 1998 and 2003 Protocols
The Protocol to the African Charter on Human and Peoples' Rights on the Establishment of an African Court on Human and Peoples' Rights, adopted on 10 June 1998 in Ouagadougou, Burkina Faso and which entered into force on 25 January 2004, and the Protocol of the Court of Justice of the African Union, adopted on 11 July 2003 in Maputo, Mozambique, are hereby replaced by the present Protocol and Statute annexed as its integral part hereto, subject to the provisions of Article 5, 7 and 9 of this Protocol.

Article 2
Establishment of a single Court
The African Court on Human and Peoples' Rights established by the Protocol to the African Charter on Human and Peoples' Rights on the Establishment of an African Court on Human and Peoples' Rights and the Court of Justice of the

African Union established by the Constitutive Act of the African Union, are hereby merged into a single Court and established as "The African Court of Justice and Human Rights".

Article 3
Reference to the single Court in the Constitutive Act
References made to the "Court of Justice" in the Constitutive Act of the African Union shall be read as references to the "African Court of Justice and Human Rights" established under Article 2 of this Protocol.

Chapter II Transitional Provisions

Article 4
Term of Office of the Judges of the African Court on Human and Peoples' Rights
The term of office of the Judges of the African Court on Human and Peoples' Rights shall end following the election of the Judges of the African Court of Justice and Human Rights. However, the Judges shall remain in office until the newly elected Judges of the African Court of Justice and Human Rights are sworn in.

Article 5
Cases Pending before the African Court on Human and Peoples' Rights
Cases pending before the African Court on Human and Peoples' Rights, that have not been concluded before the entry into force of the present Protocol, shall be transferred to the Human Rights Section of the African Court of Justice and Human Rights on the understanding that such cases shall be dealt with in accordance with the protocol to the ACHPR on the establishment of the African Court on Human and Peoples' Rights.

Article 6
Registry of the Court
The Registrar of the African Court on Human and Peoples' Rights shall remain in office until the appointment of a new Registrar for the African Court of Justice and Human Rights.

Article 7
Provisional validity of the 1998 Protocol
The Protocol to the African Charter on Human and Peoples' Rights on the Establishment of an African Court on Human and Peoples' Rights shall remain in force for a transitional period not exceeding one (1) year or any other period determined by the Assembly, after entry into force of the present Protocol, to enable the African Court on Human and Peoples' Rights to take the necessary measures for the transfer of its prerogatives, assets, rights and obligations to the African Court of Justice and Human Rights.

Chapter III Final Provisions

Article 8
Signature, Ratification and Accession
1. The present Protocol shall be open for signature, ratification or accession by Member States, in accordance with their respective constitutional procedures.
2. The instruments of ratification or accession to the present Protocol shall be deposited with the Chairperson of the Commission of the African Union.
3. Any Member State may, at the time of signature or when depositing its instrument of ratification or accession, or at any time thereafter, make a declaration accepting the competence of the Court to receive cases under Article 30 (f) involving a State which has not made such a declaration.

Article 9
Entry into force
1. The present Protocol and the Statute annexed to it shall enter into force thirty (30) days after the deposit of the instruments of ratification by fifteen (15) Member States.
2. For each Member State which shall ratify or accede to it subsequently, the present Protocol shall enter into force on the date on which the instruments of ratification or accession are deposited,
3. The Chairperson of the Commission shall inform all Member States of the entry into force of the present Protocol.
ADOPTED BY THE ELEVENTH ORDINARY SESSION OF THE ASSEMBLY, HELD IN SHARM EL-SHEIKH, EGYPT,
1ST JULY 2008

ANNEX

STATUTE OF THE AFRICAN COURT OF JUSTICE AND HUMAN RIGHTS

Chapter I General Provisions

Article 1
Definitions
In this Statute, except otherwise indicated, the following shall mean:
"African Charter" means the African Charter on Human and Peoples' Rights;
"African Commission" means the African Commission on Human and Peoples' Rights;
"African Committee of Experts" means the African Committee of Experts on the Rights and Welfare of the Child;
"African Intergovernmental Organisations" means an organisation that has been established with the aim of ensuring socio-economic integration, and to which some Member States have ceded certain competences to act on their behalf, as well as other sub-regional, regional or inter-African Organisations;

"African Non-Governmental Organizations" means Non-Governmental Organizations at the sub-regional, regional or inter-African levels as well as those in the Diaspora as may be defined by the Executive Council;

"Agent" means a person mandated in writing to represent a party in a case before the Court;

"Assembly" means the Assembly of Heads of State and Government of the Union;

"Chamber(s)" means a Chamber established in accordance with Article 19 of the Statute.

"Constitutive Act" means the Constitutive Act of the African Union;

"Commission": means the Commission of the Union;

"Court" means the African Court of Justice and Human Rights as well as its sections and chambers;

"Executive Council" means the Executive Council of Ministers of the Union;

"Full Court" means joint sitting of the General Affairs and Human Rights Sections of the Court;

"Human Rights Section" means the Human and Peoples' Rights Section of the Court;

"Judge" means a judge of the Court;

"Member State" means a Member State of the Union;

"National Human Rights Institutions" means public institutions established by a state to promote and protect human rights;

"President" means the President of the Court elected in accordance with Article 22(1) of the Statute;

"Protocol" means the Protocol to the Statute of the African Court of Justice and Human Rights;

"Registrar" means the person appointed as such in accordance with Article 22 (4) of the Statute;

"Rules" means the Rules of the Court;

"Section" means the General Affairs or the Human Rights Section of the Court;

"Senior Judge" means the person defined as such in the Rules of Court;

"States Parties" means Member States, which have ratified or acceded to this Protocol;

"Statute" means the present Statute;

"Union" means the African Union established by the Constitutive Act;

"Vice President" means the Vice President of the Court elected in accordance with Article 22 (1) of the Statute.

Article 2
Functions of the Court

1. The African Court of Justice and Human Rights shall be the main judicial organ of the African Union.

2. The Court shall be constituted and function in accordance with the provisions of the present Statute.

Chapter II Organization of the Court

Article 3
Composition
1. The Court shall consist of sixteen (16) Judges who are nationals of States Parties. Upon recommendation of the Court, the Assembly, may, review the number of Judges.
2. The Court shall not, at any one time, have more than one judge from a single Member State.
3. Each geographical region of the Continent, as determined by the Decisions of the Assembly shall, where possible, be represented by three (3) Judges except the Western Region which shall have four (4) Judges.

Article 4
Qualifications of Judges
The Court shall be composed of impartial and independent Judges elected from among persons of high moral character, who possess the qualifications required in their respective countries for appointment to the highest judicial offices, or are juris-consults of recognized competence and experience in international law and /or, human rights law.

Article 5
Presentation of Candidates
1. As soon as the Protocol to this Statute enters into force, the Chairperson of the Commission shall invite each State Party to submit, in writing, within a period of ninety (90) days, candidatures to the post of judge of the Court.
2. Each State Party may present up to two (2) candidates and shall take into account equitable gender representation in the nomination process.

Article 6
List of candidates
1. For the purpose of election, the Chairperson of the Commission shall establish two alphabetical lists of candidates presented as follows:
   i) List A containing the names of candidates having recognized competence and experience in International law; and
   ii) List B containing the names of candidates possessing recognized competence and experience in Human Rights law.
2. States Parties that nominate candidates possessing the competences required on the two lists shall choose the list on which their candidates may be placed.
3, At the first election, eight (8) Judges shall be elected from amongst the candidates of list A and eight (8) from among the candidates of list B. The elections shall be organized in a way as to maintain the same proportion of judges elected on the two lists.
4. The Chairperson of the Commission shall communicate the two lists to Member States, at least thirty (30) days before the Ordinary Session of the Assembly or of the Council, during which the elections shall take place.

Article 7
Election of judges

1. The Judges shall be elected by the Executive Council, and appointed by the Assembly.
2. They shall be elected through secret ballot by a two-thirds majority of Member States with voting rights, from among the candidates provided for in Article 6 of this Statute.
3. Candidates who obtain the two-thirds majority and the highest number of votes shall be elected. However, if several rounds of election are required, the candidates with the least number of votes shall withdraw.
4. The Assembly shall ensure that in the Court as a whole there is equitable representation of the regions and the principal legal traditions of the Continent.
5. In the election of the Judges, the Assembly shall ensure that there is equitable gender representation.

Article 8
Term of Office

1. The Judges shall be elected for a period of six (6) years and may be re-elected only once. However, the term of office of eight (8) judges, four (4) from each section, elected during the first election shall end after four (4) years.
2. The Judges, whose term of office shall end after the initial period of four (4) years, shall be determined for each section, by lot drawn by the Chairperson of the Assembly or the Executive Council, immediately after the first election.
3. A Judge, elected to replace another whose term of office has not expired, shall complete the term of office of his predecessor.
4. All the Judges except the President and the Vice-President, shall perform their functions on a part-time basis.

Article 9
Resignation, Suspension and Removal from Office

1. A Judge may resign his/her position in writing addressed to the President for transmission to the Chairperson of the Assembly through the Chairperson of the Commission.
2. A Judge shall not be suspended or removed from office save, where, on the recommendation of two-thirds majority of the other members, he/she no longer meets the requisite conditions to be a Judge.
3. The President shall communicate the recommendation for the suspension or removal of a Judge to the Chairperson of the Assembly through the Chairperson of the Commission.
4. Such a recommendation of the Court shall become final upon its adoption by the Assembly.

Article 10
Vacancies

1. A vacancy shall arise in the Court under the following circumstances:

a. Death;

b. Resignation;

c. Removal from office.

2. In the case of death or resignation of a Judge, the President shall immediately inform the Chairperson of the Assembly through the Chairperson of the Commission in writing, who shall declare the seat vacant.

3. The same procedure and consideration for the election of a Judge shall also be followed in filling the vacancies.

Article 11
Solemn Declaration

1. After the first election, the Judges shall, at the first session of the Court and in the presence of the Chairperson of the Assembly, make a Solemn Declaration as follows:

   " I ... Do solemnly swear (or affirm or declare) that I shall faithfully exercise the duties of my office as Judge of the African Court of Justice and Human Rights of the African Union impartially and conscientiously, without fear or favour, affection or ill will and that I will preserve the integrity of the Court.

2. The Chairperson of the Assembly or his/her duly authorized representative shall administer the Solemn Declaration.

3. Subsequently, the Solemn Declaration shall be made before the President of the Court.

Article 12
Independence

1. The independence of the judges shall be fully ensured in accordance with international law.

2. The Court shall act impartially, fairly and justly.

3. In performance of the judicial functions and duties, the Court and its Judges shall not be subject to the direction or control of any person or body.

Article 13
Conflict of Interest

1. Functions of a Judge are incompatible with all other activities, which might infringe on the need for independence or impartiality of the judicial profession. In case of doubt, the Court shall decide.

2. A Judge shall not exercise the function of agent, or counsel, or lawyer in any case before the Court.

Article 14
Conditions Governing the Participation of Members in the Settlement of a Specific Case

1. Where a particular judge feels he/she has a conflicting interest in a particular case, he/she shall so declare. In any event, he/she shall not participate in the settlement of a case

for which he/she was previously involved as agent, counsel or lawyer of one of the parties, or as a member of a national or international Court or Tribunal, or a Commission of enquiry or in any other capacity.

2. If the President considers that a Judge should not participate in a particular case, he/she shall notify the judge concerned. Such notification from the President shall, after agreement by the Court, exclude that Judge from participating in that particular case.

3. A Judge of the nationality of a State Party to a case before the full Court or one of its Sections shall not have the right to sit on the case.

4. Where there is doubt on these points, the Court shall decide.

Article 15
Privileges and Immunities

1. The Judges shall enjoy, from the time of their election and throughout their term of office, the full privileges and immunities extended to diplomatic agents in accordance with international law.

2. The Judges shall be immune from legal proceedings for any act or omission committed in the discharge of their judicial functions.

3. The Judges shall continue, after they have ceased to hold office, to enjoy immunity in respect of acts performed by them when engaged in their official capacity.

Article 16
Sections of the Court

The Court shall have two (2) Sections; a General Affairs Section composed of eight (8) Judges and a Human Rights Section composed of eight (8) Judges.

Article 17
Assignment of matters to Sections

1. The General Affairs Section shall be competent to hear all cases submitted under Article 28 of this Statute save those concerning human and/or peoples' rights issues.

2. The Human Rights Section shall be competent to hear all cases relating to human and/or peoples rights.

Article 18
Referral of matters to the Full Court

When a Section of the Court is seized with a case, it may, if it deems it necessary refer that case to the Full Court for consideration.

Article 19
Chambers

1. The General Affairs Section and the Human Rights Section may, at any time, constitute one or several chambers. The quorum required to constitute such chambers shall be determined in the Rules of Court.

2. A judgment given by any Section or Chamber shall be considered as rendered by the Court.

Article 20
Sessions
1. The Court shall hold ordinary and extraordinary sessions.
2. The Court shall decide each year on the periods of its ordinary sessions.
3. Extraordinary sessions shall be convened by the President or at the request of the majority of the Judges.

Article 21
Quorum
1. A quorum of nine (9) Judges shall be required for deliberations of the Full Court.
2. A quorum of five (5) Judges shall be required for the deliberations of the General Affairs Section.
3. A quorum of five (5) Judges shall be required for the deliberations of the Human and Peoples' Rights Section.

Article 22
Presidency, Vice-Presidency and Registry
1. At its first ordinary session after the election of the judges, the full Court shall elect its President as well as the Vice-President from the different lists for a period of three (3) years. The President and the Vice-President may be re-elected once.
2. The President shall preside over all sessions of the full Court and those of the Section to which he/she belongs; in the event of being unable to sit, the President shall be replaced by the Vice-President for the full Court and by the most Senior Judge for the sessions of his/her Section.
3. The Vice-President shall preside over all sessions of the Section to which he/she belongs. In the event of being unable to sit, the Vice-President shall be replaced by the most Senior Judge of that Section.
4. The Court shall appoint a Registrar and may provide for the appointment of such other officers as may be necessary.
5. The President, the Vice-President and the Registrar shall reside at the seat of the Court.

Article 23
Remuneration of Judges
1. The President and the Vice-President shall receive an annual salary and other benefits.
2. The other Judges shall receive a sitting allowance for each day on which he/she exercises his/her functions.
3. These salaries, allowances and compensation shall be determined by the Assembly, on the proposal of the Executive Council. They may not be decreased during the term of office of the Judges.
4. Regulations adopted by the Assembly on the proposal of the Executive Council shall determine the conditions under which retirement pensions shall be given to the Judges as well as the conditions under which their travel expenses shall be paid.
5. The above-mentioned salaries, allowances and compensation shall be free from all taxation.

Article 24
Conditions of Service of the Registrar and Members of the Registry
The salaries and conditions of service of the Registrar and other Court Officials shall be determined by the Assembly on the proposal of the Court, through the Executive Council.

Article 25
Seat and Seal of the Court
1. The Seat of the Court shall be same as the Seat of the African Court on Human and Peoples' Rights. However, the Court may sit in any other Member State, if circumstances warrant, and with the consent of the Member State concerned. The Assembly may change the seat of the Court after due consultations with the Court.
2. The Court shall have a seal bearing the inscription "The African Court of Justice and Human Rights".

Article 26
Budget
1. The Court shall prepare its draft annual budget and shall submit it to the Assembly through the Executive Council.
2. The budget of the Court shall be borne by the African Union.
3. The Court shall be accountable for the execution of its budget and shall submit report thereon to the Executive Council in conformity with the Financial Rules and Regulations of the African Union.

Article 27
Rules of Court
1. The Court shall adopt rules for carrying out its functions and the implementation of the present Statute. In particular, it shall lay down its own Rules.
2. In elaborating its Rules, the Court shall bear in mind the complementarity it maintains with the African Commission and the African Committee of Experts.

Chapter III Competence of the Court

Article 28
Jurisdiction of the Court
The Court shall have jurisdiction over all cases and all legal disputes submitted to it in accordance with the present Statute which relate to:
  a) the interpretation and application of the Constitutive Act;
  b) the interpretation, application or validity of other Union Treaties and all subsidiary legal instruments adopted within the framework of the Union or the Organization of African Unity;
  c) the interpretation and the application of the African Charter, the Charter on the Rights and Welfare of the Child, the Protocol to the African Charter on

Human and Peoples' Rights on the Rights of Women in Africa, or any other legal instrument relating to human rights, ratified by the States Parties concerned;

d) any question of international law;

e) all acts, decisions, regulations and directives of the organs of the Union;

f) all matters specifically provided for in any other agreements that States Parties may conclude among themselves, or with the Union and which confer jurisdiction on the Court;

g) the existence of any fact which, if established, would constitute a breach of an obligation owed to a State Party or to the Union;

h) the nature or extent of the reparation to be made for the breach of an international obligation.

Article 29
Entities Eligible to Submit Cases to the Court

1. The following entities shall be entitled to submit cases to the Court on any issue or dispute provided for in Article 28:

a) State Parties to the present Protocol;

b) The Assembly, the Parliament and other organs of the Union authorized by the Assembly;

c) A staff member of the African Union on appeal, in a dispute and within the limits and under the terms and conditions laid down in the Staff Rules and Regulations of the Union;

2. The Court shall not be open to States, which are not members of the Union. The Court shall also have no jurisdiction to deal with a dispute involving a Member State that has not ratified the Protocol.

Article 30
Other Entities Eligible to Submit Cases to the Court

The following entities shall also be entitled to submit cases to the Court on any violation of a right guaranteed by the African Charter, by the Charter on the Rights and Welfare of the Child, the Protocol to the African Charter on Human and Peoples' Rights on the Rights of Women in Africa, or any other legal instrument relevant to human rights ratified by the States Parties concerned:

a) State Parties to the present Protocol;

b) the African Commission on Human and Peoples' Rights;

c) the African Committee of Experts on the Rights and Welfare of the Child;

d) African Intergovernmental Organizations accredited to the Union or its organs;

e) African National Human Rights Institutions;

f) Individuals or relevant Non-Governmental Organizations accredited to the African Union or to its organs, subject to the provisions of Article 8 of the Protocol.

Article 31
Applicable Law
1. In carrying out its functions, the Court shall have regard to:
   a) The Constitutive Act;
   b) International treaties, whether general or particular, ratified by the contesting States;
   c) International custom, as evidence of a general practice accepted as law;
   d) The general principles of law recognized universally or by African States;
   e) Subject to the provisions of paragraph 1, of Article 46 of the present Statute, judicial decisions and writings of the most highly qualified publicists of various nations as well as the regulations, directives and decisions of the Union, as subsidiary means for the determination of the rules of law;
   f) Any other law relevant to the determination of the case.
2. This Article shall not prejudice the power of the Court to decide a case ex aequo et bono, if the parties agree thereto.

Chapter IV Procedure

Article 32
Official Languages
The official and working languages of the Court shall be those of the Union.

Article 33
Institution of Proceedings before the General Affairs Section
1. Cases brought before the Court by virtue of Article 29 of the present Statute shall be submitted by written application addressed to the Registrar. The subject of the dispute, the applicable law and basis of jurisdiction shall be indicated.
2. The Registrar shall forthwith give notice of the application to the Parties concerned.
3. The Registrar shall also notify, through the Chairperson of the Commission, all Member States and, if necessary, the organs of the Union whose decisions are in dispute.

Article 34
Institution of Proceedings before the Human Rights Section
1. Cases brought before the Court relating to an alleged violation of a human or peoples' right shall be submitted by a written application to the Registrar. The application shall indicate the right(s) alleged to have been violated, and, insofar as it is possible, the provision or provisions of the African Charter on Human and Peoples' Rights, the Charter on the Rights and Welfare of the Child, Protocol to the African Charter on Human and Peoples' Rights on the Rights of Women in Africa or any other relevant human rights instrument, ratified by the State concerned, on which it is based.
2. The Registrar shall forthwith give notice of the application to all parties concerned, as well as the Chairperson of the Commission.

Article 35
Provisional Measures
1. The Court shall have the power, on its own motion or on application by the parties, to indicate, if it considers that circumstances so require any provisional measures which ought to be taken to preserve the respective rights of the parties.
2. Pending the final decision, notice of the provisional measures shall forthwith be given to the parties and the Chairperson of the Commission, who shall inform the Assembly.

Article 36
Representation of Parties
1. The States, parties to a case, shall be represented by agents.
2. They may, if necessary, have the assistance of counsel or advocates before the Court.
3. The organs of the Union entitled to appear before the Court shall be represented by the Chairperson of the Commission or his/her representative.
4. The African Commission, the African Committee of Experts, African Inter Governmental Organizations accredited to the Union or its organs and African National Human Rights Institutions entitled to appear before the Court shall be represented by any person they choose for that purpose.
5. Individuals and Non-Governmental Organizations accredited to the Union or its organs may be represented or assisted by a person of their choice.
6. The agents and other representatives of parties before the Court, their counsel or advocates, witnesses, and any other persons whose presence is required at the Court shall enjoy the privileges and immunities necessary to the independent exercise of their duties or the smooth functioning of the Court.

Article 37
Communications and Notices
1. Communications and notices addressed to agents or counsel of parties to a case shall be considered as addressed to the parties.
2. For the service of all communications or notices upon persons other than the agents, counsel or advocates of parties concerned, the Court shall direct its request to the government of the State upon whose territory the communication or notice has to be served.
3. The same provision shall apply whenever steps are to be taken to procure evidence on the spot.

Article 38
Procedure before the Court
The procedures before the Court shall be laid out in the Rules of Court, taking into account the complementarity between the Court and other treaty bodies of the Union.

Article 39
Public Hearing
The hearing shall be public, unless the Court, on its own motion or upon application by the parties, decides that the session shall be closed.

Article 40
Record of Proceedings
1. A record of proceedings shall be made at each hearing and shall be signed by the Registrar and the presiding Judge of the session.
2. This record alone shall be authentic.

Article 41
Default Judgment
1. Whenever one of the parties does not appear before the Court, or fails to defend the case against it, the Court shall proceed to consider the case and to give its judgment.
2. The Court shall before doing so, satisfy itself, not only that it has jurisdiction in accordance with Articles 28, 29 and 30 of the present Statute, but also that the claim is well founded in fact and law, and that the other party had due notice.
3. An objection by the party concerned may be lodged against the judgment within ninety (90) days of it being notified of the default judgment. Unless there is a decision to the contrary by the Court, the objection shall not have effect of staying the enforcement of the default judgment.

Article 42
Majority Required for Decision of the Court
1. Without prejudice to the provisions of Article 50(4) of the present Statute, the decisions of the Court shall be decided by a majority of the Judges present.
2. In the event of an equality of votes, the presiding Judge shall have a casting vote.

Article 43
Judgments and Decisions
1. The Court shall render its judgment within ninety (90) days of having completed its deliberations.
2. All judgments shall state the reasons on which they are based.
3. The judgment shall contain the names of the Judges who have taken part in the decision.
4. The judgment shall be signed by all the Judges and certified by the Presiding Judge and the Registrar. It shall be read in open session, due notice having been given to the agents.
5. The Parties to the case shall be notified of the judgment of the Court and it shall be transmitted to the Member States and the Commission.

6. The Executive Council shall also be notified of the judgment and shall monitor its execution on behalf of the Assembly

Article 44
Dissenting Opinion
If the judgment does not represent in whole or in part the unanimous opinion of the Judges, any Judge shall be entitled to deliver a separate or dissenting opinion.

Article 45
Compensation
Without prejudice to its competence to rule on issues of compensation at the request of a party by virtue of paragraph 1(h), of Article 28 of the present Statute, the Court may, if it considers that there was a violation of a human or peoples' right, order any appropriate measures in order to remedy the situation, including granting fair compensation.

Article 46
Binding Force and Execution of Judgments
1. The decision of the Court shall be binding on the parties.
2. Subject to the provisions of paragraph 3, Article 41 of the present Statute, the judgment of the Court is final.
3. The parties shall comply with the judgment made by the Court in any dispute to which they are parties within the time stipulated by the Court and shall guarantee its execution.
4. Where a party has failed to comply with a judgment, the Court shall refer the matter to the Assembly, which shall decide upon measures to be taken to give effect to that judgment.
5. The Assembly may impose sanctions by virtue of paragraph 2 of Article 23 of the Constitutive Act.

Article 47
Interpretation
In the event of any dispute as to the meaning or scope of a judgment, the Court shall construe it upon the request of any party.

Article 48
Revision
1. An application for revision of a judgment may be made to the Court only when it is based upon discovery of a new fact of such nature as to be a decisive factor, which fact was, when the judgment was given, unknown to the Court and also to the party claiming revision, provided that such ignorance was not due to negligence.

2. The proceedings for revision shall be opened by a ruling of the Court expressly recording the existence of the new fact, recognizing that it has such a character as to lay the case open to revision, and declaring the revision admissible on this ground.

3. The Court may require prior compliance with the terms of the judgment before it admits proceedings in revision.

4. The application for revision shall be made within six (6) months of the discovery of the new fact.

5. No application may be made after the lapse of ten (10) years from the date of the judgment.

Article 49
Intervention

1. Should a Member State or organ of the Union consider that it has an interest of a legal nature which may be affected by the decision in the case, it may submit a request to the Court to be permitted to intervene. It shall be for the Court to decide upon this request.

2. If a Member State or organ of the Union should exercise the option offered under paragraph 1 of the present Article, the interpretation contained in the decision shall be equally binding upon it.

3. In the interest of the effective administration of justice, the Court may invite any Member State that is not a party to the case, any organ of the Union or any person concerned other than the claimant, to present written observations or take part in hearings.

Article 50
Intervention in a Case Concerning the Interpretation of the Constitutive Act

1. Whenever the question of interpretation of the Constitutive Act arises, in a case in which Member States other than the parties to the dispute have expressed an interest, the Registrar shall notify all such States and organs of the Union forthwith.

2. Every State Party and organ of the Union so notified has the right to intervene in the proceedings.

3. The decisions of the Court concerning the interpretation and application of the Constitutive Act shall be binding on Member States and organs of the Union, notwithstanding the provisions of paragraph 1, of Article 46 of this Statute.

4. Any decision made by virtue of this Article shall be made by a qualified majority of at least two (2) votes and in the presence of at least two-thirds of the Judges.

Article 51
Intervention in a Case concerning the Interpretation of Other Treaties

1. Whenever the question is that of interpretation of other treaties ratified by Member States other than the parties to a dispute, the Registrar shall notify all such States and the organs of the Union forthwith.

2. Every State Party and organ of the Union so notified has the right to intervene in the proceedings, and if it exercises this right, the interpretation given by the judgment shall be equally binding upon it.

3. This Article shall not be applicable to cases relating to alleged violations of a human or peoples' right, submitted by virtue of Articles 29 or 30 of the present Statute.

Article 52
Costs

1. Unless otherwise decided by the Court, each party shall bear its own costs.
2. Should it be required in the interest of justice, free legal aid may be provided for the person presenting an individual communication, under conditions to be set out in the Rules of Court.

Chapter V Advisory Opinion

Article 53
Request for Advisory Opinion

1. The Court may give an advisory opinion on any legal question at the request of the Assembly, the Parliament, the Executive Council, the Peace and Security Council, the Economic, Social and Cultural Council (ECOSOCC), the Financial Institutions or any other organ of the Union as may be authorized by the Assembly.
2. A request for an advisory opinion shall be in writing and shall contain an exact statement of the question upon which the opinion is required and shall be accompanied by all relevant documents.
3. A request for an advisory opinion must not be related to a pending application before the African Commission or the African Committee of Experts.

Article 54
Service of Notice

1. The Registrar shall forthwith give notice of the request for an advisory opinion to all States or organs entitled to appear before the Court by virtue of Article 30 of the present Statute.
2. The Registrar shall also, by means of a special and direct communication, notify any State entitled to appear before the Court or any Intergovernmental Organization considered by the Court, or should it not be sitting, by the President, as likely to be able to furnish information on the question, that the Court will be prepared to receive, within a time limit to be fixed by the President, written statements, or to hear, at a public sitting to be held for the purpose, oral statements relating to the question.
3. Should any such State entitled to appear before the Court have failed to receive the special communication referred to in paragraph 2 of this Article, such State may express the desire to submit a written statement or to be heard, and the Court shall decide.

4. States and organizations having presented written or oral statements or both shall be permitted to comment on the statements made by other States or organizations in the form, to the extent, and within the time limits which the Court, or should it not be sitting, the President, shall decide in each particular case. Accordingly, the Registrar shall in due course communicate any such written statements to States and organizations having submitted similar statements.

Article 55
Delivery of Advisory Opinion
The Court shall deliver its advisory opinion in open court, notice having been given to the Chairperson of the Commission and Member States, and other International Organizations directly concerned.

Article 56
Application by Analogy of the Provisions of the Statute
Applicable to Contentious Cases
In the exercise of its advisory functions, the Court shall further be guided by the provisions of the present Statute which apply in contentious cases to the extent to which it recognizes them to be applicable.

Chapter VI Report to the Assembly

Article 57
Annual Activity Report
The Court shall submit to the Assembly, an annual report on its work during the previous year. The report shall specify, in particular, the cases in which a party has not complied with the judgment of the Court.

Chapter VII Procedure for Amendments

Article 58
Proposed Amendments from a State Party
1. The present Statute may be amended if a State Party makes a written request to that effect to the Chairperson of the Commission, who shall transmit same to Member States within thirty (30) days of receipt thereof.
2. The Assembly may adopt by a simple majority, the proposed amendment after the Court has given its opinion on it.

Article 59
Proposed Amendments from the Court
The Court may propose such amendments to the present Statute as it may deem necessary, to the Assembly through written communication to the Chairperson of the

Commission, for consideration in conformity with the provisions of Article 58 of the present Statute.

Article 60
Entry into Force of Amendments
The amendment shall enter into force for every State which has accepted it in conformity with its Constitutional laws thirty (30) days after the Chairperson of the Commission is notified of this acceptance.

68

Protocol on Amendments to the Protocol on the Statute of the African Court of Justice and Human Rights, 2014

Note: Protocol on Amendments to the Protocol on the Statute of the African Court of Justice and Human Rights. Adopted 27 June 2014. Not in force.

PREAMBLE

The Member States of the African Union parties to the Constitutive Act of the African Union;

RECALLING the objectives and principles enunciated in the Constitutive Act of the African Union, adopted on 11 July 2000 in Lome, Togo, in particular the commitment to settle their disputes through peaceful means;

FURTHER RECALLING the provisions of the Protocol on the Statute of the African Court of Justice and Human Rights and the Statute annexed to it adopted on 1 July 2008 in Sharm-El-Sheikh, Egypt;

RECOGNIZING that the Protocol on the Statute of the African Court of Justice and Human Rights had merged the African Court on Human and Peoples' Rights and the Court of Justice of the African Union into a single Court;

BEARING IN MIND their commitment to promote peace, security and stability on the continent, and to protect human and peoples' rights in accordance with the African Charter on Human and Peoples' Rights and other relevant instruments;

FURTHER RECOGNIZING the efforts and contribution of the African Commission on Human and Peoples' Rights in the promotion and protection of human and peoples' rights since its inception in 1987;

NOTING the steady growth of the African Court on Human and Peoples' Rights and the contribution it has made in protecting human and peoples' rights on the African continent as well as the progress towards the establishment of the African Court of Justice and Human and Peoples' Rights;

FURTHER BEARING IN MIND the complementary relationship between the African Commission on Human and Peoples' Rights and the African Court on Human and Peoples' Rights, as well as its successor, the African Court of Justice and Human and Peoples' Rights;

FURTHER RECALLING their commitment to the right of the Union to intervene in a Member State pursuant to a decision of the Assembly in respect of grave circumstances, namely: war crimes, genocide and crimes against humanity as well as a serious threat to legitimate order to restore peace and stability to the Member State of the Union upon the recommendation of the Peace and Security Council;

REITERATING their respect for democratic principles, human and peoples' rights, the rule of law and good governance;

FURTHER REITERATING their respect for the sanctity of human life, condemnation and rejection of impunity and political assassination, acts of terrorism and subversive activities, unconstitutional changes of governments and acts of aggression;

FURTHER REITERATING their commitment to fighting impunity in conformity with the provisions of Article 4(o) of the Constitutive Act of the African Union;

ACKNOWLEDGING the pivotal role that the African Court of Justice and Human and Peoples' Rights can play in strengthening the commitment of the African Union to promote sustained peace, security and stability on the Continent and to promote justice and human and peoples' rights as an aspect of their efforts to promote the objectives of the political and socio-economic integration and development of the Continent with a view to realizing the ultimate objective of a United States of Africa;

FURTHER RECALLING Assembly Decision Assembly/AU/Dec.213 (Xll) adopted by the Twelfth Ordinary Session of the Assembly in Addis Ababa, Federal Democratic Republic of Ethiopia, on 3 February 2009 on the implementation of the Assembly's Decision on the Abuse of the Principle of Universal Jurisdiction;

FURTHER RECALLING Assembly Decision Assembly/AU/Dec.263 (Xlll) adopted by the Thirteenth Ordinary Session of the Assembly in Sirte, Libya, on 3 July 2009 on the transformation of the African Union Commission to the African Union Authority;

FURTHER RECOGNIZING the need to take the necessary measures to amend the legal instruments of the principal organs of the African Union in the light of the aforementioned Assembly Decisions;

CONVINCED that the present Protocol will complement national, regional and continental bodies and institutions in preventing serious and massive violations of human and peoples' rights in keeping with Article 58 of the Charter and ensuring accountability for them wherever they occur;

HAVE AGREED to adopt the present amendments to the Protocol on the Statute of the African Court of Justice and Human Rights and the Statute annexed thereto as follows: -

CHAPTER I

In CHAPTER I of the Protocol (MERGER OF THE AFRICAN COURT ON HUMAN AND PEOPLES' RIGHTS AND THE COURT OF JUSTICE OF THE AFRICAN UNION) the deletion of the existing title, Articles and their provisions in their entirety and the insertion in their place of the following:

"CHAPTER I GENERAL PROVISIONS

Article 1
Definitions
In this Protocol:
"Assembly" means the Assembly of Heads of State and Government of the African Union;
"Chairperson" means the Chairperson of the Assembly;
"Charter" means the African Charter on Human and Peoples' Rights;
"Commission" means the Commission of the African Union;
"Court" means the African Court of Justice and Human and Peoples' Rights;
"Member State" means a Member State of the Union;
"President" means the President of the Court;
"Protocol" means the Protocol on the Statute of the African Court of Justice and Human Rights;
"Single Court" has the same meaning as the Court;
"Statute" means the present Statute;
"Union" means the African Union established by the Constitutive Act of the African Union;
"Vice President" means the Vice President of the Court.

Article 2
Organs of the Court
The Court shall be composed of the following organs:
1. The Presidency;
2. The Office of the Prosecutor;
3. The Registry;
4. The Defence Office.

Article 3
Jurisdiction of the Court
1. The Court is vested with an original and appellate jurisdiction, including international criminal jurisdiction, which it shall exercise in accordance with the provisions of the Statute annexed hereto.
2. The Court has jurisdiction to hear such other matters or appeals as may be referred to it in any other agreements that the Member States or the Regional Economic Communities or other international organizations recognized by the African Union may conclude among themselves, or with the Union.

Article 4
Relationship between the Court and the African Commission on Human and Peoples Rights
The Court shall, in accordance with the Charter and this Protocol, complement the protective mandate of the African Commission on Human and Peoples' Rights.

Chapter II Transitional Provisions

Article 5
Term of Office of the Judges of the African Court on Human and Peoples' Rights
In Article 4 (Term of Office of the Judges of the African Court on Human and Peoples' Rights), replace the existing provision including its title, with:

"Article 4
Term of Office of the Judges of the African Court on Human and Peoples' Rights
1. Upon the coming into force of the Protocol on the Statute of the African Court of Justice and Human Rights, the terms and appointment of the Judges of the African Court on Human and Peoples' Rights shall terminate.
2. Without prejudice to paragraph 1, the Judges of the African Court on Human and Peoples' Rights shall remain in office until the judges of the African Court of Justice and Human and Peoples' Rights are sworn in."

Article 6
Pending Cases
At the entry into force of this Protocol, where any matter affecting any State had already been commenced before either the African Court on Human and Peoples' Rights or the African Court of Justice and Human Rights, if in force, such a matter shall be continued before the relevant Section of the African Court of Justice and Human and Peoples' Rights, pursuant to such Rules as may be made by the Court.

Article 6*bis*
Temporary Jurisdiction
At the entry into force of this Protocol, until a Member State ratifies it, any jurisdiction which has hitherto been accepted by such Member State with respect to either the African Court on Human and Peoples' Rights or the African Court of Justice and Human Rights shall be exercisable by this Court.

Article 7
Registry of the Court
1. The Registrar of the African Court on Human and Peoples' Rights shall remain in office until the appointment of a new Registrar for the African Court of Justice and Human and Peoples' Rights.
2. The staff of the African Court on Human and Peoples' Rights shall be absorbed into the Registry of the African Court of Justice and Human and Peoples' Rights, for the remainder of their subsisting contracts of employment.

Chapter III Final Provisions

Article 8
Nomenclature

In the Protocol and the Statute wherever it occurs "African Court of Justice and Human Rights" is deleted and replaced with "African Court of Justice and Human and Peoples' Rights."

Article 9
Signature, Ratification and Accession

1. This Protocol and the Statute annexed to it shall be open for signature, ratification or accession by Member States, in accordance with their respective constitutional procedures.
2. The instruments of ratification or accession to this Protocol and the Statute annexed to it shall be deposited with the Chairperson of the Commission.
3. Any Member State may, at the time of signature or when depositing its instrument of ratification or accession, or at any time thereafter, make a declaration accepting the competence of the Court to receive cases under Article 30 (f).

Article 10
Depository Authority

1. This Protocol and the Statute annexed to it, drawn up in four (4) original texts in the Arabic, English, French and Portuguese languages, all four (4) texts being equally authentic, shall be deposited with the Chairperson of the Commission, who shall transmit a certified true copy to the Government of each Member State.
2. The Chairperson of the Commission, shall notify all Member States of the dates of deposit of the instruments of ratification or accession, and shall, upon the entry into force of this Protocol, register the same with the Secretariat of the United Nations.

Article 11
Entry into force

1. This Protocol and the Statute annexed to it shall enter into force thirty (30) days after the deposit of instruments of ratification by fifteen (15) Member States.
2. For each Member State which shall accede to it subsequently, this Protocol and Annexed Statute shall enter into force on the date on which the instruments of ratification or accession are deposited.
3. The Chairperson of the Commission shall notify all Member States of the entry into force of this Protocol.

Article 12
Amendments

1. This Protocol and the Statute annexed to it may be amended if a State Party to the Protocol makes a written request to that effect to the Chairperson of the Commission. The Assembly may adopt, by simple majority, the draft amendment after all the States parties to the present Protocol have been duly informed of it and the Court has given its opinion on the amendment.

2. The Court shall also be entitled to propose such amendments to the present Protocol or the Statute annexed to it as it may deem necessary, through the Chairperson of the Commission.

3. The amendments shall come into force for each State Party which has accepted it thirty (30) days after the Chairperson of the Commission has received notice of the acceptance.

ADOPTED BY THE TWENTY-THIRD ORDINARY SESSION OF THE ASSEMBLY, HELD IN MALABO, EQUATORIAL GUINEA

27TH JUNE 2014
ANNEX:
(omitted).

69

Pretoria Declaration on Economic, Social and Cultural Rights in Africa, 2004

Note: Adopted by the African Commission on Human and Peoples' Rights, 17 September 2004.

PREAMBLE

Recalling that the African Charter enshrines economic, social and cultural rights, in particular in its article 14, article 15, article 16, article 17, article 18, article 21 and article 22;

Recognising the existence of regional and international human rights standards that stress the indivisibility, interdependence and universality of all human rights. Among these are the African Charter, the African Charter on the Rights and Welfare of the Child, the Protocol to the African Charter on Human and Peoples' Rights on the Rights of Women in Africa, the Universal Declaration of Human Rights, the Declaration on the Right to Development, the International Covenant on Economic, Social and Cultural Rights and the Convention for the Elimination of All Forms of Discrimination Against Women;

Recognising also that the objectives and principles of the Constitutive Act include a commitment to the promotion and protection human and peoples' rights, respect for democratic principles, human rights, the rule of law and good governance and the promotion of social justice to ensure balanced economic development;

Noting that despite the consensus on the indivisibility of human rights, economic, social and cultural rights remain marginalised in their implementation;

Concerned that there is resistance to recognising economic, social and cultural rights that results in the continued marginalisation of these rights, which excludes the majority of Africans from the enjoyment of human rights;

Appreciating the positive impact that information and communication technologies (ICTs) can have on the promotion, protection and realisation of economic, social and cultural rights;

Recognising that there are several constraints that preclude the full realisation of economic, social and cultural rights in Africa;

Deeply disturbed by the ongoing and longstanding conflicts in the regions of Africa, which impede the realisation of economic, social and cultural rights;

Adopted at a seminar in Pretoria, South Africa in September 2004 at which representatives of the Commission, 12 African states, national human rights institutions and NGOs participated. The Declaration was adopted by the Commission at its 36th session in December 2004.

Concerned further by the lack of human security in Africa due to the prevailing conditions of poverty and under-development and the failure to address poverty through development;

Further recognising the urgent need for human rights, judicial and administrative institutions in Africa to promote human dignity based on equality and to tackle the core human rights issues facing Africans including, food security, sustainable livelihoods, human survival and the prevention of violence;

The participants state that:

1. States parties to the African Charter on Human and Peoples' Rights have solemnly undertaken to respect, protect, promote and fulfil all the rights in the Charter including economic, social and cultural rights.
2. By doing so, states parties have agreed to adopt legislative and other measures, individually or through international co-operation and assistance, to give full effect to the economic, social and cultural rights contained in the African Charter, by using the maximum of their resources. States parties have an obligation to ensure the satisfaction of, at the very least, the minimum essential levels of each of the economic, social and cultural rights contained in the African Charter.
3. States are therefore called upon to address with all appropriate measures their obligations in relation to the full realisation of economic, social and cultural rights as well as tackling the following constraints:
   a. Lack of good governance and planning and failure to allocate sufficient resources for implementation of economic, social and cultural rights;
   b. Lack of political will;
   c. Corruption, misuse and misdirection of financial resources;
   d. Poor utilisation of human resources and absence of effective measures to curtail brain drain;
   e. Failure to ensure equitable distribution of income from natural resources;
   f. Trafficking in women and children;
   g. Continued outflow and existence of refugees and internally displaced persons;
   h. Illiteracy and lack of awareness,
   i. Conditionality of aid and unserviceable debt burdens,
   j. Privatisation of essential services
   k. Cost recovery including access fees and charges for essential services;
   l. Lack of support for and recognition of the work of civil society organisations;
   m. Lack of implementation of obligations assumed under international law into national law,
   n. Under development of social amenities;
   o. Limited engagement with human rights on the part of some judges;
   p. Lack of protection of African indigenous knowledge;
   q. Failure to enforce some judicial decisions against the state;
   r. The adverse effects of globalisation.

4. States parties have also undertaken to eliminate all forms of discrimination, including all forms of discrimination against women, and to promote the equal enjoyment of all human rights. Non-discrimination and equal treatment are the key components of economic, social and cultural rights since vulnerable and marginal groups including refugees and internally displaced persons are disproportionately affected by a failure of the state to respect, protect and fulfill these rights.

5. The right to property in article 14 of the Charter relating to land and housing entails among other things the following:

   a. Protection from arbitrary deprivation of property;
   b. Equitable and non-discriminatory access, acquisition, ownership, inheritance and control of land and housing, especially by women;
   c. Adequate compensation for public acquisition, nationalisation or expropriation;
   d. Equitable and non-discriminatory access to affordable loans for the acquisition of property;
   e. Equitable redistribution of land through due process of law to redress historical and gender injustices;
   f. Recognition and protection of lands belonging to indigenous communities;
   g. Peaceful enjoyment of property and protection from arbitrary eviction;
   h. Equal access to housing and to acceptable living conditions in a healthy environment.

6. The right to work in article 15 of the Charter entails among other things the following:

   a. Equality of opportunity of access to gainful work, including access for refugees, disabled and other disadvantaged persons;
   b. Conducive investment environment for the private sector to participate in creating gainful work;
   c. Effective and enhanced protections for women in the workplace including parental leave;
   d. Fair remuneration, a minimum living wage for labour, and equal remuneration for work of equal value;
   e. Equitable and satisfactory conditions of work, including effective and accessible remedies for work place-related injuries, hazards and accidents;
   f. Creation of enabling conditions and taking measures to promote the rights and opportunities of those in the informal sector, including in subsistence agriculture and in small scale enterprises activities;
   g. Promotion and protection of equitable and satisfactory conditions of work of women engaged in household labour;
   h. The right to freedom of association, including the rights to collective bargaining, strike and other related trade union rights;
   i. Prohibition against forced labour and economic exploitation of children, and other vulnerable persons;
   j. The right to rest and leisure, including reasonable limitation of working hours, periodic holidays with pay and remuneration for public holidays.

7. The right to health in article 16 of the Charter entails among other things the following:

   a. Availability of accessible and affordable health facilities, goods and services of reasonable quality for all;

b. Access to the minimum essential food which is nutritionally adequate and safe to ensure freedom from hunger to everyone and to prevent malnutrition;

c. Access to basic shelter, housing and sanitation and adequate supply of safe and potable water;

d. Access to reproductive, maternal and child health care based on the life cycle approach to health;

e. Immunisation against major infectious diseases;

f. Education, prevention and treatment of HIV/AIDS, malaria, tuberculosis and other major killer diseases;

g. Education and access to information concerning the main health problems in the community including methods of preventing and controlling them;

h. Training for health personnel including education on health and human rights;

i. Access to humane and dignified care of the elderly and for persons with mental and physical disabilities;

8. The right to education in article 17 of the African Charter entails among other things the following:

a. Provision of free and compulsory basic education that will also include a programme in psycho-social education for orphans and vulnerable children;

b. Provision of special schools and facilities for physically and mentally disabled children;

c. Access to affordable secondary and higher education;

d. Accessible and affordable vocational training and adult education;

e. Addressing social, economic and cultural practices and attitudes that hinder access to education by girl children;

f. Availability of educational institutions that are physically and economically accessible to everyone;

g. Development of curricula that address diverse social, economic and cultural settings and which inculcate human rights norms and values for responsible citizens;

h. Liberty of parents and guardians to choose for their children schools, other than those established by the public authorities, which conform to such minimum educational standards as may be laid down by the state, and to ensure the religious and moral education of their children in conformity with their own convictions;

i. Continued education for teachers and instructors including education on human rights and the continuous improvement of the conditions of work of teaching staff;

j. Education for development that links school curricula to the labour market and society's demands for technology and self-reliance.

9. The right to culture in articles 17 and 18 of the African Charter entail among other things the following:

a. Positive African values consistent with international human rights realities and standards;

b. Eradication of harmful traditional practices that negatively affect human rights;

c. Participation at all levels in the determination of cultural policies and in cultural and artistic activities;

     d.   Measures for safeguarding, protecting and building awareness of tangible and intangible cultural heritage, including traditional knowledge systems;

     e.   Recognition and respect of the diverse cultures existing in Africa;

10. The social, economic and cultural rights explicitly provided for under the African Charter, read together with other rights in the Charter, such as the right to life and respect for inherent human dignity, imply the recognition of other economic and social rights, including the right to shelter, the right to basic nutrition and the right to social security.

11. Having highlighted the core contents of economic, social and cultural rights under the African Charter, participants make the following recommendations:

    a.   States parties should:

       i.   Ratify, if they have not done so, the treaties mentioned in the Preamble, especially the Protocol on the Rights of Women in Africa;

      ii.   Incorporate into domestic law and fully implement the provisions of regional and international treaties on economic, social and cultural rights;

     iii.   Establish constitutional protection of economic, social and cultural rights subject to non-discrimination and equality;

     iv.   Come up with National Action Plans, which set out benchmark indicators for the progressive realisation of social economic and cultural rights;

      v.   Take effective measure to ensure budgetary processes are transparent and consultative;

     vi.   Involve civil society in meaningful consultations in policymaking and in the implementation of economic, social and cultural rights generally;

    vii.   Review all national policies, which undermine the realisation of specific economic, social and cultural rights;

   viii.   Provide reports under article 62 of the Charter on how far they have gone in making economic, social and cultural rights both accessible and non-discriminatory;

     ix.   Adopt measures for the prudent use of resources, including the investigation of affordable alternatives for health drugs e.g. generic vs. patent medicines

      x.   Ensure effective citizen participation in government through credible electoral processes, liberalisation of the mass media and in the formulation of legislation and policies;

     xi.   Adopt special measures for women and address the economic, social and cultural rights of vulnerable and marginalised groups including children, indigenous peoples, displaced persons, refugees, persons living with HIV/AIDS and the disabled;

    xii.   Develop mechanisms to hold non-state actors especially multi-national corporations and businesses accountable for violations of economic, social and cultural rights in such matters relating to child labour, industrial safety standards, protection against forced evictions and low wages, protection of the environment, including global warming and its impact on ecosystems, livelihood and food security;

xiii.   Strengthen the capacity of state institutions to produce disaggregate data that would provide an accurate assessment of the implementation of economic, social and cultural rights;

xiv.   Promulgate and implement comprehensive ICT policies and programmes;

xv.   Consult with civil society organisations in the nomination and election of members of the African Commission and judges of the African Court;

xvi.   Ratify the Protocol on the African Human Rights Court and make the declaration under article 34(6) of the Protocol allowing individuals and nongovernmental organisations to file cases, if they have not done so;

xvii.   Nominate and elect judges of the African Human Rights Court so that it may be established without further delay;

xviii.   Take necessary measures to reduce military spending significantly in favour of increasing spending on the implementation of economic, social and cultural rights;

xix.   Ensure that economic, social and cultural rights take primacy in the negotiations of bilateral and multilateral trade and economic agreements;

xx.   Create independent, impartial and well-resourced national human rights institutions and if they already exist to strengthen their independence and impartiality.

b.   The African Union should:

i.   Urge member states that have not done so, to ratify the human rights treaties mentioned in the Preamble, in particular the Protocol on the Rights of Women in Africa;

ii.   Provide sufficient funds for African human rights institutions to enable them to effectively fulfil their mandate;

iii.   Establish the African Court on Human and Peoples' Rights without further delay;

iv.   Urge member states that have not done so to ratify the Protocol to the African Charter on Human and Peoples' Rights on the Establishment of the African Court on Human and Peoples' Rights, and to make the necessary declaration under article 34(6) of the Protocol;

v.   Establish the Human Rights Fund as recommended by the First AU Ministerial Conference on Human Rights held in Kigali, Rwanda, in May 2003;

vi.   Strengthen the Secretariat to enhance the functioning of the African Commission;

vii.   Urge the AU Peace and Security Council to adopt urgent measures to address the conflicts in Africa in order to create a conducive environment for the respect of economic, social and cultural rights;

viii.   Call upon the organs of the AU to encourage member states to uphold economic, social and cultural rights and to hold them accountable for violations of economic, social and cultural rights;

ix.   Integrate the monitoring of economic, social and cultural rights into the work of relevant AU institutions as well as the CSSDCA Peer Review Mechanism and New Partnership for Africa's Development (NEPAD) African Peer Review Mechanism process;

        x.   Follow up recommendations of the African Commission to ensure implementation of its decisions by member states.

    c.   The African Commission should:

        i.   Elaborate principles and guidelines on economic, social and cultural rights and establish a working group for this purpose;

        ii.   Integrate economic, social and cultural rights into the mandates of existing Special Rapporteurs and Working Groups;

        iii.   Urge states to duly submit their reports to the African Commission under article 62 of the African Charter;

        iv.   Address economic, social and cultural rights during the examination of State Reports under article 62 during questions and concluding observations;

        v.   Review its guidelines for state reporting pertaining to economic, social and cultural rights;

        vi.   Consider alternative means of examining implementation of provisions of the Charter by a state that is in perpetual default of its reporting obligations under article 62 of the Charter.

        vii.   Provide substantive recommendations to the AU Assembly on economic, social and cultural rights;

        viii.   Undertake studies and research under article 45 on specific economic, social and cultural rights;

        ix.   Pay special attention to economic, social and cultural rights during promotional visits to states;

        x.   Ensure effective dissemination of relevant decisions and resolutions of the Commission in collaboration with relevant governmental and nongovernmental national and sub-regional institutions;

        xi.   Further elaborate the economic and social rights implicit in the African Charter;

        xii.   Urge the AU to establish the African Human Rights Court without further delay and those states that have not done so, to ratify the Protocol establishing the Court and to make the necessary declaration under article 34(6) of the Protocol.

    d.   Civil Society should:

        i.   Play a more pro-active role in the nomination of and lobby for the election of candidates to the African Commission who are conversant with economic, social and cultural rights;

        ii.   Advocate for states to ratify the Protocol of the African Human Rights Court and to make the declaration allowing NGOs and individuals to file cases;

        iii.   Advocate for the African Human Rights Court to be established without further delay;

        iv.   Prioritise monitoring of economic, social and cultural rights in their advocacy work;

        v.   Play a role in raising public awareness of economic, social and cultural rights and the obstacles to fulfilment of these rights in particular harmful cultural practices;

vi.   Actively participate in the budgetary process, both in terms of formulation and analysis;

vii.   Develop partnerships with both the state and private sector, where possible, for the protection of economic, social and cultural rights;

viii.   Compile and submit to the African Commission shadow reports on economic, social and cultural rights;

ix.   Improve networking amongst NGOs and their support activities of the African Commission and its Special Rapporteurs and Working Groups;

x.   Bring more cases on economic, social and cultural rights to the African Commission, the African Committee on the Rights and Welfare of the Child, national courts, and the African Human Rights Court, when it is established;

xi.   Become involved in specific projects in the implementation of economic, social and cultural rights especially in the rural areas;

xii.   Advocate for comprehensive national and regional ICT policies and programmes, and to incorporate ICT training, provision and access in their work plans.

e.   National Human Rights Institutions should:

i.   Undertake studies, monitor and report on economic, social and cultural rights;

ii.   Scrutinise existing laws and administrative acts and make submissions to Parliament on bills relating to economic, social and cultural rights;

iii.   Publish and distribute their reports on economic, social and cultural rights;

iv.   Establish regional networks/coalitions and involve NGOs in these coalitions;

v.   Apply for affiliate status with the African Commission, if they have not done so;

vi.   Raise awareness on economic, social and cultural rights among particular groups such as the public service, the judiciary, the private sector and the labour movement and encourage the Government to integrate human rights in the school curricula;

vii.   Examine complaints of infringements of economic, social and cultural rights and make recommendations on redress, and where possible file cases before national courts;

viii.   Conduct follow up activities in the implementation of recommendations of international treaty bodies and publicise their reports, especially on economic, social and cultural rights;

ix.   Advocate for states to ratify the Protocol of the African Human Rights Court and to make the declaration allowing NGOs and individuals to file cases;

x.   Advocate for the African Human Rights Court to be established without further delay;

f.   International and regional entities should:

i.   Pay particular attention to African needs related to development and the realisation of economic, social and cultural rights;

    ii.   Cancel the unserviceable debt burdens of African states;

    iii.   Ensure that bilateral and multilateral trade and economic agreements conform to international treaty obligations relating to economic, social and cultural rights;

    iv.   Play a role in the implementation of economic, social and cultural rights including through assistance and co-operation with African states;

    v.   Take measures to regulate trade in extractive industries (such as oil, mining) that are exploitative, corrupt and fuel conflicts in Africa;

    vi.   Co-operate with African countries in their efforts to repatriate money and cultural artefacts that have been unlawfully removed from African countries;

    vii.   Ensure compliance with the principles of corporate social responsibility.

12. In conclusion, the African Union, its member states, international and national organisations and non-state actors should fully recognise human rights as a fundamental objective of development and that development has to achieve the full realisation of all human rights. Economic, social and cultural rights should therefore be integrated into development planning and implementation so that African needs and aspirations are fully addressed.

70

OAU Convention Governing the Specific Aspects of Refugee Problems in Africa, 1969

Note: OAU Convention Governing the Specific Aspects of Refugee Problems in Africa. Adopted 10 September 1969, Addis Ababa, Ethiopia, 1001 UNTS 45. Entry into force: 20 June 1974.

PREAMBLE

We, the Heads of State and Government assembled in the city of Addis Ababa, from 6–10 September 1969,

NOTING with concern the constantly increasing numbers of refugees in Africa and desirous of finding ways and means of alleviating their misery and suffering as well as providing them with a better life and future,

RECOGNIZING the need for and essentially humanitarian approach towards solving the problems of refugees,

AWARE, however, that refugee problems are a source of friction among many Member States, and desirous of eliminating the source of such discord,

ANXIOUS to make a distinction between a refugee who seeks a peaceful and normal life and a person fleeing his country for the sole purpose of fomenting subversion from outside,

DETERMINED that the activities of such subversive elements should be discouraged, in accordance with the Declaration on the Problem of Subversion and Resolution on the Problem of Refugees adopted at Accra in 1965,

BEARING IN MIND that the Charter of the United Nations and the Universal Declaration of Human Rights have affirmed the principle that human beings shall enjoy fundamental rights and freedoms without discrimination,

RECALLING Resolution 2312 (XXII) of 14 December 1967 of the United Nations General Assembly, relating to the Declaration on Territorial Asylum,

CONVINCED that all the problems of our continent must be solved in the spirit of the Charter of the Organization of African Unity and in the African context,

RECOGNIZING that the United Nations Convention of 28 July 1951, as modified by the Protocol of 31 January 1967, constitutes the basic and universal instrument relating to the status of refugees and reflects the deep concern of States for refugees and their desire to establish common standards for their treatment,

RECALLING Resolutions 26 and 104 of the OAU Assemblies of Heads of State and Government, calling upon Member States of the Organization who had not already done so to accede to the United Nations Convention of 1951 and to the Protocol of 1967 relating to the Status of Refugees, and meanwhile to apply their provisions to refugees in Africa,

CONVINCED that the efficiency of the measures recommended by the present Convention to solve the problem of refugees in Africa necessitates close and continuous collaboration between the Organization of African Unity and the Office of the United Nations High Commissioner for Refugees,

HAVE AGREED as follows:

Article I
Definition of the term "Refugee"

1. For the purposes of this Convention, the term "refugee" shall mean every person who, owing to well-founded fear of being persecuted for reasons of race, religion, nationality, membership of a particular social group or political opinion, is outside the country of his nationality and is unable or, owing to such fear, is unwilling to avail himself of the protection of that country, or who, not having a nationality and being outside the country of his former habitual residence as a result of such events is unable or, owing to such fear, is unwilling to return to it.

2. The term "refugee" shall also apply to every person who, owing to external aggression, occupation, foreign domination or events seriously disturbing public order in either part or the whole of his country of origin or nationality, is compelled to leave his place of habitual residence in order to seek refuge in another place outside his country of origin or nationality.

3. In the case of a person who has several nationalities, the term "a country of which he is a national" shall mean each of the countries of which he is a national, and a person shall not be deemed to be lacking the protection of the country of which he is a national if, without any valid reason based on well-founded fear, he has not availed himself of the protection of one of the countries of which he is a national.

4. This Convention shall cease to apply to any refugee if:
   (a) he has voluntarily re-availed himself of the protection of the country of his nationality, or,
   (b) having lost his nationality, he has voluntarily reacquired it, or,
   (c) he has acquired a new nationality, and enjoys the protection of the country of his new nationality, or,
   (d) he has voluntarily re-established himself in the country which he left or outside which he remained owing to fear of persecution, or,

(e) he can no longer, because the circumstances in connection with which he was recognized as a refugee have ceased to exist, continue to refuse to avail himself of the protection of the country of his nationality, or,

(f) he has committed a serious non-political crime outside his country of refuge after his admission to that country as a refugee, or,

(g) he has seriously infringed the purposes and objectives of this Convention.

5. The provisions of this Convention shall not apply to any person with respect to whom the country of asylum has serious reasons for considering that:

(a) he has committed a crime against peace, a war crime, or a crime against humanity, as defined in the international instruments drawn up to make provision in respect of such crimes;

(b) he committed a serious non-political crime outside the country of refuge prior to his admission to that country as a refugee;

(c) he has been guilty of acts contrary to the purposes and principles of the Organization of African Unity;

(d) he has been guilty of acts contrary to the purposes and principles of the United Nations.

6. For the purposes of this Convention, the Contracting State of Asylum shall determine whether an applicant is a refugee.

Article II
Asylum

1. Member States of the OAU shall use their best endeavours consistent with their respective legislations to receive refugees and to secure the settlement of those refugees who, for well-founded reasons, are unable or unwilling to return to their country of origin or nationality.

2. The grant of asylum to refugees is a peaceful and humanitarian act and shall not be regarded as an unfriendly act by any Member State.

3. No person shall be subjected by a Member State to measures such as rejection at the frontier, return or expulsion, which would compel him to return to or remain in a territory where his life, physical integrity or liberty would be threatened for the reasons set out in Article I, paragraphs 1 and 2.

4. Where a Member State finds difficulty in continuing to grant asylum to refugees, such Member State may appeal directly to other Member States and through the OAU, and such other Member States shall in the spirit of African solidarity and international co-operation take appropriate measures to lighten the burden of the Member State granting asylum.

5. Where a refugee has not received the right to reside in any country of asylum, he may be granted temporary residence in any country of asylum in which he first presented himself as a refugee pending arrangement for his resettlement in accordance with the preceding paragraph.

6. For reasons of security, countries of asylum shall, as far as possible, settle refugees at a reasonable distance from the frontier of their country of origin.

Article III
Prohibition of Subversive Activities

1. Every refugee has duties to the country in which he finds himself, which require in particular that he conforms with its laws and regulations as well as with measures taken for the maintenance of public order. He shall also abstain from any subversive activities against any Member State of the OAU.
2. Signatory States undertake to prohibit refugees residing in their respective territories from attacking any State Member of the OAU, by any activity likely to cause tension between Member States, and in particular by use of arms, through the press, or by radio.

Article IV
Non-Discrimination

Member States undertake to apply the provisions of this Convention to all refugees without discrimination as to race, religion, nationality, membership of a particular social group or political opinions.

Article V
Voluntary Repatriation

1. The essentially voluntary character of repatriation shall be respected in all cases and no refugee shall be repatriated against his will.
2. The country of asylum, in collaboration with the country of origin, shall make adequate arrangements for the safe return of refugees who request repatriation.
3. The country of origin, on receiving back refugees, shall facilitate their resettlement and grant them the full rights and privileges of nationals of the country, and subject them to the same obligations.
4. Refugees who voluntarily return to their country shall in no way be penalized for having left it for any of the reasons giving rise to refugee situations. Whenever necessary, an appeal shall be made through national information media and through the Administrative Secretary-General of the OAU, inviting refugees to return home and giving assurance that the new circumstances prevailing in their country of origin will enable them to return without risk and to take up a normal and peaceful life without fear of being disturbed or punished, and that the text of such appeal should be given to refugees and clearly explained to them by their country of asylum.
5. Refugees who freely decide to return to their homeland, as a result of such assurances or on their own initiative, shall be given every possible assistance by the country of asylum, the country of origin, voluntary agencies and international and intergovernmental organizations, to facilitate their return.

Article VI
Travel Documents

1. Subject to Article III, Member States shall issue to refugees lawfully staying in their territories travel documents in accordance with the United Nations Convention relating to the Status of Refugees and the Schedule and Annex thereto, for the purpose of

travel outside their territory, unless compelling reasons of national security or public order otherwise require. Member States may issue such a travel document to any other refugee in their territory.

2. Where an African country of second asylum accepts a refugee from a country of first asylum, the country of first asylum may be dispensed from issuing a document with a return clause.

3. Travel documents issued to refugees under previous international agreements by States Parties thereto shall be recognized and treated by Member States in the same way as if they had been issued to refugees pursuant to this Article.

Article VII
Co-operation of the National Authorities with the Organization of African Unity

In order to enable the Administrative Secretary-General of the Organization of African Unity to make reports to the competent organs of the Organization of African Unity, Member States undertake to provide the Secretariat in the appropriate form with information and statistical data requested concerning:

(a) the condition of refugees,

(b) the implementation of this Convention, and

(c) laws, regulations and decrees which are, or may hereafter be, in force relating to refugees.

Article VIII
Cooperation with the Office of the United Nations High Commissioner for Refugees

1. Member States shall co-operate with the Office of the United Nations High Commissioner for Refugees.

2. The present Convention shall be the effective regional complement in Africa of the 1951 United Nations Convention on the Status of Refugees.

Article IX
Settlement of Disputes

Any dispute between States signatories to this Convention relating to its interpretation or application, which cannot be settled by other means, shall be referred to the Commission for Mediation, Conciliation and Arbitration of the Organization of African Unity, at the request of any one of the Parties to the dispute.

Article X
Signature and Ratification

1. This Convention is open for signature and accession by all Member States of the Organization of African Unity and shall be ratified by signatory States in accordance with their respective constitutional processes. The instruments of ratification shall be deposited with the Administrative Secretary-General of the Organization of African Unity.

2. The original instrument, done if possible in African languages, and in English and French, all texts being equally authentic, shall be deposited with the Administrative Secretary-General of the Organization of African Unity.

3. Any independent African State, Member of the Organization of African Unity, may at any time notify the Administrative Secretary-General of the Organization of African Unity of its accession to this Convention.

Article XI
Entry into force
This Convention shall come into force upon deposit of instruments of ratification by one-third of the Member States of the Organization of African Unity.

Article XII
Amendment
This Convention may be amended or revised if any member State makes a written request to the Administrative Secretary-General to that effect, provided however that the proposed amendment shall not be submitted to the Assembly of Heads of State and Government for consideration until all Member States have been duly notified of it and a period of one year has elapsed. Such an amendment shall not be effective unless approved by at least two-thirds of the Member States Parties to the present Convention.

Article XIII
Denunciation
1. Any Member State Party to this Convention may denounce its provisions by a written notification to the Administrative Secretary-General.

2. At the end of one year from the date of such notification, if not withdrawn, the Convention shall cease to apply with respect to the denouncing State.

Article XIV
Upon entry into force of this Convention, the Administrative Secretary-General of the OAU shall register it with the Secretary-General of the United Nations, in accordance with Article 102 of the Charter of the United Nations.

Article XV
Notifications by the Administrative Secretary-General of the Organization of African Unity
The Administrative Secretary-General of the Organization of African Unity shall inform all Members of the Organization:

    (a) of signatures, ratifications and accessions in accordance with Article X;

(b) of entry into force, in accordance with Article XI;

(c) of requests for amendments submitted under the terms of Article XII;

(d) of denunciations, in accordance with Article XIII.

IN WITNESS WHEREOF WE, the Heads of African State and Government, have signed this Convention.

DONE in the City of Addis Ababa this 10th day of September 1969

71

African Union Convention for the Protection and Assistance of Internally Displaced Persons in Africa (Kampala Convention), 2009

Note: African Union Convention for the Protection and Assistance of Internally Displaced Persons in Africa (Kampala Convention). Adopted 23 October 2009, Kampala, Uganda. Entry into force: 6 December 2012.

PREAMBLE

We, the Heads of State and Government of the Member States of the African Union;

CONSCIOUS of the gravity of the situation of internally displaced persons as a source of continuing instability and tension for African states;

ALSO CONSCIOUS of the suffering and specific vulnerability of internally displaced persons; REITERATING the inherent African custom and tradition of hospitality by local host communities for persons in distress and support for such communities;

COMMITTED to sharing our common vision of providing durable solutions to situations of internally displaced persons by establishing an appropriate legal framework for their protection and assistance;

DETERMINED to adopt measures aimed at preventing and putting an end to the phenomenon of internal displacement by eradicating the root causes, especially persistent and recurrent conflicts as well as addressing displacement caused by natural disasters, which have a devastating impact on human life, peace, stability, security, and development;

CONSIDERING the 2000 Constitutive Act of the African Union and the 1945 Charter of the United Nations;

REAFFIRMING the principle of the respect of the sovereign equality of States Parties, their territorial integrity and political independence as stipulated in the Constitutive Act of the African Union and the United Nations Charter;

RECALLING the 1948 Universal Declaration of Human Rights, the 1948 Convention on the Prevention and Punishment of the Crime of Genocide, the 1949 Four Geneva Conventions and the 1977 Additional Protocols to the Geneva Conventions, the 1951 United Nations Convention Relating to the Status of Refugees and the 1967 Protocol Relating to the Status of Refugees, the 1969 OAU Convention Governing the Specific Aspects of Refugee Problems in Africa, the 1979 Convention on the Elimination of All Forms of Discrimination Against Women, the 1981 African Charter on Human and

Peoples' Rights and the 2003 Protocol to the African Charter on Human and Peoples' Rights on the Rights of Women in Africa, the 1990 African Charter on the Rights and Welfare of the Child, the 1994 Addis Ababa Document on Refugees and Forced Population Displacement in Africa, and other relevant United Nations and African Union human rights instruments, and relevant Security Council Resolutions;

MINDFUL that Member States of the African Union have adopted democratic practices and adhere to the principles of non-discrimination, equality and equal protection of the law under the 1981 African Charter on Human and Peoples' Rights, as well as under other regional and international human rights law instruments;

RECOGNISING the inherent rights of internally displaced persons as provided for and protected in international human rights and humanitarian law and as set out in the 1998 United Nations Guiding Principles on Internal Displacement, which are recognized as an important international framework for the protection of internally displaced persons;

AFFIRMING our primary responsibility and commitment to respect, protect and fulfill the rights to which internally displaced persons are entitled, without discrimination of any kind;

NOTING the specific roles of international Organizations and agencies within the framework of the United Nations inter-agency collaborative approach to internally displaced persons, especially the protection expertise of the Office of the United Nations High Commissioner for Refugees (UNHCR) and the invitation extended to it by the Executive Council of the African Union in Decision EX/CL.413 (XIII) of July 2008 at Sharm El Sheikh, Egypt, to continue and reinforce its role in the protection of and assistance to internally displaced persons, within the United Nations coordination mechanism; and noting also the mandate of the International Committee of the Red Cross to protect and assist persons affected by armed conflict and other situations of violence, as well as the work of civil society organizations, in conformity with the laws of the country in which they exercise such roles and mandates;

RECALLING the lack of a binding African and international legal and institutional framework specifically, for the prevention of internal displacement and the protection of and assistance to internally displaced persons;

REAFFIRMING the historical commitment of the AU Member States to the protection of and assistance to refugees and displaced persons and, in particular, the implementation of Executive Council Decisions EX.CL/Dec.129 (V) and EX.CL/127 (V) of July 2004 in Addis Ababa, to the effect that the specific needs of internally displaced persons (IDPs) such as protection and assistance should be addressed through a separate legal instrument, and to collaborate with relevant cooperating partners and other stakeholders to ensure that internally displaced persons are provided with an appropriate legal framework to ensure their adequate protection and assistance as well as with durable solutions, respectively;

CONVINCED that the present Convention for the Protection and Assistance of Internally Displaced Persons presents such a legal framework;

HAVE AGREED AS FOLLOWS:

Article 1
Definitions

For the purpose of the present Convention:

a. "African Charter" means the African Charter on Human and Peoples' Rights;

b. "African Commission" means the African Commission on Human and Peoples' Rights;

c. "African Court of Justice and Human Rights" means the African Court of Justice and Human Rights;

d. Arbitrary displacement means arbitrary displacement as referred to in Article 4 (4) (a) to (h);

e. "Armed Groups" means dissident armed forces or other organized armed groups that are distinct from the armed forces of the state;

f. "AU" means the African Union;

g. "AU Commission" means the Secretariat of the African Union, which is the depository of the regional instruments;

h. "Child" means every human being below the age of 18 years;

i. "Constitutive Act" means the Constitutive Act of the African Union;

j. "Harmful Practices" means all behaviour, attitudes and/or practices which negatively affect the fundamental rights of persons, such as but not limited to their right to life, health, dignity, education, mental and physical integrity and education;

k. "Internally Displaced Persons" means persons or groups of persons who have been forced or obliged to flee or to leave their homes or places of habitual residence, in particular as a result of or in order to avoid the effects of armed conflict, situations of generalized violence, violations of human rights or natural or human-made disasters, and who have not crossed an internationally recognized State border;

l. "Internal displacement" means the involuntary or forced movement, evacuation or relocation of persons or groups of persons within internationally recognized state borders;

m. "Member State" means a Member State of the African Union;

n. "Non-state actors" means private actors who are not public officials of the State, including other armed groups not referred to in article 1(d) above, and whose acts cannot be officially attributed to the State;

o. "OAU" means the Organization of African Unity;

p. "Women" mean persons of the female gender, including girls;

q. "Sphere standards" mean standards for monitoring and evaluating the effectiveness and impact of humanitarian assistance; and

r. "States Parties" means African States which have ratified or acceded to this Convention.

Article 2
Objectives

The objectives of this Convention are to:

a. Promote and strengthen regional and national measures to prevent or mitigate, prohibit and eliminate root causes of internal displacement as well as provide for durable solutions;

b. Establish a legal framework for preventing internal displacement, and protecting and assisting internally displaced persons in Africa;

c. Establish a legal framework for solidarity, cooperation, promotion of durable solutions and mutual support between the States Parties in order to combat displacement and address its consequences;

d. Provide for the obligations and responsibilities of States Parties, with respect to the prevention of internal displacement and protection of, and assistance, to internally displaced persons;

e. Provide for the respective obligations, responsibilities and roles of armed groups, non-state actors and other relevant actors, including civil society organizations, with respect to the prevention of internal displacement and protection of, and assistance to, internally displaced persons;

Article 3
General Obligations Relating to States Parties

1. States Parties undertake to respect and ensure respect for the present Convention. In particular, States Parties shall:

a. Refrain from, prohibit and prevent arbitrary displacement of populations;

b. Prevent political, social, cultural and economic exclusion and marginalisation, that are likely to cause displacement of populations or persons by virtue of their social identity, religion or political opinion;

c. Respect and ensure respect for the principles of humanity and human dignity of internally displaced persons;

d. Respect and ensure respect and protection of the human rights of internally displaced persons, including humane treatment, non-discrimination, equality and equal protection of law;

e. Respect and ensure respect for international humanitarian law regarding the protection of internally displaced persons;

f. Respect and ensure respect for the humanitarian and civilian character of the protection of and assistance to internally displaced persons, including ensuring that such persons do not engage in subversive activities;

g. Ensure individual responsibility for acts of arbitrary displacement, in accordance with applicable domestic and international criminal law;

h. Ensure the accountability of non-State actors concerned, including multinational companies and private military or security companies, for acts of arbitrary displacement or complicity in such acts;

i. Ensure the accountability of non-State actors involved in the exploration and exploitation of economic and natural resources leading to displacement;

j. Ensure assistance to internally displaced persons by meeting their basic needs as well as allowing and facilitating rapid and unimpeded access by humanitarian organizations and personnel;

k. Promote self-reliance and sustainable livelihoods amongst internally displaced persons, provided that such measures shall not be used as a basis for neglecting the protection of and assistance to internally displaced persons, without prejudice to other means of assistance;

2. States Parties shall:
   a. Incorporate their obligations under this Convention into domestic law by enacting or amending relevant legislation on the protection of, and assistance to, internally displaced persons in conformity with their obligations under international law;
   b. Designate an authority or body, where needed, responsible for coordinating activities aimed at protecting and assisting internally displaced persons and assign responsibilities to appropriate organs for protection and assistance, and for cooperating with relevant international organizations or agencies, and civil society organizations, where no such authority or body exists;
   c. Adopt other measures as appropriate, including strategies and policies on internal displacement at national and local levels, taking into account the needs of host communities;
   d. Provide, to the extent possible, the necessary funds for protection and assistance without prejudice to receiving international support;
   e. Endeavour to incorporate the relevant principles contained in this Convention into peace negotiations and agreements for the purpose of finding sustainable solutions to the problem of internal displacement.

Article 4
Obligations of States Parties relating to Protection from Internal Displacement

1. States Parties shall respect and ensure respect for their obligations under international law, including human rights and humanitarian law, so as to prevent and avoid conditions that might lead to the arbitrary displacement of persons;
2. States Parties shall devise early warning systems, in the context of the continental early warning system, in areas of potential displacement, establish and implement disaster risk reduction strategies, emergency and disaster preparedness and management measures and, where necessary, provide immediate protection and assistance to internally displaced persons;
3. States Parties may seek the cooperation of international organizations or humanitarian agencies, civil society organizations and other relevant actors;
4. All persons have a right to be protected against arbitrary displacement. The prohibited categories of arbitrary displacement include but are not limited to:
   a. Displacement based on policies of racial discrimination or other similar practices aimed at/or resulting in altering the ethnic, religious or racial composition of the population;
   b. Individual or mass displacement of civilians in situations of armed conflict, unless the security of the civilians involved or imperative military reasons so demand, in accordance with international humanitarian law;
   c. Displacement intentionally used as a method of warfare or due to other violations of international humanitarian law in situations of armed conflict;
   d. Displacement caused by generalized violence or violations of human rights;
   e. Displacement as a result of harmful practices;
   f. Forced evacuations in cases of natural or human made disasters or other causes if the evacuations are not required by the safety and health of those affected;

g. Displacement used as a collective punishment;

h. Displacement caused by any act, event, factor, or phenomenon of compara-ble gravity to all of the above and which is not justified under international law, including human rights and international humanitarian law.

5. States Parties shall endeavour to protect communities with special attachment to, and dependency, on land due to their particular culture and spiritual values from being displaced from such lands, except for compelling and overriding public interests;

6. States Parties shall declare as offences punishable by law acts of arbitrary displacement that amount to genocide, war crimes or crimes against humanity.

Article 5
Obligations of States Parties relating to Protection and Assistance

1. States Parties shall bear the primary duty and responsibility for providing protection of and humanitarian assistance to internally displaced persons within their territory or jurisdiction without discrimination of any kind.

2. States Parties shall cooperate with each other upon the request of the concerned State Party or the Conference of State Parties in protecting and assisting internally displaced persons.

3. States Parties shall respect the mandates of the African Union and the United Nations, as well as the roles of international humanitarian organizations in providing protec-tion and assistance to internally displaced persons, in accordance with international law.

4. States Parties shall take measures to protect and assist persons who have been inter-nally displaced due to natural or human made disasters, including climate change.

5. States Parties shall assess or facilitate the assessment of the needs and vulnerabilities of internally displaced persons and of host communities, in cooperation with interna-tional organizations or agencies.

6. States Parties shall provide sufficient protection and assistance to internally displaced persons, and where available resources are inadequate to enable them to do so, they shall cooperate in seeking the assistance of international organizations and humani-tarian agencies, civil society organizations and other relevant actors. Such organiza-tions may offer their services to all those in need.

7. States Parties shall take necessary steps to effectively organize, relief action that is humanitarian, and impartial in character, and guarantee security. States Parties shall allow rapid and unimpeded passage of all relief consignments, equipment and person-nel to internally displaced persons. States Parties shall also enable and facilitate the role of local and international organizations and humanitarian agencies, civil society organizations and other relevant actors, to provide protection and assistance to inter-nally displaced persons. States Parties shall have the right to prescribe the technical arrangements under which such passage is permitted.

8. States Parties shall uphold and ensure respect for the humanitarian principles of humanity, neutrality, impartiality and independence of humanitarian actors.

9. States Parties shall respect the right of internally displaced persons to peacefully request or seek protection and assistance, in accordance with relevant national and interna-tional laws, a right for which they shall not be persecuted, prosecuted or punished.

10. States Parties shall respect, protect and not attack or otherwise harm humanitarian personnel and resources or other materials deployed for the assistance or benefit of internally displaced persons.

11. States Parties shall take measures aimed at ensuring that armed groups act in conformity with their obligations under Article 7.

12. Nothing in this Article shall prejudice the principles of sovereignty and territorial integrity of states.

Article 6
Obligations Relating to International Organizations and Humanitarian Agencies

1. International organizations and humanitarian agencies shall discharge their obligations under this Convention in conformity with international law and the laws of the country in which they operate.

2. In providing protection and assistance to Internally Displaced Persons, international organizations and humanitarian agencies shall respect the rights of such persons in accordance with international law.

3. International organizations and humanitarian agencies shall be bound by the principles of humanity, neutrality, impartiality and independence of humanitarian actors, and ensure respect for relevant international standards and codes of conduct.

Article 7
Protection and Assistance to Internally Displaced Persons in Situations of Armed Conflict

1. The provisions of this Article shall not, in any way whatsoever, be construed as affording legal status or legitimizing or recognizing armed groups and are without prejudice to the individual criminal responsibility of the members of such groups under domestic or international criminal law.

2. Nothing in this Convention shall be invoked for the purpose of affecting the sovereignty of a State or the responsibility of the Government, by all legitimate means, to maintain or re-establish law and order in the State or to defend the national unity and territorial integrity of the State.

3. The protection and assistance to internally displaced persons under this Article shall be governed by international law and in particular international humanitarian law.

4. Members of Armed groups shall be held criminally responsible for their acts which violate the rights of internally displaced persons under international law and national law.

5. Members of armed groups shall be prohibited from:
   a. Carrying out arbitrary displacement;
   b. Hampering the provision of protection and assistance to internally displaced persons under any circumstances;
   c. Denying internally displaced persons the right to live in satisfactory conditions of dignity, security, sanitation, food, water, health and shelter; and separating members of the same family;

d.   Restricting the freedom of movement of internally displaced persons within and outside their areas of residence;

e.   Recruiting children or requiring or permitting them to take part in hostilities under any circumstances;

f.   Forcibly recruiting persons, kidnapping, abduction or hostage taking, engaging in sexual slavery and trafficking in persons especially women and children;

g.   Impeding humanitarian assistance and passage of all relief consignments, equipment and personnel to internally displaced persons;

h.   Attacking or otherwise harming humanitarian personnel and resources or other materials deployed for the assistance or benefit of internally displaced persons and shall not destroy, confiscate or divert such materials; and

i.   Violating the civilian and humanitarian character of the places where internally displaced persons are sheltered and shall not infiltrate such places.

Article 8
Obligations relating to the African Union

1. The African Union shall have the right to intervene in a Member State pursuant to a decision of the Assembly in accordance with Article 4(h) of the Constitutive Act in respect of grave circumstances, namely: war crimes, genocide, and crimes against humanity;

2. The African Union shall respect the right of States Parties to request intervention from the Union in order to restore peace and security in accordance with Article 4(j) of the Constitutive Act and thus contribute to the creation of favourable conditions for finding durable solutions to the problem of internal displacement;

3. The African Union shall support the efforts of the States Parties to protect and assist internally displaced persons under this Convention. In particular, the Union shall:

   a.   Strengthen the institutional framework and capacity of the African Union with respect to protection and assistance to internally displaced persons;

   b.   Coordinate the mobilisation of resources for protection and assistance to internally displaced persons;

   c.   Collaborate with international organizations and humanitarian agencies, civil society organizations and other relevant actors in accordance with their mandates, to support measures taken by States Parties to protect and assist internally displaced persons.

   d.   Cooperate directly with African States and international organizations and humanitarian agencies, civil society organizations and other relevant actors, with respect to appropriate measures to be taken in relation to the protection of and assistance to internally displaced persons;

   e.   Share information with the African Commission on Human and Peoples' Rights on the situation of displacement, and the protection and assistance accorded to internally displaced persons in Africa; and

   f.   Cooperate with the Special Rapporteur of the African Commission on Human and Peoples' Rights for Refugees, Returnees, IDPs and Asylum Seekers in addressing issues of internally displaced persons.

Article 9

Obligations of States Parties Relating to Protection and Assistance during Internal Displacement

1. States Parties shall protect the rights of internally displaced persons regardless of the cause of displacement by refraining from, and preventing, the following acts, amongst others:

   a. Discrimination against such persons in the enjoyment of any rights or freedoms on the grounds that they are internally displaced persons;

   b. Genocide, crimes against humanity, war crimes and other violations of international humanitarian law against internally displaced persons;

   c. Arbitrary killing, summary execution, arbitrary detention, abduction, enforced disappearance or torture and other forms of cruel, inhuman or degrading treatment or punishment;

   d. Sexual and gender based violence in all its forms, notably rape, enforced prostitution, sexual exploitation and harmful practices, slavery, recruitment of children and their use in hostilities, forced labour and human trafficking and smuggling; and

   e. Starvation.

2. States Parties shall:

   a. Take necessary measures to ensure that internally displaced persons are received, without discrimination of any kind and live in satisfactory conditions of safety, dignity and security;

   b. Provide internally displaced persons to the fullest extent practicable and with the least possible delay, with adequate humanitarian assistance, which shall include food, water, shelter, medical care and other health services, sanitation, education, and any other necessary social services, and where appropriate, extend such assistance to local and host communities;

   c. Provide special protection for and assistance to internally displaced persons with special needs, including separated and unaccompanied children, female heads of households, expectant mothers, mothers with young children, the elderly, and persons with disabilities or with communicable diseases;

   d. Take special measures to protect and provide for the reproductive and sexual health of internally displaced women as well as appropriate psycho-social support for victims of sexual and other related abuses;

   e. Respect and ensure the right to seek safety in another part of the State and to be protected against forcible return to or resettlement in any place where their life, safety, liberty and/or health would be at risk;

   f. Guarantee the freedom of movement and choice of residence of internally displaced persons, except where restrictions on such movement and residence are necessary, justified and proportionate to the requirements of ensuring security for internally displaced persons or maintaining public security, public order and public health;

   g. Respect and maintain the civilian and humanitarian character of the places where internally displaced persons are sheltered and safeguard such locations against infiltration by armed groups or elements and disarm and separate such groups or elements from internally displaced persons;

h. Take necessary measures, including the establishment of specialized mechanisms, to trace and reunify families separated during displacement and otherwise facilitate the re-establishment of family ties;

i. Take necessary measures to protect individual, collective and cultural property left behind by displaced persons as well as in areas where internally displaced persons are located, either within the jurisdiction of the State Parties, or in areas under their effective control;

j. Take necessary measures to safeguard against environmental degradation in areas where internally displaced persons are located, either within the jurisdiction of the State Parties, or in areas under their effective control;

k. States Parties shall consult internally displaced persons and allow them to participate in decisions relating to their protection and assistance;

l. Take necessary measures to ensure that internally displaced persons who are citizens in their country of nationality can enjoy their civic and political rights, particularly public participation, the right to vote and to be elected to public office; and

m. Put in place measures for monitoring and evaluating the effectiveness and impact of the humanitarian assistance delivered to internally displaced persons in accordance with relevant practice, including the Sphere Standards.

3. States Parties shall discharge these obligations, where appropriate, with assistance from international organizations and humanitarian agencies, civil society organizations, and other relevant actors.

Article 10
Displacement induced by Projects

1. States Parties, as much as possible, shall prevent displacement caused by projects carried out by public or private actors;

2. States Parties shall ensure that the stakeholders concerned will explore feasible alternatives, with full information and consultation of persons likely to be displaced by projects;

3. States parties shall carry out a socio-economic and environmental impact assessment of a proposed development project prior to undertaking such a project.

Article 11
Obligations of States Parties relating to Sustainable Return, Local Integration or Relocation

1. States Parties shall seek lasting solutions to the problem of displacement by promoting and creating satisfactory conditions for voluntary return, local integration or relocation on a sustainable basis and in circumstances of safety and dignity.

2. States Parties shall enable internally displaced persons to make a free and informed choice on whether to return, integrate locally or relocate by consulting them on these and other options and ensuring their participation in finding sustainable solutions.

3. States Parties shall cooperate, where appropriate, with the African Union and international organizations or humanitarian agencies and civil society organizations, in providing protection and assistance in the course of finding and implementing solutions for sustainable return, local integration or relocation and long-term reconstruction.

4. States Parties shall establish appropriate mechanisms providing for simplified procedures where necessary, for resolving disputes relating to the property of internally displaced persons.

5. States Parties shall take all appropriate measures, whenever possible, to restore the lands of communities with special dependency and attachment to such lands upon the communities' return, reintegration, and reinsertion.

Article 12
Compensation

1. States Parties shall provide persons affected by displacement with effective remedies.

2. States Parties shall establish an effective legal framework to provide just and fair compensation and other forms of reparations, where appropriate, to internally displaced persons for damage incurred as a result of displacement, in accordance with international standards.

3. A State Party shall be liable to make reparation to internally displaced persons for damage when such a State Party refrains from protecting and assisting internally displaced persons in the event of natural disasters.

Article 13
Registration and Personal Documentation

1. States Parties shall create and maintain an up-dated register of all internally displaced persons within their jurisdiction or effective control. In doing so, States Parties may collaborate with international organizations or humanitarian agencies or civil society organizations.

2. States Parties shall ensure that internally displaced persons shall be issued with relevant documents necessary for the enjoyment and exercise of their rights, such as passports, personal identification documents, civil certificates, birth certificates and marriage certificates.

3. States Parties shall facilitate the issuance of new documents or the replacement of documents lost or destroyed in the course of displacement, without imposing unreasonable conditions, such as requiring return to one's area of habitual residence in order to obtain these or other required documents. The failure to issue internally displaced persons with such documents shall not in any way impair the exercise or enjoyment of their human rights.

4. Women and men as well as separated and unaccompanied children shall have equal rights to obtain such necessary identity documents and shall have the right to have such documentation issued in their own names.

Article 14
Monitoring Compliance

1. States Parties agree to establish a Conference of States Parties to this Convention to monitor and review the implementation of the objectives of this Convention.
2. States Parties shall enhance their capacity for cooperation and mutual support under the auspices of the Conference of the States Parties.
3. States Parties agree that the Conference of the States Parties shall be convened regularly and facilitated by the African Union.
4. States Parties shall, when presenting their reports under Article 62 of the African Charter on Human and Peoples' Rights as well as, where applicable, under the African Peer Review Mechanism indicate the legislative and other measures that have been taken to give effect to this Convention.

Final Provisions

Article 15
Application

1. States Parties agree that except where expressly stated in this Convention, its provisions apply to all situations of internal displacement regardless of its causes.
2. States Parties agree that nothing in this Convention shall be construed as affording legal status or legitimizing or recognizing armed groups and that its provisions are without prejudice to the individual criminal responsibility of their members under domestic or international criminal law.

Article 16
Signature, ratification and membership

1. This Convention shall be open to signature, ratification or accession by Member States of the AU in accordance with their respective constitutional procedures.
2. The instruments of ratification or accession shall be deposited with the Chairperson of the African Union Commission.

Article 17
Entry into force

1. This Convention shall enter into force thirty (30) days after the deposit of the instruments of ratification or accession by fifteen (15) Member States.
2. The Chairperson of the AU Commission shall notify Member States of the coming into force of this Convention.

Article 18
Amendment and Revision

1. States Parties may submit proposals for the amendment or revision of this Convention.
2. Proposals for amendment or revision shall be submitted, in writing, to the Chairperson of the Commission of the AU who shall transmit the same to the States Parties within thirty (30) days of receipt thereof.

3. The Conference of States Parties, upon advice of the Executive Council, shall examine these proposals within a period of one (1) year following notification of States Parties, in accordance with the provisions of paragraph 2 of this Article.

4. Amendments or revision shall be adopted by the Conference of States Parties by a simple majority of the States Parties present and voting.

5. Amendments shall come into force thirty (30) days following the depositing of the fifteenth (15) instrument of ratification by the States Parties with the Chairperson of the AU Commission.

Article 19
Denunciation

1. A State Party may denounce this Convention by sending a written notification addressed to the Chairperson of the AU Commission, while indicating the reasons for such a denunciation.

2. The denunciation shall take effect one (1) year from the date when the notification was received by the Chairperson of the AU Commission, unless a subsequent date has been specified.

Article 20
Saving Clause

1. No provision in this Convention shall be interpreted as affecting or undermining the right of internally displaced persons to seek and be granted asylum within the framework of the African Charter on Human and Peoples' Rights, and to seek protection, as a refugee, within the purview of the 1969 OAU Convention Governing the Specific Aspects of Refugee Problems in Africa or the 1951 UN Convention Relating to the Status of Refugees as well as the 1967 Protocol Relating to the Status of Refugees.

2. This Convention shall be without prejudice to the human rights of internally displaced persons under the African Charter on Human and Peoples' Rights and other applicable instruments of international human rights law or international humanitarian law. Similarly, it shall in no way be understood, construed or interpreted as restricting, modifying or impeding existing protection under any of the instruments mentioned herein.

3. The right of internally displaced persons to lodge a complaint with the African Commission on Human and Peoples' Rights or the African Court of Justice and Human Rights, or any other competent international body shall in no way be affected by this Convention.

4. The provisions of this Convention shall be without prejudice to the individual criminal responsibility of internally displaced persons, within the framework of national or international criminal law and their duties by virtue of the African Charter on Human and Peoples' Rights.

Article 21
Reservations

States Parties shall not make or enter reservations to this Convention that are incompatible with the object and purpose of this Convention.

Article 22

Settlement of Disputes

1. Any dispute or differences arising between the States Parties with regard to the interpretation or application of this Convention shall be settled amicably through direct consultations between the States Parties concerned. In the event of failure to settle the dispute or differences, either State may refer the dispute to the African Court of Justice and Human Rights.

2. Until such time as and when the latter shall have been established, the dispute or differences shall be submitted to the Conference of the States Parties, which will decide by consensus or, failing which, by a two-third (2/3) majority of the States Parties present and voting.

Article 23

Depository

1. This Convention shall be deposited with the Chairperson of the AU Commission, who shall transmit a certified true copy of the Convention to the Government of each signatory State.

2. The Chairperson of the AU Commission shall register this Convention with the United-Nations Secretary-General as soon as it comes into force.

3. This Convention is drawn up in four (4) original texts; in the Arabic, English, French and Portuguese languages, all four (4) being equally authentic.

   ADOPTED BY THE SPECIAL SUMMIT OF THE UNION

   HELD IN KAMPALA, UGANDA,

   23rd OCTOBER 2009

PART VIII
Association of Southeast Asian Nations (ASEAN) Documents

72

Cha-Am Hua Hin Declaration on the Inauguration of the ASEAN Intergovernmental Commission on Human Rights, 2009

Note: Adopted Cha-am Hua Hin, Thailand, 23 October 2009.

WE, the Heads of State/Government of the Member States of the Association of Southeast Asian Nations (ASEAN), on the occasion of the 15th ASEAN Summit in Thailand;

RECALLING Article 14 of the ASEAN Charter on the establishment of an ASEAN human rights body and ASEAN's commitment to the promotion and protection of human rights and fundamental freedoms;

WELCOMING the entry into force of the Terms of Reference (TOR) on the basis of which the ASEAN Intergovernmental Commission on Human Rights (AICHR) shall operate;

DO HEREBY:

1. APPLAUD the inauguration of the AICHR as giving concrete expression to the implementation of Article 14 of the ASEAN Charter and ASEAN's commitment to pursue forward-looking strategies to strengthen regional cooperation on human rights;
2. ENDORSE the implementation of the TOR of the AICHR as prepared by the High Level Panel and formally determined by the ASEAN Foreign Ministers;
3. CONGRATULATE the Representatives to the AICHR on their appointment by ASEAN Member States;
4. EMPHASISE the importance of the AICHR as a historic milestone in ASEAN community-building process, and as a vehicle for progressive social development and justice, the full realisation of human dignity and the attainment of a higher quality of life for ASEAN peoples;
5. ASSURE the AICHR of full support and provision of adequate resources by ASEAN Member States;
6. ACKNOWLEDGE the contribution of stakeholders in the promotion and protection of human rights in ASEAN, and encourage their continuing engagement and dialogue with the AICHR;
7. RECOGNISE that the TOR of the AICHR shall be reviewed every five years after its entry into force to strengthen the mandate and functions of the AICHR in order to further develop mechanisms on both the protection and promotion of human rights. This review and subsequent reviews shall be undertaken by the ASEAN Foreign Ministers Meeting;
8. EXPRESS confidence that ASEAN cooperation on human rights will continue to evolve and develop so that the AICHR will be the overarching institution responsible for the promotion and protection of human rights in ASEAN.

ADOPTED in Cha-am Hua Hin, Thailand, this Twenty-Third Day of October in the Year Two Thousand and Nine.

73

Terms of Reference of the ASEAN Intergovernmental Commission on Human Rights, 2009

Note: Adopted Cha-am Hua Hin, Thailand, 23 October 2009.

Pursuant to Article 14 of the ASEAN Charter, the ASEAN Intergovernmental Commission on Human Rights (AICHR) shall operate in accordance with the following Terms of Reference (TOR):

1. PURPOSES

The purposes of the AICHR are:

1.1 To promote and protect human rights and fundamental freedoms of the peoples of ASEAN;

1.2 To uphold the right of the peoples of ASEAN to live in peace, dignity and prosperity;

1.3 To contribute to the realisation of the purposes of ASEAN as set out in the ASEAN Charter in order to promote stability and harmony in the region, friendship and cooperation among ASEAN Member States, as well as the well-being, livelihood, welfare and participation of ASEAN peoples in the ASEAN Community building process;

1.4 To promote human rights within the regional context, bearing in mind national and regional particularities and mutual respect for different historical, cultural and religious backgrounds, and taking into account the balance between rights and responsibilities;

1.5 To enhance regional cooperation with a view to complementing national and international efforts on the promotion and protection of human rights; and

1.6 To uphold international human rights standards as prescribed by the Universal Declaration of Human Rights, the Vienna Declaration and Programme of Action, and international human rights instruments to which ASEAN Member States are parties.

2. PRINCIPLES

The AICHR shall be guided by the following principles:

2.1 Respect for principles of ASEAN as embodied in Article 2 of the ASEAN Charter, in particular:

a) respect for the independence, sovereignty, equality, territorial integrity and national identity of all ASEAN Member States;

b) non-interference in the internal affairs of ASEAN Member States;

c) respect for the right of every Member State to lead its national existence free from external interference, subversion and coercion;

d) adherence to the rule of law, good governance, the principles of democracy and constitutional government;

e) respect for fundamental freedoms, the promotion and protection of human rights, and the promotion of social justice;

f) upholding the Charter of the United Nations and international law, including international humanitarian law, subscribed to by ASEAN Member States; and

g) respect for different cultures, languages and religions of the peoples of ASEAN, while emphasising their common values in the spirit of unity in diversity.

2.2 Respect for international human rights principles, including universality, indivisibility, interdependence and interrelatedness of all human rights and fundamental freedoms, as well as impartiality, objectivity, non-selectivity, non-discrimination, and avoidance of double standards and politicisation;

2.3 Recognition that the primary responsibility to promote and protect human rights and fundamental freedoms rests with each Member State;

2.4 Pursuance of a constructive and non-confrontational approach and cooperation to enhance promotion and protection of human rights; and

2.5 Adoption of an evolutionary approach that would contribute to the development of human rights norms and standards in ASEAN.

3. CONSULTATIVE INTER-GOVERNMENTAL BODY

The AICHR is an inter-governmental body and an integral part of the ASEAN organisational structure. It is a consultative body.

4. MANDATE AND FUNCTIONS

4.1. To develop strategies for the promotion and protection of human rights and fundamental freedoms to complement the building of the ASEAN Community;

4.2. To develop an ASEAN Human Rights Declaration with a view to establishing a framework for human rights cooperation through various ASEAN conventions and other instruments dealing with human rights;

4.3. To enhance public awareness of human rights among the peoples of ASEAN through education, research and dissemination of information;

4.4. To promote capacity building for the effective implementation of international human rights treaty obligations undertaken by ASEAN Member States;

4.5. To encourage ASEAN Member States to consider acceding to and ratifying international human rights instruments;

4.6. To promote the full implementation of ASEAN instruments related to human rights;

4.7. To provide advisory services and technical assistance on human rights matters to ASEAN sectoral bodies upon request;

4.8. To engage in dialogue and consultation with other ASEAN bodies and entities associated with ASEAN, including civil society organisations and other stakeholders, as provided for in Chapter V of the ASEAN Charter;

4.9. To consult, as may be appropriate, with other national, regional and international institutions and entities concerned with the promotion and protection of human rights;

4.10. To obtain information from ASEAN Member States on the promotion and protection of human rights;

4.11. To develop common approaches and positions on human rights matters of interest to ASEAN;

4.12. To prepare studies on thematic issues of human rights in ASEAN;

4.13. To submit an annual report on its activities, or other reports if deemed necessary, to the ASEAN Foreign Ministers Meeting; and

4.14. To perform any other tasks as may be assigned to it by the ASEAN Foreign Ministers Meeting.

5. COMPOSITION

Membership

5.1 The AICHR shall consist of the Member States of ASEAN.

5.2 Each ASEAN Member State shall appoint a Representative to the AICHR who shall be accountable to the appointing Government.

Qualifications

5.3 When appointing their Representatives to the AICHR, Member States shall give due consideration to gender equality, integrity and competence in the field of human rights.

5.4 Member States should consult, if required by their respective internal processes, with appropriate stakeholders in the appointment of their Representatives to the AICHR.

Term of Office

5.5 Each Representative serves a term of three years and may be consecutively re-appointed for only one more term.

5.6 Notwithstanding paragraph 5.5, the appointing Government may decide, at its discretion, to replace its Representative.

Responsibility

5.7 Each Representative, in the discharge of his or her duties, shall act impartially in accordance with the ASEAN Charter and this TOR.

5.8 Representatives shall have the obligation to attend AICHR meetings. If a Representative is unable to attend a meeting due to exceptional circumstances, the Government concerned shall formally notify the Chair of the AICHR of the appointment of a temporary representative with a full mandate to represent the Member State concerned.

Chair of the AICHR

5.9   The Chair of the AICHR shall be the Representative of the Member State holding the Chairmanship of ASEAN.

5.10   The Chair of the AICHR shall exercise his or her role in accordance with this TOR, which shall include:

a) leading in the preparation of reports of the AICHR and presenting such reports to the ASEAN Foreign Ministers Meeting;

b) coordinating with the AICHR's Representatives in between meetings of the AICHR and with the relevant ASEAN bodies;

c) representing the AICHR at regional and international events pertaining to the promotion and protection of human rights as entrusted by the AICHR; and

d) undertaking other specific functions entrusted by the AICHR in accordance with this TOR.

Immunities and Privileges

5.11   In accordance with Article 19 of the ASEAN Charter, Representatives participating in official activities of the AICHR shall enjoy such immunities and privileges as are necessary for the exercise of their functions.

6. MODALITIES

Decision-making

6.1   Decision-making in the AICHR shall be based on consultation and consensus in accordance with Article 20 of the ASEAN Charter.

Number of Meetings

6.2   The AICHR shall convene two regular meetings per year. Each meeting shall normally be not more than five days.

6.3   Regular meetings of the AICHR shall be held alternately at the ASEAN Secretariat and the Member State holding the Chair of ASEAN.

6.4   As and when appropriate, the AICHR may hold additional meetings at the ASEAN Secretariat or at a venue to be agreed upon by the Representatives.

6.5   When necessary, the ASEAN Foreign Ministers may instruct the AICHR to meet.

Line of Reporting

6.6   The AICHR shall submit an annual report and other appropriate reports to the ASEAN Foreign Ministers Meeting for its consideration.

Public Information

6.7   The AICHR shall keep the public periodically informed of its work and activities through appropriate public information materials produced by the AICHR.

Relationship with Other Human Rights Bodies within ASEAN

6.8   The AICHR is the overarching human rights institution in ASEAN with overall responsibility for the promotion and protection of human rights in ASEAN.

6.9   The AICHR shall work with all ASEAN sectoral bodies dealing with human rights to expeditiously determine the modalities for their ultimate alignment with the AICHR. To this end, the AICHR shall closely consult, coordinate and collaborate with such bodies in order to promote synergy and coherence in ASEAN's promotion and protection of human rights.

7. ROLE OF THE SECRETARY-GENERAL AND ASEAN SECRETARIAT

7.1   The Secretary-General of ASEAN may bring relevant issues to the attention of the AICHR in accordance with Article 11.2 (a) and (b) of the ASEAN Charter. In so doing, the Secretary-General of ASEAN shall concurrently inform the ASEAN Foreign Ministers of these issues.

7.2   The ASEAN Secretariat shall provide the necessary secretarial support to the AICHR to ensure its effective performance. To facilitate the Secretariat's support to the AICHR, ASEAN Member States may, with the concurrence of the Secretary-General of ASEAN, second their officials to the ASEAN Secretariat.

8. WORK PLAN AND FUNDING

8.1   The AICHR shall prepare and submit a Work Plan of programmes and activities with indicative budget for a cycle of five years to be approved by the ASEAN Foreign Ministers Meeting, upon the recommendation of the Committee of Permanent Representatives to ASEAN.

8.2   The AICHR shall also prepare and submit an annual budget to support high priority programmes and activities, which shall be approved by the ASEAN Foreign Ministers Meeting, upon the recommendation of the Committee of Permanent Representatives to ASEAN.

8.3   The annual budget shall be funded on equal sharing basis by ASEAN Member States.

8.4   The AICHR may also receive resources from any ASEAN Member States for specific extra-budgetary programmes from the Work Plan.

8.5   The AICHR shall also establish an endowment fund which consists of voluntary contributions from ASEAN Member States and other sources.

8.6.   Funding and other resources from non-ASEAN Member States shall be solely for human rights promotion, capacity building and education.

8.7   All funds used by the AICHR shall be managed and disbursed in conformity with the general financial rules of ASEAN.

8.8   Secretarial support for the AICHR shall be funded by the ASEAN Secretariat's annual operational budget.

9. GENERAL AND FINAL PROVISIONS

9.1.   This TOR shall come into force upon the approval of the ASEAN Foreign Ministers Meeting.

Amendments

9.2. Any Member State may submit a formal request for an amendment of this TOR.

9.3. The request for amendment shall be considered by the Committee of Permanent Representatives to ASEAN in consultation with the AICHR, and presented to the ASEAN Foreign Ministers Meeting for approval.

9.4. Such amendments shall enter into force upon the approval of the ASEAN Foreign Ministers Meeting.

9.5. Such amendments shall not prejudice the rights and obligations arising from or based on this TOR before or up to the date of such amendments.

Review

9.6. This TOR shall be initially reviewed five years after its entry into force. This review and subsequent reviews shall be undertaken by the ASEAN Foreign Ministers Meeting, with a view to further enhancing the promotion and protection of human rights within ASEAN.

9.7. In this connection, the AICHR shall assess its work and submit recommendations for the consideration of the ASEAN Foreign Ministers Meeting on future efforts that could be undertaken in the promotion and protection of human rights within ASEAN consistent with the principles and purposes of the ASEAN Charter and this TOR.

Interpretation

9.8. Any difference concerning the interpretation of this TOR which cannot be resolved shall be referred to the ASEAN Foreign Ministers Meeting for a decision.

74

ASEAN Human Rights Declaration (AHRD) 2012

Note: Adopted Phnom Penh, Cambodia 18 November 2012.

WE, the Heads of State/Government of the Member States of the Association of Southeast Asian Nations (hereinafter referred to as "ASEAN"), namely Brunei Darussalam, the Kingdom of Cambodia, the Republic of Indonesia, the Lao People's Democratic Republic, Malaysia, the Republic of the Union of Myanmar, the Republic of the Philippines, the Republic of Singapore, the Kingdom of Thailand and the Socialist Republic of Viet Nam, on the occasion of the 21st ASEAN Summit in Phnom Penh, Cambodia.

REAFFIRMING our adherence to the purposes and principles of ASEAN as enshrined in the ASEAN Charter, in particular the respect for and promotion and protection of human rights and fundamental freedoms, as well as the principles of democracy, the rule of law and good governance;

REAFFIRMING FURTHER our commitment to the Universal Declaration of Human Rights, the Charter of the United Nations, the Vienna Declaration and Programme of Action, and other international human rights instruments to which ASEAN Member States are parties;

REAFFIRMING ALSO the importance of ASEAN's efforts in promoting human rights, including the Declaration of the Advancement of Women in the ASEAN Region and the Declaration on the Elimination of Violence against Women in the ASEAN Region;

CONVINCED that this Declaration will help establish a framework for human rights cooperation in the region and contribute to the ASEAN community building process;

HEREBY DECLARE AS FOLLOWS:

General Principles

1. All persons are born free and equal in dignity and rights. They are endowed with reason and conscience and should act towards one another in a spirit of humanity.
2. Every person is entitled to the rights and freedoms set forth herein, without distinction of any kind, such as race, gender, age, language, religion, political or other opinion, national or social origin, economic status, birth, disability or other status.
3. Every person has the right of recognition everywhere as a person before the law. Every person is equal before the law. Every person is entitled without discrimination to equal protection of the law.
4. The rights of women, children, the elderly, persons with disabilities, migrant workers, and vulnerable and marginalised groups are an inalienable, integral and indivisible part of human rights and fundamental freedoms.

5. Every person has the right to an effective and enforceable remedy, to be determined by a court or other competent authorities, for acts violating the rights granted to that person by the constitution or by law.

6. The enjoyment of human rights and fundamental freedoms must be balanced with the performance of corresponding duties as every person has responsibilities to all other individuals, the community and the society where one lives. It is ultimately the primary responsibility of all ASEAN Member States to promote and protect all human rights and fundamental freedoms.

7. All human rights are universal, indivisible, interdependent and interrelated. All human rights and fundamental freedoms in this Declaration must be treated in a fair and equal manner, on the same footing and with the same emphasis. At the same time, the realisation of human rights must be considered in the regional and national context bearing in mind different political, economic, legal, social, cultural, historical and religious backgrounds.

8. The human rights and fundamental freedoms of every person shall be exercised with due regard to the human rights and fundamental freedoms of others. The exercise of human rights and fundamental freedoms shall be subject only to such limitations as are determined by law solely for the purpose of securing due recognition for the human rights and fundamental freedoms of others, and to meet the just requirements of national security, public order, public health, public safety, public morality, as well as the general welfare of the peoples in a democratic society.

9. In the realisation of the human rights and freedoms contained in this Declaration, the principles of impartiality, objectivity, non-selectivity, non-discrimination, non-confrontation and avoidance of double standards and politicisation, should always be upheld. The process of such realisation shall take into account peoples' participation, inclusivity and the need for accountability.

Civil and Political Rights

10. ASEAN Member States affirm all the civil and political rights in the Universal Declaration of Human Rights. Specifically, ASEAN Member States affirm the following rights and fundamental freedoms:

11. Every person has an inherent right to life which shall be protected by law. No person shall be deprived of life save in accordance with law.

12. Every person has the right to personal liberty and security. No person shall be subject to arbitrary arrest, search, detention, abduction or any other form of deprivation of liberty.

13. No person shall be held in servitude or slavery in any of its forms, or be subject to human smuggling or trafficking in persons, including for the purpose of trafficking in human organs.

14. No person shall be subject to torture or to cruel, inhuman or degrading treatment or punishment.

15. Every person has the right to freedom of movement and residence within the borders of each State. Every person has the right to leave any country including his or her own, and to return to his or her country.

16. Every person has the right to seek and receive asylum in another State in accordance with the laws of such State and applicable international agreements.

17. Every person has the right to own, use, dispose of and give that person's lawfully acquired possessions alone or in association with others. No person shall be arbitrarily deprived of such property.

18. Every person has the right to a nationality as prescribed by law. No person shall be arbitrarily deprived of such nationality nor denied the right to change that nationality.

19. The family as the natural and fundamental unit of society is entitled to protection by society and each ASEAN Member State. Men and women of full age have the right to marry on the basis of their free and full consent, to found a family and to dissolve a marriage, as prescribed by law.

20. (1) Every person charged with a criminal offence shall be presumed innocent until proved guilty according to law in a fair and public trial, by a competent, independent and impartial tribunal, at which the accused is guaranteed the right to defence.

    (2) No person shall be held guilty of any criminal offence on account of any act or omission which did not constitute a criminal offence, under national or international law, at the time when it was committed and no person shall suffer greater punishment for an offence than was prescribed by law at the time it was committed.

    (3) No person shall be liable to be tried or punished again for an offence for which he or she has already been finally convicted or acquitted in accordance with the law and penal procedure of each ASEAN Member State.

21. Every person has the right to be free from arbitrary interference with his or her privacy, family, home or correspondence including personal data, or to attacks upon that person's honour and reputation. Every person has the right to the protection of the law against such interference or attacks.

22. Every person has the right to freedom of thought, conscience and religion. All forms of intolerance, discrimination and incitement of hatred based on religion and beliefs shall be eliminated.

23. Every person has the right to freedom of opinion and expression, including freedom to hold opinions without interference and to seek, receive and impart information, whether orally, in writing or through any other medium of that person's choice.

24. Every person has the right to freedom of peaceful assembly.

25. (1) Every person who is a citizen of his or her country has the right to participate in the government of his or her country, either directly or indirectly through democratically elected representatives, in accordance with national law.

    (2) Every citizen has the right to vote in periodic and genuine elections, which should be by universal and equal suffrage and by secret ballot, guaranteeing the free expression of the will of the electors, in accordance with national law.

Economic, Social and Cultural Rights

26. ASEAN Member States affirm all the economic, social and cultural rights in the Universal Declaration of Human Rights. Specifically, ASEAN Member States affirm the following:

27. (1) Every person has the right to work, to the free choice of employment, to enjoy just, decent and favourable conditions of work and to have access to assistance schemes for the unemployed.

(2) Every person has the right to form trade unions and join the trade union of his or her choice for the protection of his or her interests, in accordance with national laws and regulations.

(3) No child or any young person shall be subjected to economic and social exploitation. Those who employ children and young people in work harmful to their morals or health, dangerous to life, or likely to hamper their normal development, including their education should be punished by law. ASEAN Member States should also set age limits below which the paid employment of child labour should be prohibited and punished by law.

28. Every person has the right to an adequate standard of living for himself or herself and his or her family including:

a. The right to adequate and affordable food, freedom from hunger and access to safe and nutritious food;

b. The right to clothing;

c. The right to adequate and affordable housing;

d. The right to medical care and necessary social services;

e. The right to safe drinking water and sanitation;

f. The right to a safe, clean and sustainable environment.

29 (1) Every person has the right to the enjoyment of the highest attainable standard of physical, mental and reproductive health, to basic and affordable health-care services, and to have access to medical facilities.

(2) The ASEAN Member States shall create a positive environment in overcoming stigma, silence, denial and discrimination in the prevention, treatment, care and support of people suffering from communicable diseases, including HIV/AIDS.

30. (1) Every person shall have the right to social security, including social insurance where available, which assists him or her to secure the means for a dignified and decent existence.

(2) Special protection should be accorded to mothers during a reasonable period as determined by national laws and regulations before and after childbirth. During such period, working mothers should be accorded paid leave or leave with adequate social security benefits.

(3) Motherhood and childhood are entitled to special care and assistance. Every child, whether born in or out of wedlock, shall enjoy the same social protection.

31. (1) Every person has the right to education.

(2) Primary education shall be compulsory and made available free to all. Secondary education in its different forms shall be available and accessible to all through every appropriate means. Technical and vocational education shall be made generally available. Higher education shall be equally accessible to all on the basis of merit.

(3) Education shall be directed to the full development of the human personality and the sense of his or her dignity. Education shall strengthen the respect for human rights and fundamental freedoms in ASEAN Member States. Furthermore, education shall enable all persons to participate effectively in their respective

societies, promote understanding, tolerance and friendship among all nations, racial and religious groups, and enhance the activities of ASEAN for the maintenance of peace.

32. Every person has the right, individually or in association with others, to freely take part in cultural life, to enjoy the arts and the benefits of scientific progress and its applications and to benefit from the protection of the moral and material interests resulting from any scientific, literary or appropriate artistic production of which one is the author.

33. ASEAN Member States should take steps, individually and through regional and international assistance and cooperation, especially economic and technical, to the maximum of its available resources, with a view to achieving progressively the full realisation of economic, social and cultural rights recognised in this Declaration.

34. ASEAN Member States may determine the extent to which they would guarantee the economic and social rights found in this Declaration to non-nationals, with due regard to human rights and the organisation and resources of their respective national economies.

Right to Development

35. The right to development is an inalienable human right by virtue of which every human person and the peoples of ASEAN are entitled to participate in, contribute to, enjoy and benefit equitably and sustainably from economic, social, cultural and political development. The right to development should be fulfilled so as to meet equitably the developmental and environmental needs of present and future generations. While development facilitates and is necessary for the enjoyment of all human rights, the lack of development may not be invoked to justify the violations of internationally recognised human rights.

36. ASEAN Member States should adopt meaningful people-oriented and gender responsive development programmes aimed at poverty alleviation, the creation of conditions including the protection and sustainability of the environment for the peoples of ASEAN to enjoy all human rights recognised in this Declaration on an equitable basis, and the progressive narrowing of the development gap within ASEAN.

37. ASEAN Member States recognise that the implementation of the right to development requires effective development policies at the national level as well as equitable economic relations, international cooperation and a favourable international economic environment. ASEAN Member States should mainstream the multidimensional aspects of the right to development into the relevant areas of ASEAN community building and beyond, and shall work with the international community to promote equitable and sustainable development, fair trade practices and effective international cooperation.

Right to Peace

38. Every person and the peoples of ASEAN have the right to enjoy peace within an ASEAN framework of security and stability, neutrality and freedom, such that

the rights set forth in this Declaration can be fully realised. To this end, ASEAN Member States should continue to enhance friendship and cooperation in the furtherance of peace, harmony and stability in the region.

Cooperation in the Promotion and Protection of Human Rights

39. ASEAN Member States share a common interest in and commitment to the promotion and protection of human rights and fundamental freedoms which shall be achieved through, inter alia, cooperation with one another as well as with relevant national, regional and international institutions/organisations, in accordance with the ASEAN Charter.

40. Nothing in this Declaration may be interpreted as implying for any State, group or person any right to perform any act aimed at undermining the purposes and principles of ASEAN, or at the destruction of any of the rights and fundamental freedoms set forth in this Declaration and international human rights instruments to which ASEAN Member States are parties.

Adopted by the Heads of State/Government of ASEAN Member States at Phnom Penh, Cambodia, this Eighteenth Day of November in the Year Two Thousand and Twelve, in one single original copy in the English Language.

75

Phnom Penh Statement on the Adoption of the ASEAN Human Rights Declaration (AHRD), 2012

Note: Adopted Phnom Penh, Cambodia, 18 November 2012.

WE, the Heads of State/Government of the Member States of the Association of Southeast Asian Nations (ASEAN), on the occasion of the 21st ASEAN Summit in Phnom Penh, Cambodia;

REAFFIRMING ASEAN's commitment to the promotion and protection of human rights and fundamental freedoms as well as the purposes and the principles as enshrined in the ASEAN Charter, including the principles of democracy, rule of law and good governance;

REITERATING ASEAN and its Member States' commitment to the Charter of the United Nations, the Universal Declaration of Human Rights, the Vienna Declaration and Programme of Action, and other international human rights instruments to which ASEAN Member States are parties as well as to relevant ASEAN declarations pertaining to human rights;

ACKNOWLEDGING the importance of the role of the ASEAN Intergovernmental Commission on Human Rights (AICHR), as the overarching institution responsible for the promotion and protection of human rights in ASEAN, that contributes towards the building of a people-oriented ASEAN Community and as a vehicle for progressive social development and justice, the full realization of human dignity and the attainment of a higher quality of life for ASEAN peoples;

COMMENDING AICHR for developing a comprehensive declaration on human rights, in consultation with ASEAN Sectoral Bodies and other relevant stakeholders;

ACKNOWLEDGING the meaningful contribution of ASEAN Sectoral Bodies and other relevant stakeholders in the promotion and protection of human rights in ASEAN, and encourage their continuing engagement and dialogue with the AICHR;

DO HEREBY:
1. ADOPT the ASEAN Human Rights Declaration (AHRD); and
2. AFFIRM our commitment to the full implementation of the AHRD to advance the promotion and protection of human rights in the region.
3. REAFFIRM further our commitment to ensure that the implementation of the AHRD be in accordance with our commitment with the Charter of the United Nation, the Universal Declaration of Human Rights, the Vienna Declaration and its Program of Action, and other international human rights instrument to which ASEAN Members States are parties, as well as relevant ASEAN declarations and instruments pertaining to human rights.
   DONE at Phnom Penh, Kingdom of Cambodia this Eighteenth Day of November in the Year Two Thousand and Twelve, in a single original in the English language.

PART IX
Council of Europe Documents

76

Convention for the Protection of Human Rights and Fundamental Freedoms, 1950

Note: Convention for the Protection of Human Rights and Fundamental Freedoms, adopted Rome, 4 November 1950. ETS No. 5. Entry into force: 3 September, 1953 as amended by Protocol Number 14 (CETS No. 194); which entered into force on 1 June 2010.

The Governments signatory hereto, being members of the Council of Europe,

Considering the Universal Declaration of Human Rights proclaimed by the General Assembly of the United Nations on 10th December 1948;

Considering that this Declaration aims at securing the universal and effective recognition and observance of the Rights therein declared;

Considering that the aim of the Council of Europe is the achievement of greater unity between its members and that one of the methods by which that aim is to be pursued is the maintenance and further realisation of Human Rights and Fundamental Freedoms;

Reaffirming their profound belief in those fundamental freedoms which are the foundation of justice and peace in the world and are best maintained on the one hand by an effective political democracy and on the other by a common understanding and observance of the Human Rights upon which they depend;

Being resolved, as the governments of European countries which are likeminded and have a common heritage of political traditions, ideals, freedom and the rule of law, to take the first steps for the collective enforcement of certain of the rights stated in the Universal Declaration,

Have agreed as follows:

Article 1 Obligation to respect Human Rights

The High Contracting Parties shall secure to everyone within their jurisdiction the rights and freedoms defined in Section I of this Convention.

Section I Rights and Freedoms

Article 2 Right to life

1. Everyone's right to life shall be protected by law. No one shall be deprived of his life intentionally save in the execution of a sentence of a court following his conviction of a crime for which this penalty is provided by law.
2. Deprivation of life shall not be regarded as inflicted in contravention of this Article when it results from the use of force which is no more than absolutely necessary:
    (a) in defence of any person from unlawful violence;
    (b) in order to effect a lawful arrest or to prevent the escape of a person lawfully detained;
    (c) in action lawfully taken for the purpose of quelling a riot or insurrection.

Article 3 Prohibition of torture

No one shall be subjected to torture or to inhuman or degrading treatment or punishment.

Article 4 Prohibition of slavery and forced labour

1. No one shall be held in slavery or servitude.
2. No one shall be required to perform forced or compulsory labour.
3. For the purpose of this Article the term "forced or compulsory labour" shall not include:
   (a) any work required to be done in the ordinary course of detention imposed according to the provisions of Article 5 of this Convention or during conditional release from such detention;
   (b) any service of a military character or, in case of conscientious objectors in countries where they are recognised, service exacted instead of compulsory military service;
   (c) any service exacted in case of an emergency or calamity threatening the life or wellbeing of the community;
   (d) any work or service which forms part of normal civic obligations.

Article 5 Right to liberty and security

1. Everyone has the right to liberty and security of person. No one shall be deprived of his liberty save in the following cases and in accordance with a procedure prescribed by law:
   (a) the lawful detention of a person after conviction by a competent court;
   (b) the lawful arrest or detention of a person for noncompliance with the lawful order of a court or in order to secure the fulfilment of any obligation prescribed by law;
   (c) the lawful arrest or detention of a person effected for the purpose of bringing him before the competent legal authority on reasonable suspicion of having committed an offence or when it is reasonably considered necessary to prevent his committing an offence or fleeing after having done so;
   (d) the detention of a minor by lawful order for the purpose of educational supervision or his lawful detention for the purpose of bringing him before the competent legal authority;
   (e) the lawful detention of persons for the prevention of the spreading of infectious diseases, of persons of unsound mind, alcoholics or drug addicts or vagrants;
   (f) the lawful arrest or detention of a person to prevent his effecting an unauthorised entry into the country or of a person against whom action is being taken with a view to deportation or extradition.
2. Everyone who is arrested shall be informed promptly, in a language which he understands, of the reasons for his arrest and of any charge against him.
3. Everyone arrested or detained in accordance with the provisions of paragraph 1 (c) of this Article shall be brought promptly before a judge or other officer authorised by law to exercise judicial power and shall be entitled to trial within a reasonable time or to release pending trial. Release may be conditioned by guarantees to appear for trial.
4. Everyone who is deprived of his liberty by arrest or detention shall be entitled to take proceedings by which the lawfulness of his detention shall be decided speedily by a court and his release ordered if the detention is not lawful.
5. Everyone who has been the victim of arrest or detention in contravention of the provisions of this Article shall have an enforceable right to compensation.

Article 6 Right to a fair trial

1. In the determination of his civil rights and obligations or of any criminal charge against him, everyone is entitled to a fair and public hearing within a reasonable time by an independent and impartial tribunal established by law. Judgment shall be pronounced publicly but the press and public may be excluded from all or part of the trial in the interests of morals, public order or national security in a democratic society, where the interests of juveniles or the protection of the private life of the parties so require, or to the extent strictly necessary in the opinion of the court in special circumstances where publicity would prejudice the interests of justice.
2. Everyone charged with a criminal offence shall be presumed innocent until proved guilty according to law.
3. Everyone charged with a criminal offence has the following minimum rights:
   (a) to be informed promptly, in a language which he understands and in detail, of the nature and cause of the accusation against him;
   (b) to have adequate time and facilities for the preparation of his defence;
   (c) to defend himself in person or through legal assistance of his own choosing or, if he has not sufficient means to pay for legal assistance, to be given it free when the interests of justice so require;
   (d) to examine or have examined witnesses against him and to obtain the attendance and examination of witnesses on his behalf under the same conditions as witnesses against him;
   (e) to have the free assistance of an interpreter if he cannot understand or speak the language used in court.

Article 7 No punishment without law

1. No one shall be held guilty of any criminal offence on account of any act or omission which did not constitute a criminal offence under national or international law at the time when it was committed. Nor shall a heavier penalty be imposed than the one that was applicable at the time the criminal offence was committed.
2. This Article shall not prejudice the trial and punishment of any person for any act or omission which, at the time when it was committed, was criminal according to the general principles of law recognised by civilised nations.

Article 8 Right to respect for private and family life

1. Everyone has the right to respect for his private and family life, his home and his correspondence.
2. There shall be no interference by a public authority with the exercise of this right except such as is in accordance with the law and is necessary in a democratic society in the interests of national security, public safety or the economic wellbeing of the country, for the prevention of disorder or crime, for the protection of health or morals, or for the protection of the rights and freedoms of others.

Article 9 Freedom of thought, conscience and religion

1. Everyone has the right to freedom of thought, conscience and religion; this right includes freedom to change his religion or belief and freedom, either alone or in

community with others and in public or private, to manifest his religion or belief, in worship, teaching, practice and observance.

2. Freedom to manifest one's religion or beliefs shall be subject only to such limitations as are prescribed by law and are necessary in a democratic society in the interests of public safety, for the protection of public order, health or morals, or for the protection of the rights and freedoms of others.

Article 10 Freedom of expression

1. Everyone has the right to freedom of expression. This right shall include freedom to hold opinions and to receive and impart information and ideas without interference by public authority and regardless of frontiers. This Article shall not prevent States from requiring the licensing of broadcasting, television or cinema enterprises.

2. The exercise of these freedoms, since it carries with it duties and responsibilities, may be subject to such formalities, conditions, restrictions or penalties as are prescribed by law and are necessary in a democratic society, in the interests of national security, territorial integrity or public safety, for the prevention of disorder or crime, for the protection of health or morals, for the protection of the reputation or rights of others, for preventing the disclosure of information received in confidence, or for maintaining the authority and impartiality of the judiciary.

Article 11 Freedom of assembly and association

1. Everyone has the right to freedom of peaceful assembly and to freedom of association with others, including the right to form and to join trade unions for the protection of his interests.

2. No restrictions shall be placed on the exercise of these rights other than such as are prescribed by law and are necessary in a democratic society in the interests of national security or public safety, for the prevention of disorder or crime, for the protection of health or morals or for the protection of the rights and freedoms of others. This Article shall not prevent the imposition of lawful restrictions on the exercise of these rights by members of the armed forces, of the police or of the administration of the State.

Article 12 Right to marry

Men and women of marriageable age have the right to marry and to found a family, according to the national laws governing the exercise of this right.

Article 13 Right to an effective remedy

Everyone whose rights and freedoms as set forth in this Convention are violated shall have an effective remedy before a national authority notwithstanding that the violation has been committed by persons acting in an official capacity.

Article 14 Prohibition of discrimination

The enjoyment of the rights and freedoms set forth in this Convention shall be secured without discrimination on any ground such as sex, race, colour, language, religion, political or other opinion, national or social origin, association with a national minority, property, birth or other status.

Article 15 Derogation in time of emergency

1. In time of war or other public emergency threatening the life of the nation any High Contracting Party may take measures derogating from its obligations under this Convention to the extent strictly required by the exigencies of the situation, provided that such measures are not inconsistent with its other obligations under international law.
2. No derogation from Article 2, except in respect of deaths resulting from lawful acts of war, or from Articles 3, 4 (paragraph 1) and 7 shall be made under this provision.
3. Any High Contracting Party availing itself of this right of derogation shall keep the Secretary General of the Council of Europe fully informed of the measures which it has taken and the reasons therefor. It shall also inform the Secretary General of the Council of Europe when such measures have ceased to operate and the provisions of the Convention are again being fully executed.

Article 16 Restrictions on political activity of aliens

Nothing in Articles 10, 11 and 14 shall be regarded as preventing the High Contracting Parties from imposing restrictions on the political activity of aliens.

Article 17 Prohibition of abuse of rights

Nothing in this Convention may be interpreted as implying for any State, group or person any right to engage in any activity or perform any act aimed at the destruction of any of the rights and freedoms set forth herein or at their limitation to a greater extent than is provided for in the Convention.

Article 18 Limitation on use of restrictions on rights

The restrictions permitted under this Convention to the said rights and freedoms shall not be applied for any purpose other than those for which they have been prescribed.

Section II European Court of Human Rights

Article 19 Establishment of the Court

To ensure the observance of the engagements undertaken by the High Contracting Parties in the Convention and the Protocols thereto, there shall be set up a European Court of Human Rights, hereinafter referred to as "the Court". It shall function on a permanent basis.

Article 20 Number of judges

The Court shall consist of a number of judges equal to that of the High Contracting Parties.

Article 21 Criteria for office

1. The judges shall be of high moral character and must either possess the qualifications required for appointment to high judicial office or be jurisconsults of recognised competence.
2. The judges shall sit on the Court in their individual capacity.
3. During their term of office the judges shall not engage in any activity which is incompatible with their independence, impartiality or with the demands of a fulltime office; all questions arising from the application of this paragraph shall be decided by the Court.

Article 22 Election of judges

The judges shall be elected by the Parliamentary Assembly with respect to each High Contracting Party by a majority of votes cast from a list of three candidates nominated by the High Contracting Party.

Article 23 Terms of office and dismissal

1. The judges shall be elected for a period of nine years. They may not be reelected.
2. The terms of office of judges shall expire when they reach the age of 70.
3. The judges shall hold office until replaced. They shall, however, continue to deal with such cases as they already have under consideration.
4. No judge may be dismissed from office unless the other judges decide by a majority of two thirds that that judge has ceased to fulfil the required conditions.

Article 24 Registry and rapporteurs

1. The Court shall have a Registry, the functions and organisation of which shall be laid down in the rules of the Court.
2. When sitting in a single judge formation, the Court shall be assisted by rapporteurs who shall function under the authority of the President of the Court. They shall form part of the Court's Registry.

Article 25 Plenary Court

The plenary Court shall

    (a) elect its President and one or two Vice-Presidents for a period of three years; they may be reelected;
    (b) set up Chambers, constituted for a fixed period of time;
    (c) elect the Presidents of the Chambers of the Court; they may be reelected;
    (d) adopt the rules of the Court;
    (e) elect the Registrar and one or more Deputy Registrars;
    (f) make any request under Article 26, paragraph 2.

Article 26 Single-judge formation, Committees, Chambers and Grand Chamber

1. To consider cases brought before it, the Court shall sit in a single-judge formation, in committees of three judges, in Chambers of seven judges and in a Grand Chamber of seventeen judges. The Court's Chambers shall set up committees for a fixed period of time.
2. At the request of the plenary Court, the Committee of Ministers may, by a unanimous decision and for a fixed period, reduce to five the number of judges of the Chambers.
3. When sitting as a single judge, a judge shall not examine any application against the High Contracting Party in respect of which that judge has been elected.
4. There shall sit as an exofficio member of the Chamber and the Grand Chamber the judge elected in respect of the High Contracting Party concerned. If there is none or if that judge is unable to sit, a person chosen by the President of the Court from a list submitted in advance by that Party shall sit in the capacity of judge.
5. The Grand Chamber shall also include the President of the Court, the Vice-Presidents, the Presidents of the Chambers and other judges chosen in accordance with the rules

of the Court. When a case is referred to the Grand Chamber under Article 43, no judge from the Chamber which rendered the judgment shall sit in the Grand Chamber, with the exception of the President of the Chamber and the judge who sat in respect of the High Contracting Party concerned.

Article 27 Competence of single judges

1. A single judge may declare inadmissible or strike out of the Court's list of cases an application submitted under Article 34, where such a decision can be taken without further examination.
2. The decision shall be final.
3. If the single judge does not declare an application inadmissible or strike it out, that judge shall forward it to a committee or to a Chamber for further examination.

Article 28 Competence of Committees

1. In respect of an application submitted under Article 34, a committee may, by a unanimous vote,
   (a) declare it inadmissible or strike it out of its list of cases, where such decision can be taken without further examination; or
   (b) declare it admissible and render at the same time a judgment on the merits, if the underlying question in the case, concerning the interpretation or the application of the Convention or the Protocols thereto, is already the subject of well-established case law of the Court.
2. Decisions and judgments under paragraph 1 shall be final.
3. If the judge elected in respect of the High Contracting Party concerned is not a member of the committee, the committee may at any stage of the proceedings invite that judge to take the place of one of the members of the committee, having regard to all relevant factors, including whether that Party has contested the application of the procedure under paragraph 1(b).

Article 29 Decisions by Chambers on admissibility and merits

1. If no decision is taken under Article 27 or 28, or no judgment rendered under Article 28, a Chamber shall decide on the admissibility and merits of individual applications submitted under Article 34. The decision on admissibility may be taken separately.
2. A Chamber shall decide on the admissibility and merits of inter-State applications submitted under Article 33. The decision on admissibility shall be taken separately unless the Court, in exceptional cases, decides otherwise.

Article 30 Relinquishment of jurisdiction to the Grand Chamber

Where a case pending before a Chamber raises a serious question affecting the interpretation of the Convention or the Protocols thereto, or where the resolution of a question before the Chamber might have a result inconsistent with a judgment previously delivered by the Court, the Chamber may, at any time before it has rendered its judgment, relinquish jurisdiction in favour of the Grand Chamber, unless one of the parties to the case objects.

Article 31 Powers of the Grand Chamber

The Grand Chamber shall

    (a) determine applications submitted either under Article 33 or Article 34 when a Chamber has relinquished jurisdiction under Article 30 or when the case has been referred to it under Article 43;

    (b) decide on issues referred to the Court by the Committee of Ministers in accordance with Article 46, paragraph 4; and

    (c) consider requests for advisory opinions submitted under Article 47.

Article 32 Jurisdiction of the Court

1. The jurisdiction of the Court shall extend to all matters concerning the interpretation and application of the Convention and the Protocols thereto which are referred to it as provided in Articles 33, 34, 46 and 47.
2. In the event of dispute as to whether the Court has jurisdiction, the Court shall decide.

Article 33 Inter-State cases

Any High Contracting Party may refer to the Court any alleged breach of the provisions of the Convention and the Protocols thereto by another High Contracting Party.

Article 34 Individual applications

The Court may receive applications from any person, nongovernmental organisation or group of individuals claiming to be the victim of a violation by one of the High Contracting Parties of the rights set forth in the Convention or the Protocols thereto. The High Contracting Parties undertake not to hinder in any way the effective exercise of this right.

Article 35 Admissibility criteria

1. The Court may only deal with the matter after all domestic remedies have been exhausted, according to the generally recognised rules of international law, and within a period of six months from the date on which the final decision was taken.
2. The Court shall not deal with any application submitted under Article 34 that

    (a) is anonymous; or

    (b) is substantially the same as a matter that has already been examined by the Court or has already been submitted to another procedure of international investigation or settlement and contains no relevant new information.

3. The Court shall declare inadmissible any individual application submitted under Article 34 if it considers that:

    (a) the application is incompatible with the provisions of the Convention or the Protocols thereto, manifestly ill-founded, or an abuse of the right of individual application; or

    (b) the applicant has not suffered a significant disadvantage, unless respect for human rights as defined in the Convention and the Protocols thereto requires an examination of the application on the merits and provided that no case may be rejected on this ground which has not been duly considered by a domestic tribunal.

4. The Court shall reject any application which it considers inadmissible under this Article. It may do so at any stage of the proceedings.

Article 36 Third party intervention

1. In all cases before a Chamber or the Grand Chamber, a High Contracting Party one of whose nationals is an applicant shall have the right to submit written comments and to take part in hearings.
2. The President of the Court may, in the interest of the proper administration of justice, invite any High Contracting Party which is not a party to the proceedings or any person concerned who is not the applicant to submit written comments or take part in hearings.
3. In all cases before a Chamber or the Grand Chamber, the Council of Europe Commissioner for Human Rights may submit written comments and take part in hearings.

Article 37 Striking out applications

1. The Court may at any stage of the proceedings decide to strike an application out of its list of cases where the circumstances lead to the conclusion that
   (a) the applicant does not intend to pursue his application; or
   (b) the matter has been resolved; or
   (c) for any other reason established by the Court, it is no longer justified to continue the examination of the application.

   However, the Court shall continue the examination of the application if respect for human rights as defined in the Convention and the Protocols thereto so requires.
2. The Court may decide to restore an application to its list of cases if it considers that the circumstances justify such a course.

Article 38 Examination of the case

The Court shall examine the case together with the representatives of the parties and, if need be, undertake an investigation, for the effective conduct of which the High Contracting Parties concerned shall furnish all necessary facilities.

Article 39 Friendly settlements

1. At any stage of the proceedings, the Court may place itself at the disposal of the parties concerned with a view to securing a friendly settlement of the matter on the basis of respect for human rights as defined in the Convention and the Protocols thereto.
2. Proceedings conducted under paragraph 1 shall be confidential.
3. If a friendly settlement is effected, the Court shall strike the case out of its list by means of a decision which shall be confined to a brief statement of the facts and of the solution reached.
4. This decision shall be transmitted to the Committee of Ministers, which shall supervise the execution of the terms of the friendly settlement as set out in the decision.

Article 40 Public hearings and access to documents

1. Hearings shall be in public unless the Court in exceptional circumstances decides otherwise.
2. Documents deposited with the Registrar shall be accessible to the public unless the President of the Court decides otherwise.

Article 41 Just satisfaction

If the Court finds that there has been a violation of the Convention or the Protocols thereto, and if the internal law of the High Contracting Party concerned allows only partial reparation to be made, the Court shall, if necessary, afford just satisfaction to the injured party.

Article 42 Judgments of Chambers

Judgments of Chambers shall become final in accordance with the provisions of Article 44, paragraph 2.

Article 43 Referral to the Grand Chamber

1. Within a period of three months from the date of the judgment of the Chamber, any party to the case may, in exceptional cases, request that the case be referred to the Grand Chamber.
2. A panel of five judges of the Grand Chamber shall accept the request if the case raises a serious question affecting the interpretation or application of the Convention or the Protocols thereto, or a serious issue of general importance.
3. If the panel accepts the request, the Grand Chamber shall decide the case by means of a judgment.

Article 44 Final judgments

1. The judgment of the Grand Chamber shall be final.
2. The judgment of a Chamber shall become final:
   (a) when the parties declare that they will not request that the case be referred to the Grand Chamber; or
   (b) three months after the date of the judgment, if reference of the case to the Grand Chamber has not been requested; or
   (c) when the panel of the Grand Chamber rejects the request to refer under Article 43.
3. The final judgment shall be published.

Article 45 Reasons for judgments and decisions

1. Reasons shall be given for judgments as well as for decisions declaring applications admissible or inadmissible.
2. If a judgment does not represent, in whole or in part, the unanimous opinion of the judges, any judge shall be entitled to deliver a separate opinion.

Article 46 Binding force and execution of judgments

1. The High Contracting Parties undertake to abide by the final judgment of the Court in any case to which they are parties.
2. The final judgment of the Court shall be transmitted to the Committee of Ministers, which shall supervise its execution.
3. If the Committee of Ministers considers that the supervision of the execution of a final judgment is hindered by a problem of interpretation of the judgment, it may refer the matter to the Court for a ruling on the question of interpretation. A referral decision shall require a majority vote of two thirds of the representatives entitled to sit on the committee.

4. If the Committee of Ministers considers that a High Contracting Party refuses to abide by a final judgment in a case to which it is a party, it may, after serving formal notice on that Party and by decision adopted by a majority vote of two thirds of the representatives entitled to sit on the committee, refer to the Court the question whether that Party has failed to fulfil its obligation under paragraph 1.
5. If the Court finds a violation of paragraph 1, it shall refer the case to the Committee of Ministers for consideration of the measures to be taken. If the Court finds no violation of paragraph 1, it shall refer the case to the Committee of Ministers, which shall close its examination of the case.

Article 47 Advisory opinions
1. The Court may, at the request of the Committee of Ministers, give advisory opinions on legal questions concerning the interpretation of the Convention and the Protocols thereto.
2. Such opinions shall not deal with any question relating to the content or scope of the rights or freedoms defined in Section I of the Convention and the Protocols thereto, or with any other question which the Court or the Committee of Ministers might have to consider in consequence of any such proceedings as could be instituted in accordance with the Convention.
3. Decisions of the Committee of Ministers to request an advisory opinion of the Court shall require a majority vote of the representatives entitled to sit on the committee.

Article 48 Advisory jurisdiction of the Court
The Court shall decide whether a request for an advisory opinion submitted by the Committee of Ministers is within its competence as defined in Article 47.

Article 49 Reasons for advisory opinions
1. Reasons shall be given for advisory opinions of the Court.
2. If the advisory opinion does not represent, in whole or in part, the unanimous opinion of the judges, any judge shall be entitled to deliver a separate opinion.
3. Advisory opinions of the Court shall be communicated to the Committee of Ministers.

Article 50 Expenditure on the Court
The expenditure on the Court shall be borne by the Council of Europe.

Article 51 Privileges and immunities of judges
The judges shall be entitled, during the exercise of their functions, to the privileges and immunities provided for in Article 40 of the Statute of the Council of Europe and in the agreements made thereunder.

Section III Miscellaneous Provisions

Article 52 Inquiries by the Secretary General
On receipt of a request from the Secretary General of the Council of Europe any High Contracting Party shall furnish an explanation of the manner in which its internal law ensures the effective implementation of any of the provisions of the Convention.

Article 53 Safeguard for existing human rights
Nothing in this Convention shall be construed as limiting or derogating from any of the human rights and fundamental freedoms which may be ensured under the laws of any High Contracting Party or under any other agreement to which it is a party.

Article 54 Powers of the Committee of Ministers
Nothing in this Convention shall prejudice the powers conferred on the Committee of Ministers by the Statute of the Council of Europe.

Article 55 Exclusion of other means of dispute settlement
The High Contracting Parties agree that, except by special agreement, they will not avail themselves of treaties, conventions or declarations in force between them for the purpose of submitting, by way of petition, a dispute arising out of the interpretation or application of this Convention to a means of settlement other than those provided for in this Convention.

Article 56 Territorial application
1. Any State may at the time of its ratification or at any time thereafter declare by notification addressed to the Secretary General of the Council of Europe that the present Convention shall, subject to paragraph 4 of this Article, extend to all or any of the territories for whose international relations it is responsible.
2. The Convention shall extend to the territory or territories named in the notification as from the thirtieth day after the receipt of this notification by the Secretary General of the Council of Europe.
3. The provisions of this Convention shall be applied in such territories with due regard, however, to local requirements.
4. Any State which has made a declaration in accordance with paragraph 1 of this Article may at any time thereafter declare on behalf of one or more of the territories to which the declaration relates that it accepts the competence of the Court to receive applications from individuals, nongovernmental organisations or groups of individuals as provided by Article 34 of the Convention.

Article 57 Reservations
1. Any State may, when signing this Convention or when depositing its instrument of ratification, make a reservation in respect of any particular provision of the Convention to the extent that any law then in force in its territory is not in conformity with the provision. Reservations of a general character shall not be permitted under this Article.
2. Any reservation made under this Article shall contain a brief statement of the law concerned.

Article 58 Denunciation
1. A High Contracting Party may denounce the present Convention only after the expiry of five years from the date on which it became a party to it and after six months' notice contained in a notification addressed to the Secretary General of the Council of Europe, who shall inform the other High Contracting Parties.
2. Such a denunciation shall not have the effect of releasing the High Contracting Party concerned from its obligations under this Convention in respect of any act which,

being capable of constituting a violation of such obligations, may have been performed by it before the date at which the denunciation became effective.

3. Any High Contracting Party which shall cease to be a member of the Council of Europe shall cease to be a Party to this Convention under the same conditions.

4. The Convention may be denounced in accordance with the provisions of the preceding paragraphs in respect of any territory to which it has been declared to extend under the terms of Article 56.

Article 59 Signature and ratification

1. This Convention shall be open to the signature of the members of the Council of Europe. It shall be ratified. Ratifications shall be deposited with the Secretary General of the Council of Europe.

2. The European Union may accede to this Convention.

3. The present Convention shall come into force after the deposit of ten instruments of ratification.

4. As regards any signatory ratifying subsequently, the Convention shall come into force at the date of the deposit of its instrument of ratification.

5. The Secretary General of the Council of Europe shall notify all the members of the Council of Europe of the entry into force of the Convention, the names of the High Contracting Parties who have ratified it, and the deposit of all instruments of ratification which may be effected subsequently.

Done at Rome this 4th day of November 1950, in English and French, both texts being equally authentic, in a single copy which shall remain deposited in the archives of the Council of Europe. The Secretary General shall transmit certified copies to each of the signatories.

77

Protocol to the Convention for the Protection of Human Rights and Fundamental Freedoms, 1952 (First Protocol)

Note: Adopted, Paris, 20 March 1952. ETS No. 9. Entry into force: 18 May 1954.

The Governments signatory hereto, being members of the Council of Europe,

Being resolved to take steps to ensure the collective enforcement of certain rights and freedoms other than those already included in Section I of the Convention for the Protection of Human Rights and Fundamental Freedoms signed at Rome on 4 November 1950 (hereinafter referred to as "the Convention"),

Have agreed as follows:

Article 1 Protection of property

Every natural or legal person is entitled to the peaceful enjoyment of his possessions. No one shall be deprived of his possessions except in the public interest and subject to the conditions provided for by law and by the general principles of international law.

The preceding provisions shall not, however, in any way impair the right of a State to enforce such laws as it deems necessary to control the use of property in accordance with the general interest or to secure the payment of taxes or other contributions or penalties.

Article 2 Right to education

No person shall be denied the right to education. In the exercise of any functions which it assumes in relation to education and to teaching, the State shall respect the right of parents to ensure such education and teaching in conformity with their own religious and philosophical convictions.

Article 3 Right to free elections

The High Contracting Parties undertake to hold free elections at reasonable intervals by secret ballot, under conditions which will ensure the free expression of the opinion of the people in the choice of the legislature.

Article 4 Territorial application

Any High Contracting Party may at the time of signature or ratification or at any time thereafter communicate to the Secretary General of the Council of Europe a declaration stating the extent to which it undertakes that the provisions of the present Protocol shall apply to such of the territories for the international relations of which it is responsible as are named therein.

Any High Contracting Party which has communicated a declaration in virtue of the preceding paragraph may from time to time communicate a further declaration modifying the terms of any former declaration or terminating the application of the provisions of this Protocol in respect of any territory.

A declaration made in accordance with this Article shall be deemed to have been made in accordance with paragraph 1 of Article 56 of the Convention.

Article 5 Relationship to the Convention
As between the High Contracting Parties the provisions of Articles 1, 2, 3 and 4 of this Protocol shall be regarded as additional Articles to the Convention and all the provisions of the Convention shall apply accordingly.

Article 6 Signature and ratification
This Protocol shall be open for signature by the members of the Council of Europe, who are the signatories of the Convention; it shall be ratified at the same time as or after the ratification of the Convention. It shall enter into force after the deposit of ten instruments of ratification. As regards any signatory ratifying subsequently, the Protocol shall enter into force at the date of the deposit of its instrument of ratification.

The instruments of ratification shall be deposited with the Secretary General of the Council of Europe, who will notify all members of the names of those who have ratified.

Done at Paris on the 20th day of March 1952, in English and French, both texts being equally authentic, in a single copy which shall remain deposited in the archives of the Council of Europe.

The Secretary General shall transmit certified copies to each of the signatory governments.

78

Protocol No. 4 to the Convention for the Protection of Human Rights and Fundamental Freedoms, 1963 (Fourth Protocol)

Note: Protocol No. 4 to the Convention for the Protection of Human Rights and Fundamental Freedoms Securing Certain Rights and Freedoms Other Than Those Already Included in the Convention and in the First Protocol thereto. Adopted Strasbourg, 16 September 1963. ETS No. 46. Entry into force: 2 May 1968.

The Governments signatory hereto, being members of the Council of Europe,

Being resolved to take steps to ensure the collective enforcement of certain rights and freedoms other than those already included in Section I of the Convention for the Protection of Human Rights and Fundamental Freedoms signed at Rome on 4th November 1950 (hereinafter referred to as the "Convention") and in Articles 1 to 3 of the First Protocol to the Convention, signed at Paris on 20th March 1952,

Have agreed as follows:

Article 1 Prohibition of imprisonment for debt
No one shall be deprived of his liberty merely on the ground of inability to fulfil a contractual obligation.

Article 2 Freedom of movement
1. Everyone lawfully within the territory of a State shall, within that territory, have the right to liberty of movement and freedom to choose his residence.
2. Everyone shall be free to leave any country, including his own.
3. No restrictions shall be placed on the exercise of these rights other than such as are in accordance with law and are necessary in a democratic society in the interests of national security or public safety, for the maintenance of ordre public, for the prevention of crime, for the protection of health or morals, or for the protection of the rights and freedoms of others.
4. The rights set forth in paragraph 1 may also be subject, in particular areas, to restrictions imposed in accordance with law and justified by the public interest in a democratic society.

Article 3 Prohibition of expulsion of nationals
1. No one shall be expelled, by means either of an individual or of a collective measure, from the territory of the State of which he is a national.
2. No one shall be deprived of the right to enter the territory of the State of which he is a national.

Article 4 Prohibition of collective expulsion of aliens
Collective expulsion of aliens is prohibited.

Article 5 Territorial application

1. Any High Contracting Party may, at the time of signature or ratification of this Protocol, or at any time thereafter, communicate to the Secretary General of the Council of Europe a declaration stating the extent to which it undertakes that the provisions of this Protocol shall apply to such of the territories for the international relations of which it is responsible as are named therein.
2. Any High Contracting Party which has communicated a declaration in virtue of the preceding paragraph may, from time to time, communicate a further declaration modifying the terms of any former declaration or terminating the application of the provisions of this Protocol in respect of any territory.
3. A declaration made in accordance with this Article shall be deemed to have been made in accordance with paragraph 1 of Article 56 of the Convention.
4. The territory of any State to which this Protocol applies by virtue of ratification or acceptance by that State, and each territory to which this Protocol is applied by virtue of a declaration by that State under this Article, shall be treated as separate territories for the purpose of the references in Articles 2 and 3 to the territory of a State.
5. Any State which has made a declaration in accordance with paragraph 1 or 2 of this Article may at any time thereafter declare on behalf of one or more of the territories to which the declaration relates that it accepts the competence of the Court to receive applications from individuals, nongovernmental organisations or groups of individuals as provided in Article 34 of the Convention in respect of all or any of Articles 1 to 4 of this Protocol.

Article 6 Relationship to the Convention
As between the High Contracting Parties the provisions of Articles 1 to 5 of this Protocol shall be regarded as additional Articles to the Convention, and all the provisions of the Convention shall apply accordingly.

Article 7 Signature and ratification

1. This Protocol shall be open for signature by the members of the Council of Europe who are the signatories of the Convention; it shall be ratified at the same time as or after the ratification of the Convention. It shall enter into force after the deposit of five instruments of ratification. As regards any signatory ratifying subsequently, the Protocol shall enter into force at the date of the deposit of its instrument of ratification.
2. The instruments of ratification shall be deposited with the Secretary General of the Council of Europe, who will notify all members of the names of those who have ratified.

In witness whereof the undersigned, being duly authorised thereto, have signed this Protocol.

Done at Strasbourg, this 16th day of September 1963, in English and in French, both texts being equally authoritative, in a single copy which shall remain deposited in the archives of the Council of Europe. The Secretary General shall transmit certified copies to each of the signatory states.

79

Protocol No. 6 to the Convention for the Protection of Human Rights and Fundamental Freedoms, 1983 (Sixth Protocol)

Note: Protocol No. 6 to the Convention for the Protection of Human Rights and Fundamental Freedoms Concerning the Abolition of the Death Penalty. Adopted at Strasbourg, 28 April 1983. ETS No. 114. Entry into force: 1 March 1985.

The Member States of the Council of Europe, signatory to this Protocol to the Convention for the Protection of Human Rights and Fundamental Freedoms, signed at Rome on 4 November 1950 (hereinafter referred to as "the Convention"),

Considering that the evolution that has occurred in several member States of the Council of Europe expresses a general tendency in favour of abolition of the death penalty;

Have agreed as follows:

Article 1 Abolition of the death penalty

The death penalty shall be abolished. No one shall be condemned to such penalty or executed.

Article 2 Death penalty in time of war

A State may make provision in its law for the death penalty in respect of acts committed in time of war or of imminent threat of war; such penalty shall be applied only in the instances laid down in the law and in accordance with its provisions. The State shall communicate to the Secretary General of the Council of Europe the relevant provisions of that law.

Article 3 Prohibition of derogations

No derogation from the provisions of this Protocol shall be made under Article 15 of the Convention.

Article 4 Prohibition of reservations

No reservation may be made under Article 57 of the Convention in respect of the provisions of this Protocol.

Article 5 Territorial application

1. Any State may at the time of signature or when depositing its instrument of ratification, acceptance or approval, specify the territory or territories to which this Protocol shall apply.
2. Any State may at any later date, by a declaration addressed to the Secretary General of the Council of Europe, extend the application of this Protocol to any other territory

specified in the declaration. In respect of such territory the Protocol shall enter into force on the first day of the month following the date of receipt of such declaration by the Secretary General.

3. Any declaration made under the two preceding paragraphs may, in respect of any territory specified in such declaration, be withdrawn by a notification addressed to the Secretary General.

The withdrawal shall become effective on the first day of the month following the date of receipt of such notification by the Secretary General.

Article 6 Relationship to the Convention

As between the States Parties the provisions of Articles 1 to 5 of this Protocol shall be regarded as additional Articles to the Convention and all the provisions of the Convention shall apply accordingly.

Article 7 Signature and ratification

The Protocol shall be open for signature by the member States of the Council of Europe, signatories to the Convention. It shall be subject to ratification, acceptance or approval. A member State of the Council of Europe may not ratify, accept or approve this Protocol unless it has, simultaneously or previously, ratified the Convention. Instruments of ratification, acceptance or approval shall be deposited with the Secretary General of the Council of Europe.

Article 8 Entry into force

1. This Protocol shall enter into force on the first day of the month following the date on which five member States of the Council of Europe have expressed their consent to be bound by the Protocol in accordance with the provisions of Article 7.

2. In respect of any member State which subsequently expresses its consent to be bound by it, the Protocol shall enter into force on the first day of the month following the date of the deposit of the instrument of ratification, acceptance or approval.

Article 9 Depositary functions

The Secretary General of the Council of Europe shall notify the member States of the Council of:

(a) any signature;

(b) the deposit of any instrument of ratification, acceptance or approval;

(c) any date of entry into force of this Protocol in accordance with Articles 5 and 8;

(d) any other act, notification or communication relating to this Protocol.

In witness whereof the undersigned, being duly authorised thereto, have signed this Protocol.

Done at Strasbourg, this 28th day of April 1983, in English and in French, both texts being equally authentic, in a single copy which shall be deposited in the archives of the Council of Europe. The Secretary General of the Council of Europe shall transmit certified copies to each member State of the Council of Europe.

80

Protocol No. 7 to the Convention for the Protection of Human Rights and Fundamental Freedoms, 1984 (Seventh Protocol)

Note: Protocol No. 7 to the 1950 European Convention for the Protection of Human Rights and Fundamental Freedoms. Adopted Strasbourg, 22 November 1984. ETS No. 117. Entry into force: 1 November 1988.

The Member States of the Council of Europe, signatory hereto,

Being resolved to take further steps to ensure the collective enforcement of certain rights and freedoms by means of the Convention for the Protection of Human Rights and Fundamental Freedoms signed at Rome on 4 November 1950 (hereinafter referred to as "the Convention"),

Have agreed as follows:

Article 1 Procedural safeguards relating to expulsion of aliens

1. An alien lawfully resident in the territory of a State shall not be expelled therefrom except in pursuance of a decision reached in accordance with law and shall be allowed:
   (a) to submit reasons against his expulsion,
   (b) to have his case reviewed, and
   (c) to be represented for these purposes before the competent authority or a person or persons designated by that authority.
2. An alien may be expelled before the exercise of his rights under paragraph 1(a), (b) and (c) of this Article, when such expulsion is necessary in the interests of public order or is grounded on reasons of national security.

Article 2 Right of appeal in criminal matters

1. Everyone convicted of a criminal offence by a tribunal shall have the right to have his conviction or sentence reviewed by a higher tribunal. The exercise of this right, including the grounds on which it may be exercised, shall be governed by law.
2. This right may be subject to exceptions in regard to offences of a minor character, as prescribed by law, or in cases in which the person concerned was tried in the first instance by the highest tribunal or was convicted following an appeal against acquittal.

Article 3 Compensation for wrongful conviction

When a person has by a final decision been convicted of a criminal offence and when subsequently his conviction has been reversed, or he has been pardoned, on the ground that a new or newly discovered fact shows conclusively that there has been a miscarriage of justice, the person who has suffered punishment as a result of such conviction shall be compensated according to the law or the practice of the State concerned, unless it is proved that the nondisclosure of the unknown fact in time is wholly or partly attributable to him.

Article 4 Right not to be tried or punished twice

1. No one shall be liable to be tried or punished again in criminal proceedings under the jurisdiction of the same State for an offence for which he has already been finally acquitted or convicted in accordance with the law and penal procedure of that State.
2. The provisions of the preceding paragraph shall not prevent the reopening of the case in accordance with the law and penal procedure of the State concerned, if there is evidence of new or newly discovered facts, or if there has been a fundamental defect in the previous proceedings, which could affect the outcome of the case.
3. No derogation from this Article shall be made under Article15 of the Convention.

Article 5 Equality between spouses

Spouses shall enjoy equality of rights and responsibilities of a private law character between them, and in their relations with their children, as to marriage, during marriage and in the event of its dissolution. This Article shall not prevent States from taking such measures as are necessary in the interests of the children.

Article 6 Territorial application

1. Any State may at the time of signature or when depositing its instrument of ratification, acceptance or approval, specify the territory or territories to which the Protocol shall apply and State the extent to which it undertakes that the provisions of this Protocol shall apply to such territory or territories.
2. Any State may at any later date, by a declaration addressed to the Secretary General of the Council of Europe, extend the application of this Protocol to any other territory specified in the declaration. In respect of such territory the Protocol shall enter into force on the first day of the month following the expiration of a period of two months after the date of receipt by the Secretary General of such declaration.
3. Any declaration made under the two preceding paragraphs may, in respect of any territory specified in such declaration, be withdrawn or modified by a notification addressed to the Secretary General. The withdrawal or modification shall become effective on the first day of the month following the expiration of a period of two months after the date of receipt of such notification by the Secretary General.
4. A declaration made in accordance with this Article shall be deemed to have been made in accordance with paragraph 1 of Article 56 of the Convention.
5. The territory of any State to which this Protocol applies by virtue of ratification, acceptance or approval by that State, and each territory to which this Protocol is applied by virtue of a declaration by that State under this Article, may be treated as separate territories for the purpose of the reference in Article 1 to the territory of a State.
6. Any State which has made a declaration in accordance with paragraph 1 or 2 of this Article may at any time thereafter declare on behalf of one or more of the territories to which the declaration relates that it accepts the competence of the Court to receive applications from individuals, nongovernmental organisations or groups of individuals as provided in Article 34 of the Convention in respect of Articles 1 to 5 of this Protocol.

Article 7 Relationship to the Convention

As between the States Parties, the provisions of Article 1 to 6 of this Protocol shall be regarded as additional Articles to the Convention, and all the provisions of the Convention shall apply accordingly.

Article 8 Signature and ratification

This Protocol shall be open for signature by member States of the Council of Europe which have signed the Convention. It is subject to ratification, acceptance or approval. A member State of the Council of Europe may not ratify, accept or approve this Protocol without previously or simultaneously ratifying the Convention. Instruments of ratification, acceptance or approval shall be deposited with the Secretary General of the Council of Europe.

Article 9 Entry into force

1. This Protocol shall enter into force on the first day of the month following the expiration of a period of two months after the date on which seven member States of the Council of Europe have expressed their consent to be bound by the Protocol in accordance with the provisions of Article 8.
2. In respect of any member State which subsequently expresses its consent to be bound by it, the Protocol shall enter into force on the first day of the month following the expiration of a period of two months after the date of the deposit of the instrument of ratification, acceptance or approval.

Article 10 Depositary functions

The Secretary General of the Council of Europe shall notify all the member States of the Council of Europe of:

  (a) any signature;
  (b) the deposit of any instrument of ratification, acceptance or approval;
  (c) any date of entry into force of this Protocol in accordance with Articles 6 and 9;
  (d) any other act, notification or declaration relating to this Protocol.

In witness whereof the undersigned, being duly authorised thereto, have signed this Protocol.

Done at Strasbourg, this 22nd day of November 1984, in English and French, both texts being equally authentic, in a single copy which shall be deposited in the archives of the Council of Europe.

The Secretary General of the Council of Europe shall transmit certified copies to each member State of the Council of Europe.

81

Protocol No. 12 to the Convention for the Protection of Human Rights and Fundamental Freedoms, 2000 (Twelfth Protocol)

Note: Protocol No. 12 to the Convention for the Protection of Human Rights and Fundamental Freedom, adopted Rome, 4 November 2000. ETS No. 177. Entry into force: 1 April 2005.

The Member States of the Council of Europe, signatory hereto,

Having regard to the fundamental principle according to which all persons are equal before the law and are entitled to the equal protection of the law;

Being resolved to take further steps to promote the equality of all persons through the collective enforcement of a general prohibition of discrimination by means of the Convention for the Protection of Human Rights and Fundamental Freedoms signed at Rome on 4 November 1950 (hereinafter referred to as "the Convention");

Reaffirming that the principle of non-discrimination does not prevent States Parties from taking measures in order to promote full and effective equality, provided that there is an objective and reasonable justification for those measures,

Have agreed as follows:

Article 1 General prohibition of discrimination

1. The enjoyment of any right set forth by law shall be secured without discrimination on any ground such as sex, race, colour, language, religion, political or other opinion, national or social origin, association with a national minority, property, birth or other status.
2. No one shall be discriminated against by any public authority on any ground such as those mentioned in paragraph 1.

Article 2 Territorial application

1. Any State may, at the time of signature or when depositing its instrument of ratification, acceptance or approval, specify the territory or territories to which this Protocol shall apply.
2. Any State may at any later date, by a declaration addressed to the Secretary General of the Council of Europe, extend the application of this Protocol to any other territory specified in the declaration. In respect of such territory the Protocol shall enter into force on the first day of the month following the expiration of a period of three months after the date of receipt by the Secretary General of such declaration.
3. Any declaration made under the two preceding paragraphs may, in respect of any territory specified in such declaration, be withdrawn or modified by a notification addressed to the Secretary General of the Council of Europe. The withdrawal or

modification shall become effective on the first day of the month following the expiration of a period of three months after the date of receipt of such notification by the Secretary General.

4. A declaration made in accordance with this Article shall be deemed to have been made in accordance with paragraph 1 of Article 56 of the Convention.

5. Any State which has made a declaration in accordance with paragraph 1 or 2 of this Article may at any time thereafter declare on behalf of one or more of the territories to which the declaration relates that it accepts the competence of the Court to receive applications from individuals, nongovernmental organisations or groups of individuals as provided by Article 34 of the Convention in respect of Article 1 of this Protocol.

Article 3 Relationship to the Convention

As between the States Parties, the provisions of Articles 1 and 2 of this Protocol shall be regarded as additional Articles to the Convention, and all the provisions of the Convention shall apply accordingly.

Article 4 Signature and ratification

This Protocol shall be open for signature by member States of the Council of Europe which have signed the Convention. It is subject to ratification, acceptance or approval. A member State of the Council of Europe may not ratify, accept or approve this Protocol without previously or simultaneously ratifying the Convention. Instruments of ratification, acceptance or approval shall be deposited with the Secretary General of the Council of Europe.

Article 5 Entry into force

1. This Protocol shall enter into force on the first day of the month following the expiration of a period of three months after the date on which ten member States of the Council of Europe have expressed their consent to be bound by the Protocol in accordance with the provisions of Article 4.

2. In respect of any member State which subsequently expresses its consent to be bound by it, the Protocol shall enter into force on the first day of the month following the expiration of a period of three months after the date of the deposit of the instrument of ratification, acceptance or approval.

Article 6 Depositary functions

The Secretary General of the Council of Europe shall notify all the member States of the Council of Europe of:

(a) any signature;

(b) the deposit of any instrument of ratification, acceptance or approval;

(c) any date of entry into force of this Protocol in accordance with Articles 2 and 5;

(d) any other act, notification or communication relating to this Protocol.

In witness whereof the undersigned, being duly authorised thereto, have signed this Protocol.

Done at Rome, this 4th day of November 2000, in English and in French, both texts being equally authentic, in a single copy which shall be deposited in the archives of the Council of Europe. The Secretary General of the Council of Europe shall transmit certified copies to each member State of the Council of Europe.

82

Protocol No. 13 to the Convention for the Protection of Human Rights and Fundamental Freedoms, 2002 (Thirteenth Protocol)

Note: Protocol No. 13 to the Convention for the Protection of Human Rights and Fundamental Freedoms Concerning the Abolition of the Death Penalty in all Circumstances. Adopted Vilnius, 3 May 2002. ETS No. 187. Entry into force: 1 July 2003.

The Member States of the Council of Europe, signatory hereto,

Convinced that everyone's right to life is a basic value in a democratic society and that the abolition of the death penalty is essential for the protection of this right and for the full recognition of the inherent dignity of all human beings;

Wishing to strengthen the protection of the right to life guaranteed by the Convention for the Protection of Human Rights and Fundamental Freedoms signed at Rome on 4 November 1950 (hereinafter referred to as "the Convention");

Noting that Protocol No. 6 to the Convention, concerning the Abolition of the Death Penalty, signed at Strasbourg on 28 April 1983, does not exclude the death penalty in respect of acts committed in time of war or of imminent threat of war;

Being resolved to take the final step in order to abolish the death penalty in all circumstances,

Have agreed as follows:

Article 1 Abolition of the death penalty
The death penalty shall be abolished. No one shall be condemned to such penalty or executed.

Article 2 Prohibition of derogations
No derogation from the provisions of this Protocol shall be made under Article 15 of the Convention.

Article 3 Prohibition of reservations
No reservation may be made under Article 57 of the Convention in respect of the provisions of this Protocol.

Article 4 Territorial application
1. Any State may, at the time of signature or when depositing its instrument of ratification, acceptance or approval, specify the territory or territories to which this Protocol shall apply.
2. Any State may at any later date, by a declaration addressed to the Secretary General of the Council of Europe, extend the application of this Protocol to any other territory

specified in the declaration. In respect of such territory the Protocol shall enter into force on the first day of the month following the expiration of a period of three months after the date of receipt by the Secretary General of such declaration.

3. Any declaration made under the two preceding paragraphs may, in respect of any territory specified in such declaration, be withdrawn or modified by a notification addressed to the Secretary General. The withdrawal or modification shall become effective on the first day of the month following the expiration of a period of three months after the date of receipt of such notification by the Secretary General.

Article 5 Relationship to the Convention

As between the States Parties the provisions of Articles 1 to 4 of this Protocol shall be regarded as additional Articles to the Convention, and all the provisions of the Convention shall apply accordingly.

Article 6 Signature and ratification

This Protocol shall be open for signature by member States of the Council of Europe which have signed the Convention. It is subject to ratification, acceptance or approval. A member State of the Council of Europe may not ratify, accept or approve this Protocol without previously or simultaneously ratifying the Convention. Instruments of ratification, acceptance or approval shall be deposited with the Secretary General of the Council of Europe.

Article 7 Entry into force

1. This Protocol shall enter into force on the first day of the month following the expiration of a period of three months after the date on which ten member States of the Council of Europe have expressed their consent to be bound by the Protocol in accordance with the provisions of Article 6.

2. In respect of any member State which subsequently expresses its consent to be bound by it, the Protocol shall enter into force on the first day of the month following the expiration of a period of three months after the date of the deposit of the instrument of ratification, acceptance or approval.

Article 8 Depositary functions

The Secretary General of the Council of Europe shall notify all the member States of the Council of Europe of:

(a) any signature;

(b) the deposit of any instrument of ratification, acceptance or approval;

(c) any date of entry into force of this Protocol in accordance with Articles 4 and 7;

(d) any other act, notification or communication relating to this Protocol.

In witness whereof the undersigned, being duly authorised thereto, have signed this Protocol.

Done at Vilnius, this 3rd day of May 2002, in English and in French, both texts being equally authentic, in a single copy which shall be deposited in the archives of the Council of Europe. The Secretary General of the Council of Europe shall transmit certified copies to each member State of the Council of Europe.

83

Protocol No. 15 Amending the Convention on the Protection of Human Rights and Fundamental Freedoms, 2013 (Fifteenth Protocol)

Note: Protocol No. 15 Amending the Convention for the Protection of Human Rights and Fundamental Freedoms. Adopted Strasbourg, 24 June 2013. Council of Europe Treaty Series No. 213. Not yet in force.

PREAMBLE

The member States of the Council of Europe and the other High Contracting Parties to the Convention for the Protection of Human Rights and Fundamental Freedoms, signed at Rome on 4 November 1950 (hereinafter referred to as "the Convention"), signatory hereto,

Having regard to the declaration adopted at the High Level Conference on the Future of the European Court of Human Rights, held in Brighton on 19 and 20 April 2012, as well as the declarations adopted at the conferences held in Interlaken on 18 and 19 February 2010 and İzmir on 26 and 27 April 2011;

Having regard to Opinion No. 283 (2013) adopted by the Parliamentary Assembly of the Council of Europe on 26 April 2013;

Considering the need to ensure that the European Court of Human Rights (hereinafter referred to as "the Court") can continue to play its pre-eminent role in protecting human rights in Europe,

Have agreed as follows:

Article 1
At the end of the preamble to the Convention, a new recital shall be added, which shall read as follows:

> "Affirming that the High Contracting Parties, in accordance with the principle of subsidiarity, have the primary responsibility to secure the rights and freedoms defined in this Convention and the Protocols thereto, and that in doing so they enjoy a margin of appreciation, subject to the supervisory jurisdiction of the European Court of Human Rights established by this Convention,"

Article 2

1. In Article 21 of the Convention, a new paragraph 2 shall be inserted, which shall read as follows:

   "Candidates shall be less than 65 years of age at the date by which the list of three candidates has been requested by the Parliamentary Assembly, further to Article 22."

2. Paragraphs 2 and 3 of Article 21 of the Convention shall become paragraphs 3 and 4 of Article 21 respectively.
3. Paragraph 2 of Article 23 of the Convention shall be deleted. Paragraphs 3 and 4 of Article 23 shall become paragraphs 2 and 3 of Article 23 respectively.

Article 3

In Article 30 of the Convention, the words "unless one of the parties to the case objects" shall be deleted.

Article 4

In Article 35, paragraph 1 of the Convention, the words "within a period of six months" shall be replaced by the words "within a period of four months".

Article 5

In Article 35, paragraph 3, sub-paragraph b of the Convention, the words "and provided that no case may be rejected on this ground which has not been duly considered by a domestic tribunal" shall be deleted.

Final and transitional provisions

Article 6

1. This Protocol shall be open for signature by the High Contracting Parties to the Convention, which may express their consent to be bound by:
   (a) signature without reservation as to ratification, acceptance or approval; or
   (b) signature subject to ratification, acceptance or approval, followed by ratification, acceptance or approval.
2. The instruments of ratification, acceptance or approval shall be deposited with the Secretary General of the Council of Europe.

Article 7

This Protocol shall enter into force on the first day of the month following the expiration of a period of three months after the date on which all High Contracting Parties to the Convention have expressed their consent to be bound by the Protocol, in accordance with the provisions of Article 6.

Article 8

1. The amendments introduced by Article 2 of this Protocol shall apply only to candidates on lists submitted to the Parliamentary Assembly by the High Contracting Parties under Article 22 of the Convention after the entry into force of this Protocol.

2. The amendment introduced by Article 3 of this Protocol shall not apply to any pending case in which one of the parties has objected, prior to the date of entry into force of this Protocol, to a proposal by a Chamber of the Court to relinquish jurisdiction in favour of the Grand Chamber.

3. Article 4 of this Protocol shall enter into force following the expiration of a period of six months after the date of entry into force of this Protocol. Article 4 of this Protocol shall not apply to applications in respect of which the final decision within the meaning of Article 35, paragraph 1 of the Convention was taken prior to the date of entry into force of Article 4 of this Protocol.

4. All other provisions of this Protocol shall apply from its date of entry into force, in accordance with the provisions of Article 7.

Article 9

The Secretary General of the Council of Europe shall notify the member States of the Council of Europe and the other High Contracting Parties to the Convention of:

a. any signature;

b. the deposit of any instrument of ratification, acceptance or approval;

c. the date of entry into force of this Protocol in accordance with Article 7; and

d. any other act, notification or communication relating to this Protocol.

In witness whereof, the undersigned, being duly authorised thereto, have signed this Protocol.

Done at Strasbourg, this 24th day of June 2013, in English and in French, both texts being equally authentic, in a single copy which shall be deposited in the archives of the Council of Europe. The Secretary General of the Council of Europe shall transmit certified copies to each member State of the Council of Europe and to the other High Contracting Parties to the Convention.

84

Protocol No. 16 to the Convention on the Protection of Human Rights and Fundamental Freedoms, 2013 (Sixteenth Protocol)

Note: Protocol No. 16 to the Convention on the Protection of Human Rights and Fundamental Freedoms. Adopted Strasbourg, 2 October 2013. Council of Europe Treaty Series No. 214. Not yet in force.

PREAMBLE

The member States of the Council of Europe and other High Contracting Parties to the Convention for the Protection of Human Rights and Fundamental Freedoms, signed at Rome on 4 November 1950 (hereinafter referred to as "the Convention"), signatories hereto,

Having regard to the provisions of the Convention and, in particular, Article 19 establishing the European Court of Human Rights (hereinafter referred to as "the Court");

Considering that the extension of the Court's competence to give advisory opinions will further enhance the interaction between the Court and national authorities and thereby reinforce implementation of the Convention, in accordance with the principle of subsidiarity;

Having regard to Opinion No. 285 (2013) adopted by the Parliamentary Assembly of the Council of Europe on 28 June 2013,

Have agreed as follows:

Article 1

1. Highest courts and tribunals of a High Contracting Party, as specified in accordance with Article 10, may request the Court to give advisory opinions on questions of principle relating to the interpretation or application of the rights and freedoms defined in the Convention or the protocols thereto.
2. The requesting court or tribunal may seek an advisory opinion only in the context of a case pending before it.
3. The requesting court or tribunal shall give reasons for its request and shall provide the relevant legal and factual background of the pending case.

Article 2

1. A panel of five judges of the Grand Chamber shall decide whether to accept the request for an advisory opinion, having regard to Article 1. The panel shall give reasons for any refusal to accept the request.
2. If the panel accepts the request, the Grand Chamber shall deliver the advisory opinion.

3. The panel and the Grand Chamber, as referred to in the preceding paragraphs, shall include ex officio the judge elected in respect of the High Contracting Party to which the requesting court or tribunal pertains. If there is none or if that judge is unable to sit, a person chosen by the President of the Court from a list submitted in advance by that Party shall sit in the capacity of judge.

Article 3
The Council of Europe Commissioner for Human Rights and the High Contracting Party to which the requesting court or tribunal pertains shall have the right to submit written comments and take part in any hearing. The President of the Court may, in the interest of the proper administration of justice, invite any other High Contracting Party or person also to submit written comments or take part in any hearing.

Article 4
1. Reasons shall be given for advisory opinions.
2. If the advisory opinion does not represent, in whole or in part, the unanimous opinion of the judges, any judge shall be entitled to deliver a separate opinion.
3. Advisory opinions shall be communicated to the requesting court or tribunal and to the High Contracting Party to which that court or tribunal pertains.
4. Advisory opinions shall be published.

Article 5
Advisory opinions shall not be binding.

Article 6
As between the High Contracting Parties the provisions of Articles 1 to 5 of this Protocol shall be regarded as additional articles to the Convention, and all the provisions of the Convention shall apply accordingly.

Article 7
1. This Protocol shall be open for signature by the High Contracting Parties to the Convention, which may express their consent to be bound by:
   a   signature without reservation as to ratification, acceptance or approval; or
   b   signature subject to ratification, acceptance or approval, followed by ratification, acceptance or approval.
2. The instruments of ratification, acceptance or approval shall be deposited with the Secretary General of the Council of Europe.

Article 8
1. This Protocol shall enter into force on the first day of the month following the expiration of a period of three months after the date on which ten High Contracting Parties to the Convention have expressed their consent to be bound by the Protocol in accordance with the provisions of Article 7.
2. In respect of any High Contracting Party to the Convention which subsequently expresses its consent to be bound by it, the Protocol shall enter into force on the first day of the month following the expiration of a period of three months after the date

of the expression of its consent to be bound by the Protocol in accordance with the provisions of Article 7.

Article 9

No reservation may be made under Article 57 of the Convention in respect of the provisions of this Protocol.

Article 10

Each High Contracting Party to the Convention shall, at the time of signature or when depositing its instrument of ratification, acceptance or approval, by means of a declaration addressed to the Secretary General of the Council of Europe, indicate the courts or tribunals that it designates for the purposes of Article 1, paragraph 1, of this Protocol. This declaration may be modified at any later date and in the same manner.

Article 11

The Secretary General of the Council of Europe shall notify the member States of the Council of Europe and the other High Contracting Parties to the Convention of:

a   any signature;
b   the deposit of any instrument of ratification, acceptance or approval;
c   any date of entry into force of this Protocol in accordance with Article 8;
d   any declaration made in accordance with Article 10; and
e   any other act, notification or communication relating to this Protocol.

In witness whereof the undersigned, being duly authorised thereto, have signed this Protocol.

Done at Strasbourg, this 2nd day of October 2013, in English and French, both texts being equally authentic, in a single copy which shall be deposited in the archives of the Council of Europe. The Secretary General of the Council of Europe shall transmit certified copies to each member State of the Council of Europe and to the other High Contracting Parties to the Convention.

85

European Social Charter, 1961

Note: European Social Charter. Adopted Turin, 18 October 1961. ETS No. 35. Entry in force: 26 February 1965.

PREAMBLE

The governments signatory hereto, being members of the Council of Europe,

Considering that the aim of the Council of Europe is the achievement of greater unity between its members for the purpose of safeguarding and realising the ideals and principles which are their common heritage and of facilitating their economic and social progress, in particular by the maintenance and further realisation of human rights and fundamental freedoms;

Considering that in the European Convention for the Protection of Human Rights and Fundamental Freedoms signed at Rome on 4th November 1950, and the Protocol thereto signed at Paris on 20th March 1952, the member States of the Council of Europe agreed to secure to their populations the civil and political rights and freedoms therein specified;

Considering that the enjoyment of social rights should be secured without discrimination on grounds of race, colour, sex, religion, political opinion, national extraction or social origin;

Being resolved to make every effort in common to improve the standard of living and to promote the social wellbeing of both their urban and rural populations by means of appropriate institutions and action,

Have agreed as follows:

PART I

The Contracting Parties accept as the aim of their policy, to be pursued by all appropriate means, both national and international in character, the attainment of conditions in which the following rights and principles may be effectively realised:
1. Everyone shall have the opportunity to earn his living in an occupation freely entered upon.
2. All workers have the right to just conditions of work.

3. All workers have the right to safe and healthy working conditions.

4. All workers have the right to a fair remuneration sufficient for a decent standard of living for themselves and their families.

5. All workers and employers have the right to freedom of association in national or international organisations for the protection of their economic and social interests.

6. All workers and employers have the right to bargain collectively.

7. Children and young persons have the right to a special protection against the physical and moral hazards to which they are exposed.

8. Employed women, in case of maternity, and other employed women as appropriate, have the right to a special protection in their work.

9. Everyone has the right to appropriate facilities for vocational guidance with a view to helping him choose an occupation suited to his personal aptitude and interests.

10. Everyone has the right to appropriate facilities for vocational training.

11. Everyone has the right to benefit from any measures enabling him to enjoy the highest possible standard of health attainable.

12. All workers and their dependents have the right to social security.

13. Anyone without adequate resources has the right to social and medical assistance.

14. Everyone has the right to benefit from social welfare services.

15. Disabled persons have the right to vocational training, rehabilitation and resettlement, whatever the origin and nature of their disability.

16. The family as a fundamental unit of society has the right to appropriate social, legal and economic protection to ensure its full development.

17. Mothers and children, irrespective of marital status and family relations, have the right to appropriate social and economic protection.

18. The nationals of any one of the Contracting Parties have the right to engage in any gainful occupation in the territory of any one of the others on a footing of equality with the nationals of the latter, subject to restrictions based on cogent economic or social reasons.

19. Migrant workers who are nationals of a Contracting Party and their families have the right to protection and assistance in the territory of any other Contracting Party.

PART II

The Contracting Parties undertake, as provided for in Part III, to consider themselves bound by the obligations laid down in the following articles and paragraphs.

Article 1 – The right to work

With a view to ensuring the effective exercise of the right to work, the Contracting Parties undertake:

1. to accept as one of their primary aims and responsibilities the achievement and maintenance of as high and stable a level of employment as possible, with a view to the attainment of full employment;

2. to protect effectively the right of the worker to earn his living in an occupation freely entered upon;

3. to establish or maintain free employment services for all workers;

4. to provide or promote appropriate vocational guidance, training and rehabilitation.

Article 2 – The right to just conditions of work

With a view to ensuring the effective exercise of the right to just conditions of work, the Contracting Parties undertake:

1. to provide for reasonable daily and weekly working hours, the working week to be progressively reduced to the extent that the increase of productivity and other relevant factors permit;
2. to provide for public holidays with pay;
3. to provide for a minimum of two weeks annual holiday with pay;
4. to provide for additional paid holidays or reduced working hours for workers engaged in dangerous or unhealthy occupations as prescribed;
5. to ensure a weekly rest period which shall, as far as possible, coincide with the day recognised by tradition or custom in the country or region concerned as a day of rest.

Article 3 – The right to safe and healthy working conditions

With a view to ensuring the effective exercise of the right to safe and healthy working conditions, the Contracting Parties undertake:

1. to issue safety and health regulations;
2. to provide for the enforcement of such regulations by measures of supervision;
3. to consult, as appropriate, employers' and workers' organisations on measures intended to improve industrial safety and health.

Article 4 – The right to a fair remuneration

With a view to ensuring the effective exercise of the right to a fair remuneration, the Contracting Parties undertake:

1. to recognise the right of workers to a remuneration such as will give them and their families a decent standard of living;
2. to recognise the right of workers to an increased rate of remuneration for overtime work, subject to exceptions in particular cases;
3. to recognise the right of men and women workers to equal pay for work of equal value;
4. to recognise the right of all workers to a reasonable period of notice for termination of employment;
5. to permit deductions from wages only under conditions and to the extent prescribed by national laws or regulations or fixed by collective agreements or arbitration awards.

The exercise of these rights shall be achieved by freely concluded collective agreements, by statutory wage fixing machinery, or by other means appropriate to national conditions.

Article 5 – The right to organise

With a view to ensuring or promoting the freedom of workers and employers to form local, national or international organisations for the protection of their economic and social interests and to join those organisations, the Contracting Parties undertake that national law shall not be such as to impair, nor shall it be so applied as to impair, this freedom. The extent to which the guarantees provided for in this article shall apply to the police shall be determined by national laws or regulations. The principle governing the application to the members of the armed forces of these guarantees and the extent to which they shall apply to persons in this category shall equally be determined by national laws or regulations.

Article 6 – The right to bargain collectively

With a view to ensuring the effective exercise of the right to bargain collectively, the Contracting Parties undertake:

1. to promote joint consultation between workers and employers;
2. to promote, where necessary and appropriate, machinery for voluntary negotiations between employers or employers' organisations and workers' organisations, with a view to the regulation of terms and conditions of employment by means of collective agreements;
3. to promote the establishment and use of appropriate machinery for conciliation and voluntary arbitration for the settlement of labour disputes; and recognise:
4. the right of workers and employers to collective action in cases of conflicts of interest, including the right to strike, subject to obligations that might arise out of collective agreements previously entered into.

Article 7 – The right of children and young persons to protection

With a view to ensuring the effective exercise of the right of children and young persons to protection, the Contracting Parties undertake:

1. to provide that the minimum age of admission to employment shall be 15 years, subject to exceptions for children employed in prescribed light work without harm to their health, morals or education;
2. to provide that a higher minimum age of admission to employment shall be fixed with respect to prescribed occupations regarded as dangerous or unhealthy;
3. to provide that persons who are still subject to compulsory education shall not be employed in such work as would deprive them of the full benefit of their education;
4. to provide that the working hours of persons under 16 years of age shall be limited in accordance with the needs of their development, and particularly with their need for vocational training;
5. to recognise the right of young workers and apprentices to a fair wage or other appropriate allowances;
6. to provide that the time spent by young persons in vocational training during the normal working hours with the consent of the employer shall be treated as forming part of the working day;
7. to provide that employed persons of under 18 years of age shall be entitled to not less than three weeks' annual holiday with pay;
8. to provide that persons under 18 years of age shall not be employed in night work with the exception of certain occupations provided for by national laws or regulations;
9. to provide that persons under 18 years of age employed in occupations prescribed by national laws or regulations shall be subject to regular medical control;
10. to ensure special protection against physical and moral dangers to which children and young persons are exposed, and particularly against those resulting directly or indirectly from their work.

Article 8 – The right of employed women to protection

With a view to ensuring the effective exercise of the right of employed women to protection, the Contracting Parties undertake:

1. to provide either by paid leave, by adequate social security benefits or by benefits from public funds for women to take leave before and after childbirth up to a total of at least 12 weeks;
2. to consider it as unlawful for an employer to give a woman notice of dismissal during her absence on maternity leave or to give her notice of dismissal at such a time that the notice would expire during such absence;
3. to provide that mothers who are nursing their infants shall be entitled to sufficient time off for this purpose;
4. (a) to regulate the employment of women workers on night work in industrial employment;
   (b) to prohibit the employment of women workers in underground mining, and, as appropriate, on all other work which is unsuitable for them by reason of its dangerous, unhealthy, or arduous nature.

Article 9 – The right to vocational guidance

With a view to ensuring the effective exercise of the right to vocational guidance, the Contracting Parties undertake to provide or promote, as necessary, a service which will assist all persons, including the handicapped, to solve problems related to occupational choice and progress, with due regard to the individual's characteristics and their relation to occupational opportunity: this assistance should be available free of charge, both to young persons, including school children, and to adults.

Article 10 – The right to vocational training

With a view to ensuring the effective exercise of the right to vocational training, the Contracting Parties undertake:
1. to provide or promote, as necessary, the technical and vocational training of all persons, including the handicapped, in consultation with employers' and workers' organisations, and to grant facilities for access to higher technical and university education, based solely on individual aptitude;
2. to provide or promote a system of apprenticeship and other systematic arrangements for training young boys and girls in their various employments;
3. to provide or promote, as necessary:
   (a) adequate and readily available training facilities for adult workers;
   (b) special facilities for the re training of adult workers needed as a result of techno-logical development or new trends in employment;
4. to encourage the full utilisation of the facilities provided by appropriate measures such as:
   (a) reducing or abolishing any fees or charges;
   (b) granting financial assistance in appropriate cases;
   (c) including in the normal working hours time spent on supplementary training taken by the worker, at the request of his employer, during employment;
   (d) ensuring, through adequate supervision, in consultation with the employers' and workers' organisations, the efficiency of apprenticeship and other training arrangements for young workers, and the adequate protection of young workers generally.

Article 11 – The right to protection of health

With a view to ensuring the effective exercise of the right to protection of health, the Contracting Parties undertake, either directly or in cooperation with public or private organisations, to take appropriate measures designed inter alia:

1. to remove as far as possible the causes of ill health;
2. to provide advisory and educational facilities for the promotion of health and the encouragement of individual responsibility in matters of health;
3. to prevent as far as possible epidemic, endemic and other diseases.

Article 12 – The right to social security

With a view to ensuring the effective exercise of the right to social security, the Contracting Parties undertake:

1. to establish or maintain a system of social security;
2. to maintain the social security system at a satisfactory level at least equal to that required for ratification of International Labour Convention (No. 102) Concerning Minimum Standards of Social Security;
3. to endeavour to raise progressively the system of social security to a higher level;
4. to take steps, by the conclusion of appropriate bilateral and multilateral agreements, or by other means, and subject to the conditions laid down in such agreements, in order to ensure:

   (a) equal treatment with their own nationals of the nationals of other Contracting Parties in respect of social security rights, including the retention of benefits arising out of social security legislation, whatever movements the persons protected may undertake between the territories of the Contracting Parties;

   (b) the granting, maintenance and resumption of social security rights by such means as the accumulation of insurance or employment periods completed under the legislation of each of the Contracting Parties.

Article 13 – The right to social and medical assistance

With a view to ensuring the effective exercise of the right to social and medical assistance, the Contracting Parties undertake:

1. to ensure that any person who is without adequate resources and who is unable to secure such resources either by his own efforts or from other sources, in particular by benefits under a social security scheme, be granted adequate assistance, and, in case of sickness, the care necessitated by his condition;
2. to ensure that persons receiving such assistance shall not, for that reason, suffer from a diminution of their political or social rights;
3. to provide that everyone may receive by appropriate public or private services such advice and personal help as may be required to prevent, to remove, or to alleviate personal or family want;
4. to apply the provisions referred to in paragraphs 1, 2 and 3 of this article on an equal footing with their nationals to nationals of other Contracting Parties lawfully within their territories, in accordance with their obligations under the European Convention on Social and Medical Assistance, signed at Paris on 11th December 1953.

Article 14 – The right to benefit from social welfare services

With a view to ensuring the effective exercise of the right to benefit from social welfare services, the Contracting Parties undertake:

1. to promote or provide services which, by using methods of social work, would contribute to the welfare and development of both individuals and groups in the community, and to their adjustment to the social environment;
2. to encourage the participation of individuals and voluntary or other organisations in the establishment and maintenance of such services.

Article 15 – The right of physically or mentally disabled persons to vocational training, rehabilitation and social resettlement

With a view to ensuring the effective exercise of the right of the physically or mentally disabled to vocational training, rehabilitation and resettlement, the Contracting Parties undertake:

1. to take adequate measures for the provision of training facilities, including, where necessary, specialised institutions, public or private;
2. to take adequate measures for the placing of disabled persons in employment, such as specialised placing services, facilities for sheltered employment and measures to encourage employers to admit disabled persons to employment.

Article 16 – The right of the family to social, legal and economic protection

With a view to ensuring the necessary conditions for the full development of the family, which is a fundamental unit of society, the Contracting Parties undertake to promote the economic, legal and social protection of family life by such means as social and family benefits, fiscal arrangements, provision of family housing, benefits for the newly married, and other appropriate means.

Article 17 – The right of mothers and children to social and economic protection

With a view to ensuring the effective exercise of the right of mothers and children to social and economic protection, the Contracting Parties will take all appropriate and necessary measures to that end, including the establishment or maintenance of appropriate institutions or services.

Article 18 – The right to engage in a gainful occupation in the territory of other Contracting Parties

With a view to ensuring the effective exercise of the right to engage in a gainful occupation in the territory of any other Contracting Party, the Contracting Parties undertake:

1. to apply existing regulations in a spirit of liberality;
2. to simplify existing formalities and to reduce or abolish chancery dues and other charges payable by foreign workers or their employers;
3. to liberalise, individually or collectively, regulations governing the employment of foreign workers; and recognise:
4. the right of their nationals to leave the country to engage in a gainful occupation in the territories of the other Contracting Parties.

Article 19 – The right of migrant workers and their families to protection and assistance

With a view to ensuring the effective exercise of the right of migrant workers and their families to protection and assistance in the territory of any other Contracting Party, the Contracting Parties undertake:

1. to maintain or to satisfy themselves that there are maintained adequate and free services to assist such workers, particularly in obtaining accurate information, and to take all appropriate steps, so far as national laws and regulations permit, against misleading propaganda relating to emigration and immigration;

2. to adopt appropriate measures within their own jurisdiction to facilitate the departure, journey and reception of such workers and their families, and to provide, within their own jurisdiction, appropriate services for health, medical attention and good hygienic conditions during the journey;

3. to promote cooperation, as appropriate, between social services, public and private, in emigration and immigration countries;

4. to secure for such workers lawfully within their territories, insofar as such matters are regulated by law or regulations or are subject to the control of administrative authorities, treatment not less favourable than that of their own nationals in respect of the following matters:
   (a) remuneration and other employment and working conditions;
   (b) membership of trade unions and enjoyment of the benefits of collective bargaining;
   (c) accommodation;

5. to secure for such workers lawfully within their territories treatment not less favourable than that of their own nationals with regard to employment taxes, dues or contributions payable in respect of employed persons;

6. to facilitate as far as possible the reunion of the family of a foreign worker permitted to establish himself in the territory;

7. to secure for such workers lawfully within their territories treatment not less favourable than that of their own nationals in respect of legal proceedings relating to matters referred to in this article;

8. to secure that such workers lawfully residing within their territories are not expelled unless they endanger national security or offend against public interest or morality;

9. to permit, within legal limits, the transfer of such parts of the earnings and savings of such workers as they may desire;

10. to extend the protection and assistance provided for in this article to self-employed migrants insofar as such measures apply.

PART III

Article 20 – Undertakings

1. Each of the Contracting Parties undertakes:
   (a) to consider Part I of this Charter as a declaration of the aims which it will pursue by all appropriate means, as stated in the introductory paragraph of that part;
   (b) to consider itself bound by at least five of the following articles of Part II of this Charter: Articles 1, 5, 6, 12, 13, 16 and 19;

(c) in addition to the articles selected by it in accordance with the preceding sub paragraph, to consider itself bound by such a number of articles or numbered paragraphs of Part II of the Charter as it may select, provided that the total number of articles or numbered paragraphs by which it is bound is not less than 10 articles or 45 numbered paragraphs.

2. The articles or paragraphs selected in accordance with sub paragraphs b and c of paragraph 1 of this article shall be notified to the Secretary General of the Council of Europe at the time when the instrument of ratification or approval of the Contracting Party concerned is deposited.

3. Any Contracting Party may, at a later date, declare by notification to the Secretary General that it considers itself bound by any articles or any numbered paragraphs of Part II of the Charter which it has not already accepted under the terms of paragraph 1 of this article. Such undertakings subsequently given shall be deemed to be an integral part of the ratification or approval, and shall have the same effect as from the thirtieth day after the date of the notification.

4. The Secretary General shall communicate to all the signatory governments and to the Director General of the International Labour Office any notification which he shall have received pursuant to this part of the Charter.

5. Each Contracting Party shall maintain a system of labour inspection appropriate to national conditions.

PART IV

Article 21 – Reports concerning accepted provisions

The Contracting Parties shall send to the Secretary General of the Council of Europe a report at two yearly intervals, in a form to be determined by the Committee of Ministers, concerning the application of such provisions of Part II of the Charter as they have accepted.

Article 22 – Reports concerning provisions which are not accepted

The Contracting Parties shall send to the Secretary General, at appropriate intervals as requested by the Committee of Ministers, reports relating to the provisions of Part II of the Charter which they did not accept at the time of their ratification or approval or in a subsequent notification. The Committee of Ministers shall determine from time to time in respect of which provisions such reports shall be requested and the form of the reports to be provided.

Article 23 – Communication of copies

1. Each Contracting Party shall communicate copies of its reports referred to in Articles 21 and 22 to such of its national organisations as are members of the international organisations of employers and trade unions to be invited under Article 27, paragraph 2, to be represented at meetings of the Subcommittee of the Governmental Social Committee.

2. The Contracting Parties shall forward to the Secretary General any comments on the aid reports received from these national organisations, if so requested by them.

Article 24 – Examination of the reports

The reports sent to the Secretary General in accordance with Articles 21 and 22 shall be examined by a Committee of Experts, who shall have also before them any comments forwarded to the Secretary General in accordance with paragraph 2 of Article 23.

Article 25 – Committee of Experts

1. The Committee of Experts shall consist of not more than seven members appointed by the Committee of Ministers from a list of independent experts of the highest integrity and of recognised competence in international social questions, nominated by the Contracting Parties.
2. The members of the committee shall be appointed for a period of six years. They may be reappointed. However, of the members first appointed, the terms of office of two members shall expire at the end of four years.
3. The members whose terms of office are to expire at the end of the initial period of four years shall be chosen by lot by the Committee of Ministers immediately after the first appointment has been made.
4. A member of the Committee of Experts appointed to replace a member whose term of office has not expired shall hold office for the remainder of his predecessor's term.

Article 26 – Participation of the International Labour Organisation

The International Labour Organisation shall be invited to nominate a representative to participate in a consultative capacity in the deliberations of the Committee of Experts.

Article 27 – Sub-committee of the Governmental Social Committee

1. The reports of the Contracting Parties and the conclusions of the Committee of Experts shall be submitted for examination to a Subcommittee of the Governmental Social Committee of the Council of Europe.
2. The Subcommittee shall be composed of one representative of each of the Contracting Parties. It shall invite no more than two international organisations of employers and no more than two international trade union organisations as it may designate to be represented as observers in a consultative capacity at its meetings. Moreover, it may consult no more than two representatives of international non-governmental organisations having consultative status with the Council of Europe, in respect of questions with which the organisations are particularly qualified to deal, such as social welfare, and the economic and social protection of the family.
3. The Subcommittee shall present to the Committee of Ministers a report containing its conclusions and append the report of the Committee of Experts.

Article 28 – Consultative Assembly

The Secretary General of the Council of Europe shall transmit to the Consultative Assembly the conclusions of the Committee of Experts. The Consultative Assembly shall communicate its views on these conclusions to the Committee of Ministers.

Article 29 – Committee of Ministers

By a majority of two thirds of the members entitled to sit on the Committee, the Committee of Ministers may, on the basis of the report of the Subcommittee, and after consultation with the Consultative Assembly, make to each Contracting Party any necessary recommendations.

PART V

Article 30 – Derogations in time of war or public emergency

1. In time of war or other public emergency threatening the life of the nation any Contracting Party may take measures derogating from its obligations under this Charter to the extent strictly required by the exigencies of the situation, provided that such measures are not inconsistent with its other obligations under international law.

2. Any Contracting Party which has availed itself of this right of derogation shall, within a reasonable lapse of time, keep the Secretary General of the Council of Europe fully informed of the measures taken and of the reasons therefor. It shall likewise inform the Secretary General when such measures have ceased to operate and the provisions of the Charter which it has accepted are again being fully executed.

3. The Secretary General shall in turn inform other Contracting Parties and the Director General of the International Labour Office of all communications received in accordance with paragraph 2 of this article.

Article 31 – Restrictions

1. The rights and principles set forth in Part I when effectively realised, and their effective exercise as provided for in Part II, shall not be subject to any restrictions or limitations not specified in those parts, except such as are prescribed by law and are necessary in a democratic society for the protection of the rights and freedoms of others or for the protection of public interest, national security, public health, or morals.

2. The restrictions permitted under this Charter to the rights and obligations set forth herein shall not be applied for any purpose other than that for which they have been prescribed.

Article 32 – Relations between the Charter and domestic law or international agreements

The provisions of this Charter shall not prejudice the provisions of domestic law or of any bilateral or multilateral treaties, conventions or agreements which are already in force, or may come into force, under which more favourable treatment would be accorded to the persons protected.

Article 33 – Implementation by collective agreements

1. In member States where the provisions of paragraphs 1, 2, 3, 4 and 5 of Article 2, paragraphs 4, 6 and 7 of Article 7 and paragraphs 1, 2, 3 and 4 of Article 10 of Part II of this Charter are matters normally left to agreements between employers or employers' organisations and workers' organisations, or are normally carried out otherwise than by law, the undertakings of those paragraphs may be given and compliance with them shall be treated as effective if their provisions are applied through such agreements or other means to the great majority of the workers concerned.

2. In member States where these provisions are normally the subject of legislation, the undertakings concerned may likewise be given, and compliance with them shall be

regarded as effective if the provisions are applied by law to the great majority of the workers concerned.

Article 34 – Territorial application

1. This Charter shall apply to the metropolitan territory of each Contracting Party. Each signatory government may, at the time of signature or of the deposit of its instrument of ratification or approval, specify, by declaration addressed to the Secretary General of the Council of Europe, the territory which shall be considered to be its metropolitan territory for this purpose.

2. Any Contracting Party may, at the time of ratification or approval of this Charter or at any time thereafter, declare by notification addressed to the Secretary General of the Council of Europe, that the Charter shall extend in whole or in part to a non metropolitan territory or territories specified in the said declaration for whose international relations it is responsible or for which it assumes international responsibility. It shall specify in the declaration the articles or paragraphs of Part II of the Charter which it accepts as binding in respect of the territories named in the declaration.

3. The Charter shall extend to the territory or territories named in the aforesaid declaration as from the thirtieth day after the date on which the Secretary General shall have received notification of such declaration.

4. Any Contracting Party may declare at a later date, by notification addressed to the Secretary General of the Council of Europe, that, in respect of one or more of the territories to which the Charter has been extended in accordance with paragraph 2 of this article, it accepts as binding any articles or any numbered paragraphs which it has not already accepted in respect of that territory or territories. Such undertakings subsequently given shall be deemed to be an integral part of the original declaration in respect of the territory concerned, and shall have the same effect as from the thirtieth day after the date of the notification.

5. The Secretary General shall communicate to the other signatory governments and to the Director General of the International Labour Office any notification transmitted to him in accordance with this article.

Article 35 – Signature, ratification and entry into force

1. This Charter shall be open for signature by the members of the Council of Europe. It shall be ratified or approved. Instruments of ratification or approval shall be deposited with the Secretary General of the Council of Europe.

2. This Charter shall come into force as from the thirtieth day after the date of deposit of the fifth instrument of ratification or approval.

3. In respect of any signatory government ratifying subsequently, the Charter shall come into force as from the thirtieth day after the date of deposit of its instrument of ratification or approval.

4. The Secretary General shall notify all the members of the Council of Europe and the director General of the International Labour Office of the entry into force of the Charter, the names of the Contracting Parties which have ratified or approved it and the subsequent deposit of any instruments of ratification or approval.

Article 36 – Amendments

Any member of the Council of Europe may propose amendments to this Charter in a communication addressed to the Secretary General of the Council of Europe. The

Secretary General shall transmit to the other members of the Council of Europe any amendments so proposed, which shall then be considered by the Committee of Ministers and submitted to the Consultative Assembly for opinion. Any amendments approved by the Committee of Ministers shall enter into force as from the thirtieth day after all the Contracting Parties have informed the Secretary General of their acceptance. The Secretary General shall notify all the members of the Council of Europe and the Director General of the International Labour Office of the entry into force of such amendments.

Article 37 – Denunciation

1. Any Contracting Party may denounce this Charter only at the end of a period of five years from the date on which the Charter entered into force for it, or at the end of any successive period of two years, and, in each case, after giving six months notice to the Secretary General of the Council of Europe who shall inform the other Parties and the Director General of the International Labour Office accordingly. Such denunciation shall not affect the validity of the Charter in respect of the other Contracting Parties provided that at all times there are not less than five such Contracting Parties.
2. Any Contracting Party may, in accordance with the provisions set out in the preceding paragraph, denounce any article or paragraph of Part II of the Charter accepted by it provided that the number of articles or paragraphs by which this Contracting Party is bound shall never be less than 10 in the former case and 45 in the latter and that this number of articles or paragraphs shall continue to include the articles selected by the Contracting Party among those to which special reference is made in Article 20, paragraph 1, sub paragraph b.
3. Any Contracting Party may denounce the present Charter or any of the articles or paragraphs of Part II of the Charter, under the conditions specified in paragraph 1 of this article in respect of any territory to which the said Charter is applicable by virtue of a declaration made in accordance with paragraph 2 of Article 34.

Article 38 – Appendix

The appendix to this Charter shall form an integral part of it.

In witness whereof, the undersigned, being duly authorised thereto, have signed this Charter.

Done at Turin, this 18th day of October 1961, in English and French, both texts being equally authoritative, in a single copy which shall be deposited within the archives of the Council of Europe. The Secretary General shall transmit certified copies to each of the Signatories.

APPENDIX TO THE SOCIAL CHARTER

Scope of the Social Charter in terms of persons protected

1. Without prejudice to Article 12, paragraph 4, and Article 13, paragraph 4, the persons covered by Articles 1 to 17 include foreigners only insofar as they are nationals of other Contracting Parties lawfully resident or working regularly within the territory of the Contracting Party concerned, subject to the understanding that these articles are to be interpreted in the light of the provisions of Articles 18 and 19. This interpretation would not prejudice the extension of similar facilities to other persons by any of the Contracting Parties.

2. Each Contracting Party will grant to refugees as defined in the Convention relating to the Status of Refugees, signed at Geneva on 28th July 1951, and lawfully staying in its territory, treatment as favourable as possible, and in any case not less favourable than under the obligations accepted by the Contracting Party under the said Convention and under any other existing international instruments applicable to those refugees.

PART I, PARAGRAPH 18, AND PART II, ARTICLE 18, PARAGRAPH 1

It is understood that these provisions are not concerned with the question of entry into the territories of the Contracting Parties and do not prejudice the provisions of the European Convention on Establishment, signed at Paris on 13th December 1955.

PART II

Article 1, paragraph 2
This provision shall not be interpreted as prohibiting or authorising any union security clause or practice.

Article 4, paragraph 4
This provision shall be so understood as not to prohibit immediate dismissal for any serious offence.

Article 4, paragraph 5
It is understood that a Contracting Party may give the undertaking required in this paragraph if the great majority of workers are not permitted to suffer deductions from wages either by law or through collective agreements or arbitration awards, the exceptions being those persons not so covered.

Article 6, paragraph 4
It is understood that each Contracting Party may, insofar as it is concerned, regulate the exercise of the right to strike by law, provided that any further restriction that this might place on the right can be justified under the terms of Article 31.

Article 7, paragraph 8
It is understood that a Contracting Party may give the undertaking required in this paragraph if it fulfils the spirit of the undertaking by providing by law that the great majority of persons under 18 years of age shall not be employed in night work.

Article 12, paragraph 4
The words "and subject to the conditions laid down in such agreements" in the introduction to this paragraph are taken to imply inter alia that with regard to benefits which are available independently of any insurance contribution a Contracting Party may require the completion of a prescribed period of residence before granting such benefits to nationals of other Contracting Parties.

Article 13, paragraph 4
Governments not Parties to the European Convention on Social and Medical Assistance may ratify the Social Charter in respect of this paragraph provided that they grant to nationals of other Contracting Parties a treatment which is in conformity with the provisions of the said Convention.

Article 19, paragraph 6
For the purpose of this provision, the term "family of a foreign worker" is understood to mean at least his wife and dependent children under the age of 21 years.

PART III

It is understood that the Charter contains legal obligations of an international character, the application of which is submitted solely to the supervision provided for in Part IV thereof.

Article 20, paragraph 1
It is understood that the "numbered paragraphs" may include articles consisting of only one paragraph.

PART V

Article 30
The term "in time of war or other public emergency" shall be so understood as to cover also the threat of war.

86

Additional Protocol to the European Social Charter, 1988

Note: Additional Protocol to the European Social Charter. Adopted Strasbourg, 5 May 1988. ETS No. 128. Entry into force: 4 September 1992.

PREAMBLE

The member States of the Council of Europe signatory hereto,

Resolved to take new measures to extend the protection of the social and economic rights guaranteed by the European Social Charter, opened for signature in Turin on 18 October 1961 (hereinafter referred to as "the Charter"),

Have agreed as follows:

PART I

The Parties accept as the aim of their policy to be pursued by all appropriate means, both national and international in character, the attainment of conditions in which the following rights and principles may be effectively realised:

1. All workers have the right to equal opportunities and equal treatment in matters of employment and occupation without discrimination on the grounds of sex.
2. Workers have the right to be informed and to be consulted within the undertaking.
3. Workers have the right to take part in the determination and improvement of the working conditions and working environment in the undertaking.
4. Every elderly person has the right to social protection.

PART II

The Parties undertake, as provided for in Part III, to consider themselves bound by the obligations laid down in the following articles:

Article 1 – Right to equal opportunities and equal treatment in matters of employment and occupation without discrimination on the grounds of sex

1. With a view to ensuring the effective exercise of the right to equal opportunities and equal treatment in matters of employment and occupation without discrimination on the grounds of sex, the Parties undertake to recognise that right and to take appropriate measures to ensure or promote its application in the following fields:

- access to employment, protection against dismissal and occupational resettlement;
- vocational guidance, training, retraining and rehabilitation;
- terms of employment and working conditions including remuneration;
- career development including promotion.

2. Provisions concerning the protection of women, particularly as regards pregnancy, confinement and the post-natal period, shall not be deemed to be discrimination as referred to in paragraph 1 of this article.

3. Paragraph 1 of this article shall not prevent the adoption of specific measures aimed at removing de facto inequalities.

4. Occupational activities which, by reason of their nature or the context in which they are carried out, can be entrusted only to persons of a particular sex may be excluded from the scope of this article or some of its provisions.

Article 2 – Right to information and consultation

1. With a view to ensuring the effective exercise of the right of workers to be informed and consulted within the undertaking, the Parties undertake to adopt or encourage measures enabling workers or their representatives, in accordance with national legislation and practice:

   a   to be informed regularly or at the appropriate time and in a comprehensible way about the economic and financial situation of the undertaking employing them, on the understanding that the disclosure of certain information which could be prejudicial to the undertaking may be refused or subject to confidentiality; and

   b   to be consulted in good time on proposed decisions which could substantially affect the interests of workers, particularly on those decisions which could have an important impact on the employment situation in the undertaking.

2. The Parties may exclude from the field of application of paragraph 1 of this article, those undertakings employing less than a certain number of workers to be determined by national legislation or practice.

Article 3 – Right to take part in the determination and improvement of the working conditions and working environment

1. With a view to ensuring the effective exercise of the right of workers to take part in the determination and improvement of the working conditions and working environment in the undertaking, the Parties undertake to adopt or encourage measures enabling workers or their representatives, in accordance with national legislation and practice, to contribute:

   a   to the determination and the improvement of the working conditions, work organisation and working environment;

   b   to the protection of health and safety within the undertaking;

   c   to the organisation of social and socio-cultural services and facilities within the undertaking;

   d   to the supervision of the observance of regulations on these matters.

2. The Parties may exclude from the field of application of paragraph 1 of this article, those undertakings employing less than a certain number of workers to be determined by national legislation or practice.

Article 4 – Right of elderly persons to social protection

With a view to ensuring the effective exercise of the right of elderly persons to social protection, the Parties undertake to adopt or encourage, either directly or in co-operation with public or private organisations, appropriate measures designed in particular:

1. to enable elderly persons to remain full members of society for as long as possible, by means of:
   a   adequate resources enabling them to lead a decent life and play an active part in public, social and cultural life;
   b   provision of information about services and facilities available for elderly persons and their opportunities to make use of them;
2. to enable elderly persons to choose their life-style freely and to lead independent lives in their familiar surroundings for as long as they wish and are able, by means of:
   a   provision of housing suited to their needs and their state of health or of adequate support for adapting their housing;
   b   the health care and the services necessitated by their state;
3. to guarantee elderly persons living in institutions appropriate support, while respecting their privacy, and participation in decisions concerning living conditions in the institution.

PART III

Article 5 – Undertakings

1. Each of the Parties undertakes:
   a   to consider Part I of this Protocol as a declaration of the aims which it will pursue by all appropriate means, as stated in the introductory paragraph of that part;
   b   to consider itself bound by one or more articles of Part II of this Protocol.
2. The article or articles selected in accordance with sub-paragraph b of paragraph 1 of this article, shall be notified to the Secretary General of the Council of Europe at the time when the instrument of ratification, acceptance or approval of the Contracting State concerned is deposited.
3. Any Party may, at a later date, declare by notification to the Secretary General that it considers itself bound by any articles of Part II of this Protocol which it has not already accepted under the terms of paragraph 1 of this article. Such undertakings subsequently given shall be deemed to be an integral part of the ratification, acceptance or approval, and shall have the same effect as from the thirtieth day after the date of the notification.

PART IV

Article 6 – Supervision of compliance with the undertakings given

The Parties shall submit reports on the application of those provisions of Part II of this Protocol which they have accepted in the reports submitted by virtue of Article 21 of the Charter.

PART V

Article 7 – Implementation of the undertakings given

1. The relevant provisions of Articles 1 to 4 of Part II of this Protocol may be implemented by:

   a laws or regulations;

   b agreements between employers or employers' organisations and workers' organisations;

   c a combination of those two methods; or

   d other appropriate means.

2. Compliance with the undertakings deriving from Articles 2 and 3 of Part II of this Protocol shall be regarded as effective if the provisions are applied, in accordance with paragraph 1 of this article, to the great majority of the workers concerned.

Article 8 – Relations between the Charter and this Protocol

1. The provisions of this Protocol shall not prejudice the provisions of the Charter.

2. Articles 22 to 32 and Article 36 of the Charter shall apply, mutatis mutandis, to this Protocol.

Article 9 – Territorial application

1. This Protocol shall apply to the metropolitan territory of each Party. Any State may, at the time of signature or when depositing its instrument of ratification, acceptance or approval, specify by declaration addressed to the Secretary General of the Council of Europe, the territory which shall be considered to be its metropolitan territory for this purpose.

2. Any Contracting State may, at the time of ratification, acceptance or approval of this Protocol or at any time thereafter, declare by notification addressed to the Secretary General of the Council of Europe that the Protocol shall extend in whole or in part to a non-metropolitan territory or territories specified in the said declaration for whose international relations it is responsible or for which it assumes international responsibility. It shall specify in the declaration the article or articles of Part II of this Protocol which it accepts as binding in respect of the territories named in the declaration.

3. This Protocol shall enter into force in respect of the territory or territories named in the aforesaid declaration as from the thirtieth day after the date on which the Secretary General shall have notification of such declaration.

4. Any Party may declare at a later date by notification addressed to the Secretary General of the Council of Europe, that, in respect of one or more of the territories to which this Protocol has been extended in accordance with paragraph 2 of this article, it accepts as binding any articles which it has not already accepted in respect of that territory or territories. Such undertakings subsequently given shall be deemed to be an integral part of the original declaration in respect of the territory concerned, and shall have the same effect as from the thirtieth day after the date on which the Secretary General shall have notification of such declaration.

Article 10 – Signature, ratification, acceptance, approval and entry into force

1. This Protocol shall be open for signature by member States of the Council of Europe who are signatories to the Charter. It is subject to ratification, acceptance or approval.

No member State of the Council of Europe shall ratify, accept or approve this Protocol except at the same time as or after ratification of the Charter. Instruments of ratification, acceptance of approval shall be deposited with the Secretary General of the Council of Europe.

2. This Protocol shall enter into force on the thirtieth day after the date of deposit of the third instrument of ratification, acceptance or approval.

3. In respect of any signatory State ratifying subsequently, this Protocol shall come into force as from the thirtieth day after the date of deposit of its instrument of ratification, acceptance or approval.

Article 11 – Denunciation

1. Any Party may denounce this Protocol only at the end of a period of five years from the date on which the Protocol entered into force for it, or at the end of any successive period of two years, and, in each case, after giving six months' notice to the Secretary General of the Council of Europe. Such denunciation shall not affect the validity of the Protocol in respect of the other Parties provided that at all times there are not less than three such Parties.

2. Any Party may, in accordance with the provisions set out in the preceding paragraph, denounce any article of Part II of this Protocol accepted by it, provided that the number of articles by which this Party is bound shall never be less than one.

3. Any Party may denounce this Protocol or any of the articles of Part II of the Protocol, under the conditions specified in paragraph 1 of this article, in respect of any territory to which the Protocol is applicable by virtue of a declaration made in accordance with paragraphs 2 and 4 of Article 9.

4. Any Party bound by the Charter and this Protocol which denounces the Charter in accordance with the provisions of paragraph 1 of Article 37 thereof, will be considered to have denounced the Protocol likewise.

Article 12 – Notifications

The Secretary General of the Council of Europe shall notify the member States of the Council and the Director General of the International Labour Office of:

a any signature;

b the deposit of any instrument of ratification, acceptance or approval;

c any date of entry into force of this Protocol in accordance with Articles 9 and 10;

d any other act, notification or communication relating to this Protocol.

Article 13 – Appendix

The appendix to this Protocol shall form an integral part of it.

In witness whereof the undersigned, being duly authorised thereto, have signed this Protocol.

Done at Strasbourg, this 5th day of May, 1988, in English and French, both texts being equally authentic, in a single copy which shall be deposited in the archives of the Council of Europe. The Secretary General of the Council in Europe shall transmit certified copies to each member State of the Council of Europe.

87

Protocol Amending the European Social Charter, 1991

Note: Protocol Amending the European Social Charter, adopted Turin, 21 October 1991. ETS No. 142. Entry into force: not formally in force although all key amendments are reflected in practice or in force via the 1996 Revised Charter.

The member States of the Council of Europe, signatory to this Protocol to the European Social Charter, opened for signature in Turin on 18 October 1961 (hereinafter referred to as "the Charter"),

Being resolved to take some measures to improve the effectiveness of the Charter, and particularly the functioning of its supervisory machinery;

Considering therefore that it is desirable to amend certain provisions of the Charter,

Have agreed as follows:

Article 1
Article 23 of the Charter shall read as follows:

"Article 23 – Communication of copies of reports and comments
1. When sending to the Secretary General a report pursuant to Articles 21 and 22, each Contracting Party shall forward a copy of that report to such of its national organisations as are members of the international organisations of employers and trade unions invited, under Article 27, paragraph 2, to be represented at meetings of the Governmental Committee. Those organisations shall send to the Secretary General any comments on the reports of the Contracting Parties. The Secretary General shall send a copy of those comments to the Contracting Parties concerned, who might wish to respond.
2. The Secretary General shall forward a copy of the reports of the Contracting Parties to the international non-governmental organisations which have consultative status with the Council of Europe and have particular competence in the matters governed by the present Charter.
3. The reports and comments referred to in Articles 21 and 22 and in the present article shall be made available to the public on request."

Article 2
Article 24 of the Charter shall read as follows:

"Article 24 – Examination of the reports
1. The reports sent to the Secretary General in accordance with Articles 21 and 22 shall be examined by a Committee of Independent Experts constituted pursuant to

Article 25. The committee shall also have before it any comments forwarded to the Secretary General in accordance with paragraph 1 of Article 23. On completion of its examination, the Committee of Independent Experts shall draw up a report containing its conclusions.

2. With regard to the reports referred to in Article 21, the Committee of Independent Experts shall assess from a legal standpoint the compliance of national law and practice with the obligations arising from the Charter for the Contracting Parties concerned.

3. The Committee of Independent Experts may address requests for additional information and clarification directly to Contracting Parties. In this connection the Committee of Independent Experts may also hold, if necessary, a meeting with the representatives of a Contracting Party, either on its own initiative or at the request of the Contracting Party concerned. The organisations referred to in paragraph 1 of Article 23 shall be kept informed.

4. The conclusions of the Committee of Independent Experts shall be made public and communicated by the Secretary General to the Governmental Committee, to the Parliamentary Assembly and to the organisations which are mentioned in paragraph 1 of Article 23 and paragraph 2 of Article 27."

Article 3
Article 25 of the Charter shall read as follows:

"Article 25 – Committee of Independent Experts
1. The Committee of Independent Experts shall consist of at least nine members elected by the Parliamentary Assembly by a majority of votes cast from a list of experts of the highest integrity and of recognised competence in national and international social questions, nominated by the Contracting Parties. The exact number of members shall be determined by the Committee of Ministers.

2. The members of the committee shall be elected for a period of six years. They may stand for re-election once.

3. A member of the Committee of Independent Experts elected to replace a member whose term of office has not expired shall hold office for the remainder of his predecessor's term.

4. The members of the committee shall sit in their individual capacity. Throughout their term of office, they may not perform any function incompatible with the requirements of independence, impartiality and availability inherent in their office."

Article 4
Article 27 of the Charter shall read as follows:

"Article 27 – Governmental Committee
1. The reports of the Contracting Parties, the comments and information communicated in accordance with paragraphs 1 of Article 23 and 3 of Article 24, and the reports of the Committee of Independent Experts shall be submitted to a Governmental Committee.

2. The committee shall be composed of one representative of each of the Contracting Parties. It shall invite no more than two international organisations of employers and no more than two international trade union organisations to send observers in

a consultative capacity to its meetings. Moreover, it may consult representatives of international nongovernmental organisations which have consultative status with the Council of Europe and have particular competence in the matters governed by the present Charter.

3. The Governmental Committee shall prepare the decisions of the Committee of Ministers. In particular, in the light of the reports of the Committee of Independent Experts and of the Contracting Parties, it shall select, giving reasons for its choice, on the basis of social, economic and other policy considerations the situations which should, in its view, be the subject of recommendations to each Contracting Party concerned, in accordance with Article 28 of the Charter. It shall present to the Committee of Ministers a report which shall be made public.

4. On the basis of its findings on the implementation of the Social Charter in general, the Governmental Committee may submit proposals to the Committee of Ministers aiming at studies to be carried out on social issues and on articles of the Charter which possibly might be updated."

Article 5
Article 28 of the Charter shall read as follows:

"Article 28 – Committee of Ministers

1. The Committee of Ministers shall adopt, by a majority of two-thirds of those voting, with entitlement to voting limited to the Contracting Parties, on the basis of the report of the Governmental Committee, a resolution covering the entire supervision cycle and containing individual recommendations to the Contracting Parties concerned.

2. Having regard to the proposals made by the Governmental Committee pursuant to paragraph 4 of Article 27, the Committee of Ministers shall take such decisions as it deems appropriate."

Article 6
Article 29 of the Charter shall read as follows:

"Article 29 – Parliamentary Assembly

The Secretary General of the Council of Europe shall transmit to the Parliamentary Assembly, with a view to the holding of periodical plenary debates, the reports of the Committee of Independent Experts and of the Governmental Committee, as well as the resolutions of the Committee of Ministers."

Article 7

1. This Protocol shall be open for signature by member States of the Council of Europe signatories to the Charter, which may express their consent to be bound by:
   a   signature without reservation as to ratification, acceptance or approval; or
   b   signature subject to ratification, acceptance or approval, followed by ratification, acceptance or approval.

2. Instruments of ratification, acceptance or approval shall be deposited with the Secretary General of the Council of Europe.

Article 8
This Protocol shall enter into force on the thirtieth day after the date on which all Contracting Parties to the Charter have expressed their consent to be bound by the Protocol in accordance with the provisions of Article 7.

Article 9
The Secretary General of the Council of Europe shall notify the member States of the Council of:

a   any signature;

b   the deposit of any instrument of ratification, acceptance or approval;

c   the date of entry into force of this Protocol in accordance with Article 8;

d   any other act, notification or communication relating to this Protocol.

In witness whereof the undersigned, being duly authorised thereto, have signed this Protocol.

Done at Turin, this 21st day of October 1991, in English and French, both texts being equally authentic, in a single copy which shall be deposited in the archives of the Council of Europe.

The Secretary General of the Council of Europe shall transmit certified copies to each member State of the Council of Europe.

88

Additional Protocol to the European Social Charter Providing for a System of Collective Complaints, 1995

Note: Additional Protocol to the European Social Charter Providing for a System of Collective Complaints, adopted Strasbourg, 9 November 1995. ETS No. 158. Entry into force: 1 July 1998.

PREAMBLE

The member States of the Council of Europe, signatories to this Protocol to the European Social Charter, opened for signature in Turin on 18 October 1961 (hereinafter referred to as "the Charter"),

Resolved to take new measures to improve the effective enforcement of the social rights guaranteed by the Charter;

Considering that this aim could be achieved in particular by the establishment of a collective complaints procedure, which, inter alia, would strengthen the participation of management and labour and of non-governmental organisations,

Have agreed as follows:

Article 1

The Contracting Parties to this Protocol recognise the right of the following organisations to submit complaints alleging unsatisfactory application of the Charter:

    a   international organisations of employers and trade unions referred to in paragraph 2 of Article 27 of the Charter;

    b   other international non-governmental organisations which have consultative status with the Council of Europe and have been put on a list established for this purpose by the Governmental Committee;

    c   representative national organisations of employers and trade unions within the jurisdiction of the Contracting Party against which they have lodged a complaint.

Article 2

1. Any Contracting State may also, when it expresses its consent to be bound by this Protocol, in accordance with the provisions of Article 13, or at any moment thereafter, declare that it recognises the right of any other representative national non-governmental organisation within its jurisdiction which has particular competence in the matters governed by the Charter, to lodge complaints against it.

2. Such declarations may be made for a specific period.
3. The declarations shall be deposited with the Secretary General of the Council of Europe who shall transmit copies thereof to the Contracting Parties and publish them.

Article 3

The international non-governmental organisations and the national non-governmental organisations referred to in Article 1.b and Article 2 respectively may submit complaints in accordance with the procedure prescribed by the aforesaid provisions only in respect of those matters regarding which they have been recognised as having particular competence.

Article 4

The complaint shall be lodged in writing, relate to a provision of the Charter accepted by the Contracting Party concerned and indicate in what respect the latter has not ensured the satisfactory application of this provision.

Article 5

Any complaint shall be addressed to the Secretary General who shall acknowledge receipt of it, notify it to the Contracting Party concerned and immediately transmit it to the Committee of Independent Experts.

Article 6

The Committee of Independent Experts may request the Contracting Party concerned and the organisation which lodged the complaint to submit written information and observations on the admissibility of the complaint within such time-limit as it shall prescribe.

Article 7

1. If it decides that a complaint is admissible, the Committee of Independent Experts shall notify the Contracting Parties to the Charter through the Secretary General. It shall request the Contracting Party concerned and the organisation which lodged the complaint to submit, within such time-limit as it shall prescribe, all relevant written explanations or information, and the other Contracting Parties to this Protocol, the comments they wish to submit, within the same time-limit.
2. If the complaint has been lodged by a national organisation of employers or a national trade union or by another national or international non-governmental organisation, the Committee of Independent Experts shall notify the international organisations of employers or trade unions referred to in paragraph 2 of Article 27 of the Charter, through the Secretary General, and invite them to submit observations within such time-limit as it shall prescribe.
3. On the basis of the explanations, information or observations submitted under paragraphs 1 and 2 above, the Contracting Party concerned and the organisation which lodged the complaint may submit any additional written information or observations within such time-limit as the Committee of Independent Experts shall prescribe.
4. In the course of the examination of the complaint, the Committee of Independent Experts may organise a hearing with the representatives of the parties.

Article 8

1. The Committee of Independent Experts shall draw up a report in which it shall describe the steps taken by it to examine the complaint and present its conclusions as to whether or not the Contracting Party concerned has ensured the satisfactory application of the provision of the Charter referred to in the complaint.
2. The report shall be transmitted to the Committee of Ministers. It shall also be transmitted to the organisation that lodged the complaint and to the Contracting Parties to the Charter, which shall not be at liberty to publish it.It shall be transmitted to the Parliamentary Assembly and made public at the same time as the resolution referred to in Article 9 or no later than four months after it has been transmitted to the Committee of Ministers.

Article 9

1. On the basis of the report of the Committee of Independent Experts, the Committee of Ministers shall adopt a resolution by a majority of those voting. If the Committee of Independent Experts finds that the Charter has not been applied in a satisfactory manner, the Committee of Ministers shall adopt, by a majority of two-thirds of those voting, a recommendation addressed to the Contracting Party concerned. In both cases, entitlement to voting shall be limited to the Contracting Parties to the Charter.
2. At the request of the Contracting Party concerned, the Committee of Ministers may decide, where the report of the Committee of Independent Experts raises new issues, by a two-thirds majority of the Contracting Parties to the Charter, to consult the Governmental Committee.

Article 10

The Contracting Party concerned shall provide information on the measures it has taken to give effect to the Committee of Ministers' recommendation, in the next report which it submits to the Secretary General under Article 21 of the Charter.

Article 11

Articles 1 to 10 of this Protocol shall apply also to the articles of Part II of the first Additional Protocol to the Charter in respect of the States Parties to that Protocol, to the extent that these articles have been accepted.

Article 12

The States Parties to this Protocol consider that the first paragraph of the appendix to the Charter, relating to Part III, reads as follows: "It is understood that the Charter contains legal obligations of an international character, the application of which is submitted solely to the supervision provided for in Part IV thereof and in the provisions of this Protocol."

Article 13

1. This Protocol shall be open for signature by member States of the Council of Europe signatories to the Charter, which may express their consent to be bound by:
   a   signature without reservation as to ratification, acceptance or approval; or
   b   signature subject to ratification, acceptance or approval, followed by ratification, acceptance or approval.

2. A member State of the Council of Europe may not express its consent to be bound by this Protocol without previously or simultaneously ratifying the Charter.
3. Instruments of ratification, acceptance or approval shall be deposited with the Secretary General of the Council of Europe.

Article 14

1. This Protocol shall enter into force on the first day of the month following the expiration of a period of one month after the date on which five member States of the Council of Europe have expressed their consent to be bound by the Protocol in accordance with the provisions of Article 13.
2. In respect of any member State which subsequently expresses its consent to be bound by it, the Protocol shall enter into force on the first day of the month following the expiration of a period of one month after the date of the deposit of the instrument of ratification, acceptance or approval.

Article 15

1. Any Party may at any time denounce this Protocol by means of a notification addressed to the Secretary General of the Council of Europe.
2. Such denunciation shall become effective on the first day of the month following the expiration of a period of twelve months after the date of receipt of such notification by the Secretary General.

Article 16

The Secretary General of the Council of Europe shall notify all the member States of the Council of:

a any signature;
b the deposit of any instrument of ratification, acceptance or approval;
c the date of entry into force of this Protocol in accordance with Article 14;
d any other act, notification or declaration relating to this Protocol.

In witness whereof the undersigned, being duly authorised thereto, have signed this Protocol.

Done at Strasbourg, this 9th day of November 1995, in English and French, both texts being equally authentic, in a single copy which shall be deposited in the archives of the Council of Europe. The Secretary General of the Council of Europe shall transmit certified copies to each member State of the Council of Europe.

89

European Social Charter (Revised), 1996

Note: European Social Charter (Revised). Adopted Strasbourg, 3 May 1996. ETS No. 163. Entry into force: 7 January 1999.

PREAMBLE

The governments signatory hereto, being members of the Council of Europe,

Considering that the aim of the Council of Europe is the achievement of greater unity between its members for the purpose of safeguarding and realising the ideals and principles which are their common heritage and of facilitating their economic and social progress, in particular by the maintenance and further realisation of human rights and fundamental freedoms;

Considering that in the Convention for the Protection of Human Rights and Fundamental Freedoms signed at Rome on 4 November 1950, and the Protocols thereto, the member States of the Council of Europe agreed to secure to their populations the civil and political rights and freedoms therein specified;

Considering that in the European Social Charter opened for signature in Turin on 18 October 1961 and the Protocols thereto, the member States of the Council of Europe agreed to secure to their populations the social rights specified therein in order to improve their standard of living and their social well-being;

Recalling that the Ministerial Conference on Human Rights held in Rome on 5 November 1990 stressed the need, on the one hand, to preserve the indivisible nature of all human rights, be they civil, political, economic, social or cultural and, on the other hand, to give the European Social Charter fresh impetus;

Resolved, as was decided during the Ministerial Conference held in Turin on 21 and 22 October 1991, to update and adapt the substantive contents of the Charter in order to take account in particular of the fundamental social changes which have occurred since the text was adopted;

Recognising the advantage of embodying in a Revised Charter, designed progressively to take the place of the European Social Charter, the rights guaranteed by the Charter as amended, the rights guaranteed by the Additional Protocol of 1988 and to add new rights,

Have agreed as follows:

PART I

The Parties accept as the aim of their policy, to be pursued by all appropriate means both national and international in character, the attainment of conditions in which the following rights and principles may be effectively realised:

1. Everyone shall have the opportunity to earn his living in an occupation freely entered upon.
2. All workers have the right to just conditions of work.
3. All workers have the right to safe and healthy working conditions.
4. All workers have the right to a fair remuneration sufficient for a decent standard of living for themselves and their families.
5. All workers and employers have the right to freedom of association in national or international organisations for the protection of their economic and social interests.
6. All workers and employers have the right to bargain collectively.
7. Children and young persons have the right to a special protection against the physical and moral hazards to which they are exposed.
8. Employed women, in case of maternity, have the right to a special protection.
9. Everyone has the right to appropriate facilities for vocational guidance with a view to helping him choose an occupation suited to his personal aptitude and interests.
10. Everyone has the right to appropriate facilities for vocational training.
11. Everyone has the right to benefit from any measures enabling him to enjoy the highest possible standard of health attainable.
12. All workers and their dependents have the right to social security.
13. Anyone without adequate resources has the right to social and medical assistance.
14. Everyone has the right to benefit from social welfare services.
15. Disabled persons have the right to independence, social integration and participation in the life of the community.
16. The family as a fundamental unit of society has the right to appropriate social, legal and economic protection to ensure its full development.
17. Children and young persons have the right to appropriate social, legal and economic protection.
18. The nationals of any one of the Parties have the right to engage in any gainful occupation in the territory of any one of the others on a footing of equality with the nationals of the latter, subject to restrictions based on cogent economic or social reasons.
19. Migrant workers who are nationals of a Party and their families have the right to protection and assistance in the territory of any other Party.
20. All workers have the right to equal opportunities and equal treatment in matters of employment and occupation without discrimination on the grounds of sex.
21. Workers have the right to be informed and to be consulted within the undertaking.
22. Workers have the right to take part in the determination and improvement of the working conditions and working environment in the undertaking.
23. Every elderly person has the right to social protection.
24. All workers have the right to protection in cases of termination of employment.
25. All workers have the right to protection of their claims in the event of the insolvency of their employer.

26. All workers have the right to dignity at work.
27. All persons with family responsibilities and who are engaged or wish to engage in employment have a right to do so without being subject to discrimination and as far as possible without conflict between their employment and family responsibilities.
28. Workers' representatives in undertakings have the right to protection against acts prejudicial to them and should be afforded appropriate facilities to carry out their functions.
29. All workers have the right to be informed and consulted in collective redundancy procedures.
30. Everyone has the right to protection against poverty and social exclusion.
31. Everyone has the right to housing.

PART II

The Parties undertake, as provided for in Part III, to consider themselves bound by the obligations laid down in the following articles and paragraphs.

Article 1 – The right to work
With a view to ensuring the effective exercise of the right to work, the Parties undertake:
1. to accept as one of their primary aims and responsibilities the achievement and maintenance of as high and stable a level of employment as possible, with a view to the attainment of full employment;
2. to protect effectively the right of the worker to earn his living in an occupation freely entered upon;
3. to establish or maintain free employment services for all workers;
4. to provide or promote appropriate vocational guidance, training and rehabilitation.

Article 2 – The right to just conditions of work
With a view to ensuring the effective exercise of the right to just conditions of work, the Parties undertake:
1. to provide for reasonable daily and weekly working hours, the working week to be progressively reduced to the extent that the increase of productivity and other relevant factors permit;
2. to provide for public holidays with pay;
3. to provide for a minimum of four weeks' annual holiday with pay;
4. to eliminate risks in inherently dangerous or unhealthy occupations, and where it has not yet been possible to eliminate or reduce sufficiently these risks, to provide for either a reduction of working hours or additional paid holidays for workers engaged in such occupations;
5. to ensure a weekly rest period which shall, as far as possible, coincide with the day recognised by tradition or custom in the country or region concerned as a day of rest;
6. to ensure that workers are informed in written form, as soon as possible, and in any event not later than two months after the date of commencing their employment, of the essential aspects of the contract or employment relationship;
7. to ensure that workers performing night work benefit from measures which take account of the special nature of the work.

Article 3 – The right to safe and healthy working conditions

With a view to ensuring the effective exercise of the right to safe and healthy working conditions, the Parties undertake, in consultation with employers' and workers' organisations:

1. to formulate, implement and periodically review a coherent national policy on occupational safety, occupational health and the working environment. The primary aim of this policy shall be to improve occupational safety and health and to prevent accidents and injury to health arising out of, linked with or occurring in the course of work, particularly by minimising the causes of hazards inherent in the working environment;
2. to issue safety and health regulations;
3. to provide for the enforcement of such regulations by measures of supervision;
4. to promote the progressive development of occupational health services for all workers with essentially preventive and advisory functions.

Article 4 – The right to a fair remuneration

With a view to ensuring the effective exercise of the right to a fair remuneration, the Parties undertake:

1. to recognise the right of workers to a remuneration such as will give them and their families a decent standard of living;
2. to recognise the right of workers to an increased rate of remuneration for overtime work, subject to exceptions in particular cases;
3. to recognise the right of men and women workers to equal pay for work of equal value;
4. to recognise the right of all workers to a reasonable period of notice for termination of employment;
5. to permit deductions from wages only under conditions and to the extent prescribed by national laws or regulations or fixed by collective agreements or arbitration awards.

The exercise of these rights shall be achieved by freely concluded collective agreements, by statutory wage-fixing machinery, or by other means appropriate to national conditions.

Article 5 – The right to organise

With a view to ensuring or promoting the freedom of workers and employers to form local, national or international organisations for the protection of their economic and social interests and to join those organisations, the Parties undertake that national law shall not be such as to impair, nor shall it be so applied as to impair, this freedom. The extent to which the guarantees provided for in this article shall apply to the police shall be determined by national laws or regulations. The principle governing the application to the members of the armed forces of these guarantees and the extent to which they shall apply to persons in this category shall equally be determined by national laws or regulations.

Article 6 – The right to bargain collectively

With a view to ensuring the effective exercise of the right to bargain collectively, the Parties undertake:

1. to promote joint consultation between workers and employers;
2. to promote, where necessary and appropriate, machinery for voluntary negotiations between employers or employers' organisations and workers' organisations, with a view to the regulation of terms and conditions of employment by means of collective agreements;

3. to promote the establishment and use of appropriate machinery for conciliation and voluntary arbitration for the settlement of labour disputes;
   and recognise:
4. the right of workers and employers to collective action in cases of conflicts of interest, including the right to strike, subject to obligations that might arise out of collective agreements previously entered into.

Article 7 – The right of children and young persons to protection

With a view to ensuring the effective exercise of the right of children and young persons to protection, the Parties undertake:
1. to provide that the minimum age of admission to employment shall be 15 years, subject to exceptions for children employed in prescribed light work without harm to their health, morals or education;
2. to provide that the minimum age of admission to employment shall be 18 years with respect to prescribed occupations regarded as dangerous or unhealthy;
3. to provide that persons who are still subject to compulsory education shall not be employed in such work as would deprive them of the full benefit of their education;
4. to provide that the working hours of persons under 18 years of age shall be limited in accordance with the needs of their development, and particularly with their need for vocational training;
5. to recognise the right of young workers and apprentices to a fair wage or other appropriate allowances;
6. to provide that the time spent by young persons in vocational training during the normal working hours with the consent of the employer shall be treated as forming part of the working day;
7. to provide that employed persons of under 18 years of age shall be entitled to a minimum of four weeks' annual holiday with pay;
8. to provide that persons under 18 years of age shall not be employed in night work with the exception of certain occupations provided for by national laws or regulations;
9. to provide that persons under 18 years of age employed in occupations prescribed by national laws or regulations shall be subject to regular medical control;
10. to ensure special protection against physical and moral dangers to which children and young persons are exposed, and particularly against those resulting directly or indirectly from their work.

Article 8 – The right of employed women to protection of maternity

With a view to ensuring the effective exercise of the right of employed women to the protection of maternity, the Parties undertake:
1. to provide either by paid leave, by adequate social security benefits or by benefits from public funds for employed women to take leave before and after childbirth up to a total of at least fourteen weeks;
2. to consider it as unlawful for an employer to give a woman notice of dismissal during the period from the time she notifies her employer that she is pregnant until the end of her maternity leave, or to give her notice of dismissal at such a time that the notice would expire during such a period;

3. to provide that mothers who are nursing their infants shall be entitled to sufficient time off for this purpose;
4. to regulate the employment in night work of pregnant women, women who have recently given birth and women nursing their infants;
5. to prohibit the employment of pregnant women, women who have recently given birth or who are nursing their infants in underground mining and all other work which is unsuitable by reason of its dangerous, unhealthy or arduous nature and to take appropriate measures to protect the employment rights of these women.

Article 9 – The right to vocational guidance

With a view to ensuring the effective exercise of the right to vocational guidance, the Parties undertake to provide or promote, as necessary, a service which will assist all persons, including the handicapped, to solve problems related to occupational choice and progress, with due regard to the individual's characteristics and their relation to occupational opportunity: this assistance should be available free of charge, both to young persons, including schoolchildren, and to adults.

Article 10 – The right to vocational training

With a view to ensuring the effective exercise of the right to vocational training, the Parties undertake:
1. to provide or promote, as necessary, the technical and vocational training of all persons, including the handicapped, in consultation with employers' and workers' organisations, and to grant facilities for access to higher technical and university education, based solely on individual aptitude;
2. to provide or promote a system of apprenticeship and other systematic arrangements for training young boys and girls in their various employments;
3. to provide or promote, as necessary:
   a   adequate and readily available training facilities for adult workers;
   b   special facilities for the retraining of adult workers needed as a result of technological development or new trends in employment;
4. to provide or promote, as necessary, special measures for the retraining and reintegration of the long-term unemployed;
5. to encourage the full utilisation of the facilities provided by appropriate measures such as:
   a   reducing or abolishing any fees or charges;
   b   granting financial assistance in appropriate cases;
   c   including in the normal working hours time spent on supplementary training taken by the worker, at the request of his employer, during employment;
   d   ensuring, through adequate supervision, in consultation with the employers' and workers' organisations, the efficiency of apprenticeship and other training arrangements for young workers, and the adequate protection of young workers generally.

Article 11 – The right to protection of health

With a view to ensuring the effective exercise of the right to protection of health, the Parties undertake, either directly or in cooperation with public or private organisations, to take appropriate measures designed inter alia:
1. to remove as far as possible the causes of ill-health;

2. to provide advisory and educational facilities for the promotion of health and the encouragement of individual responsibility in matters of health;
3. to prevent as far as possible epidemic, endemic and other diseases, as well as accidents.

Article 12 – The right to social security

With a view to ensuring the effective exercise of the right to social security, the Parties undertake:

1. to establish or maintain a system of social security;
2. to maintain the social security system at a satisfactory level at least equal to that necessary for the ratification of the European Code of Social Security;
3. to endeavour to raise progressively the system of social security to a higher level;
4. to take steps, by the conclusion of appropriate bilateral and multilateral agreements or by other means, and subject to the conditions laid down in such agreements, in order to ensure:
   (a) equal treatment with their own nationals of the nationals of other Parties in respect of social security rights, including the retention of benefits arising out of social security legislation, whatever movements the persons protected may undertake between the territories of the Parties;
   (b) the granting, maintenance and resumption of social security rights by such means as the accumulation of insurance or employment periods completed under the legislation of each of the Parties.

Article 13 – The right to social and medical assistance

With a view to ensuring the effective exercise of the right to social and medical assistance, the Parties undertake:

1. to ensure that any person who is without adequate resources and who is unable to secure such resources either by his own efforts or from other sources, in particular by benefits under a social security scheme, be granted adequate assistance, and, in case of sickness, the care necessitated by his condition;
2. to ensure that persons receiving such assistance shall not, for that reason, suffer from a diminution of their political or social rights;
3. to provide that everyone may receive by appropriate public or private services such advice and personal help as may be required to prevent, to remove, or to alleviate personal or family want;
4. to apply the provisions referred to in paragraphs 1, 2 and 3 of this article on an equal footing with their nationals to nationals of other Parties lawfully within their territories, in accordance with their obligations under the European Convention on Social and Medical Assistance, signed at Paris on 11 December 1953.

Article 14 – The right to benefit from social welfare services

With a view to ensuring the effective exercise of the right to benefit from social welfare services, the Parties undertake:

1. to promote or provide services which, by using methods of social work, would contribute to the welfare and development of both individuals and groups in the community, and to their adjustment to the social environment;
2. to encourage the participation of individuals and voluntary or other organisations in the establishment and maintenance of such services.

Article 15 – The right of persons with disabilities to independence, social integration and participation in the life of the community

With a view to ensuring to persons with disabilities, irrespective of age and the nature and origin of their disabilities, the effective exercise of the right to independence, social integration and participation in the life of the community, the Parties undertake, in particular:

1. to take the necessary measures to provide persons with disabilities with guidance, education and vocational training in the framework of general schemes wherever possible or, where this is not possible, through specialised bodies, public or private;

2. to promote their access to employment through all measures tending to encourage employers to hire and keep in employment persons with disabilities in the ordinary working environment and to adjust the working conditions to the needs of the disabled or, where this is not possible by reason of the disability, by arranging for or creating sheltered employment according to the level of disability. In certain cases, such measures may require recourse to specialised placement and support services;

3. to promote their full social integration and participation in the life of the community in particular through measures, including technical aids, aiming to overcome barriers to communication and mobility and enabling access to transport, housing, cultural activities and leisure.

Article 16 – The right of the family to social, legal and economic protection

With a view to ensuring the necessary conditions for the full development of the family, which is a fundamental unit of society, the Parties undertake to promote the economic, legal and social protection of family life by such means as social and family benefits, fiscal arrangements, provision of family housing, benefits for the newly married and other appropriate means.

Article 17 – The right of children and young persons to social, legal and economic protection

With a view to ensuring the effective exercise of the right of children and young persons to grow up in an environment which encourages the full development of their personality and of their physical and mental capacities, the Parties undertake, either directly or in co-operation with public and private organisations, to take all appropriate and necessary measures designed:

1. a to ensure that children and young persons, taking account of the rights and duties of their parents, have the care, the assistance, the education and the training they need, in particular by providing for the establishment or maintenance of institutions and services sufficient and adequate for this purpose;
   b to protect children and young persons against negligence, violence or exploitation;
   c to provide protection and special aid from the state for children and young persons temporarily or definitively deprived of their family's support;

2. to provide to children and young persons a free primary and secondary education as well as to encourage regular attendance at schools.

Article 18 – The right to engage in a gainful occupation in the territory of other Parties

With a view to ensuring the effective exercise of the right to engage in a gainful occupation in the territory of any other Party, the Parties undertake:

1. to apply existing regulations in a spirit of liberality;

2. to simplify existing formalities and to reduce or abolish chancery dues and other charges payable by foreign workers or their employers;

3. to liberalise, individually or collectively, regulations governing the employment of foreign workers;

and recognise:

4. the right of their nationals to leave the country to engage in a gainful occupation in the territories of the other Parties.

Article 19 – The right of migrant workers and their families to protection and assistance

With a view to ensuring the effective exercise of the right of migrant workers and their families to protection and assistance in the territory of any other Party, the Parties undertake:

1. to maintain or to satisfy themselves that there are maintained adequate and free services to assist such workers, particularly in obtaining accurate information, and to take all appropriate steps, so far as national laws and regulations permit, against misleading propaganda relating to emigration and immigration;

2. to adopt appropriate measures within their own jurisdiction to facilitate the departure, journey and reception of such workers and their families, and to provide, within their own jurisdiction, appropriate services for health, medical attention and good hygienic conditions during the journey;

3. to promote co-operation, as appropriate, between social services, public and private, in emigration and immigration countries;

4. to secure for such workers lawfully within their territories, insofar as such matters are regulated by law or regulations or are subject to the control of administrative authorities, treatment not less favourable than that of their own nationals in respect of the following matters:

    a   remuneration and other employment and working conditions;

    b   membership of trade unions and enjoyment of the benefits of collective bargaining;

    c   accommodation;

5. to secure for such workers lawfully within their territories treatment not less favourable than that of their own nationals with regard to employment taxes, dues or contributions payable in respect of employed persons;

6. to facilitate as far as possible the reunion of the family of a foreign worker permitted to establish himself in the territory;

7. to secure for such workers lawfully within their territories treatment not less favourable than that of their own nationals in respect of legal proceedings relating to matters referred to in this article;

8. to secure that such workers lawfully residing within their territories are not expelled unless they endanger national security or offend against public interest or morality;

9. to permit, within legal limits, the transfer of such parts of the earnings and savings of such workers as they may desire;

10. to extend the protection and assistance provided for in this article to self-employed migrants insofar as such measures apply;

11. to promote and facilitate the teaching of the national language of the receiving state or, if there are several, one of these languages, to migrant workers and members of their families;

12. to promote and facilitate, as far as practicable, the teaching of the migrant worker's mother tongue to the children of the migrant worker.

Article 20 – The right to equal opportunities and equal treatment in matters of employment and occupation without discrimination on the grounds of sex

With a view to ensuring the effective exercise of the right to equal opportunities and equal treatment in matters of employment and occupation without discrimination on the grounds of sex, the Parties undertake to recognise that right and to take appropriate measures to ensure or promote its application in the following fields:

a access to employment, protection against dismissal and occupational reintegration;
b vocational guidance, training, retraining and rehabilitation;
c terms of employment and working conditions, including remuneration;
d career development, including promotion.

Article 21 – The right to information and consultation

With a view to ensuring the effective exercise of the right of workers to be informed and consulted within the undertaking, the Parties undertake to adopt or encourage measures enabling workers or their representatives, in accordance with national legislation and practice:

(a) to be informed regularly or at the appropriate time and in a comprehensible way about the economic and financial situation of the undertaking employing them, on the understanding that the disclosure of certain information which could be prejudicial to the undertaking may be refused or subject to confidentiality; and
(b) to be consulted in good time on proposed decisions which could substantially affect the interests of workers, particularly on those decisions which could have an important impact on the employment situation in the undertaking.

Article 22 – The right to take part in the determination and improvement of the working conditions and working environment

With a view to ensuring the effective exercise of the right of workers to take part in the determination and improvement of the working conditions and working environment in the undertaking, the Parties undertake to adopt or encourage measures enabling workers or their representatives, in accordance with national legislation and practice, to contribute:

(a) to the determination and the improvement of the working conditions, work organisation and working environment;
(b) to the protection of health and safety within the undertaking;
(c) to the organisation of social and socio-cultural services and facilities within the undertaking;
(d) to the supervision of the observance of regulations on these matters.

Article 23 – The right of elderly persons to social protection

With a view to ensuring the effective exercise of the right of elderly persons to social protection, the Parties undertake to adopt or encourage, either directly or in co-operation with public or private organisations, appropriate measures designed in particular:

- to enable elderly persons to remain full members of society for as long as possible, by means of:
  a adequate resources enabling them to lead a decent life and play an active part in public, social and cultural life;
  b provision of information about services and facilities available for elderly persons and their opportunities to make use of them;
- to enable elderly persons to choose their life-style freely and to lead independent lives in their familiar surroundings for as long as they wish and are able, by means of:
  a provision of housing suited to their needs and their state of health or of adequate support for adapting their housing;
  b the health care and the services necessitated by their state;
- to guarantee elderly persons living in institutions appropriate support, while respecting their privacy, and participation in decisions concerning living conditions in the institution.

Article 24 – The right to protection in cases of termination of employment

With a view to ensuring the effective exercise of the right of workers to protection in cases of termination of employment, the Parties undertake to recognise:
  a the right of all workers not to have their employment terminated without valid reasons for such termination connected with their capacity or conduct or based on the operational requirements of the undertaking, establishment or service;
  b the right of workers whose employment is terminated without a valid reason to adequate compensation or other appropriate relief.

To this end the Parties undertake to ensure that a worker who considers that his employment has been terminated without a valid reason shall have the right to appeal to an impartial body.

Article 25 – The right of workers to the protection of their claims in the event of the insolvency of their employer

With a view to ensuring the effective exercise of the right of workers to the protection of their claims in the event of the insolvency of their employer, the Parties undertake to provide that workers' claims arising from contracts of employment or employment relationships be guaranteed by a guarantee institution or by any other effective form of protection.

Article 26 – The right to dignity at work

With a view to ensuring the effective exercise of the right of all workers to protection of their dignity at work, the Parties undertake, in consultation with employers' and workers' organisations:
  1. to promote awareness, information and prevention of sexual harassment in the workplace or in relation to work and to take all appropriate measures to protect workers from such conduct;
  2. to promote awareness, information and prevention of recurrent reprehensible or distinctly negative and offensive actions directed against individual workers in the workplace or in relation to work and to take all appropriate measures to protect workers from such conduct.

Article 27 – The right of workers with family responsibilities to equal opportunities and equal treatment

With a view to ensuring the exercise of the right to equality of opportunity and treatment for men and women workers with family responsibilities and between such workers and other workers, the Parties undertake:

1. to take appropriate measures:
   a   to enable workers with family responsibilities to enter and remain in employment, as well as to reenter employment after an absence due to those responsibilities, including measures in the field of vocational guidance and training;
   b   to take account of their needs in terms of conditions of employment and social security;
   c   to develop or promote services, public or private, in particular child daycare services and other childcare arrangements;
2. to provide a possibility for either parent to obtain, during a period after maternity leave, parental leave to take care of a child, the duration and conditions of which should be determined by national legislation, collective agreements or practice;
3. to ensure that family responsibilities shall not, as such, constitute a valid reason for termination of employment.

Article 28 – The right of workers' representatives to protection in the undertaking and facilities to be accorded to them

With a view to ensuring the effective exercise of the right of workers' representatives to carry out their functions, the Parties undertake to ensure that in the undertaking:
   a   they enjoy effective protection against acts prejudicial to them, including dismissal, based on their status or activities as workers' representatives within the undertaking;
   b   they are afforded such facilities as may be appropriate in order to enable them to carry out their functions promptly and efficiently, account being taken of the industrial relations system of the country and the needs, size and capabilities of the undertaking concerned.

Article 29 – The right to information and consultation in collective redundancy procedures

With a view to ensuring the effective exercise of the right of workers to be informed and consulted in situations of collective redundancies, the Parties undertake to ensure that employers shall inform and consult workers' representatives, in good time prior to such collective redundancies, on ways and means of avoiding collective redundancies or limiting their occurrence and mitigating their consequences, for example by recourse to accompanying social measures aimed, in particular, at aid for the redeployment or retraining of the workers concerned.

Article 30 – The right to protection against poverty and social exclusion

With a view to ensuring the effective exercise of the right to protection against poverty and social exclusion, the Parties undertake:
a   to take measures within the framework of an overall and co-ordinated approach to promote the effective access of persons who live or risk living in a situation of social

exclusion or poverty, as well as their families, to, in particular, employment, housing, training, education, culture and social and medical assistance;

b to review these measures with a view to their adaptation if necessary.

Article 31 – The right to housing

With a view to ensuring the effective exercise of the right to housing, the Parties undertake to take measures designed:

1. to promote access to housing of an adequate standard;
2. to prevent and reduce homelessness with a view to its gradual elimination;
3. to make the price of housing accessible to those without adequate resources.

PART III

Article A – Undertakings

1. Subject to the provisions of Article B below, each of the Parties undertakes:
   a to consider Part I of this Charter as a declaration of the aims which it will pursue by all appropriate means, as stated in the introductory paragraph of that part;
   b to consider itself bound by at least six of the following nine articles of Part II of this Charter: Articles 1, 5, 6, 7, 12, 13, 16, 19 and 20;
   c to consider itself bound by an additional number of articles or numbered paragraphs of Part II of the Charter which it may select, provided that the total number of articles or numbered paragraphs by which it is bound is not less than sixteen articles or sixty-three numbered paragraphs.
2. The articles or paragraphs selected in accordance with sub-paragraphs b and c of paragraph 1 of this article shall be notified to the Secretary General of the Council of Europe at the time when the instrument of ratification, acceptance or approval is deposited.
3. Any Party may, at a later date, declare by notification addressed to the Secretary General that it considers itself bound by any articles or any numbered paragraphs of Part II of the Charter which it has not already accepted under the terms of paragraph 1 of this article. Such undertakings subsequently given shall be deemed to be an integral part of the ratification, acceptance or approval and shall have the same effect as from the first day of the month following the expiration of a period of one month after the date of the notification.
4. Each Party shall maintain a system of labour inspection appropriate to national conditions.

Article B – Links with the European Social Charter and the 1988 Additional Protocol

1. No Contracting Party to the European Social Charter or Party to the Additional Protocol of 5 May 1988 may ratify, accept or approve this Charter without considering itself bound by at least the provisions corresponding to the provisions of the European Social Charter and, where appropriate, of the Additional Protocol, to which it was bound.
2. Acceptance of the obligations of any provision of this Charter shall, from the date of entry into force of those obligations for the Party concerned, result in the corresponding provision of the European Social Charter and, where appropriate, of its Additional Protocol of 1988 ceasing to apply to the Party concerned in the event of that Party being bound by the first of those instruments or by both instruments.

PART IV

Article C – Supervision of the implementation of the undertakings contained in this Charter

The implementation of the legal obligations contained in this Charter shall be submitted to the same supervision as the European Social Charter.

Article D – Collective complaints

1. The provisions of the Additional Protocol to the European Social Charter providing for a system of collective complaints shall apply to the undertakings given in this Charter for the States which have ratified the said Protocol.
2. Any State which is not bound by the Additional Protocol to the European Social Charter providing for a system of collective complaints may when depositing its instrument of ratification, acceptance or approval of this Charter or at any time thereafter, declare by notification addressed to the Secretary General of the Council of Europe, that it accepts the supervision of its obligations under this Charter following the procedure provided for in the said Protocol.

PART V

Article E – Non-discrimination

The enjoyment of the rights set forth in this Charter shall be secured without discrimination on any ground such as race, colour, sex, language, religion, political or other opinion, national extraction or social origin, health, association with a national minority, birth or other status.

Article F – Derogations in time of war or public emergency

1. In time of war or other public emergency threatening the life of the nation any Party may take measures derogating from its obligations under this Charter to the extent strictly required by the exigencies of the situation, provided that such measures are not inconsistent with its other obligations under international law.
2. Any Party which has availed itself of this right of derogation shall, within a reasonable lapse of time, keep the Secretary General of the Council of Europe fully informed of the measures taken and of the reasons therefor. It shall likewise inform the Secretary General when such measures have ceased to operate and the provisions of the Charter which it has accepted are again being fully executed.

Article G – Restrictions

1. The rights and principles set forth in Part I when effectively realised, and their effective exercise as provided for in Part II, shall not be subject to any restrictions or limitations not specified in those parts, except such as are prescribed by law and are necessary in a democratic society for the protection of the rights and freedoms of others or for the protection of public interest, national security, public health, or morals.
2. The restrictions permitted under this Charter to the rights and obligations set forth herein shall not be applied for any purpose other than that for which they have been prescribed.

Article H – Relations between the Charter and domestic law or international agreements

The provisions of this Charter shall not prejudice the provisions of domestic law or of any bilateral or multilateral treaties, conventions or agreements which are already in force, or may come into force, under which more favourable treatment would be accorded to the persons protected.

Article I – Implementation of the undertakings given

1. Without prejudice to the methods of implementation foreseen in these articles the relevant provisions of Articles 1 to 31 of Part II of this Charter shall be implemented by:
   a   laws or regulations;
   b   agreements between employers or employers' organisations and workers' organisations;
   c   a combination of those two methods;
   d   other appropriate means.
2. Compliance with the undertakings deriving from the provisions of paragraphs 1, 2, 3, 4, 5 and 7 of Article 2, paragraphs 4, 6 and 7 of Article 7, paragraphs 1, 2, 3 and 5 of Article 10 and Articles 21 and 22 of Part II of this Charter shall be regarded as effective if the provisions are applied, in accordance with paragraph 1 of this article, to the great majority of the workers concerned.

Article J – Amendments

1. Any amendment to Parts I and II of this Charter with the purpose of extending the rights guaranteed in this Charter as well as any amendment to Parts III to VI, proposed by a Party or by the Governmental Committee, shall be communicated to the Secretary General of the Council of Europe and forwarded by the Secretary General to the Parties to this Charter.
2. Any amendment proposed in accordance with the provisions of the preceding paragraph shall be examined by the Governmental Committee which shall submit the text adopted to the Committee of Ministers for approval after consultation with the Parliamentary Assembly. After its approval by the Committee of Ministers this text shall be forwarded to the Parties for acceptance.
3. Any amendment to Part I and to Part II of this Charter shall enter into force, in respect of those Parties which have accepted it, on the first day of the month following the expiration of a period of one month after the date on which three Parties have informed the Secretary General that they have accepted it. In respect of any Party which subsequently accepts it, the amendment shall enter into force on the first day of the month following the expiration of a period of one month after the date on which that Party has informed the Secretary General of its acceptance.
4. Any amendment to Parts III to VI of this Charter shall enter into force on the first day of the month following the expiration of a period of one month after the date on which all Parties have informed the Secretary General that they have accepted it.

PART VI

Article K – Signature, ratification and entry into force

1. This Charter shall be open for signature by the member States of the Council of Europe. It shall be subject to ratification, acceptance or approval. Instruments of ratification,

acceptance or approval shall be deposited with the Secretary General of the Council of Europe.

2. This Charter shall enter into force on the first day of the month following the expiration of a period of one month after the date on which three member States of the Council of Europe have expressed their consent to be bound by this Charter in accordance with the preceding paragraph.

3. In respect of any member State which subsequently expresses its consent to be bound by this Charter, it shall enter into force on the first day of the month following the expiration of a period of one month after the date of the deposit of the instrument of ratification, acceptance or approval.

Article L – Territorial application

1. This Charter shall apply to the metropolitan territory of each Party. Each signatory may, at the time of signature or of the deposit of its instrument of ratification, acceptance or approval, specify, by declaration addressed to the Secretary General of the Council of Europe, the territory which shall be considered to be its metropolitan territory for this purpose.

2. Any signatory may, at the time of signature or of the deposit of its instrument of ratification, acceptance or approval, or at any time thereafter, declare by notification addressed to the Secretary General of the Council of Europe, that the Charter shall extend in whole or in part to a non-metropolitan territory or territories specified in the said declaration for whose international relations it is responsible or for which it assumes international responsibility. It shall specify in the declaration the articles or paragraphs of Part II of the Charter which it accepts as binding in respect of the territories named in the declaration.

3. The Charter shall extend its application to the territory or territories named in the aforesaid declaration as from the first day of the month following the expiration of a period of one month after the date of receipt of the notification of such declaration by the Secretary General.

4. Any Party may declare at a later date by notification addressed to the Secretary General of the Council of Europe that, in respect of one or more of the territories to which the Charter has been applied in accordance with paragraph 2 of this article, it accepts as binding any articles or any numbered paragraphs which it has not already accepted in respect of that territory or territories. Such undertakings subsequently given shall be deemed to be an integral part of the original declaration in respect of the territory concerned, and shall have the same effect as from the first day of the month following the expiration of a period of one month after the date of receipt of such notification by the Secretary General.

Article M – Denunciation

1. Any Party may denounce this Charter only at the end of a period of five years from the date on which the Charter entered into force for it, or at the end of any subsequent period of two years, and in either case after giving six months' notice to the Secretary General of the Council of Europe who shall inform the other Parties accordingly.

2. Any Party may, in accordance with the provisions set out in the preceding paragraph, denounce any article or paragraph of Part II of the Charter accepted by it provided that the number of articles or paragraphs by which this Party is bound shall never be less

than sixteen in the former case and sixty-three in the latter and that this number of articles or paragraphs shall continue to include the articles selected by the Party among those to which special reference is made in Article A, paragraph 1, sub-paragraph b.

3. Any Party may denounce the present Charter or any of the articles or paragraphs of Part II of the Charter under the conditions specified in paragraph 1 of this article in respect of any territory to which the said Charter is applicable, by virtue of a declaration made in accordance with paragraph 2 of Article L.

Article N – Appendix
The appendix to this Charter shall form an integral part of it.

Article O – Notifications
The Secretary General of the Council of Europe shall notify the member States of the Council and the Director General of the International Labour Office of:

a   any signature;
b   the deposit of any instrument of ratification, acceptance or approval;
c   any date of entry into force of this Charter in accordance with Article K;
d   any declaration made in application of Articles A, paragraphs 2 and 3, D, paragraphs 1 and 2, F, paragraph 2, L, paragraphs 1, 2, 3 and 4;
e   any amendment in accordance with Article J;
f   any denunciation in accordance with Article M;
g   any other act, notification or communication relating to this Charter.

In witness whereof, the undersigned, being duly authorised thereto, have signed this revised Charter.

Done at Strasbourg, this 3rd day of May 1996, in English and French, both texts being equally authentic, in a single copy which shall be deposited in the archives of the Council of Europe.

The Secretary General of the Council of Europe shall transmit certified copies to each member State of the Council of Europe and to the Director General of the International Labour Office.

90

European Convention for the Prevention of Torture and Inhuman or Degrading Treatment or Punishment, 1987

Note: European Convention for the Prevention of Torture and Inhuman or Degrading Treatment or Punishment. Adopted Strasbourg, 26 November 1987. ETS No. 126. Entry into force: 1 February 1989. Text amended according to the provisions of Protocols No. 1 (ETS No. 151) and No. 2 (ETS No. 152), which entered into force 1 March 2002.

The member States of the Council of Europe, signatory hereto,

Having regard to the provisions of the Convention for the Protection of Human Rights and Fundamental Freedoms,

Recalling that, under Article 3 of the same Convention, "no one shall be subjected to torture or to inhuman or degrading treatment or punishment";

Noting that the machinery provided for in that Convention operates in relation to persons who allege that they are victims of violations of Article 3;

Convinced that the protection of persons deprived of their liberty against torture and inhuman or degrading treatment or punishment could be strengthened by non-judicial means of a preventive character based on visits,

Have agreed as follows:

CHAPTER I

Article 1

There shall be established a European Committee for the Prevention of Torture and Inhuman or Degrading Treatment or Punishment (hereinafter referred to as "the Committee"). The Committee shall, by means of visits, examine the treatment of persons deprived of their liberty with a view to strengthening, if necessary, the protection of such persons from torture and from inhuman or degrading treatment or punishment.

Article 2

Each Party shall permit visits, in accordance with this Convention, to any place within its jurisdiction where persons are deprived of their liberty by a public authority.

Article 3

In the application of this Convention, the Committee and the competent national authorities of the Party concerned shall co-operate with each other.

CHAPTER II

Article 4
1. The Committee shall consist of a number of members equal to that of the Parties.
2. The members of the Committee shall be chosen from among persons of high moral character, known for their competence in the field of human rights or having professional experience in the areas covered by this Convention.
3. No two members of the Committee may be nationals of the same State.
4. The members shall serve in their individual capacity, shall be independent and impartial, and shall be available to serve the Committee effectively.

Article 5
1. The members of the Committee shall be elected by the Committee of Ministers of the Council of Europe by an absolute majority of votes, from a list of names drawn up by the Bureau of the Consultative Assembly of the Council of Europe; each national delegation of the Parties in the Consultative Assembly shall put forward three candidates, of whom two at least shall be its nationals. Where a member is to be elected to the Committee in respect of a non-member State of the Council of Europe, the Bureau of the Consultative Assembly shall invite the Parliament of that State to put forward three candidates, of whom two at least shall be its nationals. The election by the Committee of Ministers shall take place after consultation with the Party concerned.
2. The same procedure shall be followed in filling casual vacancies.
3. The members of the Committee shall be elected for a period of four years. They may be re-elected twice. However, among the members elected at the first election, the terms of three members shall expire at the end of two years. The members whose terms are to expire at the end of the initial period of two years shall be chosen by lot by the Secretary General of the Council of Europe immediately after the first election has been completed.
4. In order to ensure that, as far as possible, one half of the membership of the Committee shall be renewed every two years, the Committee of Ministers may decide, before proceeding to any subsequent election, that the term or terms of office of one or more members to be elected shall be for a period other than four years but not more than six and not less than two years.
5. In cases where more than one term of office is involved and the Committee of Ministers applies the preceding paragraph, the allocation of the terms of office shall be effected by the drawing of lots by the Secretary General, immediately after the election.

Article 6
1. The Committee shall meet in camera. A quorum shall be equal to the majority of its members. The decisions of the Committee shall be taken by a majority of the members present, subject to the provisions of Article 10, paragraph 2.
2. The Committee shall draw up its own rules of procedure.
3. The Secretariat of the Committee shall be provided by the Secretary General of the Council of Europe.

CHAPTER III

Article 7

1. The Committee shall organise visits to places referred to in Article 2. Apart from periodic visits, the Committee may organise such other visits as appear to it to be required in the circumstances.
2. As a general rule, the visits shall be carried out by at least two members of the Committee. The Committee may, if it considers it necessary, be assisted by experts and interpreters.

Article 8

1. The Committee shall notify the Government of the Party concerned of its intention to carry out a visit. After such notification, it may at any time visit any place referred to in Article 2.
2. A Party shall provide the Committee with the following facilities to carry out its task:
   a   access to its territory and the right to travel without restriction;
   b   full information on the places where persons deprived of their liberty are being held;
   c   unlimited access to any place where persons are deprived of their liberty, including the right to move inside such places without restriction;
   d   other information available to the Party which is necessary for the Committee to carry out its task. In seeking such information, the Committee shall have regard to applicable rules of national law and professional ethics.
3. The Committee may interview in private persons deprived of their liberty.
4. The Committee may communicate freely with any person whom it believes can supply relevant information.
5. If necessary, the Committee may immediately communicate observations to the competent authorities of the Party concerned.

Article 9

1. In exceptional circumstances, the competent authorities of the Party concerned may make representations to the Committee against a visit at the time or to the particular place proposed by the Committee. Such representations may only be made on grounds of national defence, public safety, serious disorder in places where persons are deprived of their liberty, the medical condition of a person or that an urgent interrogation relating to a serious crime is in progress.
2. Following such representations, the Committee and the Party shall immediately enter into consultations in order to clarify the situation and seek agreement on arrangements to enable the Committee to exercise its functions expeditiously. Such arrangements may include the transfer to another place of any person whom the Committee proposed to visit. Until the visit takes place, the Party shall provide information to the Committee about any person concerned.

Article 10

1. After each visit, the Committee shall draw up a report on the facts found during the visit, taking account of any observations which may have been submitted by the Party

concerned. It shall transmit to the latter its report containing any recommendations it considers necessary. The Committee may consult with the Party with a view to suggesting, if necessary, improvements in the protection of persons deprived of their liberty.

2. If the Party fails to co-operate or refuses to improve the situation in the light of the Committee's recommendations, the Committee may decide, after the Party has had an opportunity to make known its views, by a majority of two-thirds of its members to make a public statement on the matter.

Article 11

1. The information gathered by the Committee in relation to a visit, its report and its consultations with the Party concerned shall be confidential.
2. The Committee shall publish its report, together with any comments of the Party concerned, whenever requested to do so by that Party.
3. However, no personal data shall be published without the express consent of the person concerned.

Article 12

Subject to the rules of confidentiality in Article 11, the Committee shall every year submit to the Committee of Ministers a general report on its activities which shall be transmitted to the Consultative Assembly and to any non-member State of the Council of Europe which is a party to the Convention, and made public.

Article 13

The members of the Committee, experts and other persons assisting the Committee are required, during and after their terms of office, to maintain the confidentiality of the facts or information of which they have become aware during the discharge of their functions.

Article 14

1. The names of persons assisting the Committee shall be specified in the notification under Article 8, paragraph 1.
2. Experts shall act on the instructions and under the authority of the Committee. They shall have particular knowledge and experience in the areas covered by this Convention and shall be bound by the same duties of independence, impartiality and availability as the members of the Committee.
3. A Party may exceptionally declare that an expert or other person assisting the Committee may not be allowed to take part in a visit to a place within its jurisdiction.

CHAPTER IV

Article 15

Each Party shall inform the Committee of the name and address of the authority competent to receive notifications to its Government, and of any liaison officer it may appoint.

Article 16

The Committee, its members and experts referred to in Article 7, paragraph 2 shall enjoy the privileges and immunities set out in the annex to this Convention.

Article 17

1. This Convention shall not prejudice the provisions of domestic law or any international agreement which provide greater protection for persons deprived of their liberty.
2. Nothing in this Convention shall be construed as limiting or derogating from the competence of the organs of the European Convention on Human Rights or from the obligations assumed by the Parties under that Convention.
3. The Committee shall not visit places which representatives or delegates of Protecting Powers or the International Committee of the Red Cross effectively visit on a regular basis by virtue of the Geneva Conventions of 12 August 1949 and the Additional Protocols of 8 June 1977 thereto.

CHAPTER V

Article 18

1. This Convention shall be open for signature by the member States of the Council of Europe. It is subject to ratification, acceptance or approval. Instruments of ratification, acceptance or approval shall be deposited with the Secretary General of the Council of Europe.
2. The Committee of Ministers of the Council of Europe may invite any non-member State of the Council of Europe to accede to the Convention.

Article 19

1. This Convention shall enter into force on the first day of the month following the expiration of a period of three months after the date on which seven member States of the Council of Europe have expressed their consent to be bound by the Convention in accordance with the provisions of Article 18.
2. In respect of any State which subsequently expresses its consent to be bound by it, the Convention shall enter into force on the first day of the month following the expiration of a period of three months after the date of the deposit of the instrument of ratification, acceptance, approval or accession.

Article 20

1. Any State may at the time of signature or when depositing its instrument of ratification, acceptance, approval or accession, specify the territory or territories to which this Convention shall apply.
2. Any State may at any later date, by a declaration addressed to the Secretary General of the Council of Europe, extend the application of this Convention to any other territory specified in the declaration. In respect of such territory the Convention shall enter into force on the first day of the month following the expiration of a period of three months after the date of receipt of such declaration by the Secretary General.
3. Any declaration made under the two preceding paragraphs may, in respect of any territory specified in such declaration, be withdrawn by a notification addressed to the Secretary General. The withdrawal shall become effective on the first day of the month following the expiration of a period of three months after the date of receipt of such notification by the Secretary General.

Article 21

No reservation may be made in respect of the provisions of this Convention.

Article 22

1. Any Party may, at any time, denounce this Convention by means of a notification addressed to the Secretary General of the Council of Europe.
2. Such denunciation shall become effective on the first day of the month following the expiration of a period of twelve months after the date of receipt of the notification by the Secretary General.

Article 23

The Secretary General of the Council of Europe shall notify the member States and any non-member State of the Council of Europe party to the Convention of:

a   any signature;
b   the deposit of any instrument of ratification, acceptance, approval or accession;
c   any date of entry into force of this Convention in accordance with Articles 19 and 20;
d   any other act, notification or communication relating to this Convention, except for action taken in pursuance of Articles 8 and 10.

In witness whereof, the undersigned, being duly authorised thereto, have signed this Convention.

Done at Strasbourg, the 26 November 1987, in English and in French, both texts being equally authentic, in a single copy which shall be deposited in the archives of the Council of Europe. The Secretary General of the Council of Europe shall transmit certified copies to each member State of the Council of Europe.

ANNEX – PRIVILEGES AND IMMUNITIES

(Article 16)

1. For the purpose of this annex, references to members of the Committee shall be deemed to include references to experts mentioned in Article 7, paragraph 2.
2. The members of the Committee shall, while exercising their functions and during journeys made in the exercise of their functions, enjoy the following privileges and immunities:
   a   immunity from personal arrest or detention and from seizure of their personal baggage and, in respect of words spoken or written and all acts done by them in their official capacity, immunity from legal process of every kind;
   b   exemption from any restrictions on their freedom of movement on exit from and return to their country of residence, and entry into and exit from the country in which they exercise their functions, and from alien registration in the country which they are visiting or through which they are passing in the exercise of their functions.
3. In the course of journeys undertaken in the exercise of their functions, the members of the Committee shall, in the matter of customs and exchange control, be accorded:
   a   by their own Government, the same facilities as those accorded to senior officials travelling abroad on temporary official duty;
   b   by the Governments of other Parties, the same facilities as those accorded to representatives of foreign Governments on temporary official duty.

4. Documents and papers of the Committee, in so far as they relate to the business of the Committee, shall be inviolable. The official correspondence and other official communications of the Committee may not be held up or subjected to censorship.

5. In order to secure for the members of the Committee complete freedom of speech and complete independence in the discharge of their duties, the immunity from legal process in respect of words spoken or written and all acts done by them in discharging their duties shall continue to be accorded, notwithstanding that the persons concerned are no longer engaged in the discharge of such duties.

6. Privileges and immunities are accorded to the members of the Committee, not for the personal benefit of the individuals themselves but in order to safeguard the independent exercise of their functions. The Committee alone shall be competent to waive the immunity of its members; it has not only the right, but is under a duty, to waive the immunity of one of its members in any case where, in its opinion, the immunity would impede the course of justice, and where it can be waived without prejudice to the purpose for which the immunity is accorded.

91

European Charter for Regional or Minority Languages, 1992

Note: European Charter for Regional or Minority Languages, adopted Strasbourg, 5 November 1992. ETS No. 148. Entry into force: 1 March 1998.

PREAMBLE

The member States of the Council of Europe signatory hereto,

Considering that the aim of the Council of Europe is to achieve a greater unity between its members, particularly for the purpose of safeguarding and realising the ideals and principles which are their common heritage;

Considering that the protection of the historical regional or minority languages of Europe, some of which are in danger of eventual extinction, contributes to the maintenance and development of Europe's cultural wealth and traditions;

Considering that the right to use a regional or minority language in private and public life is an inalienable right conforming to the principles embodied in the United Nations International Covenant on Civil and Political Rights, and according to the spirit of the Council of Europe Convention for the Protection of Human Rights and Fundamental Freedoms;

Having regard to the work carried out within the CSCE and in particular to the Helsinki Final Act of 1975 and the document of the Copenhagen Meeting of 1990;

Stressing the value of interculturalism and multilingualism and considering that the protection and encouragement of regional or minority languages should not be to the detriment of the official languages and the need to learn them;

Realising that the protection and promotion of regional or minority languages in the different countries and regions of Europe represent an important contribution to the building of a Europe based on the principles of democracy and cultural diversity within the framework of national sovereignty and territorial integrity;

Taking into consideration the specific conditions and historical traditions in the different regions of the European States,

Have agreed as follows:

PART I GENERAL PROVISIONS

Article 1 – Definitions
For the purposes of this Charter:
- a "regional or minority languages" means languages that are:
    - i traditionally used within a given territory of a State by nationals of that State who form a group numerically smaller than the rest of the State's population; and
    - ii different from the official language(s) of that State;

    it does not include either dialects of the official language(s) of the State or the languages of migrants;
- b "territory in which the regional or minority language is used" means the geographical area in which the said language is the mode of expression of a number of people justifying the adoption of the various protective and promotional measures provided for in this Charter;
- c "non-territorial languages" means languages used by nationals of the State which differ from the language or languages used by the rest of the State's population but which, although traditionally used within the territory of the State, cannot be identified with a particular area thereof.

Article 2 – Undertakings
1. Each Party undertakes to apply the provisions of Part II to all the regional or minority languages spoken within its territory and which comply with the definition in Article 1.
2. In respect of each language specified at the time of ratification, acceptance or approval, in accordance with Article 3, each Party undertakes to apply a minimum of thirty-five paragraphs or sub-paragraphs chosen from among the provisions of Part III of the Charter, including at least three chosen from each of the Articles 8 and 12 and one from each of the Articles 9, 10, 11 and 13.

Article 3 – Practical arrangements
1. Each Contracting State shall specify in its instrument of ratification, acceptance or approval, each regional or minority language, or official language which is less widely used on the whole or part of its territory, to which the paragraphs chosen in accordance with Article 2, paragraph 2, shall apply.
2. Any Party may, at any subsequent time, notify the Secretary General that it accepts the obligations arising out of the provisions of any other paragraph of the Charter not already specified in its instrument of ratification, acceptance or approval, or that it will apply paragraph 1 of the present article to other regional or minority languages, or to other official languages which are less widely used on the whole or part of its territory.
3. The undertakings referred to in the foregoing paragraph shall be deemed to form an integral part of the ratification, acceptance or approval and will have the same effect as from their date of notification.

Article 4 – Existing regimes of protection
1. Nothing in this Charter shall be construed as limiting or derogating from any of the rights guaranteed by the European Convention on Human Rights.

2. The provisions of this Charter shall not affect any more favourable provisions concerning the status of regional or minority languages, or the legal regime of persons belonging to minorities which may exist in a Party or are provided for by relevant bilateral or multilateral international agreements.

Article 5 – Existing obligations

Nothing in this Charter may be interpreted as implying any right to engage in any activity or perform any action in contravention of the purposes of the Charter of the United Nations or other obligations under international law, including the principle of the sovereignty and territorial integrity of States.

Article 6 – Information

The Parties undertake to see to it that the authorities, organisations and persons concerned are informed of the rights and duties established by this Charter.

PART II OBJECTIVES AND PRINCIPLES PURSUED IN ACCORDANCE WITH ARTICLE 2, PARAGRAPH 1

Article 7 – Objectives and principles

1. In respect of regional or minority languages, within the territories in which such languages are used and according to the situation of each language, the Parties shall base their policies, legislation and practice on the following objectives and principles:
   a   the recognition of the regional or minority languages as an expression of cultural wealth;
   b   the respect of the geographical area of each regional or minority language in order to ensure that existing or new administrative divisions do not constitute an obstacle to the promotion of the regional or minority language in question;
   c   the need for resolute action to promote regional or minority languages in order to safeguard them;
   d   the facilitation and/or encouragement of the use of regional or minority languages, in speech and writing, in public and private life;
   e   the maintenance and development of links, in the fields covered by this Charter, between groups using a regional or minority language and other groups in the State employing a language used in identical or similar form, as well as the establishment of cultural relations with other groups in the State using different languages;
   f   the provision of appropriate forms and means for the teaching and study of regional or minority languages at all appropriate stages;
   g   the provision of facilities enabling non-speakers of a regional or minority language living in the area where it is used to learn it if they so desire;
   h   the promotion of study and research on regional or minority languages at universities or equivalent institutions;
   i   the promotion of appropriate types of transnational exchanges, in the fields covered by this Charter, for regional or minority languages used in identical or similar form in two or more States.
2. The Parties undertake to eliminate, if they have not yet done so, any unjustified distinction, exclusion, restriction or preference relating to the use of a regional or minority

language and intended to discourage or endanger the maintenance or development of it. The adoption of special measures in favour of regional or minority languages aimed at promoting equality between the users of these languages and the rest of the population or which take due account of their specific conditions is not considered to be an act of discrimination against the users of more widely-used languages.

3. The Parties undertake to promote, by appropriate measures, mutual understanding between all the linguistic groups of the country and in particular the inclusion of respect, understanding and tolerance in relation to regional or minority languages among the objectives of education and training provided within their countries and encouragement of the mass media to pursue the same objective.

4. In determining their policy with regard to regional or minority languages, the Parties shall take into consideration the needs and wishes expressed by the groups which use such languages. They are encouraged to establish bodies, if necessary, for the purpose of advising the authorities on all matters pertaining to regional or minority languages.

5. The Parties undertake to apply, mutatis mutandis, the principles listed in paragraphs 1 to 4 above to non-territorial languages. However, as far as these languages are concerned, the nature and scope of the measures to be taken to give effect to this Charter shall be determined in a flexible manner, bearing in mind the needs and wishes, and respecting the traditions and characteristics, of the groups which use the languages concerned.

PART III MEASURES TO PROMOTE THE USE OF REGIONAL OR MINORITY LANGUAGES IN PUBLIC LIFE IN ACCORDANCE WITH THE UNDERTAKINGS ENTERED INTO UNDER ARTICLE 2, PARAGRAPH 2

Article 8 – Education

1. With regard to education, the Parties undertake, within the territory in which such languages are used, according to the situation of each of these languages, and without prejudice to the teaching of the official language(s) of the State:

   a i   to make available pre-school education in the relevant regional or minority languages; or

   ii   to make available a substantial part of pre-school education in the relevant regional or minority languages; or

   iii   to apply one of the measures provided for under i and ii above at least to those pupils whose families so request and whose number is considered sufficient; or

   iv   if the public authorities have no direct competence in the field of pre-school education, to favour and/or encourage the application of the measures referred to under i to iii above;

   b i   to make available primary education in the relevant regional or minority languages; or

   ii   to make available a substantial part of primary education in the relevant regional or minority languages; or

   iii   to provide, within primary education, for the teaching of the relevant regional or minority languages as an integral part of the curriculum; or

   iv   to apply one of the measures provided for under i to iii above at least to those pupils whose families so request and whose number is considered sufficient;

c i to make available secondary education in the relevant regional or minority languages; or

    ii to make available a substantial part of secondary education in the relevant regional or minority languages; or

   iii to provide, within secondary education, for the teaching of the relevant regional or minority languages as an integral part of the curriculum; or

   iv to apply one of the measures provided for under i to iii above at least to those pupils who, or where appropriate whose families, so wish in a number considered sufficient;

d i to make available technical and vocational education in the relevant regional or minority languages; or

    ii to make available a substantial part of technical and vocational education in the relevant regional or minority languages; or

   iii to provide, within technical and vocational education, for the teaching of the relevant regional or minority languages as an integral part of the curriculum; or

   iv to apply one of the measures provided for under i to iii above at least to those pupils who, or where appropriate whose families, so wish in a number considered sufficient;

e i to make available university and other higher education in regional or minority languages; or

    ii to provide facilities for the study of these languages as university and higher education subjects; or

   iii if, by reason of the role of the State in relation to higher education institutions, sub-paragraphs i and ii cannot be applied, to encourage and/or allow the provision of university or other forms of higher education in regional or minority languages or of facilities for the study of these languages as university or higher education subjects;

f i to arrange for the provision of adult and continuing education courses which are taught mainly or wholly in the regional or minority languages; or

    ii to offer such languages as subjects of adult and continuing education; or

   iii if the public authorities have no direct competence in the field of adult education, to favour and/or encourage the offering of such languages as subjects of adult and continuing education;

g to make arrangements to ensure the teaching of the history and the culture which is reflected by the regional or minority language;

h to provide the basic and further training of the teachers required to implement those of paragraphs a to g accepted by the Party;

i to set up a supervisory body or bodies responsible for monitoring the measures taken and progress achieved in establishing or developing the teaching of regional or minority languages and for drawing up periodic reports of their findings, which will be made public.

2. With regard to education and in respect of territories other than those in which the regional or minority languages are traditionally used, the Parties undertake, if the number of users of a regional or minority language justifies it, to allow, encourage or provide teaching in or of the regional or minority language at all the appropriate stages of education.

Article 9 – Judicial authorities

1. The Parties undertake, in respect of those judicial districts in which the number of residents using the regional or minority languages justifies the measures specified below, according to the situation of each of these languages and on condition that the use of the facilities afforded by the present paragraph is not considered by the judge to hamper the proper administration of justice:

   a in criminal proceedings:

      i   to provide that the courts, at the request of one of the parties, shall conduct the proceedings in the regional or minority languages; and/or

      ii   to guarantee the accused the right to use his/her regional or minority language; and/or

      iii   to provide that requests and evidence, whether written or oral, shall not be considered inadmissible solely because they are formulated in a regional or minority language; and/or

      iv   to produce, on request, documents connected with legal proceedings in the relevant regional or minority language, if necessary by the use of interpreters and translations involving no extra expense for the persons concerned;

   b in civil proceedings:

      i   to provide that the courts, at the request of one of the parties, shall conduct the proceedings in the regional or minority languages; and/or

      ii   to allow, whenever a litigant has to appear in person before a court, that he or she may use his or her regional or minority language without thereby incurring additional expense; and/or

      iii   to allow documents and evidence to be produced in the regional or minority languages, if necessary by the use of interpreters and translations;

   c in proceedings before courts concerning administrative matters:

      i   to provide that the courts, at the request of one of the parties, shall conduct the proceedings in the regional or minority languages; and/or

      ii   to allow, whenever a litigant has to appear in person before a court, that he or she may use his or her regional or minority language without thereby incurring additional expense; and/or

      iii   to allow documents and evidence to be produced in the regional or minority languages, if necessary by the use of interpreters and translations;

   d to take steps to ensure that the application of sub-paragraphs i and iii of paragraphs b and c above and any necessary use of interpreters and translations does not involve extra expense for the persons concerned.

2. The Parties undertake:

   a not to deny the validity of legal documents drawn up within the State solely because they are drafted in a regional or minority language; or

   b not to deny the validity, as between the parties, of legal documents drawn up within the country solely because they are drafted in a regional or minority language, and to provide that they can be invoked against interested third parties who are not users of these languages on condition that the contents of the document are made known to them by the person(s) who invoke(s) it; or

   c not to deny the validity, as between the parties, of legal documents drawn up within the country solely because they are drafted in a regional or minority language.

3. The Parties undertake to make available in the regional or minority languages the most important national statutory texts and those relating particularly to users of these languages, unless they are otherwise provided.

Article 10 – Administrative authorities and public services

1. Within the administrative districts of the State in which the number of residents who are users of regional or minority languages justifies the measures specified below and according to the situation of each language, the Parties undertake, as far as this is reasonably possible:

   a i to ensure that the administrative authorities use the regional or minority languages; or

   ii to ensure that such of their officers as are in contact with the public use the regional or minority languages in their relations with persons applying to them in these languages; or

   iii to ensure that users of regional or minority languages may submit oral or written applications and receive a reply in these languages; or

   iv to ensure that users of regional or minority languages may submit oral or written applications in these languages; or

   v to ensure that users of regional or minority languages may validly submit a document in these languages;

   b to make available widely used administrative texts and forms for the population in the regional or minority languages or in bilingual versions;

   c to allow the administrative authorities to draft documents in a regional or minority language.

2. In respect of the local and regional authorities on whose territory the number of residents who are users of regional or minority languages is such as to justify the measures specified below, the Parties undertake to allow and/or encourage:

   a the use of regional or minority languages within the framework of the regional or local authority;

   b the possibility for users of regional or minority languages to submit oral or written applications in these languages;

   c the publication by regional authorities of their official documents also in the relevant regional or minority languages;

   d the publication by local authorities of their official documents also in the relevant regional or minority languages;

   e the use by regional authorities of regional or minority languages in debates in their assemblies, without excluding, however, the use of the official language(s) of the State;

   f the use by local authorities of regional or minority languages in debates in their assemblies, without excluding, however, the use of the official language(s) of the State;

   g the use or adoption, if necessary in conjunction with the name in the official language(s), of traditional and correct forms of place-names in regional or minority languages.

3. With regard to public services provided by the administrative authorities or other persons acting on their behalf, the Parties undertake, within the territory in which regional or minority languages are used, in accordance with the situation of each language and as far as this is reasonably possible:

a to ensure that the regional or minority languages are used in the provision of the service; or

b to allow users of regional or minority languages to submit a request and receive a reply in these languages; or

c to allow users of regional or minority languages to submit a request in these languages.

4. With a view to putting into effect those provisions of paragraphs 1, 2 and 3 accepted by them, the Parties undertake to take one or more of the following measures:

a translation or interpretation as may be required;

b recruitment and, where necessary, training of the officials and other public service employees required;

c compliance as far as possible with requests from public service employees having a knowledge of a regional or minority language to be appointed in the territory in which that language is used.

5. The Parties undertake to allow the use or adoption of family names in the regional or minority languages, at the request of those concerned.

Article 11 – Media

1. The Parties undertake, for the users of the regional or minority languages within the territories in which those languages are spoken, according to the situation of each language, to the extent that the public authorities, directly or indirectly, are competent, have power or play a role in this field, and respecting the principle of the independence and autonomy of the media:

a to the extent that radio and television carry out a public service mission:

   i to ensure the creation of at least one radio station and one television channel in the regional or minority languages; or

   ii to encourage and/or facilitate the creation of at least one radio station and one television channel in the regional or minority languages; or

   iii to make adequate provision so that broadcasters offer programmes in the regional or minority languages;

b i to encourage and/or facilitate the creation of at least one radio station in the regional or minority languages; or

   ii to encourage and/or facilitate the broadcasting of radio programmes in the regional or minority languages on a regular basis;

c i to encourage and/or facilitate the creation of at least one television channel in the regional or minority languages; or

   ii to encourage and/or facilitate the broadcasting of television programmes in the regional or minority languages on a regular basis;

d to encourage and/or facilitate the production and distribution of audio and audio-visual works in the regional or minority languages;

e i to encourage and/or facilitate the creation and/or maintenance of at least one newspaper in the regional or minority languages; or

   ii to encourage and/or facilitate the publication of newspaper articles in the regional or minority languages on a regular basis;

f   i   to cover the additional costs of those media which use regional or minority languages, wherever the law provides for financial assistance in general for the media; or

ii   to apply existing measures for financial assistance also to audiovisual productions in the regional or minority languages;

g   to support the training of journalists and other staff for media using regional or minority languages.

2. The Parties undertake to guarantee freedom of direct reception of radio and television broadcasts from neighbouring countries in a language used in identical or similar form to a regional or minority language, and not to oppose the retransmission of radio and television broadcasts from neighbouring countries in such a language. They further undertake to ensure that no restrictions will be placed on the freedom of expression and free circulation of information in the written press in a language used in identical or similar form to a regional or minority language. The exercise of the above-mentioned freedoms, since it carries with it duties and responsibilities, may be subject to such formalities, conditions, restrictions or penalties as are prescribed by law and are necessary in a democratic society, in the interests of national security, territorial integrity or public safety, for the prevention of disorder or crime, for the protection of health or morals, for the protection of the reputation or rights of others, for preventing disclosure of information received in confidence, or for maintaining the authority and impartiality of the judiciary.

3. The Parties undertake to ensure that the interests of the users of regional or minority languages are represented or taken into account within such bodies as may be established in accordance with the law with responsibility for guaranteeing the freedom and pluralism of the media.

Article 12 – Cultural activities and facilities

1. With regard to cultural activities and facilities – especially libraries, video libraries, cultural centres, museums, archives, academies, theatres and cinemas, as well as literary work and film production, vernacular forms of cultural expression, festivals and the culture industries, including inter alia the use of new technologies – the Parties undertake, within the territory in which such languages are used and to the extent that the public authorities are competent, have power or play a role in this field:

a   to encourage types of expression and initiative specific to regional or minority languages and foster the different means of access to works produced in these languages;

b   to foster the different means of access in other languages to works produced in regional or minority languages by aiding and developing translation, dubbing, post-synchronisation and subtitling activities;

c   to foster access in regional or minority languages to works produced in other languages by aiding and developing translation, dubbing, post-synchronisation and subtitling activities;

d   to ensure that the bodies responsible for organising or supporting cultural activities of various kinds make appropriate allowance for incorporating the knowledge and use of regional or minority languages and cultures in the undertakings which they initiate or for which they provide backing;

e   to promote measures to ensure that the bodies responsible for organising or supporting cultural activities have at their disposal staff who have a full command of the regional or minority language concerned, as well as of the language(s) of the rest of the population;

f   to encourage direct participation by representatives of the users of a given regional or minority language in providing facilities and planning cultural activities;

g   to encourage and/or facilitate the creation of a body or bodies responsible for collecting, keeping a copy of and presenting or publishing works produced in the regional or minority languages;

h   if necessary, to create and/or promote and finance translation and terminological research services, particularly with a view to maintaining and developing appropriate administrative, commercial, economic, social, technical or legal terminology in each regional or minority language.

2. In respect of territories other than those in which the regional or minority languages are traditionally used, the Parties undertake, if the number of users of a regional or minority language justifies it, to allow, encourage and/or provide appropriate cultural activities and facilities in accordance with the preceding paragraph.

3. The Parties undertake to make appropriate provision, in pursuing their cultural policy abroad, for regional or minority languages and the cultures they reflect.

Article 13 – Economic and social life

1. With regard to economic and social activities, the Parties undertake, within the whole country:

a   to eliminate from their legislation any provision prohibiting or limiting without justifiable reasons the use of regional or minority languages in documents relating to economic or social life, particularly contracts of employment, and in technical documents such as instructions for the use of products or installations;

b   to prohibit the insertion in internal regulations of companies and private documents of any clauses excluding or restricting the use of regional or minority languages, at least between users of the same language;

c   to oppose practices designed to discourage the use of regional or minority languages in connection with economic or social activities;

d   to facilitate and/or encourage the use of regional or minority languages by means other than those specified in the above sub-paragraphs.

2. With regard to economic and social activities, the Parties undertake, in so far as the public authorities are competent, within the territory in which the regional or minority languages are used, and as far as this is reasonably possible:

a   to include in their financial and banking regulations provisions which allow, by means of procedures compatible with commercial practice, the use of regional or minority languages in drawing up payment orders (cheques, drafts, etc.) or other financial documents, or, where appropriate, to ensure the implementation of such provisions;

b   in the economic and social sectors directly under their control (public sector), to organise activities to promote the use of regional or minority languages;

c   to ensure that social care facilities such as hospitals, retirement homes and hostels offer the possibility of receiving and treating in their own language persons using a regional or minority language who are in need of care on grounds of ill-health, old age or for other reasons;

d   to ensure by appropriate means that safety instructions are also drawn up in regional or minority languages;

e   to arrange for information provided by the competent public authorities concerning the rights of consumers to be made available in regional or minority languages.

Article 14 – Transfrontier exchanges

The Parties undertake:

a   to apply existing bilateral and multilateral agreements which bind them with the States in which the same language is used in identical or similar form, or if necessary to seek to conclude such agreements, in such a way as to foster contacts between the users of the same language in the States concerned in the fields of culture, education, information, vocational training and permanent education;

b   for the benefit of regional or minority languages, to facilitate and/or promote co-operation across borders, in particular between regional or local authorities in whose territory the same language is used in identical or similar form.

PART IV APPLICATION OF THE CHARTER

Article 15 – Periodical reports

1. The Parties shall present periodically to the Secretary General of the Council of Europe, in a form to be prescribed by the Committee of Ministers, a report on their policy pursued in accordance with Part II of this Charter and on the measures taken in application of those provisions of Part III which they have accepted. The first report shall be presented within the year following the entry into force of the Charter with respect to the Party concerned, the other reports at three-yearly intervals after the first report.

2. The Parties shall make their reports public.

Article 16 – Examination of the reports

1. The reports presented to the Secretary General of the Council of Europe under Article 15 shall be examined by a committee of experts constituted in accordance with Article 17.

2. Bodies or associations legally established in a Party may draw the attention of the committee of experts to matters relating to the undertakings entered into by that Party under Part III of this Charter. After consulting the Party concerned, the committee of experts may take account of this information in the preparation of the report specified in paragraph 3 below. These bodies or associations can furthermore submit statements concerning the policy pursued by a Party in accordance with Part II.

3. On the basis of the reports specified in paragraph 1 and the information mentioned in paragraph 2, the committee of experts shall prepare a report for the Committee of Ministers. This report shall be accompanied by the comments which the Parties have been requested to make and may be made public by the Committee of Ministers.

4. The report specified in paragraph 3 shall contain in particular the proposals of the committee of experts to the Committee of Ministers for the preparation of such recommendations of the latter body to one or more of the Parties as may be required.

5. The Secretary General of the Council of Europe shall make a two-yearly detailed report to the Parliamentary Assembly on the application of the Charter.

Article 17 – Committee of experts

1. The committee of experts shall be composed of one member per Party, appointed by the Committee of Ministers from a list of individuals of the highest integrity and recognised competence in the matters dealt with in the Charter, who shall be nominated by the Party concerned.

2. Members of the committee shall be appointed for a period of six years and shall be eligible for reappointment. A member who is unable to complete a term of office shall be replaced in accordance with the procedure laid down in paragraph 1, and the replacing member shall complete his predecessor's term of office.

3. The committee of experts shall adopt rules of procedure. Its secretarial services shall be provided by the Secretary General of the Council of Europe.

PART V FINAL PROVISIONS

Article 18

This Charter shall be open for signature by the member States of the Council of Europe. It is subject to ratification, acceptance or approval. Instruments of ratification, acceptance or approval shall be deposited with the Secretary General of the Council of Europe.

Article 19

1. This Charter shall enter into force on the first day of the month following the expiration of a period of three months after the date on which five member States of the Council of Europe have expressed their consent to be bound by the Charter in accordance with the provisions of Article 18.

2. In respect of any member State which subsequently expresses its consent to be bound by it, the Charter shall enter into force on the first day of the month following the expiration of a period of three months after the date of the deposit of the instrument of ratification, acceptance or approval.

Article 20

1. After the entry into force of this Charter, the Committee of Ministers of the Council of Europe may invite any State not a member of the Council of Europe to accede to this Charter.

2. In respect of any acceding State, the Charter shall enter into force on the first day of the month following the expiration of a period of three months after the date of deposit of the instrument of accession with the Secretary General of the Council of Europe.

Article 21

1. Any State may, at the time of signature or when depositing its instrument of ratification, acceptance, approval or accession, make one or more reservations to paragraphs 2 to 5 of Article 7 of this Charter. No other reservation may be made.

2. Any Contracting State which has made a reservation under the preceding paragraph may wholly or partly withdraw it by means of a notification addressed to the Secretary General of the Council of Europe. The withdrawal shall take effect on the date of receipt of such notification by the Secretary General.

Article 22

1. Any Party may at any time denounce this Charter by means of a notification addressed to the Secretary General of the Council of Europe.
2. Such denunciation shall become effective on the first day of the month following the expiration of a period of six months after the date of receipt of the notification by the Secretary General.

Article 23

The Secretary General of the Council of Europe shall notify the member States of the Council and any State which has acceded to this Charter of:

   a any signature;
   b the deposit of any instrument of ratification, acceptance, approval or accession;
   c any date of entry into force of this Charter in accordance with Articles 19 and 20;
   d any notification received in application of the provisions of Article 3, paragraph 2;
   e any other act, notification or communication relating to this Charter.

In witness whereof the undersigned, being duly authorised thereto, have signed this Charter.

Done at Strasbourg, this 5th day of November 1992, in English and French, both texts being equally authentic, in a single copy which shall be deposited in the archives of the Council of Europe. The Secretary General of the Council of Europe shall transmit certified copies to each member State of the Council of Europe and to any State invited to accede to this Charter.

PART X
Organization of American States Documents

92

American Declaration of the Rights and Duties of Man, 1948

Note: Adopted by the Ninth International Conference of American States, Bogotá, Colombia, 2 May 1948. OAS Resolution XXX.

WHEREAS:

The American peoples have acknowledged the dignity of the individual, and their national constitutions recognize that juridical and political institutions, which regulate life in human society, have as their principal aim the protection of the essential rights of man and the creation of circumstances that will permit him to achieve spiritual and material progress and attain happiness;

The American States have on repeated occasions recognized that the essential rights of man are not derived from the fact that he is a national of a certain state, but are based upon attributes of his human personality;

The international protection of the rights of man should be the principal guide of an evolving American law;

The affirmation of essential human rights by the American States together with the guarantees given by the internal regimes of the states establish the initial system of protection considered by the American States as being suited to the present social and juridical conditions, not without a recognition on their part that they should increasingly strengthen that system in the international field as conditions become more favorable,

The Ninth International Conference of American States

AGREES:

To adopt the following

AMERICAN DECLARATION OF THE RIGHTS AND DUTIES OF MAN

PREAMBLE

All men are born free and equal, in dignity and in rights, and, being endowed by nature with reason and conscience, they should conduct themselves as brothers one to another.

The fulfillment of duty by each individual is a prerequisite to the rights of all. Rights and duties are interrelated in every social and political activity of man. While rights exalt individual liberty, duties express the dignity of that liberty.

Duties of a juridical nature presuppose others of a moral nature which support them in principle and constitute their basis.

Inasmuch as spiritual development is the supreme end of human existence and the highest expression thereof, it is the duty of man to serve that end with all his strength and resources.

Since culture is the highest social and historical expression of that spiritual development, it is the duty of man to preserve, practice and foster culture by every means within his power.

And, since moral conduct constitutes the noblest flowering of culture, it is the duty of every man always to hold it in high respect.

Chapter One

Rights

Article I. Every human being has the right to life, liberty and the security of his person.

Right to life, liberty and personal security.

Article II. All persons are equal before the law and have the rights and duties established in this Declaration, without distinction as to race, sex, language, creed or any other factor.

Right to equality before law.

Article III. Every person has the right freely to profess a religious faith, and to manifest and practice it both in public and in private.

Right to religious freedom and worship.

Article IV. Every person has the right to freedom of investigation, of opinion, and of the expression and dissemination of ideas, by any medium whatsoever.

Right to freedom of investigation, opinion, expression and dissemination.

Article V. Every person has the right to the protection of the law against abusive attacks upon his honor, his reputation, and his private and family life.

Right to protection of honor, personal reputation, and private and family life.

Article VI. Every person has the right to establish a family, the basic element of society, and to receive protection therefore.

Right to a family and to protection thereof.

Article VII. All women, during pregnancy and the nursing period, and all children have the right to special protection, care and aid.

Right to protection for mothers and children.

Article VIII. Every person has the right to fix his residence within the territory of the state of which he is a national, to move about freely within such territory, and not to leave it except by his own will.

Right to residence and movement.

Article IX. Every person has the right to the inviolability of his home.

Right to inviolability of the home.

Article X. Every person has the right to the inviolability and transmission of his correspondence.

Right to the inviolability and transmission of correspondence.

Article XI. Every person has the right to the preservation of his health through sanitary and social measures relating to food, clothing, housing and medical care, to the extent permitted by public and community resources.

Right to the preservation of health and to well-being.

Article XII. Every person has the right to an education, which should be based on the principles of liberty, morality and human solidarity. Likewise every person has the right to an education that will prepare him to attain a decent life, to raise his standard of living, and to be a useful member of society. The right to an education includes the right to equality of opportunity in every case, in accordance with natural talents, merit and the desire to utilize the resources that the state or the community is in a position to provide. Every person has the right to receive, free, at least a primary education.

Right to education.

Article XIII. Every person has the right to take part in the cultural life of the community, to enjoy the arts, and to participate in the benefits that result from intellectual progress, especially scientific discoveries. He likewise has the right to the protection of his moral and material interests as regards his inventions or any literary, scientific or artistic works of which he is the author.

Right to the benefits of culture.

Article XIV. Every person has the right to work, under proper conditions, and to follow his vocation freely, insofar as existing conditions of employment permit. Every person who works has the right to receive such remuneration as will, in proportion to his capacity and skill, assure him a standard of living suitable for himself and for his family.

Right to work and to fair remuneration.

Article XV. Every person has the right to leisure time, to wholesome recreation, and to the opportunity for advantageous use of his free time to his spiritual, cultural and physical benefit.

Right to leisure time and to the use thereof.

Article XVI. Every person has the right to social security which will protect him from the consequences of unemployment, old age, and any disabilities arising from causes beyond his control that make it physically or mentally impossible for him to earn a living.

Right to social security.

Article XVII. Every person has the right to be recognized everywhere as a person having rights and obligations, and to enjoy the basic civil rights.

Right to recognition of juridical personality and civil rights.

Article XVIII. Every person may resort to the courts to ensure respect for his legal rights. There should likewise be available to him a simple, brief procedure whereby the courts will protect him from acts of authority that, to his prejudice, violate any fundamental constitutional rights.

Right to a fair trial.

Article XIX. Every person has the right to the nationality to which he is entitled by law and to change it, if he so wishes, for the nationality of any other country that is willing to grant it to him.

Right to nationality.

Article XX. Every person having legal capacity is entitled to participate in the government of his country, directly or through his representatives, and to take part in popular elections, which shall be by secret ballot, and shall be honest, periodic and free.

Right to vote and to participate in government.

Article XXI. Every person has the right to assemble peaceably with others in a formal public meeting or an informal gathering, in connection with matters of common interest of any nature.

Right of assembly.

Article XXII. Every person has the right to associate with others to promote, exercise and protect his legitimate interests of a political, economic, religious, social, cultural, professional, labor union or other nature.

Right of association.

Article XXIII. Every person has a right to own such private property as meets the essential needs of decent living and helps to maintain the dignity of the individual and of the home.

Right to property.

Article XXIV. Every person has the right to submit respectful petitions to any competent authority, for reasons of either general or private interest, and the right to obtain a prompt decision thereon.

Right of petition.

Article XXV. No person may be deprived of his liberty except in the cases and according to the procedures established by pre-existing law. No person may be deprived of liberty for nonfulfillment of obligations of a purely civil character. Every individual who has been deprived of his liberty has the right to have the legality of his detention ascertained without delay by a court, and the right to be tried without undue delay or, otherwise, to be released. He also has the right to humane treatment during the time he is in custody.

Right of protection from arbitrary arrest.

Article XXVI. Every accused person is presumed to be innocent until proved guilty. Every person accused of an offense has the right to be given an impartial and public hearing, and to be tried by courts previously established in accordance with pre-existing laws, and not to receive cruel, infamous or unusual punishment.

Right to due process of law.

Article XXVII. Every person has the right, in case of pursuit not resulting from ordinary crimes, to seek and receive asylum in foreign territory, in accordance with the laws of each country and with international agreements.

Right of asylum.

Article XXVIII. The rights of man are limited by the rights of others, by the security of all, and by the just demands of the general welfare and the advancement of democracy.

Scope of the rights of man.

Chapter Two

Duties

Article XXIX. It is the duty of the individual so to conduct himself in relation to others that each and every one may fully form and develop his personality.

Duties to society.

Article XXX. It is the duty of every person to aid, support, educate and protect his minor children, and it is the duty of children to honor their parents always and to aid, support and protect them when they need it.

Duties toward children and parents.

Article XXXI. It is the duty of every person to acquire at least an elementary education.

Duty to receive instruction.

Article XXXII. It is the duty of every person to vote in the popular elections of the country of which he is a national, when he is legally capable of doing so.

Duty to vote.

Article XXXIII. It is the duty of every person to obey the law and other legitimate commands of the authorities of his country and those of the country in which he may be.

Duty to obey the law.

Article XXXIV. It is the duty of every able-bodied person to render whatever civil and military service his country may require for its defense and preservation, and, in case of public disaster, to render such services as may be in his power. It is likewise his duty to hold any public office to which he may be elected by popular vote in the state of which he is a national.

Duty to serve the community and the nation.

Article XXXV. It is the duty of every person to cooperate with the state and the community with respect to social security and welfare, in accordance with his ability and with existing circumstances.

Duties with respect to social security and welfare.

Article XXXVI. It is the duty of every person to pay the taxes established by law for the support of public services.

Duty to pay taxes.

Article XXXVII. It is the duty of every person to work, as far as his capacity and possibilities permit, in order to obtain the means of livelihood or to benefit his community.

Duty to work.

93

American Convention on Human Rights, 'Pact of San Jose, Costa Rica', 1969

Note: American Convention on Human Rights, 'Pact of San Jose, Costa Rica' OAS Treaty Series No. 36, 1144 UNTS 123. Entry into force: 18 July 1978.

PREAMBLE

The American states signatory to the present Convention,

Reaffirming their intention to consolidate in this hemisphere, within the framework of democratic institutions, a system of personal liberty and social justice based on respect for the essential rights of man;

Recognizing that the essential rights of man are not derived from one's being a national of a certain state, but are based upon attributes of the human personality, and that they therefore justify international protection in the form of a convention reinforcing or complementing the protection provided by the domestic law of the American states;

Considering that these principles have been set forth in the Charter of the Organization of American States, in the American Declaration of the Rights and Duties of Man, and in the Universal Declaration of Human Rights, and that they have been reaffirmed and refined in other international instruments, worldwide as well as regional in scope;

Reiterating that, in accordance with the Universal Declaration of Human Rights, the ideal of free men enjoying freedom from fear and want can be achieved only if conditions are created whereby everyone may enjoy his economic, social, and cultural rights, as well as his civil and political rights; and

Considering that the Third Special Inter-American Conference (Buenos Aires, 1967) approved the incorporation into the Charter of the Organization itself of broader standards with respect to economic, social, and educational rights and resolved that an inter-American convention on human rights should determine the structure, competence, and procedure of the organs responsible for these matters,

Have agreed upon the following:

PART I STATE OBLIGATIONS AND RIGHTS PROTECTED

Chapter I General Obligations

Article 1. Obligation to Respect Rights

1. The States Parties to this Convention undertake to respect the rights and freedoms recognized herein and to ensure to all persons subject to their jurisdiction the free and full exercise of those rights and freedoms, without any discrimination for reasons of race, color, sex, language, religion, political or other opinion, national or social origin, economic status, birth, or any other social condition.
2. For the purposes of this Convention, "person" means every human being.

Article 2. Domestic Legal Effects

Where the exercise of any of the rights or freedoms referred to in Article 1 is not already ensured by legislative or other provisions, the States Parties undertake to adopt, in accordance with their constitutional processes and the provisions of this Convention, such legislative or other measures as may be necessary to give effect to those rights or freedoms.

Chapter II Civil and Political Rights

Article 3. Right to Juridical Personality

Every person has the right to recognition as a person before the law.

Article 4. Right to Life

1. Every person has the right to have his life respected. This right shall be protected by law and, in general, from the moment of conception. No one shall be arbitrarily deprived of his life.
2. In countries that have not abolished the death penalty, it may be imposed only for the most serious crimes and pursuant to a final judgment rendered by a competent court and in accordance with a law establishing such punishment, enacted prior to the commission of the crime. The application of such punishment shall not be extended to crimes to which it does not presently apply.
3. The death penalty shall not be reestablished in states that have abolished it.
4. In no case shall capital punishment be inflicted for political offenses or related common crimes.
5. Capital punishment shall not be imposed upon persons who, at the time the crime was committed, were under 18 years of age or over 70 years of age; nor shall it be applied to pregnant women.
6. Every person condemned to death shall have the right to apply for amnesty, pardon, or commutation of sentence, which may be granted in all cases. Capital punishment shall not be imposed while such a petition is pending decision by the competent authority.

Article 5. Right to Humane Treatment

1. Every person has the right to have his physical, mental, and moral integrity respected.
2. No one shall be subjected to torture or to cruel, inhuman, or degrading punishment or treatment. All persons deprived of their liberty shall be treated with respect for the inherent dignity of the human person.

3. Punishment shall not be extended to any person other than the criminal.

4. Accused persons shall, save in exceptional circumstances, be segregated from convicted persons, and shall be subject to separate treatment appropriate to their status as unconvicted persons.

5. Minors while subject to criminal proceedings shall be separated from adults and brought before specialized tribunals, as speedily as possible, so that they may be treated in accordance with their status as minors.

6. Punishments consisting of deprivation of liberty shall have as an essential aim the reform and social readaptation of the prisoners.

Article 6. Freedom from Slavery

1. No one shall be subject to slavery or to involuntary servitude, which are prohibited in all their forms, as are the slave trade and traffic in women.

2. No one shall be required to perform forced or compulsory labor. This provision shall not be interpreted to mean that, in those countries in which the penalty established for certain crimes is deprivation of liberty at forced labor, the carrying out of such a sentence imposed by a competent court is prohibited. Forced labor shall not adversely affect the dignity or the physical or intellectual capacity of the prisoner.

3. For the purposes of this article, the following do not constitute forced or compulsory labor:

   a. work or service normally required of a person imprisoned in execution of a sentence or formal decision passed by the competent judicial authority. Such work or service shall be carried out under the supervision and control of public authorities, and any persons performing such work or service shall not be placed at the disposal of any private party, company, or juridical person;

   b. military service and, in countries in which conscientious objectors are recognized, national service that the law may provide for in lieu of military service;

   c. service exacted in time of danger or calamity that threatens the existence or the well-being of the community; or

   d. work or service that forms part of normal civic obligations.

Article 7. Right to Personal Liberty

1. Every person has the right to personal liberty and security.

2. No one shall be deprived of his physical liberty except for the reasons and under the conditions established beforehand by the constitution of the State Party concerned or by a law established pursuant thereto.

3. No one shall be subject to arbitrary arrest or imprisonment.

4. Anyone who is detained shall be informed of the reasons for his detention and shall be promptly notified of the charge or charges against him.

5. Any person detained shall be brought promptly before a judge or other officer authorized by law to exercise judicial power and shall be entitled to trial within a reasonable time or to be released without prejudice to the continuation of the proceedings. His release may be subject to guarantees to assure his appearance for trial.

6. Anyone who is deprived of his liberty shall be entitled to recourse to a competent court, in order that the court may decide without delay on the lawfulness of his arrest or detention and order his release if the arrest or detention is unlawful. In States Parties

whose laws provide that anyone who believes himself to be threatened with deprivation of his liberty is entitled to recourse to a competent court in order that it may decide on the lawfulness of such threat, this remedy may not be restricted or abolished. The interested party or another person in his behalf is entitled to seek these remedies.

7. No one shall be detained for debt. This principle shall not limit the orders of a competent judicial authority issued for nonfulfillment of duties of support.

Article 8. Right to a Fair Trial

1. Every person has the right to a hearing, with due guarantees and within a reasonable time, by a competent, independent, and impartial tribunal, previously established by law, in the substantiation of any accusation of a criminal nature made against him or for the determination of his rights and obligations of a civil, labor, fiscal, or any other nature.

2. Every person accused of a criminal offense has the right to be presumed innocent so long as his guilt has not been proven according to law. During the proceedings, every person is entitled, with full equality, to the following minimum guarantees:

   a. the right of the accused to be assisted without charge by a translator or interpreter, if he does not understand or does not speak the language of the tribunal or court;

   b. prior notification in detail to the accused of the charges against him;

   c. adequate time and means for the preparation of his defense;

   d. the right of the accused to defend himself personally or to be assisted by legal counsel of his own choosing, and to communicate freely and privately with his counsel;

   e. the inalienable right to be assisted by counsel provided by the state, paid or not as the domestic law provides, if the accused does not defend himself personally or engage his own counsel within the time period established by law;

   f. the right of the defense to examine witnesses present in the court and to obtain the appearance, as witnesses, of experts or other persons who may throw light on the facts;

   g. the right not to be compelled to be a witness against himself or to plead guilty; and

   h. the right to appeal the judgment to a higher court.

3. A confession of guilt by the accused shall be valid only if it is made without coercion of any kind.

4. An accused person acquitted by a nonappealable judgment shall not be subjected to a new trial for the same cause.

5. Criminal proceedings shall be public, except insofar as may be necessary to protect the interests of justice.

Article 9. Freedom from Ex Post Facto Laws

No one shall be convicted of any act or omission that did not constitute a criminal offense, under the applicable law, at the time it was committed. A heavier penalty shall not be imposed than the one that was applicable at the time the criminal offense was committed. If subsequent to the commission of the offense the law provides for the imposition of a lighter punishment, the guilty person shall benefit therefrom.

Article 10. Right to Compensation

Every person has the right to be compensated in accordance with the law in the event he has been sentenced by a final judgment through a miscarriage of justice.

Article 11. Right to Privacy

1. Everyone has the right to have his honor respected and his dignity recognized.
2. No one may be the object of arbitrary or abusive interference with his private life, his family, his home, or his correspondence, or of unlawful attacks on his honor or reputation.
3. Everyone has the right to the protection of the law against such interference or attacks.

Article 12. Freedom of Conscience and Religion

1. Everyone has the right to freedom of conscience and of religion. This right includes freedom to maintain or to change one's religion or beliefs, and freedom to profess or disseminate one's religion or beliefs, either individually or together with others, in public or in private.
2. No one shall be subject to restrictions that might impair his freedom to maintain or to change his religion or beliefs.
3. Freedom to manifest one's religion and beliefs may be subject only to the limitations prescribed by law that are necessary to protect public safety, order, health, or morals, or the rights or freedoms of others.
4. Parents or guardians, as the case may be, have the right to provide for the religious and moral education of their children or wards that is in accord with their own convictions.

Article 13. Freedom of Thought and Expression

1. Everyone has the right to freedom of thought and expression. This right includes freedom to seek, receive, and impart information and ideas of all kinds, regardless of frontiers, either orally, in writing, in print, in the form of art, or through any other medium of one's choice.
2. The exercise of the right provided for in the foregoing paragraph shall not be subject to prior censorship but shall be subject to subsequent imposition of liability, which shall be expressly established by law to the extent necessary to ensure:
   a. respect for the rights or reputations of others; or
   b. the protection of national security, public order, or public health or morals.
3. The right of expression may not be restricted by indirect methods or means, such as the abuse of government or private controls over newsprint, radio broadcasting frequencies, or equipment used in the dissemination of information, or by any other means tending to impede the communication and circulation of ideas and opinions.
4. Notwithstanding the provisions of paragraph 2 above, public entertainments may be subject by law to prior censorship for the sole purpose of regulating access to them for the moral protection of childhood and adolescence.
5. Any propaganda for war and any advocacy of national, racial, or religious hatred that constitute incitements to lawless violence or to any other similar action against any person or group of persons on any grounds including those of race, color, religion, language, or national origin shall be considered as offenses punishable by law.

Article 14. Right of Reply

1. Anyone injured by inaccurate or offensive statements or ideas disseminated to the public in general by a legally regulated medium of communication has the right to reply or to make a correction using the same communications outlet, under such conditions as the law may establish.
2. The correction or reply shall not in any case remit other legal liabilities that may have been incurred.
3. For the effective protection of honor and reputation, every publisher, and every newspaper, motion picture, radio, and television company, shall have a person responsible who is not protected by immunities or special privileges.

Article 15. Right of Assembly

The right of peaceful assembly, without arms, is recognized. No restrictions may be placed on the exercise of this right other than those imposed in conformity with the law and necessary in a democratic society in the interest of national security, public safety or public order, or to protect public health or morals or the rights or freedom of others.

Article 16. Freedom of Association

1. Everyone has the right to associate freely for ideological, religious, political, economic, labor, social, cultural, sports, or other purposes.
2. The exercise of this right shall be subject only to such restrictions established by law as may be necessary in a democratic society, in the interest of national security, public safety or public order, or to protect public health or morals or the rights and freedoms of others.
3. The provisions of this article do not bar the imposition of legal restrictions, including even deprivation of the exercise of the right of association, on members of the armed forces and the police.

Article 17. Rights of the Family

1. The family is the natural and fundamental group unit of society and is entitled to protection by society and the state.
2. The right of men and women of marriageable age to marry and to raise a family shall be recognized, if they meet the conditions required by domestic laws, insofar as such conditions do not affect the principle of non-discrimination established in this Convention.
3. No marriage shall be entered into without the free and full consent of the intending spouses.
4. The States Parties shall take appropriate steps to ensure the equality of rights and the adequate balancing of responsibilities of the spouses as to marriage, during marriage, and in the event of its dissolution. In case of dissolution, provision shall be made for the necessary protection of any children solely on the basis of their own best interests.
5. The law shall recognize equal rights for children born out of wedlock and those born in wedlock.

Article 18. Right to a Name

Every person has the right to a given name and to the surnames of his parents or that of one of them. The law shall regulate the manner in which this right shall be ensured for all, by the use of assumed names if necessary.

Article 19. Rights of the Child
Every minor child has the right to the measures of protection required by his condition as a minor on the part of his family, society, and the state.

Article 20. Right to Nationality
1. Every person has the right to a nationality.
2. Every person has the right to the nationality of the state in whose territory he was born if he does not have the right to any other nationality.
3. No one shall be arbitrarily deprived of his nationality or of the right to change it.

Article 21. Right to Property
1. Everyone has the right to the use and enjoyment of his property. The law may subordinate such use and enjoyment to the interest of society.
2. No one shall be deprived of his property except upon payment of just compensation, for reasons of public utility or social interest, and in the cases and according to the forms established by law.
3. Usury and any other form of exploitation of man by man shall be prohibited by law.

Article 22. Freedom of Movement and Residence
1. Every person lawfully in the territory of a State Party has the right to move about in it, and to reside in it subject to the provisions of the law.
2. Every person has the right to leave any country freely, including his own.
3. The exercise of the foregoing rights may be restricted only pursuant to a law to the extent necessary in a democratic society to prevent crime or to protect national security, public safety, public order, public morals, public health, or the rights or freedoms of others.
4. The exercise of the rights recognized in paragraph 1 may also be restricted by law in designated zones for reasons of public interest.
5. No one can be expelled from the territory of the state of which he is a national or be deprived of the right to enter it.
6. An alien lawfully in the territory of a State Party to this Convention may be expelled from it only pursuant to a decision reached in accordance with law.
7. Every person has the right to seek and be granted asylum in a foreign territory, in accordance with the legislation of the state and international conventions, in the event he is being pursued for political offenses or related common crimes.
8. In no case may an alien be deported or returned to a country, regardless of whether or not it is his country of origin, if in that country his right to life or personal freedom is in danger of being violated because of his race, nationality, religion, social status, or political opinions.
9. The collective expulsion of aliens is prohibited.

Article 23. Right to Participate in Government
1. Every citizen shall enjoy the following rights and opportunities:
   a. to take part in the conduct of public affairs, directly or through freely chosen representatives;
   b. to vote and to be elected in genuine periodic elections, which shall be by universal and equal suffrage and by secret ballot that guarantees the free expression of the will of the voters; and

    c.   to have access, under general conditions of equality, to the public service of his country.
2. The law may regulate the exercise of the rights and opportunities referred to in the preceding paragraph only on the basis of age, nationality, residence, language, education, civil and mental capacity, or sentencing by a competent court in criminal proceedings.

Article 24. Right to Equal Protection

All persons are equal before the law. Consequently, they are entitled, without discrimination, to equal protection of the law.

Article 25. Right to Judicial Protection

1. Everyone has the right to simple and prompt recourse, or any other effective recourse, to a competent court or tribunal for protection against acts that violate his fundamental rights recognized by the constitution or laws of the state concerned or by this Convention, even though such violation may have been committed by persons acting in the course of their official duties.
2. The States Parties undertake:
    a.   to ensure that any person claiming such remedy shall have his rights determined by the competent authority provided for by the legal system of the state;
    b.   to develop the possibilities of judicial remedy; and
    c.   to ensure that the competent authorities shall enforce such remedies when granted.

Chapter III Economic, Social, and Cultural Rights

Article 26. Progressive Development

The States Parties undertake to adopt measures, both internally and through international cooperation, especially those of an economic and technical nature, with a view to achieving progressively, by legislation or other appropriate means, the full realization of the rights implicit in the economic, social, educational, scientific, and cultural standards set forth in the Charter of the Organization of American States as amended by the Protocol of Buenos Aires.

Chapter IV Suspension of Guarantees, Interpretation, and Application

Article 27. Suspension of Guarantees

1. In time of war, public danger, or other emergency that threatens the independence or security of a State Party, it may take measures derogating from its obligations under the present Convention to the extent and for the period of time strictly required by the exigencies of the situation, provided that such measures are not inconsistent with its other obligations under international law and do not involve discrimination on the ground of race, color, sex, language, religion, or social origin.
2. The foregoing provision does not authorize any suspension of the following articles: Article 3 (Right to Juridical Personality), Article 4 (Right to Life), Article 5 (Right to Humane Treatment), Article 6 (Freedom from Slavery), Article 9 (Freedom from Ex Post Facto Laws), Article 12 (Freedom of Conscience and Religion), Article 17 (Rights of the Family), Article 18 (Right to a Name), Article 19 (Rights of the Child), Article

20 (Right to Nationality), and Article 23 (Right to Participate in Government), or of the judicial guarantees essential for the protection of such rights.

3. Any State Party availing itself of the right of suspension shall immediately inform the other States Parties, through the Secretary General of the Organization of American States, of the provisions the application of which it has suspended, the reasons that gave rise to the suspension, and the date set for the termination of such suspension.

Article 28. Federal Clause

1. Where a State Party is constituted as a federal state, the national government of such State Party shall implement all the provisions of the Convention over whose subject matter it exercises legislative and judicial jurisdiction.

2. With respect to the provisions over whose subject matter the constituent units of the federal state have jurisdiction, the national government shall immediately take suitable measures, in accordance with its constitution and its laws, to the end that the competent authorities of the constituent units may adopt appropriate provisions for the fulfillment of this Convention.

3. Whenever two or more States Parties agree to form a federation or other type of association, they shall take care that the resulting federal or other compact contains the provisions necessary for continuing and rendering effective the standards of this Convention in the new state that is organized.

Article 29. Restrictions Regarding Interpretation

No provision of this Convention shall be interpreted as:

a. permitting any State Party, group, or person to suppress the enjoyment or exercise of the rights and freedoms recognized in this Convention or to restrict them to a greater extent than is provided for herein;

b. restricting the enjoyment or exercise of any right or freedom recognized by virtue of the laws of any State Party or by virtue of another convention to which one of the said states is a party;

c. precluding other rights or guarantees that are inherent in the human personality or derived from representative democracy as a form of government; or

d. excluding or limiting the effect that the American Declaration of the Rights and Duties of Man and other international acts of the same nature may have.

Article 30. Scope of Restrictions

The restrictions that, pursuant to this Convention, may be placed on the enjoyment or exercise of the rights or freedoms recognized herein may not be applied except in accordance with laws enacted for reasons of general interest and in accordance with the purpose for which such restrictions have been established.

Article 31. Recognition of Other Rights

Other rights and freedoms recognized in accordance with the procedures established in Articles 76 and 77 may be included in the system of protection of this Convention.

Chapter V Personal Responsibilities

Article 32. Relationship between Duties and Rights

1. Every person has responsibilities to his family, his community, and mankind.
2. The rights of each person are limited by the rights of others, by the security of all, and by the just demands of the general welfare, in a democratic society.

PART II MEANS OF PROTECTION

Chapter VI Competent Organs

Article 33

The following organs shall have competence with respect to matters relating to the fulfillment of the commitments made by the States Parties to this Convention:

   a. the Inter-American Commission on Human Rights, referred to as "The Commission;" and
   b. the Inter-American Court of Human Rights, referred to as "The Court."

Chapter VII Inter-American Commission on Human Rights

Section 1. Organization

Article 34

The Inter-American Commission on Human Rights shall be composed of seven members, who shall be persons of high moral character and recognized competence in the field of human rights.

Article 35

The Commission shall represent all the member countries of the Organization of American States.

Article 36

1. The members of the Commission shall be elected in a personal capacity by the General Assembly of the Organization from a list of candidates proposed by the governments of the member states.
2. Each of those governments may propose up to three candidates, who may be nationals of the states proposing them or of any other member state of the Organization of American States. When a slate of three is proposed, at least one of the candidates shall be a national of a state other than the one proposing the slate.

Article 37

1. The members of the Commission shall be elected for a term of four years and may be reelected only once, but the terms of three of the members chosen in the first election shall expire at the end of two years. Immediately following that election the General Assembly shall determine the names of those three members by lot.
2. No two nationals of the same state may be members of the Commission.

Article 38

Vacancies that may occur on the Commission for reasons other than the normal expiration of a term shall be filled by the Permanent Council of the Organization in accordance with the provisions of the Statute of the Commission.

Article 39

The Commission shall prepare its Statute, which it shall submit to the General Assembly for approval. It shall establish its own Regulations.

Article 40

Secretariat services for the Commission shall be furnished by the appropriate specialized unit of the General Secretariat of the Organization. This unit shall be provided with the resources required to accomplish the tasks assigned to it by the Commission.

Section 2. Functions

Article 41

The main function of the Commission shall be to promote respect for and defense of human rights. In the exercise of its mandate, it shall have the following functions and powers:

a.   to develop an awareness of human rights among the peoples of America;

b.   to make recommendations to the governments of the member states, when it considers such action advisable, for the adoption of progressive measures in favor of human rights within the framework of their domestic law and constitutional provisions as well as appropriate measures to further the observance of those rights;

c.   to prepare such studies or reports as it considers advisable in the performance of its duties;

d.   to request the governments of the member states to supply it with information on the measures adopted by them in matters of human rights;

e.   to respond, through the General Secretariat of the Organization of American States, to inquiries made by the member states on matters related to human rights and, within the limits of its possibilities, to provide those states with the advisory services they request;

f.   to take action on petitions and other communications pursuant to its authority under the provisions of Articles 44 through 51 of this Convention; and

g.   to submit an annual report to the General Assembly of the Organization of American States.

Article 42

The States Parties shall transmit to the Commission a copy of each of the reports and studies that they submit annually to the Executive Committees of the Inter-American Economic and Social Council and the Inter-American Council for Education, Science, and Culture, in their respective fields, so that the Commission may watch over the promotion of the rights implicit in the economic, social, educational, scientific, and cultural standards set forth in the Charter of the Organization of American States as amended by the Protocol of Buenos Aires.

Article 43

The States Parties undertake to provide the Commission with such information as it may request of them as to the manner in which their domestic law ensures the effective application of any provisions of this Convention.

Section 3. Competence

Article 44

Any person or group of persons, or any nongovernmental entity legally recognized in one or more member states of the Organization, may lodge petitions with the Commission containing denunciations or complaints of violation of this Convention by a State Party.

Article 45

1. Any State Party may, when it deposits its instrument of ratification of or adherence to this Convention, or at any later time, declare that it recognizes the competence of the Commission to receive and examine communications in which a State Party alleges that another State Party has committed a violation of a human right set forth in this Convention.
2. Communications presented by virtue of this article may be admitted and examined only if they are presented by a State Party that has made a declaration recognizing the aforementioned competence of the Commission. The Commission shall not admit any communication against a State Party that has not made such a declaration.
3. A declaration concerning recognition of competence may be made to be valid for an indefinite time, for a specified period, or for a specific case.
4. Declarations shall be deposited with the General Secretariat of the Organization of American States, which shall transmit copies thereof to the member states of that Organization.

Article 46

1. Admission by the Commission of a petition or communication lodged in accordance with Articles 44 or 45 shall be subject to the following requirements:
    a. that the remedies under domestic law have been pursued and exhausted in accordance with generally recognized principles of international law;
    b. that the petition or communication is lodged within a period of six months from the date on which the party alleging violation of his rights was notified of the final judgment;
    c. that the subject of the petition or communication is not pending in another international proceeding for settlement; and
    d. that, in the case of Article 44, the petition contains the name, nationality, profession, domicile, and signature of the person or persons or of the legal representative of the entity lodging the petition.
2. The provisions of paragraphs 1.a and 1.b of this article shall not be applicable when:
    a. the domestic legislation of the state concerned does not afford due process of law for the protection of the right or rights that have allegedly been violated;

b.   the party alleging violation of his rights has been denied access to the remedies under domestic law or has been prevented from exhausting them; or

c.   there has been unwarranted delay in rendering a final judgment under the aforementioned remedies.

Article 47

The Commission shall consider inadmissible any petition or communication submitted under Articles 44 or 45 if:

a.   any of the requirements indicated in Article 46 has not been met;

b.   the petition or communication does not state facts that tend to establish a violation of the rights guaranteed by this Convention;

c.   the statements of the petitioner or of the state indicate that the petition or communication is manifestly groundless or obviously out of order; or

d.   the petition or communication is substantially the same as one previously studied by the Commission or by another international organization.

Section 4. Procedure

Article 48

1. When the Commission receives a petition or communication alleging violation of any of the rights protected by this Convention, it shall proceed as follows:

   a.   If it considers the petition or communication admissible, it shall request information from the government of the state indicated as being responsible for the alleged violations and shall furnish that government a transcript of the pertinent portions of the petition or communication. This information shall be submitted within a reasonable period to be determined by the Commission in accordance with the circumstances of each case.

   b.   After the information has been received, or after the period established has elapsed and the information has not been received, the Commission shall ascertain whether the grounds for the petition or communication still exist. If they do not, the Commission shall order the record to be closed.

   c.   The Commission may also declare the petition or communication inadmissible or out of order on the basis of information or evidence subsequently received.

   d.   If the record has not been closed, the Commission shall, with the knowledge of the parties, examine the matter set forth in the petition or communication in order to verify the facts. If necessary and advisable, the Commission shall carry out an investigation, for the effective conduct of which it shall request, and the states concerned shall furnish to it, all necessary facilities.

   e.   The Commission may request the states concerned to furnish any pertinent information and, if so requested, shall hear oral statements or receive written statements from the parties concerned.

   f.   The Commission shall place itself at the disposal of the parties concerned with a view to reaching a friendly settlement of the matter on the basis of respect for the human rights recognized in this Convention.

2. However, in serious and urgent cases, only the presentation of a petition or communication that fulfills all the formal requirements of admissibility shall be necessary in

order for the Commission to conduct an investigation with the prior consent of the state in whose territory a violation has allegedly been committed.

Article 49

If a friendly settlement has been reached in accordance with paragraph 1.f of Article 48, the Commission shall draw up a report, which shall be transmitted to the petitioner and to the States Parties to this Convention, and shall then be communicated to the Secretary General of the Organization of American States for publication. This report shall contain a brief statement of the facts and of the solution reached. If any party in the case so requests, the fullest possible information shall be provided to it.

Article 50

1. If a settlement is not reached, the Commission shall, within the time limit established by its Statute, draw up a report setting forth the facts and stating its conclusions. If the report, in whole or in part, does not represent the unanimous agreement of the members of the Commission, any member may attach to it a separate opinion. The written and oral statements made by the parties in accordance with paragraph 1.e of Article 48 shall also be attached to the report.
2. The report shall be transmitted to the states concerned, which shall not be at liberty to publish it.
3. In transmitting the report, the Commission may make such proposals and recommendations as it sees fit.

Article 51

1. If, within a period of three months from the date of the transmittal of the report of the Commission to the states concerned, the matter has not either been settled or submitted by the Commission or by the state concerned to the Court and its jurisdiction accepted, the Commission may, by the vote of an absolute majority of its members, set forth its opinion and conclusions concerning the question submitted for its consideration.
2. Where appropriate, the Commission shall make pertinent recommendations and shall prescribe a period within which the state is to take the measures that are incumbent upon it to remedy the situation examined.
3. When the prescribed period has expired, the Commission shall decide by the vote of an absolute majority of its members whether the state has taken adequate measures and whether to publish its report.

Chapter VIII Inter-American Court of Human Rights

Section 1. Organization

Article 52

1. The Court shall consist of seven judges, nationals of the member states of the Organization, elected in an individual capacity from among jurists of the highest moral authority and of recognized competence in the field of human rights, who possess the qualifications required for the exercise of the highest judicial functions in conformity with the law of the state of which they are nationals or of the state that proposes them as candidates.

2. No two judges may be nationals of the same state.

Article 53

1. The judges of the Court shall be elected by secret ballot by an absolute majority vote of the States Parties to the Convention, in the General Assembly of the Organization, from a panel of candidates proposed by those states.
2. Each of the States Parties may propose up to three candidates, nationals of the state that proposes them or of any other member state of the Organization of American States. When a slate of three is proposed, at least one of the candidates shall be a national of a state other than the one proposing the slate.

Article 54

1. The judges of the Court shall be elected for a term of six years and may be reelected only once. The term of three of the judges chosen in the first election shall expire at the end of three years. Immediately after the election, the names of the three judges shall be determined by lot in the General Assembly.
2. A judge elected to replace a judge whose term has not expired shall complete the term of the latter.
3. The judges shall continue in office until the expiration of their term. However, they shall continue to serve with regard to cases that they have begun to hear and that are still pending, for which purposes they shall not be replaced by the newly elected judges.

Article 55

1. If a judge is a national of any of the States Parties to a case submitted to the Court, he shall retain his right to hear that case.
2. If one of the judges called upon to hear a case should be a national of one of the States Parties to the case, any other State Party in the case may appoint a person of its choice to serve on the Court as an ad hoc judge.
3. If among the judges called upon to hear a case none is a national of any of the States Parties to the case, each of the latter may appoint an ad hoc judge.
4. An ad hoc judge shall possess the qualifications indicated in Article 52.
5. If several States Parties to the Convention should have the same interest in a case, they shall be considered as a single party for purposes of the above provisions. In case of doubt, the Court shall decide.

Article 56

Five judges shall constitute a quorum for the transaction of business by the Court.

Article 57

The Commission shall appear in all cases before the Court.

Article 58

1. The Court shall have its seat at the place determined by the States Parties to the Convention in the General Assembly of the Organization; however, it may convene in the territory of any member state of the Organization of American States when a

majority of the Court considers it desirable, and with the prior consent of the state concerned. The seat of the Court may be changed by the States Parties to the Convention in the General Assembly by a two-thirds vote.

2. The Court shall appoint its own Secretary.

3. The Secretary shall have his office at the place where the Court has its seat and shall attend the meetings that the Court may hold away from its seat.

Article 59

The Court shall establish its Secretariat, which shall function under the direction of the Secretary of the Court, in accordance with the administrative standards of the General Secretariat of the Organization in all respects not incompatible with the independence of the Court. The staff of the Court's Secretariat shall be appointed by the Secretary General of the Organization, in consultation with the Secretary of the Court.

Article 60

The Court shall draw up its Statute which it shall submit to the General Assembly for approval. It shall adopt its own Rules of Procedure.

Section 2. Jurisdiction and Functions

Article 61

1. Only the States Parties and the Commission shall have the right to submit a case to the Court.

2. In order for the Court to hear a case, it is necessary that the procedures set forth in Articles 48 and 50 shall have been completed.

Article 62

1. A State Party may, upon depositing its instrument of ratification or adherence to this Convention, or at any subsequent time, declare that it recognizes as binding, ipso facto, and not requiring special agreement, the jurisdiction of the Court on all matters relating to the interpretation or application of this Convention.

2. Such declaration may be made unconditionally, on the condition of reciprocity, for a specified period, or for specific cases. It shall be presented to the Secretary General of the Organization, who shall transmit copies thereof to the other member states of the Organization and to the Secretary of the Court.

3. The jurisdiction of the Court shall comprise all cases concerning the interpretation and application of the provisions of this Convention that are submitted to it, provided that the States Parties to the case recognize or have recognized such jurisdiction, whether by special declaration pursuant to the preceding paragraphs, or by a special agreement.

Article 63

1. If the Court finds that there has been a violation of a right or freedom protected by this Convention, the Court shall rule that the injured party be ensured the enjoyment of his right or freedom that was violated. It shall also rule, if appropriate, that the consequences of the measure or situation that constituted the breach of such right or freedom be remedied and that fair compensation be paid to the injured party.

2. In cases of extreme gravity and urgency, and when necessary to avoid irreparable damage to persons, the Court shall adopt such provisional measures as it deems pertinent in matters it has under consideration. With respect to a case not yet submitted to the Court, it may act at the request of the Commission.

Article 64

1. The member states of the Organization may consult the Court regarding the interpretation of this Convention or of other treaties concerning the protection of human rights in the American states. Within their spheres of competence, the organs listed in Chapter X of the Charter of the Organization of American States, as amended by the Protocol of Buenos Aires, may in like manner consult the Court.
2. The Court, at the request of a member state of the Organization, may provide that state with opinions regarding the compatibility of any of its domestic laws with the aforesaid international instruments.

Article 65

To each regular session of the General Assembly of the Organization of American States the Court shall submit, for the Assembly's consideration, a report on its work during the previous year. It shall specify, in particular, the cases in which a state has not complied with its judgments, making any pertinent recommendations.

Section 3. Procedure

Article 66

1. Reasons shall be given for the judgment of the Court.
2. If the judgment does not represent in whole or in part the unanimous opinion of the judges, any judge shall be entitled to have his dissenting or separate opinion attached to the judgment.

Article 67

The judgment of the Court shall be final and not subject to appeal. In case of disagreement as to the meaning or scope of the judgment, the Court shall interpret it at the request of any of the parties, provided the request is made within ninety days from the date of notification of the judgment.

Article 68

1. The States Parties to the Convention undertake to comply with the judgment of the Court in any case to which they are parties.
2. That part of a judgment that stipulates compensatory damages may be executed in the country concerned in accordance with domestic procedure governing the execution of judgments against the state.

Article 69

The parties to the case shall be notified of the judgment of the Court and it shall be transmitted to the States Parties to the Convention.

Chapter IX Common Provisions

Article 70

1. The judges of the Court and the members of the Commission shall enjoy, from the moment of their election and throughout their term of office, the immunities extended to diplomatic agents in accordance with international law. During the exercise of their official function they shall, in addition, enjoy the diplomatic privileges necessary for the performance of their duties.

2. At no time shall the judges of the Court or the members of the Commission be held liable for any decisions or opinions issued in the exercise of their functions.

Article 71

The position of judge of the Court or member of the Commission is incompatible with any other activity that might affect the independence or impartiality of such judge or member, as determined in the respective statutes.

Article 72

The judges of the Court and the members of the Commission shall receive emoluments and travel allowances in the form and under the conditions set forth in their statutes, with due regard for the importance and independence of their office. Such emoluments and travel allowances shall be determined in the budget of the Organization of American States, which shall also include the expenses of the Court and its Secretariat. To this end, the Court shall draw up its own budget and submit it for approval to the General Assembly through the General Secretariat. The latter may not introduce any changes in it.

Article 73

The General Assembly may, only at the request of the Commission or the Court, as the case may be, determine sanctions to be applied against members of the Commission or judges of the Court when there are justifiable grounds for such action as set forth in the respective statutes. A vote of a two-thirds majority of the member states of the Organization shall be required for a decision in the case of members of the Commission and, in the case of judges of the Court, a two-thirds majority vote of the States Parties to the Convention shall also be required.

PART III GENERAL AND TRANSITORY PROVISIONS

Chapter X Signature, Ratification, Reservations, Amendments, Protocols, and Denunciation

Article 74

1. This Convention shall be open for signature and ratification by or adherence of any member state of the Organization of American States.

2. Ratification of or adherence to this Convention shall be made by the deposit of an instrument of ratification or adherence with the General Secretariat of the Organization

of American States. As soon as eleven states have deposited their instruments of ratification or adherence, the Convention shall enter into force. With respect to any state that ratifies or adheres thereafter, the Convention shall enter into force on the date of the deposit of its instrument of ratification or adherence.

3. The Secretary General shall inform all member states of the Organization of the entry into force of the Convention.

Article 75

This Convention shall be subject to reservations only in conformity with the provisions of the Vienna Convention on the Law of Treaties signed on May 23, 1969.

Article 76

1. Proposals to amend this Convention may be submitted to the General Assembly for the action it deems appropriate by any State Party directly, and by the Commission or the Court through the Secretary General.

2. Amendments shall enter into force for the States ratifying them on the date when two-thirds of the States Parties to this Convention have deposited their respective instruments of ratification. With respect to the other States Parties, the amendments shall enter into force on the dates on which they deposit their respective instruments of ratification.

Article 77

1. In accordance with Article 31, any State Party and the Commission may submit proposed protocols to this Convention for consideration by the States Parties at the General Assembly with a view to gradually including other rights and freedoms within its system of protection.

2. Each protocol shall determine the manner of its entry into force and shall be applied only among the States Parties to it.

Article 78

1. The States Parties may denounce this Convention at the expiration of a five-year period from the date of its entry into force and by means of notice given one year in advance. Notice of the denunciation shall be addressed to the Secretary General of the Organization, who shall inform the other States Parties.

2. Such a denunciation shall not have the effect of releasing the State Party concerned from the obligations contained in this Convention with respect to any act that may constitute a violation of those obligations and that has been taken by that state prior to the effective date of denunciation.

Chapter XI Transitory Provisions

Section 1. Inter-American Commission on Human Rights

Article 79

Upon the entry into force of this Convention, the Secretary General shall, in writing, request each member state of the Organization to present, within ninety days, its candidates for membership on the Inter-American Commission on Human Rights. The

Secretary General shall prepare a list in alphabetical order of the candidates presented, and transmit it to the member states of the Organization at least thirty days prior to the next session of the General Assembly.

Article 80

The members of the Commission shall be elected by secret ballot of the General Assembly from the list of candidates referred to in Article 79. The candidates who obtain the largest number of votes and an absolute majority of the votes of the representatives of the member states shall be declared elected. Should it become necessary to have several ballots in order to elect all the members of the Commission, the candidates who receive the smallest number of votes shall be eliminated successively, in the manner determined by the General Assembly.

Section 2. Inter-American Court of Human Rights

Article 81

Upon the entry into force of this Convention, the Secretary General shall, in writing, request each State Party to present, within ninety days, its candidates for membership on the Inter-American Court of Human Rights. The Secretary General shall prepare a list in alphabetical order of the candidates presented and transmit it to the States Parties at least thirty days prior to the next session of the General Assembly.

Article 82

The judges of the Court shall be elected from the list of candidates referred to in Article 81, by secret ballot of the States Parties to the Convention in the General Assembly. The candidates who obtain the largest number of votes and an absolute majority of the votes of the representatives of the States Parties shall be declared elected. Should it become necessary to have several ballots in order to elect all the judges of the Court, the candidates who receive the smallest number of votes shall be eliminated successively, in the manner determined by the States Parties.

94

Additional Protocol to the American Convention on Human Rights in the Area of Economic, Social and Cultural Rights 'Protocol of San Salvador', 1988

Note: Adopted San Salvador, 17 November 1988. OAS Treaty Series No. 69. Entry into force: 16 November 1999.

PREAMBLE

The States Parties to the American Convention on Human Rights "Pact San José, Costa Rica,"

Reaffirming their intention to consolidate in this hemisphere, within the framework of democratic institutions, a system of personal liberty and social justice based on respect for the essential rights of man;

Recognizing that the essential rights of man are not derived from one's being a national of a certain State, but are based upon attributes of the human person, for which reason they merit international protection in the form of a convention reinforcing or complementing the protection provided by the domestic law of the American States;

Considering the close relationship that exists between economic, social and cultural rights, and civil and political rights, in that the different categories of rights constitute an indivisible whole based on the recognition of the dignity of the human person, for which reason both require permanent protection and promotion if they are to be fully realized, and the violation of some rights in favor of the realization of others can never be justified;

Recognizing the benefits that stem from the promotion and development of cooperation among States and international relations;

Recalling that, in accordance with the Universal Declaration of Human Rights and the American Convention on Human Rights, the ideal of free human beings enjoying freedom from fear and want can only be achieved if conditions are created whereby everyone may enjoy his economic, social and cultural rights as well as his civil and political rights;

Bearing in mind that, although fundamental economic, social and cultural rights have been recognized in earlier international instruments of both world and regional scope, it is essential that those rights be reaffirmed, developed, perfected and protected in order to consolidate in America, on the basis of full respect for the rights of the individual, the democratic representative form of government as well as the right of its peoples to development, self-determination, and the free disposal of their wealth and natural resources; and

Considering that the American Convention on Human Rights provides that draft additional protocols to that Convention may be submitted for consideration to the States Parties, meeting together on the occasion of the General Assembly of the Organization of American States, for the purpose of gradually incorporating other rights and freedoms into the protective system thereof,

Have agreed upon the following Additional Protocol to the American Convention on Human Rights "Protocol of San Salvador:"

Article 1
Obligation to Adopt Measures

The States Parties to this Additional Protocol to the American Convention on Human Rights undertake to adopt the necessary measures, both domestically and through international cooperation, especially economic and technical, to the extent allowed by their available resources, and taking into account their degree of development, for the purpose of achieving progressively and pursuant to their internal legislations, the full observance of the rights recognized in this Protocol.

Article 2
Obligation to Enact Domestic Legislation

If the exercise of the rights set forth in this Protocol is not already guaranteed by legislative or other provisions, the States Parties undertake to adopt, in accordance with their constitutional processes and the provisions of this Protocol, such legislative or other measures as may be necessary for making those rights a reality.

Article 3
Obligation of non-discrimination

The State Parties to this Protocol undertake to guarantee the exercise of the rights set forth herein without discrimination of any kind for reasons related to race, color, sex, language, religion, political or other opinions, national or social origin, economic status, birth or any other social condition.

Article 4
Inadmissibility of Restrictions

A right which is recognized or in effect in a State by virtue of its internal legislation or international conventions may not be restricted or curtailed on the pretext that this Protocol does not recognize the right or recognizes it to a lesser degree.

Article 5
Scope of Restrictions and Limitations

The State Parties may establish restrictions and limitations on the enjoyment and exercise of the rights established herein by means of laws promulgated for the purpose of preserving the general welfare in a democratic society only to the extent that they are not incompatible with the purpose and reason underlying those rights.

Article 6
Right to Work

1. Everyone has the right to work, which includes the opportunity to secure the means for living a dignified and decent existence by performing a freely elected or accepted lawful activity.
2. The State Parties undertake to adopt measures that will make the right to work fully effective, especially with regard to the achievement of full employment, vocational guidance, and the development of technical and vocational training projects, in particular those directed to the disabled. The States Parties also undertake to implement and strengthen programs that help to ensure suitable family care, so that women may enjoy a real opportunity to exercise the right to work.

Article 7
Just, Equitable, and Satisfactory Conditions of Work

The States Parties to this Protocol recognize that the right to work to which the foregoing article refers presupposes that everyone shall enjoy that right under just, equitable, and satisfactory conditions, which the States Parties undertake to guarantee in their internal legislation, particularly with respect to:

a. Remuneration which guarantees, as a minimum, to all workers dignified and decent living conditions for them and their families and fair and equal wages for equal work, without distinction;

b. The right of every worker to follow his vocation and to devote himself to the activity that best fulfills his expectations and to change employment in accordance with the pertinent national regulations;

c. The right of every worker to promotion or upward mobility in his employment, for which purpose account shall be taken of his qualifications, competence, integrity and seniority;

d. Stability of employment, subject to the nature of each industry and occupation and the causes for just separation. In cases of unjustified dismissal, the worker shall have the right to indemnity or to reinstatement on the job or any other benefits provided by domestic legislation;

e. Safety and hygiene at work;

f. The prohibition of night work or unhealthy or dangerous working conditions and, in general, of all work which jeopardizes health, safety, or morals, for persons under 18 years of age. As regards minors under the age of 16, the work day shall be subordinated to the provisions regarding compulsory education and in no case shall work constitute an impediment to school attendance or a limitation on benefiting from education received;

g. A reasonable limitation of working hours, both daily and weekly. The days shall be shorter in the case of dangerous or unhealthy work or of night work;

h. Rest, leisure and paid vacations as well as remuneration for national holidays.

Article 8
Trade Union Rights

1. The States Parties shall ensure:

a. The right of workers to organize trade unions and to join the union of their choice for the purpose of protecting and promoting their interests. As an extension of that right, the States Parties shall permit trade unions to establish national federations or confederations, or to affiliate with those that already exist, as well as to form international trade union organizations and to affiliate with that of their choice. The States Parties shall also permit trade unions, federations and confederations to function freely;

b. The right to strike.

2. The exercise of the rights set forth above may be subject only to restrictions established by law, provided that such restrictions are characteristic of a democratic society and necessary for safeguarding public order or for protecting public health or morals or the rights and freedoms of others. Members of the armed forces and the police and of other essential public services shall be subject to limitations and restrictions established by law.

3. No one may be compelled to belong to a trade union.

Article 9
Right to Social Security

1. Everyone shall have the right to social security protecting him from the consequences of old age and of disability which prevents him, physically or mentally, from securing the means for a dignified and decent existence. In the event of the death of a beneficiary, social security benefits shall be applied to his dependents.

2. In the case of persons who are employed, the right to social security shall cover at least medical care and an allowance or retirement benefit in the case of work accidents or occupational disease and, in the case of women, paid maternity leave before and after childbirth.

Article 10
Right to Health

1. Everyone shall have the right to health, understood to mean the enjoyment of the highest level of physical, mental and social well-being.

2. In order to ensure the exercise of the right to health, the States Parties agree to recognize health as a public good and, particularly, to adopt the following measures to ensure that right:

a. Primary health care, that is, essential health care made available to all individuals and families in the community;

b. Extension of the benefits of health services to all individuals subject to the State's jurisdiction;

c. Universal immunization against the principal infectious diseases;

d. Prevention and treatment of endemic, occupational and other diseases;

e. Education of the population on the prevention and treatment of health problems, and

f. Satisfaction of the health needs of the highest risk groups and of those whose poverty makes them the most vulnerable.

Article 11
Right to a Healthy Environment

1. Everyone shall have the right to live in a healthy environment and to have access to basic public services.

2. The States Parties shall promote the protection, preservation, and improvement of the environment.

Article 12
Right to Food

1. Everyone has the right to adequate nutrition which guarantees the possibility of enjoying the highest level of physical, emotional and intellectual development.
2. In order to promote the exercise of this right and eradicate malnutrition, the States Parties undertake to improve methods of production, supply and distribution of food, and to this end, agree to promote greater international cooperation in support of the relevant national policies.

Article 13
Right to Education

1. Everyone has the right to education.
2. The States Parties to this Protocol agree that education should be directed towards the full development of the human personality and human dignity and should strengthen respect for human rights, ideological pluralism, fundamental freedoms, justice and peace. They further agree that education ought to enable everyone to participate effectively in a democratic and pluralistic society and achieve a decent existence and should foster understanding, tolerance and friendship among all nations and all racial, ethnic or religious groups and promote activities for the maintenance of peace.
3. The States Parties to this Protocol recognize that in order to achieve the full exercise of the right to education:
   a. Primary education should be compulsory and accessible to all without cost;
   b. Secondary education in its different forms, including technical and vocational secondary education, should be made generally available and accessible to all by every appropriate means, and in particular, by the progressive introduction of free education;
   c. Higher education should be made equally accessible to all, on the basis of individual capacity, by every appropriate means, and in particular, by the progressive introduction of free education;
   d. Basic education should be encouraged or intensified as far as possible for those persons who have not received or completed the whole cycle of primary instruction;
   e. Programs of special education should be established for the handicapped, so as to provide special instruction and training to persons with physical disabilities or mental deficiencies.
4. In conformity with the domestic legislation of the States Parties, parents should have the right to select the type of education to be given to their children, provided that it conforms to the principles set forth above.
5. Nothing in this Protocol shall be interpreted as a restriction of the freedom of individuals and entities to establish and direct educational institutions in accordance with the domestic legislation of the States Parties.

Article 14
Right to the Benefits of Culture

1. The States Parties to this Protocol recognize the right of everyone:
   a. To take part in the cultural and artistic life of the community;
   b. To enjoy the benefits of scientific and technological progress;
   c. To benefit from the protection of moral and material interests deriving from any scientific, literary or artistic production of which he is the author.

2. The steps to be taken by the States Parties to this Protocol to ensure the full exercise of this right shall include those necessary for the conservation, development and dissemination of science, culture and art.

3. The States Parties to this Protocol undertake to respect the freedom indispensable for scientific research and creative activity.

4. The States Parties to this Protocol recognize the benefits to be derived from the encouragement and development of international cooperation and relations in the fields of science, arts and culture, and accordingly agree to foster greater international cooperation in these fields.

Article 15
Right to the Formation and the Protection of Families

1. The family is the natural and fundamental element of society and ought to be protected by the State, which should see to the improvement of its spiritual and material conditions.

2. Everyone has the right to form a family, which shall be exercised in accordance with the provisions of the pertinent domestic legislation.

3. The States Parties hereby undertake to accord adequate protection to the family unit and in particular:
   a. To provide special care and assistance to mothers during a reasonable period before and after childbirth;
   b. To guarantee adequate nutrition for children at the nursing stage and during school attendance years;
   c. To adopt special measures for the protection of adolescents in order to ensure the full development of their physical, intellectual and moral capacities;
   d. To undertake special programs of family training so as to help create a stable and positive environment in which children will receive and develop the values of understanding, solidarity, respect and responsibility.

Article 16
Rights of Children

Every child, whatever his parentage, has the right to the protection that his status as a minor requires from his family, society and the State. Every child has the right to grow under the protection and responsibility of his parents; save in exceptional, judicially-recognized circumstances, a child of young age ought not to be separated from his mother. Every child has the right to free and compulsory education, at least in the elementary phase, and to continue his training at higher levels of the educational system.

Article 17
Protection of the Elderly

Everyone has the right to special protection in old age. With this in view the States Parties agree to take progressively the necessary steps to make this right a reality and, particularly, to:
   a. Provide suitable facilities, as well as food and specialized medical care, for elderly individuals who lack them and are unable to provide them for themselves;
   b. Undertake work programs specifically designed to give the elderly the opportunity to engage in a productive activity suited to their abilities and consistent with their vocations or desires;

c. Foster the establishment of social organizations aimed at improving the quality of life for the elderly.

Article 18
Protection of the Handicapped

Everyone affected by a diminution of his physical or mental capacities is entitled to receive special attention designed to help him achieve the greatest possible development of his personality. The States Parties agree to adopt such measures as may be necessary for this purpose and, especially, to:

a. Undertake programs specifically aimed at providing the handicapped with the resources and environment needed for attaining this goal, including work programs consistent with their possibilities and freely accepted by them or their legal representatives, as the case may be;

b. Provide special training to the families of the handicapped in order to help them solve the problems of coexistence and convert them into active agents in the physical, mental and emotional development of the latter;

c. Include the consideration of solutions to specific requirements arising from needs of this group as a priority component of their urban development plans;

d. Encourage the establishment of social groups in which the handicapped can be helped to enjoy a fuller life.

Article 19
Means of Protection

1. Pursuant to the provisions of this article and the corresponding rules to be formulated for this purpose by the General Assembly of the Organization of American States, the States Parties to this Protocol undertake to submit periodic reports on the progressive measures they have taken to ensure due respect for the rights set forth in this Protocol.

2. All reports shall be submitted to the Secretary General of the OAS, who shall transmit them to the Inter-American Economic and Social Council and the Inter-American Council for Education, Science and Culture so that they may examine them in accordance with the provisions of this article. The Secretary General shall send a copy of such reports to the Inter-American Commission on Human Rights.

3. The Secretary General of the Organization of American States shall also transmit to the specialized organizations of the inter-American system of which the States Parties to the present Protocol are members, copies or pertinent portions of the reports submitted, insofar as they relate to matters within the purview of those organizations, as established by their constituent instruments.

4. The specialized organizations of the inter-American system may submit reports to the Inter-American Economic and Social Council and the Inter-American Council for Education, Science and Culture relative to compliance with the provisions of the present Protocol in their fields of activity.

5. The annual reports submitted to the General Assembly by the Inter-American Economic and Social Council and the Inter-American Council for Education, Science and Culture shall contain a summary of the information received from the States Parties to the present Protocol and the specialized organizations concerning the progressive measures adopted in order to ensure respect for the rights acknowledged in the Protocol itself and the general recommendations they consider to be appropriate in this respect.

6. Any instance in which the rights established in paragraph a) of Article 8 and in Article 13 are violated by action directly attributable to a State Party to this Protocol may give rise, through participation of the Inter-American Commission on Human Rights and, when applicable, of the Inter-American Court of Human Rights, to application of the system of individual petitions governed by Article 44 through 51 and 61 through 69 of the American Convention on Human Rights.

7. Without prejudice to the provisions of the preceding paragraph, the Inter-American Commission on Human Rights may formulate such observations and recommendations as it deems pertinent concerning the status of the economic, social and cultural rights established in the present Protocol in all or some of the States Parties, which it may include in its Annual Report to the General Assembly or in a special report, whichever it considers more appropriate.

8. The Councils and the Inter-American Commission on Human Rights, in discharging the functions conferred upon them in this article, shall take into account the progressive nature of the observance of the rights subject to protection by this Protocol.

Article 20
Reservations
The States Parties may, at the time of approval, signature, ratification or accession, make reservations to one or more specific provisions of this Protocol, provided that such reservations are not incompatible with the object and purpose of the Protocol.

Article 21
Signature, Ratification or Accession
Entry into Effect
1. This Protocol shall remain open to signature and ratification or accession by any State Party to the American Convention on Human Rights.
2. Ratification of or accession to this Protocol shall be effected by depositing an instrument of ratification or accession with the General Secretariat of the Organization of American States.
3. The Protocol shall enter into effect when eleven States have deposited their respective instruments of ratification or accession.
4. The Secretary General shall notify all the member states of the Organization of American States of the entry of the Protocol into effect.

Article 22
Inclusion of other Rights and Expansion of those Recognized
1. Any State Party and the Inter-American Commission on Human Rights may submit for the consideration of the States Parties meeting on the occasion of the General Assembly proposed amendments to include the recognition of other rights or freedoms or to extend or expand rights or freedoms recognized in this Protocol.
2. Such amendments shall enter into effect for the States that ratify them on the date of deposit of the instrument of ratification corresponding to the number representing two thirds of the States Parties to this Protocol. For all other States Parties they shall enter into effect on the date on which they deposit their respective instrument of ratification.

95

Protocol to the American Convention on Human Rights to Abolish the Death Penalty, 1990

Note: A-53: Protocol to the American Convention on Human Rights to Abolish the Death Penalty. Adopted: Asuncion, Paraguay, 8 June 1990. OAS Treaty Series No. 73 (1990). Not yet in force.

PREAMBLE

THE STATES PARTIES TO THIS PROTOCOL,

CONSIDERING:

That Article 4 of the American Convention on Human Rights recognizes the right to life and restricts the application of the death penalty;

That everyone has the inalienable right to respect for his life, a right that cannot be suspended for any reason;

That the tendency among the American States is to be in favor of abolition of the death penalty;

That application of the death penalty has irrevocable consequences, forecloses the correction of judicial error, and precludes any possibility of changing or rehabilitating those convicted;

That the abolition of the death penalty helps to ensure more effective protection of the right to life;

That an international agreement must be arrived at that will entail a progressive development of the American Convention on Human Rights, and

That States Parties to the American Convention on Human Rights have expressed their intention to adopt an international agreement with a view to consolidating the practice of not applying the death penalty in the Americas,

HAVE AGREED TO SIGN THE FOLLOWING PROTOCOL TO THE AMERICAN CONVENTION ON HUMAN RIGHTS TO ABOLISH THE DEATH PENALTY

Article 1

The States Parties to this Protocol shall not apply the death penalty in their territory to any person subject to their jurisdiction.

Article 2

1. No reservations may be made to this Protocol. However, at the time of ratification or accession, the States Parties to this instrument may declare that they reserve the right to apply the death penalty in wartime in accordance with international law, for extremely serious crimes of a military nature.
2. The State Party making this reservation shall, upon ratification or accession, inform the Secretary General of the Organization of American States of the pertinent provisions of its national legislation applicable in wartime, as referred to in the preceding paragraph.
3. Said State Party shall notify the Secretary General of the Organization of American States of the beginning or end of any state of war in effect in its territory.

Article 3

1. This Protocol shall be open for signature and ratification or accession by any State Party to the American Convention on Human Rights.
2. Ratification of this Protocol or accession thereto shall be made through the deposit of an instrument of ratification or accession with the General Secretariat of the Organization of American States.

Article 4

This Protocol shall enter into force among the States that ratify or accede to it when they deposit their respective instruments of ratification or accession with the General Secretariat of the Organization of American States.

96

Inter-American Convention to Prevent and Punish Torture, 1985

Note: A-51: Inter-American Convention to Prevent and Punish Torture. Adopted: Cartagena de Indias, Colombia, 9 December 1985. OAS Treaty Series No. 67. Entry into force: 28 February 1987.

The American States signatory to the present Convention,

Aware of the provision of the American Convention on Human Rights that no one shall be subjected to torture or to cruel, inhuman, or degrading punishment or treatment;

Reaffirming that all acts of torture or any other cruel, inhuman, or degrading treatment or punishment constitute an offense against human dignity and a denial of the principles set forth in the Charter of the Organization of American States and in the Charter of the United Nations and are violations of the fundamental human rights and freedoms proclaimed in the American Declaration of the Rights and Duties of Man and the Universal Declaration of Human Rights;

Noting that, in order for the pertinent rules contained in the aforementioned global and regional instruments to take effect, it is necessary to draft an Inter-American Convention that prevents and punishes torture;

Reaffirming their purpose of consolidating in this hemisphere the conditions that make for recognition of and respect for the inherent dignity of man, and ensure the full exercise of his fundamental rights and freedoms,

Have agreed upon the following:

Article 1

The State Parties undertake to prevent and punish torture in accordance with the terms of this Convention.

Article 2

For the purposes of this Convention, torture shall be understood to be any act intentionally performed whereby physical or mental pain or suffering is inflicted on a person for purposes of criminal investigation, as a means of intimidation, as personal punishment, as a preventive measure, as a penalty, or for any other purpose. Torture shall also be understood to be the use of methods upon a person intended to obliterate the personality of the victim or to diminish his physical or mental capacities, even if they do not cause physical pain or mental anguish.

The concept of torture shall not include physical or mental pain or suffering that is inherent in or solely the consequence of lawful measures, provided that they do not include the performance of the acts or use of the methods referred to in this article.

Article 3

The following shall be held guilty of the crime of torture:

  a. A public servant or employee who acting in that capacity orders, instigates or induces the use of torture, or who directly commits it or who, being able to prevent it, fails to do so.

  b. A person who at the instigation of a public servant or employee mentioned in subparagraph (a) orders, instigates or induces the use of torture, directly commits it or is an accomplice thereto.

Article 4

The fact of having acted under orders of a superior shall not provide exemption from the corresponding criminal liability.

Article 5

The existence of circumstances such as a state of war, threat of war, state of siege or of emergency, domestic disturbance or strife, suspension of constitutional guarantees, domestic political instability, or other public emergencies or disasters shall not be invoked or admitted as justification for the crime of torture.

Neither the dangerous character of the detainee or prisoner, nor the lack of security of the prison establishment or penitentiary shall justify torture.

Article 6

In accordance with the terms of Article 1, the States Parties shall take effective measures to prevent and punish torture within their jurisdiction.

The States Parties shall ensure that all acts of torture and attempts to commit torture are offenses under their criminal law and shall make such acts punishable by severe penalties that take into account their serious nature.

The States Parties likewise shall take effective measures to prevent and punish other cruel, inhuman, or degrading treatment or punishment within their jurisdiction.

Article 7

The States Parties shall take measures so that, in the training of police officers and other public officials responsible for the custody of persons temporarily or definitively deprived of their freedom, special emphasis shall be put on the prohibition of the use of torture in interrogation, detention, or arrest.

The States Parties likewise shall take similar measures to prevent other cruel, inhuman, or degrading treatment or punishment.

Article 8

The States Parties shall guarantee that any person making an accusation of having been subjected to torture within their jurisdiction shall have the right to an impartial examination of his case.

Likewise, if there is an accusation or well-grounded reason to believe that an act of torture has been committed within their jurisdiction, the States Parties shall guarantee that their respective authorities will proceed properly and immediately to conduct an investigation into the case and to initiate, whenever appropriate, the corresponding criminal process.

After all the domestic legal procedures of the respective State and the corresponding appeals have been exhausted, the case may be submitted to the international fora whose competence has been recognized by that State.

Article 9

The States Parties undertake to incorporate into their national laws regulations guaranteeing suitable compensation for victims of torture.

None of the provisions of this article shall affect the right to receive compensation that the victim or other persons may have by virtue of existing national legislation.

Article 10

No statement that is verified as having been obtained through torture shall be admissible as evidence in a legal proceeding, except in a legal action taken against a person or persons accused of having elicited it through acts of torture, and only as evidence that the accused obtained such statement by such means.

Article 11

The States Parties shall take the necessary steps to extradite anyone accused of having committed the crime of torture or sentenced for commission of that crime, in accordance with their respective national laws on extradition and their international commitments on this matter.

Article 12

Every State Party shall take the necessary measures to establish its jurisdiction over the crime described in this Convention in the following cases:

   a.   When torture has been committed within its jurisdiction;
   b.   When the alleged criminal is a national of that State; or
   c.   When the victim is a national of that State and it so deems appropriate.

Every State Party shall also take the necessary measures to establish its jurisdiction over the crime described in this Convention when the alleged criminal is within the area under its jurisdiction and it is not appropriate to extradite him in accordance with Article 11.

This Convention does not exclude criminal jurisdiction exercised in accordance with domestic law.

Article 13

The crime referred to in Article 2 shall be deemed to be included among the extraditable crimes in every extradition treaty entered into between States Parties. The States Parties undertake to include the crime of torture as an extraditable offence in every extradition treaty to be concluded between them.

Every State Party that makes extradition conditional on the existence of a treaty may, if it receives a request for extradition from another State Party with which it has no extradition treaty, consider this Convention as the legal basis for extradition in respect of the crime of torture. Extradition shall be subject to the other conditions that may be required by the law of the requested State.

States Parties which do not make extradition conditional on the existence of a treaty shall recognize such crimes as extraditable offences between themselves, subject to the conditions required by the law of the requested State.

Extradition shall not be granted nor shall the person sought be returned when there are grounds to believe that his life is in danger, that he will be subjected to torture or to cruel, inhuman or degrading treatment, or that he will be tried by special or ad hoc courts in the requesting State.

Article 14

When a State Party does not grant the extradition, the case shall be submitted to its competent authorities as if the crime had been committed within its jurisdiction, for the purposes of investigation, and when appropriate, for criminal action, in accordance with its national law. Any decision adopted by these authorities shall be communicated to the State that has requested the extradition.

Article 15

No provision of this Convention may be interpreted as limiting the right of asylum, when appropriate, nor as altering the obligations of the States Parties in the matter of extradition.

Article 16

This Convention shall not limit the provisions of the American Convention on Human Rights, other conventions on the subject, or the Statutes of the Inter-American Commission on Human Rights, with respect to the crime of torture.

Article 17

The States Parties undertake to inform the Inter-American Commission on Human Rights of any legislative, judicial, administrative, or other measures they adopt in application of this Convention.

In keeping with its duties and responsibilities, the Inter-American Commission on Human Rights will endeavor in its annual report to analyze the existing situation in the member states of the Organization of American States in regard to the prevention and elimination of torture.

Article 18

This Convention is open to signature by the member States of the Organization of American States.

Article 19

This Convention is subject to ratification. The instruments of ratification shall be deposited with the General Secretariat of the Organization of American States.

Article 20

This Convention is open to accession by any other American state. The instruments of accession shall be deposited with the General Secretariat of the Organization of American States.

Article 21

The States Parties may, at the time of approval, signature, ratification, or accession, make reservations to this Convention, provided that such reservations are not incompatible with the object and purpose of the Convention and concern one or more specific provisions.

Article 22

This Convention shall enter into force on the thirtieth day following the date on which the second instrument of ratification is deposited. For each State ratifying or acceding to the Convention after the second instrument of ratification has been deposited, the Convention shall enter into force on the thirtieth day following the date on which that State deposits its instrument of ratification or accession.

Article 23

This Convention shall remain in force indefinitely, but may be denounced by any State Party. The instrument of denunciation shall be deposited with the General Secretariat of the Organization of American States. After one year from the date of deposit of the instrument of denunciation, this Convention shall cease to be in effect for the denouncing State but shall remain in force for the remaining States Parties.

Article 24

The original instrument of this Convention, the English, French, Portuguese, and Spanish texts of which are equally authentic, shall be deposited with the General Secretariat of the Organization of American States, which shall send a certified copy to the Secretariat of the United Nations for registration and publication, in accordance with the provisions of Article 102 of the United Nations Charter. The General Secretariat of the Organization of American States shall notify the member states of the Organization and the States that have acceded to the Convention of signatures and of deposits of instruments of ratification, accession, and denunciation, as well as reservations, if any.

97

Inter-American Convention on the Forced Disappearance of Persons, 1994

Note: A-60: Inter-American Convention on Forced Disappearance of Persons. Adopted at Belem Do Parma, Brazil, 9 June 1994. Entry into force: 28 March 1996.

PREAMBLE

The Member States of the Organization of American States signatory to the present Convention,

DISTURBED by the persistence of the forced disappearance of persons;

REAFFIRMING that the true meaning of American solidarity and good neighborliness can be none other than that of consolidating in this Hemisphere, in the framework of democratic institutions, a system of individual freedom and social justice based on respect for essential human rights;

CONSIDERING that the forced disappearance of persons in an affront to the conscience of the Hemisphere and a grave and abominable offense against the inherent dignity of the human being, and one that contradicts the principles and purposes enshrined in the Charter of the Organization of American States;

CONSIDERING that the forced disappearance of persons of persons violates numerous non-derogable and essential human rights enshrined in the American Convention on Human Rights, in the American Declaration of the Rights and Duties of Man, and in the Universal Declaration of Human Rights;

RECALLING that the international protection of human rights is in the form of a convention reinforcing or complementing the protection provided by domestic law and is based upon the attributes of the human personality;

REAFFIRMING that the systematic practice of the forced disappearance of persons constitutes a crime against humanity;

HOPING that this Convention may help to prevent, punish, and eliminate the forced disappearance of persons in the Hemisphere and make a decisive contribution to the protection of human rights and the rule of law,

RESOLVE to adopt the following Inter-American Convention on Forced Disappearance of Persons:

Article I

The States Parties to this Convention undertake:

a. Not to practice, permit, or tolerate the forced disappearance of persons, even in states of emergency or suspension of individual guarantees;

b. To punish within their jurisdictions, those persons who commit or attempt to commit the crime of forced disappearance of persons and their accomplices and accessories;

c. To cooperate with one another in helping to prevent, punish, and eliminate the forced disappearance of persons;

d. To take legislative, administrative, judicial, and any other measures necessary to comply with the commitments undertaken in this Convention.

Article II

For the purposes of this Convention, forced disappearance is considered to be the act of depriving a person or persons of his or their freedom, in whatever way, perpetrated by agents of the state or by persons or groups of persons acting with the authorization, support, or acquiescence of the state, followed by an absence of information or a refusal to acknowledge that deprivation of freedom or to give information on the whereabouts of that person, thereby impeding his or her recourse to the applicable legal remedies and procedural guarantees.

Article III

The States Parties undertake to adopt, in accordance with their constitutional procedures, the legislative measures that may be needed to define the forced disappearance of persons as an offense and to impose an appropriate punishment commensurate with its extreme gravity. This offense shall be deemed continuous or permanent as long as the fate or whereabouts of the victim has not been determined.

The States Parties may establish mitigating circumstances for persons who have participated in acts constituting forced disappearance when they help to cause the victim to reappear alive or provide information that sheds light on the forced disappearance of a person.

Article IV

The acts constituting the forced disappearance of persons shall be considered offenses in every State Party. Consequently, each State Party shall take measures to establish its jurisdiction over such cases in the following instances:

a. When the forced disappearance of persons or any act constituting such offense was committed within its jurisdiction;

b. When the accused is a national of that state;

c. When the victim is a national of that state and that state sees fit to do so.

Every State Party shall, moreover, take the necessary measures to establish its jurisdiction over the crime described in this Convention when the alleged criminal is within its territory and it does not proceed to extradite him.

This Convention does not authorize any State Party to undertake, in the territory of another State Party, the exercise of jurisdiction or the performance of functions that are placed within the exclusive purview of the authorities of that other Party by its domestic law.

Article V

The forced disappearance of persons shall not be considered a political offense for purposes of extradition.

The forced disappearance of persons shall be deemed to be included among the extraditable offenses in every extradition treaty entered into between States Parties. The States Parties undertake to include the offense of forced disappearance as one which is extraditable in every extradition treaty to be concluded between them in the future. Every State Party that makes extradition conditional on the existence of a treaty and receives a request for extradition from another State Party with which it has no extradition treaty may consider this Convention as the necessary legal basis for extradition with respect to the offense of forced disappearance. States Parties which do not make extradition conditional on the existence of a treaty shall recognize such offense as extraditable, subject to the conditions imposed by the law of the requested state.

Extradition shall be subject to the provisions set forth in the constitution and other laws of the request state.

Article VI

When a State Party does not grant the extradition, the case shall be submitted to its competent authorities as if the offense had been committed within its jurisdiction, for the purposes of investigation and when appropriate, for criminal action, in accordance with its national law. Any decision adopted by these authorities shall be communicated to the state that has requested the extradition.

Article VII

Criminal prosecution for the forced disappearance of persons and the penalty judicially imposed on its perpetrator shall not be subject to statutes of limitations.

However, if there should be a norm of a fundamental character preventing application of the stipulation contained in the previous paragraph, the period of limitation shall be equal to that which applies to the gravest crime in the domestic laws of the corresponding State Party.

Article VIII

The defense of due obedience to superior orders or instructions that stipulate, authorize, or encourage forced disappearance shall not be admitted. All persons who receive such orders have the right and duty not to obey them.

The States Parties shall ensure that the training of public law-enforcement personnel or officials includes the necessary education on the offense of forced disappearance of persons.

Article IX

Persons alleged to be responsible for the acts constituting the offense of forced disappearance of persons may be tried only in the competent jurisdictions of ordinary law in each state, to the exclusion of all other special jurisdictions, particularly military jurisdictions.

The acts constituting forced disappearance shall not be deemed to have been committed in the course of military duties.

Privileges, immunities, or special dispensations shall not be admitted in such trials, without prejudice to the provisions set forth in the Vienna Convention on Diplomatic Relations.

Article X

In no case may exceptional circumstances such as a state of war, the threat of war, internal political instability, or any other public emergency be invoked to justify the forced disappearance of persons. In such cases, the right to expeditious and effective judicial procedures and recourse shall be retained as a means of determining the whereabouts or state of health of a person who has been deprived of freedom, or of identifying the official who ordered or carried out such deprivation of freedom.

In pursuing such procedures or recourse, and in keeping with applicable domestic law, the competent judicial authorities shall have free and immediate access to all detention centers and to each of their units, and to all places where there is reason to believe the disappeared person might be found including places that are subject to military jurisdiction.

Article XI

Every person deprived of liberty shall be held in an officially recognized place of detention and be brought before a competent judicial authority without delay, in accordance with applicable domestic law.

The States Parties shall establish and maintain official up-to-date registries of their detainees and, in accordance with their domestic law, shall make them available to relatives, judges, attorneys, any other person having a legitimate interest, and other authorities.

Article XII

The States Parties shall give each other mutual assistance in the search for, identification, location, and return of minors who have been removed to another state or detained therein as a consequence of the forced disappearance of their parents or guardians.

Article XIII

For the purposes of this Convention, the processing of petitions or communications presented to the Inter-American Commission on Human Rights alleging the forced disappearance of persons shall be subject to the procedures established in the American Convention on Human Rights and to the Statue and Regulations of the Inter-American Commission on Human Rights and to the Statute and Rules of Procedure of the Inter-American Court of Human Rights, including the provisions on precautionary measures.

Article XIV

Without prejudice to the provisions of the preceding article, when the Inter-American Commission on Human Rights receives a petition or communication regarding an alleged forced disappearance, its Executive Secretariat shall urgently and confidentially address the respective government, and shall request that government to provide as soon as possible information as to the whereabouts of the allegedly disappeared person together with any other information it considers pertinent, and such request shall be without prejudice as to the admissibility of the petition.

Article XV
None of the provisions of this Convention shall be interpreted as limiting other bilateral or multilateral treaties or other agreements signed by the Parties.

This Convention shall not apply to the international armed conflicts governed by the 1949 Geneva Conventions and its Protocol concerning protection of wounded, sick, and shipwrecked members of the armed forces; and prisoners of war and civilians in time of war.

Article XVI
This Convention is open for signature by the member states of the Organization of American States.

Article XVII
This Convention is subject to ratification. The instruments of ratification shall be deposited with the General Secretariat of the Organization of American States.

Article XVIII
This Convention shall be open to accession by any other state. The instruments of accession shall be deposited with the General Secretariat of the Organization of American States.

Article XIX
The states may express reservations with respect to this Convention when adopting, signing, ratifying or acceding to it, unless such reservations are incompatible with the object and purpose of the Convention and as long as they refer to one or more specific provisions.

Article XX
This Convention shall enter into force for the ratifying states on the thirtieth day from the date of deposit of the second instrument of ratification.

For each state ratifying or acceding to the Convention after the second instrument of ratification has been deposited, the Convention shall enter into force on the thirtieth day from the date on which that state deposited its instrument of ratification or accession.

Article XXI
This Convention shall remain in force indefinitely, but may be denounced by any State Party. The instrument of denunciation shall be deposited with the General Secretariat of the Organization of American States. The Convention shall cease to be in effect for the denouncing state and shall remain in force for the other States Parties one year from the date of deposit of the instrument of denunciation.

Article XXII

The original instrument of this Convention, the Spanish, English, Portuguese, and French texts of which are equally authentic, shall be deposited with the General Secretariat of the Organization of American States, which shall forward certified copies thereof to the United Nations Secretariat, for registration and publication, in accordance with Article 102 of the Charter of the United Nations. The General Secretariat of the Organization of American States shall notify member states of the Organization and states acceding to the Convention of the signatures and deposit of instruments of ratification, accession or denunciation, as well as of any reservations that may be expressed.

PART XI
Organisation of Islamic Cooperation,
Arab and Islamic States

98

Arab Charter on Human Rights, 2004

Noted: Adopted by the League of Arab States, 22 May 2004. Entry into force: 15 March 2008. It should be noted that there are a number of differing translations from the authentic Arabic text into English. The English version reproduced is probably the most widely used.

Based on the faith of the Arab nation in the dignity of the human person whom God has exalted ever since the beginning of creation and in the fact that the Arab homeland is the cradle of religions and civilizations whose lofty human values affirm the human right to a decent life based on freedom, justice and equality,

In furtherance of the eternal principles of fraternity, equality and tolerance among human beings consecrated by the noble Islamic religion and the other divinely-revealed religions,

Being proud of the humanitarian values and principles that the Arab nation has established throughout its long history, which have played a major role in spreading knowledge between East and West, so making the region a point of reference for the whole world and a destination for seekers of knowledge and wisdom,

Believing in the unity of the Arab nation, which struggles for its freedom and defends the right of nations to self-determination, to the preservation of their wealth and to development; believing in the sovereignty of the law and its contribution to the protection of universal and interrelated human rights and convinced that the human person's enjoyment of freedom, justice and equality of opportunity is a fundamental measure of the value of any society,

Rejecting all forms of racism and Zionism, which constitute a violation of human rights and a threat to international peace and security, recognizing the close link that exists between human rights and international peace and security, reaffirming the principles of the Charter of the United Nations, the Universal Declaration of Human Rights and the provisions of the International Covenant on Civil and Political Rights and the International Covenant on Economic, Social and Cultural Rights, and having regard to the Cairo Declaration on Human Rights in Islam,

The States parties to the Charter have agreed as follows:

Article 1

The present Charter seeks, within the context of the national identity of the Arab States and their sense of belonging to a common civilization, to achieve the following aims:

1. To place human rights at the centre of the key national concerns of Arab States, making them lofty and fundamental ideals that shape the will of the individual in Arab States and enable him to improve his life in accordance with noble human values.

2. To teach the human person in the Arab States pride in his identity, loyalty to his country, attachment to his land, history and common interests and to instill in him a culture of human brotherhood, tolerance and openness towards others, in accordance with universal principles and values and with those proclaimed in international human rights instruments.

3. To prepare the new generations in Arab States for a free and responsible life in a civil society that is characterized by solidarity, founded on a balance between awareness of rights and respect for obligations, and governed by the values of equality, tolerance and moderation.

4. To entrench the principle that all human rights are universal, indivisible, interdependent and interrelated.

Article 2

1. All peoples have the right of self-determination and to control over their natural wealth and resources, and the right to freely choose their political system and to freely pursue their economic, social and cultural development.

2. All peoples have the right to national sovereignty and territorial integrity.

3. All forms of racism, Zionism and foreign occupation and domination constitute an impediment to human dignity and a major barrier to the exercise of the fundamental rights of peoples; all such practices must be condemned and efforts must be deployed for their elimination.

4. All peoples have the right to resist foreign occupation.

Article 3

1. Each State party to the present Charter undertakes to ensure to all individuals subject to its jurisdiction the right to enjoy the rights and freedoms set forth herein, without distinction on grounds of race, colour, sex, language, religious belief, opinion, thought, national or social origin, wealth, birth or physical or mental disability.

2. The States parties to the present Charter shall take the requisite measures to guarantee effective equality in the enjoyment of all the rights and freedoms enshrined in the present Charter in order to ensure protection against all forms of discrimination based on any of the grounds mentioned in the preceding paragraph.

3. Men and women are equal in respect of human dignity, rights and obligations within the framework of the positive discrimination established in favour of women by the Islamic Shari'a, other divine laws and by applicable laws and legal instruments. Accordingly, each State party pledges to take all the requisite measures to guarantee equal opportunities and effective equality between men and women in the enjoyment of all the rights set out in this Charter.

Article 4

1. In exceptional situations of emergency which threaten the life of the nation and the existence of which is officially proclaimed, the States parties to the present Charter may take measures derogating from their obligations under the present Charter, to the extent strictly required by the exigencies of the situation, provided that such measures are not inconsistent with their other obligations under international law and do not

involve discrimination solely on the grounds of race, colour, sex, language, religion or social origin.

2. In exceptional situations of emergency, no derogation shall be made from the following articles: article 5, article 8, article 9, article 10, article 13, article 14, paragraph 6, article 15, article 18, article 19, article 20, article 22, article 27, article 28, article 29 and article 30. In addition, the judicial guarantees required for the protection of the aforementioned rights may not be suspended.

3. Any State party to the present Charter availing itself of the right of derogation shall immediately inform the other States parties, through the intermediary of the Secretary-General of the League of Arab States, of the provisions from which it has derogated and of the reasons by which it was actuated. A further communication shall be made, through the same intermediary, on the date on which it terminates such derogation.

Article 5
1. Every human being has the inherent right to life.
2. This right shall be protected by law. No one shall be arbitrarily deprived of his life.

Article 6
Sentence of death may be imposed only for the most serious crimes in accordance with the laws in force at the time of commission of the crime and pursuant to a final judgment rendered by a competent court. Anyone sentenced to death shall have the right to seek pardon or commutation of the sentence.

Article 7
1. Sentence of death shall not be imposed on persons under 18 years of age, unless otherwise stipulated in the laws in force at the time of the commission of the crime.
2. The death penalty shall not be inflicted on a pregnant woman prior to her delivery or on a nursing mother within two years from the date of her delivery; in all cases, the best interests of the infant shall be the primary consideration.

Article 8
1. No one shall be subjected to physical or psychological torture or to cruel, degrading, humiliating or inhuman treatment.
2. Each State party shall protect every individual subject to its jurisdiction from such practices and shall take effective measures to prevent them. The commission of, or participation in, such acts shall be regarded as crimes that are punishable by law and not subject to any statute of limitations. Each State party shall guarantee in its legal system redress for any victim of torture and the right to rehabilitation and compensation.

Article 9
No one shall be subjected to medical or scientific experimentation or to the use of his organs without his free consent and full awareness of the consequences and provided that ethical, humanitarian and professional rules are followed and medical procedures are observed to ensure his personal safety pursuant to the relevant domestic laws in force in each State party. Trafficking in human organs is prohibited in all circumstances.

Article 10

1. All forms of slavery and trafficking in human beings are prohibited and are punishable by law. No one shall be held in slavery and servitude under any circumstances.
2. Forced labor, trafficking in human beings for the purposes of prostitution or sexual exploitation, the exploitation of the prostitution of others or any other form of exploitation or the exploitation of children in armed conflict are prohibited.

Article 11

All persons are equal before the law and have the right to enjoy its protection without discrimination.

Article 12

All persons are equal before the courts and tribunals. The States parties shall guarantee the independence of the judiciary and protect magistrates against any interference, pressure or threats. They shall also guarantee every person subject to their jurisdiction the right to seek a legal remedy before courts of all levels.

Article 13

1. Everyone has the right to a fair trial that affords adequate guarantees before a competent, independent and impartial court that has been constituted by law to hear any criminal charge against him or to decide on his rights or his obligations. Each State party shall guarantee to those without the requisite financial resources legal aid to enable them to defend their rights.
2. Trials shall be public, except in exceptional cases that may be warranted by the interests of justice in a society that respects human freedoms and rights.

Article 14

1. Everyone has the right to liberty and security of person. No one shall be subjected to arbitrary arrest, search or detention without a legal warrant.
2. No one shall be deprived of his liberty except on such grounds and in such circumstances as are determined by law and in accordance with such procedure as is established thereby.
3. Anyone who is arrested shall be informed, at the time of arrest, in a language that he understands, of the reasons for his arrest and shall be promptly informed of any charges against him. He shall be entitled to contact his family members.
4. Anyone who is deprived of his liberty by arrest or detention shall have the right to request a medical examination and must be informed of that right.
5. Anyone arrested or detained on a criminal charge shall be brought promptly before a judge or other officer authorized by law to exercise judicial power and shall be entitled to trial within a reasonable time or to release. His release may be subject to guarantees to appear for trial. Pre-trial detention shall in no case be the general rule.
6. Anyone who is deprived of his liberty by arrest or detention shall be entitled to petition a competent court in order that it may decide without delay on the lawfulness of his arrest or detention and order his release if the arrest or detention is unlawful.
7. Anyone who has been the victim of arbitrary or unlawful arrest or detention shall be entitled to compensation.

Article 15

No crime and no penalty can be established without a prior provision of the law. In all circumstances, the law most favorable to the defendant shall be applied.

Article 16

Everyone charged with a criminal offence shall be presumed innocent until proved guilty by a final judgment rendered according to law and, in the course of the investigation and trial, he shall enjoy the following minimum guarantees:

1. The right to be informed promptly, in detail and in a language which he understands, of the charges against him.
2. The right to have adequate time and facilities for the preparation of his defense and to be allowed to communicate with his family.
3. The right to be tried in his presence before an ordinary court and to defend himself in person or through a lawyer of his own choosing with whom he can communicate freely and confidentially.
4. The right to the free assistance of a lawyer who will defend him if he cannot defend himself or if the interests of justice so require, and the right to the free assistance of an interpreter if he cannot understand or does not speak the language used in court.
5. The right to examine or have his lawyer examine the prosecution witnesses and to on defense according to the conditions applied to the prosecution witnesses.
6. The right not to be compelled to testify against himself or to confess guilt.
7. The right, if convicted of the crime, to file an appeal in accordance with the law before a higher tribunal.
8. The right to respect for his security of person and his privacy in all circumstances.

Article 17

Each State party shall ensure in particular to any child at risk or any delinquent charged with an offence the right to a special legal system for minors in all stages of investigation, trial and enforcement of sentence, as well as to special treatment that takes account of his age, protects his dignity, facilitates his rehabilitation and reintegration and enables him to play a constructive role in society.

Article 18

No one who is shown by a court to be unable to pay a debt arising from a contractual obligation shall be imprisoned.

Article 19

1. No one may be tried twice for the same offence. Anyone against whom such proceedings are brought shall have the right to challenge their legality and to demand his release.
2. Anyone whose innocence is established by a final judgment shall be entitled to compensation for the damage suffered.

Article 20

1. All persons deprived of their liberty shall be treated with humanity and with respect for the inherent dignity of the human person.

2. Persons in pre-trial detention shall be separated from convicted persons and shall be treated in a manner consistent with their status as unconvicted persons.

3. The aim of the penitentiary system shall be to reform prisoners and effect their social rehabilitation.

Article 21

1. No one shall be subjected to arbitrary or unlawful interference with regard to his privacy, family, home or correspondence, nor to unlawful attacks on his honour or his reputation.

2. Everyone has the right to the protection of the law against such interference or attacks.

Article 22

Everyone shall have the right to recognition as a person before the law.

Article 23

Each State party to the present Charter undertakes to ensure that any person whose rights or freedoms as herein recognized are violated shall have an effective remedy, notwithstanding that the violation has been committed by persons acting in an official capacity.

Article 24

Every citizen has the right:

1. To freely pursue a political activity.

2. To take part in the conduct of public affairs, directly or through freely chosen representatives.

3. To stand for election or choose his representatives in free and impartial elections, in conditions of equality among all citizens that guarantee the free expression of his will.

4. To the opportunity to gain access, on an equal footing with others, to public office in his country in accordance with the principle of equality of opportunity.

5. To freely form and join associations with others.

6. To freedom of association and peaceful assembly.

7. No restrictions may be placed on the exercise of these rights other than those which are prescribed by law and which are necessary in a democratic society in the interests of national security or public safety, public health or morals or the protection of the rights and freedoms of others.

Article 25

Persons belonging to minorities shall not be denied the right to enjoy their own culture, to use their own language and to practice their own religion. The exercise of these rights shall be governed by law.

Article 26

1. Everyone lawfully within the territory of a State party shall, within that territory, have the right to freedom of movement and to freely choose his residence in any part of that territory in conformity with the laws in force.

2. No State party may expel a person who does not hold its nationality but is lawfully in its territory, other than in pursuance of a decision reached in accordance with law and

after that person has been allowed to submit a petition to the competent authority, unless compelling reasons of national security preclude it. Collective expulsion is prohibited under all circumstances.

Article 27

1. No one may be arbitrarily or unlawfully prevented from leaving any country, including his own, nor prohibited from residing, or compelled to reside, in any part of that country.
2. No one may be exiled from his country or prohibited from returning thereto.

Article 28

Everyone has the right to seek political asylum in another country in order to escape persecution. This right may not be invoked by persons facing prosecution for an offence under ordinary law. Political refugees may not be extradited.

Article 29

1. Everyone has the right to nationality. No one shall be arbitrarily or unlawfully deprived of his nationality.
2. States parties shall take such measures as they deem appropriate, in accordance with their domestic laws on nationality, to allow a child to acquire the mother's nationality, having due regard, in all cases, to the best interests of the child.
3. No one shall be denied the right to acquire another nationality, having due regard for the domestic legal procedures in his country.

Article 30

1. Everyone has the right to freedom of thought, conscience and religion and no restrictions may be imposed on the exercise of such freedoms except as provided for by law.
2. The freedom to manifest one's religion or beliefs or to perform religious observances, either alone or in community with others, shall be subject only to such limitations as are prescribed by law and are necessary in a tolerant society that respects human rights and freedoms for the protection of public safety, public order, public health or morals or the fundamental rights and freedoms of others.
3. Parents or guardians have the freedom to provide for the religious and moral education of their children.

Article 31

Everyone has a guaranteed right to own private property, and shall not under any circumstances be arbitrarily or unlawfully divested of all or any part of his property.

Article 32

1. The present Charter guarantees the right to information and to freedom of opinion and expression, as well as the right to seek, receive and impart information and ideas through any medium, regardless of geographical boundaries.
2. Such rights and freedoms shall be exercised in conformity with the fundamental values of society and shall be subject only to such limitations as are required to ensure respect for the rights or reputation of others or the protection of national security, public order and public health or morals.

Article 33

1. The family is the natural and fundamental group unit of society; it is based on marriage between a man and a woman. Men and women of marrying age have the right to marry and to found a family according to the rules and conditions of marriage. No marriage can take place without the full and free consent of both parties. The laws in force regulate the rights and duties of the man and woman as to marriage, during marriage and at its dissolution.

2. The State and society shall ensure the protection of the family, the strengthening of family ties, the protection of its members and the prohibition of all forms of violence or abuse in the relations among its members, and particularly against women and children. They shall also ensure the necessary protection and care for mothers, children, older persons and persons with special needs and shall provide adolescents and young persons with the best opportunities for physical and mental development.

3. The States parties shall take all necessary legislative, administrative and judicial measures to guarantee the protection, survival, development and well-being of the child in an atmosphere of freedom and dignity and shall ensure, in all cases, that the child's best interests are the basic criterion for all measures taken in his regard, whether the child is at risk of delinquency or is a juvenile offender.

4. The States parties shall take all the necessary measures to guarantee, particularly to young persons, the right to pursue a sporting activity.

Article 34

1. The right to work is a natural right of every citizen. The State shall endeavor to provide, to the extent possible, a job for the largest number of those willing to work, while ensuring production, the freedom to choose one's work and equality of opportunity without discrimination of any kind on grounds of race, colour, sex, religion, language, political opinion, membership in a union, national origin, social origin, disability or any other situation.

2. Every worker has the right to the enjoyment of just and favourable conditions of work which ensure appropriate remuneration to meet his essential needs and those of his family and regulate working hours, rest and holidays with pay, as well as the rules for the preservation of occupational health and safety and the protection of women, children and disabled persons in the place of work.

3. The States parties recognize the right of the child to be protected from economic exploitation and from being forced to perform any work that is likely to be hazardous or to interfere with the child's education or to be harmful to the child's health or physical, mental, spiritual, moral or social development. To this end, and having regard to the relevant provisions of other international instruments, States parties shall in particular:
   (a) Define a minimum age for admission to employment;
   (b) Establish appropriate regulation of working hours and conditions;
   (c) Establish appropriate penalties or other sanctions to ensure the effective endorsement of these provisions.

4. There shall be no discrimination between men and women in their enjoyment of the right to effectively benefit from training, employment and job protection and the right to receive equal remuneration for equal work.

5. Each State party shall ensure to workers who migrate to its territory the requisite protection in accordance with the laws in force.

Article 35

1. Every individual has the right to freely form trade unions or to join trade unions and to freely pursue trade union activity for the protection of his interests.
2. No restrictions shall be placed on the exercise of these rights and freedoms except such as are prescribed by the laws in force and that are necessary for the maintenance of national security, public safety or order or for the protection of public health or morals or the rights and freedoms of others.
3. Every State party to the present Charter guarantees the right to strike within the limits laid down by the laws in force.

Article 36

The States parties shall ensure the right of every citizen to social security, including social insurance.

Article 37

The right to development is a fundamental human right and all States are required to establish the development policies and to take the measures needed to guarantee this right. They have a duty to give effect to the values of solidarity and cooperation among them and at the international level with a view to eradicating poverty and achieving economic, social, cultural and political development. By virtue of this right, every citizen has the right to participate in the realization of development and to enjoy the benefits and fruits thereof.

Article 38

Every person has the right to an adequate standard of living for himself and his family, which ensures their well-being and a decent life, including food, clothing, housing, services and the right to a healthy environment. The States parties shall take the necessary measures commensurate with their resources to guarantee these rights.

Article 39

1. The States parties recognize the right of every member of society to the enjoyment of the highest attainable standard of physical and mental health and the right of the citizen to free basic health-care services and to have access to medical facilities without discrimination of any kind.
2. The measures taken by States parties shall include the following:
   (a) Development of basic health-care services and the guaranteeing of free and easy access to the centres that provide these services, regardless of geographical location or economic status.
   (b) Efforts to control disease by means of prevention and cure in order to reduce the morality rate.
   (c) Promotion of health awareness and health education.
   (d) Suppression of traditional practices which are harmful to the health of the individual.
   (e) Provision of the basic nutrition and safe drinking water for all.
   (f) Combating environmental pollution and providing proper sanitation systems;
   (g) Combating drugs, psychotropic substances, smoking and substances that are damaging to health.

Article 40

1. The States parties undertake to ensure to persons with mental or physical disabilities a decent life that guarantees their dignity, and to enhance their self-reliance and facilitate their active participation in society.
2. The States parties shall provide social services free of charge for all persons with disabilities, shall provide the material support needed by those persons, their families or the families caring for them, and shall also do whatever is needed to avoid placing those persons in institutions. They shall in all cases take account of the best interests of the disabled person.
3. The States parties shall take all necessary measures to curtail the incidence of disabilities by all possible means, including preventive health programmes, awareness raising and education.
4. The States parties shall provide full educational services suited to persons with disabilities, taking into account the importance of integrating these persons in the educational system and the importance of vocational training and apprenticeship and the creation of suitable job opportunities in the public or private sectors.
5. The States parties shall provide all health services appropriate for persons with disabilities, including the rehabilitation of these persons with a view to integrating them into society.
6. The States parties shall enable persons with disabilities to make use of all public and private services.

Article 41

1. The eradication of illiteracy is a binding obligation upon the State and everyone has the right to education.
2. The States parties shall guarantee their citizens free education at least throughout the primary and basic levels. All forms and levels of primary education shall be compulsory and accessible to all without discrimination of any kind.
3. The States parties shall take appropriate measures in all domains to ensure partnership between men and women with a view to achieving national development goals.
4. The States parties shall guarantee to provide education directed to the full development of the human person and to strengthening respect for human rights and fundamental freedoms.
5. The States parties shall endeavour to incorporate the principles of human rights and fundamental freedoms into formal and informal education curricula and educational and training programmes.
6. The States parties shall guarantee the establishment of the mechanisms necessary to provide ongoing education for every citizen and shall develop national plans for adult education.

Article 42

1. Every person has the right to take part in cultural life and to enjoy the benefits of scientific progress and its application.
2. The States parties undertake to respect the freedom of scientific research and creative activity and to ensure the protection of moral and material interests resulting from scientific, literary and artistic production.

3. The State parties shall work together and enhance cooperation among them at all levels, with the full participation of intellectuals and inventors and their organizations, in order to develop and implement recreational, cultural, artistic and scientific programmes.

Article 43

Nothing in this Charter may be construed or interpreted as impairing the rights and freedoms protected by the domestic laws of the States parties or those set force in the international and regional human rights instruments which the States parties have adopted or ratified, including the rights of women, the rights of the child and the rights of persons belonging to minorities.

Article 44

The States parties undertake to adopt, in conformity with their constitutional procedures and with the provisions of the present Charter, whatever legislative or non-legislative measures that may be necessary to give effect to the rights set forth herein.

Article 45

1. Pursuant to this Charter, an "Arab Human Rights Committee", hereinafter referred to as "the Committee" shall be established. This Committee shall consist of seven members who shall be elected by secret ballot by the States parties to this Charter.
2. The Committee shall consist of nationals of the States parties to the present Charter, who must be highly experienced and competent in the Committee's field of work. The members of the Committee shall serve in their personal capacity and shall be fully independent and impartial.
3. The Committee shall include among its members not more than one national of a State party; such member may be re-elected only once. Due regard shall be given to the rotation principle.
4. The members of the Committee shall be elected for a four-year term, although the mandate of three of the members elected during the first election shall be for two years and shall be renewed by lot.
5. Six months prior to the date of the election, the Secretary-General of the League of Arab States shall invite the States parties to submit their nominations within the following three months. He shall transmit the list of candidates to the States parties two months prior to the date the election. The candidates who obtain the largest number of votes cast shall be elected to membership of the Committee. If, because two or more candidates have an equal number of votes, the number of candidates with the largest number of votes exceeds the number required, a second ballot will be held between the persons with equal numbers of votes. If the votes are again equal, the member or members shall be selected by lottery. The first election for membership of the Committee shall be held at least six months after the Charter enters into force.
6. The Secretary-General shall invite the States parties to a meeting at the headquarters the League of Arab States in order to elect the member of the Committee. The presence of the majority of the States parties shall constitute a quorum. If there is no quorum, the Secretary-General shall call another meeting at which at least two thirds

of the States parties must be present. If there is still no quorum, the Secretary-General shall call a third meeting, which will be held regardless of the number of States parties present.

7. The Secretary-General shall convene the first meeting of the Committee, during the course of which the Committee shall elect its Chairman from among its members, for a two-year term which may be renewed only once and for an identical period. The Committee shall establish its own rules of procedure and methods of work and shall determine how often it shall meet. The Committee shall hold its meetings at the head-quarters of the League of Arab States. It may also meet in any other State party to the present Charter at that party's invitation.

Article 46

1. The Secretary-General shall declare a seat vacant after being notified by the Chairman of a member's:
   (a) Death;
   (b) Resignation; or
   (c) If, in the unanimous, opinion of the other members, a member of the Committee has ceased to perform his functions without offering an acceptable justification or for any reason other than a temporary absence.

2. If a member's seat is declared vacant pursuant to the provisions of paragraph 1 and the term of office of the member to be replaced does not expire within six months from the date on which the vacancy was declared, the Secretary-General of the League of Arab States shall refer the matter to the States parties to the present Charter, which may, within two months, submit nominations, pursuant to article 45, in order to fill the vacant seat.

3. The Secretary-General of the League of Arab States shall draw up an alphabetical list of all the duly nominated candidates, which he shall transmit to the States parties to the present Charter. The elections to fill the vacant seat shall be held in accordance with the relevant provisions.

4. Any member of the Committee elected to fill a seat declared vacant in accordance with the provisions of paragraph 1 shall remain a member of the Committee until the expiry of the remainder of the term of the member whose seat was declared vacant pursuant to the provisions of that paragraph.

5. The Secretary-General of the League of Arab States shall make provision within the budget of the League of Arab States for all the necessary financial and human resources and facilities that the Committee needs to discharge its functions effectively. The Committee's experts shall be afforded the same treatment with respect to remuneration and reimbursement of expenses as experts of the secretariat of the League of Arab States.

Article 47

The States parties undertake to ensure that members of the Committee shall enjoy the immunities necessary for their protection against any form of harassment or moral or material pressure or prosecution on account of the positions they take or statements they make while carrying out their functions as members of the Committee.

Article 48

1. The States parties undertake to submit reports to the Secretary-General of the League of Arab States on the measures they have taken to give effect to the rights and freedoms recognized in this Charter and on the progress made towards the enjoyment thereof. The Secretary-General shall transmit these reports to the Committee for its consideration.
2. Each State party shall submit an initial report to the Committee within one year from the date on which the Charter enters into force and a periodic report every three years thereafter. The Committee may request the States parties to supply it with additional information relating to the implementation of the Charter.
3. The Committee shall consider the reports submitted by the States parties under paragraph 2 of this article in the presence of the representative of the State party whose report is being considered.
4. The Committee shall discuss the report, comment thereon and make the necessary recommendations in accordance with the aims of the Charter.
5. The Committee shall submit an annual report containing its comments and recommendations to the Council of the League, through the intermediary of the Secretary-General.
6. The Committee's reports, concluding observations and recommendations shall be public documents which the Committee shall disseminate widely.

Article 49

1. The Secretary-General of the League of Arab States shall submit the present Charter, once it has been approved by the Council of the League, to the States members for signature, ratification or accession.
2. The present Charter shall enter into effect two months from the date on which the seventh instrument of ratification is deposited with the secretariat of the League of Arab States.
3. After its entry into force, the present Charter shall become effective for each State two months after the State in question has deposited its instrument of ratification or accession with the secretariat.
4. The Secretary-General shall notify the States members of the deposit of each instrument of ratification or accession.

Article 50

Any State party may submit written proposals, though the Secretary-General, for the amendment of the present Charter. After these amendments have been circulated among the States members, the Secretary-General shall invite the States parties to consider the proposed amendments before submitting them to the Council of the League for adoption.

Article 51

The amendments shall take effect, with regard to the States parties that have approved them, once they have been approved by two thirds of the States parties.

Article 52

Any State party may propose additional optional protocols to the present Charter and they shall be adopted in accordance with the procedures used for the adoption of amendments to the Charter.

Article 53

1. Any State party, when signing this Charter, depositing the instruments of ratification or acceding hereto, may make a reservation to any article of the Charter, provided that such reservation does not conflict with the aims and fundamental purposes of the Charter.

2. Any State party that has made a reservation pursuant to paragraph 1 of this article may withdraw it at any time by addressing a notification to the Secretary-General of the League of Arab States.

99

Covenant on the Rights of the Child in Islam, 2004

Note: The Covenant was finalised in 2004 (see OIC/9-IGGE/HRI/2004/Rep.Final) and was formally adopted at the 32nd Islamic Conference of Foreign Ministers, Sana'a, Yemen, 28–30 June 2005 under the auspices of the Organisation of the Islamic Conference. Not yet in force. The English language text reproduced is the official version provided by the OIC.

The States Parties to this Covenant,

Believing that the values and principles constitute the patterns of behavior of Muslim society in such a way as to realize security, stability, development and progress for the society within the family environment, which is the cornerstone of the social edifice,

Proceeding from Islamic efforts on issues of childhood, which contributed to the development of the 1989 United Nations Convention on the Rights of the Child,

Cognizant of the objectives of the Organization of the Islamic Conference enshrined in its Charter and its Summit and Ministerial Conferences resolutions and of international conventions signed by its Member States;

Affirming the principles contained in the Dhaka Declaration on Human Rights in Islam adopted by the 14th Islamic Conference of Foreign Ministers in December 1983 and the Cairo Declaration on Human Rights in Islam adopted by the 14th ICFM under resolution No. 49/19-P (1990) and in the Declaration on the Rights and Care of the Child in Islam adopted by the Seventh Islamic Summit Conference under resolution No. 16/7-C (1994),

Affirming the civilisational and historic role of the Islamic Ummah and in contributing to the international efforts on human rights,

Believing that basic rights and public freedoms in Islam are an integral part thereof that no one has a prerogative to interrupt, violate, or disregard;

Aware of the enormous responsibility towards the Child in particular as the vanguard and maker of the future of the Ummah;

Seeking to enhance Islamic performance in the Child sector so as to adapt frameworks and mechanisms to face the ever-accelerating changes and transformations and their repercussions on that sector;

Realizing that the first order of serious work is to gain a conscious insight into the accumulating and expected challenges facing the Ummah, particularly the adverse effects of economic and social transformations, the waning role of the family, the weakening feeling of belonging, the breaking-down of family-ties, the decline of values and ideals, the diminishing health and educational services, the growing illiteracy rate, as well as the effects of the accelerating advances in sciences and fields of knowledge and the information revolution in addition to the continuing persistence of negative and old-fashioned cultural models;

Considering that children, as part of the vulnerable sector of society, bear the burden of the greater suffering as a result of natural and man-made disasters leading to tragic consequences, such as orphanage, homelessness, and exploitation of children in military, harsh, hazardous, or illegitimate labor, and considering also the suffering of refugee children and those living under the yoke of occupation or languishing or displaced as a result of armed conflicts and famines thus fostering the spread of violence among children and increasing the number of physically, mentally, and socially disabled children;

Believing that the situation requires a stand that establishes a commitment to the Rights of the Child and confirms the determination to continue the efforts to activate these rights and overcome the obstacles standing in the way of the Ummah;

Confident that the Ummah has sufficient capabilities and resources to ensure a victory over the hurdles facing it, building on the lofty religious and social values with the family enjoying pride of place on the basis of love and mercy as well as human and material resources which afford it a real opportunity for comprehensive and sustainable development;

Recognizing the Child's right to grow up within a family environment governed by established values, love, and understanding so as to enable him to exercise his rights without discrimination;

Supporting the plans, programs, and projects aimed at improving the conditions of childhood in the Islamic world, including the elaboration of national legislations or regimes ensuring the child's exercise of his full rights;

Considering that the present Covenant affirms the rights of the child in the provisions of the Islamic Shari'a, taking into account the domestic laws of states and the rights of children of minorities and non-Muslim communities, in affirmation of the human rights shared by the Muslim and non-Muslim child,

Have agreed as follows:

Article One
Definition of the Child
For the purposes of the present Covenant, a child means every human being who, according to the law applicable to him/her, has not attained maturity.

Article Two
Objectives
This Covenant seeks to realize the following objectives:
1. To care for the family, strengthen its capabilities, and extend to it the necessary support to prevent the deterioration of its economic, social, or health conditions, and to habilitate the husband and wife to ensure their fulfillment of their role of raising children physically, psychologically, and behaviorally.
2. To ensure a balanced and safe childhood and ensure the raising of generations of Muslim children who believe in their creator, adhere to their faith, are loyal to their country, committed to the principles of truth and goodness in thoughts and in deeds, and to the sense of belonging to the Islamic civilization.
3. To generalize and deepen interest in the phases of childhood and adolescence and to provide full care for them so as to raise worthy generations for society.

4. To provide free, compulsory primary and secondary education for all children irre-spective of gender, color, nationality, religion, birth, or any other consideration, to develop education through enhancement of school curricula, training of teachers, and providing opportunities for vocational training.

5. To provide opportunities for the child to discover his/her talents and to recognize his/her importance and place in the society through the family and relevant institutions, and to encourage children to participate in the cultural life of society.

6. To provide the necessary care for children with special needs and for those who live in difficult conditions as well as address the causes that lead to such conditions.

7. To provide all possible assistance and support for Muslim children in all parts of the world in coordination with governments or through international mechanisms.

Article Three
Principles
To achieve the objectives contained in Article Two it is incumbent to:

1. Respect the provisions of the Islamic Shari'a, and observe the domestic legislations of the Member States.

2. Respect the objectives and principles of the Organization of the Islamic Conference.

3. Attach high priority to the rights, interests, protection, and development of children.

4. Ensure equality in care, rights, and duties for all children.

5. Observe non-interference in the internal affairs of any State.

6. Observe the cultural and civilizational constants of the Islamic Ummah.

Article Four
Obligations of States
States Parties to this Covenant shall observe the following:

1. Respect the rights stipulated in this Covenant, and take the necessary steps to enforce it in accordance with their domestic regulations.

2. Respect the responsibilities and duties of parents, legal guardians, or other persons that are legally responsible for the child in accordance with existing domestic regula-tions as required by the child's interest.

3. End action based on customs, traditions or practices that are in conflict with the rights and duties stipulated in this Covenant.

Article Five
Equality
States Parties shall guarantee equality of all children as required by law to enjoy their rights and freedoms stipulated in this Covenant regardless of sex, birth, race, religion, language, political affiliation, or any other consideration affecting the right of the child, the family, or his/her representative under the law or Shari'a.

Article Six
The Right to Life

1. The child shall have the right to life from when he is a fetus in his/her mother's womb or in the case of his/her mother's death; abortion should be prohibited except under necessity warranted by the interests of the mother, the fetus, or both of them. The child shall have the right to descent, ownership, inheritance, and child support.

2. States Parties to the Covenant shall guarantee the basics necessary for the survival and development of the child and for his/her protection from violence, abuse, exploitation, and deterioration of his/her living and health conditions.

Article Seven
Identity

1. A child shall, from birth, have right to a good name, to be registered with authorities concerned, to have his nationality determined and to know his/her parents, all his/her relatives and foster mother.
2. States Parties to the Covenant shall safeguard the elements of the child's identity, including his/her name, nationality, and family relations in accordance with their domestic laws and shall make every effort to resolve the issue of statelessness for any child born on their territories or to any of their citizens outside their territory.
3. The child of unknown descent or who is legally assimilated to this status shall have the right to guardianship and care but without adoption. He shall have a right to a name, title and nationality.

Article Eight
Family Cohesion

1. States Parties shall protect the family from causes of weakness and disintegration and shall work, within their available resources, to care for the family members and cause cohesion and balance among them.
2. No child shall be separated from his/her parents against their will and parents shall not have their guardianship revoked save under extreme necessity, in the interest of the child and with a legal justification, in accordance with domestic procedures, and subject to judicial rules where the opportunity is provided for both the child, one or both parents, or a family member to make their views known.
3. States Parties shall take into account in their social policies the child's best interests and if separation from his/her or her parents is necessary, no child shall be deprived of maintaining relations with them.
4. The child shall be permitted to leave his/her state to stay with his/her parents/or with either of them in another country provided he is not separated from them in accordance with Paragraph 2 of this Article, or his/her leaving does not violate the restrictions imposed by virtue of applicable procedures in the state concerned.

Article Nine
Personal Freedoms

1. Every child capable of forming his/her own personal views, according to his/her age and maturity, shall have the right to express them freely in all matters affecting him/her either orally, in writing, or through any other lawful means in a manner not contradictory to the Shari'a and ethics.
2. Every child is entitled to the respect of his/her personal life. Nevertheless the parents or legal representative are entitled to exercise Islamic and humane supervision over the conduct of the child who shall not be subject to any restrictions other than those imposed in conformity with law and are necessary for the protection of public order, public security, public morals, public health, or the protection of the fundamental rights and freedoms of others.

Article Ten
Freedom of Assembly

Every child shall have the right to form and join any peaceful, civilian gathering in accordance with legal and statutory provisions in his/her society and in a way that is compatible with his/her age and does not affect his/her behavior, health or heritage.

Article Eleven
Upbringing

1. A sound upbringing is a right of the child and shall be the responsibility of his/her parents or legal guardian, as the case may be, and in which the institutions of the state, within their means, shall assist them.
2. The upbringing of the child shall aim at the following objectives:
    i.   To develop the personality, religious and moral value, and sense of citizenship and Islamic and human solidarity of the child and to instill in him/her a spirit of understanding, dialogue, tolerance, and friendship among peoples.
    ii. To encourage the child to acquire skills and capabilities to face new situations and overcome negative customs, and to grow up grounded in scientific and objective reasoning.

Article Twelve
Education and Culture

1. Every child has a right to free compulsory basic education by learning the principles of Islamic education (as well as belief and Shari'a according to the situation) and to the provision of the necessary means to develop his/her mental, psychological and physical abilities, to allow him/her to be open to the common standards of human culture.
2. States Parties to the present Covenant shall provide:
    i.   Compulsory, free primary education for all children on an equal footing.
    ii. Free and compulsory secondary education on a progressive basis so that, within ten years, it is made available to all children.
    iii. Higher education, while observing the capability and interest of each child, in accordance with the education system in each State.
    iv. The right of every child to wear clothes "compatible with her beliefs", while complying with Islamic Shari'a, public etiquette, and modesty.
    v.   Effective treatment of the problem of illiteracy, drop-outs and those who miss basic education.
    vi. Taking care of outstanding and gifted students in all stages of education.
    vii. Producing and publishing children's books, setting up children's libraries, and making use of the mass media in propagating cultural, social, and artistic materials relating to children and encouraging childrens' education.
3. For the right of the child approaching puberty to receive proper sex education distinguishing between the lawful and unlawful.
4. The provisions of this Article and Article 11 immediately preceding it shall not be in conflict with the freedom of the Muslim child to joint private educational institutions, provided that such institutions respect the provisions of the Islamic Shari'a and that the education given in such institutions observe the rules laid down by the State.

Article Thirteen
Rest and Activity Times
1. The child is entitled to times for rest and play, and to exercise legitimate activities that are suitable to his/her age during his/her free time.
2. The child is entitled to participate in cultural, artistic and social spheres.
3. Parents or the one legally responsible for the child, have the right to oversee the child while exercising the activities he desires in accordance with this Article in the framework of the educational, religious and moral controls.

Article Fourteen
Social Living Standard
1. Every child is entitled to custody and maintenance in order to save him/her from perishing due to his/her inability to preserve and maintain himself/herself.
2. States Parties shall recognize the right of every child to benefit from social security in accordance with their national laws.
3. States Parties shall be obliged to reduce the prices of services and exempt children from tariffs and taxes.
4. Every child is entitled to a living standard suitable to his/her mental, psychological, physical and social development.
5. The States Parties shall guarantee for the child mandatory measures to compel his/her parents or legal guardian under Shari'a law to offer him/her support according to their abilities.

Article Fifteen
Child Health
The child is entitled to physical and psychological care. This shall be realized through:
1. Providing care for the mother since the onset of pregnancy and during natural nursing either by the mother or someone else if the mother is unable to suckle the baby.
2. The right of the child to mitigate some Shari'a and judicial rules in favour of his/her legitimate wet-nurse under Shari'a law, and to postpone some punishments given against her as well as lessening work assignments of a nursing and pregnant woman and reduce their working hours.
3. His/her right to necessary measures to reduce infant and child mortality rates.
4. A compulsory medical examination for prospective couples in order to ensure the absence or causes of hereditary or contagious diseases which portend danger for the child.
5. The right of a male child to circumcision.
6. Non-interference of both parents or others in medically altering the colour, shape, features or sex of the fetus except for medical necessities.
7. Providing preventive medical care, disease and malnutrition control, as well as providing the necessary health care for him/her and for his/her mother.
8. The right of the child from the State and society to extend medical information and services for mothers in order to raise awareness and help them improve the health of their children.
9. Guaranteeing the right of the child to be protected from narcotics, intoxicants and other harmful substances as well as from infectious and endemic diseases.

Article Sixteen
Disabled Children and Children with Special Needs

1. A disabled child, or one with special needs, is entitled to receive a special care that guarantees his/her full rights and is commensurate with his/her case and the conditions of his/her parents or of the one responsible for him/her, as well as with available capabilities; the services should, as much as possible, be provided free of charge or with nominal fees.
2. The objectives of care for a disabled child, or one with special needs are education, rehabilitation and training; providing appropriate mobility means (medical, psychological, social, educational, professional, and entertainment services); to enable him/her to be integrated into society.

Article Seventeen
Child Protection

States Parties shall take necessary measures to protect the child from:

1. Illegal use of drugs, intoxicants and harmful substances, or participation in their production, promotion, or trafficking.
2. All forms of torture or inhumane or humiliating treatment in all circumstances and conditions, or his/her smuggling, kidnapping, or trafficking in him/her.
3. All forms of abuse, particularly sexual abuse.
4. Cultural, ideological, information and communication invasion which contradicts the Islamic Shari'a or the national interests of States Parties.
5. To protect children by not involving them in armed conflicts or wars.

Article Eighteen
Child Labour

1. No child shall exercise any risky work, or work which obstructs his/her education or which is at the expense of his/her health as well as physical or spiritual growth.
2. Domestic regulations of every State shall fix a minimum working age, as well as working conditions and hours. Sanctions shall be imposed against those who contravene these regulations.

Article Nineteen
Justice

1. No child shall be deprived of his/her freedom, save in accordance with the law and for a reasonable and a specific period.
2. A child deprived of his/her freedom shall be treated in a way consistent with dignity, respect for human rights and basic freedoms. Needs of persons of his/her age shall be observed.
3. States Parties to the Covenant shall observe the following:
   (a) A child deprived of his/her freedom shall be separated from adults in special places for delinquent children.
   (b) A child shall be informed immediately and directly about the charges against him/her upon his/her summoning or apprehension, and his/her parents, guardian or lawyer shall be invited to be present with him/her.
   (c) The child shall be provided with legal and humanitarian assistance where needed including access to a lawyer and an interpreter if necessary.

(d) Expeditious consideration of the case by a specialized juvenile court, with the possibility of the judgment being contested by a higher court, once the child is convicted.

(e) No child shall be compelled to plead guilty or to offer testimony.

(f) Punishment shall be considered as a means of reform and care in order to rehabilitate the child and reintegrate him/her into the society.

(g) A minimum age under which the child may not be tried shall be determined.

(h) Respect for the child's privacy during all stages of the lawsuit shall be ensured.

Article Twenty
Parents' Responsibility and Protection from Detrimental Practices

1. Parents or the one legally responsible shall be obliged to provide good education and upbringing for the child.

2. Parents or the one legally responsible and States Parties to the Covenant shall protect the child from practices and traditions which are socially or culturally detrimental or harmful to the health, and from practices which have negative effects on his/her welfare, dignity or growth, as well as those leading to discrimination between children on basis of sex or other grounds in accordance with the regulations and without prejudice to Islamic Shari' a.

Article Twenty-One
Child Refugees

States Parties to this Covenant shall ensure, as much as possible, that refugee children, or those legally assimilated to this status, enjoy the rights provided for in this Covenant within their national legislation.

Article Twenty-Two
Signing, ratification and/or accession to the Covenant

1. The present Covenant shall be open for signature by all Member States of the Organisation of the Islamic Conference.

2. The present Covenant shall be open for ratification and/or accession by all Member States.

3. The instruments of ratification shall be deposited with the Secretary General of the Organisation of the Islamic Conference.

Article Twenty-Three
The Covenant's Entry in force

1. The present Covenant shall enter into force on the thirtieth day following the date of deposit with the Secretary General of the Organization of the Islamic Conference of the twentieth instrument of ratification.

2. For each State acceding to this Covenant, the Covenant shall enter into force on the thirtieth day after the deposit by such State of its instrument of accession.

Article Twenty-Four
Implementation Mechanism of the Covenant

1. States Parties to the present Covenant agree to establish an Islamic Committee on the Rights of the Child. The Committee shall be composed of the representatives of all the States Parties to the present Covenant and shall meet every two years, starting from

the date of entry into force of this Covenant, at the headquarters of the Organisation of the Islamic Conference, to examine the progress made in the implementation of this Covenant.

2. The proceedings of the meeting, for which two thirds of the States Parties to the present Covenant shall constitute a quorum, shall be governed by the rules of procedure for the meeting of the conferences of the Organization of the Islamic Conference.

Article Twenty-Five
Reservation, Withdrawal and Amendment

1. Member States shall have the right to make reservation on some sections of this Covenant or to withdraw their reservation after notifying the Secretary General.

2. Every Member State shall have the right to withdraw from this Covenant whenever they so wish. The withdrawal shall become effective on the thirtieth day following the Secretary General's receipt of the notice.

3. Any State Party may present a request to amend this Covenant through a written notice; the amendment will only enter into force with the approval of two-thirds of the OIC Member States.

Article Twenty-Six
Official Languages

The present Covenant has been done in the Arabic, English, and French languages, all of which are equally authentic.

PART XII
Miscellaneous Documents

100

OECD Guidelines for Multinational Corporations (excerpt), 2011

Note: The OECD Guidelines for Multinational Corporations are a part of the OECD Declaration and Decisions on International Investment and Multinational Enterprises. First adopted in 1976, the excerpt below is from the fifth update of 2011.

...

IV. HUMAN RIGHTS

States have the duty to protect human rights. Enterprises should, within the framework of internationally recognised human rights, the international human rights obligations of the countries in which they operate as well as relevant domestic laws and regulations:

1. Respect human rights, which means they should avoid infringing on the human rights of others and should address adverse human rights impacts with which they are involved.
2. Within the context of their own activities, avoid causing or contributing to adverse human rights impacts and address such impacts when they occur.
3. Seek ways to prevent or mitigate adverse human rights impacts that are directly linked to their business operations, products or services by a business relationship, even if they do not contribute to those impacts.
4. Have a policy commitment to respect human rights.
5. Carry out human rights due diligence as appropriate to their size, the nature and context of operations and the severity of the risks of adverse human rights impacts.
6. Provide for or co-operate through legitimate processes in the remediation of adverse human rights impacts where they identify that they have caused or contributed to these impacts.

Index